INTERNATIONAL COURTS AND TRIBUNALS SERIES

General Editors: Philippe Sands, Ruth Mackenzie, and Cesare Romano

A COMMON LAW OF INTERNATIONAL ADJUDICATION

INTERNATIONAL COURTS AND TRIBUNALS SERIES

A distinctive feature of modern international society is the increase in the number of international judicial bodies and dispute settlement and implementation control bodies; in their case-loads; and in the range and importance of the issues that they are called upon to address. These factors reflect a new stage in the delivery of international justice. The International Courts and Tribunals series has been established to encourage the publication of independent and scholarly works which address, in critical and analytical fashion, the legal and policy aspects of the functioning of international courts and tribunals, including their institutional, substantive and procedural aspects.

A COMMON LAW OF INTERNATIONAL ADJUDICATION

CHESTER BROWN

THE PROJECT ON PICT
INTERNATIONAL COURTS AND TRIBUNALS

This series has been developed in cooperation with the Project on International Courts and Tribunals

OXFORD
UNIVERSITY PRESS

OXFORD
UNIVERSITY PRESS

Great Clarendon Street, Oxford OX2 6DP

Oxford University Press is a department of the University of Oxford.
It furthers the University's objective of excellence in research, scholarship,
and education by publishing worldwide in

Oxford New York

Auckland Cape Town Dar es Salaam Hong Kong Karachi
Kuala Lumpur Madrid Melbourne Mexico City Nairobi
New Delhi Shanghai Taipei Toronto

With offices in

Argentina Austria Brazil Chile Czech Republic France Greece
Guatemala Hungary Italy Japan Poland Portugal Singapore
South Korea Switzerland Thailand Turkey Ukraine Vietnam

Published in the United States
by Oxford University Press Inc., New York

First published 2007

British Library Cataloguing in Publication Data
Data available

Library of Congress Cataloging in Publication Data
Brown, Chester.
A common law of international adjudication / Chester Brown.
p. cm. — (International courts and tribunals series)
Includes bibliographical references and index.
ISBN 978–0–19–920650–6
1. International courts. 2. Arbitration, International. 3. Law—International unification. I. Title.
KZ6250.B76 2007
341.5′5—dc22 2007024144

Typeset by Newgen Imaging Systems (P) Ltd., Chennai, India
Printed in Great Britain
on acid-free paper by
Biddles Ltd., King's Lynn

ISBN 978–0–19–920650–6

1 3 5 7 9 10 8 6 4 2

For Catherine

Foreword

The past years have seen a proliferation of scholarly works on international courts and tribunals, reflecting the growing number of such bodies and the increasing importance that is being attached to adjudicative mechanisms of dispute settlement in the international community. These works are welcome as they explore the changing character of the international system and the development of international law as a hard system of rules and principles by which States and other subjects of international law can prosecute rights, protect interests and be held to account. In the main, however, the scholarly works to date have focused on the institutions of adjudication, and how they interact, or might usefully do so. Relatively few works take a step back and cast a strategic gaze over the evolution of the adjudicatory system more generally, and what the institutional proliferation means for the development of the underlying principles of evidence and procedure, of the power to award remedies, and of other powers relevant to the adjudicatory task.

It is these aspects that are the focus of this book. It is a timely and scholarly work, which will appeal in equal measure to academics and practitioners of international law, as well as to those interested in dispute settlement more generally. It also collects within its pages, in a systematic and accessible manner, a wealth of primary material which will be a useful mine for all those who wish to think further about the subject in the future. Not least, it is likely to be a book consulted frequently by judges and arbitrators as they reflect on their competence in novel or difficult areas, and consider whether it is appropriate for them to draw on decisions by and analogous practices of other bodies of similar character.

As the author makes clear in the opening pages, the phrase 'common law of international adjudication' is not intended as a reference to the Anglo-American legal tradition or an implied suggestion that this municipal law tradition is especially relevant in the development of international law. It is rather a reference to the emergence of a homogenous body of rules and principles applicable to international adjudication.

Quite apart from the breadth of its coverage—addressing issues of evidence, the power to grant provisional measures, the power to interpret and revise judgments and awards, and the power to award remedies—the book examines closely the sources of law relating to procedure and remedies, including the elusive but vitally important concept of the powers inherent in courts and tribunals as a necessary feature of their adjudicatory function. This discussion, in chapter 2, is amongst the most interesting in the book as it is here that the creative tools of the judge and arbitrator will be found.

As an academic and the author's PhD supervisor, I was delighted to watch this work unfold and to see the emergence of a text that combined a strategic overview with a sense of practical application. As a litigation lawyer, I turned to the text on many occasions as a source of information and to aid my understanding of the evolving adjudicatory system. As a government lawyer, I now turn to the work as a touchstone on the subject of the fragmentation of international law and the issues to which this gives rise in the adjudicatory field. I confidently expect that others will turn to this work in similar vein and will find it equally stimulating and useful.

Daniel Bethlehem QC
London

17 May 2007

General Editors' Preface

In 1935 Abraham H. Feller, a young international law scholar, described the procedure of international adjudicatory bodies as 'the Antarctica of international law' (*The Mexican Claims Commissions: 1923–34* (1935) vii). Seventy years on, the number of international courts and tribunals has grown significantly, and it has fallen to Chester Brown to pick up the gauntlet and present a doctoral thesis on this challenging topic. If not exactly Antarctic-like, the subject remains open to new explorers. Dr Brown has made a significant contribution to the development of international procedural law with this diligent examination of the extent of convergence—or divergence, perhaps—of the procedures, practice and remedies of the rapidly growing body of rules relating to international adjudicative bodies.

Dr Brown's argument is that international courts often—but not always—adopt common approaches to questions of procedure and remedies. The turn towards common approaches gives rise to an increasing commonality in the practice and case law of international courts, in relation to the identification and application of procedural and remedial powers. Dr Brown considers that this has given rise to a 'common law of international adjudication', or what might perhaps be referred to as international customary procedural law.

Those charged with the study and practice of international law have probably long suspected this tendency. Dr Brown's study describes circumstances in which some procedural practices migrate between courts and tribunals, and can in this way contribute to the development of a more structured and systemic international judicial architecture. His study also indicates the limits of that migratory tendency, describing also the occasions in which the different courts and tribunals retain an insular character. These efforts constitute an important contribution, examining the effects of the multiplication of international adjudicative bodies on the coherence—or incoherence—of the larger international legal order.

The International Courts and Tribunals series intends to provide an outlet for new scholarly works that examine, in a critical and analytical fashion, aspects of the substantive or procedural international law across several international courts and tribunals. We are very pleased that *A Common Law of International Adjudication* can be a part of this series.

Cesare P.R. Romano
Loyola Law School Los Angeles

Philippe Sands
University College London
10 April 2007

Acknowledgements

This book is a revised and expanded version of a PhD dissertation which was submitted to the Law Faculty at the University of Cambridge in November 2004. While the process of writing a doctoral dissertation is largely a solitary task, many people supported and contributed to this undertaking in many ways. The encouragement and guidance of my supervisor, Daniel Bethlehem QC, Legal Adviser to the Foreign and Commonwealth Office, is greatly appreciated, and I am also indebted to him for writing the Foreword for this resulting publication. My PhD dissertation was examined by Professor Philippe Sands QC and Dr Guglielmo Verdirame, who subjected it to a thorough and searching analysis, and made thoughtful and perceptive comments which are gratefully acknowledged.

Friends and colleagues have also read and commented on various sections of this book, and sincere thanks are due to Dr Matthew Conaglen, Dr Caroline Foster, and Dr Christian Tams. Many others were willing to correspond and discuss the ideas developed in it, and also assist in other ways. I am grateful in particular to Dr Isabella Alexander, Professor Mads Andenas, Dr John Barker, Dr Lorand Bartels, Professor John Bell QC, Professor Chi Carmody, Professor James Crawford SC, Zachary Douglas, Professor Christine Gray, Dr Felix Ho, Professor Sir Elihu Lauterpacht QC, Richard Nolan, Ben Olbourne, Dr Alexander Orakhelashvili, Dr Federico Ortino, Professor Cesare Romano, Professor Shabtai Rosenne, Dr David Scannell, Professor Iain Scobbie, Professor Yuval Shany, Professor Christoph Schreuer, and Professor Ole Spiermann.

Some parts of this book draw on and develop material first published elsewhere. A section of chapter 2 has appeared as Chester Brown, 'The Inherent Powers of International Courts and Tribunals' (2005) 76 *British Yearbook of International Law* 195. In addition, sections of chapter 1 develop ideas first presented in Chester Brown, 'The Proliferation of International Courts and Tribunals: Finding Your Way through the Maze' (2002) 3 *Melbourne Journal of International Law* 453.

St John's College, the Squire Law Library and the Lauterpacht Research Centre for International Law at the University of Cambridge proved to be excellent working environments during my time in Cambridge. I am grateful to the Director of the British Institute of International and Comparative Law, Professor Gillian Triggs, for granting me a Visiting Fellowship during the summer of 2006, which facilitated the revision and updating of the manuscript. I also wish to record my thanks to the partners in the International Law and International Arbitration Group of Clifford Chance LLP, in particular Audley Sheppard and John Beechey, for supporting my further work on this text and for affording the many practical insights that have enriched it. Thanks are also due to the General Editors of Oxford University Press's International Courts and Tribunals Series; to John Louth, Fiona Stables, Rebecca Smith and others at Oxford University Press; and to the external reviewer who provided many useful comments on the manuscript.

This book would not have been possible without the generosity and support of the Sir Robert Menzies Memorial Foundation, Australia; the British Council; the Cambridge Commonwealth Trust; the McMahon Fund, St John's College; and the Lauterpacht Fund of the Law Faculty, University of Cambridge. I am also indebted to those who supported my applications to undertake postgraduate study, particularly Professors Michael Bryan, Tim McCormack and Gillian Triggs of the University of Melbourne.

Finally, I am especially grateful to my parents, David and Judith Brown, who have constantly supported all my endeavours in many ways. My warmest thanks are reserved for my wife, Catherine Brown, not only for reading and commenting on countless drafts of this book, but more importantly, for providing unstinting support for me and for this project. It is to her that this book is dedicated.

The views in this book are expressed in a personal capacity, and do not necessarily reflect those of the Foreign and Commonwealth Office. The law stated is as it appeared to me on 31 January 2007, although it has been possible to include some later developments.

Dr Chester Brown
London
17 May 2007

Summary Contents

Contents

Table of Cases

Permanent Court of International Justice

International Court of Justice

GATT and World Trade Organisation

International Tribunal for the Law of the Sea and UNCLOS Tribunals

International Centre for the Settlement of Investment Disputes

Permanent Court of Arbitration

European Court of Justice

European Court of Human Rights

European Commission of Human Rights

Inter-American Court of Human Rights

Iran–US Claims Tribunal

NAFTA Tribunals

International Criminal Tribunal for the Former Yugoslavia

International Criminal Tribunal for Rwanda

Mixed Claims Commissions

Mixed Arbitral Tribunals

Other Arbitral Decisions

United Nations Administrative Tribunal

ILO Administrative Tribunal

UN Human Rights Committee

UN Committee against Torture

Central American Court of Justice

United Nations Compensation Commission

National Courts

Table of International Instruments

Conventions

United Nations Resolutions

Resolutions of Other International Organisations

Rules of Procedure

Practice Directions

ICJ Practice Directions:

ICTY Practice Directions:

List of Abbreviations

AAA	American Arbitration Association
AB	WTO Appellate Body
ABR	WTO Appellate Body Report
AC	Appeal Cases (UK)
ACHPR	African Court of Human and Peoples' Rights
ACommHPR	African Commission on Human and Peoples' Rights
AJIL	*American Journal of International Law*
All ER	All England Law Reports (UK)
App Cas	Law Reports Appeal Cases, House of Lords 1875–90
ASIL	American Society of International Law
BIICL	British Institute of International and Comparative Law
BIT	Bilateral Investment Treaty
CC	Claims Commission
CLJ	*Cambridge Law Journal*
CLP	*Current Legal Problems*
CLR	Commonwealth Law Reports (Australia)
CML Rev	*Common Market Law Review*
Conc Op	Concurring Opinion
CR	*Compte Rendu* (oral proceedings of the ICJ)
CRR	Canadian Rights Reporter
Dec & Rep	Decisions and Reports of the ECommHR
Decl	Declaration
Diss Op	Dissenting Opinion
DSB	WTO Dispute Settlement Body
DSR	Dispute Settlement Reports of the WTO
DSU	*Understanding on Rules and Procedures Governing the Settlement of Disputes*
EC	European Communities
ECHR	European Court of Human Rights
ECommHR	European Commission of Human Rights
ECJ	Court of Justice of the European Communities
ECR	Reports of the Court of Justice of the European Communities
EHRR	European Human Rights Reports
ELR	*European Law Review*
GA	United Nations General Assembly
GATT	*General Agreement on Tariffs and Trade*
GB	Great Britain

GCC	General Claims Commission
IACHR	Inter-American Court of Human Rights
IACommHR	Inter-American Commission of Human Rights
ICC	International Chamber of Commerce
ICCPR	*International Covenant on Civil and Political Rights*
ICCt	International Criminal Court
ICJ	International Court of Justice
ICJ Rep	Reports of the International Court of Justice
ICLQ	*International and Comparative Law Quarterly*
ICSID	International Centre for the Settlement of Investment Disputes
ICSID Rep	Reports of ICSID Awards
ICSID Review–FILJ	*ICSID Review–Foreign Investment Law Journal*
ICTR	International Criminal Tribunal for Rwanda
ICTY	International Criminal Tribunal for the former Yugoslavia
ILA	International Law Association
ILC	International Law Commission
ILM	International Legal Materials
ILO	International Labour Organization
ILOAT	International Labour Organization Administrative Tribunal
ILR	International Law Reports
Ir–USCTR	Reports of the Iran–United States Claims Tribunal
ITLOS	International Tribunal for the Law of the Sea
KB	King's Bench (England)
LCIA	London Court of International Arbitration
LNAT	League of Nations Administrative Tribunal
LNTS	League of Nations Treaty Series
LQR	*Law Quarterly Review*
MAT	Mixed Arbitral Tribunal
MCC	Mixed Claims Commission
Mercosur	Common Market between Argentina, Brazil, Paraguay and Uruguay
MLJ	Malaysian Law Journal
MLR	*Modern Law Review*
Mod Rep	Modern Reports (England 1669–1755)
Moore	*History and Digest of the International Arbitrations to which the United States has been a Party* (1898)
NAFTA	*North American Free Trade Agreement*
NATO	North Atlantic Treaty Organization
NCP	Non-Compliance Procedure
NLJ	*New Law Journal*
NZLR	New Zealand Law Reports
OSCE	Organization for Security and Cooperation in Europe

OSPAR Convention	*Convention for the Protection of the Marine Environment of the North-East Atlantic*
PCA	Permanent Court of Arbitration
PCIJ	Permanent Court of International Justice
PICT	Project on International Courts and Tribunals
PR	WTO Panel Report
PV	*Procès Verbaux* (oral proceedings of the ITLOS)
QB	Queen's Bench (England)
QBD	Queen's Bench Division Law Reports (1875–90)
RIAA	UN Reports of International Arbitral Awards
SC	UN Security Council
SCM Agreement	*Agreement on Subsidies and Countervailing Measures*
Sep Op	Separate Opinion
Ser A	PCIJ Documents, Series A (Judgments)
Ser A/B	PCIJ Documents, Series A/B (Judgments and Advisory Opinions)
Ser B	PCIJ Documents, Series B (Advisory Opinions)
Ser C	PCIJ Documents, Series C (Pleadings)
Ser D	PCIJ Documents, Series D (Documents concerning the Jurisdiction of the Court)
TAM	Reports of the Mixed Arbitral Tribunals
Times LR	Times Law Reports
UK	United Kingdom
UN	United Nations
UNAT	United Nations Administrative Tribunal
UNCC	United Nations Compensation Commission
UNCITRAL	United Nations Commission on International Trade Law
UNCLOS	*United Nations Convention on the Law of the Sea*
UNGA	United Nations General Assembly
UNSC	United Nations Security Council
UNTS	United Nations Treaty Series
US	United States (of America)
VCLT	Vienna Convention on the Law of Treaties
WBAT	World Bank Administrative Tribunal
WIPO	World Intellectual Property Organization
WLR	Weekly Law Reports
WP	Working Procedures of WTO Panels
WPAR	Working Procedures for Appellate Review of the WTO Appellate Body
WTO	World Trade Organization
YbECHR	*Yearbook of the European Convention on Human Rights*
YbILC	*Yearbook of the International Law Commission*
ZaöRV	*Zeitschrift für ausländisches öffentliches Recht und Völkerrecht*

Introduction

I. Introduction to the Research Theme

The obligation on states to settle disputes peacefully is contained in article 2(3) of the UN Charter, one of its cornerstone provisions.[1] Article 33(1) further specifies that one of the methods of peaceful settlement of disputes is adjudication.[2] Despite the significance of these stipulations, the creation of procedures for the settlement of disputes by adjudication is a relatively recent development in international relations. Whilst international arbitration was not unknown amongst the Ancient Greeks, and was resorted to in medieval Europe,[3] the first instance of modern international adjudication is regarded as having taken place just over 200 years ago following the conclusion of the Jay Treaty between Great Britain and the United States in 1794.[4] Today, there are over 120 different international dispute settlement bodies.[5] The creation of this multitude of international courts is known as the 'proliferation' of international courts and tribunals. Proliferation has raised several

[1] *Charter of the United Nations*, opened for signature 26 June 1945, 3 Bevans 1153, art 2(3) (entered into force 24 October 1945).

[2] UN Charter, art 33(1). See further UNGA Res 2625 (XXV) (1970).

[3] See, e.g., Louis Sohn, 'International Arbitration in Historical Perspective: Past and Present' in A H A Soons (ed), *International Arbitration: Past and Prospects* (1990) 9, 9–11; R P Anand, *International Courts and Contemporary Conflicts* (1974) 11–15; Jackson Ralston, *International Arbitration from Athens to Locarno* (1929) 153–89; Marcus Niebuhr Tod, *International Arbitration amongst the Greeks* (1913); A Ræder, *L'arbitrage international chez les Hellènes* (1912).

[4] *Treaty of Amity, Commerce and Navigation*, signed 19 November 1794 (GB–US), 12 Bevans 13 (entered into force 28 October 1795) ('Jay Treaty').

[5] See especially the 'Synoptic Chart' prepared by PICT: Cesare Romano, 'PICT Synoptic Chart' at <http://www.pict-pcti.org> under 'Materials and Publications' (last visited 25 November 2006).

issues concerning the administration of international justice. One which has gone somewhat unnoticed by writers is the subject of this book: namely, whether the many international courts and tribunals adopt common approaches to issues of procedure and remedies that arise in the course of international adjudication.

The constitutive instruments of early arbitral tribunals made little provision for the applicable procedure and available remedies. The Jay Treaty, for instance, was silent as to procedure, other than the location of the commissions, the time limit for the hearing of claims, and the evidence the commissions were expected to consider.[6] A significant advance in the codification of international procedure was made in 1875 when the Institut de Droit International prepared a 'Règlement pour la procédure arbitrale internationale'.[7] This 'Règlement' later informed the procedural provisions of the Hague Conventions of 1899 and 1907 which created the Permanent Court of Arbitration ('PCA'), but these conventions left much discretion to the individual tribunals that were established under its auspices. The awards of these early arbitral tribunals were, in the words of Professor Merrills:

> instrumental in developing the rules and principles of international law concerned with the conduct of litigation, including those relating to a variety of procedural matters, to evidence, to the review of awards and to judicial remedies.[8]

Even so, there was a lack of uniformity in the rules applied by early international tribunals. In 1935, A H Feller described procedure as 'the Antarctica of international law',[9] and the practice of international courts in awarding remedies was also a much neglected subject for many years.[10] Today, it is no longer true to say that international procedural law can be regarded as 'Antarctica';[11] many substantial works have been published on the procedure obtaining before various international tribunals,[12] and significant studies have been made on the availability of

[6] Jay Treaty, arts V–VII.

[7] L Goldschmidt, 'Projet de règlement pour tribunaux arbitraux internationaux, présenté à l'Institut de Droit International (Session de Genève, 1874)' (1874) 6 *Revue de Droit International et de Législation Comparée* 421; Institut de Droit International, 'Procès-verbal de la session de Genève: Procès-verbal No 1: Séance du 31 août 1874' (1874) 6 *Revue de Droit International et de Législation Comparée* 583; L Goldschmidt, 'Examen des Conclusions de la 2me Commission (Projet de Règlement pour la procédure arbitrale internationale' (1877) 1 *Annuaire de l'Institut de Droit International* 84; Institut de Droit International, 'Projet de règlement pour la procédure arbitrale internationale' (1877) 1 *Annuaire de l'Institut de Droit International* 126.

[8] John Merrills, 'The Contribution of the PCA to International Law and the Settlement of Disputes by Peaceful Means' in P Hamilton, H C Requena, L van Scheltinga and B Schifman (eds), *The Permanent Court of Arbitration: International Arbitration and Dispute Resolution* (1999) 3, 17–18.

[9] A H Feller, *The Mexican Claims Commissions: 1923–34* (1935) vii. For the expression of similar sentiments, see Philip Jessup, 'The Palmas Island Arbitration' (1928) 22 AJIL 735, 748–52.

[10] Ian Brownlie, 'Remedies in the International Court of Justice' in Vaughan Lowe and Malgosia Fitzmaurice (eds), *Fifty Years of the International Court of Justice* (1996) 557, 557.

[11] This point is also made by Mojtaba Kazazi and Bette Shifman, 'Evidence before International Tribunals: Introduction' (1999) 1 *International Law FORUM du Droit International* 193, 193.

[12] E.g., Shabtai Rosenne, *The Law and Practice of the International Court, 1920–2005* (2006); Andreas Zimmermann, Christian Tomuschat and Karin Oellers-Frahm (eds), *The Statute of the International Court of Justice: A Commentary* (2006); see also the works cited below at nn 14–15.

judicial remedies in international law.[13] Yet what is lacking is an examination of procedure and remedies before different international courts, and an answer to the question of whether the same procedural rules obtain and the same remedies are available before different international judicial bodies. The existing studies on international procedure focus on the procedure applicable before the limited number of tribunals which were operational in the early part of the twentieth century, such as early ad hoc arbitral tribunals, the mixed claims commissions ('MCCs'), the interwar mixed arbitral tribunals ('MATs') and the Permanent Court of International Justice ('PCIJ').[14] Other works focus largely on the law and procedure of the PCIJ and International Court of Justice ('ICJ').[15] One contribution examined the existence of general principles of law relating to procedure and evidence in national legal systems.[16] None of these, however, addresses the effects of proliferation on the international legal order, and nor do they examine the practices of a range of international courts in order to ascertain the degree of convergence—or divergence—in their approaches to issues of procedure and remedies. The present book aims to fill this gap in the literature.

Essentially, the argument developed in this book is that international courts often adopt common approaches to questions of procedure and remedies. These common approaches lead in turn to increasing commonality in the case law of international courts. These common features include both the existence of procedural and remedial powers, and the manner in which those powers are exercised. This practice is seeing the emergence of what might be called a 'common law of international adjudication'.

The emergence of common features in the practice of international courts is significant, for it was not clear that the proliferation of international tribunals

[13] Christine Gray, *Judicial Remedies in International Law* (1987); Christine Gray, 'Is there an International Law of Remedies?' (1985) 56 *British Yearbook of International Law* 25. For studies of remedies in specialized fields of international adjudication, see Dinah Shelton, *Remedies in International Human Rights Law* (2nd ed, 2005); John Barker, 'The Valuation of Income-Producing Property in International Law' (PhD dissertation, University of Cambridge, 1998).

[14] E.g., J L Simpson and Hazel Fox, *International Arbitration* (1959); Kenneth Carlston, *Process of International Arbitration* (1946); Manley Hudson, *International Tribunals: Past and Future* (1944); J C Witenberg, *L'Organisation Judiciaire: La Procédure et la Sentence Internationales* (1937); Feller, above n 9; Ralston, above n 3; Jackson Ralston, *The Law and Procedure of International Tribunals* (rev ed, 1926).

[15] E.g., Rosenne, above n 12; Zimmermann, Tomuschat and Oellers-Frahm (eds), above n 12; Shabtai Rosenne, *Procedure in the International Court* (1983); Sir Gerald Fitzmaurice, *The Law and Procedure of the International Court of Justice* (1986); V S Mani, *International Adjudication: Procedural Aspects* (1980); J H W Verzijl, *The Jurisprudence of the World Court* (1965); Manley Hudson, *The Permanent Court of International Justice 1920–1942* (1943); Manley Hudson, *The Permanent Court of International Justice: A Treatise* (1934); Alexander Fachiri, *The Permanent Court of International Justice* (1932); Antonio Sanchez de Bustamante, *The World Court* (1925); for an exception, see Sir Elihu Lauterpacht, *Aspects of the Administration of International Justice* (1991).

[16] A Sereni, *Principi generali di diretto e processo internazionali* (1955). Professor Sereni concluded that there were no general principles that were applicable in international adjudication: ibid 93; see, however, Bin Cheng, *General Principles of Law as Applied by International Courts and Tribunals* (first published 1953, 1987 ed).

would give rise to any convergence in their approach to procedure and remedies. Indeed, in light of concerns that have been expressed about the 'fragmentation' of international law, on which proliferation might have had an exacerbating effect, the multiplication of international courts and tribunals could conceivably have led to the atomization of these legal categories. This is highlighted by the dictum of the Appeals Chamber of the International Criminal Tribunal for the former Yugoslavia ('ICTY') in *Prosecutor v Tadic*, where it stated that:

> International law, because it lacks a centralised structure, does not provide for an integrated judicial system operating an orderly division of labour among a number of tribunals, where certain aspects or components of jurisdiction as a power could be centralised or vested in one of them but not the others. In international law, every tribunal is a self-contained system (unless otherwise provided).[17]

In contrast, international courts have often demonstrated their readiness to allow their procedures and remedies to be informed by the practice of other international tribunals. This is exemplified in the approach of the Appellate Body of the World Trade Organisation ('WTO') in *EC—Bananas* to the question of whether member states were permitted to use private counsel in dispute settlement proceedings. It held that:

> We can find nothing in the [WTO Agreement], the DSU or the Working Procedures, nor in customary international law or the prevailing practice of international tribunals, which prevents a WTO Member from determining the composition of its delegation in Appellate Body proceedings.[18]

The approach of the Appellate Body reflects a readiness to reach out and have regard to the experience and practice of other international tribunals, and to develop its own procedures consistently with that practice. Similar statements can be found in the jurisprudence of a wide range of international courts in the context of numerous issues of procedure and remedies.

II. Definitions and Scope

A. On the Term 'Common Law of International Adjudication'

At the outset, it is useful to provide a detailed explanation of the term 'common law of international adjudication'. It is stressed that the expression 'common law' is not a reference to the Anglo-American legal tradition. Nor is it a suggestion that the common law legal system is exerting an influence—or that it should be influential—in international dispute settlement. Rather, the expression 'common

[17] *Prosecutor v Tadic* (1996) 35 ILM 32, 39.

[18] *EC—Regime for the Importation, Sale and Distribution of Bananas*, DSR 1997–II, 591, 599, para 10 (ABR).

law of international adjudication' refers to the emergence of an increasingly homogeneous body of rules applied by international courts and tribunals relating to issues of procedure and remedies, both in cases where their constitutive instruments make provision for certain procedures and remedies, and also in cases where there are *lacunae* in their statutes and rules. This emerging body of rules, which is being developed through a process of 'cross-fertilization' of principles by international courts,[19] is what is meant by the term 'common law of international adjudication'.

Three justifications are proposed for the choice of the term 'common law of international adjudication'. First, the idea of a 'common law of international adjudication' aptly reflects the suggestion that international courts and tribunals are increasingly adopting 'common' approaches to the exercise of their powers over procedure and remedies which can result in 'commonality', and that in cases where their statutes and rules of procedure make provision for the application of a certain procedure or remedy (which may be subject to interpretation), and also in cases where they contain *lacunae*, international courts can, in certain circumstances, draw on a 'common' body of rules.

Second, other international lawyers have in the past employed this term, or a variant of it, to refer to similar developments in international adjudication. Allusion to the existence of a 'common law of international adjudication' was made as early as the First Hague Peace Conference in 1899 by Baron Descamps, the Rapporteur for the Third Commission on Pacific Settlement of International Disputes. During the proceedings which led to the adoption of the 1899 Convention, he observed that arbitration was assuming 'the character of an institution of international common law'.[20] The term 'common law' has also been used in connection with the law of international institutions. In his Hague lectures in 1976, Sir Elihu Lauterpacht considered the question of whether there were common rules applicable to different international organizations.[21] After considering examples of the practice of the PCIJ and ICJ, Sir Elihu concluded that the instances demonstrated 'quite clearly' that:

> a similar approach has been applied to the interpretation both of international constituent instruments and of other legal documents relevant to the structure and operation of international organisation. In this not inconsiderable sense one may properly speak of a 'common law of international organisation'.[22]

[19] For use of this term, see especially Philippe Sands, 'Treaty, Custom and the Cross-fertilisation of International Law' (1998) 1 *Yale Human Rights and Development Law Journal* 85.

[20] Baron Descamps, 'Report to the Conference from the Third Commission on Pacific Settlement of International Disputes' in James Brown Scott (ed), *The Reports to the Hague Conferences of 1899 and 1907* (1917) 42, 83. See also the *Convention for the Pacific Settlement of International Disputes*, opened for signature 29 July 1899 ('1899 Convention') 1 Bevans 230 (entered into force 4 September 1900).

[21] Sir Elihu Lauterpacht, 'The Development of the Law of International Organisations by the Decisions of International Tribunals' (1976) 152 *Recueil des cours* 377, 396–402.

[22] Ibid 402.

The third reason for choosing this term is the perceived unsuitability of many of the alternatives. In the past other writers have used different terms to refer to a broadly similar concept. Shabtai Rosenne, in his treatment of the law and practice of the PCIJ and ICJ, refers to the concept of 'international procedural law',[23] as does Professor Thirlway.[24] However, this arguably would exclude any discussion of remedies in international dispute settlement, which have largely been developed in the practice of international courts and tribunals.[25] In addition, reaching a satisfactory definition of 'procedure' is a difficult exercise in itself, as will be discussed below; in its wider sense the term might be said to encompass all aspects of law which are not substantive; a narrower meaning would limit its scope to the conduct of international litigation.[26] Another possibility would be to use the term 'adjective international law', which is occasionally used in the literature in reference to questions of procedure.[27] But this falls into the same difficulty as the term 'international procedural law', in that it would tend to exclude consideration of the remedies available before different international courts.[28] As a further alternative, Professor Schwarzenberger preferred the nomenclature 'international judicial law'.[29] Using this term, however, could be interpreted as excluding the wealth of jurisprudence that has been generated by international arbitral tribunals.[30] Rather than 'international judicial law', it has been decided to use the term 'international adjudication', as this can be said to include international courts and tribunals engaged in the resolution of disputes both by judicial settlement and by arbitration.[31]

B. On 'Procedure' and 'Remedies'

Having explained the use of the term 'common law of international adjudication', and clarified its meaning as referring to the emergence of an increasingly homogeneous body of rules applied by international courts and tribunals relating to issues of procedure and remedies, it is necessary to explain the development of 'procedure' and 'remedies' in international adjudication, and define what is understood by those terms.

23 Rosenne, *Law and Practice*, above n 12, vol III, 1021.

24 Hugh Thirlway, 'Procedure of International Courts and Tribunals', in Rudolf Bernhardt (ed), *Encyclopedia of Public International Law* (1992) vol III, 1128, 1128; see also Hugh Thirlway, 'Procedural Law and the International Court of Justice' in Lowe and Fitzmaurice, above n 10, 389, 389.

25 See, e.g., James Crawford, *The International Law Commission's Articles on State Responsibility* (2002) 201–6, 211–34.

26 See especially Robert Kolb, 'General Principles of Procedural Law', in Zimmermann, Tomuschat and Oellers-Frahm (eds), above n 12, 793; Georg Schwarzenberger, *International Law as Applied by International Courts and Tribunals* (1986) vol IV, 17.

27 E.g., Rosenne, *Law and Practice*, above n 12, vol III, 1021. The division into 'adjective' and 'substantive' law is said to originate in the writings of Jeremy Bentham: Schwarzenberger, ibid, vol IV, 17; Sir Henry Maine, *Dissertations on Early Law and Custom* (1883) 389.

28 See further Schwarzenberger, ibid, vol IV, 17.

29 Ibid 3–4, 17.

30 See ibid 3–4.

31 See further John Bassett Moore, *International Adjudications: Ancient and Modern —History and Documents* (1929) vol I, xii–xiii.

1. 'Procedure' in International Adjudication

There is no universally accepted definition of what constitutes 'procedural law'.[32] Different legal systems give it different meanings. In common law systems, 'procedural law' is often referred to as being mutually exclusive to law that relates to 'substance'.[33] However, writers have sought to distinguish between the two for over a century, only to find that it is very difficult to draw a clear line.[34] In English law, only the most general definitions of 'procedural law' have been given. The best-known definition was provided in 1881 by Lush LJ in *Poyser v Minors*:

> 'Practice' ... like 'procedure' ... denotes the mode of proceeding by which a legal right is enforced, as distinguished from the law which gives or defines the right, and by which means of the proceeding the Court is to administer the machinery as distinguished from its product.[35]

Later, in *Re Fuld's Estate*, Scarman J was less certain that the distinction was as clear-cut:

> When is a question one of substantive law? When is a question merely one of evidence or procedure? I attempt no general answer to these questions; for answer can only be made after an analysis of the specific questions calling for decision, its legal background and factual context.[36]

In a civil law system, that of France, 'procedure' is defined broadly, to include not only the rules according to which the court is seised, and according to which it conducts the proceedings and delivers judgment, 'but also the rules governing judicial organisation, establishing the composition and operation of the courts, and the rules determining the competence of these various courts'.[37] French procedural law also includes 'part of the law of evidence', and 'the rules governing the methods of execution of judgments'.[38] Nevertheless, other aspects which one might expect to find discussed under this broad heading of procedure, such as the

[32] See also Schwarzenberger, above n 26, vol IV, 17.

[33] See, e.g., Janeen Carruthers, 'Substance and Procedure in the Conflict of Laws: A Continuing Debate in Relation to Damages' (2004) 53 *ICLQ* 691, 694–6; Lawrence Collins (ed), *Dicey & Morris: The Conflict of Laws* (13th ed, 2000) 157ff; Sir Peter North and J J Fawcett, *Cheshire and North's Private International Law* (13th ed, 1999) 67.

[34] Mauro Cappelletti and Bryant Garth, 'Introduction—Policies, Trends and Ideas in Civil Procedure' in *International Encyclopaedia of Comparative Law, Civil Procedure* (1987) vol XVI, ch 1, 14; Carruthers, ibid, 694–6.

[35] (1881) 7 QBD 329, 333; see also *Re Shoesmith* [1938] 2 KB 637, 648.

[36] [1968] P 675, 695.

[37] Xavier Blanc-Jouvan and Jean Boulois, 'France' in International Association of Legal Science, *International Encyclopedia of Comparative Law* (1972) vol I, paras F–47, F–81; Jean Vincent and Serge Guinchard, *Procédure civile* (1999) 7.

[38] Blanc-Jouvan and Boulois, ibid, para F–81.

rules on admissibility of evidence, are not included.[39] On the distinction between substance and procedure, Professors Cappelletti and Bryant state:

> If one tries to argue that procedure becomes substance when it determines the particular 'outcome' of a legal dispute, then it appears necessary to concede that almost everything is substance. On the other hand, if procedure is confined to the methods by which legal claims are initiated and proved, there is little doubt that much of the substantive law governs procedure.[40]

Similarly the distinction between substance and procedure is not straightforward in public international law. As Sir Hersch Lauterpacht argued, procedural rules 'represent the element of convenience and certainty in law, and in the prosecution of rights. Thus conceived, they are often regarded as embodying an element of substantive justice.'[41] Shabtai Rosenne has also observed that international law makes 'no sharp distinction' between substantive law and procedural law:

> In so far as regular legal procedures exist for the judicial settlement of international disputes, their norms are indistinguishable, in their creation as in their effect, from those substantive norms through the application of which that dispute will be settled.[42]

Despite these definitional difficulties, one can still seek a common-sense understanding of what can be included in 'procedure'. For the purposes of this book, 'procedure' is understood in a broad sense as including all elements of the adjudicatory process other than the application of primary rules of international law which determine the rights and obligations in dispute, and the application of secondary rules of international law which determine the consequences of breaches of primary rules. Thus, 'procedure' includes not only the conduct of proceedings, including the power of international courts to rule on preliminary objections, the adduction of evidence, and the exercise of incidental powers, during and after the adjudication on the merits, but also the constitution of international tribunals, and questions relating to their jurisdiction.[43]

It is emphasized that this is not an exhaustive definition of procedure, but rather a working appreciation of the many aspects of adjudication which can be regarded as procedural in nature. Admittedly, it could be accused of running into the problem highlighted by Professors Cappelletti and Bryant, being that if the criterion is whether the final outcome of the litigation is affected, then most rules can be characterized as substantive. However, procedure should be regarded as a fluid concept; the elements listed above can be regarded as procedural, although they may have substantive rules which govern their application.

[39] Crawford, above n 25, 201–6, 211–34.

[40] Cappelletti and Bryant, above n 34, 14.

[41] Sir Hersch Lauterpacht, *The Development of International Law by the International Court* (1958) 209; see also Schwarzenberger, above n 26, vol IV, 17.

[42] Rosenne, *Law and Practice*, above n 12, vol III, 1024.

[43] See also Kolb, above n 26, 795–6.

2. *'Remedies' in International Adjudication*

This book also considers common approaches in the awarding of remedies in international adjudication. Remedies do not form part of procedure, but are governed by secondary rules of international law which are treated as part of the law of state responsibility.[44] There are several reasons for including an examination of remedies in this book. First, the constitutive instruments of international courts rarely make provision for the remedies that they have the power to award. The secondary rules of international law concerning the consequences of an internationally wrongful act, including the awarding of remedies, have been developed in the practice of states and also to a large extent in the jurisprudence of international tribunals.[45] In this sense, the awarding of remedies is an aspect of adjudication in which judges on international courts have some measure of discretion in forming the appropriate rules for the consequences of breaches of international law, and common approaches might not be unexpected. It may be that states responsible for the commission of an internationally wrongful act are under an obligation to make 'full reparation', but if the dispute is referred to adjudication, judges on an international court can exercise some control over the suitability of the different forms of reparation. In this sense, both the regulation of procedure and the awarding of remedies are aspects of international adjudication where judicial discretion plays a role, unlike the pre-ordained nature (at least in theory) of substantive law. Second, the obtaining of a remedy is one of the primary reasons why states embark on dispute settlement proceedings. Admittedly, it may not be the only reason; states might also wish to obtain publicity and international support for their cause, or use the initiation of judicial proceedings as an additional source of pressure in dispute settlement negotiations. Yet obtaining a remedy is the *raison d'être* for the commencement of most proceedings. Likewise, awarding a remedy for the commission of an internationally wrongful act is the purpose of the creation of most international courts.

C. Scope of the Book

1. *Aspects of International Adjudication*

It is beyond the scope of this book to examine exhaustively all aspects of international adjudication. Instead, several aspects have been chosen which are thought to be representative of the issues that typically arise in international dispute settlement proceedings, and they are also issues for which constitutive instruments usually do not make exhaustive provision. These are: aspects of the rules of evidence applied by international courts; the power of international courts to grant provisional measures; the power of international courts to interpret and revise judgments and awards; and the availability of remedies in international adjudication.

[44] See, e.g., Crawford, above n 25, 191–241.

[45] Ibid 201–6, 211–34.

Restricting the scope of the book in this manner will, of course, place limitations on the generality of the conclusions that can be drawn. Nonetheless, an examination of whether international courts adopt a common approach to these questions will indicate whether there is any broad commonality on these issues. It will also provide evidence as to whether international courts exercise powers other than those expressly conferred on them, whether they regard themselves as having the same functions as other international courts, and whether they are prepared to refer to the case law and practice of other international judicial bodies. If they do so on these issues, then common approaches might also be found in other issues as well.

2. *Coverage of International Courts and Tribunals*

Having detailed the aspects of international adjudication which are to be considered in this book, the selection of international courts whose practice will be considered needs to be determined. This selection is important, as it impacts greatly on the conclusions that may be reached, and different methods of making this selection should be considered. For the avoidance of doubt, the terms 'international courts and tribunals', 'international courts', 'international tribunals', 'international adjudicatory bodies', 'international judicial bodies' and 'international dispute settlement bodies' are used interchangeably.[46]

There are several methods which can be used in deciding which international courts should be considered. One is to identify criteria and formulate a definition of the term 'international court' or 'international tribunal', and then select all bodies which satisfy that definition. There are, however, no universally accepted criteria.[47] Professor Brownlie states that the international character of a tribunal is a question of both its organization and its jurisdiction.[48] Professor Tomuschat has suggested that for a body to be designated an 'international court', it must be permanent, it must be established by an international legal instrument, it must apply international law, it must apply rules of procedure that cannot be modified by the parties, and its judgment must be binding.[49] Professor Romano has suggested similar

[46] For discussion of possible differences in these terms, see Cesare Romano, 'The Proliferation of International Judicial Bodies: The Pieces of the Puzzle' (1999) 31 *New York University Journal of International Law and Politics* 709, 712.

[47] Ibid 713; see also Yuval Shany, *The Competing Jurisdictions of International Courts and Tribunals* (2003) 12–17, especially fn 44; Mani, above n 15, 10.

[48] Ian Brownlie, *Principles of Public International Law* (6th ed, 2003) 676.

[49] Christian Tomuschat, 'International Courts and Tribunals with Regionally Restricted and/or Specialised Jurisdiction' in Max-Planck Institut für ausländisches öffentliches Recht und Völkerrecht, *Judicial Settlement of International Disputes—International Court of Justice, Other Courts and Tribunals, Arbitration and Conciliation: An International Symposium* (1974) 299–312; see also Romano, 'The Pieces of the Puzzle', above n 46, 713–14; see also Christian Tomuschat, 'International Courts and Tribunals' in Rudolf Bernhardt (ed), *Encyclopaedia of Public International Law* (1981) 92, 92–9.

criteria: he argues that the body must be permanent; that it must be composed of independent judges; that it must adjudicate disputes between two or more entities, one of which is a state or international organization; that it must work on the basis of predetermined rules of procedure; and that it must render decisions that are binding.[50]

Another method is to identify the aspects of international adjudication which this book will examine, and then consider only those bodies which apply those as part of their procedure and remedies. Adopting this approach for the present inquiry can be justified at a certain level; it would, for instance, be relatively unproductive to examine the procedures and remedies obtaining before two international dispute settlement bodies which serve different purposes. For instance, if the approaches applicable under the non-compliance procedure ('NCP') of a multilateral environmental agreement were considered along with those pertaining to arbitration under the Convention for the Settlement of Investment Disputes between States and Nationals of Other States,[51] wide variances would not be unexpected. But if the only bodies compared were those which are very similar in nature, such as the PCIJ and the ICJ, then the probable conclusion would be that common practices exist.

The foregoing paragraphs show that various approaches can be proffered. It is decided that for an international court to be included, it must be engaged in international adjudication, or at least have the capacity to adjudicate in international disputes. An 'international dispute' is understood as one in which at least one party is a state or international organization. Other factors deemed relevant are that the courts should be the product of an international instrument, and that they should have jurisdiction to apply international law. The international courts which have been selected are those which could be described as the 'principal' international dispute settlement bodies. These are the PCIJ and the ICJ; the International Tribunal for the Law of the Sea ('ITLOS') and tribunals constituted under the United Nations Convention on the Law of the Sea;[52] tribunals constituted under the auspices of the Permanent Court of Arbitration ('PCA'); ad hoc international tribunals; the Iran–US Claims Tribunal; WTO panels and the WTO Appellate Body; the European Court of Human Rights ('ECHR'); the Inter-American Court of Human Rights ('IACHR'); the ICTY; the International Criminal Tribunal for Rwanda ('ICTR'); the International Criminal Court ('ICCt'); and tribunals formed under the ICSID Convention,[53] or under bilateral and multilateral investment treaties.

50 Romano, 'PICT Synoptic Chart', above n 5.

51 Opened for signature 18 March 1965, 575 UNTS 159 (entered into force 14 October 1966) ('ICSID Convention').

52 Opened for signature 10 December 1982, 21 ILM 1261 (entered into force 16 November 1994) ('UNCLOS').

53 Above n 51.

III. Outline of the Book

This book proceeds in the following way. First, chapter 1 describes the relevant background, being the 'fragmentation' of international law through the creation of specialized regimes and the proliferation of international courts and tribunals, and addresses specific concerns regarding the effect of proliferation on the unity of international law. In considering whether international courts are in fact harmonizing their approaches to the application of legal norms concerning procedure and remedies, it is apparent that the sources of law for the rules applied by international courts on these issues are relevant. These issues are considered in chapter 2. The primary source can be found in the constitutive instruments and rules of procedure of international courts. Where the statutes and rules of different international courts are drafted in similar terms, it is naturally likely that they will be interpreted and applied consistently with each other. Where the statutes and rules are not similar, however, or where they leave gaps, international courts are able to employ rules of treaty interpretation which can operate as powerful techniques for the harmonization of parallel legal regimes. These are: the principle of effectiveness in treaty interpretation; the evolutive approach to treaty interpretation; and the application of article 31(3)(c) of the Vienna Convention on the Law of Treaties,[54] which provides that in interpreting treaties 'there shall be taken into account, together with the context...any relevant rules of international law applicable in the relations between the parties'.[55] Second, the statutes and rules of procedure of international tribunals frequently make only scant provision for the regulation of procedural questions, and are often silent on the question of the available remedies. In order to fill such gaps, international courts can draw on 'general principles of law', which are recognized as a source of international law in article 38(1)(c) of the ICJ Statute.[56] Third, where the constitutive instruments and rules of procedure of international courts contain gaps on issues of procedure and remedies, international courts might have the ability to fill in such gaps by the exercise of inherent powers, which are powers that international courts can exercise in order to carry out their functions.

Chapters 3–6 then proceed to an examination of the issues related to procedure and remedies which have been selected for scrutiny. These issues are: aspects of the rules of evidence and the evidence-gathering powers of international courts (chapter 3); the power of international courts to grant provisional measures (chapter 4); the power of international courts to interpret and revise judgments and awards (chapter 5); and the availability of remedies in international adjudication

[54] Opened for signature 23 May 1969, 1155 UNTS 311 (entered into force 27 January 1980) ('VCLT').

[55] VCLT, art 31(3)(c).

[56] *Statute of the International Court of Justice*, opened for signature 26 June 1945, 3 Bevans 1153 (entered into force 24 October 1945).

(chapter 6). In reviewing the practice of international courts concerning each of these aspects, it is apparent that the factors noted as relevant in the emerging common law of international adjudication are of varying degrees of importance. For instance, general principles of law are more relevant in assessing the rules of evidence, while the methods of treaty interpretation and the existence of inherent powers take greater prominence in examining the powers to grant provisional measures, and the interpretation and revision of judgments.

Having reviewed these aspects of the international adjudication process, it is concluded that there is, on the whole, broad commonality in the approach of international courts and tribunals, and that this can be described as an emerging common law of international adjudication. In chapter 7, the possible reasons for this development are explored. It is not suggested, however, that there is a universally applicable corpus of rules that all international courts and tribunals can apply to all questions of procedure and remedies in every case. Rather, there are limitations on the development of the common law of international adjudication. These limitations can be found in the specific provisions of an international court's statute or rules of procedure, which that international court is bound to follow; the specific functions of an international tribunal; the particular relationship between each international court and the parties before it; and finally, the question of the desirability of common features for all aspects of the adjudication process. In this sense, common approaches cannot be expected for all international courts in all cases; some issues of procedure and remedies are more likely to give rise to common approaches than others.

The implications of the emerging common law of international adjudication are addressed in chapter 8. It is suggested that the practical implications can be significant. The adoption by international courts of increasingly common approaches to a number of procedural and remedial issues demonstrates that international courts are generally amenable to the suggestion that, in interpreting the provisions of their statutes and rules, the practice of other international courts is relevant, and that where their statutes and rules are silent, international courts might exercise inherent powers and refer to the practice of other international courts on how those powers could and should be exercised. It is further suggested that the emerging common law of international adjudication could have some prescriptive effect in determining the resolution of other issues of procedure and remedies for which the constitutive instruments and rules of procedure of international courts make no provision. Three such issues are examined, being the power to dismiss proceedings summarily; the power to suspend proceedings; and the power to enjoin parties from pursuing other proceedings.

The emerging common law of international adjudication also has theoretical implications, especially in light of the criticisms levelled at the administration of international justice as being effected by international courts that operate as self-contained regimes. If international courts apply similar norms for procedure and remedies, and if they have regard to the jurisprudence of other international courts, this might indicate that the community of international courts resembles an international legal system, or international judicial system, even if it does not satisfy the often-cited criteria of normative coherence and institutional linkages. It is not suggested that an international legal system exists in the same way that national legal systems exist. Nonetheless, the emergence of common elements in the way that international courts and tribunals approach certain questions of procedure and remedies demonstrates the existence of systemic features in the international legal order which have previously been ignored.

1

The Emergence of a Common Law of International Adjudication against a Background of Proliferation and Fragmentation

Introduction

This chapter sets out the background to this book, namely the proliferation of international courts and tribunals, and the perceived problem of 'fragmentation' in international law. The proliferation of international judicial bodies makes this study timely, not only because a raft of new international courts is in the process of developing their procedures and will possibly look to the practice of existing international courts for inspiration, but also because recent years have seen a significant increase in the volume of international litigation. This is placing demands on more established international courts, and often causes them to take new approaches to aspects of their procedure, including methods of handling their workload. Proliferation can also increase the likelihood of multiple proceedings before different international courts, which can result in these courts being confronted with new procedural questions. In resolving these issues, international courts may also consider the way in which other international tribunals deal with these situations, and might adopt those practices, leading to increased commonality on a number of issues. The emergence of a common law of international adjudication could, then, be a by-product of proliferation.

The proliferation of international courts and tribunals has taken place contemporaneously with the expression of concerns about the 'fragmentation' of international law.[1] This is said to be caused by multiple factors, one of which is the creation of regional and specialized international organizations, including judicial bodies, which operate in parallel with other international institutions of a universal or general character. The existence of overlap in the sphere of operation of different institutions may lead to divergences in the ways those institutions approach legal issues, resulting in conflicting norms. This can be seen where states have inconsistent obligations under different treaties which cover the same field, and also where different international tribunals reach inconsistent decisions on the same issue. Proliferation is, therefore, one of the root causes of fragmentation, and in this sense, the question posed in this book—whether international courts adopt common approaches to issues of procedure and remedies—is located within the context of the broader issue of fragmentation.

The problematic feature of proliferation is that the multitude of new international courts has been created in the absence of a systemic framework; there are no formal links between different international courts, and there is no structural hierarchy within which they work, meaning that international tribunals essentially operate in isolation from each other, increasing the possibility of inconsistent decisions. If it is the case, however, that international courts are adopting similar approaches to certain issues, this might suggest not only that, in fact, international law is not 'fragmenting'; it might also foretell the emergence of some form of 'system' of international adjudication, in which international judicial bodies consider themselves to be operating as part of a 'community of courts',[2] to whose practice they should have regard.

This chapter first describes the proliferation of international courts and tribunals, and then explains the reasons for this phenomenon. It next considers the context in which this has occurred, namely the perceived 'fragmentation' of international law, reviewing the work of the International Law Commission ('ILC') on this subject, and considers whether this fragmentation has been exacerbated by the multitude of international courts rendering inconsistent decisions. It also

[1] See generally the various contributions to 'Symposium: Diversity or Cacophony? New Sources of Norms in International Law' (2004) 25 *Michigan Journal of International Law* 845–1375; and 'Symposium: The Proliferation of International Courts and Tribunals: Piecing Together the Puzzle' (1999) 31 *New York University Journal of International Law and Politics* 679–933.

[2] For previous use of this phrase, see especially Anne-Marie Slaughter, 'A Global Community of Courts' (2003) 44 *Harvard International Law Journal* 191, who describes the 'community' as including both international and domestic courts.

briefly considers another effect of proliferation, being the creation of overlapping jurisdictions. Finally it highlights the methods identified by the ILC which might be used to address the problems posed by conflicting norms, and suggests that some of these methods may be employed by international courts in confronting issues of procedure and remedies for which their constitutive instruments make no provision, and in adopting consistent approaches to those issues.

I. Proliferation of International Courts and Tribunals

Writers generally refer to the Jay Treaty of 1794 as representing the origins of modern international adjudication.[3] This provided for the establishment of mixed commissions, consisting of members appointed by Great Britain and the United States, to decide claims by nationals of each state, with an impartial umpire deciding a claim in the event of disagreement.[4] Although the process was a diplomatic exercise inasmuch as it involved the application of any legal rules, the constitution of such commissions under the Jay Treaty was an important precedent. The next watershed was the conclusion of the 1871 Washington Treaty between Great Britain and the United States,[5] under which the *Alabama* claims of 1872 were decided by an arbitral tribunal.[6] In these claims, an 'essentially judicial process' was followed, and the tribunal delivered 'a reasoned decision clearly based on law', marking a significant development.[7] It was not until 1899 that a permanent institution for the settlement of international disputes was founded, the Permanent Court of Arbitration ('PCA'), which was to serve as a framework institution for the constitution of ad hoc arbitral tribunals.[8]

In contrast to the situation at the beginning of the twentieth century, there is today a multitude of bodies which can be classified as 'international courts and tribunals', namely bodies established by international instrument with the capacity

[3] *Treaty of Amity, Commerce and Navigation*, signed 19 November 1794, (Great Britain–United States), 12 Bevans 13 (entered into force 28 October 1795). See, e.g. Ian Brownlie, *Principles of Public International Law* (6th ed, 2003) 672; John Collier and Vaughan Lowe, *The Settlement of Disputes in International Law: Institutions and Procedures* (1999) 32; Christine Gray and Benedict Kingsbury, 'Developments in Dispute Settlement: Inter-state Arbitration Since 1945'(1992) 63 *British Yearbook of International Law* 97, 97; Georg Schwarzenberger, *International Law as Applied by International Courts and Tribunals* (1986) vol IV, 21; J H W Verzijl, *International Law in Historical Perspective* (1976) vol VIII, 71–3; J L Simpson and Hazel Fox, *International Arbitration* (1959) 1.

[4] Collier and Lowe, ibid, 32.

[5] Signed 8 May 1871 (Great Britain–United States), 12 Bevans 170 (entered into force 17 June 1871).

[6] Moore, vol I, 495 (Great Britain–United States, 1875); J G Wetter, *The International Arbitral Process: Public and Private* (1979) vol I, 27.

[7] Collier and Lowe, above n 3, 32.

[8] *Convention for the Pacific Settlement of International Disputes*, opened for signature 29 July 1899, 1 Bevans 230 (entered into force 4 September 1900) ('1899 Convention'); see also *Convention for the Pacific Settlement of International Disputes*, opened for signature 18 October 1907, 1 Bevans 577 (entered into force 26 January 1910) ('1907 Convention').

to settle international disputes.[9] This proliferation has provoked much scholarly and judicial debate, which is well documented.[10] The dramatic increase in the number of such bodies can be contrasted with the fact that prior to 1990 there were only six permanent international courts in existence.[11] These were the ICJ,[12] the Court of Justice of the European Communities ('ECJ'),[13] the ECHR,[14] the Court of Justice of the Benelux Economic Union,[15] the IACHR,[16] and the Court

[9] See especially Cesare Romano, 'PICT Synoptic Chart', available at <http://www.pict-pcti.org> under 'Materials and Publications' (last visited 25 November 2006).

[10] See, e.g. Giorgio Gaja, 'Relationship of the ICJ with Other International Courts and Tribunals', in Andreas Zimmermann, Christian Tomuschat and Karin Oellers-Frahm (eds), *The Statute of the International Court of Justice: A Commentary* (2006) 532, 543–4; Shabtai Rosenne, *The Law and Practice of the International Court, 1920–2005* (2006) vol I, 32–42; Pemmaraju Sreenivasa Rao, 'Multiple International Judicial Forums: A Reflection of the Growing Strength of International Law or its Fragmentation?' (2004) 25 *Michigan Journal of International Law* 929; Gilbert Guillaume, 'Advantages and Risks of Proliferation: A Blueprint for Action' (2004) 2 *Journal of International Criminal Justice* 300; Société Française pour le Droit International, *Colloque de Lille: La juridictionnalisation du droit international* (2003); Yuval Shany, *The Competing Jurisdictions of International Courts and Tribunals* (2003) 1–11; Nathan Miller, 'An International Jurisprudence? The Operation of "Precedent" across International Tribunals' (2002) 15 *Leiden Journal of International Law* 483; Chester Brown, 'The Proliferation of International Courts and Tribunals: Finding Your Way Through the Maze' (2002) 3 *Melbourne Journal of International Law* 453; Mireille Couston, 'La Multiplication des Juridictions Internationales: Sens et Dynamiques' (2002) 129 *Journal du Droit International* 5; Thomas Buergenthal, 'Proliferation of International Courts and Tribunals: Is It Good or Bad?' (2001) 14 *Leiden Journal of International Law* 267; Gilbert Guillaume, 'The Proliferation of International Judicial Bodies—The Outlook for the International Legal Order: Speech to the Sixth Committee of the General Assembly' (27 October 2000), available at <http://www.icj-cij.org> (last visited 25 November 2006); Philippe Sands, Ruth Mackenzie and Yuval Shany (eds), *Manual on International Courts and Tribunals* (1999); Symposium, 'Piecing Together the Puzzle', above n 1; Hugh Thirlway, 'The Proliferation of International Judicial Organs and the Formation of International Law' in W P Heere (ed), *International Law and the Hague's 750th Anniversary* (1999) 433; Gerhard Hafner, 'Should One Fear the Proliferation of Mechanisms for the Peaceful Settlement of Disputes?' in Lucius Caflisch (ed), *The Peaceful Settlement of Disputes Between States: Universal and European Perspectives* (1998) 25; Jonathan Charney, 'Is International Law Threatened by Multiple International Tribunals?' (1998) 271 *Recueil des Cours* 101; Alan Boyle, 'The Proliferation of International Jurisdiction and its Implications for the Court' in D W Bowett *et al* (eds), *The International Court of Justice: Process, Practice and Procedure* (1997) 124; Gilbert Guillaume, 'The Future of International Judicial Institutions' (1995) 44 *ICLQ* 848; and Laurence Boisson de Chazournes (ed), *ASIL Proceedings: Implications of the Proliferation of International Adjudicatory Bodies for Dispute Resolution* (1995).

[11] Shany, ibid, 5.

[12] *Statute of the International Court of Justice*, opened for signature 26 June 1945, 3 Bevans 1153 (entered into force 24 October 1945).

[13] *Treaty Establishing the European Coal and Steel Community*, opened for signature 18 April 1951, 261 UNTS 140 (entered into force 25 July 1952) ('ECSC Treaty'); *Treaty Establishing the European Economic Community*, opened for signature 25 March 1957, 298 UNTS 3 (entered into force 1 January 1958) ('EEC Treaty'); *Treaty Establishing the European Atomic Energy Community*, opened for signature 25 March 1957, 298 UNTS 167 (entered into force 1 January 1958) ('Euratom Treaty'); see also *Treaty Establishing the European Community* (2002) *OJ* C 325 (entered into force) ('EC Treaty').

[14] *Convention for the Protection of Human Rights and Fundamental Freedoms*, opened for signature 4 November 1950, 213 UNTS 221 (entered into force 3 September 1953) ('European HR Convention').

[15] *Treaty Concerning the Establishment and Statute of the Benelux Court of Justice*, opened for signature 31 March 1965, 924 UNTS 1 (entered into force 1 January 1974).

[16] *American Convention on Human Rights*, opened for signature 22 November 1969, 1144 UNTS 123 (entered into force 18 July 1978).

of Justice of the Andean Community.[17] There were, of course, also arbitral tribunals that could be constituted on an ad hoc basis; this could be done without an institutional framework, or under the auspices of the PCA. Further, ad hoc arbitral tribunals have been available under the ICSID Convention since 1966,[18] and panels could be established to settle disputes arising under the GATT 1947.[19] In addition, the Iran-US Claims Tribunal has been functioning on a semi-permanent basis since 1981.[20] But these were not permanent institutions; tribunals and panels constituted under the auspices of the PCA, ICSID, and GATT 1947 had to be created specifically for each dispute, and the Iran-US Claims Tribunal, while it has dealt with a large number of claims, is not a permanent body.

In the past two decades, more than a dozen international judicial or quasi-judicial bodies have been established. These include the Court of First Instance of the European Communities,[21] the panels and the Appellate Body of the WTO,[22] the Court of Conciliation and Arbitration of the Organization for Security and Cooperation in Europe,[23] the Court of Justice of the Common Market for Eastern and Southern Africa,[24] and the ITLOS.[25] Many international agreements have also been adopted that provide for the establishment of arbitral tribunals, such as the NAFTA,[26] the Energy Charter Treaty,[27] the Protocol of Brasilia, establishing the Mercosur dispute settlement system,[28] and other regional investment treaties and

[17] *Treaty Creating the Court of Justice of the Cartagena Agreement*, opened for signature 28 May 1979, (1979) 18 ILM 1203 (entered into force 1984).

[18] *Convention for the Settlement of Investment Disputes between States and Nationals of Other States*, opened for signature 18 March 1965, 575 UNTS 159 (entered into force 14 October 1966) ('ICSID Convention'). The first dispute to be registered under the ICSID Convention was in 1972: *Holiday Inns SA v Morocco*, ICSID Case No ARB/72/1: Pierre Lalive, 'The First World Bank Arbitration (*Holiday Inns v Morocco*): Some Legal Problems' (1980) 51 *British Yearbook of International Law* 123.

[19] *General Agreement on Tariffs and Trade*, opened for signature 30 October 1947, 55 UNTS 194 (entered into force 1 January 1948) ('GATT 1947'); Ernst-Ulrich Petersmann, *The GATT/WTO Dispute Settlement System* (1997) 70–72.

[20] *Algiers Accords* (US–Iran), signed 19 January 1981, (1981) 20 ILM 223. The Iran–US Claims Tribunal held its first meeting on 1 July 1981: <http://www.iusct.org/background-english.html> (last visited 25 November 2006).

[21] EC Treaty (as amended by the *Treaty Establishing the European Union*, opened for signature 7 February 1992, (1992) OJ (C 224) 6), art 225; Sands, Mackenzie and Shany (eds), above n 10, 125.

[22] *Marrakesh Agreement Establishing the WTO*, opened for signature 15 April 1994, 1867–9 UNTS 1 (entered into force 1 January 1995) ('WTO Agreement').

[23] *Convention on Conciliation and Arbitration within the Conference on Security and Cooperation in Europe/Organization for Security and Cooperation in Europe*, 15 December 1992, (1993) 32 ILM 557 (entered into force 1995).

[24] *Treaty Establishing the Common Market for Eastern and Southern Africa*, opened for signature 5 November 1993, 33 ILM 1067 (entered into force 8 December 1994).

[25] UNCLOS, opened for signature 10 December 1982, 1833 UNTS 3, Annex VI ('ITLOS Statute') (entered into force 16 November 1994).

[26] *North American Free Trade Agreement*, signed 17 December 1992 (USA–Canada–Mexico), (1993) 32 ILM 289, 605 (entered into force 1 January 1994).

[27] Opened for signature 17 December 1994, (1995) 34 ILM 360 (entered into force 16 April 1998).

[28] *Treaty Establishing a Common Market between Argentina, Brazil, Paraguay and Uruguay* (*Treaty of Asunción*), opened for signature 26 March 1991, (1991) 30 ILM 1041 (entered into force

BITs.[29] Arbitral tribunals can also be constituted under Annexes VII and VIII of UNCLOS.[30] In addition, several international criminal tribunals have been established: these include the ICTY,[31] the ICTR,[32] the Special Court for Sierra Leone,[33] and the International Criminal Court.[34] Other newly established dispute settlement bodies are the United Nations Compensation Commission ('UNCC'),[35] the World Bank Inspection Panel[36] and its Asian and Inter-American Development Bank counterparts,[37] the European Free Trade Association ('EFTA') Court of Justice,[38] the African Commission of Human and Peoples' Rights ('ACommHPR'),[39] the African Court of Human and Peoples' Rights ('ACHPR'),[40] and the Economic Court of the Commonwealth of Independent States.[41] Additionally, an agreement

29 November 1991); *Protocol of Brasilia for the Settlement of Disputes*, opened for signature 17 December 1991, (1997) 36 ILM 691 (entered into force 1993).

[29] For example, *ASEAN Agreement for the Promotion and Protection of Investments*, opened for signature 15 December 1987, (1988) 27 ILM 612 (entered into force). There are in excess of 2,000 bilateral investment treaties (BITs): Zachary Douglas, 'The Hybrid Foundations of Investment Treaty Arbitration' (2003) 74 *British Yearbook of International Law* 151, 156.

[30] Opened for signature 10 December 1982, 1833 UNTS 3, Annexes VII–VIII (entered into force 16 November 1994).

[31] *International Tribunal for the Prosecution of Persons Responsible for Serious Violations of International Humanitarian Law Committed in the Territory of the Former Yugoslavia Since 1991*, adopted by SC Res 827 (1993), UN Doc S/RES/827 (1993).

[32] *International Tribunal for the Prosecution of Persons Responsible for Genocide and Other Serious Violations of International Humanitarian Law Committed in the Territory of Rwanda and Rwandan Citizens Responsible for Genocide and Other Such Violations Committed in the Territory of Neighbouring States, between 1 January 1994 and 31 December 1994*, adopted by SC Res 955 (1994), UN Doc S/RES/955 (1994).

[33] *Agreement between the United Nations and the Government of Sierra Leone on the Establishment of a Special Court for Sierra Leone*, signed 16 January 2002, (entered into force) <http://www.sc-sl.org> (last visited 25 November 2006).

[34] *Rome Statute of the International Criminal Court*, opened for signature 17 July 1998, (1998), 2187 UNTS 3 (entered into force 1 July 2002).

[35] SC Resolution 692 (20 May 1991), (1991) 30 ILM 846.

[36] 'The World Bank Inspection Panel' (1995) 34 ILM 520.

[37] Inter-American Development Bank Board of Executive Directors, Decision on Independent Investigation Mechanism, 10 August 1994, Minutes DEA/94/34/sec 142; Asian Development Bank Inspection Procedures, Decision of Inspection Committee of the Board of Directors, 9 October 1996; referred to in Sands, Mackenzie and Shany (eds), above n 10, 313, 317.

[38] *Agreement between the EFTA States on the Establishment of a Surveillance Authority and a Court of Justice*, signed 2 May 1992, available at <http://www.eftacourt.lu> (entered into force) (last visited 25 November 2006).

[39] *African Charter on Human and Peoples' Rights*, opened for signature 27 June 1981, available at <http://www.achpr.org/english/_info/charter_en.html> (entered into force 21 October 1986) (last visited 25 November 2006).

[40] *Protocol to the African Charter on Human and Peoples' Rights on the Establishment of an African Court of Human and Peoples' Rights*, opened for signature 8 June 1998, (1998) 58 ZaöR 727 (entered into force 25 January 2004).

[41] *Agreement on the Statute of the Economic Court of the Commonwealth of Independent States*, 6 July 1992, (1992) 6 *Sodruzhestvo: Informatsionnii Vestnik* 53 (entered into force 1994); referred to in Gennady Danilenko, 'The Economic Court of the Commonwealth of Independent States' (1999) 31 *New York University Journal of International Law and Politics* 893, 895.

establishing the Caribbean Court of Justice was adopted in 2001, and this body was inaugurated on 16 April 2005.[42]

In addition to the creation of these international courts, numerous quasi-judicial procedures have been adopted in recent years. Examples of these are the non-compliance procedures ('NCPs') of the Montreal Protocol on Substances that Deplete the Ozone Layer,[43] the 1994 Protocol to the Convention on Long Range Transboundary Air Pollution,[44] and the Chemical Weapons Convention,[45] as well as those of the Kyoto Protocol to the Framework Convention on Climate Change,[46] and the Cartagena Protocol on Biosafety to the Convention on Biological Diversity.[47] Several petition procedures have also recently been adopted under human rights agreements. In addition to those already existing under the International Covenant on Civil and Political Rights ('ICCPR')[48] and the Convention Against Torture,[49] an Optional Protocol to the Convention on the Elimination of Discrimination Against Women has been adopted, allowing for complaints by individuals,[50] as has a 'collective complaints procedure' under the European Social Charter.[51] Another recently established

[42] *Agreement Establishing the Caribbean Court of Justice*, opened for signature 14 February 2001, available at <http://www.caribbeancourtofjustice.org > (entered into force 23 July 2002) (last visited 25 November 2006).

[43] Opened for signature 16 September 1987, (1987) 26 ILM 1550 (entered into force 1 January 1989); Non-Compliance Procedure, Decision II/5, Report of the Second Meeting of the Parties to the Montreal Protocol, UN Doc UNEP/Oz L Pro 2/3 (29 June 1990).

[44] *UN Economic Commission for Europe Convention on Long Range Transboundary Air Pollution*, opened for signature 13 November 1979, (1979) 18 ILM 1442 (entered into force 16 March 1983); *Protocol on Further Reduction of Sulphur Emissions*, opened for signature 14 June 1994, (1994) 33 ILM 1542 (entered into force 5 August 1998).

[45] *Convention on the Prohibition of the Development, Production, Stockpiling and Use of Chemical Weapons and on their Destruction*, opened for signature 13 January 1993, 1974 UNTS 45 (entered into force 29 April 1997).

[46] Opened for signature 16 March 1998, (1998) 37 ILM 22 (entered into force 16 February 2005); 'Procedures and Mechanisms Relating to Compliance under the Kyoto Protocol', Decision 24/CP.7, UN Doc FCCC/CP/2001/13/Add.3 (10 November 2001), available at <http://www.unfccc.de> (last visited 25 November 2006).

[47] Opened for signature 29 January 2000, (2000) 39 ILM 1027 (entered into force 11 September 2003); see also Conference of the Parties to the Convention on Biological Diversity/Meeting of the Parties to the Cartagena Protocol on Biosafety, 'Compliance (Article 34): Procedures and Mechanisms on Compliance under the Cartagena Protocol on Biosafety', UN Doc UNEP/CBD/BS/COP-MOP/1/8 (18 November 2003).

[48] *First Optional Protocol to the ICCPR*, opened for signature 16 December 1966, 999 UNTS 302 (entered into force 23 March 1976).

[49] *Convention against Torture and other Cruel, Inhuman or Degrading Treatment or Punishment*, opened for signature 10 December 1984, 1465 UNTS 85 (entered into force 26 June 1987).

[50] Opened for signature 6 October 1999, (2000) 39 ILM 281 (entered into force 22 December 2000).

[51] *Additional Protocol to the European Social Charter Providing for a System of Collective Complaints*, opened for signature 9 November 1995, (1995) 34 ILM 1453 (entered into force 7 January 1998); see especially Robin Churchill and Urfan Khaliq, 'The Collective Complaints System of the European Social Charter: An Effective Mechanism for Ensuring Compliance with Economic and Social Rights?' (2004) 15 *European Journal of International Law* 417.

quasi-judicial procedure is the 'citizens' submissions procedure' under the North American Agreement on Environmental Cooperation.[52]

This proliferation has occurred at the same time as a substantial increase in the recourse by many states and non-state parties to international dispute settlement procedures.[53] For instance, in contrast to the 1970s, when the ICJ had on average one or two cases on its docket, there are currently 13 disputes pending before the ICJ.[54] Over 300 disputes have been referred to WTO dispute settlement since its commencement in 1995, eclipsing the number of disputes that were submitted to GATT panels in over 40 years between 1948 and 1994.[55] Further, between 1966 and 1996, only 38 disputes were referred to tribunals constituted under the ICSID Convention. In contrast, 106 cases are currently pending before ICSID tribunals, 26 of which were registered by the ICSID Secretary-General in 2005, and 23 of which were registered in 2006.[56]

II. Reasons for Proliferation

Two primary reasons for the recent proliferation can be identified.[57] The first of these is an erosion of the traditional reluctance of states to submit disputes to third-party adjudication. This may be due in part to the emergence of a 'greater commitment to the rule of law in international relations, at the expense of power-oriented diplomacy',[58] and the end of the Cold War, which has seen an easing in international tensions; these tensions had 'hampered in the past the growth of international adjudicative procedures'.[59] The increased willingness of states and other non-state parties to refer disputes to international adjudication might also be due to the positive experiences which they have had with some international courts in the past; this may have 'inspired the creation of more such bodies'.[60]

[52] Signed 14 September 1993, (1993) 32 ILM 1480 (entered into force 1 January 1994).

[53] Philippe Sands, 'Treaty, Custom and the Cross-fertilisation of International Law' (1998) 1 *Yale Human Rights and Development Law Journal* 85, 91–3.

[54] Figures taken from <http://www.icj-cij.org> (last visited 31 December 2006). Until 15 December 2004, there were over 20 cases pending before the ICJ; this was reduced when the ICJ disposed of eight cases with its judgments in the *Legality of Use of Force* cases: (2005) 44 ILM 299.

[55] There have been 356 WTO disputes (the most recent being *Chile—Definitive Safeguard Measures on Certain Milk Products*, in which Argentina's Request for Consultations is dated 28 December 2006), compared with 131 GATT disputes: figures taken from <http://www.wto.org> under 'Disputes' (last visited 31 December 2006). See also Debra Steger and Susain Hainsworth, 'World Trade Organisation Dispute Settlement: The First Three Years' (1998) 1 *Journal of International Economic Law* 199, 203–4; Robert Hudec, *Enforcing International Trade Law: The Evolution of the Modern GATT Legal System* (1993) viii.

[56] Figures taken from <http://www.worldbank.org/icsid> (last visited 31 December 2006).

[57] See especially Rao, above n 10, 944–6; Shany, above n 10, 3–4; Sands, Mackenzie and Shany (eds), above n 10, xxv–xxx; Cesare Romano, 'The Proliferation of International Judicial Bodies: The Pieces of the Puzzle' (1999) 31 *New York University Journal of International Law and Politics* 709, 728–38.

[58] Shany, above n 10, 3–4.

[59] Ibid 4.

[60] Ibid 4; Romano, 'The Pieces of the Puzzle', above n 57, 729–33.

Further, states may also consider that the submission of disputes to international adjudication lends legitimacy to actions taken by them in the course of their international relations;[61] or perceive that their resort to these mechanisms enhances their credibility as members of the international community.

A second reason for the proliferation can be found in the effects of globalization. Globalization and the increasing interdependence of the international community have resulted in complex problems. This has arguably led to an increase in the 'density, volume, and complexity of international norms', which can often require correspondingly sophisticated dispute settlement institutions.[62] The increase in the number of international agreements dealing with a specialized subject-matter, such as the protection of human rights, international economic law, international investment law, and the protection of the international environment, have resulted in the need for specialized dispute settlement arrangements. These specialized tribunals have been established due to 'the functional needs and special features of the legal regime in question',[63] and also due to the realization that the ICJ was unsuitable for the resolution of all types of disputes in these specialized areas.[64]

III. Proliferation and Fragmentation

A. International Law as an '"Anarchical" Domain'?

Proliferation can have both positive and negative implications for the international legal order. It may be regarded as a positive development because it signifies a trend towards the peaceful settlement of disputes in international relations by means of adjudication, in preference to the resort to non-peaceful means of regulating differences, such as the threat or use of force. Yet it has not come without complications. The growth in the number of international courts has occurred in the absence of an overarching framework within which the international judicial bodies operate. This was observed by the ICTY Appeals Chamber in its famous dictum in *Prosecutor v Tadic*, to which reference has already been made:

> International law, because it lacks a centralised structure, does not provide for an integrated judicial system operating an orderly division of labour among a number of tribunals, where certain aspects or components of jurisdiction as a power could be centralised or vested in one of them but not the others. In international law, every tribunal is a self-contained system (unless otherwise provided).[65]

61 See generally Thomas Franck, 'Legitimacy in the International System' (1988) 82 *AJIL* 705.

62 Shany, above n 10, 3; Sands, Mackenzie and Shany (eds), above n 10, xxviii–xxx.

63 Rao, above n 10, 946.

64 Shany, above n 10, 4.

65 *Prosecutor v Tadic* (Jurisdiction), (1996) 35 ILM 32, 39; see also the comment of the ECHR in *Loizidou v Turkey* (1995) 20 EHRR 99, 133: '[t]he International Court is a free-standing international tribunal which has no links to a standard-setting treaty such as the Convention.'

Proliferation has served to highlight this decentralized nature of the international legal order. Writers have criticized the existence of international law not as a coherent legal system but as an '"anarchical" domain' consisting of a set of unconnected self-contained regimes.[66] Writers point in particular to the differences that exist between the international legal order and domestic legal systems.[67] These include the absence of a hierarchical normative structure;[68] the 'horizontal' relationship that exists between the primary law-makers and the subjects of international law, which are states;[69] the absence of a supreme legislator; and the lack of a centralized court of appeal.[70] Any appellate structures which exist in international judicial bodies form part of those same 'self-contained systems',[71] and there are today no formal institutional linkages between international courts. The ICJ is the 'principal judicial organ' of the UN, but there is no formalized procedure enabling it to answer questions of international law referred to it by other international tribunals, despite this having been suggested by writers,[72] and, indeed, successive Presidents of the ICJ.[73] Although article 87 of the ICJ Rules contemplates questions of international law arising in dispute settlement proceedings before other international bodies being brought before the ICJ, the ICJ can only take jurisdiction over such preliminary reference questions if it is referred under a treaty or convention in force, such as a special agreement between the parties; the other international court cannot refer a question *proprio motu*.[74] Another possibility is for an international court to suggest that the UN General Assembly ('GA'), the UN Security Council ('SC') or another 'authorized body' request the ICJ for an advisory opinion on a point of international law,[75] but it is doubted whether such an unwieldy and cumbersome procedure would be utilized.

[66] Michel van de Kerchove and François Ost, *Legal System between Order and Disorder* (1994) 68; see also Jean Combacau, 'Le Droit International: Bric-à-Brac ou Système?' (1986) 31 *Archives de Philosophie du Droit* 85, 90; and discussion in Shany, above n 10, 95.

[67] See, e.g. the discussion in Shany, ibid 94–9. [68] Ibid 94–6. [69] Ibid 96–7.

[70] Ibid 97–8.

[71] For example, the possibility of appealing WTO panel reports to the WTO Appellate Body, and the existence of the ICTY and ICTR Appeals Chamber.

[72] Jonathan Charney, 'The Impact on the International Legal System of the Growth of International Courts and Tribunals' (1999) 31 *New York University Journal of International Law and Politics* 697, 698–9; Georges Abi-Saab, 'Fragmentation or Unification: Some Concluding Remarks' (1999) 31 *New York University Journal of International Law and Politics* 919, 929–30; Charney, 'Is International Law Threatened?', above n 10, 126–31, 134, 373.

[73] For example, Gilbert Guillaume, 'The Current Situation of the International Court of Justice and its Future' (Address to the Lauterpacht Research Centre for International Law, University of Cambridge, 9 November 2001) 14, available at <http://lcil.cam.ac.uk/lectures/lecture_papers.php> (last visited 25 November 2006); Gilbert Guillaume, 'Speech to the General Assembly of the United Nations' (30 October 2001) 5, available at <http://www.icj-cij.org> under 'Statements of the President of the Court' (last visited 25 November 2006); Guillaume, 'The Proliferation of International Judicial Bodies' above n 10, 6–7; Stephen Schwebel, 'Address to the Plenary Session of the General Assembly of the United Nations' (26 October 1999) 4, available at <http://www.icj-cij.org> under 'Statements of the President of the Court' (last visited 25 November 2006).

[74] ICJ Rules, art 87.

[75] Guillaume, 'Current Situation of the ICJ', above n 73, 14; Guillaume, 'The Proliferation of International Judicial Bodies', above n 10, 6–7.

In light of these criticisms and potential problems, proliferation raises the question of whether the multitude of international courts merely exist as self-contained regimes, as suggested by the ICTY Appeals Chamber, or, rather, whether they form an informal 'system' or 'community' of courts. In the absence of formal institutional links, it is in the jurisprudence of international courts and tribunals that the answers to these questions might be found. If international courts have applied rules of international law consistently, and in doing so, have referred to the practice of other international tribunals, this may suggest that international courts do not consider themselves as operating in isolation from each other, but do operate within a framework where some regard—perhaps in the form of an international judicial 'comity'—is had for the practice and jurisprudence of other international judicial bodies.

B. Proliferation as a Cause of Jurisdictional Competition and Fragmentation

It has already been noted that proliferation has taken place in the context of concerns regarding the 'fragmentation' of international law. The multiplicity of international courts has arguably had an exacerbating effect on the threats to the unity and integrity of international law. With the increasing number of international tribunals which do not form part of a structural hierarchy, the likelihood exists that international courts will reach inconsistent decisions; this has heightened concerns among international legal scholars and practitioners anxious to curb the effect of proliferation on 'fragmentation'.[76] Yet the problem of fragmentation is not linked solely to the possibility of inconsistent decisions by international courts. Rather, several possible causes of the threat to the unity of international law can be identified, as can be seen from the report of Professor Hafner, who prepared an initial study on fragmentation for consideration by the ILC in 2000.[77] One cause noted by Professor Hafner is the emergence of specialized areas of international legal regulation, which could lead to 'topic autonomy'.[78] This

[76] See, e.g., Martti Koskenniemi and Paivi Leino, 'Fragmentation of International Law? Postmodern Anxieties' (2002) 15 *Leiden Journal of International Law* 553; Gilbert Guillaume, 'Statement of the President of the Court to the UN General Assembly' (26 October 2000), available at <http://www.icj-cij.org> under 'Statements of the President of the Court' (last visited 25 November 2006); Sir Robert Jennings, 'The Role of the International Court of Justice' (1997) 68 *British Yearbook of International Law* 1, 60; Guillaume, 'The Future of International Judicial Institutions', above n 10; Shigeru Oda, 'The International Court of Justice Viewed from the Bench (1976–93)' (1993) 244 *Recueil des cours* 12, 153–4.

[77] Gerhard Hafner, 'Risks Ensuing from the Fragmentation of International Law', *Official Records of the General Assembly, Fifty-fifth Session*, Supplement No 10, 321 (UN Doc A/55/10); a revised version of this study has been published as Gerhard Hafner, 'Pros and Cons Ensuing from Fragmentation of International Law' (2004) 25 *Michigan Journal of International Law* 849.

[78] Hafner, 'Risks Ensuing from the Fragmentation of International Law', ibid, 326.

problematic feature of the modern international legal order was observed by Professor Brownlie in 1988, who commented on:

> the tendency to fragmentation of law which characterises the enthusiastic legal literature. The assumption is made that there are discrete subjects, such as 'international human rights law' or an 'international law on development'. As a consequence the quality and coherence of international law as a whole is threatened.[79]

Professor Hafner also identified another cause of fragmentation as lying in international law's recognition of 'three different legal structures' of norms; these are reciprocal norms of a synallagmatic nature, such as bilateral obligations; international obligations owed by states towards individuals; and obligations owed to 'the community of states participating in a given legal system'.[80] Further causes of fragmentation could be found in 'the parallel regulation on the universal or regional level relating to the same subject matter'; and also 'the elaboration of different legal regimes in different international negotiating bodies, both addressing the same group of states'.[81] At a more general level, Professor Hafner noted that fragmentation was caused in part by 'the enlargement of the material scope of international law', in particular in the fields of human rights, international economic law, international trade law, and international environmental law.[82] Relatedly, he also observed the emergence of different regimes of 'secondary rules', such as remedies for breaches of international obligations in specialized sub-systems of international law.[83]

But the first—and perhaps the primary—cause cited by Professor Hafner for fragmentation was 'the lack of centralised institutions which would ensure homogeneity and conformity of legal regulations'.[84] This absence of a specialized authority to which decisions of international courts and tribunals could be appealed, such as an international 'supreme court', lies at the heart of the problems engendered by proliferation.

[79] Ian Brownlie, 'The Rights of Peoples in Modern International Law', in James Crawford (ed), *The Rights of Peoples* (1988) 1, 15; see also Ian Brownlie, 'Problems Concerning the Unity of International Law', in *Le droit international à l'heure de sa codification: Études en l'honneur de Roberto Ago* (1987) vol I, 153.

[80] Hafner, 'Risks Ensuing from the Fragmentation of International Law', above n 77, 326–7; to this list might be added international obligations *erga omnes*: *Barcelona Traction* [1970] ICJ Rep 3, 32; see especially Christian Tams, *Enforcing Obligations* Erga Omnes *in International Law* (2005).

[81] Hafner, ibid, 328.

[82] Ibid 329, referring to Pierre-Marie Dupuy, 'The Danger of Fragmentation or Unification of the International Legal System and the International Court of Justice' (1999) 31 *New York University Journal of International Law and Politics* 791, 795.

[83] Hafner, ibid, 330; see, e.g., the possibility of compartmentalization of various international legal categories in *Tehran Hostages*, where the ICJ held that the rules of diplomatic law relating to the conduct of diplomatic and consular officials, and, in particular, the right of the receiving state to designate diplomatic officials as *persona non grata*, constituted 'a self-contained regime': *US Diplomatic and Consular Staff in Tehran (US v Iran) (Merits)* [1980] ICJ Rep 3, 40; see further Bruno Simma, 'Self-Contained Regimes' (1985) 16 *Netherlands Yearbook of International Law* 111, 112–3.

[84] Hafner, 'Risks Ensuing from the Fragmentation of International Law', above n 77, 326.

Concerns about the negative effects of proliferation and its threat to the unity of international law were expressed by the former President of the ICJ, Judge Gilbert Guillaume, in his extrajudicial writings in 1995.[85] This issue was taken up by the then President of the ICJ, Judge Stephen Schwebel, in his address to the General Assembly in 1998, where he recognized that the ICJ was not 'a supreme court of appeal from other international judicial bodies, and still less a court of appeal from national courts', and that 'proliferation risks conflict'.[86] Judge Schwebel raised this issue again in his annual address to the General Assembly in 1999;[87] and it was raised again in 2000 and 2001 by Judge Guillaume when he assumed the presidency of the ICJ.[88] It is noteworthy that concerns arising out of the creation of new international courts are not novel; the former American PCIJ judge, Manley Hudson, appreciated these dangers as early as 1944, when he opposed a suggestion that an 'Inter-American Court of International Justice' be constituted, for he wanted to avoid 'the danger of a particularistic development of international law'.[89] Hudson argued that:

> in the field of adjudication . . . it is important to safeguard the primacy of the general international law, to protect the universality of its application, and to assure uniformity in its administration.[90]

In this connection, it should be noted that it was never envisaged, even at the time of the creation of the PCIJ, that there would only be one international tribunal to which interstate disputes could be referred. Indeed, the PCIJ operated in tandem with ad hoc arbitration tribunals constituted under the auspices of the PCA, and on an ad hoc basis, and this continued with the creation of the ICJ in 1945. But it is the multiplicity of international courts with similar—and even overlapping—jurisdictions that has given rise to concerns.[91] There are, in fact, two principal problematic effects of the disparate nature of the multitude of international judicial bodies: the first is that proliferation has created overlapping jurisdictions among international tribunals; and the second is that different international courts can come to conflicting decisions, thus arguably exacerbating 'fragmentation'. These will now briefly be considered.

[85] Guillaume, 'The Future of International Judicial Institutions', above n 10, 849.

[86] Stephen Schwebel, 'Address to the General Assembly of the United Nations' (27 October 1998) 2, 4, available at <http://www.icj-cij.org> under 'Statements of the President of the Court' (last visited 25 November 2006).

[87] Schwebel, 'Address to the Plenary Session of the General Assembly', above n 73, 3–4.

[88] Guillaume, 'Statement to the United Nations General Assembly', above n 76, 5–6; see also Guillaume, 'The Proliferation of International Judicial Bodies', above n 10; Guillaume, 'Speech to the General Assembly of the United Nations', above n 73, 5; Gilbert Guillaume, 'Speech to the Sixth Committee of the General Assembly of the United Nations' (31 October 2001), all available at <http://www.icj-cij.org> under 'Statements of the President of the Court' (last visited 25 November 2006).

[89] Manley Hudson, *International Tribunals: Past and Future* (1944) 179.

[90] Ibid.

[91] Rosenne, above n 10, vol I, 32–5.

1. *Overlapping Jurisdictions of International Courts*

The creation of overlapping jurisdictions can be problematic because general international law lacks clear rules of coordination for the resolution of jurisdictional conflicts between different international tribunals.[92] This can give rise to one dispute being referred to more than one international court, and this has already occurred on several occasions.[93] The *Southern Bluefin Tuna* dispute between Australia/New Zealand and Japan could have been submitted to any of three fora: the ICJ, as all parties had made optional clause declarations; a dispute settlement body under UNCLOS, such as the ITLOS or an arbitral tribunal established under Annex VII of UNCLOS, or an arbitral tribunal established under a regional convention, the Convention for the Conservation of Southern Bluefin Tuna.[94] Australia and New Zealand ultimately made a request for provisional measures to the ITLOS, and the dispute was then referred to an UNCLOS tribunal.[95] The *Swordfish* dispute between Spain and Chile, which concerned Chile's refusal to permit Spanish vessels to tranship their catch of protected swordfish in Chilean ports, was simultaneously referred both to a panel of the WTO (by the EC),[96] and to a Special Chamber of the ITLOS (by Chile).[97] The parties to the dispute have agreed to a provisional settlement, thus avoiding, to date, a jurisdictional ruling by either of the tribunals.[98] In addition, the *MOX Plant* dispute

[92] See especially Shany, above n 10; Vaughan Lowe, 'Overlapping Jurisdiction in International Tribunals' (1999) 20 *Australian Yearbook of International Law* 191.

[93] Brown, 'The Proliferation of International Courts and Tribunals', above n 10, 465–70.

[94] Opened for signature 10 May 1993, 1819 UNTS 359 (entered into force 20 May 1994). On the different fora available to Australia and New Zealand in the *Southern Bluefin Tuna* case, see especially Cesare Romano, 'The Southern Bluefin Tuna Dispute: Hints of a World to Come . . . Like It or Not' (2001) *Ocean Development & International Law* 313.

[95] *Southern Bluefin Tuna (Australia and New Zealand v Japan) (Provisional Measures)* (1999) 38 ILM 1624; *Southern Bluefin Tuna (Australia and New Zealand v Japan) (Jurisdiction and Admissibility)* (2000) 39 ILM 1359.

[96] *Chile—Measures Affecting the Transit and Importation of Swordfish*, WT/DS193/2, available at <http://www.wto.org> under 'Disputes' (last visited 25 November 2006).

[97] *Conservation and Sustainable Exploitation of Swordfish Stocks in the South-Eastern Pacific Ocean (Chile v European Community)*, ITLOS Case No 7, <http://www.itlos.org> under 'Proceedings and Judgments' (last visited 25 November 2006).

[98] *Chile—Measures Affecting the Transit and Importation of Swordfish*, WT/DS193/3, (Arrangement between EC and Chile, 6 April 2001); see also the parties' agreement to maintain the suspension of the process for the constitution of the WTO panel, at WT/DS193/3/Add.2 (17 November 2003) and WT/DS193/3/Add.3 (22 December 2005), available at <http://www.wto.org> under 'Disputes' (last visited 25 November 2006); and *Conservation and Sustainable Exploitation of Swordfish Stocks in the South-Eastern Pacific Ocean (Chile v European Community)* (ITLOS Order of 15 March 2001); see also the ITLOS's Orders reflecting the parties' agreement to maintain the suspension of proceedings: Order of 16 December 2003, and Order of 29 December 2005, available at <http://www.itlos.org> under 'Proceedings and Judgments' (last visited 25 November 2006). On this dispute, see Marcos Orellana, 'The Swordfish Dispute between the EU and Chile at the ITLOS and the WTO' (2002) 71 *Nordic Journal of International Law* 55; Andrew Serdy, 'See You in Port: Australia and New Zealand as Third Parties in the Dispute between Chile and the European Community over Chile's Denial of Port Access to Spanish Vessels Fishing for Swordfish on the High Seas' (2002) 3 *Melbourne Journal of International Law* 79.

between Ireland and the United Kingdom has been the subject of decisions by the ITLOS,[99] a PCA tribunal,[100] an UNCLOS tribunal,[101] and the ECJ, which, in its judgment of 30 May 2006, held that Ireland had breached its obligation under article 292 of the EC Treaty by bringing proceedings against the United Kingdom under the framework of UNCLOS, rather than before the ECJ.[102] Article 292 of the EC Treaty requires Member States not to submit disputes concerning the interpretation or application of that treaty to any method of settlement 'other than those provided for therein'; this is one of the few exceptions to the absence of rules of jurisdictional coordination in international law.[103]

The difficulty with more than one court being seised of the same dispute is that general international law does not provide for any jurisdiction-regulating rules, such as litispendence, or *forum non conveniens*, and this means that it is difficult to resolve such issues before the different international tribunals proceed to render possibly inconsistent judgments, unless there is a clearly agreed treaty rule, such as article 292 of the EC Treaty.[104] It appears that in the absence of such rules, it is through judicial restraint and comity that such problems might be avoided.[105]

A further issue is that the availability of multiple courts tends to encourage the practice of forum shopping.[106] It should be stressed that forum shopping need not be a problem in itself; it does become an issue, however, if more than one court becomes seised of the same dispute and those courts issue inconsistent decisions.[107]

2. *Doctrinal Inconsistencies in the Jurisprudence of International Courts*

The second problematic effect of proliferation is that different international tribunals may be seised of disputes concerning the same legal issues, and might render

[99] *MOX Plant* (*Ireland v UK*) (*Provisional Measures*) (2002) 41 ILM 405.

[100] *Access to Information under Article 9 of the OSPAR Convention* (*Ireland v UK*) (2003) 42 ILM 1118.

[101] *MOX Plant* (*Ireland v UK*) (Procedural Order No 3) (2003) 42 ILM 1187; see generally Robin Churchill and Joanne Scott, 'The *MOX Plant* Litigation: The First Half-Life' (2004) 53 *ICLQ* 643.

[102] *Commission v Ireland* (Case C–459/03), Judgment of 30 May 2006, paras 120–39 (ECJ, 2006); see also para 61 (Op A-G Poiares Maduro) (18 January 2006), available at <http://www.curia.europa.eu > under 'Case Law' (last visited 25 November 2006).

[103] See especially Shany, above n 10, 180–3, 226–8.

[104] Professor Lowe has argued that while it is arguable that the doctrines of *res judicata*, *lis alibi pendens* and abuse of process might be applied as jurisdiction-regulating rules, there is little evidence of a doctrine of *forum non conveniens* in international law: Lowe, above n 92, 198–203; Professor Shany also concluded that there is little evidence of any generally applicable principles on choice of forum in public international law: Shany, above n 10, 269–71.

[105] See, e.g. Buergenthal, above n 10, 274–5; Charney, 'Is International Law Threatened?', above n 10, 371–3; Shany, above n 10, 278–81. Such judicial restraint was demonstrated, for instance, by the UNCLOS tribunal in *MOX Plant*, above n 101, 1191, and by the ICSID tribunal in *SPP v Egypt*, 3 ICSID Rep 112, 129–30 (1985); see further below, chapter 8.

[106] Shany, above n 10, 10; Guillaume, 'The Current Situation of the ICJ', above n 73, 11–14; Guillaume, 'The Proliferation of International Judicial Bodies', above n 10, 3; Tullio Treves, 'Conflicts between the International Tribunal for the Law of the Sea and the International Court of Justice' (1999) 31 *New York University Journal of International Law and Politics* 809, 811; Laurence Helfer, 'Forum Shopping for Human Rights' (1999) 148 *University of Pennsylvania Law Review* 285, 290–6, 304–40.

[107] See, e.g., Shany, above n 10, 133–4.

conflicting decisions. Several such instances can be found.[108] The most well-known is the ICTY Appeals Chamber's judgment in *Prosecutor v Tadic*, where it expressly disregarded ICJ jurisprudence on an aspect of the law of state responsibility.[109] At issue was whether the acts of the accused, Dusko Tadic, could be attributed to the Federal Republic of Yugoslavia. The responsibility of states for the acts of private individuals had previously been the subject of judicial consideration by the ICJ. In *Nicaragua*, the ICJ had held that the US could not be held responsible for acts committed by the *Contras* in Nicaragua unless it had exercised 'effective control of the military or paramilitary operations in the course of which the alleged violations were committed'.[110] In *Tadic*, the ICTY Appeals Chamber disagreed with the ICJ's approach.[111] The Appeals Chamber failed to see 'why in each and every circumstance international law should require a high threshold for the test of control'.[112] It distinguished between:

> the situation of individuals acting on behalf of a State without specific instructions, . . . [and] that of individuals making up *an organised and hierarchically structured group*, such as a military unit, or, in case of war or civil strife, armed bands or irregulars or rebels.[113]

The Appeals Chamber summarized its position by stating that international law did not always require 'the same degree of control over armed groups or private individuals for the purpose of determining whether an individual not having the status of a State official under internal legislation can be regarded as a *de facto* organ of the State'.[114] Rather, the extent of the required degree of control varied. Where the acts of a private individual were at issue, the Appeals Chamber held that 'specific instructions concerning the commission of that particular act' were required in order to establish state responsibility; this conformed with the ICJ's approach in *Nicaragua*.[115] In contrast, where attribution was sought for the acts of 'subordinate *armed forces or militias or paramilitary units*', the requirement was that the state's control be of 'an overall character'; this degree of control did not require the issuing of specific orders.[116]

[108] See, e.g., ibid 112–13; Brown, above n 10, 460–4; Guillaume, 'The Current Situation of the ICJ', above n 73, 11–14; see also Charney, 'Is International Law Threatened?', above n 10.

[109] (1999) 38 ILM 1518.

[110] *Military and Paramilitary Activities in and against Nicaragua (Nicaragua v US) (Merits)* [1986] ICJ Rep 14, 65.

[111] Above n 109, 1540–5; see especially Koskenniemi and Leino, above n 76, 562–7.

[112] *Tadic*, ibid, 1541.

[113] Ibid (emphasis in original).

[114] Ibid, 1544.

[115] Ibid, 1544–5.

[116] Ibid. See Rosenne, above n 10, vol I, 36, who observes that the ICTY Appeals Chamber's disregard of the ICJ's judgment in *Nicaragua* 'has since to some extent been corrected', referring to the ICTY Appeals Chambers' statements in *Prosecutor v Delalic* (Judgment of 20 February 2001), para 24; and *Prosecutor v Kvocka* (Decision on Interlocutory Appeal by the Accused Zoran Zigic of 25 May 2001), paras 16–18 (ICTY, 2001), both available at <http://www.un.org/icty/> (last visited 25 November 2006). Note: *Delalic* is available under the name *Prosecutor v Mucic* et al ('Celibici') (IT–96–21). See also the ICJ's judgment in *Application of the Genocide Convention (Bosnia and Herzegovina v Serbia and Montenegro) (Merits)* (ICJ Judgment of 26 February 2007), paras 396–407, where the Court did not follow the ICTY Appeals Chamber's decision in *Prosecutor v Tadic*.

Another issue on which divergent approaches can be found is the permissibility of reservations to treaties. In *Reservations to the Convention on the Prevention and Punishment of the Crime of Genocide*, the ICJ held that a state making a reservation to the Genocide Convention could still be considered a party to the convention, so long as the reservation was compatible with its 'object and purpose'.[117] As was observed by Judges Higgins, Kooijmans, Elaraby, Owada and Simma in their Joint Separate Opinion in *Armed Activities on the Territory of the Congo (New Application: 2002)*, the ECHR and the IACHR 'have not followed the "laissez-faire" approach attributed to the International Court's Advisory Opinion of 1951'.[118] One instance of this can be found in *Loizidou v Turkey*, in which the ECHR was faced with the question whether a condition could be attached to a declaration accepting its compulsory jurisdiction which had the effect of restricting the territorial scope of that acceptance.[119] Turkey argued that article 36(3) of the ICJ Statute, on which the relevant provisions of the European HR Convention were based, permitted 'the attachment of substantive, territorial and temporal restrictions to the optional recognition of the [ICJ's] jurisdictional competence'.[120] However, the ECHR decided that the practice of the ICJ 'afforded no assistance in the present case because of the substantial differences between the two systems'.[121] It held that the ICJ was 'a free-standing international tribunal which has no links to a standard-setting treaty such as the Convention',[122] and that the ICJ's jurisdiction was general, and not limited 'to direct supervisory functions in respect of a law-making treaty such as the Convention'.[123] It concluded that the territorial restrictions attached to Turkey's declaration were invalid.[124]

These are not the only instances of divergent jurisprudence; others have also arisen,[125] such as the use of advisory proceedings in order to bring an interstate dispute before an international tribunal;[126] the margin of discretion accorded to

[117] [1951] ICJ Rep 15, 24; see also, generally, Catherine Redgwell, 'Universality or Integrity? Some Reflections on Reservations to General Multilateral Treaties' (1993) 64 *British Yearbook of International Law* 245. See also *Armed Activities on the Territory of the Congo (New Application: 2002) (DRC v Rwanda)* (Judgment of 3 February 2006), paras 64–70, where the ICJ held that it could not conclude that Rwanda's reservation to article IX of the Genocide Convention was incompatible with the convention's object and purpose (*Convention on the Prevention and Punishment of the Crime of Genocide*, opened for signature 9 December 1948, 78 UNTS 277, entered into force 12 January 1951). See, however, paras 11–29 (Diss Op Koroma); paras 1–29 (Joint Sep Op Higgins, Kooijmans, Elaraby, Owada and Simma), available at <http://www.icj-cij.org> under 'Decisions' (last visited 31 December 2006).

[118] *Armed Activities* (*New Application: 2002*), ibid, para 15 (Joint Sep Op Higgins, Kooijmans, Elaraby, Owada and Simma). For the suggestion that the ICJ's advisory opinion of 1951 should not be read in such a '*laissez-faire*' manner, see ibid, paras 4–13.

[119] Above n 65.

[120] Ibid, 132.

[121] Ibid, 132–3.

[122] Ibid, 133.

[123] Ibid, 136; see also Koskenniemi and Leino, above n 76, 567–70.

[124] Above n 65, 137.

[125] See, e.g., Shany, above n 10, 123–4; Brown, above n 10, 460–4; see also, in particular, Charney, 'The Impact of the Growth of International Courts and Tribunals', above n 72; and Charney, 'Is International Law Threatened', above n 10.

[126] *Status of Eastern Carelia* (*Advisory Opinion*), Ser B, (No 5), 28–9 (PCIJ, 1923); see also *The Right to Information on Consular Assistance in the Framework of the Guarantees of the Due Process of Law* (*Advisory Opinion*), Ser A, No 16, para 61 (IACHR, 1999).

authorities of an expropriating state in determining the level of compensation;[127] and the application of the rule of 'proportionality' in continental shelf delimitation cases.[128] Yet despite some instances of doctrinal inconsistencies, by and large international courts have applied international law relatively consistently. In his extensive review of the case law of a number of different international courts on a variety of different issues, Professor Charney concluded that on those issues, 'the different international tribunals do share a coherent understanding of that law', although he conceded that '[t]he increasing number of international law tribunals without a fully effective hierarchical system makes complete uniformity of decisions impossible'.[129] If, in the words of Professor Charney, international courts and tribunals also share a 'coherent understanding' on issues of procedure and remedies, this might lend weight to the suggestion that the threat to the unity of international law posed by proliferation is minimal, and it might also suggest the existence of informal systemic links between international courts.

C. The International Law Commission's Consideration of Fragmentation

In the ILC's consideration of fragmentation, which was included in its long-term programme of work under the title 'Fragmentation of International Law: Difficulties Arising from the Diversification and Expansion of International Law', the ILC Study Group, chaired by Professor Martti Koskenniemi, has undertaken the task of producing 'critical analyses of the experience of fragmentation in various international organs and institutions'.[130] The ILC Study Group aimed to 'yield an outcome that will be helpful in providing resources for judges and administrators coping with questions such as conflicting or overlapping obligations emerging from different legal sources.'[131] Although the ILC Study Group recognized that fragmentation gives rise to both 'institutional and substantive problems', it chose not to address the institutional issues, which 'have to do with the jurisdiction

[127] *Lithgow v UK* (1986) 8 EHRR 329, 372–3; but see *SEDCO Inc v NIOC* (1986) 10 Ir–USCTR 180, 187; cited in Shany, above n 10, 124.

[128] *Continental Shelf* (*Tunisia/Libya*) [1982] ICJ Rep 18, 61–76, 91; but see *Delimitation of the Continental Shelf*, 54 ILR 6, 67–8, (UK–France, 1977), referred to in Charney, 'Is International Law Threatened?', above n 10, 331–2.

[129] Charney, ibid, 347.

[130] ILC, 'Report of the Study Group on Fragmentation of International Law: Difficulties arising from the Diversification and Expansion of International Law', UN Doc A/CN.4/L.676, para 7 (29 July 2005) ('Report of the Study Group 2005'); ILC, 'Report of the Study Group on Fragmentation of International Law: Difficulties arising from the Diversification and Expansion of International Law', UN Doc A/CN.4/L.682 (4 April 2006) ('Consolidated Report 2006'); see also ILC, 'Fragmentation of International Law: Difficulties arising from the Diversification and Expansion of International Law', in ILC, *Report of the International Law Commission: Fifty-eighth Session (1 May–9 June and 3 July–11 August 2006)*, UNGAOR Sixty-first Session, Supplement No 10 (UN Doc A/61/10); available at <http://www.un.org> under 'International Law > International Law Commission' (last visited 25 November 2006).

[131] ILC, 'Report of the Study Group 2005', ibid, para 7.

and competence of various institutions applying international legal rules and their hierarchical relations *inter se*', as this issue was, in the view of the ILC, 'best dealt with by the institutions themselves'.[132] The approach adopted by the ILC Study Group has been to focus on the substantive aspects of fragmentation; the justification for this is the fact that 'although fragmentation is inevitable, it is desirable to have a framework through which it may be assessed and managed'.[133] The ILC Study Group considered that such a framework may be found in the Vienna Convention on the Law of Treaties,[134] and the ILC Study Group examined several aspects of the law of treaties that are relevant to the problem of fragmentation. As summarized in the ILC's *Report of its Fifty-eighth Session* in 2006, these aspects include the function and scope of the *lex specialis* rule;[135] the question of 'self-contained regimes';[136] the operation of article 31(3)(c) of the VCLT;[137] the application of successive treaties relating to the same subject matter;[138] and the question of hierarchy in international law: *jus cogens*, obligations *erga omnes*, and article 103 of the UN Charter as conflict rules.[139]

The work of the ILC Study Group, in particular its consideration of the operation of article 31(3)(c) of the VCLT, is relevant to an examination of the ways in which international courts can harmonize their approaches to the interpretation of their statutes and rules of procedure, the tools which international tribunals can employ to have regard to the practice of other international courts and tribunals, and how international courts can act when faced with procedural issues for which their constitutive instruments make no provision. These methods, which might foster the emergence of a common law of international adjudication, are considered in chapter 2.

Conclusion

This chapter has laid the foundations for the examination in subsequent chapters into the existence of a common law of international adjudication. It has described the proliferation of international courts and tribunals, which has occurred in the

[132] ILC, 'Consolidated Report 2006', above n 130, para 13; see also Rosalyn Higgins, 'A Babel of Judicial Voices? Ruminations from the Bench' (2006) 55 *ICLQ* 791, 800.

[133] ILC, 'Report, 58th Session', above n 130, para 249.

[134] *Vienna Convention on the Law of Treaties*, opened for signature 23 May 1969, 1155 UNTS 311 (entered into force 27 January 1980) ('VCLT').

[135] ILC, 'Report, 58th Session', above n 130, para 251(5)–(10).

[136] Ibid, para 251(11)–(16).

[137] Ibid, para 251(17)–(23). The ILC's work on article 31(3)(c) of the VCLT has been based on a paper prepared by William Mansfield, the New Zealand member of the ILC, which is discussed in Campbell McLachlan, 'The Principle of Systemic Integration and Article 31(3)(c) of the Vienna Convention' (2005) 54 *ICLQ* 279.

[138] ILC, 'Report, 58th Session', above n 130, para 251(24)–(30).

[139] Ibid, para 251(31)–(42).

absence of any formal institutional linkages or hierarchical system, and which has taken place in the context of concerns over the 'fragmentation' of international law. It has also noted that this proliferation has contributed to the creation of overlapping jurisdictions among international courts, and has, at times, also led to the rendering of conflicting decisions. Yet in spite of this, later chapters of this book will look at the existence of certain common features among these 'fragmented' and 'self-contained' regimes on certain aspects of the adjudication process. Before turning to these discrete issues, chapter 2 examines the sources of norms concerning procedure and remedies applied by international courts, examines what scope international courts have to interpret the provisions of their statutes and rules consistently with the practice of other international courts, and also considers the extent of the powers of international courts over procedure and remedies.

2

Methods Used by International Courts and Tribunals to Engage in Cross-Fertilization

Introduction

This chapter inquires into the procedural and remedial powers exercised by international courts, and the methods available to international courts to engage in the process of cross-fertilization on issues of procedure and remedies. This inquiry is relevant, as the sources of the rules relating to procedure and remedies—and the way that they are interpreted and applied—play a large role in determining the existence of a common law of international adjudication. The primary source of rules can be found in the statutes and rules of procedure of international courts, but these instruments do not make exhaustive provision for the myriad issues that may arise in the course of international judicial or arbitral proceedings. In interpreting and applying the provisions in their constitutive instruments, international courts can adopt a number of methods which enable them to have recourse to the practice of other international tribunals. These include various principles of treaty interpretation; the application of customary rules, rules developed in international judicial practice, and 'general principles of law'; and the exercise of inherent powers concerning procedure and remedies. In identifying these methods, this chapter addresses a number of points which are common to the more specific issues addressed in later chapters.

I. Sources of Law Relating to Procedure and Remedies

In the past, writers have expressed uncertainty about the sources of procedural law applicable before international courts.[1] According to article 38(1) of the ICJ Statute, the sources of international law applicable to proceedings before the ICJ are treaties, customary international law, general principles of law, and as a subsidiary source of law, judicial decisions and the teachings of the most highly qualified publicists.[2] Formally, this list of sources only applies to the ICJ, but it is widely regarded as having general application,[3] and it has been accepted by other

[1] For example, Hugh Thirlway, 'Procedural Law and the International Court of Justice' in Vaughan Lowe and Malgosia Fitzmaurice (eds), *Fifty Years of the International Court of Justice* (1996) 389, 389; Hugh Thirlway, 'Procedure of International Courts and Tribunals', in Rudolf Bernhardt (ed), *Encyclopedia of Public International Law* (1992) vol III, 1128, 1128.

[2] *Statute of the International Court of Justice*, opened for signature 26 June 1945, 3 Bevans 1153 (entered into force 24 October 1945), art 38(1).

[3] See, for example, Malcolm Shaw, *International Law* (5th ed, 2003) 66–7; Ian Brownlie, *Principles of Public International Law* (6th ed, 2003) 4–5; Christoph Schreuer, *The ICSID Convention: A Commentary* (2001) 609–10, 614–16; Lorand Bartels, 'Applicable Law in WTO Dispute Settlement Proceedings' (2001) 35 *Journal of World Trade Law* 499, 501–2, 504; David Palmeter and Petros Mavroidis, *Dispute Settlement in the World Trade Organisation* (1999) 35–7; David Palmeter and Petros Mavroidis, 'The WTO Legal System: Sources of Law' (1998) 92 *AJIL* 398, 398–9 (but see Gabrielle Marceau, 'A Call for Coherence in International Law' (1999) 33(5)

international tribunals.[4] These are not only the sources of substantive international law, but also the sources of procedural law obtaining before international courts. As has been observed by Shabtai Rosenne, international law makes 'no sharp distinction' between substantive law and procedural law.[5] Thus, if customary international law, general principles of law, judicial decisions and writings of publicists are sources of the substantive rules of international law, there is no reason why they might not also serve as a source of the procedural rules of international law, including those relating to the competences of international tribunals.[6] For although the norms which govern the relations of the parties to the international courts 'nominally have a conventional origin', as Rosenne states:

> they have grown out of the law and practice of international arbitration, and in the course of the history of that institution much customary law has been generated by and some underlying principles have emerged from the practice of states and the accumulation of arbitral awards following a fairly consistent underlying pattern.[7]

The sources listed in article 38(1) of the ICJ Statute also serve as sources of the law relating to remedies.

As international courts are established by treaties or other international instruments, the primary source of law for the procedure and remedies applicable before such courts is the treaty or statute which brings that body into existence.

A. Constitutive Instruments of International Courts

International courts are the product of the express will of states, and there is an 'uncontroverted principle' that no state is obliged to submit a dispute with another

Journal of World Trade 87, 109–15); Sir Robert Jennings, *Collected Writings of Sir Robert Jennings* (1998) vol I, 6; Herman Mosler, 'General Principles of Law' in Rudolf Bernhardt (ed), *Encyclopedia of Public International Law* (1995) vol II, 511, 515; Michel Virally, 'The Sources of International Law' in Max Sørensen (ed), *Manual of Public International Law* (1968) 116, 121–2; J L Brierly, *The Law of Nations* (6th ed, 1963) 56; J L Simpson and Hazel Fox, *International Arbitration* (1959) 130–1; ILC, 'Report of the Commission to the General Assembly on the Work of its Tenth Session' [1958] *YbILC*, vol II, 78, 84, art 10, UN Doc A/3859; UN Secretary-General, *Survey of International Law in Relation to the Work of Codification of the International Law Commission* (1949) UN Doc A/CN.4/1/Rev.122; Sir John Fischer Williams, *Chapters on Current International Law and the League of Nations* (1929) 20–1.

4 See, e.g., *International Thunderbird Gaming Corporation v Mexico* (NAFTA Tribunal Award of 26 January 2006), para 90; *Methanex Corporation v US* (NAFTA Tribunal Award of 3 August 2005), Part II, Chapter B, paras 2–3; *Amco Asia Corporation v Indonesia*, 1 ICSID Rep 413, 491 (1984); *Klöckner Industrie—Anlagen GmbH v United Republic of Cameroon and Société Camerounaise des Engrais* (Annulment), 114 ILR 243, 268–72 (1985); UN Secretary-General, above n 3, 22; *Responsabilité de l'Allemagne à raison des dommages causés dans les colonies portugaises du Sud de l'Afrique*, 8 TAM 409, 413 (Portugal–Germany, 1928); see also *Mihaly International Corporation v Sri Lanka*, 17 *ICSID Review—FILJ* 142, 158 (2001).

5 Shabtai Rosenne, *The Law and Practice of the International Court, 1920–2005* (2006) vol III, 1021, 1023.

6 Ibid, 1024; see also Thirlway, 'Procedural Law', above n 1, 389–90; see, however, A Sereni, *Principi generali di diretto e processo internazionali* (1955).

7 Rosenne, *Law and Practice*, above n 5, vol III, 1028.

state to an international tribunal; this can only be done with the state's consent.[8] Just as consent is the essential basis of the jurisdiction of international tribunals to decide a dispute, consent is a source of the procedural powers of such bodies. This consent to the grant of procedural powers is manifested in the constitutive instrument or *compromis*, which usually confers certain powers on international courts. Many such examples can be found; a well-known power is the competence of each international court to determine the extent of its own jurisdiction. This power finds expression, for instance, in article 36(6) of the ICJ Statute, article 288(4) of UNCLOS, and article 41(1) of the ICSID Convention.[9] Other powers which are often expressly conferred by constitutive instruments include the power to grant provisional measures;[10] the power to permit the intervention of third parties;[11] the power to give an interpretation of judgments and awards, if there is a dispute as to its meaning or scope;[12] and the power to revise judgments and awards.[13]

B. Rules of Procedure of International Courts

Many constitutive instruments of international courts do not contain detailed provisions on the applicable procedure or the available remedies. In drafting the PCIJ Statute in 1920, for instance, the Advisory Committee of Jurists did not make any concerted effort to establish the PCIJ's procedure, but merely adopted a few general rules.[14] It recognized that the question of procedure should be left

[8] Rosenne, *Law and Practice* above n 5, vol II, 549–557; Brownlie, above n 3, 680–90; Alexander Orakhelashvili, 'The Concept of International Judicial Jurisdiction: A Reappraisal' (2003) 3 *Law and Practice of International Courts and Tribunals* 501, 501; Schreuer, above n 3, 191; Hugh Thirlway, 'The Law and Procedure of the International Court of Justice 1960–89: Part Nine' (1998) 69 *British Yearbook of International Law* 1, 4, 23–30; Sir Gerald Fitzmaurice, *The Law and Procedure of the International Court of Justice* (1986) 492–5; Sir Hersch Lauterpacht, *The Development of International Law by the International Court* (1958) 91–5; e.g. *East Timor* (*Portugal v Australia*) [1995] ICJ Rep 90, 101; *Continental Shelf (Tunisia/Libya) (Revision and Interpretation)* [1985] ICJ Rep 192, 216; *Corfu Channel (UK v Albania) (Preliminary Objections)* [1948] ICJ Rep 15, 27.

[9] See also 1899 Convention, art 48; 1907 Convention, art 73; European HR Convention, art 32(2).

[10] For example, ICJ Statute, art 41; UNCLOS, art 290; *Convention for the Settlement of Invesment Disputes between States and Nationals of Other States*, opened for signature 18 March 1965, 575 UNTS 159 (entered into force 14 October 1966) ('ICSID Convention'), art 47; *American Convention on Human Rights*, opened for signature 22 November 1969, 1144 UNTS 123 (entered into force 18 July 1978) ('American Convention'), art 63(2); EC Treaty, art 243; *Protocol on the Statute of the Court of Justice, Consolidated Version of the Treaty establishing the European Economic Community*, OJ C 325/33, 167 (24 December 2002) ('ECJ Statute'), art 36.

[11] ICJ Statute, arts 62–3; ITLOS Statute, arts 31–2; European HR Convention, art 36; ECJ Statute, art 37; *Understanding on Rules and Procedures Governing the Settlement of Disputes*, opened for signature 15 April 1994, 1869 UNTS 401, 33 ILM 1226 (entered into force 1 January 1995) ('DSU'), art 10(2).

[12] ICJ Statute, art 60; ITLOS Statute, article 33(3); ICSID Convention, article 50; American Convention, art 67; ECJ Statute, art 40.

[13] ICJ Statute, art 61; ICSID Convention, art 51; 1899 Convention, art 55; 1907 Convention, art 83; ECJ Statute, art 41.

[14] *Statute of the Permanent Court of International Justice*, PCIJ Publications, Ser D (No 1), 7; Antonio Sanchez de Bustamante, *The World Court* (1925) 220.

to the PCIJ itself, and that the court should be allowed a wide freedom in framing its rules.[15] Likewise, many statutes of international courts confer on such bodies an express power to frame rules of procedure,[16] and to make procedural orders for the conduct of the proceedings.[17] International courts have often exercised this power to expand their procedural powers appreciably. For instance, the provision concerning the power of international courts to carry out on-site inspections for the gathering of evidence is found in the ICJ Rules;[18] the ECHR's power to make practice directions is located within its Rules;[19] and the power of the ITLOS to give an interpretation of its judgments is found in the ITLOS Rules.[20]

This power to make rules of procedure is often expressly conferred on international courts by the constitutive instrument, but these rules generally do not need to be ratified by the states parties.[21] Accordingly, while the rules of procedure might be regarded as a source of procedural law which is ultimately derived from the consent of states, the states have in reality little control over their provisions, and it is the members of the international courts who determine the content of these instruments. The provisions contained in the rules of procedure thus represent a source of law which is only indirectly derived from the consent of states, and reflect the international court's conception of the rules and powers needed to carry out its functions. There is, however, one possible method for states to affect the content of the rules of procedure in individual cases: under the ICJ Rules and the ITLOS Rules, the parties to a dispute may jointly propose modifications to the rules,[22] and under the ICSID Convention, parties may agree to vary the arbitration rules.[23] This gives the parties some degree of control over the rules, should they require this; in the case of the ICJ and ITLOS, such modifications will be

[15] For example, Manley Hudson, *The Permanent Court of International Justice: A Treatise* (1934) 154, 258.

[16] ICJ Statute, art 30; ITLOS Statute, art 16; 1899 Convention, art 49; 1907 Convention, art 74; European HR Convention, art 26(d); American Convention, art 60; *Statute of the Inter-American Court of Human Rights*, Organization of American States Resolution (IX–79) ('IACHR Statute'), art 25; DSU, art 17(9); EC Treaty, art 245; ICTR Statute, art 14; ICTY Statute, art 15.

[17] ICJ Statute, art 48; ITLOS Statute, art 27; DSU, app 3, para 11; ICSID Convention, art 44; 1899 Convention, art 49; 1907 Convention, art 74; see generally Rosenne, *Law and Practice*, above n 5, vol II, 584–5.

[18] International Court of Justice Rules of Court, available at <http://www.icj-cij.org>, art 66.

[19] European Court of Human Rights, Rules of Court, available at <http://www.echr.coe.int>, Rule 32.

[20] ITLOS Rules of the Tribunal, available at <http://www.itlos.org>, art 126.

[21] But see *Rome Statute of the International Criminal Court*, art 51, which provides that the International Criminal Court's Rules and amendments to the rules must be adopted by a two-thirds majority of the Assembly of States Parties; and see also the ICSID Arbitration Rules (available at <http://www.worldbank.org/ icsid>), which were adopted by the ICSID Administrative Council, and apply in the absence of agreement to the contrary 'ICSID Convention', art 44.

[22] ICJ Rules, above n 18, art 101; ITLOS Rules, above n 20, art 48.

[23] ICSID Convention, art 44.

applied if the body thinks it 'appropriate'; in the case of ICSID tribunals, such modifications are binding on the tribunal.[24]

While the constitutive instruments and the rules form a good point of departure for a discussion of the powers of international courts, such instruments do not necessarily make exhaustive provision for the procedural law or the procedural powers of such courts. Constitutive instruments, and even rules of procedure, often contain gaps or ambiguities, or other such *lacunae*.[25] The following section considers the approach of international courts in such situations.

C. Sources of Law when International Courts are Faced with *Lacunae*

Several types of *lacuna* might be identified in international constitutive instruments. A first type may be found where an issue has deliberately not been addressed by the drafters of the instrument. As Edward Gordon observed, '[w]ith the hope of reaching some accord, or gaining acceptance for some treaty rather than having none at all, drafters sometimes compromise by omitting all reference to a disputed subject.'[26] Thus, those framing the instrument might purposefully refrain from addressing certain questions. In other cases, the drafters might leave further details to be completed by the court or tribunal itself, such as the decision of the Advisory Committee of Jurists to grant the power to the PCIJ to draft its rules of procedure. Second, even if the negotiators of the constitutive instruments of international courts seek to establish a comprehensive set of procedural rules, and manage to reach complete agreement on the powers to be accorded to the court, such drafters can never completely envisage the circumstances that might arise in the future.[27] This is a common problem with constitutive treaties, although the drafters of such treaties generally hope to frame an instrument which will be able to be adapted to 'the unknown, the unforeseen, and, indeed, the unforeseeable'.[28] Third, constitutive instruments may contain ambiguities. These might be inadvertent, or intentional as an alternative to omitting any reference to a matter on which the

[24] It appears that such modifications are only very rarely made. In the case of the ITLOS Rules, this provision was invoked in *Conservation and Sustainable Exploitation of Swordfish Stocks in the South-Eastern Pacific Ocean (Chile v European Community)* (Order of 20 December 2000) (2001) 40 ILM 475.

[25] In this context, a *lacuna* is a case where the intent of the parties to the instrument is not known, and thus may include ambiguities: Joel Trachtman, 'The Domain of WTO Dispute Resolution' (1999) 40 *Harvard International Law Journal* 333, 340.

[26] Edward Gordon, 'The World Court and the Interpretation of Constitutive Treaties' (1965) 59 *AJIL* 794, 804–5; Sir Hersch Lauterpacht, 'Restrictive Interpretation and the Principle of Effectiveness in the Interpretation of Treaties' (1949) 26 *British Yearbook of International Law* 48, 53; see, e.g., *Constitution of the Maritime Safety Committee of the IMCO* [1960] ICJ Rep 150, 165–71; *Conditions of Admission of a State to Membership in the United Nations (Advisory Opinion)* [1947–48] ICJ Rep 57, 98–9 (Diss Op Zoricic).

[27] Gordon, ibid, 803.

[28] *Certain Expenses of the United Nations (Advisory Opinion)* [1962] ICJ Rep 151, 182, 185 (Sep Op Spender).

negotiating parties have not been able to reach agreement. Examples of such ambiguity can be found where the parties incorporate terms and practices which are unclear, and where there is more than one authentic language version of a constitutive instrument.[29]

Faced with *lacunae* over procedure and remedies in their constitutive instruments, a review of international jurisprudence reveals that many international courts have considered that they have a source of competence to fill in such gaps, and they have engaged in a process of cross-fertilization of principles which has had a harmonizing effect on the way they approach questions of procedure and remedies. International courts may develop their procedures by seeking the views of the parties, and they also may fill in any gaps by interpreting and applying procedural rules which are consistent with the practice of other international courts and tribunals. There are a number of methods by which international courts and tribunals might do this. First, international courts can, by applying certain rules of treaty interpretation, take account of extraneous rules of international law, including international judicial practice. Second, international courts may resort to general principles of law that are applicable in judicial proceedings, as customarily applied in the decisions and judgments of other international courts.[30] Third, international courts have also found that they can exercise inherent powers, being powers that are not expressly conferred on them by the terms of their statutes and rules of procedure. These three methods are not mutually exclusive, and in practice, it is not always clear whether international courts are relying on one or several of these methods to reach a result consistent with other international courts and tribunals. These are now considered more closely.

1. *Interpretation by International Courts of their Constitutive Instruments*

The first tool available to international courts is to interpret their statutes and rules of procedure in such a way as to take account of the practice of other international tribunals. There are three principal methods by which international courts and tribunals can do this. It should be noted at the outset that a certain amount of overlap can be found between these rules of interpretation, and there is not always complete transparency in the way that international courts interpret the terms of their statutes and rules of procedure. As Professor Schwarzenberger aptly observed, 'international courts and tribunals fight shy of laying bare the equitable

[29] Gordon, above n 26, 810–13; e.g. *LaGrand* (2001) 40 ILM 1069, 1092–3.

[30] For example, Robert Kolb, 'General Principles of Procedural Law', in Andreas Zimmermann, Christian Tomuschat and Karin Oellers-Frahm (eds), *The Statute of the International Court of Justice: A Commentary* (2006) 793; Rosenne, *Law and Practice*, above n 5, vol III, 1021–8; Mosler, above n 3, 515; Bin Cheng, *General Principles of Law as Applied by International Courts and Tribunals* (1987) 19, 22, 257–386; Durward Sandifer, *Evidence before International Tribunals* (2nd ed, 1975) 44.

and common-sense reasons on which, in fact, their interpretative work is based'.[31] Nonetheless, identifying these techniques by which international courts can have recourse to the practice of other international courts is useful, as they represent a 'gateway' through which international courts may reach out to international judicial practice and develop their procedures and remedies in harmony with those applicable before other international courts.[32]

As a starting point, it is trite to note that international courts generally go about the business of treaty interpretation in accordance with the rules that have been codified in the Vienna Convention on the Law of Treaties, which originated in a draft prepared by the ILC.[33] Article 31(1) of the VCLT of course provides that:

> [A] treaty shall be interpreted in good faith in accordance with the ordinary meaning to be given to the terms of the treaty in their context and in the light of its object and purpose.[34]

Article 31(2) stipulates that the 'context', for the purpose of treaty interpretation, shall comprise, in addition to the text, its preamble and annexes, 'any agreement relating to the treaty which was made between all the parties in connection with the conclusion of the treaty', and 'any instrument which was made by one or more of the parties in connection with the conclusion of the treaty and accepted by the other parties as an instrument related to the treaty'.[35] Article 31(3) then provides that:

> there shall be taken into account, together with the context:
>
> (a) any subsequent agreement between the parties regarding the interpretation of the treaty or the application of its provisions;
> (b) any subsequent practice in the application of the treaty which establishes the agreement of the parties regarding its interpretation; and
> (c) any relevant rules of international law applicable in the relations between the parties.[36]

Under article 31(4), special meaning can be given to a term if it is shown that the parties so intended.[37] Article 32 provides that 'recourse may be had to supplementary means of interpretation', such as the *travaux préparatoires*, 'in order to confirm the meaning' resulting from the application of article 31, or 'to determine the meaning' if the interpretation according to article 31 is 'ambiguous or obscure', or 'leads to a result which is manifestly absurd or unreasonable'.[38] International tribunals have repeatedly confirmed that the provisions of the VCLT concerning treaty interpretation reflect customary international law.[39]

[31] Georg Schwarzenberger, *A Manual of International Law* (4th ed, 1960) vol I, 153; cited by Duncan French, 'Treaty Interpretation and the Incorporation of Extraneous Legal Rules' (2006) 55 *ICLQ* 281, 281.

[32] See also French, ibid, 292.

[33] *Vienna Convention on the Law of Treaties*, opened for signature 23 May 1969, 1155 UNTS 311 (entered into force 27 January 1980) ('VCLT').

[34] Ibid, art 31(1).

[35] Ibid, art 31(2).

[36] Ibid, art 31(3).

[37] Ibid, art 31(4).

[38] Ibid, art 32.

[39] See, e.g., *Saluka Investments BV v Czech Republic* (PCA, Partial Award of 17 March 2006), para 296; *Iron Rhine Railway* (PCA, Award of 24 May 2005), para 45, both available at <http://www.

In drafting these provisions of the VCLT, the ILC essentially took the view that what mattered was the parties' intentions, as expressed in the terms of the treaty.[40] This code of interpretation, however, is not exhaustive. In its Report to the General Assembly, the ILC noted that:

> Most cases submitted to international adjudication involve the interpretation of treaties, and the jurisprudence of international tribunals is rich in reference to principles and maxims of interpretation. In fact, statements can be found in the decisions of international tribunals to support the use of almost every principle or maxim of which use is made in national systems of law in the interpretation of statutes and contracts.[41]

Faced with this task, the ILC observed that it would be 'inadvisable' to try to codify the conditions for application of the many possible principles of interpretation, and reported that it had decided to '[confine] itself to trying to isolate and codify the comparatively few general principles which appear to constitute general rules for the interpretation of treaties'.[42]

There are three rules of treaty interpretation which can be employed by international courts as harmonizing tools. Two of these are not expressly included in the VCLT; these are the principle of effectiveness in treaty interpretation, and the evolutive approach to treaty interpretation. The third rule is found in the VCLT, in article 31(3)(c). These will now be considered.

a) Principle of Effectiveness

The first relevant rule is the principle of effectiveness in treaty interpretation. This principle assumes that the parties to a treaty intended its provisions 'to have a certain effect, and not to be meaningless'.[43] It was described by Sir Gerald Fitzmaurice in 1951 as one of the six key principles of treaty interpretation.[44] He wrote that the principle of effectiveness required that:

> Particular provisions are to be interpreted so as to give them the fullest weight and effect consistent with the normal meaning of the words and with other parts of the text.[45]

pca-cpa.org> under 'Recent and Pending Cases' (last visited 25 November 2006); *Camuzzi International SA v Argentina* (ICSID Case No ARB/03/2, Decision on Jurisdiction of 11 May 2005), para 133; *Sovereignty over Pulau Ligitan and Pulau Sipadan* [2002] ICJ Rep 625, 645–6; *Kasikili/Sedudu Island* [1999]-II ICJ Rep 1045, 1059; *Territorial Dispute (Libya/Chad)* [1994] ICJ Rep 6, 21–22; see also the cases cited by Campbell McLachlan, 'The Principle of Systemic Integration and Article 31(3)(c) of the Vienna Convention' (2005) 54 *ICLQ* 279, 293, fn 61: *Golder v UK*, Ser A (No 18), para 29 (ECHR, 1975); *Restrictions to the Death Penalty Case*, 70 ILR 449, 466 (IACHR, 1983); and *US—Standards for Reformulated and Conventional Gasoline*, DSR 1996-I, 3, 16 (ABR); see also Hugh Thirlway, 'The Law and Procedure of the International Court of Justice 1960–1989: Part Three' (1991) 62 *British Yearbook of International Law* 1, 16–17.

[40] Brownlie, above n 3, 602.

[41] ILC, 'Report of the Commission on the Work of its Eighteenth Session' [1966] *Yearbook of the ILC*, vol II, 172, 218.

[42] Ibid, 218–19; see also Brownlie, above n 3, 602.

[43] Sir Robert Jennings and Sir Arthur Watts (eds), *Oppenheim's International Law* (9th ed, 1992) vol I, 1280.

[44] Fitzmaurice, above n 8, 50.

[45] Ibid.

Professor Thirlway has observed that the principle of effectiveness actually contains two separate rules:

> The first is the rule that all provisions of the treaty or other instrument must be supposed to have been intended to have significance and be necessary to convey the intended meaning... The second is the rule that the instrument as a whole, and each of its provisions, must be taken to have been intended to have some end, and that an interpretation which would make the text ineffective to achieve the object in view is, again, prima facie suspect.[46]

In the present context, it is the second of these rules with which this book is concerned, and which is known as the principle *ut res magis valeat quam pereat*.[47] This principle has been applied on numerous occasions by the PCIJ and the ICJ in finding that international organizations have powers that can be implied from their constitutive instruments. In *Reparation for Injuries*, for example, the ICJ observed that the UN Charter did not empower the UN to bring a claim for injuries sustained by one of its employees. Nonetheless, the ICJ held that in light of the functions of the UN, the provisions of the Charter imply that the UN had the power to bring such a claim. The ICJ stated that:

> Under international law, the Organisation must be deemed to have those powers which, though not expressly provided for in the Charter, are conferred upon it by necessary implication as being essential to the performance of its duties.[48]

This principle has been employed by international courts not only to find that international organizations have powers and capacities other than those expressly conferred on them, but also in order to ensure the effective exercise of their own functions.[49] Thus, in *Mavrommatis Palestine Concessions*, the PCIJ held that a clause conferring jurisdiction on it can be applied to disputes arising both prior and subsequent to the entry into force of the clause in question.[50] In *The Right to Information on Consular Assistance*, the IACHR held that when interpreting the American Convention, 'the Court must do it in such a way that the system for the

[46] Thirlway, 'Part Three', above n 39, 44, referring to Georges Berlia, 'Contribution à l'interprétation des traités' (1965) 114 *Recueil des cours* 287, 306–11.

[47] Thirlway, ibid, 44.

[48] [1949] ICJ Rep 174, 182; see, however, the more restrictive view in ibid, 196, 198 (Diss Op Hackworth): 'powers not expressed cannot freely be implied. Implied powers flow from a grant of express powers, and are limited to those that are "necessary" to the exercise of powers expressly granted'. The majority position was confirmed in *Certain Expenses*, above n 28, 168. See also *Competence of the ILO*, Ser B, (No 2) (PCIJ, 1922); *Competence of the ILO*, Ser B, (No 3) (PCIJ, 1922); *Competence of the ILO*, Ser B, (No 13) 18 (PCIJ, 1926); *Jurisdiction of the European Commission of the Danube between Galatz and Braila*, Ser B, (No 14) 64–7 (PCIJ, 1927); *Effect of Awards of Compensation of the UN Administrative Tribunal* [1954] ICJ Rep 47, 56–8; *Legality of the Use by a State of Nuclear Weapons* (WHO Request) [1996] ICJ Rep 66, 78–9.

[49] But see Paola Gaeta, 'Inherent Powers of International Courts and Tribunals' in Lal Chand Vohrar *et al* (eds), *Man's Inhumanity to Man: Essays on International Law in Honour of Antonio Cassese* (2003) 353, 360, 362–3, who suggests that 'the only clear instance' of the invocation of the doctrine of implied powers by an international court regarding its own powers can be found in the case of *Prosecutor v Blaskic*, 110 ILR 608 (ICTY, 1997).

[50] Ser A, (No 2), 35 (PCIJ, 1924).

protection of human rights has all its appropriate effects (*effet utile*)'.[51] In *LaGrand*, the ICJ was faced with the question of whether it had the power to order provisional measures that were binding. There, the ICJ also adopted an interpretation of article 41 of the ICJ Statute in accordance with the principle of effectiveness to find that its provisional measures had mandatory force.[52] The ECHR has also adopted this approach to the question of the binding nature of its own provisional measures. In *Mamatkulov*, the ECHR held that '[t]he... Court reiterates that the provisions of treaties must be interpreted in good faith in the light of the object and purpose of the treaty and in accordance with the principle of effectiveness'.[53]

In addition, the source of the jurisdiction of international courts to award remedies can be regarded as an application of the principle of effectiveness in treaty interpretation. In *Factory at Chorzów*, Poland argued that the compromissory clause giving the PCIJ jurisdiction did not confer on it the jurisdiction to decide the quantum and form of the reparation to be made.[54] The PCIJ rejected this argument, stating that reparation was 'the indispensable complement of a failure to apply a convention and there is no necessity for this to be stated in the convention itself'.[55] The PCIJ justified its approach as follows:

> An interpretation [of the compromissory clause] which would confine the Court simply to recording that the Convention had been incorrectly applied or that it had not been applied, without being able to lay down the conditions for the re-establishment of the treaty rights affected, would be contrary to what would, *prima facie*, be the natural object of the clause; for a jurisdiction of this kind, instead of settling a dispute once and for all, would leave open the possibility of further disputes.[56]

This attitude of the PCIJ was consistent with previous arbitral practice. In earlier arbitrations, tribunals which had the express power to 'settle all claims' often also saw no obstacle to their making awards of damages; in some cases where the arbitral tribunal was in fact only expressly charged with the task of determining the question of liability, the arbitrators also assumed that they had the power to award damages.[57]

[51] *The Right to Information on Consular Assistance in the Framework of the Guarantees of the Due Process of Law*, Ser A, No 16, para 58 (IACHR, 1999).

[52] Above n 29, 1093; Martin Mennecke and Christian Tams, '*LaGrand* Case (*Germany v United States of America*)' (2002) 51 *ICLQ* 449.

[53] *Mamatkulov and Abdurasulovic v Turkey* (Appl. Nos. 46827/99, 46951/99) (ECHR Judgment of 6 February 2003), para 109; confirmed by the ECHR Grand Chamber (Judgment of 4 February 2005), available at <http://www.echr.coe.int> (last visited 26 November 2006); see generally Christian Tams, 'Interim Orders by the European Court of Human Rights: Comments on *Mamatkulov and Abdurasulovic v Turkey*' (2003) 63 *ZaöRV* 681; Chester Brown, 'Strasbourg Follows Suit on Provisional Measures' (2003) 62 *CLJ* 532.

[54] *Factory at Chorzów (Germany v Poland) (Jurisdiction)* Ser A (No 9), 20–1 (PCIJ, 1927); James Crawford, *The International Law Commission's Articles on State Responsibility* (2002) 201.

[55] Ser A (No 9), 21 (PCIJ, 1927). [56] Ibid, 25.

[57] Christine Gray, *Judicial Remedies in International Law* (1987) 12, 60; referring, e.g. to *Van Bokkelen*, Moore, vol II, 1807 (US–Haiti, 1888); *Forests of Central Rhodope*, 3 RIAA 1389, 1431 (Greece–Bulgaria, 1931).

The ICJ and other international tribunals have maintained the same approach. In *Corfu Channel*, under a *compromis* concluded between the UK and Albania the ICJ had jurisdiction to decide, first, whether Albania was responsible for damage to UK naval vessels and loss of human life, and second, whether the UK had violated the sovereignty of Albania.[58] The UK claimed monetary compensation; Albania argued that the ICJ had no power to decide the amount of damages, but only the question of responsibility. The ICJ rejected Albania's argument:

> If the Court should limit itself to saying that there is a duty to pay compensation without deciding what amount of compensation is due, the dispute would not be finally decided. An important part of it would remain unsettled.... It would not give full effect to the Resolutions but would leave open the possibility of a further dispute.[59]

This approach, which has been confirmed in later ICJ jurisprudence,[60] can be regarded as an application of the principle of effectiveness. As the PCIJ and the ICJ noted, if they found that they lacked the power to award reparation, the dispute would be left unresolved; they therefore adopted an interpretation of their powers which made it possible for them to carry out their functions and ensure the settlement of the disputes.[61]

The principle of effectiveness does have its limits, however; as Sir Percy Spender and Sir Gerald Fitzmaurice observed in their joint dissenting opinion in *South West Africa*, 'the principle of interpretation directed to giving provisions their maximum effect cannot legitimately be employed in order to introduce what would amount to a revision of the treaty'.[62] The PCA Tribunal in *Iron Rhine Railway* agreed, noting that the application of the principle of effectiveness in treaty interpretation did not 'entitle a Tribunal to revise a treaty'.[63] This principle is a useful tool, allowing international courts to have regard to the practice of other international courts with respect to procedural issues, for it enables tribunals to consider how similarly—if not identically—drafted provisions have been applied by other tribunals.

b) Evolutive Approach to Treaty Interpretation

A second method adopted by international courts to reach out and borrow from the practice of other international courts is the adoption of an evolutive approach to treaty interpretation, also referred by Professor Thirlway as the 'intertemporal *renvoi*'.[64] This approach appears to conflict with the principle of intertemporal

[58] *Corfu Channel (United Kingdom/Albania) (Merits)* [1949] ICJ Rep 4. [59] Ibid, 26.

[60] *Fisheries Jurisdiction (Germany v Iceland) (Merits)* [1974] ICJ Rep 175, 203–5; *Military and Paramilitary Activities in and against Nicaragua* [1986] ICJ Rep 14, 142; *LaGrand*, above n 29, 1082; *Avena (Merits)*, (2004) 43 ILM 581, 598. [61] Lauterpacht, *Development*, above n 8, 246–7.

[62] [1962] ICJ Rep 319, 465, 468 (Joint Diss Op Spender and Fitzmaurice); see also Thirlway, 'Part Three', above n 39, 47–8.

[63] Above n 39, para 49; see also Jennings and Watts (eds), above n 43, 1280–1.

[64] Hugh Thirlway, 'The Law and Procedure of the International Court of Justice: Part One' (1989) 60 *British Yearbook of International Law* 1, 135; see also French, above n 31, 284, 295–300.

law, being the concept developed by Judge Huber in *Island of Palmas* that 'a juridical fact must be appreciated in the light of the law contemporary with it, and not of the law in force at the time when a dispute in regard to it arises or falls to be settled'.[65] However, as Dr French notes, while the principle of intertemporal law is often determinative, it 'may, in other cases, only be a starting point and be displaced by subsequent developments'.[66] The ICJ recognized this in its advisory opinion in *Namibia* where, in its consideration of the Covenant establishing the League of Nations in 1919, it held that:

> Mindful as it is of the primary necessity of interpreting an instrument in accordance with the intentions of the parties at the time of its conclusion, the Court is bound to take into account the fact that the concepts embodied in Article 22 of the Covenant—'the strenuous conditions of the modern world' and the 'well-being and development' of the peoples concerned—were not static, but were by definition evolutionary, as also, therefore, was the concept of the 'sacred trust'. The parties to the Covenant must subsequently be deemed to have accepted them as such. That is why, viewing the institutions of 1919, the Court must take into consideration the changes which have occurred in the supervening half-century, and its interpretation cannot remain unaffected by the subsequent development of law, through the Charter of the United Nations and by way of customary international law. Moreover, an international instrument has to be interpreted and applied within the framework of the entire legal system prevailing at the time of the interpretation.[67]

Many instances can be found where international courts have adopted this approach to treaty interpretation, such as in the recent award of the PCA Tribunal in *Iron Rhine Railway*. There, the Tribunal held that:

> It has long been established that the understanding of conceptual or generic terms in a treaty may be seen as 'an essentially relative question; it depends upon the development of international relations' ... Some terms are 'not static, but were by definition evolutionary'.[68]

The Tribunal referred to the ICJ's judgment in *Gabcikovo–Nagymaros Project*, where the ICJ had held that 'the Treaty is not static, and is open to adapt to emerging norms of international law'.[69] The Tribunal in *Iron Rhine Railway* held that:

> [I]t seems that an evolutive interpretation, which would ensure an application of the treaty that would be effective in terms of its object and purpose, will be preferred to a strict application of the intertemporal rule.[70]

[65] *Island of Palmas*, 2 RIAA 829, 845 (US–Netherlands, 1928).

[66] French, above n 31, 295.

[67] *Legal Consequences for States of the Continued Presence of South Africa in Namibia (South-West Africa) Notwithstanding Security Council Resolution 726 (1970) (Advisory Opinion)* [1971] ICJ Rep 16, 31.

[68] Above n 39, para 79, citing *Nationality Decrees Issued in Tunis and Morocco*, Ser B (No 4), 24 (PCIJ, 1923), and *Namibia*, ibid, 31.

[69] *Gabcikovo–Nagymaros Project* [1997] ICJ Rep 7, 67–8.

[70] Above n 39, para 80.

It also noted:

a general support among the leading writers today for evolutive interpretation of treaties. The editors of the 9th edition of *Oppenheim* agree that, notwithstanding the intertemporal rule, 'in some respects the interpretation of a treaty's provisions cannot be divorced from developments in the law subsequent to its adoption... the concepts embodied in a treaty may not be static but evolutionary'.[71]

Consistent with this principle, the ECHR has also repeatedly confirmed that the European HR Convention is 'a living instrument which must be interpreted in light of present-day conditions',[72] and has stressed that 'a failure by the Court to maintain a dynamic and evolutive approach would indeed risk rendering it a bar to reform or improvement'.[73] The WTO Appellate Body has also adopted an evolutive approach to treaty interpretation. In *US—Shrimp*, at issue was whether the term 'exhaustible natural resource', found in article XX(g) of the GATT, could be read as including both living and non-living natural resources.[74] In its report, the Appellate Body observed that:

The words of Article XX(g), 'exhaustible natural resource', were actually crafted more than 50 years ago. They must be read by a treaty interpreter in the light of contemporary concerns of the community of nations about the protection and conservation of the environment. While Article XX(g) was not modified in the Uruguay Round, the preamble attached to the WTO Agreement shows that the signatories to that Agreement were, in 1994, fully aware of the importance and legitimacy of environmental protection as a goal of national and international policy.... [W]e note that the generic term 'natural resource' in Article XX(g) is not 'static' in its content or reference but is rather 'by definition, evolutionary'.[75]

The Appellate Body concluded that:

Given the recent acknowledgment by the international community of the importance of concerted bilateral or multilateral action to protect living natural resources, and recalling the explicit recognition by WTO Members of the objective of sustainable development in the preamble of the WTO Agreement, we believe it is too late in the day to suppose that Article XX(g) of the GATT 1994 may be read as referring only to the conservation of exhaustible mineral or other non-living natural resources. Moreover, two adopted GATT 1947 panel reports previously found fish to be an 'exhaustible natural resource' within the meaning of Article XX(g). We hold that, in line with the principle of effectiveness in treaty

[71] Above n 39, para 81, referring to Jennings and Watts (eds), above n 43, vol I, 1282. The Tribunal also referred to the writings of Eduardo Jiménez de Arachaga, 'International Law in the Past Third of a Century' (1978) 159 *Recueil des cours* 1, 48–50; and Rudolf Bernhardt, 'Evolutive Treaty Interpretation, Especially of the European Convention on Human Rights' (1999) 42 *German Yearbook of International Law* 11, 16–17.

[72] See, e.g. *Mamatkulov*, above n 53, (Judgment of 2003), para 94; see also *Bankovic v Belgium*, 123 ILR 94, 110, para 64 (ECHR, 2001); see also *Soering v UK*, Ser A (No 161), para 102 (ECHR, 1989).

[73] *Mamatkulov*, ibid, para 105.

[74] *US—Import Prohibition of Certain Shrimp and Shrimp Products*, DSR 1998–VII, 2755 (ABR).

[75] Ibid, 2794–5.

interpretation, measures to conserve exhaustible natural resources, *whether living or non-living*, may fall within Article XX(g).[76]

This decision by the Appellate Body combines the evolutive approach to treaty interpretation with the principle of effectiveness, in order to reach its finding on the interpretation of article XX(g) of the GATT; the Appellate Body also referred to article 31(3)(c) of the VCLT in interpreting the chapeau of that provision.[77] It is not clear which of these methods was decisive, or if the Appellate Body relied on the cumulative effect of the various approaches. This decision nonetheless provides an excellent illustration of how these methods may be used to take account of other rules of international law, even if the Appellate Body's decision can be criticized for coming to a conclusion 'through an amalgam of a variety of very different approaches... without any real attempt to isolate individual theoretical positions'.[78]

In addition to the practice of international tribunals adopting this approach to treaty interpretation, international courts have also applied this principle to the interpretation of their own statutes. For instance, the ECHR in *Mamatkulov* adopted an evolutive approach to treaty interpretation in finding that it had the power to grant provisional measures with mandatory force, even though the ECHR Rules only confer the power to 'indicate' provisional measures, which does not necessarily imply that they are binding.[79] Further, it may be argued that ICSID Tribunals have also adopted an evolutive approach to their power to grant provisional measures. Three different ICSID tribunals have found that their power under article 47 of the ICSID Convention, being the power to 'recommend' provisional measures, should be interpreted as meaning that such measures have binding force, even though such measures are not 'ordered' or 'prescribed'.[80]

c) Article 31(3)(c) of the VCLT

A third method open to international courts to have regard to the practice of other international courts in interpreting their constitutive instruments is provided by article 31(3)(c) of the VCLT, which requires that, in interpreting a treaty, 'there shall be taken into account, together with the context:... (c) any relevant rules of international law applicable in the relations between the parties'.[81] This does not

[76] Ibid, 2796–7 (footnotes omitted); for criticism, see French, above n 31, 297–9.

[77] *US—Shrimp*, above n 74, 2807 (ABR).

[78] French, above n 31, 298.

[79] *Mamatkulov*, above n 53 (Judgment of 2003), para 105; see also Tams, above n 53; Brown, above n 53.

[80] *Maffezini v Spain (Provisional Measures)*, 5 ICSID Rep 393, 394 (1999); *Victor Pey Casado and Fondation Président Allende v Chile* (2001) 16 *ICSID Review—FILJ* 567, 578; and *Tokios Tokeles v Ukraine* (ICSID Case No ARB/02/18, Procedural Order No 1 of 1 July 2003), para 4; ibid, (Procedural Order No 3 of 18 January 2005), paras 6–7, fn 12; see further chapter 4, part III(C). These decisions may, equally, be regarded as an application of the *effet utile*.

[81] VCLT, above n 33, art 31(3)(c). For a review of the drafting history of this provision, see ILC Study Group, 'Fragmentation of International Law: Difficulties Arising from the Diversification and Expansion of International Law', UN Doc A/CN.4/L.682 (4 April 2006) paras 429–32 ('Consolidated Report 2006'); McLachlan, above n 39, 291–3; Sir Humphrey Waldock, 'Third Report on the Law of Treaties' [1964] *Yearbook of the International Law Commission*, vol II, 52–62.

mean, however, that other rules of international law can be applied in place of the treaty provision, as Dr Orakhelashvili has noted:

> [T]he purpose of interpreting by reference to 'relevant rules' is, normally, not to defer the provisions being interpreted to the scope and effect of those 'relevant rules', but to clarify the content of the former by referring to the latter. Relevant rules may not, generally speaking, override or limit the scope or effect of a provision for whose clarification they are referred.[82]

For many years, article 31(3)(c) 'languished' in 'obscurity'.[83] Professor Sands has observed that there was a 'general reluctance' to refer to it in doctrine and in international judicial practice,[84] and Professor McLachlan has noted that, as of 1998, only the ECHR and the Iran–US Claims Tribunal had made express reference to article 31(3)(c).[85] In 1991, Professor Thirlway even expressed the view that it was 'doubtful whether this sub-paragraph [would] be of any assistance in the task of treaty interpretation'.[86] However, this provision appears to have been rediscovered, and has been applied—both implicitly and expressly—by international tribunals on several occasions in recent years.[87]

The WTO Appellate Body referred to it in *US—Shrimp*, in interpreting the chapeau of Article XX(g) of the GATT, as noted above,[88] and in 2006, a WTO panel in *EC—Biotechnical Products* considered the application of article 31(3)(c) in response to an argument by the EC that the relevant WTO covered agreement should be interpreted in light of the Convention on Biological Diversity, the Cartagena Biosafety Protocol, and the precautionary principle; essentially, the EC had argued that taking these rules of international law into account justified its ban on the importation of genetically modified organisms. The WTO Panel interpreted article 31(3)(c) of the VCLT as requiring 'consideration of those rules of international law which are applicable in the relations between all parties to the

[82] Alexander Orakhelashvili, 'Restrictive Interpretation of Human Rights Treaties in Recent Jurisprudence of the European Court of Human Rights' (2003) 14 *European Journal of International Law* 529, 537.

[83] McLachlan, above n 39, 279; see also Orakhelashvili, 'Restrictive Interpretation', ibid, 536.

[84] Philippe Sands, 'Treaty, Custom and the Cross-Fertilisation of International Law' (1998) 1 *Yale Human Rights and Development Law Journal* 85, 95; see also Philippe Sands, 'Sustainable Development: Treaty, Custom and the Cross-Fertilisation of International Law' in Alan Boyle and David Freestone (eds), *International Law and Sustainable Development: Past Achievements and Future Challenges* (1999) 39, 49–50. Dr Orakhelashvili has observed that in the 'Report of the ILC on its Eighteenth Session', above n 41, 222, the ILC does not provide any references to doctrine or international judicial practice in support of this provision: Orakhelashvili, 'Restrictive Interpretation', above n 82, 536.

[85] McLachlan, above n 39, 294, referring to *Golder v UK*, above n 39, para 35; *Loizidou v Turkey (Merits)*, 108 ILR 443, 461, para 43 (ECHR, 1996); *Grimm v Iran* (1983) 2 Ir-USCTR 78, 81, 82 (Diss Op Holtzmann); *Case A–18*, 75 ILR 176, 188, 194; (1984) 5 Ir-USCTR 251, 260, 265; and *Esphahanian v Bank Tejarat*, 72 ILR 478, 483; (1983) 2 Ir-USCTR 157, 161. See also Sands, 'Sustainable Development', above n 84, 50.

[86] Thirlway, 'Part Three', above n 39, 58.

[87] For a review of those cases, see ILC, 'Consolidated Report 2006', above n 81, paras 433–60; McLachlan, above n 39, 295–309.

[88] Above n 74, 2807, para 158 (ABR).

treaty which is being interpreted'.[89] The Panel therefore held that in the context of the instant dispute, 'if a rule of international law is not applicable to one of the four WTO Members which are parties to the present dispute, the rule is not applicable in the relations between all WTO Members'.[90] The Panel therefore declined to take account of the Biodiversity Convention, to which the United States was not a state party, or the Cartagena Protocol, which had entered into force after the date of the constitution of the panel.[91] It also declined to apply the precautionary principle, leaving open the question whether that principle was a rule of international law for the purposes of article 31(3)(c).[92] The Panel held, however, that 'other relevant rules of international law may in some cases aid a treaty interpreter in establishing, or confirming, the ordinary meaning of treaty terms in the specific context in which they are used.'[93]

For its part, the ECHR referred to article 31(3)(c) in three cases—*Al-Adsani v UK*, *Fogarty v UK*, and *McElhinney v Ireland*—in deciding whether the defence of state immunity was a proportionate (and permissible) restriction to the right of individuals to have access to a court for civil claims, as protected by article 6(1) of the European HR Convention.[94] The ECHR also made reference to this provision in *Bankovic v Belgium* in stressing that it was under a duty to interpret the European HR Convention 'as far as possible in harmony with other principles of international law of which it forms part'.[95] In *Access to Information under Article 9 of the OSPAR Convention*, the PCA Tribunal relied on article 31(3)(c) in finding that it could draw on 'international law and practice' in interpreting provisions of the OSPAR Convention, although it ultimately declined to do so, because the law on which Ireland sought to rely was *in statu nascendi*.[96] In 2003, the ICJ deployed it in the *Oil Platforms* case 'as a bridge between the provisions of a treaty of friendship and the customary international law of armed conflict';[97] and in 2005, the PCA Tribunal in *Iron Rhine Railway* expressly referred to article 31(3)(c) in order to take account of European law and developments in international environmental law in

[89] *EC—Measures Affecting the Approval and Marketing of Biotech Products*, WT/DS291–293, para 7.70 (PR of 29 September 2006); *Cartagena Protocol on Biosafety to the Convention on Biological Diversity*, opened for signature 29 January 2000, (2000) 39 ILM 1027 (entered into force 11 September 2003).

[90] *EC—Biotech*, ibid, para 7.71.

[91] Ibid, paras 7.73–7.75; *Convention on Biological Diversity*, opened for signature 5 June 1992, 1760 UNTS 79 (entered into force 29 December 1993).

[92] Ibid, paras 7.76–7.89.

[93] Ibid, para 7.92.

[94] *Al-Adsani v UK*, 123 ILR 24, 40 (ECHR, 2001); *Fogarty v UK*, 123 ILR 54, 65 (ECHR, 2001); and *McElhinney v Ireland*, 123 ILR 73, 85 (ECHR, 2001): see also McLachlan, above n 39, 304–6.

[95] Above n 72, 108.

[96] (2003) 42 ILM 1118, 1138, para 101; see also the dissenting opinion of Gavan Griffith QC: (2003) 42 ILM 1161, 1162–5; *Convention for the Protection of the Marine Environment of the North-East Atlantic*, opened for signature 22 September 1992 (1993) 32 ILM 1068 (entered into force 25 March 1998) ('OSPAR Convention').

[97] McLachlan, above n 39, 280, 306–9; *Oil Platforms* (2003) 42 ILM 1334, 1352, para 41; see also ibid, 1428, 1432, para 9 (Sep Op Simma); for criticism of the ICJ's approach, see ibid, 1379, 1386–88, paras 40–54 (Sep Op Higgins); and ibid, 1404, 1409–1413, paras 20–32 (Sep Op Buergenthal).

determining the obligations of the Netherlands under the 1839 Treaty of Separation with Belgium.[98]

International courts have also referred to article 31(3)(c) in order to interpret provisions of their constitutive instruments, although it does not appear that this has occurred with great frequency. One instance can be found in the ECHR's judgment in *Mamatkulov*, where it examined the question of the binding nature of its provisional measures 'by reference to general principles of international law, in particular those concerning the binding force of interim measures indicated by other international courts'.[99] This provision is, then, another means by which international courts can have reference to the practice of other international adjudicatory bodies.

d) Limitations to these Approaches to Treaty Interpretation

There are two principal limitations to the application of these interpretative techniques—one has been noted in the context of each of these rules; namely, that international courts cannot, by application of the principle of effectiveness, the evolutive approach, or article 31(3)(c) of the VCLT, revise the content of a constitutive instrument or any other treaty.[100] The ICJ has noted that it cannot interpret a treaty in such a way that 'would go beyond the scope of its declared purposes and objects'.[101] Dr French has also warned that the approach to treaty interpretation which permits the objective revision of treaties provides tribunals 'with too much latitude, with too few safeguards, for discretionary decision-making'.[102] Moreover, 'such objective revision also undermines the fundamental notion of consent, both at the treaty adoption stage and, subsequently, during dispute settlement.'[103]

A second limiting factor on the application of these interpretative techniques is that some international courts might be more willing than others to refer to the jurisprudence of other international tribunals on questions of procedure and remedies. It is not possible to find universal practice in this regard; the ICJ, for instance, is well known for only very rarely referring to the jurisprudence of other international courts.[104] Many other international tribunals, however, do not

[98] *Iron Rhine Railway*, above n 39, paras 58, 79.

[99] *Mamatkulov*, above n 53 (Judgment of 2003), paras 98–99.

[100] See, e.g., *South West Africa*, above n 62, 465, 468 (Joint Diss Op Spender and Fitzmaurice); *Rights of Nationals of the United States in Morocco* [1952] ICJ Rep 176, 196; *Iron Rhine Railway*, above n 39, para 49; Thirlway, 'Part Three', above n 39, 47–8; and Orakhelashvili, 'Restrictive Interpretation', above n 82, 537.

[101] See, e.g., *Rights of US Nationals in Morocco*, ibid, 196; see also at 199: 'the Court cannot, by way of interpretation, derive from the Act a general rule as to full consular jurisdiction which it does not contain'; see also Waldock, above n 81, 56, noting that the ICJ has stressed that 'it is not the function of interpretation to revise treaties or to read into them what they do not expressly or by necessary implication contain'.

[102] French, above n 31, 300.

[103] Ibid.

[104] For a discussion of the ICJ's practice of referring to its own case law, and the few instances in which the PCIJ and ICJ have referred to the decisions of other international tribunals, see Judge Gilbert Guillaume, 'The Proliferation of International Judicial Bodies—The Outlook for the

operate under the same strictures, and frequently refer to the case law of other international courts. This practice encourages the cross-fertilization of principles, and supports the development of a common law of international adjudication.

2. *Custom, International Judicial Practice, and General Principles of Law*

Another method by which international courts and tribunals can fill gaps in their statutes and rules of procedure and develop their procedures and remedies in line with other international courts is to have reference to customary international law, rules developed in international judicial and arbitral practice, and general principles of law. Customary international law can represent a source of procedural law, even though it is usually thought to be generated by the practice of states and their expressions of *opinio juris*,[105] and not the practice of international courts and tribunals.[106] Writers have nonetheless emphasized the relevance of custom as a source of procedural law.[107] The role of custom is also evinced by references to the practice of international courts in international jurisprudence. For instance, in *Factory at Chorzów*, the PCIJ held that the obligation to make full reparation for an internationally wrongful act was 'established by international practice and in particular by the decisions of arbitral tribunals'.[108] In *US—Shirts and Blouses*, the WTO Appellate Body referred to the practice of 'various international tribunals, including the International Court of Justice' in applying the rule on the allocation of the burden of proof.[109] In a further example, the UNCLOS tribunal in *MOX Plant* referred to 'international judicial practice' on the general requirements for the granting of provisional measures.[110]

The application of 'general principles of law' by international courts as a source of judicial procedure is well established.[111] These 'general principles' are those

International Legal Order: Speech to the Sixth Committee of the General Assembly', 4–5 (27 October 2000) available at <http://www.icj-cij.org> (last visited 25 November 2006); Mohamed Shahabuddeen, *Precedent in the World Court* (1996) 23–31, 35–9.

105 Brownlie, above n 3, 6–10; ILA, *Report of the Committee on the Formation of Customary (General) International Law* (London Conference, 2000); *North Sea Continental Shelf* [1969] ICJ Rep 3, 43–4; *Nicaragua*, above n 60, 108–9.

106 It might be argued, however, that state practice can be found in the acceptance by states of the decisions of international courts and tribunals.

107 See especially Hugh Thirlway, 'Dilemma or Chimera? Admissibility of Illegally Obtained Evidence in International Adjudication' (1984) 78 *AJIL* 622, 623; Rosenne, *Law and Practice*, above n 5, vol III, 1027–8.

108 *Factory at Chorzów (Merits)*, Ser A, (No 17), 47 (PCIJ, 1928).

109 *US—Measure Affecting Imports of Woven Wool Shirts and Blouses from India*, DSR 1997–I, 323, 335 (ABR).

110 *MOX Plant* (Procedural Order No 3 of 24 June 2003), 42 ILM 1187, 1197. For further examples, see, e.g., *Nottebohm* [1953] ICJ Rep 111, 119; and *Interhandel* [1957] ICJ Rep 105, 117, 118 (Sep Op Lauterpacht).

111 See especially Kolb, above n 30; Rosenne, *Law and Practice*, above n 5, vol III, 1022–3; Cheng, above n 30, 299–386; Georg Schwarzenberger, *International Law as Applied by International Courts and Tribunals* (1986) vol IV, 584–5; see also Thirlway, 'Dilemma or Chimera?', above n 107, 624.

referred to as a source of international law in article 38(1)(c) of the ICJ Statute. One of the motivations for the inclusion of this provision in the original PCIJ Statute was the fear that the PCIJ would state a *non liquet*, in light of the incomplete nature of the other sources of international law, namely treaty obligations and customary international law.[112] It appears that this concept was originally intended to refer exclusively to general principles applicable in domestic legal orders,[113] although general principles of international relations have also been applied by international courts, including principles which derive from the features of the international legal order, such as the sovereign equality of states, state immunity, and principles of territorial jurisdiction.[114] There is a somewhat blurred distinction between a rule deriving from the 'customary practice' of international tribunals, and a rule constituting a 'general principle of law'.[115] The overlap in these categories is evident from Professor Cheng, in his work on general principles of law, having included rules such as that relating to *audi alteram partem*, the rule on the allocation of the burden of proof, and *res judicata*,[116] which rules might equally be said to have been developed as customary rules of practice.[117] There is also much overlap in the use of judicial decisions as a subsidiary source of international law; as noted above, international courts frequently refer to international judicial practice as a source of procedural rules.[118]

Professor Kolb has noted that the general principles which are relevant to judicial procedure before the ICJ can be classified into three types. First, there are 'structural and constitutional principles', such as 'the equality of the parties' and 'the principle of the proper administration of justice'.[119] Second, there are 'procedural principles *stricto sensu*', which 'relate to the division of work between the parties and the Court'.[120] These principles include the rule on the allocation on the burden of proof, or *actori incumbit probatio*; the rule that international courts are deemed to know the law, or *iura novit curia*; the principle that 'the object of the

[112] Cheng, above n 30, 18–19; Mosler, above n 3, 516.

[113] See, e.g. the discussion of the proposals of Baron Descamps, Lord Phillimore and Elihu Root in the Advisory Committee of Jurists, referred to in Cheng, above n 30, 11–17. See also especially Sir Hersch Lauterpacht, *Private Law Sources and Analogies of International Law* (1927) 71, who states that general principles of law are 'for most practical purposes identical with general principles of private law'; see, however, Dionisio Anzilotti, *Cours de Droit International* (French trans Gilbert Gidel, 3rd ed, 1929) vol I, 117, who argues that this provision refers primarily to 'les principes généraux de l'ordre juridique international, et, en second lieu, les principes universellement admis dans les législations des peuples civilisés'. For a consideration of the Advisory Committee of Jurists' debate on the sources of international law, see especially Ole Spiermann, ' "Who Attempts too Much Does Nothing Well": The 1920 Advisory Committee of Jurists and the Statute of the Permanent Court of International Justice' (2002) 73 *British Yearbook of International Law* 187, 212–18.

[114] On the application of general principles of international relations, see Mosler, above n 3, 511–12, 513, 522–4.

[115] Thirlway, 'Dilemma or Chimera?', above n107, 624.

[116] Cheng, above n 30, 290–8, 302–35, 336–72.

[117] For example, for the suggestion that *res judicata* might be treated as a rule of customary international law, see Yuval Shany, *The Competing Jurisdictions of International Courts and Tribunals* (2003) 245.

[118] See above nn 108–110 and accompanying text.

[119] Kolb, above n 30, 798.

[120] Ibid, 799.

dispute on which the judge can award executory rights is limited by the submission of the plaintiff... and of the defendant', or *ne ultra petita*;[121] and the principle that international courts have 'a wide discretion in the assessment of the evidence'.[122] Third, Professor Kolb states that there are some substantive principles that relate to international judicial and arbitral proceedings. These include 'the principle of *res judicata* and the duty to state the reasons upon which the decision is based', and also some 'substantive principles of general international law applicable also to procedural aspects' which describe the conduct expected of the parties.[123] These principles stem from 'the general duty of good faith the parties owe to one another when engaging in judicial proceedings',[124] and include the prohibition on abuse of process, the doctrine of estoppel, and the principle that 'a party claiming a certain fact or a certain legal point will not be admitted to benefit from it because of a previous fault committed in the context of the argument in question', or *nemo commodum capere potest de sua propria injuria*.[125]

These general principles have all been applied by international courts in international dispute settlement proceedings, and represent a method by which international tribunals can develop their procedures in harmony with those applicable before other international courts, where their own constitutive instruments are silent.

3. *Inherent Powers*

In addition to employing the tools of treaty interpretation, drawing on customary rules developed in international judicial practice, and having recourse to general principles of law, international courts have also relied on another source of law relating to procedure and remedies; that is, the exercise of powers that are not expressly conferred on them by their constitutive instruments, but which are nonetheless necessary for the performance of their functions. These powers are inherent powers. As these powers are somewhat more controversial than the harmonizing effect of the above-mentioned approaches to treaty interpretation, and the application of customary rules and general principles of law, the remainder of this chapter considers the concept of inherent powers in more detail.[126]

II. Inherent Powers in International Adjudication

A. The Concept of 'Inherent Powers'

The adjective 'inherent' is used to describe something which 'exist[s] in something as a permanent attribute or quality; forming an element, esp. a characteristic or essential element of something; belonging to the intrinsic nature of that which is

[121] Ibid, 810. [122] Ibid, 818. [123] Ibid, 799. [124] Ibid. [125] Ibid, 834.

[126] See also Chester Brown, 'The Inherent Powers of International Courts and Tribunals' (2005) 76 *British Yearbook of International Law* 195.

spoken of'.[127] An 'inherent power' might thus be said to be one that derives from an office, position or status;[128] an inherent power of a court might then be thought to derive 'from its nature as a court of law'.[129]

As a source of judicial power, 'inherent powers' appear to have their origin in the practice of English courts. English courts have invoked their inherent jurisdiction to exercise certain procedural powers 'from early times'.[130] The exercise of inherent powers has not been limited to English courts, however. The courts of many other common law jurisdictions have also claimed 'inherent powers'. These courts have variously invoked inherent powers in a wide variety of situations, such as to make rules of court and practice directions,[131] to prevent abuse of the court's process,[132] to stay proceedings,[133] to correct any injustice caused by an earlier order, such as where an individual is subjected to a lack of procedural fairness,[134] and to exercise control over persons before them, such as persons who are in contempt of court.[135] In addition, domestic superior courts have employed inherent powers in order to exercise control over inferior courts and tribunals.[136] While the use of inherent powers is certainly more widespread in common law countries, the exercise by courts of jurisdictional powers which are not expressly provided for in legislation or statutory rules is not unknown in civil law countries.[137]

[127] *Oxford English Dictionary* (1933 ed) vol V, 293.

[128] *Black's Law Dictionary* (abridged 7th ed, 2000) 953.

[129] I H Jacob, 'The Inherent Jurisdiction of the Court' (1970) 23 *CLP* 23, 24; on the inherent powers of domestic courts generally, see also Robert Pushaw, 'The Inherent Powers of the Federal Courts and the Structural Constitution' (2001) 86 *Iowa Law Review* 735; J A Jolowicz, 'Practice Directions and the Civil Procedure Rules' (2000) 59 *CLJ* 53; M S Dockray, 'The Inherent Jurisdiction to Regulate Civil Proceedings' (1997) 113 *LQR* 120; Jeffrey Pinsler, 'The Inherent Powers of the Court' (1997) *Singapore Journal of Legal Studies* 1; Keith Mason, 'The Inherent Jurisdiction of the Court' (1983) 57 *Australian Law Journal* 449.

[130] *Metropolitan Bank v Pooley* (1885) 10 App Cas 210, 220–1 (Lord Blackburn); see also *Civil Procedure* (2002) vol 2, 1539–40; Pushaw, ibid, 800–6; Jacob, ibid, 25–7.

[131] Jolowicz, above n 129; Jacob, above n 129, 33–7; e.g. *Thomas v Arn*, 474 US 140, 146–7 (1985); *Connelly v DPP* [1964] AC 1254, 1347; *Practice Direction (Trials in Middlesex)* [1958] 1 WLR 1291.

[132] *Connelly v DPP*, ibid, 1301; *R v Forbes; ex p Bevan* (1972) 127 CLR 1, 7–8; *Taylor v Taylor* (1979) 143 CLR 1, 6; *Re Regina and Unnamed Person* (1985) 20 CRR 188, 190–1; *Emilia Shipping Inc v State Enterprise for Pulp and Paper Industries* [1991] 2 MLJ 379.

[133] *R v Duval* [1995] 3 NZLR 202, 205; *Spiliada Maritime Corporation v Cansulex* [1987] AC 460, 476.

[134] *R v Bow Street Metropolitan Stipendiary Magistrate; ex p Pinochet Ugarte (No 2)* [2000] 1 AC 119, 132.

[135] *Connelly v DPP*, above n 131, 1301; *R v Forbes; ex p Bevan*, above n 132, 7; *Young v United States*, 481 US 787, 793 (1987); *Re Regina and Unnamed Person*, above n 132, 190–1.

[136] Jacob, above n 129, 48–9; *R v Parke* [1903] 2 KB 432, 443–4.

[137] For example, French procedural law derives not only from statutory instruments, but also from general principles of law and constitutional principles relating to fundamental rights: Serge Guinchard *et al*, *Droit processuel: Droit Commun et droit comparé du procès* (2e ed, 2003) 53–8, 286–96; the jurisdiction of administrative law courts in Germany is not prescribed by statute: Werner Ebke and Matthew Finkin (eds), *Introduction to German Law* (1996) 101–2; Nigel Foster and Satish Sute, *German Legal Systems and Laws* (3rd ed, 2002) 267–91; in Norway, custom represents a source of procedure: Anders Bratholm and Jo Hov, *Sivil Retergang* (1973) 10–11; and in Sweden, judicial

Despite the widespread exercise of inherent powers by domestic courts, there appears to be no consensus on the source of these powers.[138] Two views can be discerned in the literature and case law. On one view, only 'superior' courts can exercise inherent powers; this theory was advanced by Sir Jack Jacob, who wrote that:

> [T]he essential character of a superior court is that it should be invested with a power to maintain its authority and to prevent its process being obstructed and abused. Such a power is intrinsic in a superior court; it is its very life-blood, its very essence, its immanent attribute. Without such a power, the court would have form but lack substance. The jurisdiction which is inherent in a superior court of law is that which enables it to fulfil itself as a court of law. The juridical basis of this jurisdiction is therefore the authority of the judiciary to uphold, to protect and to fulfil the judicial function of administering justice according to law in a regular, orderly and effective manner.[139]

The view that only 'superior' courts possess inherent powers appears to be based on the origin of such bodies as exercising an 'unlimited jurisdiction' in the administration of the Sovereign's judicial power.[140] In order to carry out their functions, judges on such courts were able to rely on the existence of powers conferred by the exercise of royal prerogative.[141] In contrast, the jurisdiction of inferior courts is considered to be limited to that conferred on them by their founding statutes.

According to another view, all courts—whether superior or inferior—endowed with a particular jurisdiction have those powers which are necessary to enable them to act effectively. Those espousing this view regard courts as having inherent powers, to use the words of Lord Morris of Borth-y-Gest in *Connelly v DPP*, 'in order to enforce [their] rules of practice and to suppress any abuses of [their] process'.[142] Although it is unnecessary for present purposes to resolve completely the conceptual debate between these competing positions, it is noteworthy that the latter view appears to reflect the reality more accurately; many inferior courts have asserted inherent powers,[143] and those superior courts that assert inherent powers tend not to justify their exercise of such powers on the basis of their status as 'superior courts'.

decisions may be a source of procedural law: Ruth Bader Ginsburg and Anders Bruzelius, *Civil Procedure in Sweden* (1965) 39–40. Generally, on the existence of inherent powers in civil law countries, see further Jacob, above n 129, 23; Anthony Arnull, 'Does the Court of Justice Have Inherent Jurisdiction?' (1990) 27 *CML Rev* 683, 701; see, however, Gaeta, above n 49, 365.

138 Dockray, above n 129, 120.

139 Jacob, above n 129, 27–8.

140 Sir William Blackstone, *Commentaries on the Laws of England* (first published 1765, Stanley Katz ed, 1979) vol I, 257; Pushaw, above n 129, 800.

141 Blackstone, ibid, vol I, 257; Pushaw, ibid, 800–6.

142 Above n 131, 1301.

143 For example, Pushaw, above n 129, 822, 850–67; Charles Plant (ed), *Blackstone's Civil Practice* (2003) 4; Johnnie Kovacevich, 'The Inherent Power of the District Court' [1989] *New Zealand Law Journal* 184, 185–6; *Langley v North West Water Authority* [1991] 1 WLR 697, 709; *Chambers v NASCO, Inc*, 501 US 32, 43–51 (1991); *R v Saville* [1981] 1 QB 12, 17–18; *Jackson v Sterling Industries Ltd*, paras 47, 53–54 (Unreported, Federal Court of Australia, 15 October 1986); *R v Moke and Lawrence* [1996] 1 NZLR 263.

Before turning to the practice of international courts concerning inherent powers, it should be observed that certain theoretical objections have been made to the exercise of inherent powers by international courts. These objections are based on the fundamental differences that exist between the functions of national courts and international courts. Admittedly, there are dangers in importing concepts from domestic legal systems into international law, where those concepts might not be relevant. Sir Hersch Lauterpacht warned of these dangers in 1927, when he criticized

> the tendency on the part of many writers to resort to notions peculiar to their own municipal law or to some other system of private law regardless of the fact that conceptions of that kind cannot, owing to their technical character or the altogether special reason of their creation, claim that degree of cogency which is conditioned by the actual universality of a legal rule, from the point of view either of juridical logic or of legal justice, and which alone may serve as a basis of analogy.[144]

These words of caution have been repeated by Professor Thirlway with specific reference to the argument that the ICJ can exercise inherent powers in the context of the power to grant binding provisional measures. He referred to:

> the dangers of attributing to an international tribunal such as the Court inherent powers traced on the basis of municipal analogies. It needs to be recalled once more that the essence of jurisdiction is consent: if the Statute expresses the consent of States to a limited power to indicate provisional measures, it is self-contradictory to argue that, by creating a *court*, they implicitly consented to a wider power.[145]

Mindful of these warnings, the validity of the objections to the exercise of inherent powers by international courts is examined in the following section.

B. Arguments against the Exercise of Inherent Powers by International Courts

1. *The Exercise of Inherent Powers Depends on Unlimited Compulsory Jurisdiction*

The first objection to the exercise of inherent powers by international courts relates to the absence of unlimited compulsory jurisdiction in international dispute settlement. In contrast to the national courts which exercise inherent powers, international courts do not have unlimited compulsory jurisdiction derived from a sovereign prerogative. As Dr Orakhelashvili explains:

> National courts are established by the law and possess *ipso facto* compulsory jurisdiction within the ambit of their subject-matter competence. International tribunals, on the other

[144] Lauterpacht, *Private Law Sources and Analogies*, above n 113, 84–5.

[145] Thirlway, 'Part Nine', above n 8, 21 (emphasis in original); see also Rosenne, *Law and Practice*, above n 5, vol II, 517–19.

hand, are established by international agreements and their jurisdiction is based on the consent of States.[146]

In light of these differences, the objection might be made that international courts cannot exercise inherent powers. This can, however, be rejected. National courts which assert the existence of inherent powers only rarely justify such powers by reference to unlimited jurisdictional powers derived from a Sovereign. Rather, they generally state that these powers are necessary for the carrying out of their functions and the administration of justice.[147] In addition, it is not only superior national courts that have exercised powers other than those conferred on them: statutory courts—being municipal courts with limited jurisdiction—have also done so.[148] Furthermore, the fact that judges on international courts are not acting in pursuance of a sovereign grant of unlimited jurisdiction need not deprive them of powers needed to ensure the carrying out of their functions. Once the states party to the dispute have consented to the creation of the international court and the referral of the dispute to that body, it is then up to that body to decide how it is to carry out its functions; in this sense, the method of creation of a particular jurisdiction does not necessarily explain the legal effects of that jurisdiction.[149]

2. *International Courts can only exercise Expressly Conferred Powers*

The second objection that can be made to the exercise of inherent powers by international courts is related to the first; this objection is that the international instruments that establish international courts are constitutive of their powers; and accordingly, such courts can only exercise those powers which are expressly conferred by the consent of states. This objection is exemplified in the following statement by Professor Thirlway:

> When jurisdiction is referred to, it must always be asked, 'jurisdiction to do what?'. Jurisdiction or competence is not, in the sense in which those terms are used in relation to a dispute, a general property vested in the court or tribunal contemplated: it is the power, conferred by the consent of the parties, to make a determination on specified disputed issues which will be binding on the parties because that is what they have consented to.[150]

The view that the statutes of international courts are constitutive of their powers reflects the 'doctrine of attribution', as it is known in the context of the law of international organizations, according to which institutions can only work on the

[146] Orakhelashvili, 'International Judicial Jurisdiction', above n 8, 504–5.

[147] For example, *R v Moke and Lawrence*, above n 143, 266–7; *Connelly v DPP*, above n 131, 1301.

[148] See above n 143 and accompanying text.

[149] See especially Orakhelashvili, 'International Judicial Jurisdiction', above n 8, 505, who argues that the distinction between national courts and international courts is, in a practical sense, 'merely descriptive rather than prescriptive. It clarifies only the different ways in which national and international jurisdictions came into being. But it is unable to explain the nature of a jurisdiction as such, in particular its legal effects.'

[150] Thirlway, 'Part Nine', above n 8, 6.

basis of powers specifically attributed to them.[151] In the early twentieth century, this doctrine accorded with the prevailing positivist mode of thinking in international law.[152] It also received judicial support in the famous dictum of the PCIJ in *SS Lotus*, where it said that restrictions on the independence of states were not to be presumed.[153] In line with this dictum, the powers of international organizations are to be interpreted restrictively,[154] and, accordingly, it has been suggested that the powers of international courts are strictly limited to those that are expressly conferred on them by states in their constitutive instruments.[155]

This objection can likewise be rejected for two reasons. First, it has been observed that the constitutive instruments of international courts often contain *lacunae*; some constitutive instruments might make provision for a given situation, while others are silent. As Professor Crawford has argued, just because the constitutive instrument of one international court contains an express power where another does not, this 'should not be used to justify, *a contrario*, a failure to develop necessary or desirable rules of general international law'.[156] Second, the view that international courts can only exercise those powers which are expressly conferred on them is not borne out by substantial judicial and arbitral practice. It is to examples of the practice of international courts and tribunals that this chapter now turns.

III. Inherent Powers in the Practice of International Courts

The existence of inherent powers has been asserted in the case law of many international courts. The ICJ discussed the nature of its inherent powers most extensively in *Nuclear Tests*, in which it held that:

> [I]t should be emphasised that the Court possesses an inherent jurisdiction enabling it to take such action as may be required, on the one hand, to ensure that the exercise of its jurisdiction over the merits, if and when established, shall not be frustrated, and on the other, to provide for the orderly settlement of all matters in dispute, to ensure the observance of

[151] Jan Klabbers, *An Introduction to International Institutional Law* (2001) 64; see especially *Jurisdiction of the European Commission of the Danube between Galatz and Braila*, above n 48, PCIJ.

[152] Klabbers, ibid, 64.

[153] Ser A, (No 10), 18–19 (PCIJ, 1927).

[154] See, e.g., Klabbers, above n 151, 78–80; Georg Schwarzenberger, *International Law as Applied by International Courts and Tribunals* (1976) vol III, 52: 'If parties to an agreement establishing an international institution intend to grant any particular powers to the institution, they may be expected to define these powers in articulate language. If they fail to do so, the presumption must be in favour of the freedom of member states' (references omitted); Hans Kelsen, *The Law of the United Nations* (1950) 329–30.

[155] See especially *Lehigh Valley Railroad Company (United States) v Germany*, 8 RIAA 160, 170–1 (Op Comm Kiesselbach) (US–German MCC, 1933) ('*Sabotage Claims*'); see also, more recently, *Camera Care Ltd v Commission* [1980] ECR–I 119, 135 (Op A-G Warner): 'A body that is created by a legal instrument does not have "inherent" powers. It has only the powers that are conferred on it by that instrument, either expressly or by necessary implication.'

[156] James Crawford, 'International Law as an Open System' in James Crawford, *International Law as an Open System: Selected Essays* (2002) 17, 35.

the 'inherent limitations on the exercise of the judicial function' of the Court, and to 'maintain its judicial character'.... Such inherent jurisdiction, on the basis of which the Court is fully empowered to make whatever findings may be necessary for the purposes just indicated, derives from the mere existence of the Court as a judicial organ established by the consent of states, and is conferred upon it in order that its basic judicial functions may be safeguarded.[157]

Here, arguably the ICJ was continuing the theme which was considered by Sir Gerald Fitzmaurice in his separate opinion in *Northern Cameroons*.[158] There, he observed that the substantive jurisdiction of an international court, being its jurisdiction to hear and determine the merits, is distinct from its 'incidental' jurisdiction over procedural issues, such as granting provisional measures, admitting counterclaims, or permitting third party intervention; Fitzmaurice argued that:

[A]lthough much (though not all) of this incidental jurisdiction is specifically provided for in the Court's Statute, or in Rules of Court which the Statute empowers the Court to make, it is really an inherent jurisdiction, the power to exercise which is a necessary condition of the Court—or any court of law—being able to function at all.[159]

In pursuance of their 'inherent jurisdiction', international courts have on many occasions exercised powers not expressly conferred on them. In addition, international courts have exercised powers which are expressly conferred on them, but have noted that in doing so, they are exercising inherent powers, lending weight to Fitzmaurice's suggestion that such provisions really do no more than declare the existence of powers which international courts already possess.[160]

It is helpful to illustrate the existence of inherent powers in international adjudication with a series of examples. From the earliest days of modern international arbitration, international tribunals have found that they have the *compétence de la compétence*, or the power to determine the extent of their jurisdiction. For instance, the two American-appointed commissioners in the *Betsey* case, an arbitration

157 *Nuclear Tests (Australia v France)* [1974] ICJ Rep 253, 259–60 (references omitted).

158 [1963] ICJ Rep 15.

159 Ibid, 97, 103 (Sep Op Fitzmaurice) (references omitted); see also Fitzmaurice, above n 8, 542.

160 See, e.g., Gaeta, above n 49, 356; Orakhelashvili, 'International Judicial Jurisdiction', above n 8, 538–49; see also discussion in Hugh Thirlway, 'The Law and Procedure of the International Court of Justice 1960–1989: Part Ten' 70 *British Yearbook of International Law* 1, 2–5; Thirlway, 'Part Nine', above n 8, 18–19, 65; Fitzmaurice, above n 8, 451–7; Rosenne, *Law and Practice*, above n 5, vol II, 584–5, 812–17; Sir Elihu Lauterpacht, '"Partial" Judgments and the Inherent Jurisdiction of the International Court of Justice' in Vaughan Lowe and Malgosia Fitzmaurice (eds), *Fifty Years of the International Court of Justice* (1996) 465, 477; Ibrahim Shihata, *The Power of the International Court to Determine Its Own Jurisdiction* (1965) 47–56; Simpson and Fox, above n 3, 68–72; Georges Scelle, 'Draft on Arbitral Procedure Adopted by the Commission at its Fifth Session, Report by Georges Scelle, Special Rapporteur' [1958] *Yearbook of the International Law Commission*, vol II, 1, 8, UN Doc A/CN.4/113; Georges Scelle, 'Arbitral Procedure' [1950] *Yearbook of the International Law Commission*, vol II, 114, 136, UN Doc A/CN.4/18; Kenneth Carlston, *Process of International Arbitration* (1946) 74–81; Jackson Ralston, *Supplement to 1926 Revised Edition of The Law and Procedure of International Tribunals* (1936) 29; Jackson Ralston, *The Law and Procedure of International Tribunals* (rev ed, 1926) 44–8.

under article VII of the Jay Treaty, filed separate opinions in which they defended 'the right of the majority of the board to determine the board's own jurisdiction',[161] which was 'inherent in its very Constitution, and indispensably necessary to the discharge of any of its duties',[162] even though that power was not expressly provided for in the Jay Treaty. Subsequent arbitrations, in particular the *Alabama Arbitrations*, tended to confirm the existence of this power,[163] and the PCIJ considered it to be inherent in any body possessing jurisdictional powers.[164] In *Nottebohm*, the ICJ held that:

> [A]n international tribunal has the right to decide as to its own jurisdiction and has the power to interpret for this purpose the instruments which govern that jurisdiction.[165]

The ICJ further held that although the ICJ Statute provides in article 36(6) for this power, it also possesses the power as an inherent power; this was because article 36(6) of the Statute merely adopted 'a rule consistently accepted by general international law in the matter of international arbitration'.[166] The ICJ explained that the Rapporteur to the 1899 Convention had 'emphasised the necessity of this principle, presented by him as being "of the very essence of the arbitral function and one of the inherent requirements for the exercise of this function." '[167] The ICJ concluded that '[t]he judicial character of the Court and the rule of general international law referred to above are sufficient to establish that the court is competent to adjudicate on its own jurisdiction in the present case.'[168] In another case, the ICJ has held that other international tribunals also have this power; in *Arbitral Award of 31 July 1989*, the ICJ held that 'Article 4, paragraph 2, of the Arbitration Agreement *confirmed* that the Tribunal had power to determine its own jurisdiction'.[169] Most recently, in *Legality of Use of Force*, the ICJ described its *compétence de la compétence* as being '*reflected* in Article 36, paragraph 6 of the Statute',[170] rather than being '*conferred*' by that provision. The *compétence de la compétence* has been recognized in the jurisprudence of many other international courts, such as the WTO Appellate Body,[171]

[161] Moore, vol III, 2277. [162] Moore, vol III, 2278, 2278.

[163] Moore, vol I, 495, 646 (Great Britain–United States, 1875); see also *Pious Fund of the Californias*, 9 RIAA 11, 12–13 (US–Mexico, 1902) (PCA); *Flutie*, 9 RIAA 148, 151 (US–Venezuela MCC, 1903); *Preferential Treatment of Claims of Blockading Powers against Venezuela*, 9 RIAA 99, 108 (PCA, 1904); *Rio Grande Irrigation and Land Company*, 6 RIAA 131, 135–6 (UK–US, 1923).

[164] *Interpretation of the Greco-Turkish Agreement*, Ser B, (No 16), 20 (PCIJ, 1928).

[165] Above n 110, 119–20; on this point, see also *Certain Norwegian Loans* [1957] ICJ Rep 9, 34, 44 (Sep Op Lauterpacht). [166] *Nottebohm*, ibid 119.

[167] Ibid. [168] Ibid, 120.

[169] *Arbitral Award of 31 July 1989* [1991] ICJ Rep 53, 69 (emphasis added); Thirlway, 'Part Nine', above n 8, 19.

[170] *Legality of Use of Force (Serbia and Montenegro v Belgium) (Preliminary Objections)* (2005) 44 ILM 299, 312, para 34 (emphasis added).

[171] *US—Anti-Dumping Act of 1916*, WT/DS136/AB/R, para 54, fn 30 (ABR); see also *Mexico—Corn Syrup (Article 21(5))*, WT/DS132/ABR/RW, paras 35–7 (ABR); *Mexico—Taxes on Soft Drinks*, WT/DS308/AB/R, para 45 (ABR); Joost Pauwelyn, *Conflict of Norms in Public International Law*

the IACHR,[172] the Iran–US Claims Tribunal,[173] an ICSID tribunal,[174] the ICTY,[175] and in the separate opinion of a judge of the ITLOS.[176]

Although the *compétence de la compétence* is perhaps the best known example of an inherent power, it is by no means the only such example. Another power which is commonly exercised by international courts is the power to frame rules of procedure and to make procedural orders. It has been observed above that most international courts have an express power in their constitutive instruments to frame such rules. However, even in the absence of express authority, all international courts have the power to make rules of procedure and procedural orders as a necessary incident of their judicial functions.[177] Naturally, such rules of procedure must not contradict the provisions of the constitutive instrument or the *compromis*.[178] This has been expressly recognized by tribunals constituted under the NAFTA and the ICSID Convention,[179] and in a dissenting opinion of Judge Shahabuddeen of the ICTR Appeals Chamber.[180]

Another example is provided by the practice in many international courts of hearing preliminary objections regarding the court's jurisdiction and the admissibility of the claim separately from the merits. In *Mavrommatis Palestine Concessions*,

(2003) 448–9; Joost Pauwelyn, 'The Role of Public International Law in the WTO: How Far Can We Go?' (2001) 95 *AJIL* 535, 555–6.

172 *Ivcher Bronstein v Peru (Competence)*, Ser C, (No 54), paras 31–3 (IACHR, 24 September 1999); *Constitutional Court (Competence)*, Ser C, (No 55), paras 31–3 (IACHR, 24 September 1999); Gaeta, above n 49, 356.

173 *Marks & Umann v Iran*, 8 Ir–USCTR 290, 296–7 (1985).

174 *Klöckner v Cameroon*, above n 4, 251–2 (1985).

175 *Prosecutor v Tadic* (1996) 35 ILM 32, 40.

176 *M/V 'Saiga' (No 2) (Admissibility and Merits)*, 120 ILR 143, 239, 241 (Sep Op Nelson) (ITLOS, 1999).

177 Sir Arthur Watts, 'New Practice Directions of the International Court of Justice' (2002) 1 *Law and Practice of International Courts and Tribunals* 247, 255; Sir Arthur Watts, 'Burden of Proof, and Evidence before the ICJ' in Friedl Weiss (ed), *Improving WTO Dispute Settlement Procedures: Issues and Lessons from the Practice of Other International Courts and Tribunals* (2000) 289, 289; Rosenne, *Law and Practice*, above n 5, vol II, 584–5; Scelle, 'Draft on Arbitral Procedure', above n 160, 8–9, art 13; Manley Hudson, *International Tribunals: Past and Future* (1944) 86; Jackson Ralston, *International Arbitration from Athens to Locarno* (1929) 76–7; Ralston, *Law and Procedure*, above n 160, 197; Institut de Droit International, 'Projet de règlement pour la procédure arbitrale internationale' (1877) 1 *Annuaire de l'Institut de Droit International* 126, 130, art 15(1), (2), (4).

178 Ralston, *Athens to Locarno*, ibid, 76–7.

179 *United Parcel Services of America, Inc v Canada* (Order on Amici Curiae of 17 October 2001), para 38, observing that article 15(1) of the UNCITRAL Rules, which confers the power on the tribunal to 'conduct the arbitration in such a manner as it considers appropriate', was 'essential to the very process of dispute settlement by way of arbitration and might be thought to be inherent even if not expressly stated'; see also *Aguas Provinciales de Santa Fe SA, Suez, Sociedad General de Aguas de Barcelona SA and InterAguas Servicios Integrales del Agua SA v Argentina* (ICSID Case No ARB/03/17, Order on Amicus Curiae of 17 March 2006), para 7: '[a]lthough the Tribunal, as the Petition asserts, does have certain inherent powers with respect to arbitral procedure, it has no authority to exercise such power in opposition to a clear directive in the Arbitration Rules, which both Claimant and Respondent have agreed will govern the procedure in this case.'

180 *Kanyabashi v Prosecutor* (ICTR App Ch, 1999) 17 (Diss Op Shahabuddeen) (references omitted), referred to in Gaeta, above n 49, 358.

the PCIJ was confronted with a preliminary objection to its jurisdiction.[181] The PCIJ Statute and Rules provided no guidance on how this should be dealt with. The PCIJ stated that:

> Neither the Statute nor the Rules of Court contain any rule regarding the procedure to be followed in the event of an objection being taken *in limine litis* to the Court's jurisdiction. The Court therefore is at liberty to adopt the principle which it considers best calculated to ensure the administration of justice, most suited to procedure before an international tribunal and most in conformity with the fundamental principles of international law.[182]

Another power which has been asserted as an inherent power is the competence of international courts to reformulate the submissions of the applicants.[183] In *Nuclear Tests*, Australia and New Zealand had brought separate actions against France to restrain it from carrying out further atmospheric nuclear tests in the South Pacific. The relief sought included a declaration that such tests were unlawful.[184] Prior to judgment being handed down, France announced that it planned to halt its nuclear testing programme. The ICJ concluded that the relief sought by Australia and New Zealand was actually the cessation of the nuclear testing program, and that as a result of the French unilateral declaration, the applications of Australia and New Zealand were rendered 'moot'.[185] The ICJ's exercise of its inherent powers to interpret the parties' submissions in *Nuclear Tests* was not uncontroversial; the ICJ had, in effect, ignored Australia's and New Zealand's requests for a declaratory judgment on the illegality of France's atmospheric nuclear testing, and based its decision on public statements by the French Government on which neither Australia nor New Zealand had an opportunity to comment.[186] In this respect, limitations on the inherent power must be recognized, as noted by Judges Onyeama, Dillard, Jimenez de Aréchaga and Sir Humphrey Waldock in their Joint Dissenting Opinion.[187]

181 *Mavrommatis*, above n 50; see also discussion in Gaeta, above n 49, 371, fn 42.

182 *Mavrommatis*, ibid, 1, 16 (PCIJ, 1924); referred to in Gaeta, above n 49, 371. The PCIJ later adopted a provision in its Rules to regulate preliminary objections: PCIJ Rules, art 26 (1926); *Aerial Incident of 3 July 1988* [1989] ICJ Rep 132, 145, 146–7 (Sep Op Shahabuddeen). This practice of the PCIJ has been followed by a WTO panel in *Guatemala—Cement II*, DSR 2000–XI, 5295, 5638 (PR).

183 Thirlway, 'Part Nine', above n 8, 19.

184 See written submissions of Australia: above n 157, 256; and of New Zealand: [1974] ICJ Rep 457, 460.

185 *Nuclear Tests (Australia v France)*, above n 157, 271–2; and *Nuclear Tests (New Zealand v France)*, ibid, 475–7; Thirlway, 'Part Nine', above n 8, 18–19. The IACHR has also asserted an inherent power to arrive at its own understanding of the parties' submissions: *Character and Scope of the Right to Reply or Correction* (1986) 7 *Human Rights Law Journal* 238, 239; see also *The Right to Information*, above n 51, 37.

186 See, e.g., *Nuclear Tests*, above n 157, 312, and above n 184, 494 (Joint Diss Op Onyeama, Dillard, Jimenez de Aréchaga and Waldock); F A Mann, 'The Consequences of an International Wrong in International and National Law' (1976–7) 48 *British Yearbook of International Law* 1, 10–11.

187 *Nuclear Tests (Australia v France)*, ibid, 312, 316, and *(New Zealand v France)*, ibid, 494, 498 (Joint Diss Op Onyeama, Dillard, Jimenez de Aréchaga and Waldock): 'While the Court is entitled to interpret the submissions of the Parties, it is not entitled to introduce into them radical alterations'.

Another example can be found in the exercise by international tribunals of powers over the management of proceedings. Mention has been made in chapter 1 of the increased volume of interstate litigation. This higher workload of international tribunals, combined with a relative stagnation in the amount of financial support provided to such bodies, has required international tribunals to adopt methods of managing their workload to cope with these pressures.[188] To this end, several international courts, including the ICJ, the ICTY, the ICTR, the ECJ and the ECHR have in recent years modified their working procedures and adopted Practice Directions.[189] While the ICTY, ICTR and the ECHR have granted themselves in their rules of procedure the power to promulgate Practice Directions, the ICJ has no textual basis for doing so.[190] One possible basis might be found in article 30 of the ICJ Statute which empowers the ICJ to 'frame rules for carrying out its functions'. It is suggested, however, that the issuing of Practice Directions goes beyond the framing of rules, and that it can be based on the ICJ's inherent power to take action to ensure the proper administration of international justice.[191]

Relatedly, international tribunals have held that they are masters of their own procedure even in instances where the parties prefer the adoption of another method of handling the case. In *Larsen/Hawaiian Kingdom*, the parties concluded a revised *compromis*, in which they requested the PCA tribunal to verify 'the

[188] See, e.g., Shabtai Rosenne, 'Updates to Law and Practice of the International Court of Justice' (2002) 1 *Law and Practice of International Courts and Tribunals* 129, 139–40; Dietmar Prager, 'The 2001 Amendments to the Rules of Procedure of the International Court of Justice' (2002) 1 *Law and Practice of International Courts and Tribunals* 155; Judge Rosalyn Higgins, 'Respecting Sovereign States and Running a Tight Courtroom' (2001) 50 *ICLQ* 121, 122–32; see also 'The International Court of Justice Revises its Working Methods to Expedite the Examination of Contested Cases' (Press Communiqué 98/14, 6 April 1998); and 'Response of the International Court of Justice to GA Resolution 52/161 of 15 December 1997' (1998) 37 ILM 1466.

[189] See, e.g., Philippe Couvreur, 'L'organisation et les moyens des juridictions internationales face au contentieux international' in Société Française pour le Droit International, *Colloque de Lille: La juridictionnalisation du droit international* (2003) 467, 506; ICJ Practice Directions of 31 October 2001 (Press Release 2001/32), 4 April 2002: (2002) 41 ILM 998, 30 July 2004 (Press Release 2004/30), and 13 December 2006 (Press Release 2006/43) (12 in total); ICTY Practice Directions of 9 July 1998, 18 December 1998 (revised on 4 May 2001, and on 24 January 2002), 7 April 1999, 1 October 1999 (revised on 7 March 2002, on 21 February 2005, and again on 16 September 2005), 12 July 2000, 19 January 2001 (revised on 5 March 2002, and on 16 September 2005), 20 July 2001, 7 March 2002, 6 May 2004, 14 November 2005, and 15 August 2006 (13 in total); ICTR Practice Directions of 16 September 2002, 24 April 2004, and 4 July 2005 (4 in total); ECHR Practice Directions of 5 March 2003 and 1 November 2003 (3 in total), based on ECHR Rules, Rule 32; and, e.g. ECJ Practice Directions of 15 October 2004: OJ L361/15 (8 December 2004). See further Watts, 'New Practice Directions', above n 177, 248; Shabtai Rosenne, 'International Court of Justice: Practice Directions on Judges Ad Hoc; Agents; Counsel and Advocates; and Submission of New Documents' (2002) 1 *Law and Practice of International Courts and Tribunals* 223, 223; Higgins, above n 188, 124; and also, more generally, Shabtai Rosenne, 'Controlling Interlocutory Aspects of Proceedings in the International Court of Justice' (2000) 94 *AJIL* 307.

[190] ECHR Rules, above n 19, Rule 32; ICTY Rules, available from <http://www.un.org/icty> Rule 19(B); ICTR Rules, available from <http://www.ictr.org> Rules 19(B), 107*bis*.

[191] For the expression of a similar view, see Watts, 'New Practice Directions', above n 177, 255; see also more generally Higgins, above n 188, 131–2.

continued existence of Hawaiian Statehood' in an interlocutory award. The PCA tribunal refused to accede to this request, holding that:

> [i]t is not open to the parties by way of an Amendment to the Special Agreement to seek to redefine the essential issues, so as to convert them into 'interim' or 'interlocutory' issues. In accordance with Article 32 of the UNCITRAL Rules, and with the general principles of arbitral procedure, it is for the Tribunal to determine which issues need to be dealt with and in what order.[192]

It is also well established that notwithstanding the absence of an express power to award remedies, international courts having jurisdiction over a dispute also have as an essential part of that jurisdiction the power to award remedies.[193] This has already been referred to above in the context of the principle of effectiveness in treaty interpretation. While the jurisdiction of an international court to award remedies can be regarded as an application of the *effet utile*, it is suggested that the awarding of remedies can also be considered as an example of the exercise by these bodies of an inherent power, which lies at the heart of the judicial function in the settlement of disputes. It is noteworthy in this connection that other international tribunals, such as the ITLOS, *ad hoc* arbitral tribunals, PCA, ICSID and NAFTA tribunals, have simply assumed that they have the power to award remedies without expressly relying on the *Factory at Chorzów* and *Corfu Channel* jurisprudence.[194]

The foregoing section is not an exhaustive review of the exercise of inherent powers in international adjudication, but it illustrates the existence of these powers in several notable situations. In light of this practice, and in order to judge better when international courts can exercise such powers as a method of cross-fertilizing their procedures and remedies with those of other international tribunals, there is a need to arrive at a proper understanding of these powers' source, and the limitations of their use.

IV. Source of Inherent Powers

In the past writers have lamented the failure of international courts to clarify the source of inherent powers.[195] Sir Elihu Lauterpacht has observed that the ICJ has 'simply assumed' the existence of an inherent jurisdiction,[196] and added that it

[192] 119 ILR 566, 579–80 (PCA, 2001).

[193] Crawford, *ILC Articles on State Responsibility*, above n 54, 218.

[194] For example, *M/V 'Saiga' (No 2)*, above n 176, 199–200 (ITLOS); *Protection of the Rhine against Pollution by Chlorides*, (Award of 12 March 2004) paras 133–43 (Netherlands–France, 2004), available at <http://www.pca-cpa.org> (last visited 25 November 2006); *Feldman v Mexico* (ICSID Case No ARB(AF)/99/1, Award of 16 December 2002), paras 189–207 (NAFTA Tribunal); *Maffezini v Spain* (2001) 16 *ICSID Review—FILJ* 248, paras 94–7; *Amco v Indonesia* (Award), above n 4, 498–501.

[195] See, e.g., Gaeta, above n 49, 354–5, 358–61.

[196] Lauterpacht, '"Partial" Judgments', above n 160, 477.

would be to the general advantage of all if the ICJ were to identify the use and source of inherent powers in any relevant case.[197] In its dictum in *Nuclear Tests*, the ICJ arguably indicated three different sources of its 'inherent jurisdiction':

> Such inherent jurisdiction, on the basis of which the Court is fully empowered to make whatever findings may be necessary for the purposes just indicated, derives from the mere existence of the Court as a judicial organ established by the consent of states, and is conferred upon it in order that its basic judicial functions may be safeguarded.[198]

Here, the ICJ states that its inherent jurisdiction derives from 'the mere existence of the Court as a judicial organ'; this suggests that any judicial organ possesses inherent powers. The ICJ then appears immediately to contradict this assertion with the statement that the inherent jurisdiction is 'conferred upon it'. This does not sit comfortably with the idea of an 'inherent power', for if a power is 'inherent', then there is no need for any conferral, whether express or implied. Finally, the ICJ states that the inherent jurisdiction exists in order to safeguard 'its basic judicial functions'; this suggests that the inherent jurisdiction derives from the existence of expressly conferred functions and powers, and that the inherent powers exist in order to ensure that the expressly conferred powers can be exercised.

Essentially, four possible sources of inherent powers can be discerned in the jurisprudence of international courts and the writings of publicists. These are: the concept of 'general principles of law'; the doctrine of implied powers; the identity of international courts as judicial bodies; and a functional justification.[199] There is a degree of overlap between these sources, and some of the distinctions between them may seem artificial. Nevertheless, there are subtle conceptual differences, and it is important to distinguish these possible sources in order to find the most appropriate justification for the exercise of inherent powers in international adjudication. This is because it is the source of inherent powers that provides guidance as to the limitations that exist to restrict the exercise of such powers. If the source is located in the concept of general principles of law, for instance, inherent powers might be few in number, given the relative scarcity of such principles. If inherent powers are justified by the function of international courts, on the other hand, they are likely to be more abundant, and careful limiting factors need to be identified to curb their use.

A. Inherent Powers are Derived from General Principles of Law

The first suggestion is that the source of inherent powers of international courts can be found in 'general principles of law'. In a few cases, international tribunals have explained the inherent character of a power by pointing to the existence of a

[197] Ibid, 483. [198] Above n 157, 259–60.

[199] But see Gaeta, above n 49, 354–5, who suggests that only three possible sources can be identified: general principles of law, the doctrine of implied powers, and the judicial nature of international courts.

'general principle of law' specifically providing for such a power.[200] For instance, in *Genie Lacayo (Judicial Review)*, the IACHR held that it had an inherent power to revise its judgments, noting that this finding accorded with 'the general principles of both domestic and international procedural law'.[201] In another example, the PCIJ held, in the context of its power to indicate provisional measures, that there was a general principle of law that parties must abstain from action which would prejudice the rights which are the subject of proceedings.[202] This approach has also been adopted by some writers who have sought to explain the source of some inherent powers, such as the *compétence de la compétence*,[203] and the power to grant provisional measures,[204] as lying in general principles of law.

This basis for the existence of inherent powers is attractive, and does provide a sound explanation for the exercise of some inherent powers by international courts. It is suggested, however, that general principles of law are unlikely to provide a basis for all cases where international courts seek to exercise an inherent power, as there are relatively few general principles which are widely applicable in domestic legal orders, and they do not always relate to the existence of procedural powers. It is difficult to substantiate as a general principle of law, for instance, that all courts have the power to make cost orders, or order the preparation of an expert report, when those procedures might not be known to all legal systems. The non-universality of many legal principles has also been recognised by a NAFTA Tribunal. In response to an argument that the doctrine of *laches* should bar a request for the consolidation of a series of claims, the NAFTA Tribunal observed that:

> [T]he forms of equity known to Anglo-American common law do not form part of the corpus of public international law. While there is a borrowing of principles derived from domestic legal systems in public international law, this takes the form of general principles of law that do not necessarily replicate the rules of domestic law from which they derive their common origin.[205]

Moreover, when international courts have invoked procedural powers that are not expressly conferred on them, they have only rarely done so by reference to a general

[200] See also Gaeta, above n 49, 359.

[201] *Genie Lacayo (Judicial Review)*, Ser C, (No 45), para 9 (IACHR, 1997).

[202] *Electricity Company of Sofia and Bulgaria*, Ser A/B, (No 79), 194, 199 (PCIJ, 1939); see also *LaGrand*, above n 29, 1093–4; *Aegean Sea (Greece v Turkey)* [1976] ICJ Rep 3, 15–16 (Sep Op Aréchaga); *Casado and Fondation Allende*, above n 80, 579; *Amco v Indonesia* (Provisional Measures), 89 ILR 402, 404–5 (1983); see also the decision of a national court, the Cour d'appel de Rennes, in *Guinea v Atlantic Triton Co*, 3 ICSID Rep 3, 8–9 (1984).

[203] Cheng, above n 30, 275–8; Carlston, above n 160, 74–5.

[204] Lawrence Collins, 'Provisional and Protective Measures in International Litigation' (1992) 234 *Recueil des cours* 9, 23–4, 214–16; Cheng, above n 30, 267–9; E Dumbauld, *Interim Measures of Protection in International Controversies* (1932) 42–81; see also Francis Jacobs and Rudolf Bernhardt (reported comments), in Rudolf Bernhardt (ed), *Interim Measures Indicated by International Courts* (1994) 137–9, 140.

[205] *Canfor Corporation v US*, *Tembec* et al *v US* and *Terminal Forest Products v US* (Order of the Consolidation Tribunal of 7 September 2005), para 165 (footnote omitted).

principle of law. In other words, their methodological approach is not one which is consistent with the application of general principles of law within the meaning of article 38(1)(c) of the ICJ Statute. For these reasons, other possible sources of inherent powers are examined.

B. Inherent Powers are Implied Powers

Another possible basis for the exercise of inherent powers can be found in the doctrine of implied powers.[206] Like express powers, implied powers are considered to be conferred by the terms of a constitutive instrument, but they are not made express; rather, they are conferred by implication. This doctrine essentially rests on the principle of effectiveness in treaty interpretation, which has been described above.[207]

The doctrine of implied powers certainly has some appeal as a justification for the exercise of inherent powers. The ICJ's approach to the implication of powers of international organizations in *Reparation for Injuries*, where it stated the test as being whether the power was necessary for the functions of the international organization, certainly appears to accord with much international judicial practice on the exercise of inherent powers.[208] Yet it is suggested that to regard inherent powers as identical with implied powers is not entirely accurate. The doctrine of implied powers has been used by international courts far more frequently in the context of the powers of international organizations.[209] In contrast, when they have claimed powers for themselves which are not expressly provided for in their constitutive instruments, international courts, in general, have not sought to imply powers from the express terms of their statutes. This suggests that international courts themselves find the doctrine of implied powers inappropriate.[210] In her consideration of inherent powers, Professor Gaeta even states that there is only one example of an international court exercising an 'implied power', being the judgment of the ICTY Trial Chamber in *Prosecutor v Blaskic* that it had an 'implied power' to issue a *subpoena duces tecum* to a state or state official for the production of government documents.[211] On appeal, the ICTY Appeals Chamber, in overturning the Trial Chamber's decision, held that it preferred to speak of 'inherent

[206] For example, for the view that it is difficult to distinguish an inherent power from an implied one in the context of the powers of international organizations, see Blain Sloan, 'General Assembly Resolutions Revisited (Forty Years Later)' (1987) 58 *British Yearbook of International Law* 39, 55.

[207] See above part I(C)(1)(a) of this chapter; see also Lauterpacht, *Development*, above n 8, 227–8; Hugo Grotius, *On the Law of War and Peace* (first published 1625, 1964 ed, Francis Kelsey trans) 857; Emmerich de Vattel, *The Law of Nations, or, Principles of the Law of Nature, Applied to the Conduct and Affairs of Nations and Sovereigns* (first published 1758, 4th ed, 1811) 234.

[208] *Reparation for Injuries* [1949] ICJ Rep 174, 182.

[209] Gaeta, above n 49, 360, 362.

[210] For example, *Nuclear Tests* above n 157, 259–60; *Continental Shelf (Revision and Interpretation)*, above n 8, 198; *Request for an Examination—Nuclear Tests* [1995] ICJ Rep 288, 303–4; see also Judge Koroma's dissenting opinion at [1995] ICJ Rep 363, 369 (referring to 'the Court's inherent power to accommodate the particular requirements of the case.').

[211] *Prosecutor v Blaskic*, above n 49, 624–7, 630, 637–40 (ICTY, 1997); Gaeta, above n 49, 360.

powers' rather than 'implied powers'.[212] It is unlikely that this is the only instance of international courts relying on the doctrine of 'implied powers'; the instances mentioned above, where international courts have found that they are competent to award remedies, and order binding provisional measures, arguably offer further examples, as do the reports of the WTO Appellate Body on its authority, and that of WTO panels, to receive *amicus curiae* briefs.[213] Yet Professor Gaeta's point remains a valid one; while the basic methodology of implied powers might provide a solid basis for the exercise of inherent powers, it is not one that international courts often invoke.

C. Inherent Powers are Derived from the Identity of Courts as Judicial Bodies

In some cases, international courts have found that they have inherent powers simply because the relevant powers are usually attributed to judicial bodies.[214] For instance, in an early decision, the arbitral tribunal in *Rio Grande Irrigation and Land Company* noted that 'there is inherent in this and in every legal Tribunal a power, and indeed a duty, to entertain, and, in proper cases, to raise for themselves, preliminary points going to their jurisdiction to entertain the claim'.[215] The ICJ has also used this language in *Nuclear Tests*,[216] and also in *Effect of Awards of Compensation Made by the UNAT* in characterising the UNAT as a judicial body and its power to make final and binding awards.[217]

The view that certain rules of procedure can be attributed to international judicial bodies on the basis of their being called 'courts' has attracted some doctrinal support. In discussing the existence of a procedural norm which requires international tribunals to hear both parties to a dispute, Professor Thirlway has argued that the principle of *audi alteram partem* could be regarded as a general principle of law, but could also 'be considered to be contained within the concept of a "court" ', for 'a "court" that was not required to hear both sides would generally be regarded as not worthy of the name'.[218]

[212] *Prosecutor v Blaskic*, 110 ILR 688, 698, fn 27 (ICTY App Ch, 1997); Danesh Sarooshi, 'The Powers of the United Nations International Criminal Tribunals' (1998) 2 *Max Planck Yearbook of United Nations Law* 141, 150; Gaeta, ibid, 360.

[213] See, e.g., *US—Shrimp*, above n 74, 2783–7 (ABR) (concerning the power of WTO panels to receive *amicus curiae* briefs); *US—Hot Rolled Steel*, WT/DS138/AB/R, paras 36–42 (ABR) (concerning the power of the WTO Appellate Body to receive *amicus curiae* briefs); see also *EC—Asbestos*, WT/DS135/AB/R, paras 50–7 (ABR) (outlining procedures for the submission of *amicus curiae* briefs).

[214] Gaeta, above n 49, 360, 364–5.

[215] Above n 163, 135–6.

[216] Above n 157, 259–60.

[217] Above n 48, 52. In referring to the provisions of the UNAT Statute, the ICJ held that 'these provisions and the terminology used are evidence of the judicial nature of the Tribunal. Such terms as "tribunal", "judgment", competence to "pass judgment on applications", are generally used with respect to judicial bodies. The above mentioned provisions . . . are of an essentially judicial character and conform with rules generally laid down in statutes or laws issued from courts of justice'. *Statute of the Administrative Tribunal of the United Nations*, UNGA Res 315–A(IV), 24 November 1949.

[218] Thirlway, 'Dilemma or Chimera?', above n 107, 626 (references omitted).

But the identity of international courts as judicial bodies is also less than satisfactory as a source of inherent powers, for relying on a body's name as a source for competences is problematic. In particular, it is difficult to maintain that courts and tribunals, whether national or international, can exercise certain powers on the basis of their being called 'courts' or 'tribunals', simply because certain procedural powers, which are sought to be established as inherent powers, are the types of power that courts usually have. To argue that a court has certain powers because it is called a 'court' is a circular argument; it is to deduce from the word 'court' the existence of certain characteristics without which the body in question could not be referred to as a 'court'.[219] Moreover, to say that a power is inherent 'in a court' is unhelpful when one does not take account of the nature or function of the court or legal system in question.[220]

D. Inherent Powers are Necessary to Ensure the Performance of the Functions of International Courts

A better view of the source of the inherent powers of international courts is their need to ensure the carrying out of the functions that have been expressly conferred upon them. This 'functional justification' for the existence of inherent powers finds support in judicial decisions; it accords with one of the ICJ's asserted bases for inherent powers in *Nuclear Tests*, where the court referred to the need to safeguard its judicial functions, and it also accords with the finding of the ICTY Appeals Chamber in *Blaskic*, where it held that 'the International Tribunal must possess the power to make all those judicial determinations that are necessary for the exercise of its primary jurisdiction'.[221] The WTO Appellate Body has also stated that 'WTO panels have certain powers that are inherent in their adjudicative function'.[222] In addition, the functional justification for the existence of inherent powers has found support in doctrinal writings.[223]

The conclusion that the source of inherent powers can be found in the necessity of international courts to carry out their functions raises the question of the extent of those functions. This is because the functions of international courts define which powers international courts may exercise as inherent powers. Equally, the extent of the functions of international courts imposes certain limitations on the exercise of such powers. In order to examine the scope of inherent powers, an identification of the functions of international courts is crucial, and it is to this question that this chapter now turns.

219 Karl Zemanek (reported comments), in Bernhardt (ed), above n 204, 129; Hartmut Schiedermair (reported comments), in Bernhardt, ibid, 142–3; but see also Thirlway, (reported comments) in Bernhardt, ibid, 137.

220 See also Iain Scobbie, *Legal Reasoning and the Judicial Function in the International Court* (PhD Dissertation, University of Cambridge, 1990) 67–71.

221 Above n 212, 704.

222 *Mexico—Taxes on Soft Drinks*, above n 171, para 45.

223 Gaeta, above n 49, 364–8; Thirlway, 'Part Nine', above n 8, 41; Lauterpacht, '"Partial" Judgments', above n 160, 480.

V. Extent of the Inherent Powers of International Courts

A. Functions of International Adjudication

There is an active debate about the functions of international adjudication,[224] and two main schools of thought can be distinguished. On one view, the function of international courts is a private function, that is, that international courts are created in order to settle disputes referred to them. In other words, their task is 'to do justice' between the litigant states, and to render a judgment or award which takes account of all relevant facts, which is limited to the *petitum* of the dispute, and which is made with final and binding force.[225] This function can be discerned from the constitutive instruments and the jurisprudence of many international courts. For instance, arbitration under the auspices of the PCA has as its object the settlement of disputes between states by judges of their own choice, and on the basis of respect for law.[226] This private function is also reflected in article 42(1) of the ICSID Convention, which stipulates that the function of arbitral tribunals established under that convention is to 'decide a dispute in accordance with such rules of law as may be agreed by the parties'.[227] It is also summed up in the statement of the WTO panel in *EC—Bananas*, which considers the role of WTO dispute settlement: 'first and foremost, that system is designed to settle disputes.'[228] Article 38(1) of the ICJ Statute also states the function of that body as being 'to decide in accordance with international law such disputes as are submitted to it'.[229] In its case law, the ICJ has repeatedly confirmed that its judicial function is the resolution of questions which must be answered in accordance with law.[230]

On another view, international adjudication also has a public function, which goes beyond the settlement of the dispute. This view regards the goal of settling disputes as being too focused on the private aspect of disputes, and not conducive to the positive creation of norms which can generate obedience among members

[224] For example, on the function of the ICJ, see Rosenne, *Law and Practice*, above n 5, vol I, 97–193; Jennings, above n 3, vol I, 433–93; Sir Robert Jennings, 'The Role of the International Court of Justice' (1997) 68 *British Yearbook of International Law* 1, 1–9; A S Muller, D Raic and J M Thuransky (eds), *The International Court of Justice: Its Future Role after Fifty Years* (1997); Georges Abi-Saab, 'The International Court as a World Court' in Lowe and Fitzmaurice (eds), above n 1, 3; Nagendra Singh, *The Role and Record of the International Court of Justice* (1989).

[225] See, for example, Rosenne, *Law and Practice*, above n 5, vol II, 507.

[226] 1899 Convention, art 15; 1907 Convention, art 37; Jennings, above n 224, 5.

[227] *ICSID Convention*, above n 21, art 42(1).

[228] *EC—Regime for the Importation, Sale and Distribution of Bananas*, [1997] DSR–II 695, 711 (PR); see also *US—Shirts and Blouses*, above n 109, 340.

[229] *ICJ Statute*, above n 2, art 38(1).

[230] For example, *LaGrand*, above n 29, 1093; *Questions of Interpretation—Lockerbie* [1992] ICJ Rep 3, 50, 56 (Diss Op Weeramantry); *Nuclear Tests*, above n 157, 270–1; *Fisheries Jurisdiction* (*UK v Iceland*) [1974] ICJ Rep 3, 18–19; *Namibia*, above n 67, 23; *Northern Cameroons*, above n 158, 29–34, 38; *Haya de la Torre* [1951] ICJ Rep 71, 83; Lauterpacht, *Development*, above n 8, 3–5; Sir Hersch Lauterpacht, *The Function of Law in the International Community* (1933) 105–7, 127–31.

of the community being regulated by that system of norms.[231] This public function encompasses several considerations, each of which may be equally important. One of these is the function of ensuring the proper administration of international justice. This is distinct from the function of settling disputes, in that it emphasizes the need for effectiveness and efficiency in judicial decision-making, and it is well established in the jurisprudence of international courts, as well as in the literature.[232] This function has asserted itself recently as a result of the increased workload of international courts.[233] As noted in chapter 1, the proliferation of international courts has been matched by a sharp increase in the recourse by states to third-party dispute settlement procedures. This has required such bodies to take greater control over the management of disputes.[234] Judge Higgins has noted extrajudicially that in order to cope with this increase in activity, a modernization of ICJ procedures is required concerning 'the timetable for the speedy resolution of disputes', and which would enhance the ICJ's integrity in permitting it 'the *normal* control . . . of its own procedures'.[235] The recognition that an international court such as the ICJ is a 'normal' court underlines the importance of this function. One manifestation of international courts taking greater control over their procedures is the issuing of practice directions, which has been noted above.[236] Other inherent powers have been justified on the basis of the need to carry out this function, such as the power to dismiss proceedings summarily,[237] and the power to hear preliminary objections.[238]

Another manifestation of the public function of international adjudication is the role that international courts play in the clarification and the progressive development of international law.[239] Sir Hersch Lauterpacht saw a broader role for the ICJ than the mere settlement of disputes; he argued that 'the development of international law by international tribunals was, in the long run, one of the important conditions of their continued successful functioning and of their jurisdiction'.[240] Professor de Visscher was also of this view. He stated that '[m]uch

231 In the context of domestic adjudication, see especially Owen Fiss, 'Against Settlement' (1983–4) 93 *Yale Law Journal* 1073, 1089.

232 See, e.g., *Mavrommatis Palestine Concessions*, above n 50, 1, 16; *Legality of Use of Force (Yugoslavia v Spain)* [1999] ICJ Rep 761, 773–4; *Legality of Use of Force (Yugoslavia v US)* [1999] ICJ Rep 916, 925–6; see also Kolb, above n 30, 806–9; John Bassett Moore, *International Adjudications: Ancient and Modern—History and Documents* (1929) vol I, xxii, lviii–lix, and the references cited therein.

233 Couvreur, above n 189, 467; Higgins, above n 188, 131–2; Sir Robert Jennings, 'The International Court of Justice after Fifty Years' (1995) 89 *AJIL* 493, 497–8.

234 'Response of the ICJ to GA Resolution 52/161', above n 188, 1469–71.

235 Higgins, above n 188, 131–2 (emphasis added).

236 Couvreur, above n 189, 506; see also above n 189 and accompanying text.

237 *Legality of Use of Force, (Yugoslavia v Spain)*, above n 232, 773–4; *(Yugoslavia v US)*, above n 232, 925–6.

238 *Mavrommatis Palestine Concessions*, above n 50, 1, 16.

239 Lauterpacht, *Development*, above n 8, 5–7; see, e.g., Gilbert Guillaume, 'The Current Situation of the International Court of Justice and its Future' (Address to the Lauterpacht Research Centre for International Law, University of Cambridge, 9 November 2001) 9.

240 Lauterpacht, *Development*, above n 8, 6–7.

more than the establishment of peace, the development of international law is the essential function of judicial settlement by a permanent and institutionalised tribunal'.[241] In exercising this function, Sir Hersch Lauterpacht argued that international courts could exercise:

> in each case a creative activity, having as its background the entirety of international law and the necessities of the international community. The distinction between the making of law by judges and by the legislature is upon analysis one of degree... judicial activity is nothing else than legislation *in concreto*.[242]

As an example of Lauterpacht's position, he was opposed to the use of 'judicial economy' by international courts in the settlement of disputes. He argued that 'there are compelling considerations of international justice and of development of international law which favour a full measure of exhaustiveness of judicial pronouncements of international tribunals'.[243] He also considered that the administration of justice in a domestic legal system 'can afford to rely on purely formal and procedural grounds', but that this could not be done in interstate disputes, 'where it is of importance that justice should not only be done but that it should also appear to have been done'.[244] Yet while Lauterpacht supported international courts explaining, clarifying and developing international law, he did not propose that international courts should go beyond the confines of the four corners of the dispute in exercising this creative role; to do so would be to permit legislation by the 'backdoor of transforming the nature of the judicial function'.[245] The case for this function is strengthened if the international court in question is established within the context of a particular regime. It might be said, for instance, that the ICJ, as 'the principal judicial organ' of the UN, fills a public or constitutional role in the UN system.[246] Its role in giving advisory opinions, which have provided guidance on the powers of the UN and its different organs, bears testament to this function.[247] Many international courts clearly consider that they have a broader

[241] Charles de Visscher, *Theory and Reality in Public International Law* (1968) 390.

[242] Lauterpacht, *Function of Law*, above n 230, 319–20; for discussion of Lauterpacht's view of the international judicial function, see especially Iain Scobbie, 'The Theorist as Judge: Hersch Lauterpacht's Concept of the International Judicial Function' (1997) 8 *European Journal of International Law* 264, 277–8, 284; Sir Gerald Fitzmaurice, 'Hersch Lauterpacht and His Attitude to the Judicial Function' (1979) 50 *British Yearbook of International Law* 1, 10–11; Sir Gerald Fitzmaurice, 'Hersch Lauterpacht—The Scholar as Judge: I' (1961) 37 *British Yearbook of International Law* 1, 14–15.

[243] Lauterpacht, *Development*, above n 8, 37.

[244] Ibid, 39.

[245] Ibid, 75–7; Sir Hersch Lauterpacht, 'The Legal Aspect' in C A W Manning (ed), *Peaceful Change: An International Problem* (1937) 135, 145. See also *Barcelona Traction (Preliminary Objections)* [1964] ICJ Rep 4, 65 (Sep Op Tanaka).

[246] *Charter of the United Nations*, opened for signature 26 June 1945, 3 Bevans 1153 (entered into force 24 October 1945), art 92; see, e.g., Malcolm Shaw, 'The Security Council and the International Court of Justice: Judicial Drift and the Judicial Function' in Muller, Raic and Thuransky (eds), above n 224, 219, 219; Jennings, 'The Role of the International Court of Justice', above n 224, 1–9; Neill Alford, 'Fact finding by the World Court' (1958) 4 *Villanova Law Review* 37, 37–8.

[247] ICJ Statute, above n 2, art 65.

function which includes the development of the law. The ECHR has held that its functions were 'not only to decide those cases brought before it, but more generally, to elucidate, safeguard and develop the rules instituted by the Convention'.[248] The ECJ has also assumed a constitutional role in the EC, and has sought to clarify and develop EC law, as evidenced by its willingness to give judgments in cases which were moot, in order to clarify questions of law which could arise in other cases.[249] The WTO dispute settlement system also arguably fills a constitutional role in overseeing the implementation of the WTO Agreement and its covered agreements.[250] Under article 3(2) of the DSU, an explicit goal of the dispute settlement system is to provide jurisprudence to help ensure the predictability and stability of the world trading system.[251] WTO panels and the Appellate Body, as the GATT panels before them, have, in accordance with this function, substantially developed WTO law in the course of settling disputes.[252] The Appellate Body indicated its acceptance of this role in *US—Gasoline*, where it made reference to ICJ jurisprudence and general principles of law as a basis for interpretations of the WTO Agreement.[253] However, the WTO Appellate Body has stated that it would not go beyond the limits of what it needs to do to settle the dispute. In *US—Shirts and Blouses*, it held that it:

> [did] not consider that article 3.2 of the DSU is meant to encourage either panels or the Appellate Body to 'make law' by clarifying existing provisions of the WTO Agreement outside the context of resolving a particular dispute. A panel need only address those claims which must be addressed in order to resolve the matter in issue in the dispute.[254]

A further element of the public function of international adjudication is the practice in international courts of considering interests other than those of the parties to the dispute in reaching their decision. For instance, in the past the ICJ has demonstrated a willingness to take account of the interests of third states which have been refused permission to intervene in disputes. In *Continental Shelf (Libya/Malta)*, the ICJ refused Italy's request to intervene on the basis that it had not disclosed an interest of a legal nature which might be affected by a decision in the case, but the court noted that there could be no doubt that 'the Court will, in its future judgment in the case, take account, as a fact, of the existence of other states having claims in the region'.[255] In addition, the ICJ held in *Land, Island and*

[248] *Ireland v United Kingdom*, Ser A, (No 25), 62 (ECHR, 1978); John Collier and Vaughan Lowe, *The Settlement of Disputes in International Law: Institutions and Procedures* (1999) 13.

[249] For example, Case 26/69, *Commission v France* [1970] ECR–II, 565, 575–6; Collier and Lowe, ibid, 14.

[250] John Jackson, 'The Varied Policies of International Juridical Bodies—Reflections on Theory and Practice' (2004) 25 *Michigan Journal of International Law* 869.

[251] DSU, above n 11, art 3(2); see, e.g., Donald McRae, 'What is the Future of WTO Dispute Settlement?' (2004) 7 *Journal of International Economic Law* 3, 7–8, 14; Jackson, ibid.

[252] Ernst-Ulrich Petersmann, *The GATT/WTO Dispute Settlement System* (1997) 92–134.

[253] Above n 39, 15–16, 20–2; Petersmann, ibid, 93.

[254] Above n 109, 340.

[255] *Continental Shelf (Libya/Malta) (Application by Italy)* [1984] ICJ Rep 3, 26; see e.g., Sir Robert Jennings, 'The Judiciary, International and National, and the Development of International Law'

Maritime Frontier Dispute that a state wishing to intervene as a third party need not demonstrate a valid 'link of jurisdiction' which could be invoked in order to bring proceedings against either or both of the parties in dispute, which were, in that case, El Salvador and Honduras.[256] Rather, it could do so as a non-party simply by demonstrating that it held a 'legal interest' in the dispute, as prescribed by article 62 of the ICJ Statute.[257] This was not clear from the terms of article 62 of the ICJ Statute, which was the relevant provision governing third-party intervention in that dispute.[258] The effect of this ruling is to enhance the possibility for third-state intervention before the ICJ, and arguably it also demonstrates an awareness of a broader function which goes beyond the court's role in settling the dispute submitted by the parties.

Many international courts also occasionally take account of broader community interests. This is evinced in part by the increasing practice of certain international courts in accepting the submission of *amicus curiae* briefs, frequently in the absence of an express power to do so. This indicates their acceptance of broader functions in settling disputes and clarifying legal issues in a way that takes account of the views of other stakeholders potentially affected by the decision, rather than just the parties to the dispute. Some international courts have an express power to accept such briefs; these include the ICTY, the ICTR, the ECHR, and the International Criminal Court.[259] Other international courts and tribunals have found that despite the absence of a relevant provision in their constitutive instruments, they too have the power to accept *amicus* briefs. These include the WTO Appellate Body,[260] the

(1996) 45 *ICLQ* 5, 7–8; see also *Land, Island and Maritime Frontier Dispute (Application to Intervene)* [1990] ICJ Rep 92, 130.

256 Ibid, 135–6; *Land, Island and Maritime Frontier Dispute (Nicaragua Intervening)* [1992] ICJ Rep 351, 360; Rosenne, *Law and Practice*, above n 5, vol III, 1493–1502; Jennings, 'The Role of the International Court of Justice', above n 224, 8; Jennings, The Judiciary, International and National', above n 255, 7.

257 *Application to Intervene*, above n 255, 131–7; Rosenne, *Law and Practice*, above n 5, vol III, 1490–1.

258 See especially Rosenne, ibid vol III, 1480–93; see also the ICJ's failure to resolve this issue in *Continental Shelf (Tunisia/Libya) (Application by Malta)* [1981] ICJ Rep 3, 16–20; and *Continental Shelf (Libya/Malta) (Application by Italy)* above n 255, 27–8.

259 ICTY Rules, above n 190, Rule 74; ICTR Rules, above n 190, Rule 74; European HR Convention, art 36(2); ECHR Rules, above n 19, art 44; International Criminal Court Rules of Procedure and Evidence, Rule 103, UN Doc ICC-ASP/1/3, available at <http://www.icc-cpi.int>; see especially Christine Chinkin and Ruth Mackenzie, 'Intergovernmental Organisations as Friends of the Court', in Laurence Boisson de Chazournes, Cesare Romano and Ruth Mackenzie (eds), *International Organisations and International Dispute Settlement* (2002) 135.

260 See, e.g., *US—Shrimp*, above n 74, 2783–7 (concerning the power of WTO panels to receive *amicus curiae* briefs); *US—Hot Rolled Steel*, above n 213, para 36–42 (concerning the power of the WTO Appellate Body to receive *amicus curiae* briefs); see also *EC—Asbestos*, above n 213, paras 50–7 (concerning procedures for the submission of *amicus curiae* briefs). See Robert Howse, 'Membership and its Privileges: The WTO, Civil Society, and the *Amicus* Brief Controversy' (2003) 9 *European Law Journal* 496, 497; see also Geert Zonnekeyn, 'The Appellate Body's Communication on *Amicus Curiae* Briefs in the Asbestos Case' (2001) 35 *Journal of World Trade* 553; Gabrielle Marceau and Matthew Stilwell, 'Practical Suggestions for *Amicus Curiae* Briefs before WTO Adjudicating Bodies' (2001) 4 *Journal of International Economic Law* 155; Georg Umbricht, 'An "Amicus Curiae" Brief on Amicus Curiae Briefs at the WTO' (2001) 4 *Journal of International Economic Law* 773.

IACHR,[261] NAFTA tribunals,[262] and, more recently, ICSID tribunals.[263] The ICJ has also recently stated in a Practice Direction that briefs submitted by non-governmental organizations are not considered as part of the case file, but are available for consultation at the Peace Palace.[264]

International courts also carry out other functions. They can assist in lending legitimacy to the international arrangements of states, as the existence of a forum for the settlement of disputes by adjudication can make the meeting of international commitments less reliant on power-oriented diplomacy. At the same time, the international obligations of states can be made more acceptable to domestic constituents if an independent and impartial tribunal is created to resolve disputes.[265] International judicial bodies may also be created to fill in gaps or ambiguities in treaties which prove too intractable to be completed by negotiation. In this sense, diplomats might choose to delegate power to a dispute settlement body to settle questions which could not be resolved in the course of negotiations.[266] This may not be the case in all treaty regimes, however; article 3(2) of the DSU makes it clear that '[r]ecommendations and rulings of the DSB cannot add to or diminish the rights and obligations provided in the covered agreements'.[267] On top of these functions, individual international courts may also have certain functions specific to the regime within which they operate. The ITLOS, for instance, arguably performs a broader role regarding the objects and purposes of UNCLOS, as reflected in its power to grant provisional measures to prevent serious harm to the marine environment.[268] International human rights tribunals, such as the ECHR and IACHR, exist, *inter alia*, to promote the protection of human rights.[269] ICSID tribunals, for their part, are concerned with the protection of foreign investment;[270] WTO panels and the Appellate Body arguably have an institutional commitment

[261] See, e.g., *Mayagna (Sumo) Awas Tingni Community v Nicaragua*, Ser C (No 79), paras 38, 41–2, 61 (IACHR, 2001); Jo Pasqualucci, *The Practice and Procedure of the Inter-American Court of Human Rights* (2003) 16, 74–5, 214–15.

[262] *Methanex Corporation v United States* (Decision on *Amicus Curiae* of 15 January 2001), (NAFTA, 2001); *UPS v Canada* (Amici Curiae), above n 179.

[263] *Aguas Provinciales de Santa Fe*, above n 179, paras 17–22; *Aguas Argentinas, SA, Suez, Sociedad General de Aguas de Barcelona, SA and Vivendi Universal, SA v Argentina* (ICSID Case No ARB/03/19, Order on *Amicus Curiae* of 19 May 2005), paras 9–16. See, however, ICSID Arbitration Rule 37(2), which was introduced on 10 April 2006, which permits ICSID tribunals to accept submissions from non-disputing parties: see discussion in *Biwater Gauff (Tanzania) Ltd v Tanzania* (ICSID Case No ARB/05/22, Procedural Order No 3 of 29 September 2006), para 122.

[264] ICJ Practice Direction XII, at <http://www.icj-cij.org> (last visited 25 November 2006).

[265] See, for example, Marcel Brus, *Third Party Dispute Settlement in an Interdependent World* (1995) 102; Thomas Franck, 'Legitimacy in the International System' (1988) 82 *AJIL* 705, 727.

[266] Gordon, above n 26, 804–5.

[267] DSU, above n 11, art 3(2); see also art 19(2).

[268] *United Nations Convention on the Law of the Sea* ('UNCLOS'), opened for signature 10 December 1982, 21 ILM 1261 (entered into force 16 November 1994) art 290(1).

[269] *Loizidou v Turkey* (1995) 20 EHRR 99, 133.

[270] For example, *Tokios Tokeles v Ukraine*, above n 80 (Decision on Jurisdiction of 29 April 2004), (Diss Op Weil).

to the promotion of global free trade;[271] international human rights courts, bilateral and multilateral investment treaty tribunals, and the WTO dispute settlement bodies also perform the function of a type of 'international judicial review' of state regulatory action;[272] and international criminal tribunals have a function in determining the criminal responsibility of individuals.

These aspects of the broader public function—the proper administration of international justice, the development of the law, and the consideration of public interests—are important functions of international courts, as are the private function of settling disputes, and the performance of other functions specific to individual regimes. Yet the justification for the existence of inherent powers will most often be found in the functions of settling disputes and ensuring the proper administration of international justice. This is because inherent powers are mainly connected with the procedures applicable before international courts, and the carrying out of the more immediate functions of these bodies. There are, however, limitations on the use of inherent powers and the resort to the jurisprudence of other international tribunals, which are now addressed.

B. Limitations on the Exercise of Inherent Powers

The ability of international courts to exercise inherent powers and have regard to the jurisprudence of other international courts on questions of procedure and remedies is not unlimited. For instance, international courts cannot simply assert the existence of inherent powers as a type of carte blanche to do whatever they choose. There are certain limitations on the exercise of inherent powers, and the use of such powers to reach out and refer to the jurisprudence of other international courts.

The first of these can be found in the limitations on the judicial function.[273] As the ICJ observed in *Northern Cameroons*, even when it finds that it has jurisdiction, 'the Court is not compelled in every case to exercise that jurisdiction'.[274] An international court might decline to exercise its jurisdiction due to the absence of a dispute, the absence of a third party whose rights form the subject matter of the dispute, because the claim is otherwise inadmissible, or for reasons of judicial propriety.[275] In this sense, even though an international court might have jurisdiction

[271] For example, Chester Brown, 'The Proliferation of International Courts and Tribunals: Finding Your Way Through the Maze' (2002) 3 *Melbourne Journal of International Law* 453, 465–7.

[272] See, e.g., Benedict Kingsbury, Nico Krisch, and Richard Stewart, 'The Emergence of Global Administrative Law' (2005) 68 *Law and Contemporary Problems* 15.

[273] Thirlway, 'Part Nine', above n 8, 19; for ICJ pronouncements on the limitations of its judicial function, see especially *Nuclear Tests*, above n 157, 259; *Northern Cameroons*, above n 158, 29.

[274] Ibid, 29; see also Fitzmaurice, *Law and Procedure*, above n 8, 434.

[275] See, e.g., Brownlie, above n 3, 457–83; Collier and Lowe, above n 248, 155–62, 191–8; Thirlway, 'Part Nine', above n 8, 34–57; Rosenne, *Law and Practice*, above n 5, vol II, 505–22, 532–9; Fitzmaurice, *Law and Procedure*, above n 8, 438–40, 447–8, 555–8; Georges Abi-Saab, *Les exceptions préliminaires dans la procédure de la Cour internationale* (1967); Ian Brownlie, 'The

over a dispute, objections may be made to its competence to hear it; 'the former is a plea that the tribunal is incompetent to give any ruling at all whether as to the merits or to the admissibility of the claim', whereas the latter is a plea that while the tribunal has jurisdiction, it 'should rule the claim to be inadmissible on some ground other than its ultimate merits'.[276] This limitation to the exercise of inherent powers, then, is not due to the international court lacking jurisdiction, but rather due to it lacking competence to hear the dispute.[277] Such limitations on the exercise of inherent powers should properly be understood as bars to the exercise of international judicial jurisdiction generally, rather than limitations to the exercise of inherent powers specifically. These have been considered elsewhere, and do not need to be examined further here.[278]

The second type of limitation arising from the function of international courts, which is more relevant, is that because the source of inherent powers lies in the need for international courts to carry out their functions, the particular functions of each international court will determine the scope of its inherent powers.[279] International courts cannot claim to possess an inherent power if that power is not necessary for the performance of its particular functions. It has been observed above that different international courts, such as, say, the ICTY and the ITLOS, may have differing specific functions in addition to the common general functions of settling disputes and ensuring the proper administration of international justice. So, as Professor Gaeta has noted, an international criminal tribunal arguably has an inherent power to punish an individual for contempt of the tribunal, but this power would not necessarily be inherent in the functions of an interstate tribunal.[280] In a further example, a body which can be petitioned by individuals might exercise an inherent power to impose fines on individuals who abuse their right to petition by lodging frivolous or vexatious claims; but this power might not be exercised by dispute settlement bodies before which only states can appear.[281] The different functions of courts, and the limitations that these differences impose

Justiciability of Disputes and Issues in International Relations' (1967) 42 *British Yearbook of International Law* 123.

276 Fitzmaurice, *Law and Procedure*, above n 8, 438–9; see also Hugh Thirlway, 'The Law and Procedure of the International Court of Justice 1960–1989: Part Eleven' (2000) 71 *British Yearbook of International Law* 71, 74–5.

277 The concepts 'jurisdiction' and 'competence' appear to overlap in meaning; they are often (incorrectly) used interchangeably and are denoted by the same word in French: see, e.g., Thirlway, 'Part Nine', above n 8, 4; Rosenne, *Law and Practice*, above n 5, vol II, 522–4; Fitzmaurice, *Law and Procedure*, above n 8, 434–5.

278 See, e.g., the references cited in above n 275.

279 See also Gaeta, above n 49, 370–1.

280 Ibid; see also Sarooshi, above n 212, 152–4.

281 See, e.g., *Vollering (No 15)*, paras 8–9 (ILOAT, 1999, Judgment No 1884); *Martinuzzi*, para 4 (ILOAT, 2000, Judgment No 1962); referred to by Gaeta, above n 49, 358, 371; see also Kolb, above n 30, 637–9; see also the express provisions in the *European HR Convention*, art 35(3); *Optional Protocol to the International Covenant on Civil and Political Rights*, opened for signature 16 December 1966, 999 UNTS 302, art 3 (entered into force 23 March 1976); *Convention Against Torture and Other Cruel, Inhuman or Degrading Treatment or Punishment*, opened for signature 10 December 1984, 1465 UNTS 85, art 22(2) (entered into force 29 June 1987).

on their powers is also reflected at the national level. For instance, a domestic small claims tribunal could not claim to possess the same jurisdictional and coercive powers as a domestic criminal tribunal, and nor would it be desirable for it to do so from a normative point of view. In this way, the specific functions of each court place limitations on their ability to exercise inherent powers.

A third limitation is that inherent powers may be displaced by the express terms of a *clause contraire* in the constitutive instrument of an international court. This was recognised in *Nottebohm*, where the ICJ held that an international tribunal had an inherent power to determine the extent of its own jurisdiction 'in the absence of agreement to the contrary'.[282] Sir Hersch Lauterpacht also recognised this in his separate opinion in *Norwegian Loans*, where he held that 'clearly the Court cannot act otherwise than in accordance with its Statute'.[283] So, for instance, in *Pope & Talbot Inc v Canada*, the claimant requested in its application for provisional measures the enjoining of the application of a trade measure.[284] Under article 1134 of NAFTA, however, which confers the power to order provisional measures, '[a] Tribunal may not order attachment or enjoin the application of the measure alleged to constitute a breach referred to in Article 1116 or 1117'.[285] In accordance with article 1134, the tribunal correctly held that it had no power to grant such a provisional measure.[286]

A related type of limitation might be found where the constitutive instrument does not expressly exclude the exercise of a certain procedural power, but where the procedures actually provided for in the constitutive instrument would be inconsistent with the exercise of that power. It would be more difficult to show the existence of such an 'implicit agreement' to exclude the exercise of an inherent power. This might arise, for instance, in an application for provisional measures in the context of WTO dispute settlement, where the time frames for the settlement of the dispute are relatively short compared to those applicable in other dispute settlement systems. This question will be considered more closely in chapter 4.

A further factor which operates to restrain the exercise of inherent powers is the relationship between each particular international court and the parties, and, in particular, the degree of deference displayed by each international court to the parties. This particularly affects the exercise of powers which might be described as 'coercive'. Some international tribunals have, for instance, demonstrated a notable reluctance to order the production of evidence. This is exemplified in the practice of the ICJ, which in only a few instances has called on parties before it to

[282] Above n 110, 119; see also Gaeta, above n 49, 370; Orakhelashvili, 'International Judicial Jurisdiction', above n 8, 539; Thirlway, 'Part Ten', above n 160, 4.

[283] *Norwegian Loans*, above n 165, 34, 45 (Sep Op Lauterpacht). See also *Interhandel* [1959] ICJ Rep 6, 85, 93 (Diss Op Armand Ugon).

[284] *Pope & Talbot Inc v Canada* (Order on Interim Measures of 7 January 2000), para 1, available at <http://www.naftalaw.org> (last visited 30 November 2006).

[285] *North American Free Trade Agreement*, signed 17 December 1992, (US–Canada–Mexico), 32 ILM 289 (entered into force 1 January 1994), art 1134.

[286] *Pope & Talbot*, above n 284.

produce documents or other evidence.[287] In *Corfu Channel* and *Tehran Hostages*, the ICJ did not even draw any adverse inferences from the UK's and US's refusal to provide the documents.[288] In contrast, tribunals constituted under the auspices of the PCA, the ICSID Convention and the NAFTA to settle private or mixed disputes have proved more amenable to the exercise of this power.[289] A similar disparity can be seen in the practice among international courts of issuing mandatory or consequential orders. Traditionally, the ICJ and the ECHR have been reluctant to direct parties on how they should comply with a judgment,[290] although other international tribunals have not displayed the same reticence.[291] This inconsistent approach arguably reflects the different relationship between some international courts and the litigating parties. Thus, if the proposition is advanced that international courts have an inherent power to issue such orders, one must, nevertheless, take account of the deference displayed by each particular court towards the parties, as this will have an impact on the exercise of that power.

Conclusion

This chapter has suggested that there are various methods which international courts might adopt in order to have regard to the practice of other international courts and tribunals in exercising powers over procedure and remedies. These

[287] For some of the few instances where the PCIJ and ICJ have exercised this power, see *Corfu Channel*, above n 58; *Ambatielos*, ICJ Pleadings, 346–7, 566–7; *US Nationals in Morocco*, ICJ Pleadings, vol II, 431–4; *US Diplomatic and Consular Staff in Tehran (US v Iran) (Provisional Measures)* [1979] ICJ Rep 7, 10; *Aegean Sea Continental Shelf*, ICJ Pleadings, 296; *Diversion of Water from the Meuse*, Ser E, (No 14), 153 (PCIJ, 1937). See further Christian Tams, 'Article 49' in Zimmermann, Tomuschat and Oellers-Frahm (eds), above n 30, 1099, 1101–1105.

[288] *Corfu Channel*, ibid, 32; *Tehran Hostages*, ibid 7, 10; for further discussion, see below chapter 3, pt III(B).

[289] See, e.g., *Ceskoslovenska Obchodni Banka, AS v The Slovak Republic*, 14 *ICSID Review—FILJ* 251, 254 (1999); *Tanzania Electric Supply Co Ltd v Independent Power Tanzania* (ICSID Case No ARB/98/8, Award of 22 June 2001), paras 43–44; *Feldman v Mexico*, above n 194, paras 27–41; *Plama Consortium Ltd v Bulgaria* (ICSID Case No ARB/03/24, Decision on Jurisdiction of 8 February 2005), para 16; *GAMI Investments, Inc v Mexico* (NAFTA Tribunal) (Procedural Order No 1 of 31 January 2003), para 7.6; see also *Bank for International Settlements* (PCA) (Procedural Order No 3 of 5 March 2002), (Procedural Order No 5 of 3 May 2002), (Procedural Order No 6 of 11 June 2002), (Procedural Order No 10 of 9 March 2003).

[290] See especially *Haya de la Torre*, above n 230, 79–83; *Marckx v Belgium* Ser A, (No 31), 25 (ECHR, 1979).

[291] For example, *Loayza Tamayo (Reparations)*, 116 ILR 388, 440–2 (IACHR, 1998); *Suarez Rosero (Merits)*, 118 ILR 56, 90 (IACHR, 1997); *Suarez Rosero (Reparations)* 118 ILR 92, 113 (IACHR, 1999); but see also some recent decisions of the ICJ: *Arrest Warrant (Merits)* (2002) 41 ILM 536, 540; *LaGrand*, above n 29, 1103; *Avena*, above n 60, 624; and the ECHR: *Assanidze v Georgia* (2004) 39 EHRR 653, 698–9; *Broniowski v Poland* (2005) 40 EHRR 495, 564; see generally Alexander Orakhelashvili, 'Judicial Competence and Judicial Remedies in the *Avena* Case' (2005) 18 *Leiden Journal of International Law* 31; and Christoph Schreuer, 'Non-Pecuniary Remedies in ICSID Arbitration' (2004) 20 *Arbitration International* 325.

include: the application of principles of treaty interpretation, such as the principle of effectiveness, the evolutive approach to treaty interpretation, and the consideration of 'other rules of international law' pursuant to article 31(3)(c) of the VCLT; the application of general principles of law; and the exercise of inherent powers. These methods are clearly relevant to the ability of international courts to develop their procedures and remedies in line with those of other international courts, and thus support the emergence of a common law of international adjudication. This book now proceeds to an examination of specific areas of international adjudication; the first of these, considered in chapter 3, concerns the rules of evidence applicable before international courts.

3

Aspects of Evidence in International Adjudication

Introduction

Most fora for the adjudication of disputes receive and hear evidence concerning the facts underlying the dispute, for the finding of facts is an important part of the judicial function.[1] This is true of municipal courts as well as of international courts; the function of evidence is 'to enable the tribunal to discover the truth concerning the conflicting claims of the parties before it'.[2] As the court's capacity to dispose of

[1] J A Jolowicz, *On Civil Procedure* (2000) 211–12; Christoph Schreuer, *The ICSID Convention: A Commentary* (2001) 645; Keith Highet, 'Evidence, the Court, and the Nicaragua Case' (1987) 81 *AJIL* 1, 6; Sir Hersch Lauterpacht, *The Development of International Law by the International Court* (1958) 48.

[2] Durward Sandifer, *Evidence before International Tribunals* (2nd ed, 1975) 1.

the dispute depends on its ability to arrive at an accurate understanding of the facts, rules concerning evidence are crucial in the process of adjudication.[3] Yet the constitutive instruments and rules of procedure of most international courts do not, generally, make extensive provision for the applicable rules of evidence, and by and large international courts have been left to develop the applicable rules of evidence in their case law. The typical lack of prescription for rules of evidence in the constitutive instruments of international courts makes this subject extremely relevant to an examination of whether international courts adopt common approaches to issues of procedure and remedies, and thus justifies its inclusion in this book.

The question whether common features exist in the rules of evidence applied before international courts has been addressed previously by writers. Durward Sandifer has asserted that there is 'a notable agreement on basic principles and practice among a disparate variety of tribunals, reaching back to the early days of modern international adjudication'.[4] He concluded that a product of this agreement on the basic character and purpose of international proceedings pertaining to evidence is 'the development of what is tantamount to a customary law of evidence'.[5] This optimistic assessment is not shared by all writers, however. John Wigmore disagreed, and called for the creation of such a body of law,[6] and Charles Brower has also lamented the 'lack of standard rules of evidence to govern the submission and evaluation of evidence in international proceedings'.[7] In light of this lack of consensus, the existence or otherwise of a common set of rules of evidence in international adjudication is worth examining. Indeed, it has become all the more compelling in light of the proliferation of international courts and tribunals. Has the creation of additional international courts contributed to the emergence of common approaches by such bodies to questions of evidence? Or have apparent differences in the practice of international courts become more entrenched?

In this chapter it is suggested that many international courts, despite their varied nature, different jurisdictions and different specific functions, often adopt broadly similar approaches to evidence.[8] 'Evidence' in itself is not a type of procedure; 'evidence', properly understood, refers only to the facts and opinions put before the court.[9] But rules are needed to facilitate and control the adduction of this evidence, and, in so doing, to ensure the proper administration of international justice.

[3] British Institute of International and Comparative Law ('BIICL'), *Evidence before International Tribunals* (2002) 20; Lauterpacht, *Development*, above n 1, 48.

[4] Sandifer, above n 2, 457.

[5] Ibid.

[6] John Wigmore, *A Treatise on the Anglo-American System of Evidence in Trials at Common Law* (1940) vol I, 157.

[7] Charles Brower, 'Evidence before International Tribunals: The Need for some Standard Rules' (1994) 28 *International Lawyer* 47, 47; see also Charles Brower and Jason Brueschke, *The Iran–United States Claims Tribunal* (1998) 197–8; and Charles Brower, 'The Anatomy of Fact-Finding before International Tribunals: An Analysis and a Proposal Concerning the Evaluation of Evidence' in Richard Lillich (ed), *Fact-Finding Before International Tribunals* (1992) 147, 149.

[8] See also BIICL, above n 3, 25.

[9] Chittharanjan Amerasinghe, *Evidence in International Litigation* (2005) 31–2; Manley Hudson, *The Permanent Court of International Justice 1920–1942* (1943) 565.

Such rules relate to the different forms of proof that are admissible before international courts, whether different forms of proof are accorded varying probative value, whether there are any applicable rules concerning the burden of proof and the standard of proof, and also whether international tribunals can exercise any powers to gather evidence of their own motion. International courts have consistently treated such matters as procedural matters within their competence.[10] The role of the rules of evidence, then, is to facilitate the court's search for the facts in order to ensure the correct application of the law, and the procedural powers of courts to seek out evidence—other than that which has been submitted by the parties—are crucial in those bodies' ability to find the truth. As stated by Professor Witenberg:

> Quant aux règles de fond elles-mêmes, elles viennent imposer au juge international la recherche de la vérité . . . que le vrai—quel qu'il puisse être—est la raison d'être suprême du juge international.[11]

There are many aspects of evidence in international adjudication which could be considered, but rather than seek to produce a comprehensive treatise on the practice of international courts with regard to evidential issues,[12] this chapter makes a broader *tour d'horizon* and asks whether, in general, international courts and tribunals adopt a similar approach to certain issues. First, the sources of rules of evidence are identified. Next, the question is asked whether international courts adopt a similar approach to several central evidential issues, such as the admissibility of evidence, the burden of proof and the standard of proof. Finally, the question is asked whether international tribunals have the same powers to gather evidence of their own motion. It is concluded that there is a substantial level of agreement between many different international courts with respect to these issues, although it cannot be said that there is complete consistency in the application of these rules. Nonetheless, the broad agreement on major issues strengthens the case for the existence of an emerging common law of international adjudication.

I. Sources of Rules of Evidence in International Law

It was noted in the previous chapter that the sources of procedural rules applicable in international adjudication included the constitutive instruments of international courts, their rules of procedure, general principles of law, rules developed in international judicial practice, and the exercise by international courts of inherent powers, by which they can incorporate rules applied by other international tribunals. These sources will now be examined with respect to rules of evidence.

[10] J C Witenberg, 'La théorie des preuves devant les juridictions internationales' (1936) 56 *Recueil des cours* 5, 15; BIICL, above n 3, 29–30.

[11] J C Witenberg, '*Onus probandi* devant les juridictions arbitrales' (1951) 55 *Revue Générale du Droit International Public* 321, 340.

[12] For such an attempt, see Amerasinghe, above n 9.

A. Constitutive Instruments

A review of the constitutive instruments of international courts reveals that, in general, only the most rudimentary rules concerning evidence are included in such instruments.[13] The constitutive instrument of the commissions which were created to determine the first modern day international arbitrations under the Jay Treaty provided, for example, that the commissioners meeting under article V were to decide the questions put to them 'according to such evidence as shall respectively be laid before them on the part of the British Government and the United States'.[14] Other arbitration agreements have contained only marginally more detail on the powers of the tribunal with respect to evidence.[15] The first multilateral agreement for the settlement of international disputes, the 1899 Convention, also contained few relevant provisions; rather than be prescriptive, the drafters thought it important 'to invest the arbitrators with the most extended powers'.[16]

Under article 49 of the 1899 Convention, PCA tribunals have the power to 'decide the forms and periods within which each party must conclude its arguments, and to arrange all the formalities required for dealing with the evidence'. Under articles 39 and 40, all 'documents and acts' are to be submitted in the form and within the periods fixed by the tribunal, and are to be provided to the other party. Article 42 provides that after the conclusion of the 'preliminary examination', the tribunal can refuse discussion 'of all fresh Acts or documents which one party may desire to submit to it without the consent of the other party'. The 1907 Convention makes similar provision, and includes several new terms empowering PCA tribunals to require the production of evidence, and to require the parties to supply the tribunal with all information required for deciding the case;[17] the power to procure evidence at a location connected with the dispute;[18] and, if the procedure for

[13] See, e.g., Amerasinghe, above n 9, 47: 'no extensive rules regarding evidence are generally to be found in the agreements establishing arbitral tribunals . . . Even when the parties to arbitrations agree on rules in the *compromis* or otherwise, their agreement is usually confined to general questions and the details of the procedure are left for the tribunal to formulate.' See also Witenberg, 'La théorie des preuves', above n 10, 13–15.

[14] John Bassett Moore, *History and Digest of the International Arbitrations to which the United States has been a Party* (1898), vol I, 5–6 (art V); for the commissions established to decide claims brought under articles VI and VII, see respectively Moore, vol I, 276–7, 309–10.

[15] Sandifer, above n 2, 39; see, e.g., *Agreement of 3 August 1891* (US–Portugal), *Delagoa Bay Railway Arbitration*, Moore, vol II, 1876, 1877, art IV; *Agreement of 7 May 1903* (Germany–Venezuela), *Venezuela Preferential Claims* (1916) *Hague Court Reports* 62, 63, art 2; *Arbitral Agreement of 25 March 1965* (US–Canada), *Gut Dam Claims* (1965) 52 Department of State Bulletin 643, 645, art VI.

[16] Baron Descamps, 'Report to the Conference from the Third Commission on Pacific Settlement of International Disputes' in James Brown Scott (ed), *The Reports to the Hague Conferences of 1899 and 1907* (1917) 42, 84; *Convention for the Pacific Settlement of International Disputes*, opened for signature 29 July 1899, 1 Bevans 230 (entered into force 4 September 1900).

[17] *Convention for the Pacific Settlement of International Disputes*, opened for signature 18 October 1907, 1 Bevans 577 (entered into force 26 January 1910) arts 69, 75.

[18] Ibid, art 76.

summary arbitration in chapter IV of the Convention is being invoked, the power to obtain an expert opinion.[19]

Only the most general provisions were included in the PCIJ Statute with respect to evidence and procedure. The stipulations that were made, which were adopted in the ICJ Statute,[20] largely supported the freedom of action of the International Court—in both its incarnations—as to presentation and admission of evidence. In addition to articles 30 and 48, which empower the ICJ to frame rules for carrying out its functions and to 'make all arrangements connected with the taking of evidence', article 49 provides that the ICJ can request the production of evidence from parties, and if the requested evidence is not produced, 'formal note shall be taken of any refusal'. Under article 50, the ICJ may at any time 'entrust any individual, body, bureau, commission, or other organization that it may select, with the task of carrying out an enquiry or giving an expert opinion'. Article 51 empowers the ICJ to put 'any relevant questions' to the witnesses and experts during the hearing, and under article 52, the ICJ can refuse to admit any further oral or written evidence after the expiry of the time specified for the purpose, unless the other side consents.

Provisions on evidence in the constitutive instruments of other international courts do not differ widely from those in the Hague Conventions and the ICJ Statute; indeed, some contain far fewer provisions dealing with evidence. The ITLOS Statute[21] essentially contains only two provisions: article 16 replicates article 30 of the ICJ Statute, the rule-making power; and article 27, which reflects article 48 of the ICJ Statute, provides that the ITLOS can make procedural orders for the conduct of the case. Article 289 of UNCLOS[22] provides that in disputes involving scientific or technical matters, the ITLOS (or any court or tribunal exercising jurisdiction over a dispute arising under UNCLOS) may appoint scientific or technical experts to sit with the court or tribunal, but without the right to vote. The ICSID Convention contains only two provisions dealing with evidence. Article 43 provides that unless the parties agree otherwise, the tribunal may if it considers necessary at any stage of the proceedings, 'call upon the parties to produce documents or other evidence', and 'visit the scene connected with the dispute, and conduct such inquiries there as it may deem appropriate.' Under article 44, ICSID tribunals have the power to decide questions of procedure not covered in the conventions.[23] As with tribunals operating under the Hague Conventions, however, such rulings apply only to that tribunal.

[19] Ibid, art 90.

[20] *Statute of the International Court of Justice*, opened for signature 26 June 1945, 3 Bevans 1153 (entered into force 24 October 1945); *Statute of the Permanent Court of International Justice*, PCIJ Publications Ser D (No 1).

[21] UNCLOS (see n 22), 1833 UNTS 3, Annex VI.

[22] *United Nations Convention on the Law of the Sea*, opened for signature 10 December 1982, 1833 UNTS 3 (entered into force 16 November 1994).

[23] *Convention for the Settlement of Investment Disputes between States and Nationals of Other States*, opened for signature 18 March 1965, 575 UNTS 159 (entered into force 14 October 1966), art 44.

The DSU also provides little guidance regarding rules of evidence obtaining before WTO panels and the Appellate Body. Under article 13(1), panels have 'the right to seek information and technical advice from any individual or body which it deems appropriate.' Article 13(2) also permits panels to seek information 'from any relevant source and consult experts to obtain their opinion on certain aspects of the matter.' Article 13(1) provides that 'a Member should respond promptly and fully to any request by a panel for such information as the panel considers necessary and appropriate'. WTO panels also have some latitude to frame their rules of procedure; panels are to follow the 'Working Procedures' in Appendix 3 of the DSU 'unless the panel decides otherwise after consulting the parties to the dispute'.[24] The Appellate Body, on the other hand, is empowered to draw up working procedures 'in consultation with the Chairman of the DSB and the Director-General, and communicated to the Members for their information'.[25] In the event that an issue arises which is not dealt with in the 'Working Procedures for Appellate Review', the division of the Appellate Body can adopt a procedure 'for the purposes of that appeal only'.[26]

It can be seen that the constitutive instruments of many international courts only supply basic provisions for the procedures to be applied to the adduction and treatment of evidence. Constitutive instruments are silent on many evidential issues, such as rules concerning the form of admissible evidence, the burden of proof, and the standard of proof. Instead, these questions are left to be decided by international courts. In so doing, international courts have often drawn on other sources, including their rules of procedure, general principles of law, precedents established in earlier international practice, and their inherent powers.

B. Other Sources of Evidentiary Rules in International Adjudication

1. Rules of Procedure

Most international courts have the express power in their constitutive instruments to frame rules of procedure.[27] It has also been suggested that international courts and tribunals have an inherent power to do so, and to make orders for the management of the case and the taking of evidence, in the absence of express agreement to the contrary.[28] The rules of procedure of international courts represent a significant source of rules of evidence and often amplify the provisions of the statute. For instance, article 61 of the ICJ Rules provides more detail on the ICJ's power under article 49 of the ICJ Statute to seek further information from the parties;[29] article 56 of the ICJ Rules spells out the ICJ's power to refuse to accept further documents

[24] *Understanding on Rules and Procedures Governing the Settlement of Disputes*, opened for signature 15 April 1994, 1869 UNTS 401 (entered into force 1 January 1995), art 12(1).

[25] Ibid, art 17(9).

[26] Working Procedures for Appellate Review, art 16(1).

[27] See above chapter 2, part I(B); see also chapter 2, part III.

[28] See above chapter 2; see also Amerasinghe, above n 9, 47.

[29] Shabtai Rosenne, *Procedure in the International Court* (1983) 133–4.

'after the close of written proceedings', thus elaborating article 52 of the ICJ Statute.[30] The ICSID Arbitration Rules also expand on the rules of evidence and powers of ICSID tribunals. Yet the rules of procedure of international courts do more than provide detail on provisions of the statute; they also include new substantive provisions. The ITLOS Statute, for instance, is generally silent on questions of evidence other than the two provisions noted above.[31] So, article 73 of the ITLOS Rules provides that the ITLOS determines the order of the parties' arguments and the submission of evidence, and under article 76(2), it can put questions to the parties and their agents. The rules of procedure of each international court thus represent a significant source of its rules of evidence.

2. *General Principles of Law*

In addition to the constitutive instrument and rules of procedure of international courts, international judges have frequently resorted to other methods to devise rules of procedure and evidence.[32] These may be developed in consultation with the parties to the dispute, and in addition, international courts often turn to rules customarily applied by other international courts, and also to general principles of law, so long as these do not contradict their constitutive instrument.[33] Many international courts have applied general principles of law relating to questions of evidence, such as the principle that each party has the right to be heard (*audi alteram partem*),[34] the principle that the court knows the law, and is not dependent on the submissions of the parties (*iura novit curia*),[35] and the principle that a party asserting a fact bears the burden of providing proof of that fact (*actori incumbit probatio*).[36] Elements of these principles are generally incorporated into the constitutive instrument and rules of procedure, such as the general exclusion of new evidence after a certain specified stage in proceedings, unless the other party consents and is given an opportunity to comment on it.[37]

While general principles of law are regarded as a source of rules relating to evidence, some writers have hesitated before referring to customary international law as a source of such rules.[38] Professor Amerasinghe has observed that:

> The reason is that, while theoretically custom, residing in the practice of States accompanied by an *opinio iuris*, qualifies as a source, it has never been the case that custom has been properly so invoked by international tribunals. This is understandable, because it is difficult to

[30] Ibid, 124–5. [31] ITLOS Statute, above n 21, arts 16, 27.

[32] See chapter 2, part I(C)(2).

[33] Sandifer, above n 2, 44; see especially Bin Cheng, *General Principles of Law as Applied by International Courts and Tribunals* (first published 1953, 1987 ed) 257–386.

[34] Cheng, ibid, 291; V S Mani, *International Adjudication: Procedural Aspects* (1980) 15–16.

[35] Cheng, ibid, 299; e.g. *Fisheries Jurisdiction (Merits)* [1974] ICJ Rep 3, 9; *Military and Paramilitary Activities in and against Nicaragua (Merits)* [1986] ICJ Rep 14, 24–5.

[36] Cheng, ibid, 326–35; see below part II(B).

[37] For example, ICJ Statute, art 52; International Court of Justice Rules of Court, available at <http://www.icj-cij.org>, art 56; ITLOS Rules of the Tribunal, available at <http://www.itlos.org>, art 71.

[38] Amerasinghe, above n 9, 26.

see how custom as the practice of States, as contrasted with the general principles of law arising from applications by international and national tribunals, can give rise to evidentiary law which international tribunals can apply.[39]

But writers have emphasized the relevance of customary international law as a source of procedure,[40] and it is also possible to regard the rules of evidence that have been developed in international judicial practice as being customary rules;[41] in this sense, it is difficult to draw a clear distinction between general principles and customary international law.

3. *Inherent Powers*

In addition to the rules provided for by constitutive instruments, rules of procedure, and rules derived from general principles of law, it is suggested that international courts have inherent powers over issues of evidence. This power is derived from the need for international courts to carry out their functions in the settlement of the dispute; in order for courts to apply the law to a dispute, they need to have a full appreciation of the facts underlying that dispute. International courts have generally considered their power to decide questions of procedure as including a power to decide evidential issues, even where this power is not expressly conferred.[42]

The next section of this chapter considers some rules of evidence applied by international courts, and seeks to examine whether they are applied consistently by international courts. As stated at the outset, it does not purport to provide a complete coverage of rules of evidence. Instead, it is restricted to consideration of three central evidential issues in international adjudication: the admissibility of different forms of evidence, the burden of proof, and the standard of proof obtaining before international courts.

II. Evidential Issues in International Adjudication

A. Admission of Evidence

It is useful to begin this section with a brief *discursus* into the rules on admission of evidence in municipal legal systems, for procedure in international adjudication has been informed by experience gained in domestic legal systems. Common law legal systems traditionally impose restrictive rules on the admission of evidence.[43]

39 Ibid.

40 See above chapter 2; see, e.g., Hugh Thirlway, 'Dilemma or Chimera? Admissibility of Illegally Obtained Evidence in International Adjudication' (1984) 78 *AJIL* 622, 623; Shabtai Rosenne, *The Law and Practice of the International Court, 1920–2005* (2006) vol III, 1027–8.

41 See especially Rosenne, *Law and Practice*, ibid, vol III, 1027–8.

42 Witenberg, 'La théorie des preuves', above n 10, 15.

43 Jolowicz, above n 1, 214; see also Sandifer, above n 2, 2; Jens Evensen, 'Evidence before International Courts' (1955) 25 *Nordisk Tidskrift for International Ret* 44, 44–5; A H Feller, *The Mexican Claims Commissions: 1923–34* (1935) 251.

At the same time, once evidence has been declared admissible, no specific weight or probative value is generally attached to different forms of evidence, such as oral, affidavit, or other documentary evidence.[44] In contrast, civil law systems have comparatively fewer exclusionary rules regarding the presentation and admissibility of evidence.[45] However, different weight is attached to different forms of proof in civil law systems. For instance, documentary proof is preferred to oral testimony of witnesses, and a 'public act' such as a notarial act or deed can provide conclusive proof of certain matters. Oral proof is regarded as 'untrustworthy', because it comes into existence after the dispute has arisen.[46]

International courts adopt a similar approach to courts in civil law systems concerning the forms of proof which are admitted; Sandifer states that before international tribunals, 'evidence in written form is the rule and direct oral evidence the exception'.[47] Likewise, the admission of evidence before international tribunals has much in common with the approach of courts in countries of the civilian legal tradition in that there is a tendency to avoid a restrictive approach to the admissibility of evidence.[48] Many statements to this effect can be found in the jurisprudence of early international tribunals.[49] In *Island of Palmas*, the sole arbitrator, Dr Huber, expressed the view that:

> it would seem to be contrary to the broad principles applied in international arbitrations to exclude *a limine*, except under the explicit terms of a conventional rule, every allegation made by a Party as irrelevant, if it is not supported by evidence . . . an arbitral tribunal must have entire freedom to estimate the value of assertions made by the Parties. . . . The value and the weight of any assertion can only be estimated in the light of all the evidence and all the assertions made on either side, and of facts which are notorious for the tribunal.[50]

The PCIJ has expressed similar views on the question of its freedom to admit evidence. In *Mavrommatis Palestine Concessions*, it enunciated a famous dictum regarding its treatment of questions of procedure:

> the Court, whose jurisdiction is international, is not bound to attach to matters of form the same degree of importance which they might possess in municipal law.[51]

44 Jolowicz, ibid, 214; M Howard, *Phipson on Evidence* (15th ed, 2000) 112–14.

45 Sandifer, above n 2, 3; e.g. Ruth Bader Ginsburg and Anders Bruzelius, *Civil Procedure in Sweden* (1965) 295; see also Evensen, above n 43, 45; Feller, above n 43, 251.

46 Jolowicz, above n 1, 214.

47 Sandifer, above n 2, 197. For further consideration of the forms of proof used in international adjudication, see ibid 197–348; Mani, above n 34, 215–38; J L Simpson and Hazel Fox, *International Arbitration* (1959) 207–11; and the chapters contained in Lillich (ed), above n 7.

48 Sir Hersch Lauterpacht, 'The So-Called Anglo-American and Continental Schools of Thought in International Law' (1931) 12 *British Yearbook of International Law* 31, 41–2.

49 See, e.g., *Shufeldt*, 2 RIAA 1079, 1083 (US–Guatemala, 1930); *Parker v Mexico*, 4 RIAA 35, 39 (US–Mexico GCC, 1926); *Franqui*, 10 RIAA 751, 751 (Spain–Venezuela CC, 1903); *Lasry*, 9 RIAA 147, 148 (US–Venezuela CC, 1903); *Faber*, 10 RIAA 438, 458–9 (Germany–Venezuela CC, 1903); *Pelletier*, Moore, vol II, 1749, 1752 (US–Haiti, 1884); see also Institut de Droit International, 'Projet de règlement pour la procédure arbitrale internationale' (1877) 1 *Annuaire de l'Institut de Droit International* 126, art 15.

50 2 RIAA 829, 840–1 (US–Netherlands, PCA, 1928).

51 Ser A, (No 2), 34 (PCIJ, 1924). See, however, the discussion in *Legality of Use of Force*, CR 2004/6, paras 29–39 (Daniel Bethlehem).

This liberal approach to questions of procedure and evidence was followed in later cases.[52] In his separate opinion in *Oscar Chinn*, Judge van Eysinga encapsulated the approach of the PCIJ to evidential matters: 'the Court is not tied to any system of taking evidence, whether proceedings are begun by Special Agreement or by Application. Its task is to co-operate in the objective ascertainment of the truth'.[53] The ICJ has not deviated from this approach.[54] Other international tribunals have also adopted the same liberal attitude to questions of evidence, including ICSID tribunals,[55] WTO panels,[56] and the ICTY.[57] Indeed, Sandifer has stressed that 'no rule of evidence thus finds more frequent statement in the cases than the one that international tribunals are not bound to adhere to strict rules of evidence'.[58] In *Nicaragua*, the ICJ again confirmed that, 'within the limits of its Statute and Rules', it 'has freedom in estimating the value of the various elements of evidence, though it is clear that general principles of judicial procedure necessarily govern the determination of what can be regarded as proved'.[59] These general principles concerning when a fact is regarded as having been proved are now considered.

B. Burden of Proof

A general principle of evidence commonly applied in domestic legal systems, but not referred to in most constitutive instruments or rules of procedure of international courts, is the rule on the allocation of the burden of proof.[60] This involves identifying which party has the onus of proving an assertion made in judicial proceedings.[61]

[52] For example, *Mavrommatis Jerusalem Concessions*, Ser A (No 5), 19–21 (PCIJ, 1925); Ser C (No 7), vol II, 46–8, 95–6; *Certain German Interests in Polish Upper Silesia (Merits)*, Ser A (No 7), 72–3 (PCIJ, 1926); *Free Zones*, Ser A/B (No 46), 155–6 (PCIJ, 1932); Evensen, above n 43, 46.

[53] Ser A/B (No 63), 131, 146–7 (Sep Op van Eysinga) (PCIJ, 1934).

[54] For example, *Barcelona Traction* (*Second Phase*) [1970] ICJ Rep 3, 65, 98 (Sep Op Fitzmaurice).

[55] *Asian Agricultural Products Ltd v Sri Lanka*, 4 ICSID Rep 245, 273 (1990); see also *Tradex v Albania* (1999) 14 *ICSID Review—FILJ* 197, 220–1; ICSID Arbitration Rules, available at <http://www.worldbank.org/icsid>, Rule 34(1).

[56] *Argentina—Textiles and Apparel*, DSR 1998–III, 1033, 1159 (PR); David Palmeter and Petros Mavroidis, *Dispute Settlement in the World Trade Organisation* (1999) 76.

[57] *Prosecutor v Aleksovski* (Admissibility of Evidence), para 19 (ICTY App Ch, 1999); Richard May, 'Evidence before the International Criminal Tribunal for the Former Yugoslavia: An Overview' (1999) 1 *International Law Forum* 197, 197–8.

[58] Sandifer, above 2, 9; see also Keith Highet, 'Evidence and Proof of Facts' in Lori Damrosch (ed), *The International Court of Justice at a Crossroads* (1987) 355, 358.

[59] Above n 35, 40.

[60] Amerasinghe, above n 9, 61–95; Caroline Foster, 'The Adjudication of International Disputes Involving Scientific Uncertainty' (PhD Dissertation, University of Cambridge, 2003) 79–86; Mojtaba Kazazi, *Burden of Proof and Related Issues: A Study on Evidence before International Tribunals* (1996) 104. See also Iran–US Claims Tribunal Rules of Procedure, 1 Ir–USCTR 57, art 24(1); PCA Optional Rules for Arbitrating Disputes between Two States, available at <http://www.pca-cpa.org>, art 24(1); Model Rules of Procedure for Chapter 20 of the NAFTA, available at <http://www.nafta-sec-alena.org> (last visited 31 January 2007), Rule 33.

[61] Foster, ibid, 79–80; Sir Arthur Watts, 'Burden of Proof, and Evidence before the ICJ' in Friedl Weiss (ed), *Improving WTO Dispute Settlement Procedures: Issues and Lessons from the Practice of Other International Courts and Tribunals* (2000) 289, 291; Rosenne, *Law and Practice*, above n 40, vol III, 1039–40; Kazazi, ibid, 76, 85; Cheng, above n 33, 326–35; Georg Schwarzenberger, *International*

In accordance with this rule, which is derived from the general principle *actori incumbit probatio*, international courts require the party putting forward a claim to establish the facts on which a decision in its favour may be given.[62] Where a party makes an assertion which it cannot establish, a finding is made against this party on the point in question; if the point is essential to that party's case, the case is lost.[63]

The rule on the allocation of the burden of proof is not applied in the same way in common law and civil law systems. In common law systems, writers make a distinction between the concepts of 'evidential' and 'persuasive' burdens of proof. The 'evidential' burden, which is also known as 'the duty of passing the judge', is said initially to be on the claimant, and imposes on it the obligation to adduce sufficient evidence 'to raise an issue as to the existence or non-existence of a fact in issue'.[64] The effect of the claimant meeting the 'evidential' burden is that the question of fact is then passed to the tribunal of fact.[65] The 'persuasive' burden, also known as the 'legal' burden, rests on the party carrying the risk of losing on the issue in question if a proposition is not made out.[66] So, in a common law trial, once the claimant has met the 'evidential' burden, they then must meet the 'persuasive' burden on each allegation made. The 'persuasive' burden might also rest on the defendant if seeking to establish a defence.[67] The distinction between these two burdens is not made in civil law systems; Sandifer suggests that this is probably due to the absence of the jury, which may serve as the tribunal of fact in common law civil trials.[68] In civil law systems, the burden of proof reflects the 'persuasive burden' in common law systems; that is, it simply rests on the party alleging a fact to provide the means of proof, whether it be the claimant or the defendant.[69] Thus, it is an unadulterated application of the *actori incumbit probatio* principle.[70] International courts also tend to apply the principle in this way; as put by Sandifer, '[t]he burden of proof rests upon him who asserts the affirmative of a proposition that if not substantiated will result in a decision adverse to his contention'.[71]

Law (1986) vol IV, 190, 641–3; Sandifer, above n 2, 123–41; Witenberg, 'La théorie des preuves', above n 10, 97–8.

62 Rosenne, *Law and Practice*, above n 40, vol III, 1040.

63 Sandifer, above n 2, 127.

64 Colin Tapper, *Cross & Tapper on Evidence* (9th ed, 1999) 109–10; see also Howard, above n 44, 55, 64–8.

65 Tapper, ibid, 109; Wigmore, above n 6, vol IX, 284.

66 See, e.g., Howard, above n 44, 55–64; Tapper, above n 64, 106–9; Foster, above n 60, 81–2; Jeff Waincymer, *WTO Litigation: Procedural Aspects of Formal Dispute Settlement* (2002) 536–7; Joost Pauwelyn, 'Evidence, Proof and Persuasion in WTO Dispute Settlement: Who Bears the Burden?' (1998) 1 *Journal of International Economic Law* 227, 229.

67 Tapper, above n 64, 108–9.

68 Sandifer, above n 2, 125–6; see also Tapper, above n 64, 109–12; Glanville Williams, 'The Evidential Burden: Some Common Misapprehensions' (1977) 127 *NLJ* 156, 156; Wigmore, above n 6, vol IX, 284.

69 For example, *Nouveau Code de Procédure Civil* (96e édition, 2004), art 9; Kazazi, above n 60, 26; Sandifer, above n 2, 125–6; Claude Giverdon, 'The Problem of Proof in French Civil Law' (1956) 31 *Tulane Law Review* 29, 38–47.

70 Pauwelyn, above n 66, 229–30.

71 Sandifer, above n 2, 127, 468; see also Foster, above n 60, 82; Pauwelyn, above n 66, 232; Kazazi, above n 60, 30–1; Neill Alford, 'Fact finding by the World Court' (1958) 4 *Villanova Law Review* 37, 83.

The rule on the allocation of the burden of proof has been applied by international tribunals since the early days of international arbitration.[72] In the jurisprudence of the PCIJ and the ICJ, direct consideration of the question has often been avoided, as these courts have frequently been able to base their decisions on undisputed facts.[73] Both courts have applied the rule that a party asserting a fact bears the burden of proving it, although they seldom refer directly to that rule. As Sir Hersch Lauterpacht held in *Norwegian Loans*: 'There is, in general, a degree of unhelpfulness in the argument concerning burden of proof. Yet some prima facie distribution of the burden of proof there must be.'[74] So, in *Legal Status of Eastern Greenland*, the PCIJ held that if a disputant alleged that 'some unusual or exceptional meaning' was to be attributed to a term, then that party bore the onus of establishing its contention.[75] The ICJ followed a similar approach in *Asylum*, where it held that a party seeking to establish a 'regional custom' must prove that it is binding on the other party.[76] In cases where parties present competing claims, both parties may be regarded as bearing burdens of proof. In *Temple of Preah Vihear*, Cambodia was formally the applicant while Thailand made its own claim in its counter-memorial. Both parties based their claims on a series of facts and contentions, and each bore a burden of proof accordingly.[77] In *Oil Platforms*, in relation to the US claim that it had acted in self-defence when destroying the Iranian oil platforms, the ICJ emphasized that the US bore the burden of proving that the *Sea Isle City* and the *USS Samuel B Roberts* were the subject of attacks by Iran.[78] In *Nicaragua*, the ICJ gave perhaps its clearest statement of the burden of proof: 'ultimately . . . it is the litigant seeking to establish a fact who bears the burden of proving it'.[79] The rule on burden of proof is applied in the jurisprudence of all international tribunals, including the ECJ,[80] ICSID tribunals,[81] NAFTA

[72] Sandifer, above n 2, 127–8; Georges Scelle, 'Arbitral Procedure' [1950] *YbILC*, vol II, 114, 133, UN Doc A/CN.4/18; see, e.g., *Lighthouses Arbitration (Claim 6)*, 12 RIAA 155, 212; 23 ILR 677, 678 (Greece–France, 1956) (PCA); *Meeresauge*, 8 *Revue de Droit International et de Législation Comparée* 162, 200 (Austria–Hungary, 1906). See also *Parker*, above n 49, 39, *Archuleta v Mexico*, 4 RIAA 376, 379 (US–Mexico GCC, 1928); *Pinson v Mexico*, 5 RIAA 327, 412–14 (France–Mexico CC, 1928), where it was held that the burden of proof did not apply in international litigation. These statements have been regarded as unconvincing: Amerasinghe, above n 9, 63–5; Witenberg, 'Onus probandi', above n 11, 327–8; Sandifer, above n 2, 128–30.

[73] Rosenne, *Law and Practice*, above n 40, vol III, 1039.

[74] *Certain Norwegian Loans* [1957] ICJ Rep 9, 34, 39 (Sep Op Lauterpacht).

[75] Ser A/B, (No 53), 49 (PCIJ, 1933); Kazazi, above n 60, 76–7; Sandifer, above n 2, 132–3.

[76] *Asylum (Colombia v Peru)* [1950] ICJ Rep 266, 276.

[77] [1962] ICJ Rep 6, 15–16.

[78] (2003) 42 ILM 1334, 1356–7, 1360–2.

[79] [1984] ICJ Rep 392, 437; see also *Frontier Dispute* [1986] ICJ Rep 554, 587; *Land and Maritime Boundary (Preliminary Objections)* [1998] ICJ Rep 275, 319. See further Rosenne, *Law and Practice*, above n 40, vol III, 1040; Kazazi, above n 60, 83–6; Keith Highet, 'Evidence, the Chamber, and the *ELSI* Case' in Lillich (ed), above n 7, 33, 34; Highet, 'Evidence, the Court', above n 1; Sandifer, above n 2, 132–41.

[80] *Blackspur DIY v Council and Commission* [1997] ECR–I 4775, 4784–5 (A-G Tesauro); Jacquelyn MacLennan, 'Evidence, Standard and Burden of Proof and the Use of Experts in Procedure before the Luxembourg Courts' in Weiss (ed), above n 61, 265, 266–8.

[81] *AAPL v Sri Lanka*, above n 55, 272; see also *Tradex v Albania*, above n 55, 219–21; *Plama Consortium Ltd v Bulgaria* (ICSID Case No ARB/03/24, Decision on Jurisdiction of 8 February 2005), paras 118–20, 167.

tribunals,[82] WTO panels and the WTO Appellate Body,[83] the IACHR,[84] the UN Human Rights Committee,[85] and the Iran–US Claims Tribunal.[86]

Despite its universal application, aspects of international dispute settlement proceedings can raise problems regarding the allocation of the burden of proof. For instance, cases may be brought before the ICJ by application or by special agreement. In cases brought by application, it is clear that the onus is on the applicant to establish the facts necessary to support its claim; yet what of the cases brought by *compromis*, where there is no clear applicant or respondent? The ICJ has clarified that the rule on the burden of proof also applies in such cases: in *Corfu Channel*, which was ultimately submitted by *compromis*, the UK bore the burden of proving Albania's responsibility for the mines,[87] and Albania bore the burden of proving that the UK had violated Albanian sovereignty by reason of its naval activities in the Corfu Channel.[88] In *Minquiers and Ecrehos*, the ICJ subjected both parties to an equal burden of proof, holding that 'each party has to prove its alleged title and the facts upon which it relies';[89] the ICJ was thus called on to appraise the relative strength of opposing claims.[90] In such cases, international courts have the power to determine which party bears the burden of proof; as Professor Amerasinghe has explained, '[t]his is an inherent power which is essential for the proper functioning of international tribunals'.[91]

A distinction in the treatment of burden of proof issues appears to have arisen in its invocation in WTO dispute settlement. There is no question that the principle of *actori incumbit probatio* applies in WTO adjudication; in an early decision, *US—Shirts and Blouses*, the Appellate Body held that:

> various international tribunals, including the International Court of Justice, have generally and consistently accepted and applied the rule that the party who asserts a fact, whether the claimant or the respondent, is responsible for providing proof thereof. Also, it is a generally-accepted canon of evidence in civil law, common law and, in fact, most jurisdictions, that the burden of proof rests upon the party, whether complaining or defending, who asserts the affirmative of a particular claim or defence.[92]

82 See, e.g., *Canfor Corporation v US*, *Tembec* et al *v US* and *Terminal Forest Products v US* (Order of the Consolidation Tribunal of 7 September 2005), para 93, and also n 45.

83 For example, *EC—Tariff Preferences*, WT/DS246/AB/R, paras 87–8 (ABR); *US—Shirts and Blouses*, DSR 1997–I, 323, 333–8 (ABR); *US—Shirts and Blouses*, DSR 1997–I, 343, 429–30 (PR).

84 *Velásquez Rodríguez* (1989) 28 ILM 291, 315.

85 *Bordes and Temeharo*, HRC Decision No 645/1995, para 5.5 (1996).

86 *Iran v US (Case A-20)*, 11 Ir–USCTR 271, 274 (1986); Kazazi, above n 60, 104.

87 For example, [1949] ICJ Rep 4, 13–17.

88 For example, ibid, 26–35.

89 [1953] ICJ Rep 47, 52.

90 Ibid, 67; Rosenne, *Law and Practice*, above n 40, vol III, 1041–2.

91 Amerasinghe, above n 9, 75.

92 Above n 83 (ABR), 335 (footnotes omitted); see also *Turkey—Textiles*, DSR 1999–VI, 2363, 2507–8 (PR); *Argentina—Textiles and Apparel*, above n 56, 1158–9 (PR); *US—Shirts and Blouses*, above n 83 (PR), 429–30; *India—Patent*, DSR 1998-I, 41, 115–16, (PR); *India—Patent*, DSR 1998–I, 9, 32–3 (ABR); see also *EC—Asbestos*, WT/DS135/R, para 8.79 (PR); *EC—Tariff Preferences*, above n 83, paras 87–8, 104–5; Mitsuo Matsushita, Thomas Schoenbaum and Petros Mavroidis, *The World Trade Organisation: Law, Practice, and Policy* (2nd ed, 2006) 125–7; Waincymer, above n 66, 550; BIICL, above n 3, 67; Palmeter and Mavroidis, above n 56, 81–2; Pauwelyn, above n 66, 237–8.

The distinction pertains to the use in WTO adjudication of the concept of a prima facie case.[93] The Appellate Body observed in *US—Shirts and Blouses* that once the asserting party has presumptively established a fact—that is, made it out on a prima facie basis—it is the responsibility of the other party to provide evidence and argument sufficient to rebut the presumption.[94] It confirmed the use of this concept in *EC—Hormones*:

> The initial burden lies on the complaining party, which must establish a *prima facie* case of inconsistency with a particular provision of the SPS Agreement on the part of the defending party, or more precisely, of its SPS measure or measures complained about. When that *prima facie* case is made, the burden of proof moves to the defending party, which must in turn counter or refute the claimed inconsistency.[95]

The prima facie case rule has been applied consistently by WTO panels and the Appellate Body.[96] In *Canada—Aircraft*, the Appellate Body identified the standard required to make out a prima facie case as one which 'in the absence of effective refutation by the defending party . . . requires a panel, as a matter of law, to rule in favour of the complaining party presenting the prima facie case'.[97]

This approach appears to be at variance with the manner in which most other international courts deal with the allocation of the burden of proof. While it cannot be maintained that the use of the prima facie case concept is unique to WTO dispute settlement,[98] most other international tribunals do not expressly employ this concept in determining whether the burden of proof has been discharged. Given the wide discretion WTO panels enjoy in deciding when the prima facie case has been established, concerns have been raised that the shifting of the burden of proof can too arbitrarily be justified by WTO panels, and that this can disadvantage states seeking to implement trade measures which respond to scientific risks.[99] But subsequent WTO practice has sought to refine the approach to burden of proof and avoid the 'shift' of the burden once a prima facie case is established. In *Korea—Dairy Products*, a panel held that:

> As a matter of law, the burden of proof rests with the European Communities, as complainant, and does not shift during the panel process. As a matter of process before the

[93] This appears to have been argued for the first time by the US in *Japan—Alcohol*, DSR 1996–I, 125, 159 (PR); Pauwelyn, above n 66, 243.

[94] Above n 83 (ABR) 335.

[95] DSR 1998–I, 135, 174 (ABR); see also *EC—Hormones (Canada Complaint)*, DSR 1998–II, 235, 480–1 (PR).

[96] Foster, above n 60, 97–104.

[97] *Canada—Aircraft*, DSR 1999–III, 1377, 1428 (ABR); see also *EC—Hormones* (ABR), above n 95, 173; *US—Shirts and Blouses* (ABR), above n 83, 335.

[98] See, e.g., *Feldman v Mexico* (ICSID Case No ARB(AF)/99/1, Award of 16 December 2002), para 177, in which the NAFTA Tribunal cites the WTO Appellate Body report in *US—Shirts and Blouses*, (ABR), above n 83, 335; see also *AAPL v Sri Lanka* (1991) 30 ILM 577, 604; *Tariffs Applied by Canada to Certain US–Origin Agricultural Products*, paras 125–8 (NAFTA Ch 20 Panel, 1996); *Kling*, 4 RIAA 575 (US–Mexico CC, 1930); *Mexico City Bombardment Claims*, 5 RIAA 76, 80 (GB–Mexico CC, 1930); and *Bowerman*, 5 RIAA 104, 106 (GB–Mexico CC, 1930). See also Amerasinghe, above n 9, 87–8; Foster, above n 60, 97; and J C Witenberg, *L'Organisation Judiciaire: La Procédure et la Sentence Internationales* (1937) 235.

[99] Foster, above n 60, 102; Pauwelyn, above n 66, 258.

Panel, the European Communities will submit its arguments and evidence and Korea will respond to rebut the EC claims. At the end of this process, it is for the Panel to weigh and assess the evidence and arguments submitted by both parties in order to reach conclusions as to whether the EC claims are well-founded.[100]

The Appellate Body confirmed in *Japan—Apples* that the burden of proof did not 'shift' or 'move', stating that:

It is important to distinguish, on the one hand, the principle that the complainant must establish a *prima facie* case of inconsistency with a provision of a covered agreement from, on the other hand, the principle that the party that asserts a fact is responsible for providing proof thereof.[101]

Thus, while maintaining the use of the rule that the complainant must establish a prima facie case,[102] the Appellate Body clarified that the application of the burden of proof in WTO dispute settlement is no different from the approach adopted by other international tribunals: that is, that any party—be it the applicant or respondent state—has the burden of proving any factual assertion which they make.[103]

While the prima facie case rule appears to be more frequently applied in WTO adjudication than by other international courts, it is possible that its greater prominence is due to the greater level of complex scientific evidence which is led in WTO disputes.[104] It is possible that some other international courts adopt a similar approach—albeit at a subconscious level—to the rule on the allocation of the burden of proof, but that this is not expressed due to the reluctance of international courts to discuss questions of competing evidence. Given the persistence of the rule in WTO dispute settlement, it is possible that use of the prima facie case rule might be transplanted to other international courts.

C. Standard of Proof

The standard of proof is connected to the burden of proof, for the party that has this burden must discharge it by convincing the tribunal of its claim to the requisite standard.[105] As is the case with burden of proof, the applicable standard of proof differs between common law and civil law systems. In common law systems, the standard of proof in civil actions is known as the 'balance of probabilities';[106]

100 DSR 2000–I, 49, 242 (PR); James Cameron and Stephen Orava, 'GATT/WTO Panels between Recording and Finding Facts' in Weiss (ed), above n 61, 195, 234.

101 WT/DS245/AB/R, para 157 (ABR) (references omitted).

102 Ibid, paras 152–3.

103 For particular application of the prima facie case rule in the context of disputes involving the 'Enabling Clause', which authorizes developed WTO member states to grant enhanced market access to products from developing countries beyond that granted to products from developed countries, see *EC—Tariff Preferences*, above n 83 (ABR), paras 106–110; see also Matsushita, Schoenbaum and Mavroidis, above n 92, 127.

104 For other suggestions as to the justification for the rule, and the conclusion that it operates so as to create a presumption 'that what is claimed is true', see Pauwelyn, above n 66, 244–6.

105 Kazazi, above n 60, 323.

106 Tapper, above n 64, 141; Kazazi, above n 60, 324.

in civil law systems, the standard of proof in civil actions is the 'conviction of the judge', known as the '*intime conviction*' or '*freie richterliche Überzeugung*'.[107] Yet in international proceedings, there is no clear standard; the statutes and rules of procedure of international courts are generally silent on the required standard of proof, and international courts apply a degree of flexibility.[108] Referring to jurisprudence of the ICJ, the IACHR held in *Velásquez Rodríguez* that 'international jurisprudence has recognised the power of the courts to weigh the evidence freely, although it has always avoided a rigid rule regarding the amount of proof necessary to support the judgment'.[109] Thus, in *US—Shirts and Blouses*, the WTO Appellate Body held that:

> in the context of the GATT 1994 and the WTO Agreement, precisely how much and precisely what kind of evidence will be required to establish such a presumption will necessarily vary from measure to measure, provision to provision, and case to case.[110]

There are, possibly, five different standards of proof which have been applied in international judicial proceedings.[111] One standard is the requirement to show prima facie evidence.[112] This is the lowest degree of proof; failure to make a prima facie case can result in a claim being dismissed.[113] International tribunals have accepted this standard of proof at times, most frequently in situations where the other party fails to produce any evidence rebutting the prima facie evidence produced by the claimant.[114] In *Corfu Channel*, the ICJ noted that in general, the

[107] For example, Bernard Hanotiau, 'Satisfying the Burden of Proof: The Viewpoint of a "Civil Law" Lawyer' (1994) 10 *Arbitration International* 341, 341; Andreas Reiner, 'Burden and General Standards of Proof' (1994) 10 *Arbitration International* 329, 335; Jochen Frowein, 'Fact-Finding by the European Commission of Human Rights' in Lillich (ed), above n 7, 237, 248; see also Waincymer, above n 66, 539; Kazazi, above n 60, 324.

[108] Amerasinghe, above n 9, 232; Foster, above n 60, 87; BIICL, above n 3, 98, 119; Kazazi, above n 60, 325; see also *Armed Activities (DRC v Uganda)*, CR 2005/3, 12 April 2005, 25–6 (Philippe Sands).

[109] *Velásquez Rodríguez (Merits)*, 95 ILR 259, 285 (IACHR, 1988) referring to *Corfu Channel*, above n 87, and *Nicaragua*, above n 35, 24–5, 39–40; see also Kazazi, above n 60, 351.

[110] Above n 83, 335 (ABR); BIICL, above n 3, 64.

[111] See especially Amerasinghe, above n 9, 232–58; and Kazazi, above n 60, 326; see, however, *M/V 'Saiga' (No 2)*, 120 ILR 143, 220, 222 (Sep Op Wolfrum) (ITLOS, 1999), where the view was expressed that there were only two possible standards of proof in international adjudication, being 'proof beyond reasonable doubt, which requires a high degree of cogency, and preponderance of evidence'. One standard identified by Professor Amerasinghe, being a standard of 'reasonableness' (at 243), is, however, not a standard of proof as such, but rather a standard for the ICTY Appeals Chamber's review of the Trial Chamber's findings on fact. In *Prosecutor v Tadic*, the Appeals Chamber held that 'the standard to be used when determining whether the Trial Chamber's factual finding should stand is that of unreasonableness, that is, a conclusion which no reasonable person could have reached. . . . It is only where the evidence relied on by the Trial Chamber could not reasonably have been accepted by any reasonable person that the Appeals Chamber can substitute its own finding for that of the Trial Chamber': (1999) 38 ILM 1518, 1532.

[112] Kazazi, above n 60, 326–43.

[113] For example, *Golshani v Iran*, 29 Ir–USCTR 78, 116 (1993); *Pomeroy v Iran*, 2 Ir–USCTR 372, 382 (1983); *Batchelder*, 22 ILR 864, 866 (Italy–US CC, 1954); Kazazi, above n 60, 327–8.

[114] For example, *Canada—Aircraft*, above n 97, 1428 (ABR); *EC—Hormones*, above n 95, 173 (ABR); Waincymer, above n 66, 538; *Lockheed Corporation v Iran*, 18 Ir–USCTR 292, 318 (1988); *Time Inc v Iran*, 7 Ir–USCTR 8, 11 (1984); *International Technical Products v Iran*, 9 Ir–USCTR 10, 28–9 (1985); Kazazi, above n 60, 333–9.

characteristics of interstate litigation permit reliance on a lower standard of proof and recourse to inferences, stating that:

> the victim of a breach of international law, is often unable to furnish direct proof of facts giving rise to responsibility. Such a State should be allowed a more liberal recourse to inferences of fact and circumstantial evidence. This indirect evidence is admitted in all systems of law, and its use is recognised by international decisions.[115]

While the ICJ did not expressly refer to the prima facie case standard in its dictum, it recognized that parties to international disputes often encounter difficulty in obtaining evidence, and that in such cases, a lower standard of proof can be appropriate. In addition, in the context of requests for provisional measures, applicants before many international courts and tribunals are only required to show that the international court has a prima facie basis of jurisdiction to determine the merits of the dispute.[116]

A second possible standard of proof is the need to prove facts 'beyond reasonable doubt'.[117] This standard is generally applied by criminal courts in common law systems.[118] The ICJ appeared to apply this standard in *Corfu Channel* in responding to the UK argument that a minefield which caused damage to two British naval vessels had been laid with the connivance of the Albanian government. The ICJ held that '[a] charge of such exceptional gravity against a State would require a high degree of certainty that has not been reached here'.[119] In another aspect of the case, the ICJ admitted that inferences may be drawn, only if 'they leave *no room* for reasonable doubt'.[120] The ECommHR and the ECHR have also applied this standard in several cases.[121]

A third possible standard is 'proof in a convincing manner', which appears to be a standard of proof located somewhere between 'proof beyond reasonable doubt' and 'the preponderance of evidence'.[122] It was applied by the IACHR in *Velásquez Rodríguez*, in which it considered that the case, which involved allegations of state torture by Honduras, required the application of 'a standard of proof which considers the seriousness of the charge and which, notwithstanding what has already been said, is capable of establishing the truth of the allegations in a convincing

[115] Above n 87, 18; see also Chittharanjan Amerasinghe, 'Presumptions and Inferences in Evidence in International Litigation' (2004) 3 *Law and Practice of International Courts and Tribunals* 395, 405–6.

[116] See, e.g., *Interhandel* [1957] ICJ Rep 105, 117, 118 (Sep Op Lauterpacht); *Fisheries Jurisdiction (UK v Iceland) (Interim Protection)* [1972] ICJ Rep 12, 15; *Fisheries Jurisdiction (Federal Republic of Germany v Iceland) (Interim Protection)* [1972] ICJ Rep 29, 33; *Nuclear Tests (Interim Protection) (Australia v France)* [1973] ICJ Rep 99, 101; *Nuclear Tests (New Zealand v France) (Interim Protection)* [1973] ICJ Rep 135, 137; UNCLOS, above n 22, arts 290(1), 290(5); *Victor Pey Casado and Fondation Président Allende v Chile*, 16 *ICSID Review—FILJ* 567, 574–6 (2001); *Component Builders, Inc v Iran*, 8 Ir–USCTR 3, 4 (1985); see further below chapter 4, part III(A).

[117] Kazazi, above n 60, 344–7.

[118] Ibid, 344; Tapper, above n 64, 140.

[119] Above n 87, 17.

[120] Ibid, 18 (emphasis in original); Watts, above n 61, 295.

[121] *Aydin v Turkey* [1997] 6 ECHR Rep (No 50) 1867, 1889; *Sevtap Veznedaroglu v Turkey* (ECHR Judgment of 11 April 2000), para 30; *Ireland v UK* [1976] *YbECHR* 512, 796 (ECommHR); 58 ILR 188, 264 (ECHR, 1978); *Denmark, Norway, Sweden and the Netherlands v Greece* [1969] 12 *YbECHR* 1, 196; Frowein, above n 107, 246–7.

[122] Amerasinghe, above n 9, 239–41.

manner'.[123] This standard was also applied by the ICJ in *Nicaragua*, where it noted its obligation under article 53 of the ICJ Statute, in light of the US's non-appearance in the merits phase of the case, to 'satisfy itself... that the claim is well-founded in fact and law'.[124] The ICJ held that this provision of the ICJ Statute implied that 'the Court must attain the same degree of certainty as in any other case that the claim of the party appearing is sound in law, and, so far as the nature of the case permits, that the facts on which it is based are supported by convincing evidence'.[125] Further support for the application of this standard which is relevant in cases of non-appearance might be found in the Separate Opinion of Vice-President Wolfrum in *M/V 'Saiga' (No 2)*, before the ITLOS. In his Separate Opinion, he held that the equivalent provision of the ITLOS Statute, article 28, which provides that in cases of non-appearance, the ITLOS 'must satisfy itself not only that it has jurisdiction over the dispute, but also that the claim is well founded in fact and in law',[126] implied 'that this was the standard of proof to be applied by the [ITLOS] in general'.[127] However, in Vice-President Wolfrum's view, the standard in article 28 was 'not a standard of proof in the sense of "preponderance of evidence", it [was] rather comparable to the standard of proof in the sense of "proof beyond reasonable doubt" as applied in many national legal systems'.[128] This view does not appear to be entirely consistent with that of the ICJ in *Nicaragua*, which did not clearly assimilate the requirement of 'convincing evidence' with the standard of proving facts 'beyond reasonable doubt'. Support for the standard of 'convincing evidence' can also be found in the many partial awards of the Eritrea–Ethiopia Claims Commission, which has repeatedly held, 'in light of the gravity of some of the claims' being advanced, involving widespread violations of international law, that it requires 'clear and convincing evidence in support of its findings'.[129]

A fourth possible standard applied by some international tribunals is a 'preponderance of evidence', or 'balance of probabilities' standard.[130] It has been suggested that this standard is more appropriate in international proceedings where evidence is not always easily obtainable, or is under the exclusive control of a state, and the production of that evidence cannot be compelled; in this sense, it is not greatly dissimilar to the prima facie case standard.[131] The 'preponderance of evidence'

[123] Above n 109, 285; Kazazi, above n 60, 346. [124] ICJ Statute, above n 20, art 53.

[125] *Nicaragua*, above n 35, 24. [126] ITLOS Statute, above n 21, art 28.

[127] *M/V 'Saiga' (No 2)*, above n 111, 220, 220–3 (Sep Op Wolfrum). [128] Ibid, 222.

[129] See, e.g., *Prisoners of War: Eritrea's Claim No 17* (Partial Award of 1 July 2003), para 46 (Eritrea–Ethiopia CC, 2003); *Prisoners of War: Ethiopia's Claim 4* (Partial Award of 1 July 2003), para 37 (Eritrea–Ethiopia CC, 2003); *Central Front: Eritrea's Claims 2, 4, 6, 7, 8 & 22* (Partial Award of 28 April 2004), para 6 (Eritrea–Ethiopia CC, 2004); *Central Front: Ethiopia's Claim 2* (Partial Award of 28 April 2004), para 7 (Eritrea–Ethiopia CC, 2004); *Diplomatic Claim: Ethiopia's Claim 8* (Partial Award of 19 December 2005), para 27 (Eritrea–Ethiopia CC, 2005); *Western and Eastern Fronts: Ethiopia's Claims 1 & 3* (Partial Award of 19 December 2005), para 7 (Eritrea–Ethiopia CC, 2005); *Diplomatic Claim: Eritrea's Claim 20* (Partial Award of 19 December 2005), para 24 (Eritrea–Ethiopia CC, 2005), all available at <http://www.pca-cpa.org> (last visited 25 November 2006).

[130] See, e.g., *Land, Island and Maritime Frontier Dispute* [1992] ICJ Rep 351, 506; Kazazi, above n 60, 347–50; *Pereira Associates, Inc v Iran*, 5 Ir–USCTR 198, 230, 231 (1984) (Sep Op Mosk).

[131] See also *Armed Activities*, above n 108, 25–6 (Philippe Sands).

standard was recognized by Sir Hersch Lauterpacht in *Norwegian Loans*, in which he stated 'the degree of burden of proof... to be adduced ought not to be so stringent as to render the proof unduly exacting'.[132]

The 'preponderance of evidence' standard is similar to a fifth possible standard, being the exercise of judicial discretion to determine if the evidence produced by the parties is 'sufficient' to satisfy the burden of proof.[133] It is suggested that this is the approach most commonly applied. In *Oil Platforms*, the ICJ appeared to apply such a test in considering whether the US had proved that its vessels had been attacked by Iran; it held that 'if at the end of the day the evidence available is insufficient to establish that the missile was fired by Iran, then the necessary burden of proof has not been discharged by the United States'.[134] The ITLOS also appeared to apply this standard in *M/V 'Saiga'*; there, it held that it had to determine whether certain allegations made were 'arguable' or 'of a sufficiently plausible character'.[135]

It can be seen that there is a general lack of consensus on the appropriate standard of proof in international adjudication. International courts apply different tests depending on the facts and circumstances of each case. The most commonly asserted standard is whether the evidence submitted is 'sufficient'; yet, as noted by Judges Higgins and Buergenthal in their separate opinions in *Oil Platforms*, this standard lacks clear guidance for litigants.[136] There appears to be 'general agreement', in the words of Judge Higgins, that 'the graver the charge the more confidence there must be in the evidence relied on',[137] although precisely when an allegation reaches the gravity for the standard to shift from the 'preponderance of evidence' standard, to one which requires evidence 'beyond reasonable doubt', remains opaque. This lack of a clear standard has drawn some criticism from members of the international judiciary.[138] Dr Foster has concluded that:

> Standards of proof are not a focus of attention in international tribunals... In effect the standard of proof usually used in international tribunals comes down to whether a tribunal considers that the evidence supports one proposition better than it does another.[139]

D. Conclusion

The foregoing section considers three evidential issues arising in international courts: the admission of evidence, the burden of proof and the standard of proof. International courts have often adopted a similar approach to these three questions. With respect to the admission of evidence, international courts have adopted a

132 Above n 74, 34, 39–40 (Sep Op Lauterpacht).

133 Kazazi, above n 60, 350–2.

134 Above n 78, 1356–7.

135 *M/V 'Saiga'*, 110 ILR 736, 750; see, however, 750, 761 (Diss Op Mensah); 767, 767–8 (Diss Op Wolfrum and Yamamoto); 773, 773–4 (Diss Op Anderson) (ITLOS, 1998).

136 Above n 78, 1379, 1384–6 (Sep Op Higgins), 1404, 1412–15 (Sep Op Buergenthal).

137 Ibid, 1385 (Sep Op Higgins).

138 See, e.g., ibid; *M/V 'Saiga' (No 2)*, above n 111, 220, 222 (Sep Op Wolfrum); *Schering Corporation v Iran* (1984) 5 Ir–USCTR 361, 374, 375 (Diss Op Mosk).

139 Foster, above n 60, 87 (references omitted); see also Schwarzenberger, above n 61, 192, 643.

liberal approach. As regards questions of proof, international courts have adopted the rule that each party making an assertion bears the burden of proving it. International courts have failed to articulate a clear standard of proof; usually, the question whether a party has discharged its burden of proof will depend on whether the evidence led has been sufficient. The evidence of a common approach regarding the first two issues, however, does not mean that there is complete consistency in the application of these rules by international tribunals. There is, nonetheless, an instinct towards convergence in the practice of international courts. The attention of this chapter is now directed towards the powers of international courts to procure evidence *proprio motu*.

III. Powers of International Courts Regarding Evidence

An international court may desire further evidence or explanations if it is faced with an inadequacy of evidence. It is often stated that the powers of international courts regarding evidence are very wide,[140] but it is also frequently lamented that international courts are handicapped due to their lack of coercive powers to compel the production of evidence and the attendance of witnesses.[141] Questions relating to the evidence-gathering powers of international courts are pertinent, as the ability of international courts to gather evidence other than that submitted by the parties might be crucial to their ability to carry out their functions in finding the truth and, by the correct application of law to those facts, settling the dispute. This aspect of how international courts treat issues of evidence will also lend further insights into whether international courts have the same powers over evidence, and whether those powers are exercised consistently. International courts have various evidence-gathering powers, such as taking judicial notice of notorious facts, appointing experts, and asking questions to the parties in the course of hearings. The following paragraphs are not intended as an exhaustive consideration of these methods, but merely seek to illustrate the ways in which international courts can seek evidence. If it can be shown that there are common features in the exercise by international courts of evidential powers, this will complement the broad commonality that has been shown to exist regarding the admissibility of evidence, the allocation of the burden of proof, and, to a lesser extent, the standard of proof.

A. Judicial Notice of Facts

One example which can briefly be noted is the technique whereby international courts take 'judicial notice' of evidence which is available as a matter of public

[140] For example, Highet, 'Evidence, the Court', above n 1, 7.

[141] Kazazi, above n 60, 170; Michael Reisman and Eric Freedman, 'The Plaintiff's Dilemma: Illegally Obtained Evidence and Admissibility in International Adjudication' (1982) 76 *AJIL* 737, 737–8; Highet, ibid, 10; Alford, above n 71, 53; 'Harvard Research Draft Convention on Judicial Assistance' (1939) AJIL Supplement 15, 104.

knowledge.[142] Early international tribunals assumed this power,[143] and the ICJ has also exercised this power in several cases. In *Tehran Hostages*, the ICJ considered that:

The essential facts of the present case are, for the most part, matters of public knowledge which have received extensive coverage in the world press and in radio and television broadcasts from Iran and other countries... The result is that the Court has available to it a massive body of information from various sources concerning the facts and circumstances of the present case, including numerous official statements of both Iranian and United States authorities.[144]

In *Nicaragua*, the ICJ confirmed that 'public knowledge of a fact may... be established by means of these sources',[145] and did rely on press reports to establish certain facts, such as the existence of joint military manoeuvres between the United States and Honduras near the Nicaraguan border; the ICJ held that 'since there was no secrecy about the holding of the manoeuvres, the Court considers that it may treat the matter as one of public knowledge, and as such, sufficiently established'.[146] But the ICJ noted that:

The Court has however to show particular caution in this area. Widespread reports of a fact may prove on closer examination to derive from a single source, and such reports, however numerous, will in such case have no greater value as evidence than the original source. It is with this important reservation that the newspaper reports submitted to the Court should be examined in order to assess the facts of the case, and in particular to ascertain whether such facts were matters of public knowledge.[147]

In *Nuclear Tests*, the ICJ went to 'curious lengths' in exercising its power to find evidence not adduced by the parties,[148] and ultimately based its decision that the Australian and New Zealand claims were inadmissible on statements made by the French government after the close of the proceedings.[149] This power has also been exercised by other international tribunals: in *Tadic*, the ICTY took judicial notice of conclusions of the Appeals Chamber and the Security Council concerning the nature of the conflict,[150] and in *Delalic*, the ICTY took notice of 'many public documents', including UN Security Council resolutions, concerning the conflict

[142] Amerasinghe, above n 9, 160–1; Highet, 'Evidence, the Court', above n 1, 39–40, 49; Sandifer, above n 2, 382–97; Scelle, above n 72, 133.

[143] Sandifer, ibid, 382–97; Cheng, above n 33, 303.

[144] *US Diplomatic and Consular Staff in Tehran* [1980] ICJ Rep 3, 9–10. Earlier, in *Anglo-Norwegian Fisheries*, the ICJ had referred to the concept of 'notoriety of facts': [1951] ICJ Rep 116, 138–9: see *Application of the Genocide Convention* [1993] ICJ Rep 407, 423 (Sep Op Lauterpacht).

[145] Above n 35, 40. [146] Ibid, 53. [147] Ibid, 41.

[148] Judge Philip Jessup, 'Foreword' in Sandifer, above n 2, x–xi.

[149] [1974] ICJ Rep 253, 259, 261–72; see also 312–71 (Joint Diss Op Onyeama, Dillard, Jiménez de Aréchaga, and Waldock); F A Mann, 'The Consequences of an International Wrong in International and National Law' (1976–7) 48 *British Yearbook of International Law* 1, 11–12; and see chapter 2 above. See also *Application of the Genocide Convention* [1993] ICJ Rep 325, 423 (Sep Op Lauterpacht).

[150] *Prosecutor v Tadic*, para 583 (ICTY Trial Chamber Judgement, 1997).

in Bosnia and Herzegovina.[151] It is suggested that all international courts may exercise the power to take judicial notice of 'notorious facts' in order to supplement evidence adduced by the parties, and this appears to be generally accepted.

B. Power to Order the Production of Evidence

It is uncontroversial that international courts have the power to request the production of further information or to investigate the facts *proprio motu*.[152] The power to request evidence is expressly conferred on many international courts by their constitutive instruments, and others have included it in their rules of procedure.[153] Moreover, the fact-finding powers of international courts represent an essential part of their adjudicative function, and so where the power is not expressly included in the constitutive instrument, international courts arguably have an inherent power to request the production of further evidence.[154] More controversial is the existence of a coercive power to *demand* or *order* the production of evidence. Certain international tribunals have in the past been given powers to 'require' or 'compel' the production of evidence or witnesses, but such powers remain exceptional.[155] In the face of a recalcitrant state's refusal to hand over evidence, be it requested or demanded, a question arises regarding the consequences of such refusal. The present section examines the nature of the power of international courts to seek further evidence from the parties, and the consequences of non-compliance.

[151] *Prosecutor v Delalic* et al, para 90 (ICTY Trial Chamber Judgment, 1998); see generally Eugene O'Sullivan, 'Judicial Notice' in Richard May *et al* (eds), *Essays on ICTY Procedure and Evidence* (2001) 329.

[152] Kazazi, above n 60, 165; see generally *Prosecutor v Blaskic (Subpoenae duces tecum)*, 110 ILR 607, 634–7 (ICTY Trial Chamber Decision, 1997).

[153] 1899 Convention, above n 16, art 44; 1907 Convention, above n 17, art 69; ICJ Statute, above n 20, arts 34(2), 49; ICJ Rules, above n 37, art 62(1); ITLOS Rules, above n 37, art 77; ICSID Convention, above n 23, art 43(a); ICSID Rules, above n 55, Rules 34(2)–(3), 37; DSU, art 13(1); *Protocol on the Statute of the Court of Justice, Consolidated Version of the EEC Treaty*, OJ C 325/33, 167 ('ECJ Statute'), art 21; *Convention for the Protection of Human Rights and Fundamental Freedoms*, opened for signature 4 November 1950, 213 UNTS 221 (entered into force 3 September 1953) ('European HR Convention') art 38(1)(a); see also European Court of Human Rights, Rules of Court, available at <http://www.echr.coe.int>, art 42(1); American Convention, art 48; Inter-American Court of Human Rights, Rules of Procedure, available at <http://www.corteidh.or.cr> art 44(2).

[154] Kazazi, above n 60, 166.

[155] *Rome Statute of the International Criminal Court*, opened for signature 17 July 1998, 37 ILM 999 (entered into force 1 July 2002) art 69(3); International Criminal Court Rules of Procedure and Evidence, Rule 65, 171 UN Doc ICC–ASP/1/3; ICTY Rules of Procedure and Evidence, Rule 98; ICTR Rules, Rule 98; see especially *Prosecutor v Blaskic*, above n 152, 636–76; *Prosecutor v Blaskic*, 110 ILR 688 (ICTY App Ch, 1997). For further examples, see, e.g., Ir–USCT Rules, above n 60, art 24(3); Arbitral Commission on Property, Rights and Interests in Germany Rules, reprinted in *Decisions of the Arbitral Commission on Property, Rights and Interests in Germany* (1958) vol 1, 298, art 22; and see also the Rules of Procedure of various MATs, e.g. German-Belgian MAT Rules, 1 TAM 33, arts 54, 57; and those of the Franco-German MAT, 1 TAM 44, art 90; the Greco-German MAT, 1 TAM 61, art 87; the Anglo-German MAT, 1 TAM 109, art 27; and the Franco-Bulgarian MAT, 1 TAM 121, art 44; *International Joint Commission Treaty* (US–UK) signed 11 January 1909, USTS, No 548, art XII; see also Harvard Draft, above n 141, 105.

It is apparent that there are fewer common features in the exercise of powers concerning this aspect of evidence, than in the other elements under consideration in the present chapter. This is because the exercise of a coercive power depends not only on whether the court has a power to act, be it express or inherent, or on the functions of that international court, but also, perhaps most importantly, on the nature of the relationship between the international court and the parties before it. For the existence of a power to order the production of evidence will be of little assistance to a party to international proceedings if the international court in question is unwilling to exercise that power out of deference to the parties.

It is widely accepted that parties to international litigation have a general obligation of disclosure which requires them to produce evidence which is in their possession and which is not available to the opposing party.[156] This was established in *Parker*, where the US-Mexican GCC held that the respondent government was under an 'obligation to lay before the Commission all evidence within its possession to establish the truth, whatever it may be'.[157] This rule has been followed by other international tribunals,[158] and an obligation to make a high standard of disclosure is reflected in many constitutive instruments. In *Argentina—Textiles and Apparel*, the WTO panel held that:

> the most important result of the rule of collaboration appears to be that the adversary is obligated to provide the tribunal with relevant documents which are in its sole possession. This obligation does not arise until the claimant has done its best to secure evidence and has actually produced some *prima facie* evidence in support of its case.[159]

Whether this obligation extends to full compliance with requests from international courts is uncertain, however; some have described the obligation as an 'empty piety'.[160] An examination of the source of this obligation might shed light on the effects of non-compliance. In the case of the ICJ, the obligation might be said to derive from states' obligations to comply with the UN Charter, of which the ICJ Statute forms an integral part.[161] Under the UN Charter, states parties have an obligation to comply with 'decisions' of the ICJ.[162] A request by the ICJ for the production of evidence under article 49 of the ICJ Statute is unlikely to be regarded as a 'decision', however. Yet it is arguable that states parties, having accepted the jurisdiction of the ICJ, or other international courts, are under an obligation of

[156] *Ireland v UK*, above n 121, 259; *Fairen Garbi and Solis Corrales*, Ser C, (No 6), 31, para 160 (IACHR, 1989); Amerasinghe, above n 9, 96–8; Göran Sluiter, *International Criminal Adjudication and the Collection of Evidence: Obligations of States* (2002) 140–5; Kazazi, above n 60, 119; Sandifer, above n 2, 153; Michael Reisman, *Nullity and Revision* (1971) 593; Reisman and Freedman, above n 141, 738; Scelle, 'Arbitral Procedure', above n 72, 134; Witenberg, 'La théorie des preuves', above n 10, 97–8.

[157] Above n 49, 39.

[158] For example, *Kling*, above n 98, 581–4; *Pinson*, above n 72, 411–14; see also *Ambatielos*, 12 RIAA 83, 112–13, 117–18 (Greece–UK, 1956).

[159] Above n 56, 1159 (PR); Palmeter and Mavroidis, above n 56, 83.

[160] Reisman and Freedman, above n 141, 738.

[161] *Charter of the United Nations*, opened for signature 26 June 1945, 3 Bevans 1153 (entered into force 24 October 1945) art 92.

[162] Ibid, art 94(1).

good faith to comply with such requests. This analysis is strengthened by other provisions of the constitutive instruments of such courts, such as their power to 'make all arrangements connected with the taking of evidence' and to put any relevant questions to witnesses.[163]

However, this question needs to be examined in light of the terms of each statutory provision or rule of procedure empowering the international court to seek further information. Article 49 of the ICJ Statute is not expressed in mandatory terms: the ICJ can only 'call upon' parties to produce evidence, rather than 'demand', 'compel', or 'require' the production of evidence. This suggests that such requests only have exhortative effect. Additionally, the consequences of non-compliance are expressly stated: far from suggesting that offending parties have committed an internationally wrongful act, such as could give rise to state responsibility, article 49 merely provides that the ICJ 'takes formal note'. This indicates that the intention of the drafters was not that there should be a more serious outcome. Hudson has observed that very little discussion attended the adoption of article 49 by the Advisory Committee of Jurists.[164] One would imagine that the debate might have been more vigorous were article 49 to have the effect of creating a binding obligation. The same analysis applies to the relevant provisions in the ITLOS Rules: article 77(1) provides that the ITLOS can 'call upon' parties to produce evidence, which implies that this is to have exhortative force only. In the case of the 1907 Convention, article 69 provides that the tribunal can 'require' from the parties the production of all papers, and 'demand' all necessary explanations; but here, the consequences of non-compliance are that the tribunal merely 'takes note' of any refusal. Article 43(a) of the ICSID Convention is couched in terms of the tribunal having the power merely to 'call upon' parties to produce documents and other evidence, and the same language can be found in article 34(2)(a) of the ICSID Arbitration Rules. Again, this does not inspire a belief that such requests are to be treated as having mandatory force. Nonetheless, an ICSID Tribunal held in *Biwater Gauff (Tanzania) Ltd v Tanzania* that the respondent state was under an obligation to produce documents if ordered to do so by the Tribunal, and that this was 'an international legal obligation arising from the State's consent by way of the BIT to ICSID arbitration.'[165]

[163] For example, ICJ Statute, above n 20, arts 48, 51. Professor Reisman goes so far as to argue that this analysis would apply *a fortiori* in the case of requests for further information made by a PCA tribunal under article 69 of the 1907 Convention due to the presence of article 75, which he interprets as imposing an express obligation of good faith on parties to PCA proceedings: Reisman, above n 156, 599.

[164] Hudson, above n 9, 202.

[165] *Biwater Gauff (Tanzania) Ltd v Tanzania* (ICSID Case No ARB/05/22, Procedural Order No 2 of 24 May 2006), 8–9. The Tribunal further held that 'the public interest immunity exception invoked by the Respondent [was] not a valid objection to the production of documents requested by the Claimant'. The Tribunal held that 'the only ground which might justify a refusal by the Republic to produce documents to this Tribunal is the protection of privileged or politically sensitive information, including State secrets, as pointed out by the Arbitral Tribunal in *Pope & Talbot, Inc v Government of Canada*, Ruling on Claim of Crown Privileges dated 6 September 2000 (2005) 7 ICSID Rep 99, para 1.4, and restated in article 9(2)(f) of the IBA Rules of Evidence'. See also *Biwater Gauff (Tanzania) Ltd v*

In contrast to the ICJ, the ITLOS, PCA and ICSID tribunals, the Appeals Chamber of the ICTY has held that it has the power to issue binding orders to states, including orders for the production of evidence, and subpoenas to individuals acting in their private capacity.[166] This power is derived from the fact that the ICTY was established by a SC Resolution made under Chapter VII of the UN Charter. Paragraph 4 of this Resolution, together with article 29 of the ICTY Statute, imposes on all states 'the obligation to lend cooperation and judicial assistance' to the ICTY.[167] The binding force of the obligation, in the words of the ICTY Appeals Chamber,

> derives from the provisions of Chapter VII and Article 25 of the United Nations Charter and from the Security Council Resolution adopted pursuant to those provisions. The exceptional legal basis of Article 29 accounts for the novel and indeed unique power granted to the International Tribunal to issue orders to sovereign states.[168]

This power is, then, specific to the method of creation of the ICTY (and, presumably the ICTR, as it was created by Security Council Resolution), and is of little assistance in the search for a general rule.

Another international tribunal which has considered the existence of an obligation to produce requested evidence is the WTO Appellate Body, which construed DSU article 13(1) in *Canada—Aircraft*.[169] In its report, the Appellate Body noted the content of article 13(1), which provides that '[a] member *should* respond promptly and fully to any request for such information'.[170] The Appellate Body observed that while the word 'should' is often used to imply an 'exhortation', it could also be used to express 'a duty or obligation', and in the present case, the Appellate Body held that 'should' was being used in the 'normative' rather than the 'exhortative' sense.[171] Consequently, the Appellate Body concluded that members are 'under a duty and an obligation to "respond promptly and fully" to requests made by panels for information'.[172] It explained further that if article 13(1) did not connote a duty, then the Panel's 'right to seek information' would be devoid of meaning, and a party to a dispute could

> thwart the panel's fact-finding powers and take control itself of the information-gathering process that articles 12 and 13 place in the hands of the panel. A Member could, in other

Tanzania (ICSID Case No ARB/05/22, Procedural Order No 1 of 31 March 2006), para 106, where the ICSID Tribunal expressed its direction on production of documents under article 43 of the ICSID Convention as an 'order'.

166 *Prosecutor v Blaskic*, above n 155, 698–704, 713–16.

167 Ibid, 699. See also UN Charter, above n 161, and *International Tribunal for the Prosecution of Persons Responsible for Serious Violations of International Humanitarian Law Committed in the Territory of the former Yugoslavia since 1991*, adopted by SC Res 827(1993), UN Doc S/RES/827 (1993).

168 *Prosecutor v Blaskic*, ibid, 699.

169 Above n 97.

170 DSU, above n 24, art 13(1) (emphasis added).

171 *Canada—Aircraft*, above n 97, 1427.

172 Ibid; Rambod Behboodi, '"Should" means "Shall": A Critical Analysis of the Obligation to Submit Information under Article 13.1 of the DSU in the *Canada—Aircraft* Case' (2000) 3 *Journal of International Economic Law* 563.

words, prevent a panel from carrying out its task of finding the facts constituting the dispute before it and, inevitably, from going forward with the legal characterisation of those facts.[173]

Further, the Appellate Body held that if it concluded that a member state had no such obligation, this would be, in effect:

to declare that Member legally free to preclude a panel from carrying out its mandate and responsibility under the DSU. So to rule would be to reduce to an illusion and a vanity the fundamental right of Members to have disputes arising between them resolved through the system and proceedings for which they bargained in concluding the DSU.[174]

Accordingly, states parties to dispute settlement proceedings before WTO panels are under an obligation to comply with requests for further information from the panel. The question remains, however, as to the consequences of non-compliance with such a request.

One possible consequence is that the award or judgment can be treated as a nullity. This suggestion finds its origins in the *Lazare* arbitration of 1884–5 between the US and Haiti.[175] In this case, counsel for the US failed to disclose a US State Department document which would 'materially have affected' the award rendered.[176] Haiti subsequently claimed that the award was a 'nullity'. Yet it is questionable whether this case actually represents authority for the proposition that awards made after lack of full disclosure should be treated as a nullity, for the US merely declined to enforce the award.[177] In addition, this outcome has not been followed by other international courts.

Furthermore, as previously stated, many constitutive instruments spell out the consequences of non-compliance; article 49 of the ICJ Statute provides that the ICJ shall take 'formal note' of any refusal to provide requested information. This is a stronger measure than simply ignoring the state's non-production of evidence, but, as noted by Professor Amerasinghe, 'it does not have any particular teeth in itself'.[178] Taking 'formal note', however, suggests that the international court might be able to draw an adverse inference from the failure of a state to produce requested evidence. The drawing of 'adverse inferences' is premised on the view that, if evidence is not produced, it is because the disclosure of such evidence might be contrary to the interests of the party in possession of that evidence.[179] International courts have adopted this approach since early international arbitrations.[180] It appears

173 *Canada—Aircraft*, above n 97, 1427, para 188 (footnotes omitted). 174 Ibid, para 189.

175 Moore, vol II, 1749–50 (US–Haiti, 1886); Reisman, above n 156, 594–7.

176 Moore, vol II, 1800–1. 177 Ibid, 1804. 178 Amerasinghe, above n 9, 132.

179 *Barcelona Traction*, above n 54, 162, 215 (Sep Op Jessup).

180 See, e.g., *Parker*, above n 49, 39; *Hatton*, 4 RIAA 329, 331–2 (US–Mexico GCC, 1928); *Kalklosch*, 4 RIAA 412, 414 (US–Mexico GCC, 1928); *Kling*, above n 98, 581–2; *Melczer Mining Co*, 4 RIAA 481, 485 (US–Mexico GCC, 1929); *Mexico City Bombardment*, above n 98, 83–4 (Diss Op Comm Percival); *Tinoco*, 1 RIAA 375, 393 (UK–Costa Rica, 1923); *Island of Palmas*, above n 50, 841–2; Reisman, above n 156, 596; Sandifer, above n 2, 150–2; Feller, above n 43, 262–3.

that no such instance arose before the PCIJ,[181] but there have been several cases before the ICJ in which parties have refused to produce requested documents. In *Corfu Channel*, the ICJ requested that the UK produce a certain document, 'Document XCU', for the use of the Court. The UK refused to produce the document, pleading 'naval secrecy', and refused to answer questions relating to it.[182] The ICJ noted the UK's refusal, but did not draw any inferences adverse to the UK's case.[183] In *Tehran Hostages*, the ICJ also put questions to the US Government, one of which the US did not answer, but in this case too, the ICJ made no comment.[184] These cases demonstrate that it is up to the discretion of the international tribunal whether or not an adverse inference is actually drawn.[185] The Iran–US Claims Tribunal has also noted that it can draw adverse inferences from the failure to provide requested evidence.[186] In the case of ICSID tribunals, Professor Schreuer has observed that failure to produce a document would probably lead to an inference being drawn by the tribunal.[187]

The question of adverse inferences came under the scrutiny of the WTO Appellate Body in *Canada—Aircraft*, referred to above.[188] It has already been noted that Canada refused to provide information requested by the panel. Canada sought to justify its refusal to provide the information on two grounds, both of which the Appellate Body rejected. The Appellate Body considered the question of whether the panel had the power to draw adverse inferences from a refusal to provide requested information. It noted that the DSU did not state 'in what detailed circumstances inferences, adverse or otherwise, may be drawn by panels from infinitely varying combinations of facts'.[189] The Appellate Body held that the drawing of inferences was 'an inherent and unavoidable aspect of a panel's basic task of finding and characterising the facts making up a dispute', and referred to the practice of other international courts and tribunals in this regard.[190] 'Clearly', in the view of the Appellate Body, 'the Panel had the legal authority and the discretion to draw inferences from the facts before it—including the fact that Canada had refused to provide information sought by the Panel.'[191]

181 Amerasinghe, above n 9, 132; Reisman, above n 156, 599; but see *Electricity Company of Sofia and Bulgaria*, Ser A/B (No 77), 109, 115 (Diss Op van Eysinga) (PCIJ, 1939).

182 Above n 87, 32; Rosenne, *Procedure*, above n 29, 134. Compare the UK's attitude with that of Sweden in *Guardianship Convention* [1958] ICJ Rep 55, 59, where that country placed on record its willingness to provide further documents.

183 *Corfu Channel*, ibid, 32, (Diss Op Ecer) 115, 129; Sandifer, above n 2, 148–9. The Document 'XCU' is now publicly available: Anthony Carty, 'The *Corfu Channel* Case—And the Missing Admiralty Orders' (2004) 2 *Law and Practice of International Courts and Tribunals* 1.

184 Rosenne, *Procedure*, above n 29, 134; *Tehran Hostages (Provisional Measures)* [1979] ICJ Rep 7, 10.

185 See also Feller, above n 43, 262, fn 29; *Pomeroy's El Paso Transfer Co*, 4 RIAA 551, 553–5 (US–Mexico GCC, 1930); *Melczer Mining Co*, above n 180, 485.

186 *ITT Industries Inc, v Iran*, 2 Ir–USCTR 348, 349, 355 (Conc Op Aldrich) (1983).

187 Schreuer, above n 1, 656; see also *Biwater Gauff*, above n 165 (Procedural Order No 2), 8–9. Although the Tribunal did not draw adverse inferences from Tanzania's failure to produce documents, it ordered the production of those documents and held that Tanzania could not rely on public interest immunity to refuse production.

188 Above n 97.

189 Ibid, 1430.

190 Ibid, 1431–3.

191 Ibid, 1433.

It is concluded that international courts hold broadly similar views concerning both the existence of a power to request further information from the parties, and also the consequences for parties of non-compliance with such a request; that is, the possible drawing of an adverse inference. This commonality, however, does not extend to the question of how those provisions are actually used in practice, and whether parties to international proceedings comply with such requests. Some international tribunals that deal with interstate disputes have shown particular reluctance to order the production of evidence. For instance, the ICJ has called on parties before it to produce documents or other evidence in only a few instances.[192] In *Corfu Channel* and *Tehran Hostages*, the ICJ did not even draw any adverse inferences from the refusals of the UK and US to provide the documents.[193] The ITLOS, for its part, has not yet issued an order exercising its power to call upon parties to produce evidence. In contrast to the ICJ and the ITLOS, tribunals constituted under the auspices of the PCA, the ICSID Convention and the NAFTA to settle private or mixed disputes have proved more amenable to the exercise of this power.[194] The lack of common examples of the exercise of this power arguably reflects the different relationship between some international courts and the litigating parties. Some international courts accord a degree of deference to the parties to the dispute, particularly where those parties are sovereign states, while other international courts, such as ad hoc tribunals which operate in a similar fashion to international commercial arbitration tribunals, do not display the same deference.[195] The relationship between an international court and the parties, then, is relevant in assessing the potential for a certain practice to be adopted. Even if the statutes provide for the same power, and the courts are equally able to fill gaps in their statutes and rules, the deference displayed by the court towards the parties will have an impact on the application of a certain rule.

[192] See, e.g., *Corfu Channel*, above n 87; *Ambatielos*, ICJ Pleadings, 346–7, 566–7; *US Nationals in Morocco*, ICJ Pleadings, vol II, 431–4; *Tehran Hostages*, above n 184, 10; *Aegean Sea Continental Shelf*, ICJ Pleadings, 296; *Diversion of Water from the Meuse*, Ser E, (No 14), 153 (PCIJ, 1937); see also Christian Tams, 'Article 49' in Andreas Zimmermann, Christian Tomuschat and Karin Oellers-Frahm (eds), *The Statute of the International Court of Justice: A Commentary* (2006) 1099, 1101–1105.

[193] *Corfu Channel*, ibid, 32; *Tehran Hostages*, ibid, 10.

[194] See, e.g., *Biwater Gauff*, above n 165, (Procedural Order No 1 of 31 March 2006), paras 104–6, (Procedural Order No 2 of 24 May 2006), 8–9; *CSOB v Slovakia*, 14 *ICSID Review—FILJ* 251, 254 (2001); *Tanzania Electric Supply Co Ltd v Independent Power Tanzania* (ICSID Case No ARB/98/8, Award of 22 June 2001), paras 43–44; *Feldman v Mexico*, above n 98, paras 27–41; *Plama Consortium Ltd v Bulgaria*, above n 81, para 16; *GAMI Investments, Inc v Mexico* (Procedural Order No 1 of 31 January 2003), para 7.6; see also *Bank for International Settlements* (Procedural Order No 3 of 5 March 2002), (Procedural Order No 5 of 3 May 2002), (Procedural Order No 6 of 11 June 2002), (Procedural Order No 10 of 9 March 2003), available at <http://www.pca-cpa.org> (last visited 25 November 2006).

[195] See, e.g., the failure of the UNCLOS tribunal to order the production of documents in an interstate dispute: *Barbados/Trinidad and Tobago* (Procedural Order No 4 of 26 October 2004), available at <http://www.pca-cpa.org> (last visited 25 November 2006).

C. Power to Make Site Visits

Another procedural power which has been developed in the practice of international tribunals is the *descente sur les lieux*, or a visit by members of a court to sites connected with a dispute for the purpose of gathering evidence and familiarizing themselves with the location.[196] This is another possible means for international courts to overcome an inadequacy of evidence. This power is only rarely provided for in the constitutive instruments of international courts. Article 76 of the 1907 Convention empowers PCA tribunals to procure evidence on the spot, although they must obtain the permission of the state on whose territory the inspection would take place. This power was alluded to in article 44(2) of the PCIJ Statute, which is retained in the ICJ Statute, and provides that the ICJ is to apply to the government of the state 'whenever steps are to be taken to procure evidence on the spot'. ICSID tribunals have an express power under the ICSID Convention to 'visit any place connected with the dispute or conduct enquiries there'.[197] In addition, the ECommHR exercised this power in several cases, in which it sent missions of its members to carry out on-site visits, interview witnesses, and take relevant evidence.[198] The ECHR has arrogated to itself the power under its Rules to make site visits to gather evidence,[199] as has the ITLOS.[200]

This power is also an inherent power, which international courts may exercise in order to carry out their functions in gathering evidence and settling a dispute, although it is not one which all international courts choose to exercise.[201] Site visits have been conducted by several arbitral tribunals in the absence of an express power.[202] A PCA tribunal constituted under the 1907 Convention exercised its power to conduct a site visit in *Grisbådarna* in 1909.[203] The arbitrator in *Ben Tillett* also visited the prison where the British national, Mr Tillett, was detained for several days in 1896, in order to gather evidence.[204] The earliest exercise of

196 Amerasinghe, above n 9, 159; Watts, above n 61, 301; C Wilfred Jenks, *The Prospects of International Adjudication* (1964) 137; Manley Hudson, 'Visit by International Tribunals to Places Concerned in Proceedings' (1937) 31 *AJIL* 696.

197 ICSID Convention, above n 23, art 43(b); ICSID Arbitration Rules, above n 55, Rule 37; exercise of this power was contemplated in *Compania del Desarrollo de Santa Elena*, 15 *ICSID Review—FILJ* 169, 174 (2000).

198 *Denmark, Norway, Sweden and the Netherlands v Greece*, above n 121, 189–92; *France, Norway, Denmark, Sweden, and the Netherlands v Turkey* (1985) 44 Dec & Rep 31, 36–7; *B v UK* (1981) 32 Dec & Rep 5, 8; Frowein, above n 107, 244–5; BIICL, above n 3, 84.

199 ECHR Rules, above n 153, Rule 42(2). 200 ITLOS Rules, above n 37, art 81.

201 Mohammed Bedjaoui, 'La "Descente sur les Lieux" dans la Pratique de la Cour Internationale de Justice et de sa Devancière' in Gerhard Hafner *et al* (eds), *Liber Amicorum Professor Ignaz Seidl-Hohenveldern* (1998) 1, 1–2; Shabtai Rosenne, 'Visit to the Site by the International Court' in Emile Yakpo and Tahar Boumedra (eds), *Liber Amicorum Mohammed Bedjaoui* (1999) 461, 461.

202 *Meeresauge*, above n 72; see further Bedjaoui, ibid, 4.

203 *Grisbådarna*, 11 RIAA 147, 157 (Norway–Sweden, 1909).

204 *Ben Tillett*, in Henri La Fontaine, *Pasicrisie Internationale 1794–1900: Histoire Documentaire des Arbitrages Internationaux* (1997) 581, 584–5 (GB–Belgium, 1898).

the power by the PCIJ can be found in *Diversion of Water from the Meuse*.[205] Interestingly, in that case, the relevant Order did not refer to article 44(2) of the PCIJ Statute, which directs the PCIJ to apply to the government concerned 'whenever steps are taken to procure evidence on the spot', but rather to articles 48 and 50 of the PCIJ Statute, being the powers to make orders for the conduct of proceedings, and the power to consult experts.[206] This suggests that the PCIJ might not have viewed article 44(2) as contemplating site visits by the court itself, but rather merely the gathering of testimony of witnesses by agents of the PCIJ; this precedent was, perhaps, the exercise of an inherent power. Later, the ICJ arranged for experts to visit the site in *Corfu Channel* to gather evidence.[207] Somewhat remarkably, one ICJ judge, Judge Moreno Quintana, seems to have inspected the disputed area in *Frontier Land* at his own initiative.[208] Site visits were proposed in *South West Africa*, but the ICJ, this time acting under article 48 of the ICJ Statute, did not think it necessary to accede to this suggestion.[209] In 1978, the ICJ included article 66 in its Rules of Court, which gave a more concrete textual basis for this practice.[210] A site visit was also suggested in *Land, Island and Maritime Frontier Dispute*, but the ICJ did not accede to this request.[211] It next exercised the power in *Gabcikovo-Nagymaros Project*.[212] Other arbitral practice, involving a series of boundary disputes between Argentina and Chile, also supports the existence of a power to make site visits.[213]

Site visits are a useful way for international courts to procure evidence of their own motion. The principal limitation to the exercise of this power is that the consent of the state on whose territory the site visit is to take place must be obtained before it can proceed; and in practice, site visits have never taken place in the absence of the agreement of the parties to the dispute.

D. Power to Order Expert Reports

In many international disputes the parties submit large volumes of complex technical, scientific or financial material in support of their case.[214] This evidence may

[205] Ser A/B, (No 70), 9 (PCIJ, 1937). An on-site inspection was suggested in *Free Zones*, but the PCIJ rejected the request: *Free Zones*, above n 52, 162–3; Bedjaoui, above n 201, 9.

[206] Ser C, (No 81), 553–4.

[207] Above n 87, 21.

[208] [1959] ICJ Rep 209, 252 (Diss Op Moreno Quintana).

[209] [1965] ICJ Rep 9, 9–10; Highet, 'Evidence, the Court', above n 1, 30; Sandifer, above n 2, 345–8.

[210] Rosenne, *Procedure*, above n 29, 139.

[211] Above n 130, 361–2. A site visit was also discussed by the parties in *Gulf of Maine* [1984] ICJ Rep 246, but no agreement was reached: Rosenne, 'Visit to the Site', above n 201, 467–9.

[212] [1997] ICJ Rep 3, 4–5; see further Peter Tomka and Samuel Wordsworth, 'The First Site Visit of the International Court of Justice in Fulfilment of Its Judicial Function' (1998) 92 *AJIL* 133; Bedjaoui, above n 201, 9; Rosenne, 'Visit to the Site', above n 201, 461.

[213] *Palena*, 38 ILR 10, 17, 27–8, 55–8 (Argentina–Chile, 1966); *Beagle Channel*, 52 ILR 93, 115–16 (Argentina–Chile, 1977); *Dispute on the Frontier between Boundary Post 62 and Mount Fitzroy*, 22 RIAA 3, 9–10 (Argentina–Chile, 1996); Rosenne, 'Visit to the Site', above n 201, 470–3.

[214] Watts, above n 61, 298; Alford, above n 71, 73.

include expert evidence. Given the rising tendency of states to submit disputes to third party adjudication, and particularly in light of the technical nature of some disputes, international courts are increasingly being faced with such evidence. Yet expert evidence presented on behalf of parties may be conflicting, in that the different parties' experts sometimes offer differing opinions based on the same factual data.[215] In addition, expert evidence presented on behalf of the parties might also be regarded as biased: as Professor Pauwelyn has noted, even if party-appointed experts 'are presented as "neutrals", it is difficult not to see them as "hired guns"'.[216] Further, international judges are not always best positioned to deal with such expert material.[217] The technical nature of evidence in international adjudication and the inadequacies which can result from relying on the expert opinions submitted by the parties might give rise to a need for independent experts to give evidence to an international court. There are several ways in which such evidence can be brought before an international court by means other than the parties' submissions.[218] First, the court might appoint 'assessors', experts who sit with the court or tribunal during the proceedings, but do not have a vote. Second, expertise might be brought to bear on the dispute by appointing technically qualified members of the tribunal. Third, the international court itself may appoint independent experts to provide a report.

There are a number of disadvantages with the first two methods. First, international courts have relatively little experience with 'assessors'. The PCIJ Statute provided for their appointment to the special chambers formed for labour disputes and transit and communications disputes under articles 26 and 27, but these chambers were never used.[219] Article 30(2) of the ICJ Rules provides for the appointment of assessors, as does article 289 of UNCLOS, but these provisions, too, have not been utilized. A further problem is that the use of assessors by international courts in the decision-making process may be seen as lacking transparency, since the parties do not have the opportunity to participate 'at every stage of consultation';[220] this may result in a breach of the principle that each party should have the opportunity to comment on material presented before the court. Second, the appointment of technically qualified members to international courts is also potentially problematic. While such members would probably bring useful knowledge to bear on the dispute, there is a risk that they would exert influence over any non-qualified members of the tribunal. In addition, any decision made

[215] For example, *US—Shrimp*, DSR 1998–VII, 2821, 3006 (PR); Palmeter and Mavroidis, above n 56, 77–8.

[216] Joost Pauwelyn, 'The Use of Experts in WTO Dispute Settlement' (2002) 51 *ICLQ* 325, 334; see also BIICL, above n 3, 10; Jolowicz, above n 1, 234.

[217] For practice of municipal tribunals, see Jolowicz, ibid, 225–7, 229–30, 239–40; Tapper, above n 64, 521–5; Gillian White, *The Use of Experts by International Tribunals* (1965) 15–33; John Basten, 'The Court Expert in Civil Trials: A Comparative Appraisal' (1977) 40 *MLR* 174, 175; Learned Hand, 'Historical and Practical Considerations Regarding Expert Testimony' (1901) 15 *Harvard Law Review* 40, 42–3.

[218] Amerasinghe, above n 9, 156–8; Foster, above n 60, 123–53.

[219] White, above n 217, 46–7.

[220] Foster, above n 60, 139.

by a court ultimately needs to be made on the basis of law, and not solely on the technical evidence submitted by the parties.

Of the options available to international courts, the appointment of an independent expert offers a number of benefits.[221] Dr Foster has argued that this means of taking expert evidence assists in eliminating the possibility of biased expert evidence, and it also 'gives a tribunal more direct access to an expert or experts'.[222] This is because the tribunal can request reports and arrange meetings, and it 'may expect full responses on all points on which it seeks further information'.[223] In light of these perceived advantages, the power of international courts to appoint such experts *proprio motu*, and the extent of common practice among international courts, will form the focus of this section.

Many international courts and tribunals have an express power to commission expert inquiries. The first such provision can be found in the 1907 Convention. Article 90 provides that an arbitral tribunal has 'the right to demand oral explanations from the agents of the two parties, as well as from the experts and witnesses whose appearance in Court it may consider useful'.[224] However, this provision is only applicable where the arbitration is conducted under chapter IV of the Convention, which deals with summary procedure. The Advisory Committee of Jurists included the power in the PCIJ Statute. Under article 50:

> The Court may, at any time, entrust any individual, body, bureau, commission, or other organization that it may select, with the task of carrying out an enquiry or giving an expert opinion.[225]

In 1945, article 50 was adopted without amendment into the ICJ Statute. The PCIJ exercised its power to appoint experts in *Factory at Chorzów* in order to determine the compensation owing for the damages suffered by the expropriation.[226] In *Corfu Channel*, the ICJ appointed experts for the purposes of making site visits, collecting and evaluating complex evidence,[227] and assessing the quantum of compensation due to the UK.[228] The PCIJ and ICJ have, on occasion, considered an expert inquiry to be unnecessary.[229]

As well as the ICJ, WTO panels also have an express power in article 13(1) of the DSU 'to seek information and technical advice from any individual or body which it deems appropriate'. Article 13(2) clarifies that WTO panels may 'seek information from any relevant source and consult experts to obtain their opinion

[221] Foster, above n 60, 128. [222] Ibid. [223] Ibid.

[224] 1907 Convention, above n 17, art 90; White, above n 217, 35.

[225] PCIJ Statute, above n 20, art 50. In the PCIJ Rules, a provision was included ensuring that parties to a dispute would be furnished with a copy of any expert report prepared in connection with that dispute: PCIJ Rules (1922), in PCIJ Documents, Ser D, (No 1), 66, art 53.

[226] Ser A (No 17), 51–5, 99, 100–3 (PCIJ, 1928).

[227] Above n 87, 142–62; Highet, 'Evidence, the Court', above n 1, 23–4.

[228] *Corfu Channel (Compensation)* [1949] ICJ Rep 244, 258–60.

[229] For example, *Free Zones*, above n 52, 162–3; *Oscar Chinn*, above n 53, 88; *Nicaragua*, above n 35, 40.

on certain aspects of the matter'. WTO panels have exercised this power in cases involving complex scientific or technical evidence.[230] Other WTO panels have sought information from international organisations,[231] while another panel has sought expert translating skills.[232] The ECJ also has the express power to commission an expert report under article 22 of the ECJ Statute.[233] Like WTO panels, the ECJ has made extensive use of this power.[234] It has exercised it to appoint experts in cases of complex medical evidence,[235] where economic evidence is relevant for the assessment of damages,[236] expert evidence on markets, prices and costs,[237] and expert evidence on the translation of documents.[238]

It might seem, then, that the question of the existence of the power is relatively uncontroversial. Yet not all international courts are expressly endowed with it, and this raises the question whether international courts can nonetheless exercise a power to order an expert report. It is suggested that international courts do have an inherent power of this kind.[239] This was posited by Judge Anzilotti during the 1936 revision of the PCIJ Rules, where he expressed the view that article 50 of the PCIJ Statute, and the attendant provisions in the Rules, were not really necessary.[240]

230 See, e.g., *Japan—Apples*, WT/DS245/R, paras 6.1–6.194; *EC—Asbestos*, above n 92, para 5.1–5.659; *Australia—Salmon*, DSR 2000–IV, 2031, 2119–50 (Art 21(5) PR); *Japan—Agricultural Products*, DSR 1999–I, 315, 401–27; *Australia—Salmon*, DSR 1998-VIII, 3407, 3534–83 (PR); *US—Shrimp*, above n 215, 3006–93 (PR); *EC—Hormones*, (PR), above n 95, 408–64; Pauwelyn, 'The Use of Experts', above n 216, 325.

231 *US—Section 211*, WT/DS176/R, paras 8.11–8.13, 6.1–6.49 (PR); *US—Copyright Act* (Recourse to Arbitration), DSR 2000–VIII, 3769, 3779–80, 4051–65 (PR); *India—Quantitative Restrictions*, DSR 1999–V, 1799, 1927–62, (PR); see also the GATT panel report in *Thailand—Restrictions on Importation of and Internal Taxes on Cigarettes*, paras 50–7 (GATT Doc DS10/R—37S/200 (1990)); see also Pauwelyn, 'The Use of Experts', above n 216, 325.

232 *Japan—Film*, DSR 1998–IV, 1179, 1192–3, paras 1.8–1.11 (PR); Pauwelyn, ibid, 325.

233 ECJ Statute, art 22; Court of Justice of the European Communities Rules of Procedure, available at <http://curia.europa.eu>, art 49; see also *Agreement between the EFTA States on the Establishment of a Surveillance Authority and a Court of Justice*, signed 2 May 1992; available at <http:www.eftacourt.lu> (entered into force) ('EFTA Statute'), art 22; *Protocol of the Statute of Justice of the European Atomic Energy Community, Treaty establishing the European Atomic Energy Community*, signed 25 March 1957, 298 UNTS 167 (entered into force 1 January 1958) ('Euratom Statute'), art 23; *Protocol of the Statute of Justice of the European Coal and Steel Community, Treaty establishing the European Coal and Steel Community*, opened for signature 18 April 1951, 26 UNTS 140 (entered into force 25 July 1952) ('ECSC Statute'), art 25.

234 Richard Plender (ed), *European Courts: Practice and Precedents* (1997) 386–95.

235 *X v Audit Board* [1969] ECR 109, 118–19; *Nijman v Commission* [1991] ECR–II 699, 703–6.

236 *Frederiksen v Parliament* [1991] ECR–II 1403, 1421–2.

237 *Chambre Syndicale de la Sidérurgie v High Authority* [1960] ECR 281, 291–3; *ICI v Commission* [1972] ECR–II, 619, 647–8; *Société CdF Chimie Azote et Fertilisants v Commission* [1990] ECR–I, 3083, 3085, 3098–100.

238 *Mirossevich v High Authority* [1954–6] ECR 333, 336, 343.

239 See White, above n 217, 73; see, however, Sandifer, above n 2, 329. Some municipal courts regard themselves as having an inherent power: *Ex p Peterson*, 253 US 300, 312–13 (1920); *Johnson v US*, 333 US 46, 54 (1948); referred to in White, above n 217, 78–9.

240 'It was of no great consequence whether these powers were derived from Article 50 or from a general principle of procedure not stated in the Statute. In any case, the Court had power to order an expert report. That was a power which it might or might not exercise at its discretion': Ser D, (No 2), 3rd Add, 247; see also White, above n 217, 41–2.

Professor White has noted that the other judges did not dissent from his 'clearly expressed view that the court possessed an inherent discretionary power to order an inquiry or expert report, irrespective of the consent of all the parties'.[241] Many other international courts have since assumed this power even though it was not expressly granted; this has been done either by inclusion of the power in their rules of procedure, or by ordering an expert inquiry even in the absence of such a rule.[242]

The ITLOS Statute does not contain a provision conferring an express power to order an expert inquiry, but article 82 of the ITLOS Rules states in part that the ITLOS can order an expert report.[243] This expert report is communicated to the parties, who are given the opportunity to comment on it.[244] The Iran–US Claims Tribunal also has the power to commission an expert opinion under article 27 of its Rules of Procedure.[245] In contrast to the ITLOS and UNCLOS tribunals, the Iran–US Claims Tribunal has had much experience with this power.[246] In addition, many of the MATs of the interwar period included the power to commission an expert opinion in their rules of procedure.[247] This power was exercised on many occasions, mainly in order to obtain a valuation of goods which had been expropriated or damaged.[248]

It is not surprising that international courts have exercised the power to seek expert opinions in similar situations where there is complex evidence of a technical or scientific nature. An interesting development, however, is that some international courts are finding new methods of exercising this power in collaboration with the parties. In *Gulf of Maine*, for instance, Canada and the US requested the ICJ Chamber to appoint a jointly nominated expert.[249] This was also done in *Frontier Dispute*, where Burkina Faso and Mali requested the ICJ Chamber 'to

[241] White, above n 217, 42.

[242] Ibid, 74–5; see, e.g., *Lighthouses Arbitration*, 12 RIAA 155, 228–9, 245, 256–7 (Greece–France, 1956) (PCA); *Benvenuti & Bonfant v Congo*, 1 ICSID Rep 330, 342, 358–9 (1980); *SOABI v Senegal*, 2 ICSID Rep 164, 265–6 (1988); *LETCO v Liberia*, 2 ICSID Rep 343, 348 (1986); *AMT v DRC*, (1997) 36 ILM 1531, 1554.

[243] ITLOS Rules, above n 37, art 82(1).

[244] Ibid, art 82(2).

[245] Brower and Bruschke, above n 7, 182ff; M Straus, 'The Practice of the Iran–US Claims Tribunal in Receiving Evidence from Parties and from Experts' (1986) 3 *Journal of International Arbitration* 57; Stewart Baker and Mark Davis, *The UNCITRAL Arbitration Rules in Practice* (1992) 126–30.

[246] See, e.g., *Richard D Harza v Iran*, 1 Ir–USCTR 234, 235 (1982); 2 Ir–USCTR 68, 71–7 (1983); *Chas T Main International Inc, v Khuzestan Water and Power Authority and Iran*, 3 Ir–USCTR 156, 164–7 (1983); *Bechtel Inc v Iran*, 14 Ir–USCTR 149, 156 (1987); *Behring International v Iranian Air Force*, 4 Ir–USCTR 89, 91–2 (1983); *International Technical Products Corporation v Iran*, above n 114, 34–5; and see also Brower and Brueschke, ibid, 199, 201.

[247] See, e.g., Rules of Procedure of the German–Belgian MAT, above n 155, art 56; and those of the Franco–German MAT, above n 155, art 57.

[248] See, e.g., *Huret v État allemand*, 1 TAM 98, 487 (Franco–German MAT, 1921); *Chamant v État allemand*, 1 TAM 361, 370–1, 745 (Franco–German MAT, 1921–2); *Compagnie d'Electricité de Sofia et de Bulgarie v État Bulgare*, 3 TAM 308, 323 (Bulgar–Belgian MAT, 1923).

[249] Above n 211, 252.

nominate, in its judgment, three experts to assist them in the demarcation operation'. The Chamber noted that this was a different procedure to ordering an expert opinion under article 50 of the ICJ Statute, but held that:

> there is nothing in the Statute of the Court nor in the settled jurisprudence to prevent the Chamber from exercising this power, the very purpose of which is to enable the Parties to achieve a final settlement of their dispute in implementation of the Judgment which it has delivered.[250]

More recently, the ITLOS in *Land Reclamation* ordered Malaysia and Singapore to establish 'a group of independent experts', charged with the task of '[conducting] a study . . . to determine . . . the effects of Singapore's land reclamation and to propose, as appropriate, measures to deal with any adverse effects of such reclamation'.[251] There are certain advantages to this collaborative approach to the use of experts. It promotes party contact, and encourages the parties to engage in negotiation, thus increasing the likelihood of the dispute being resolved amicably. Indeed, the collaboration of the parties in agreeing on the group of independent experts in *Land Reclamation* may have been a contributing factor towards the settlement of that dispute in January 2005.[252] This procedure was also employed by the PCA Tribunal in *Iron Rhine Railway*, where it stated that it was not the task of the Tribunal:

> to investigate questions of considerable scientific complexity as to which measures will be sufficient to achieve compliance with the required levels of environmental protection. These issues are appropriately left to technical experts. To that effect, the Tribunal recommends that the Parties promptly, and in any case not later than 4 months from the date of this Award, put into effect the conditions necessary for a committee of independent experts to be set up within the same time frame, unless the Parties agree otherwise.[253]

The PCA Tribunal directed that '[t]he committee of independent experts should conclude its findings as soon as possible, and in any case no later than 6 months from the date of its establishment'.[254]

In addition, assuming that the parties are able to agree on the experts who are to be commissioned, it can reduce the time needed for the expert report to be produced. Finally, it eliminates the possibility of the international court or tribunal being faced with three possibly conflicting expert reports. This is, then, a procedure that should be considered by international courts and tribunals facing complex technical disputes.

250 [1987] ICJ Rep 7, 8.

251 *Land Reclamation by Singapore in and around the Straits of Johor* (ITLOS Order of 8 October 2003), para 106(1)(a)(i).

252 'Case Concerning Land Reclamation by Singapore in and around the Straits of Johor', (14 January 2005), at <http://www.pca-cpa.org> (last visited 25 November 2006).

253 *Iron Rhine Railway* (Award of 24 May 2005), para 235.

254 Ibid.

Conclusion

This chapter has reviewed the approach of international courts and tribunals to several evidential issues which arise in international proceedings. It has shown that international courts have adopted a liberal approach to the admission of evidence. The rule on the allocation of the burden of proof has been adopted by all international courts as a general principle of law. With respect to the appropriate standard of proof, the practice of international tribunals demonstrates an absence of a clear standard; if a standard is referred to at all, international courts appear most often to require the production of 'sufficient' evidence, although the standard of proof appears to differ depending on the gravity of the allegations. This chapter also considers the powers of international courts to procure evidence *proprio motu*, and it demonstrates that international tribunals consider themselves empowered to take judicial notice of notorious facts; to request further evidence from parties, and to draw adverse inferences when such evidence is not provided; to make site visits; and also to order expert reports. There are, however, differences in the application of these rules by international courts; thus, while it might be said that international courts have broadly similar approaches to these questions, this does not always result in complete consistency.

4

Power of International Courts to Grant Provisional Measures

Introduction

This chapter examines the power of international courts to grant provisional measures and analyses whether there is an emerging common practice among international courts in this regard. At the outset, it should be noted that there is some variation in the terminology used in the constitutive instruments, rules and practice of international tribunals to describe provisional measures. They are variously referred to as 'provisional measures',[1] 'interim measures',[2] 'interim measures of protection',[3] and 'precautionary measures'.[4] For the sake of convenience, the measures will here be referred to as 'provisional measures', for there is no distinction between the various terms. The terminological differences also extend to the terms used to describe the manner in which these measures are granted. The ICJ and the ECHR 'indicate' provisional measures,[5] the ITLOS and UNCLOS tribunals 'prescribe' them,[6] the IACHR can both 'adopt'[7] and 'order'[8] provisional measures, ICSID tribunals 'recommend' provisional measures,[9] and the IACommHR 'request[s] that the state concerned adopt precautionary measures'.[10] Practical differences can arise depending on the verb used to describe how such measures are granted. For instance, a provisional measure which is 'prescribed' has legal force, whereas a provisional measure which is 'recommended' arguably does not. In this chapter, the power will usually be referred to as the power to 'grant' provisional measures, which is intended as a neutral term; the question of whether provisional measures are binding is addressed later in this chapter.

This chapter begins with a discussion of the purposes of the power to grant provisional measures, and then turns to the question of whether all international courts have that power. International courts with an express statutory power to grant provisional measures are examined, and the question is then asked whether international courts lacking an express power can nonetheless exercise the power as an inherent power. Finally, any common features of the exercise of the power are addressed.

[1] *Statute of the International Court of Justice*, opened for signature 26 June 1945, 3 Bevans 1153 (entered into force 24 October 1945), art 41; International Court of Justice Rules of Court, available at <http://www.icj-cij,org>, arts 73–8; *United Nations Convention on the Law of the Sea*, opened for signature 10 December 1982, 21 ILM 1261 (entered into force 16 November 1994), art 290 (1) and (5); *Convention for the Settlement of Investment Disputes between States and Nationals of Other States*, opened for signature 18 March 1965, 575 UNTS 159 (entered into force 14 October 1966) ('ICSID Convention'), art 47; *American Convention on Human Rights*, opened for signature 22 November 1969, 1144 UNTS 123 (entered into force 18 July 1978) ('American Convention'), art 63(2); IACHR Rules of Procedure, available at <http://www.corteid.or.cr>, art 25(1).

[2] Iran–US Claims Tribunal Rules of Procedure, 1 Ir–USCTR 57, art 26; European Court of Human Rights, Rules of Court, available at <http://www.echr.coe.int>, Rule 39.

[3] ICJ Rules (1946), art 61; PCIJ Rules (1922) in PCIJ Documents, Ser D, (No 1), 66, art 57; see also ICJ Rules (1978), Section D, Subsection 1; Hugh Thirlway, 'The Indication of Provisional Measures by the International Court of Justice' in Rudolf Bernhardt (ed), *Interim Measures Indicated by International Courts* (1994) 1, 3.

[4] Inter-American Commission on Human Rights, Rules of Procedure, available at <http://www.cidh. oas.org>, art 25(1).

[5] ICJ Statute, art 41; ECHR Rules, Rule 39.

[6] UNCLOS, art 290(1) and (5).

[7] American Convention, art 63(2).

[8] IACHR Rules, art 25(1).

[9] ICSID Convention, art 47.

[10] IACommHR Rules, art 25(1).

I. Purpose of Provisional Measures in International Adjudication

The essential purpose of the power of international courts to grant provisional measures is the preservation of the respective rights of the parties pending the decision on the merits, and the safeguarding of the jurisdiction of the international court to render a judgment which is effective.[11] In this regard, the ICJ has stated that its power 'has as its object to preserve the respective rights of the parties, and presupposes that irreparable prejudice should not be caused to rights which are the subject of dispute in judicial proceedings'.[12] This protective function is illustrated in the French term for provisional measures, '*mesures conservatoires*'.[13] The need for international courts to be able to grant interim relief stems from the fact that once an application is made instituting proceedings, that court might not be in a position to determine the rights in dispute for some time. In the intervening period, those rights might be prejudiced by events which would prevent the international court from being able to render an effective decision, thus rendering its jurisdiction nugatory.[14] This purpose thus reflects the function of international courts to settle disputes by adjudication.

Another purpose of provisional measures could be the maintenance of the status quo.[15] This purpose was referred to in the provision conferring the power on the Central American Court of Justice,[16] and during the discussion on the PCIJ Rules of Court in 1931, Judge Negulesco observed that provisional measures 'sometimes ... were regarded as designed to preserve rights claimed in an action at law, sometimes their object was to re-establish or safeguard the *status quo ante*'.[17] Germany argued in *LaGrand* that 'the United States should restore the *status quo ante* in the case of Walter LaGrand';[18] and Mexico made a similar argument in

[11] Shabtai Rosenne, *Provisional Measures in International Law* (2005) 3–4; John Merrills, 'Interim Measures of Protection in the Recent Jurisprudence of the International Court of Justice' (1995) 44 *ICLQ* 90, 100; see, e.g., ICJ Statute, above n 1, art 41; ICSID Convention, above n 1, art 47; UNCLOS, above n 1, art 290(1) and (5).

[12] *Fisheries Jurisdiction* (*Interim Protection*) [1972] ICJ Rep 12, 16, 30, 34.

[13] Thirlway, 'The Indication of Provisional Measures', above n 3, 3.

[14] Bernard Oxman, 'Jurisdiction and the Power to Indicate Provisional Measures' in Lori Damrosch (ed), *The International Court of Justice at a Crossroads* (1987) 323, 325; Maurice Mendelson, 'Interim Measures of Protection in Cases of Contested Jurisdiction' (1972–3) 46 *British Yearbook of International Law* 259; J C Witenberg, *L'Organisation Judiciaire: La Procédure et la Sentence Internationales* (1937) 387.

[15] For example, Thirlway, 'The Indication of Provisional Measures', above n 3, 7; Jerome Elkind, *Interim Protection: A Functional Approach* (1981) 219–20.

[16] *Convention for the Establishment of the Central American Court of Justice* [1907] 2 *US Foreign Relations* 697, art 18; Paul Guggenheim, 'Les mesures conservatoires dans la procédure arbitrale et judiciaire' (1932) 40 *Recueil des cours* 645, 660–2; E Dumbauld, *Interim Measures of Protection in International Controversies* (1932) 93–6.

[17] Ser D, (No 2) Add 2, 192.

[18] *LaGrand* (*Provisional Measures*) [1999] ICJ Rep 9, 11–12.

Avena.[19] International courts do not, however, make frequent reference to this purpose in their orders.

Yet another purpose which is often referred to by international courts is the avoidance of any aggravation or extension of a dispute.[20] This purpose was referred to in the constitutive instrument of the Central American Court of Justice,[21] and the PCIJ and ICJ have made orders with this aim in many cases in which provisional measures have been granted since the power was first exercised by the PCIJ in *Electricity Company of Sofia and Bulgaria.*[22] In granting provisional measures other international courts, including ICSID tribunals and the ITLOS, have also urged parties to avoid aggravating and extending the dispute.[23]

Other purposes of provisional measures, which are related to the preservation of the parties' rights and the safeguarding of the jurisdiction of international courts, may include the preservation of evidence, without which a party might not be able to prove its claim and the tribunal might not be able to settle the dispute;[24] the granting of discovery orders;[25] making orders to ensure the satisfactory conduct of procedure before the court;[26] and the making of orders staying domestic court proceedings.[27] Finally, under article 290 of UNCLOS, the ITLOS and

19 *Avena*, CR 2003/1, para 32 (Santiago Oñate).

20 Thirlway, 'The Indication of Provisional Measures', above n 3, 12–16.

21 Above n 16, art 18.

22 Ser A/B, (No 79) 194, 199 (PCIJ, 1939); see, e.g., *Nuclear Tests (Australia v France) (Interim Protection)* [1973] ICJ Rep 99, 106.

23 *Amco v Indonesia (Provisional Measures)*, 1 ICSID Rep 410 (1983); Paul Friedland, 'Provisional Measures and ICSID Arbitration' (1986) 2 *Arbitration International* 335, 336–9; *MOX Plant* (2002) 41 ILM 405, 415 (ITLOS); *Land Reclamation by Singapore in and around the Straits of Johore* (ITLOS Order of 8 October 2003), para 102.

24 See, e.g., *Biwater Gauff (Tanzania) Ltd v Tanzania* (ICSID Case No ARB/05/22, Procedural Order No 1 of 31 March 2006), paras 84 and 92, available at <http://ita.law.uvic.edu> (last visited 25 November 2006); *Denunciation of the Treaty of 2 November 1865*, Ser A, (No 8) 8 (PCIJ, 1927); *Frontier Dispute (Provisional Measures)* [1986] ICJ Rep 3, 9; *Land and Maritime Boundary (Provisional Measures)* [1996] ICJ Rep 13, 23; *AGIP v Congo*, 1 ICSID Rep 306, 311 (1979); *Vacuum Salt v Ghana*, 4 ICSID Rep 323, 325 (1993); see also *North American Free Trade Agreement*, signed 17 December 1992, (1993) 32 ILM 289 (entered into force 1 January 1994), art 1134; Thirlway, 'The Indication of Provisional Measures', above n 3, 16.

25 *AGIP v Congo*, ibid, 311 (1979); Friedland, above n 23, 347; see, however, *Biwater Gauff* (Procedural Order No 1) ibid, para 100, where the ICSID Tribunal held that '[a]ctual production is not usually considered within the ambit of such interim relief, partly because preservation is usually sufficient to protect the rights in question, and partly because actual production is catered for by other rules (in particular Article 43 of the ICSID Convention and Rule 34 of the ICSID Arbitration Rules). Indeed, the two procedures are aimed at different issues: Article 47 is designed to ensure that the Arbitral Tribunal can properly discharge its mandate, whilst Article 43 is one element in a range of provisions that structures how the mandate is to be discharged.'

26 *Denunciation of the Treaty*, above n 24, 11; *Aegean Sea* [1980] ICJ Pleadings 67, 75; Jerzy Sztucki, *Interim Measures in the Hague Court* (1983) 10, 73.

27 *Electricity Company of Sofia and Bulgaria*, above n 22, 197–9; *Interhandel* [1957] ICJ Rep 105, 106; *E-Systems, Inc, v Iran*, 2 Ir–USCTR 51, 55–7 (1983); *CSOB v Slovakia*, 14 *ICSID Review—FILJ* 251, 255 (1999); *Holiday Inns v Morocco*, 1 ICSID Rep 645, 655–9 (1972); Charles Brower and Jason Brueschke, *The Iran—United States Claims Tribunal* (1998) 229–35; David Caron, 'Interim

other UNCLOS tribunals have the power to grant provisional measures not only to preserve the respective rights of the parties, but also to prevent serious harm to the marine environment.[28] This purpose reflects the importance of the environmental protection function of international tribunals having jurisdiction under the dispute settlement regime of UNCLOS.[29]

II. Source of the Power to Grant Provisional Measures

A. Constitutive Instruments of International Courts

Many international courts have an express power in their constitutive instruments to grant provisional measures.[30] Following earlier precedents,[31] an express power was conferred on the PCIJ in article 41(1) of the PCIJ Statute, which was retained in the ICJ Statute in 1945:

> The Court shall have the power to indicate, if it considers that circumstances so require, any provisional measures which ought to be taken to preserve the respective rights of either party.[32]

Some multilateral agreements for the settlement of disputes also confer such a power on tribunals charged with settling disputes;[33] and the constitutive instruments of a large number of other international courts expressly confer the power.

Measures of Protection: Theory and Practice in Light of the Iran–US Claims Tribunal' (1986) 46 *ZaöRV* 466, 469; Friedland, above n 23, 339.

28 UNCLOS, above n 1, art 290; *Land Reclamation by Singapore*, above n 23, para 106(2); *Southern Bluefin Tuna (Provisional Measures)* (1999) 38 ILM 1624, 1634.

29 See also Elkind, above n 15, 220–4.

30 Rosenne, *Provisional Measures*, above n 11, 5–7; Sztucki, above n 26, 4–11.

31 On the earlier precedents, see Rosenne, ibid, 12–21; Baron Schenk von Stauffenberg, *Le statut et règlement de la Cour Permanente de Justice Internationale* (1934) 309; Manley Hudson, *The Permanent Court of International Justice 1920–1942* (1943) 198–9; Edvard Hambro, 'The Binding Character of the Provisional Measures of Protection Indicated by the International Court of Justice' in Walter Schätzel and Hans-Jürgen Schlochauer (eds), *Rechtsfragen der Internationalen Organisation—Festschrift für Hans Wehberg zu seinem 70. Geburtstag* (1956) 152, 166; and Guggenheim, above n 16, 660–75.

32 ICJ Statute, above n 1, art 41(1). On the ICJ's power, see generally Rosenne, *Provisional Measures*, above n 11; Judge Shigeru Oda, 'Provisional Measures: The Practice of the International Court of Justice' in Vaughan Lowe and Malgosia Fitzmaurice (eds), *Fifty Years of the International Court of Justice* (1996) 541; Merrills, above n 11; Thirlway, 'The Indication of Provisional Measures', above n 3; Lawrence Collins, 'Provisional and Protective Measures in International Litigation' (1992) 234 *Recueil des cours* 9; Sir Gerald Fitzmaurice, *The Law and Procedure of the International Court of Justice* (1986) 533–50; Sztucki, above n 26; Elkind, above n 15.

33 *General Act for the Pacific Settlement of International Disputes*, opened for signature 26 September 1928, 93 LNTS 343, art 33 (entered into force 16 August 1929); *European Convention for the Peaceful Settlement of Disputes*, opened for signature 29 April 1957, 320 UNTS 243, art 31 (entered into force 30 April 1958); *Pact of Bogotá*, opened for signature 30 April 1948, 30 UNTS 55, art XVI (entered into force 6 May 1949).

These include the ECJ,[34] ICSID tribunals,[35] the IACHR,[36] the ITLOS and UNCLOS tribunals,[37] NAFTA tribunals,[38] and the African Court on Human and Peoples' Rights.[39]

This list of international courts possessing an express statutory power to grant provisional measures does not include all international courts. Notable among those lacking an express power in their constitutive instruments are tribunals established under the auspices of the PCA, WTO panels and the WTO Appellate Body. It has been suggested that PCA tribunals might have a power to grant provisional measures under the Hague Conventions,[40] and WTO panels and the Appellate Body might also have the power under the terms of their Working Procedures,[41] although this is doubtful.

In the absence of an express statutory power to grant provisional measures, many international courts and tribunals have found that they have a source of competence to make such orders. This is by inclusion of the power in their rules of procedure, by reliance on a general principle of law, and by asserting the existence of an inherent power to grant interim relief.

[34] *Treaty Establishing the European Community*, (2002) OJ C325 (entered into force), arts 242–3; see generally Francis Jacobs, 'Interim Measures in the Law and Practice of the Court of Justice of the European Communities', in Bernhardt (ed), above n 3, 37; G Borchardt, 'The Award of Interim Measures by the European Court of Justice' (1985) 22 *Common Market Law Review* 203; Christine Gray, 'Interim Measures of Protection in the European Court' (1979) 4 *ELR* 80; Richard Wainwright, 'Article 186 EEC: Interim Measures and Member States' (1977) 2 *ELR* 349.

[35] ICSID Convention, above n 1, art 47; ICSID Arbitration Rules, Rule 39; ICSID Arbitration (Additional Facility) Rules, art 46; Christoph Schreuer, *The ICSID Convention: A Commentary* (2001) 744–82; Friedland, above n 23.

[36] American Convention, above n 1, art 63(2), IACHR Rules, 25(1); Jo Pasqualucci, 'Provisional Measures in the Inter-American Human Rights System: An Innovative Development in International Law' (1993) 26 *Vanderbilt Journal of Transnational Law* 803; Thomas Buergenthal, 'Interim Measures in the Inter-American Court of Human Rights' in Bernhardt (ed), above n 3, 69.

[37] UNCLOS, above n 1, art 290, UNCLOS, above n 1, Annex VI ('ITLOS Statute'), art 25(1), ITLOS Rules, art 89(1); Rosenne, *Provisional Measures*, above n 11; Thomas Mensah, 'Provisional Measures in the International Tribunal for the Law of the Sea' (2002) 62 *ZaöRV* 43; Chester Brown, 'Provisional Measures before the International Tribunal for the Law of the Sea: The *MOX Plant* Case' (2002) 17 *International Journal of Marine and Coastal Law* 267; Rüdiger Wolfrum, 'Provisional Measures of the International Tribunal for the Law of the Sea' (1997) 37 *Indian Journal of International Law* 420.

[38] NAFTA, above n 24, art 1134.

[39] *Protocol to the African Charter on Human and Peoples' Rights on the Establishment of an African Court on Human and Peoples' Rights*, opened for signature 8 June 1998, (1998) *ZaöRV* 727 (entered into force 25 January 2004) art 27(2).

[40] For example, André Cocâtre-Zilgien, 'Les mesures conservatoires décidées par le juge ou par l'arbitre international' (1966) 70 *Revue Générale de Droit International Public* 5, 10–11, who suggests that the power might be found in the 1907 Convention, arts 73–4; and the 1899 Convention, arts 48–9, which confer on tribunals the power to determine their competence and make orders for the conduct of proceedings. See, however, Guggenheim, above n 16, 654–5.

[41] Working Procedures for WTO Panels, DSU Appendix 3, para 11; and Working Procedures for Appellate Review, art 16(1), which provide that panels and the Appellate Body can adopt any additional procedures specific to the dispute.

B. Rules of Procedure of International Courts

Some international courts and tribunals have arrogated to themselves the power to grant provisional measures in their rules of procedure. Even though the power to frame rules is generally conferred by the constitutive instrument, the practice of international courts in including the power demonstrates that certain international courts consider such a power to be necessary in order to carry out their functions,[42] for the rules of procedure of these international courts are drafted by the courts themselves without the need for ratification by the states parties. These international courts need to be distinguished from those whose rules of procedure are drafted by the states parties or the administrative body of the court; thus, the power of PCA tribunals to grant provisional measures under the Optional Rules of 1992 cannot be considered as providing judicial support for the inherent nature of the power,[43] nor can the power of arbitral tribunals constituted under the ICC Rules of Arbitration or the UNCITRAL Rules.[44] In addition, the Rules of the Iran–US Claims Tribunal were essentially agreed by the parties, rather than by the Tribunal itself.[45]

Many international judicial bodies have included the power to grant provisional measures in their rules of procedure. 33 of the 36 MATs which were established after the First World War included the power to grant interim relief in their Rules of Procedure.[46] The ECommHR, prior to its dissolution in 1998, exercised a power to grant interim relief which it arrogated to itself in Rule 36 of its Rules of Procedure in 1974.[47] The ECHR has also granted itself such a power in Rule 39 of its Rules of Court,[48] as have other international judicial and quasi-judicial bodies, including the Human Rights Committee of the UN,[49] the Court of Justice of the

[42] Sztucki, above n 26, 63.

[43] PCA Optional Rules for Arbitrating Disputes between Two States, art 26.

[44] ICC Rules of Arbitration (1998), art 23(1); UNCITRAL Arbitration Rules (1976), art 26.

[45] The Algiers Accords directed the Tribunal to apply the UNCITRAL Rules, although the Tribunal was free to make modifications: Brower and Brueschke, above n 27, 12.

[46] For example, Rules of Procedure of the Franco-German MAT, 1 TAM 44, art 31; Sztucki, above n 26, 4, 63, fn 15. The rules of procedure of the MATs were laid down by the tribunals themselves, but envisaged some indirect scrutiny by the states parties, as they had to be published in their official journals: Sztucki, ibid, 65, fn 29; see, however, Bin Cheng, *General Principles of Law as Applied by International Courts and Tribunals* (first published 1953, 1987 ed) 269–70.

[47] European Commission of Human Rights Rules of Procedure, in *European Commission of Human Rights: Documents and Decisions* (1955–1956–1957) 58, Rule 36.

[48] ECHR Rules, above n 2, Rule 39; see generally R Macdonald, 'Interim Measures in International Law, with Special Reference to the European System for the Protection of Human Rights' (1992) 52 *ZaöRV* 703; Rudolf Bernhardt, 'Interim Measures of Protection under the European Convention on Human Rights', in Bernhardt (ed), above n 3, 95; Marc-André Eissen, 'Les mesures provisoires dans la Convention Européenne des Droits de l'Homme' (1969) 2 *Revue des Droits de l'Homme* 252, 255.

[49] UNHRC Rules of Procedure, UN Doc CCPR/C/3/Rev.6, (24 April 2001), art 86; Christian Tomuschat, in Bernhardt (ed), above n 3, 120; Macdonald, ibid, 723–5.

Benelux Union,[50] the IACommHR,[51] the ACommHPR,[52] the UN Tribunal in Libya,[53] and various PCA tribunals.[54] Various international administrative tribunals also have the power in their rules.[55]

C. Power to Grant Provisional Measures as a General Principle of Law

Many international courts have held that there is a general principle of law that parties to litigation must abstain from any act which might exercise a prejudicial effect on any future judgment, or aggravate or extend the dispute. This was recognised in *Electricity Company of Sofia and Bulgaria*, where the PCIJ referred to:

> the principle universally accepted by international tribunals . . . to the effect that the parties to a case must abstain from any measure capable of exercising a prejudicial effect in regard to the execution of the decision to be given.[56]

Several writers have suggested that there is also a general principle of law common to many domestic legal systems that litigants are entitled to some form of relief *pendente lite*.[57] Such procedural devices in domestic legal systems include the interlocutory injunction in English law, the temporary restraining order and the preliminary injunction in the United States, the *ordonnance de référé* in French law, the *einstweilige Verfügung* in German law, and the *provvedimenti d'urgenza* in Italian law.[58] On the basis of the widespread existence of the principle of interim relief in domestic legal systems, it is suggested that the power to grant provisional

[50] Court of Justice of the Benelux Union Rules of Procedure, art 50; Macdonald, ibid, 719.

[51] IACommHR Rules, above n 4, art 25(1).

[52] African Commission on Human and Peoples' Rights Rules of Procedure, art 111.

[53] UN Tribunal in Libya Rules, arts 25–6, extracted in *Administration of Certain Properties in the State of Libya*, 12 RIAA 359, 360–1 (UN Tribunal in Libya, 1952).

[54] For example, PCA Tribunal, *Access to Information under Article 9 of the OSPAR Convention*, Rules of Procedure, art 15; PCA Tribunal, *Arbitration between the Bank of International Settlements and Private Parties*, Rules for Arbitration, art 21; PCA Tribunal, *Larsen/Hawaiian Kingdom*, Award of 5 February 2001, 119 ILR 566 (2001), para 3.1 (selecting UNCITRAL Rules); Eritrea–Ethiopia Claims Commission Rules of Procedure, art 15; Eritrea–Ethiopia Boundary Commission Rules of Procedure, art 20; all available at <http://www.pca-cpa.org> (last visited 25 November 2006).

[55] For example, LNAT Rules of Procedure, reproduced in Chittharanjan Amerasinghe (ed), *Documents on International Administrative Tribunals* (1989), art 14; International Labour Organization Administrative Tribunal Rules, in Amerasinghe (ed) (ibid), art 19; United Nations Administrative Tribunal Rules of Procedure, in Amerasinghe (ed), ibid, art 7(3); World Bank Administrative Tribunal Rules of Procedure, in Amerasinghe (ed), ibid, art 7(3)(a); Sztucki, above n 26, 10.

[56] Above n 22, 194, 199; see also *Aegean Sea* [1976] ICJ Rep 3, 15–16; *LaGrand (Merits)* (2001) 40 ILM 1069, 1093–4; *Amco v Indonesia*, above n 23, 412; see also in the context of ICSID arbitration, *Guinea v Atlantic Triton Co* (Cour d'appel de Rennes), 3 ICSID Rep 3, 8–9 (1984).

[57] Hermann Mosler, Francis Jacobs, and Rudolf Bernhardt (reported comments), in Bernhardt (ed), above n 3, 127–9, 137–9, and 140; Collins, above n 32, 23–4, 169–71; Cheng, above n 46, 140–1, 267–9; Elkind, above n 15, 3–4; V S Mani, *International Adjudication: Procedural Aspects* (1980) 277; Dumbauld, above n 16, 180.

[58] Collins, above n 32, 24; Dumbauld, above n 16, 42–81.

measures can be characterized as a 'general principle of law' within the meaning of article 38(1)(c) of the ICJ Statute, and that international tribunals may rely on this general principle as a source of the power to grant provisional measures.

Notwithstanding the widespread availability of interim relief in municipal legal systems, the objection has been made that the existence of a general principle obliging parties to litigation to refrain from prejudicing the rights in dispute does not empower the tribunal to grant provisional measures.[59] This objection appears to be based on the premise that international courts cannot derive jurisdictional powers from general principles of law, but rather must base their powers on the consent of the parties as expressed in the constitutive instrument.[60]

This objection can be rejected. As has been seen in chapter 2, international law does not make a clear distinction between substance and procedure, and there is no reason why general principles of law should not be a source of procedural law. While there are limitations to an argument about the existence of inherent powers being based on general principles of law, the practice of domestic courts in making interim relief available is so widespread that general principles of law provide a solid basis for the existence of the power.

D. Power to Grant Provisional Measures as an Inherent Power

Finally, many international courts have asserted the power to grant provisional measures as an inherent power. The proposition that international courts have an inherent power to grant provisional measures has attracted the support of many writers.[61] For instance, Edvard Hambro, referring to the ICJ, has stated that 'the Court in exercising its authority under Article 41 does only in effect give life and blood to a rule that already exists in principle'.[62] Other writers, however, have argued that the power to grant provisional measures cannot be considered inherent.[63] For

59 Hugh Thirlway, 'The Law and Procedure of the International Court of Justice 1960–1989: Part Twelve' (2001) 72 *British Yearbook of International Law* 37, 123–4; Dumbauld, above n 16, 180–1.

60 Mathias Herdegen (reported comments), in Bernhardt (ed), above n 3, 126–7; Dumbauld, above n 16, 180–1.

61 For example, Jo Pasqualucci, *The Practice and Procedure of the Inter-American Court of Human Rights* (2003) 298–300 (re the IACHR); Alexander Orakhelashvili, 'Questions of International Judicial Jurisdiction in the *LaGrand* Case' (2002) 15 *Leiden Journal of International Law* 105, 107–8, 114 (re 'international tribunals'); MacDonald, above n 48, 726–9 (re the ECHR and 'international organs'); Caron, above n 27, 475–80 (re the Iran-US Claims Tribunal, but also noting that '[a]n inherent power to grant interim measures is generally recognised'); Fitzmaurice, *Law and Procedure*, above n 32, 542–3 (re the ICJ and 'other tribunals'); Mani, above n 57, 286–9 (re international tribunals); Cocâtre-Zilgien, above n 40, 10 (re PCA tribunals); Shabtai Rosenne, *The Law and Practice of the International Court* (1965) vol 1, 423–4 (re the ICJ); Michel Dubisson, *La Cour internationale de justice* (1964) 225 (re the ICJ); Shabtai Rosenne, *The International Court of Justice: An Essay in Political and Legal Theory* (1957) 327–8 (re the ICJ); Hambro, above n 31, 167 (re the ICJ).

62 Hambro, ibid.

63 See especially Hugh Thirlway, 'The Law and Procedure of the International Court of Justice 1960–89: Part Nine' (1998) 69 *British Yearbook of International Law* 1, 19; Heribert Golsong and Sir Ian Sinclair (reported comments), in Bernhardt (ed), above n 3, 124–5, 133; Dumbauld, above n 16, 180–2; Guggenheim, above n 16, 651–5.

instance, Shabtai Rosenne has stated that 'every international court or tribunal requires a specific provision in its constituent instrument to empower it to order provisional measures';[64] and Dumbauld argued that '[t]he mere fact that a tribunal has jurisdiction over the dispute in chief does not, without more, give it jurisdiction to order interim measures'.[65] Proponents of this view argue that since the power is specifically provided for in the constitutive instrument of some international courts and left out of others, this suggests that the power must be expressly conferred.[66] Further, it has been argued that there is no practice of international tribunals asserting this power where it has not been expressly conferred.[67]

The following paragraphs, however, suggest that the power to grant provisional measures can be exercised as an inherent power by international tribunals on the basis that such a power is necessary for the performance of their functions. This suggestion that international courts have an inherent power to grant provisional measures is also buttressed by substantial international judicial practice.

1. The Power is necessary to carry out the Functions of International Courts

It has been observed that the primary functions of international courts are twofold: the settlement of disputes by adjudication, and the proper administration of international justice; and it is suggested that the power of international courts to grant provisional measures is necessary for the carrying out of both these functions. First, the function of international courts in settling disputes by adjudication entails the rendering of an effective judgment, that is, a judgment which has not been stultified by the acts of parties prejudicing the rights in dispute. If international courts were unable to make orders preventing any prejudicial action and safeguard their jurisdiction to render an effective decision, their function in settling the dispute would be undermined. At the same time, the function of international courts in administering justice would not be served if the very ability of international courts to do justice were frustrated.[68] Sir Gerald Fitzmaurice has argued that the power to grant provisional measures should be considered an inherent power due to the necessity of the power 'in order to ensure that justice is done and that the eventual decision of the Court on the merits is not stultified by intermediate action on the part of one or other party rendering such decision unenforceable or unavailing'.[69] Significantly, he has argued that all international courts have the power to order provisional measures:

[64] Rosenne, *Provisional Measures*, above n 11, 7.

[65] Dumbauld, above n 16, 181; see also Guggenheim, above n 16, 651, fn 1, 655.

[66] Golsong and Sinclair, above n 63, 124–5, 133; and *Mamatkulov and Abdurasulovic v Turkey* (ECHR, Judgment of 6 February 2003) (Diss Op Türmen), available at <http://www.echr.coe.int> (last visited 30 November 2006).

[67] Guggenheim, above n 16, 665.

[68] See, e.g., *Frontier Dispute*, above n 24, 9.

[69] Fitzmaurice, *Law and Procedure*, above n 32, 542.

In short, if there is ever a case at all for conferring this faculty expressly on an international tribunal (be it the Court or another), there is automatically a case for regarding all international tribunals as inherently invested with it.[70]

The proposition that the power to grant provisional measures is necessary to carry out the function of international courts reflects the principle that the jurisdiction of international courts should be effective.[71] As parties to disputes have generally consented to the jurisdiction of international courts to make a determination on the merits of those disputes, it is suggested that the parties must have intended the international court to have the power to ensure the effectiveness of any future judgment and avoid the adjudicative process being rendered a futile exercise.[72]

In addition to the functions of international courts in settling the dispute by adjudication and in ensuring the proper administration of international justice, it is suggested that a further function of international adjudication is relevant in connection with their power to grant provisional measures. This is the function of international courts to manage disputes.[73] This function can be seen in the frequency with which international tribunals grant provisional measures which require the states parties to the dispute to refrain from acts which will 'aggravate or extend the dispute', even though the constitutive instruments of international courts do not foresee the granting of provisional measures for this purpose.[74] It is suggested that this practice evinces the existence of a broader underlying inherent power to grant provisional measures.[75] This suggestion was put to the ICJ by Greece in *Aegean Sea Continental Shelf*, but the ICJ did not decide the point,[76] although later, in *Frontier Dispute*, the Chamber of the ICJ claimed that such provisional measures could be made under article 41: it held that it possessed 'by virtue of Article 41 of the Statute the power to indicate provisional measures with a view to preventing the aggravation or extension of the dispute whenever it considers that circumstances so require'.[77] On its face, it is difficult to see how

[70] Ibid; see also Rosenne, *Provisional Measures*, above n 11, 4.

[71] Sir Hersch Lauterpacht, *The Development of International Law by the International Court* (1958) 243–56.

[72] Fitzmaurice, *Law and Procedure*, above n 32, 541–3; Ignaz Seidl-Hohenveldern, Rudolf Bernhardt, and Karin Oellers-Frahm (reported comments), in Bernhardt (ed), above n 3, 134, 140, 146; see especially *Avena* (*Provisional Measures*) (2003) 42 ILM 309; *LaGrand*, above n 18; *Vienna Convention on Consular Relations* [1998] ICJ Rep 248.

[73] Thirlway, 'Part Twelve', above n 59, 99–107.

[74] For example, *Electricity Company of Sofia and Bulgaria*, above n 22, 199; *Anglo-Iranian Oil Co* [1951] ICJ Rep 89; *Fisheries Jurisdiction (UK v Iceland) (Interim Protection)* [1972] ICJ Rep 12, 142; *Nuclear Tests*, above n 22, 106; *Nuclear Tests* (*New Zealand v France*) [1973] ICJ Rep 135, 142; *Tehran Hostages* [1979] ICJ Rep 7, 21; *Application of the Genocide Convention* (*Provisional Measures*) [1993] ICJ Rep 3, 24; *Application of the Genocide Convention* (*Further Requests*) [1993] ICJ Rep 325, 350; *Biwater Gauff v Tanzania*, above n 24, (Procedural Order No 3 of 29 September 2006), para 135. For the view that the ICJ does not have jurisdiction to grant such provisional measures, see Thirlway, 'Part Twelve', above n 59, 85, 99–101.

[75] But see Thirlway, 'The Indication of Provisional Measures', above n 3, 13.

[76] Above n 56, 12–13.

[77] Above n 24, 9.

article 41 confers such a power, but the Chamber's explanation can be understood as suggesting that it had the power to grant provisional measures for the management of the dispute, in addition to the narrower purpose of the preservation of rights.[78] This purpose can also be discerned in the ITLOS Order for provisional measures in *MOX Plant*, which granted a provisional measure requiring the parties to enter into consultations to exchange information, monitor the effects of the MOX Plant on the Irish Sea, and devise measures to prevent pollution.[79] It is made explicit in the ICSID Tribunal's Procedural Order No 3 in *Biwater Gauff (Tanzania) Ltd v Tanzania*, where the Tribunal observed that:

> It is now settled in both treaty and international commercial arbitration that an arbitral tribunal is entitled to direct the parties not to take any step that might (1) harm or prejudice the integrity of the proceedings, or (2) aggravate or exacerbate the dispute. Both may be seen as a particular type of provisional measure . . . or simply as a facet of the tribunal's overall procedural powers and its responsibility for its own process.[80]

It is suggested that such provisional measures are based on the function of managing the resolution of international disputes, and that this function may, in certain cases, form the basis of the power of international courts to grant such measures.

2. *Practice of International Courts supporting the Existence of the Power*

There is also substantial arbitral and judicial practice supporting the existence of an inherent power. This can be found in instances where international courts have granted such measures even though their constitutive instrument and rules of procedure do not provide for such a power. These cases include the decision of the arbitral tribunal which met under the *Treaty of Corinto* in 1907 to determine the dispute between Honduras and Nicaragua.[81] Under its constitutive instrument, this tribunal had no formal power to grant provisional measures; article 11 merely obliged parties not to extend or aggravate any dispute. Nevertheless, the tribunal declared that for it to be able to examine the dispute, it was necessary for Nicaraguan and Honduran troops to retreat from the frontier and put themselves on a footing of peace.[82] It is suggested that this order was akin to a provisional measure.[83]

A further example is provided by an order of the Anglo-German MAT in *Gramophone Co Ltd v Deutsche Grammophon AG*.[84] This MAT also lacked an express power to grant interim relief. Nonetheless, the tribunal members stated that they were 'of opinion that they have jurisdiction in this case', and it was

[78] See also Thirlway, 'Part Twelve', above n 59, 101.
[79] Above n 23, 416; see Brown, above n 37, 281–2.
[80] *Biwater Gauff*, above n 24 (Procedural Order No 3 of 29 September 2006), para 135, available at <http://ita.law.uvic.ca> (last visited 25 November 2006).
[81] [1902] *US Foreign Relations* 881.
[82] Guggenheim, above n 16, 661.
[83] Ibid, 660–2; Dumbauld, above n 16, 93–6.
[84] 1 TAM 857 (Anglo-German MAT, 1922).

'enough to say that the Tribunal are opinion [*sic*] that there are sufficient reasons for granting a provisional protection for the interests of the Claimants, which otherwise would be seriously endangered'.[85]

Another early example is provided by the *Trail Smelter* case.[86] In this arbitration, the United States sought compensation from Canada for damage caused by transboundary pollution from a smelter in British Columbia. Before it was able to render a final award, the tribunal established a 'temporary regime' with which the parties were obliged to comply, even though the parties had not expressly asked it to do so.[87] This regime was, effectively, a form of provisional measure, as it sought to preserve the rights in dispute.[88]

In addition, the ECommHR also granted provisional measures several times prior to including a specific power in its Rules of Procedure in 1974, even though its previous rules of 1955 did not contain the power.[89] As a final example, the ECJ held in *Camera Care v Commission* that a non-judicial body, the European Commission, had the power to grant interim relief, even though the EC Treaty and the relevant EC Regulation did not expressly confer such a power on the Commission.[90] The ECJ held that despite the absence of an express power, the Commission must be able 'to take protective measures to the extent to which they might appear indispensable in order to avoid the exercise of [its] power to make decisions . . . from becoming ineffectual or even illusory'.[91]

Finally, further support can be found in the jurisprudence of international courts which have expressly relied on an inherent power to provide interim relief, even though they also had a textual basis for the granting of provisional measures. For instance, the Iran–US Claims Tribunal has held that in addition to the power conferred in article 26 of its Rules, it has 'an inherent power . . . to conserve the respective rights of the parties and to ensure that this Tribunal's jurisdiction and authority are made fully effective'.[92] It has also considered that the scope of its power to grant interim protection is not limited by article 26 of the Rules, according to which interim measures must pertain to the subject matter of the dispute. The Tribunal has held that it may issue interim measures which protect its 'jurisdiction and authority'.[93] Further, it has held that it can grant 'temporary restraining

[85] Ibid, 859. [86] 3 RIAA 1911 (US–Canada, 1938). [87] Ibid, 1934–7.

[88] Ibid; Mani, above n 57, 289; Cocâtre-Zilgien, above n 40, 24–5.

[89] Rudolf Bernhardt, above n 48, 98; Hans Christian Krüger, 'The European Commission of Human Rights' (1980) 1 *Human Rights Law Journal* 66, 74; Eissen, above n 48, 253–4; Marc-André Eissen, 'La Convention Européenne des Droits de L'Homme et les Mesures Conservatoires' (1967) 71 *Revue Générale de Droit International Public* 558, 559; Application No 2143/64 (1964) *X v Austria and Yugoslavia*, 7 *YbECHR* 314, 317–21.

[90] [1980] ECR–I 119.

[91] Ibid, 131.

[92] *E-Systems, Inc, v Iran*, above n 27, 57; *Ford Aerospace and Communications Corporation v Air Force of Iran*, 6 Ir–USCTR 104, 108–9 (1984); Brower and Brueschke, above n 27, 217.

[93] *E-Systems*, ibid, 57 (1983); *RCA Global Communications Disc, Inc v Iran*, 4 Ir–USCTR 5, 7 (1983); *Rockwell International Systems v Iran*, 2 Ir–USCTR 369, 371 (1983); Brower and Brueschke, ibid, 217–19.

measures' pending consideration of the request for provisional measures, in order to preserve its ability 'to act effectively on a request for interim measures'.[94]

Additional support is found in the decision of the Third Chamber of the Arbitral Tribunal on Property, Rights and Interests in Germany in *Veerman v Germany*.[95] Here, although the tribunal had an express power to order interim measures with respect to rights which are the subject of proceedings, the tribunal referred to its 'inherent power to issue such orders as may be necessary to conserve the respective rights of the parties... and thereby to ensure that this Tribunal's jurisdiction and authority are made fully effective'.[96]

Another example can be found in the practice of the IACHR. It has, on at least one occasion, referred to the existence of an inherent power as well as express powers in granting provisional measures. In granting provisional measures in *Velásquez Rodríguez*, it relied on:

> Articles 63(2), 33 and 62(3) of the American Convention on Human Rights, Articles 1 and 2 of the Statute of the Court and Article 23 of the Rules of Procedure and its character as a judicial body and the powers which derive therefrom.[97]

Before the PCIJ and the ICJ, suggestions have been made in the course of oral argument that the International Court has an inherent power to grant provisional measures, in addition to the express power conferred in article 41 of the ICJ Statute.[98] The International Court has not made a judicial pronouncement on this question, and maintains the practice of relying expressly on article 41 in orders for provisional measures, yet individual judges have certainly expressed their views. In his separate opinion in *Northern Cameroons*, Sir Gerald Fitzmaurice stated that the power to grant provisional measures, together with the ICJ's incidental jurisdiction, is 'an inherent jurisdiction, the power to exercise which is a necessary condition of the Court—or any court of law—being able to function at all'.[99] There have also been other strong pronouncements by individual judges that the ICJ has an inherent power to grant provisional measures.[100]

The ICJ's approach to relying on article 41 of the ICJ Statute in granting provisional measures is mirrored in the practice of the ITLOS and ICSID tribunals. In

[94] *Component Builders, Inc v Iran*, 8 Ir–USCTR 3, 5 (1985); see also 5, 6–7 (Conc Op Brower).

[95] 25 ILR 522 (1957); see also *Scheidt v Germany*, 25 ILR 555 (1957); D P O'Connell, *International Law* (2nd ed, 1970) vol 2, 1093.

[96] *Veerman*, ibid 523; Sztucki, above n 26, 63.

[97] *Velásquez Rodríguez (Merits)*, 95 ILR 259, 268 (IACHR, 1988); see also Pasqualucci, *Practice and Procedure*, above n 61, 298–300; Buergenthal, above n 36, 83–4.

[98] *Legal Status of South-Eastern Greenland*, Ser C, (No 69) 32; Ser A/B, (No 48), 281 (PCIJ, 1932); *Aegean Sea* [1980] ICJ Pleadings 88, 99, 100–4; Sztucki, above n 26, 62; see also above n 76 and accompanying text.

[99] [1963] ICJ Rep 15, 97, 103 (Sep Op Fitzmaurice).

[100] *Application of the Genocide Convention (Further Requests)*, above n 74, 370, 379 (Sep Op Weeramantry), 390, 397 (Sep Op Ajibola); *Lockerbie (Provisional Measures)* [1992] ICJ Rep 3, 50, 70 (Diss Op Weeramantry), 78, 88–90 (Diss Op Ajibola); *Nuclear Tests (Australia)*, above n 22, 109; *Nuclear Tests (New Zealand)*, above n 74, 145 (Declaration Nagendra Singh).

four provisional measures cases to come before the ITLOS, it has expressly relied on article 290(1) or article 290(5) for the prescription of provisional measures.[101] ICSID tribunals also appear to have consistently relied on the power conferred by article 47 of the ICSID Convention in granting provisional measures.[102]

E. Limitations on the Power to Grant Provisional Measures

The power to grant provisional measures might not be necessary for carrying out the functions of every international court.[103] For instance, tribunals operating under the PCA and WTO panels have, so far, operated successfully without an express power, as did Conciliation Commissions under the Peace Treaty with Italy (1947), and the Mexican Claims Commissions (1923–34).[104] It is possible that provisional measures are less relevant in proceedings before PCA tribunals; this is because PCA tribunals are not permanent bodies which can be convened at short notice for the purposes of a provisional measures request. Even so, PCA tribunals routinely include a power to grant provisional measures in their rules of procedure, and those PCA tribunals selecting the PCA Optional Rules of Procedure also have the power.[105] In addition, ad hoc tribunals have in some disputes rendered an 'interim award', which is akin to provisional measures as it has had the effect of preserving rights or maintaining the status quo.[106]

The position of WTO panels and the Appellate Body is more complex. While the exercise of the power would be consistent with the functions of WTO panels and the Appellate Body in setting disputes, the existence of a power to grant provisional measures may be inconsistent with the terms of the DSU. At the outset it might be noted that an appellate court, such as the Appellate Body, is unlikely to be called upon to grant provisional measures. By the time a dispute reaches the appellate stage, the need for provisional measures will be less pressing than at the commencement of a dispute. Accordingly, this section will focus on the possibility of WTO panels granting provisional measures.

101 *M/V 'Saiga' (No 2) (Provisional Measures)*, 117 ILR 111, 124 (ITLOS, 1998); *Southern Bluefin Tuna*, above n 28, 1632–3; *MOX Plant* above n 23, 411, 416; *Land Reclamation by Singapore*, above n 23, para 106(1), available at <http://www.itlos.org> (last visited 25 November 2006).

102 For example *Tokios Tokeles v Ukraine* (ICSID Case No ARB/02/18, Procedural Order No 3 of 18 January 2005), paras 6–8, available at <http://ita.law.uvic.ca> (last visited 25 November 2006); *Atlantic Triton v Guinea*, 3 ICSID Rep 13, 35–7 (1986); *Holiday Inns v Morocco*, 1 ICSID Rep 645, 658 (1972).

103 Sir Ian Sinclair and Hartmut Schiedermair (reported comments), in Bernhardt (ed), above n 3, 133–4, 142–3; see also, more generally, Georges Abi-Saab, *Les exceptions préliminaires dans la procédure de la Cour internationale* (1967) 89.

104 Sztucki, above n 26, 63–4.

105 See, e.g., the examples in above n 54.

106 See, e.g., *Trail Smelter*, above n 86, 1934–7; and see the discussion in *Access to Information under the OSPAR Convention*, Verbatim Record (24 October 2002), 1, 30, available at <http://www.pca-cpa.org> (last visited 25 November 2006).

First, it might be argued that a power to grant provisional measures would be inconsistent with the short timeframes provided for in the DSU. The usual time between the lodging of a request for consultations to the adoption of a panel report by the DSB is between six and nine months.[107] This contrasts with the position before other international tribunals, where it could take years from the date of the institution of proceedings until final judgment.[108] But the shorter time frames involved in WTO dispute settlement need not exclude the relevance of provisional measures. Even over a short period, significant damage might be done to a state's economy.[109]

Second, it might be argued that the DSU already provides for expedited procedures in cases of 'urgency', such as where perishable goods or prohibited subsidies are concerned.[110] But this factor also need not rule out the relevance of provisional measures. Even where shorter time frames are involved, the rights of the parties can still be harmed, even though the state whose economy is suffering can levy countervailing duties on imported goods which are thought to be benefiting from prohibited subsidies.[111]

A third factor militating against a power of WTO panels to grant provisional measures is that remedies under the WTO dispute settlement system are typically forward-looking rather than retrospective.[112] That is, the right to a remedy arises on the date of adoption of the report, not the date of the alleged internationally wrongful act, or the date of the commencement of the action. This contrasts with the position under general international law, where states responsible for an internationally wrongful act are under an obligation to make 'full reparation' to the injured state,[113] and 'wipe out all the consequences' of the breach of international

[107] *Understanding on Rules and Procedures Governing the Settlement of Disputes*, opened for signature 15 April 1994, 1869 UNTS 401 (entered into force 1 January 1995) ('DSU'), Appendix 3, Working Procedures, para 12.

[108] See, e.g., *Land and Maritime Boundary between Cameroon and Nigeria*, where the dispute before the ICJ was initiated in 1994, and judgment was rendered in 2003; and *Oil Platforms*, where the proceedings were commenced in 1992 and judgment was delivered in 2003.

[109] For example in *EC—Hormones*, the DSB approved the suspension of concessions to the EC in the order of US$116,800,000 per year (for the US) and CAN$11,300,000 per year (for Canada): *EC—Hormones*, Minutes of Meeting held in the Centre William Rappard on 26 July 1999, WT/DSB/M65, 17–19.

[110] DSU, above n 107, arts 4(8)–(9), 12(8), art 17(5); David Palmeter and Petros Mavroidis, *Dispute Settlement in the World Trade Organisation* (1st ed, 1999), 144; Appellate Body, Working Procedures, above n 41, Rule 31.

[111] *Agreement on Subsides and Countervailing Measures*, opened for signature 15 April 1994, 1869 UNTS 14 (entered into force 1 January 1995) ('SCM Agreement') arts 17–21.

[112] Marco Bronckers and Naboth van den Broek, 'Financial Compensation in the WTO: Improving the Remedies of WTO Dispute Settlement' (2005) 8 *Journal of International Economic Law* 101, 102; Chi Carmody, 'Remedies and Conformity under the WTO Agreement' (2002) 5 *Journal of International Economic Law* 307, 315–21; Patricio Grané, 'Remedies under WTO Law' (2001) 4 *Journal of International Economic Law* 755, 759–63; DSU, above n 107, arts 3(7); 19(1).

[113] ILC Articles, art 31 in James Crawford, *The International Law Commission's Articles on State Responsibility* (2002) 201–6.

law.[114] The non-availability of retrospective remedies in WTO dispute settlement might permit the inference to be drawn that WTO panels do not have an inherent power to preserve the rights of the parties during the pendency of the proceedings, for there is no right to compensation for any damage to the complainant state which occurs prior to the adoption of the report.

It is suggested, however, that WTO remedies are not exclusively forward-looking. In a prohibited subsidies dispute, *Australia—Leather*, a WTO panel had held that subsidies paid by the Australian government to a local producer of automotive leather were inconsistent with Australia's obligations under the SCM Agreement, and ordered that they be withdrawn 'without delay'.[115] The panel constituted under article 21(5) of the DSU to monitor the implementation of the original panel report ordered that the subsidies be reimbursed.[116] In so doing, the panel found that an order under article 4(7) of the SCM Agreement was not limited to prospective action, but could encompass repayment of the prohibited subsidy.[117] This panel report therefore suggests that remedies in prohibited subsidies disputes can seek to 'wipe out all the consequences' of the wrongful act.[118] This provides support for the proposition that the parties' rights can be protected during the pendency of such proceedings. Nevertheless, this is an isolated case, and in the absence of further practice by WTO panels, it is difficult to characterize the function of WTO dispute settlement as reflecting the function of other international adjudicatory bodies in preserving the parties' rights pending final judgment. It might be that a power to grant provisional measures, if it exists in WTO dispute settlement, is limited to prohibited subsidies cases and anti-dumping disputes, where it is possible that a retroactive remedy might be available.[119]

III. Common Features in the Exercise of the Power

The power to grant provisional measures—whether it be as a result of an express power, a general principle of law, or an inherent power—is one that has been exercised with relative frequency by international courts, resulting in much jurisprudence.[120] There are four issues which may be considered relevant in addressing the question whether international courts exercise this power consistently. First, whether international courts need to have established jurisdiction over the merits of the dispute in order to have jurisdiction to grant provisional measures; second, what circumstances are relevant to the granting of provisional measures; third,

[114] *Factory at Chorzów*, Ser A, (No 17), 47 (PCIJ, 1928).
[115] *Australia—Leather*, DSR 1999–III, 951, 1103–4 (PR).
[116] *Australia—Leather*, DSR 2000–III 1189, 1203–11 (Art 21(5) PR). [117] Ibid, 1210.
[118] See also *Factory at Chorzów*, above n 114, 47.
[119] For example, *Guatemala—Cement II*, DSR 2000–XI, 5295 (PR); see further below chapter 6.
[120] For example, for a list of all provisional measures orders of the PCIJ and ICJ until 2004, see Rosenne, *Provisional Measures*, above n 11, 27–31.

whether provisional measures are binding; and fourth, whether international courts can grant provisional measures *ultra petita* or *proprio motu*.

A. Question of Jurisdiction over the Merits

The relationship between the power of international courts to grant provisional measures and their jurisdiction over the merits of a dispute has been a controversial question.[121] The constitutive instruments of many international tribunals do not clarify whether jurisdiction over the merits must be clearly established before that tribunal has jurisdiction to grant provisional measures. Over time, various positions have been put forward, ranging from the view that the question of jurisdiction over the merits has to be conclusively established,[122] to the view that the question of the court's jurisdiction is irrelevant to the granting of provisional measures.[123] These two extreme positions are widely regarded as unsatisfactory. On one hand, if a party has to wait until the international court's jurisdiction over the merits has been affirmatively established, the length of time involved in cases of complexity would often deprive any provisional measures of their efficacy in preserving the rights of the parties.[124] On the other hand, if international courts disregarded the question of jurisdiction before making an order restraining a party's right to act, arguably this would contravene the principle of consent, on which the jurisdiction of international courts is based.[125] Other tests regarding the relevance of jurisdiction have also been proposed.[126] The position which the ICJ has adopted is that it need not finally satisfy itself that it has jurisdiction on the merits of the case, but ought not to indicate provisional measures unless the state requesting provisional measures can show a prima facie basis on which the jurisdiction of the ICJ might be founded. This test was first proposed by Sir Hersch Lauterpacht

[121] See, e.g., Rosenne, *Provisional Measures*, ibid, 85–102; in the context of the ICJ, see Oxman, above n 14; John Merrills, 'Interim Measures of Protection and the Substantive Jurisdiction of the International Court' (1977) 36 CLJ 86; Mendelson, above n 14.

[122] *Nuclear Tests (Australia)*, above n 22, 111, 111 (Diss Op Forster), 115, 118–9 (Diss Op Gros); *Nuclear Tests (New Zealand)*, above n 74, 148, 148 (Diss Op Forster), 149, 153–4 (Diss Op Gros); *Aegean Sea* above n 56, 22 (Sep Op Morozov).

[123] See discussion in Thirlway, 'Part Twelve', above n 59, 79; Hans Gerd Niemeyer, *Einstweilige Verfügungen des Weltgerichtshofs, ihr Wesen und ihre Grenzen* (1932) 70–1.

[124] For example, John Collier and Vaughan Lowe, *The Settlement of Disputes in International Law: Institutions and Procedures* (1999) 169; Mendelson, above n 14, 261.

[125] For example, Collier and Lowe, ibid, 169; Mendelson, ibid, 261; *Interhandel*, above n 27, 117, 118 (Sep Op Lauterpacht).

[126] Collier and Lowe, ibid, 170; e.g., the view that jurisdiction is merely one of the circumstances for an international court to consider in deciding whether to grant provisional measures: *Nuclear Tests (Australia)*, above n 22, 106, 107 (Declaration Aréchaga); *Aegean Sea*, above n 56, 16 (Sep Op Aréchaga); and the view that jurisdiction must be reasonably probable: *Anglo-Iranian Oil Co*, above n 74, 96, 96 (Diss Op Winiarski and Badawi Pasha); *Fisheries Jurisdiction*, above n 12, 20, 21 (Diss Op Padilla Nervo); *Fisheries Jurisdiction* [1972] ICJ Rep 30, 37, 38 (Diss Op Padilla Nervo); *Aegean Sea*, ibid, 17 (Sep Op Nagendra Singh).

in his separate opinion in *Interhandel*, where, significantly, he based this view on uniform 'international arbitral and judicial practice':

> The correct principle which emerges from these apparently conflicting considerations and which has been uniformly adopted in international arbitral and judicial practice is as follows: The Court may properly act under the terms of Article 41 provided that there is in existence an instrument such as a Declaration of Acceptance of the Optional Clause, emanating from the Parties to the dispute, which *prima facie* confers jurisdiction upon the Court and which incorporates no reservations obviously excluding its jurisdiction.[127]

The ICJ adopted this test in *Fisheries Jurisdiction*[128] and *Nuclear Tests*,[129] and has since been regularly repeated in requests for provisional measures.[130]

Other international courts appear to have adopted this requirement of prima facie jurisdiction over the merits of the dispute. In the case of the ITLOS and other tribunals having jurisdiction under UNCLOS, the question is expressly addressed in article 290(1) and 290(5). Together, the effect of these provisions requires that the court or tribunal determining a request for provisional measures must be satisfied that the tribunal to which the merits of the dispute are ultimately submitted has a prima facie basis of jurisdiction over the dispute. This question is complicated by the choice made by states parties when signing or ratifying UNCLOS. Under article 287, parties may choose to refer disputes to the ICJ, the ITLOS or arbitral tribunals constituted in accordance with Annex VII or Annex VIII. Article 290(1) applies to requests for provisional measures to the body which will have jurisdiction over the merits of the dispute, and article 290(5) applies to requests for provisional measures made to bodies other than the tribunal which will determine the merits of the dispute.

Similarly, the jurisdiction of ICSID tribunals does not need to be conclusively established before they can grant provisional measures.[131] Under article 36(3) of the ICSID Convention, upon receipt of an application, the Secretary-General of ICSID registers the request for arbitration and constitutes a tribunal unless it is found that the dispute is manifestly outside the jurisdiction of ICSID.[132] This preliminary examination of jurisdiction before the claim even reaches the tribunal forms a type of prima facie test for whether the tribunal has jurisdiction. It is then up to the tribunal to decide whether it wants to accept the Secretary-General's registration as a sufficient basis or whether it wants to form its own prima facie

[127] Above n 27, 117, 118 (Sep Op Lauterpacht).

[128] Above n 12, 15; [1972] ICJ Rep 29, 33.

[129] Above n 22, 101; above n 74, 137.

[130] For example, *Pulp Mills on the River Uruguay* (ICJ Order of 13 July 2006), para 57, available at <http://www.icj-cij.org> (last visited 25 November 2006); *Passage Through the Great Belt* [1991] ICJ Rep 12, 15; *Application of the Genocide Convention*, (*Provisional Measures*), above n 74, 11–12; *Land and Maritime Boundary*, above n 24, 21; *Armed Activities on the Territory of the Congo* (*New Application*) (2002) 41 ILM 1175, 1190.

[131] Schreuer, above n 35, 764–6; Charles Brower and Ronald Goodman, 'Provisional Measures and the Protection of ICSID Jurisdictional Exclusivity Against Municipal Proceedings' (1991) 6 *ICSID Review—FILJ* 431, 451–6.

[132] ICSID Convention, above n 1, art 36(3); Friedland, above n 23, 341.

view on jurisdiction before recommending provisional measures.[133] ICSID tribunals have followed this practice, and at least one tribunal has made express reference to the standard of a prima facie basis of jurisdiction.[134]

Other international courts also require a jurisdictional link before granting provisional measures. The Iran–US Claims Tribunal has stated that it must be satisfied that it has prima facie jurisdiction over the dispute before granting provisional measures.[135] The IACHR also considers questions of jurisdiction in granting provisional measures, although the issue of jurisdiction is usually less complex before this body. Article 63(2) of the American Convention on Human Rights, which contains the express power, makes no mention of a specific jurisdictional requirement, but it would seem apparent that the IACHR can only grant such measures if the states parties to the litigation have accepted its jurisdiction.[136] Judge Buergenthal has suggested that it is sufficient for the IACHR to find that it has prima facie jurisdiction over the merits.[137] In practice, states appear to have challenged the jurisdiction of the IACHR to grant provisional measures on one occasion; this was in *James v Trinidad and Tobago*, where the respondent state had withdrawn its consent to the IACHR's jurisdiction, and argued that the IACHR lacked jurisdiction *ratione temporis*.[138] The IACHR nonetheless granted provisional measures, as Trinidad and Tobago had not denounced the American Convention until after its alleged violations of it.[139] Usually, however, the IACHR simply makes a finding that the respondent state is a state party to the convention, and proceeds to grant the measures, if the other criteria are satisfied.[140] Questions of jurisdiction to grant provisional measures have not arisen before the ECHR; this is perhaps due to the fact that there is no provision in the European HR Convention empowering the ECHR to grant provisional measures, and orders made under Rule 39 of its Rules have, until the *Mamatkulov* judgment in 2003, been considered non-binding.[141] The question of jurisdiction may arise in future requests for provisional measures.

[133] Schreuer, above n 35, 764–5; Friedland, ibid, 341; Pierre Lalive, 'The First World Bank Arbitration (*Holiday Inns v Morocco*): Some Legal Problems' (1980) 51 *British Yearbook of International Law* 123, 136.

[134] *Victor Pey Casado and Fondation Président Allende v Chile* (2001) 16 *ICSID Review—FILJ* 567, 574–6; see also Schreuer, ibid, 765–6.

[135] *Component Builders, Inc v Iran*, above n 94, 4; *Ford Aerospace and Communications Corporation v Air Force of Iran*, above n 92, 108–10; Brower and Brueschke, above n 27, 218–22; Brower and Goodman, above n 131, 451–2; Caron, above n 27, 488–90.

[136] Thomas Buergenthal, 'The Inter-American Court of Human Rights' (1982) 76 *AJIL* 231, 241.

[137] Buergenthal, 'Interim Measures', above n 36, 71; see also Pasqualucci, *Practice and Procedure*, above n 61, 308–9; Pasqualucci, 'Provisional Measures', above n 36, 826.

[138] *James* et al *v Trinidad and Tobago*, (IACHR Order of 25 May 1999), available at <http://www.corteidh.or.cr> (last visited 25 November 2006); Pasqualucci, *Practice and Procedure*, above n 61, 308.

[139] *James v Trinidad and Tobago*, ibid, 4–5; Pasqualucci, ibid, 308.

[140] For example, *Urso Branco Prison (Brazil)* (IACHR Order of 29 August 2002), 7; *Constitutional Court (Peru)* (IACHR Order of 7 April 2000), 2, all available at <http://www.corteidh.or.cr> (last visited 25 November 2006).

[141] *Cruz Varas v Sweden*, Ser A (No 201) (ECHR, 1991); *Conka v Belgium* (ECHR Decision of 13 March 2001); Christian Tams, 'Interim Orders by the European Court of Human Rights:

B. Circumstances Relevant to the Granting of Provisional Measures

The constitutive instruments of international courts often provide that the court may grant provisional measures if 'the circumstances so require',[142] or if to do so would be 'appropriate under the circumstances'.[143] The constitutive instruments are generally silent, however, on what these words actually mean, and international courts have accordingly developed criteria in their case law. There are many circumstances which might be considered pertinent to requests for provisional measures, but there are two criteria which have emerged as being crucial. One reflects the purpose of provisional measures, being the preservation of the parties' rights from irreparable prejudice pending the decision on the merits, and the other criterion is urgency.

1. Prevention of Irreparable Prejudice to the Rights of the Parties

The preservation of the parties' rights from irreparable prejudice is one of the two criteria widely adopted by international courts in deciding on requests for provisional measures. For example, the ICJ clarified in *Fisheries Jurisdiction* that the power to grant provisional measures 'presupposes that irreparable prejudice should not be caused to rights which are the subject of a dispute in judicial proceedings',[144] and this has been repeated almost verbatim in subsequent cases.[145] There are two comments that need to be made regarding this statement. First, the ICJ only has jurisdiction to order provisional measures which are 'needed to protect rights which might form the subject matter of a judgment under the treaty or treaties which the Court determines afford a *prima facie* basis for its jurisdiction'.[146] Second, the rights of the parties should only properly be the subject of an order for provisional measures if the probability exists that they will be damaged in a way that cannot be made good in a later judgment on the merits.[147] Prejudice is deemed to be 'irreparable' for the purpose of the indication of interim measures if it makes impossible full execution of the judgment and full restoration of the position of the party seeking preservation of its rights.[148] This test has been interpreted very restrictively by international courts and tribunals. For instance, in *Aegean Sea*, Greece sought provisional measures to prevent Turkey from carrying out seismic tests on the area of continental shelf in dispute. In its order denying

Comments on *Mamatkulov and Abdurasulovic v Turkey*' (2003) 63 *ZaöRV* 681; Chester Brown, 'Strasbourg Follows Suit on Provisional Measures' (2003) 62 *CLJ* 532.

[142] For example, ICJ Statute, above n 1 art 41; ICSID Convention, above n 1, art 47.

[143] For example, UNCLOS, above n 1, art 290(1).

[144] Above n 12, 16; above n 126, 34.

[145] For example, *Pulp Mills on the River Uruguay*, above n 130, paras 61–2; *Avena*, above n 72, 318; *LaGrand*, above n 18, 14–15; *Consular Relations*, above n 72, 257; *Passage through the Great Belt*, above n 130, 16; *Frontier Dispute*, above n 24, 8.

[146] *Armed Activities (New Application)*, above n 130, 1190; *Application of the Genocide Convention*, above n 74, 342; see also *Armed Activities (New Application)*, CR 2002/37, 13–14, 26–8 (Christopher Greenwood), CR 2002/39, 6–7 (Christopher Greenwood); Thirlway, 'Part Twelve', above n 59, 87–8.

[147] Oda, above n 32, 551.

[148] Sztucki, above n 26, 110–12.

provisional measures, the ICJ held that the 'alleged breach by Turkey . . . is one that might be capable of reparation by appropriate means', and it followed that the ICJ was unable 'to find in that alleged breach of Greece's rights such a risk of irreparable prejudice to rights in issue before the Court as might require the exercise of its power under Article 41 of the Statute to indicate interim measures for their preservation'.[149] A similar finding was made by the Iran–US Claims Tribunal in *Iran v US (Case No B-1)*, where it held that 'injury that can be made whole by monetary relief does not constitute irreparable harm'.[150] This was also accepted by the ICSID Tribunal in *Plama Consortium Ltd v Bulgaria*, which accepted Bulgaria's argument that 'harm is not irreparable if it can be compensated for by damages, which is the case in the present arbitration'.[151]

The jurisprudence of the ICJ demonstrates that the court does not require that irreparable harm should seem certain, but that there should be a probability of such prejudice.[152] In practice, the ICJ has generally indicated provisional measures in cases where events were certain because they had already taken place or on the basis of events the occurrence of which in the near future could be regarded as certain unless prevented by some diplomatic or judicial action.[153]

Tribunals having jurisdiction to grant provisional measures under UNCLOS may do so to preserve the rights of the parties or to prevent serious harm to the marine environment. With respect to the standard of harm, no guidance is given by article 290 of UNCLOS or the constitutive instruments of the ITLOS and Annex VII tribunals, and in its first three provisional measures orders, the ITLOS did not expressly adopt the standard of 'irreparable damage'.[154] In *Land Reclamation*, however, the ITLOS directed Singapore 'not to conduct its land reclamation in ways that might cause irreparable prejudice to the rights of Malaysia or serious harm to the marine environment', thereby adopting this standard.[155] Yet even prior to this

[149] Above n 56, 11. There is, however, some authority for the proposition that the test should not be drawn so narrowly: *Legal Status of South-Eastern Greenland*, Ser A/B, (No 48), 277, 284 (*PCIJ*, 1932); *Anglo-Iranian Oil Company*; above n 74, 93–4; *Fisheries Jurisdiction* above n 12, 16–17; *Behring International v Islamic Republic of Iran Air Force*, 8 Ir-USCTR 238, 276, fn 50, (1985); see also Karin Oellers-Frahm, 'Article 41', in Andreas Zimmermann, Christian Tomuschat and Karin Oellers-Frahm (eds), *The Statute of the International Court of Justice: A Commentary* (2006) 921, 939–40; and Merrills, above n 11, 108.

[150] *Iran v US (Case No B–1)*, 22 Ir–USCTR 105, 109 (1989); see also *Boeing Company* et al *v Iran*, 5 Ir–USCTR 152, 154 (1984). See also, however, *Behring International v Islamic Republic of Iran Air Force*, ibid, 276, fn 50.

[151] *Plama Consortium Ltd v Bulgaria* (ICSID Case ARB/03/24, Order on Provisional Measures of 6 September 2005), para 46.

[152] Thirlway, 'Part Twelve', above n 59, 93; Sztucki, above n 26, 105; *Tehran Hostages*, above n 74, 20; *Nuclear Tests*, above n 22, 105; *Denunciation of the Treaty of 1865*, above n 24, 7.

[153] *Arrest Warrant of 11 April 2000*, CR 2000/33, para 58 (Daniel Bethlehem); *Land and Maritime Boundary*, above n 24, 23; Judge Rosalyn Higgins, 'Interim Measures for the Protection of Human Rights' (1997) 36 *Columbia Journal of Transnational Law* 91, 98–102, 104–5; Sztucki, above n 26, 105.

[154] See, e.g., *Southern Bluefin Tuna*, above n 28, 1638, 1639 (Sep Op Laing); *M/V 'Saiga' (No 2)*, above n 101, 129, 142–3 (Sep Op Laing) (ITLOS, 1998).

[155] *Land Reclamation by Singapore*, above n 23, para 106(2).

order for provisional measures, parties had treated this standard as relevant. In *M/V 'Saiga' (No 2)*, counsel for St Vincent and the Grenadines submitted that provisional measures were necessary 'to prevent further irreparable harm'.[156] In the request for provisional measures before the ITLOS in *MOX Plant*, Ireland submitted that there was a 'serious and imminent danger of irreparable harm to Ireland's rights and of serious harm to the marine environment',[157] and the UK agreed that the required standard was that of irreparability.[158] More significantly, the UNCLOS tribunal in *MOX Plant* expressly noted the relevance of ICJ jurisprudence to requests for provisional measures under *UNCLOS*:

> Although the language of article 290 is not in all respects identical to that of article 41 of the Statute of the International Court of Justice, the Tribunal considers that it should have regard to the law and practice of that Court, as well as to the law and practice of ITLOS, in considering provisional measures.[159]

It also explicitly accepted the requirement of irreparable damage in applications for provisional measures under *UNCLOS*:

> International judicial practice confirms that a general requirement for the prescription of provisional measures to protect the rights of the parties is that there needs to be a showing both of urgency and of irreparable harm to the claimed rights (see, eg, *Certain Criminal Proceedings in France*, Order of 17 June 2003, paras 34–5.)[160]

ICSID tribunals have also made express reference to the language of 'irreparable damage' or 'irreparable prejudice' in granting provisional measures. In *Plama Consortium Ltd v Bulgaria*, the ICSID Tribunal held that '[t]he need for provisional measures must be... necessary to preserve the status quo or avoid the occurrence of irreparable harm or damage'.[161] In *Tokios Tokeles v Ukraine*, the ICSID Tribunal referred to ICJ jurisprudence, stating that '[t]he international jurisprudence on provisional measures indicates that a provisional measure is necessary where the actions of a party "are capable of causing or of threatening irreparable prejudice to the rights invoked"'.[162] In *Cases Nos A4 and A15(III)*, the Iran-US Claims Tribunal, operating under a modified version of the UNCITRAL Rules, also expressly adopted the standard of 'irreparable prejudice' set by the ICJ,[163] and the UNCITRAL Tribunal in *EnCana Corporation v Ecuador* also adopted the test of 'irreparable prejudice'.[164]

156 *M/V 'Saiga' (No 2)*, ITLOS/PV.98/1, 48–9 (Philippe Sands).

157 *MOX Plant*, ITLOS/PV.01/07, 7 (Vaughan Lowe).

158 Ibid, ITLOS/PV.01/08, 15, 19–20 (Daniel Bethlehem), 30–1 (Richard Plender); see also *MOX Plant*, above n 23, 414–15.

159 (2003) 42 ILM 1187, 1195.

160 Ibid, 1197.

161 *Plama Consortium Ltd v Bulgaria*, above n 151, para 38.

162 *Tokios Tokeles v Ukraine*, above n 102, para 8, referring to *Aegean Sea*, above n 56, 15, 15 (Sep Op Jiménez de Aréchaga); see also *Victor Pey Casado and Fondation Président Allende v Chile*, above n 134, 592; *Holiday Inns v Morocco*, above n 27, 656.

163 *Iran v US, Cases Nos A–4 and A–15*, 5 Ir–USCTR 112, 113 (1984), referring to *Aegean Sea*, ibid, 15, 16 (Sep Op Jiménez de Aréchaga); see also *United Technologies International, Inc v Iran*, 13 Ir–USCTR 254, 257–8 (1986); and Brower and Bruschke, above n 27, 226–229.

164 *EnCana Corporation v Ecuador* (Request for Interim Measures of Protection of 31 January 2004), para 13, available at <http://ita.law.uvic.ca> (last visited 25 November 2006). But see

As for the practice of the IACHR, article 63(2) of the American Convention expressly provides that the IACHR has the power to grant provisional measures 'when necessary to avoid irreparable damage to persons'.[165] Provisional measures orders typically include statements by the IACHR to the effect that 'the purpose of provisional measures . . . is to effectively protect fundamental rights, inasmuch as they seek to avoid irreparable damage to persons'.[166] As regards the ECHR, Rule 39 does not specifically mention the criterion of 'irreparable damage'. But in *Mamatkulov*, the ECHR stated that 'any State Party to the Convention to which interim measures have been indicated in order to avoid irreparable harm being caused to the victim of an alleged violation must comply with those measures'.[167] From this statement it is not clear whether 'irreparable harm' is a precondition for the granting of provisional measures, or a condition that determines whether certain provisional measures granted by the ECHR are binding.[168] In light of the methodology employed by the ECHR of referring to the practice and case law of other international courts to determine whether it had the power to order binding provisional measures,[169] it is suggested that the ECHR intended to follow the practice of other international courts, and that the probability of irreparable harm should be considered a criterion for the granting of provisional measures. Irreparable damage is also a prerequisite for the granting of interim relief by the UN Human Rights Committee,[170] and the UN Committee against Torture.[171]

2. *Urgency*

The second substantive condition necessary for international courts to grant provisional measures is that the requesting state must show that they are required as a matter of urgency. 'Urgency' is not a requirement expressed in article 41 of the ICJ Statute, but the ICJ Rules stipulate that a request for provisional measures 'shall have priority over all other cases',[172] and that the ICJ 'shall be convened forthwith for the purpose of proceeding to a decision on the request as a matter of urgency'.[173]

David Caron, Lee Caplan and Matti Pellonpää, *The UNCITRAL Arbitration Rules: A Commentary* (2006) 537, where the authors argue that the standard of 'irreparable harm' should not be applied under the UNCITRAL Rules, and suggest that 'the terms "grave" or "substantive" might be more appropriate'. See also Oellers-Frahm, above n 149, 921, 939–40.

[165] American Convention, above n 1, art 63(2).

[166] For example, *Mayagna (Sumo) Awas Tingni Community (Nicaragua)* (IACHR Order of 6 September 2002), 5; *Peace Community of San José De Apartadó (Colombia)* (IACHR Order of 18 June 2002), 9; *Velásquez Rodríguez (Honduras)* (IACHR Order of 19 January 1988), 2, all available at <http://www.corteidh.or.cr> (last visited 30 November 2006).

[167] *Mamatkulov and Abdurasulovic v Turkey*, above n 66, para 110.

[168] See also Tams, above n 141, 688.

[169] *Mamatkulov and Abdurasulovic v Turkey*, above n 66, paras 39–51, 92–111; Tams, ibid, 685–6; Brown, 'Strasbourg Follows Suit', above n 141, 533.

[170] United Nations Human Rights Committee Rules, above n 49, Rule 86.

[171] UN Committee Against Torture Rules of Procedure, CAT/C/3/Rev.4 (9 August 2002), Rule 108(9).

[172] ICJ Rules, above n 1, art 74(1).

[173] Ibid, art 74(2).

The criterion of urgency is an implicit requirement in any request for provisional measures, and is closely connected with the requirement of irreparable damage; if the request for the preservation of rights were not urgent, in the sense that the probable damage were not irreparable, then it would be acceptable to wait until such time as the court or tribunal is able to hear the dispute in full.[174] Parties requesting provisional measures have consistently sought to persuade the ICJ that the provisional measures they requested were urgently required,[175] and the ICJ has regularly recognized 'urgency' as a substantive requirement of any request for provisional measures, as expressed in its Order in *Passage through the Great Belt*:

> [P]rovisional measures under Article 41 of the Statute are indicated 'pending the final decision' of the Court on the merits of the case, and are therefore only justified if there is urgency in the sense that action prejudicial to the rights of either party is likely to be taken before such final decision is given.[176]

The temporal element of urgency is important; as the ICJ stated, provisional measures must be necessary as a matter of urgency pending the 'final decision'.[177] This factor is significant before all international courts, although it differs in requests for provisional measures under UNCLOS. Urgency is not an express criterion for requests under article 290(1) of UNCLOS, which deals with requests made to the same body that will have jurisdiction over the merits. In the case of requests made under article 290(5) of UNCLOS, however, the tribunal seised of the provisional measures request will have jurisdiction to grant such measures '[p]ending the constitution of [the] arbitral tribunal to which the dispute is being submitted... if it considers that *prima facie* the tribunal which is to be constituted would have jurisdiction and that the urgency of the situation so requires'.[178]

174 Rosenne, *Provisional Measures*, above n 11, 135; Shabtai Rosenne, *The Law and Practice of the International Court, 1920–2005* (2006) vol III, 1395–7; Merrills, 'Interim Measures/Recent Jurisprudence', above n 11, 110; Sztucki, above n 26, 113; *Interhandel*, above n 27, 117, 118 (Sep Op Lauterpacht).

175 Sztucki, above n 26, 113, fn 256; see also *Avena*, CR 2003/1, para 52 (Sandra Babcock), paras 112–14 (Donald Donovan); *LaGrand*, Request for the Indication of Provisional Measures of Protection (2 March 1999), paras 7–9; *Consular Relations*, CR 1998/7 (Donald Donovan), all available at <http://www.icj-cij.org> (last visited 25 November 2006).

176 Above n 130, 17; see also *Pulp Mills on the River Uruguay*, above n 130, para 62, available at <www.icj-cij.org> (last visited 25 November 2006).

177 See *Certain Criminal Proceedings in France*, para 35 (ICJ, 2003), where the ICJ held that 'there is at the present time no risk of irreparable prejudice, so as to justify the indication of provisional measures as a matter of urgency'. This suggests that the temporal element relevant in provisional measures applications is not necessarily 'pending the final decision', but 'at the present time', which recognizes that parties can make subsequent applications for provisional measures. This has indeed occurred in *Application of the Genocide Convention*, where Bosnia and Herzegovina made two requests for provisional measures: [1993] ICJ Rep 3 and [1993] ICJ Rep 325; and also in *Pulp Mills on the River Uruguay*, where the ICJ issued an order on provisional measures on 13 July 2006 in response to Argentina's request, and a further request for provisional measures was made, albeit by Uruguay, on 29 November 2006, in response to which the ICJ issued an Order on 23 January 2007: available at <http://www.icj-cij.org> (last visited 31 January 2007).

178 UNCLOS, above n 1, art 290(5).

Even though article 290(1) does not expressly mention a requirement of urgency, individual judges and parties have treated urgency as a requirement for the prescription of provisional measures under both articles 290(1) and 290(5). In *M/V 'Saiga' (No 2)*, St Vincent and the Grenadines submitted that although there were 'certain differences between these two paragraphs textually', these differences were 'essentially academic' and 'for all practical purposes that standards and the tests they apply are the same'.[179] It was submitted that urgency was a requirement of article 290(1),[180] a submission with which counsel for Guinea agreed.[181]

The ITLOS did not prescribe any provisional measures in that case, and did not consider the question of urgency; the three other provisional measures cases to come before the ITLOS have been applications under article 290(5), and urgency was thus, in these cases, a statutory requirement.[182] But Judge Treves, in his separate opinion in *Southern Bluefin Tuna*, observed that:

> The requirement of urgency is part of the very nature of provisional measures, as these measures are meant to preserve the rights of the parties *pending the final decision* (article 290, paragraph 1 of the Convention) (emphasis in the original).[183]

Indeed, the UNCLOS tribunal in *MOX Plant* explicitly accepted the relevance of urgency in applications for provisional measures under UNCLOS.[184] It should be noted, however, that there is one significant difference to the way in which urgency is relevant in requests for provisional measures under article 290(1) and 290(5). Under article 290(1), the provisional measures must be urgent for the preservation of the parties' rights—or the protection of the marine environment from serious harm—pending 'the final decision'. In the case of an application under article 290(5), however, the provisional measures must be urgent in the sense that they are necessary pending the constitution of the tribunal which will decide the merits.

The term 'urgency' is not found in the text of the ICSID Convention; an attempt to have a reference to urgency and imminent danger included in it was defeated.[185] However, as Professor Schreuer has argued, 'provisional measures will only be appropriate where a question cannot await the outcome of the award on the merits',[186] and ICSID tribunals have referred to the need for 'urgency' to justify the recommendation of provisional measures.[187] Likewise, urgency is also a

179 *M/V 'Saiga' (No 2)*, ITLOS/PV.98/1, 52 (Philippe Sands); see also ibid, 48–9.

180 Ibid, ITLOS/PV.98/3, 12 (Philippe Sands).

181 Ibid, ITLOS/PV.98/2, 10 (Hartmut von Brevern).

182 *Land Reclamation by Singapore*, above n 23, para 72; *MOX Plant*, above n 23, 415; *Southern Bluefin Tuna*, above n 28, 1634.

183 *Southern Bluefin Tuna*, ibid, 1644, 1644 (Sep Op Treves).

184 *MOX Plant*, above n 159, 1197; see also Rosenne, *Provisional Measures*, above n 11, 148.

185 Schreuer, above n 35, 751. 186 Ibid.

187 For example, *Plama Consortium Ltd v Bulgaria*, above n 151, para 38; *Tokios Tokeles*, above n 102, para 8; *Victor Pey Casado*, above n 134, 573; *Tanzania Electric Supply Co Ltd* (ICSID Case No ARB/98/8, Decision on Provisional Measures of 20 November 1999), para 18, available at <http://www.worldbank.org/icsid> (last visited 25 November 2006).

criterion for the granting of provisional measures before the Iran–US Claims Tribunal,[188] the IACHR,[189] and the IACommHR.[190]

3. Other Factors

In considering whether 'circumstances' require the granting of provisional measures, other factors may be relevant.[191] One factor which has been suggested is the likelihood of the international court having jurisdiction over the merits of the case,[192] but in light of the widely accepted test of prima facie jurisdiction, this is no longer seriously considered.[193] A second factor suggested by some writers is the prospect of the applicant's success on the merits.[194] This issue was considered by Judge Shahabuddeen in his separate opinion in *Passage through the Great Belt*, where he concluded that 'a State requesting interim measures... is required to establish the possible existence of the rights sought to be protected',[195] and Professor Thirlway has also argued that the applicant must show a prima facie case for the existence of the rights in dispute.[196] This was certainly a consideration of the ICJ in *Passage through the Great Belt*,[197] but while it may be accepted that the applicant must be able to demonstrate the existence of the rights in question, the suggestion that it must also establish that it would succeed on the merits is yet to receive clear endorsement as a necessary criterion by the ICJ, or any other international court.[198] A third relevant factor is the presence of activity on the international plane pertaining to the dispute.[199] In two recent cases, action by the UN Security Council arguably had an effect on the outcome of a request for provisional measures. In *Lockerbie*, SC Resolution 748 played a significant role in the ICJ's holding that the rights of Libya could not 'now be regarded as appropriate for protection by the indication of provisional measures',[200] and in *DRC v Uganda*, the ICJ referred in some detail to SC Resolution 1304 (2000), indicating that it had played some part in the ICJ's decision to indicate provisional measures.[201]

[188] Brower and Brueschke, above n 27, 218, 222–6; e.g., *Aeronutronic Overseas Services Inc v Iran*, 7 Ir–USCTR 217, 219 (1984); *Ford Aerospace and Communications Corporation v Iran*, 2 Ir–USCTR 281, 282 (1983).

[189] American Convention, above n 1, art 63(2).

[190] IACommHR Rules, above n 4, art 25(1).

[191] Merrills, 'Interim Measures/Recent Jurisprudence', above n 11, 114–25; Sztucki, above n 26, 103–4; Elkind, above n 15, 209–33.

[192] See, e.g., Mendelson, above n 14.

[193] Merrills, 'Interim Measures/Recent Jurisprudence', above n 11, 114; e.g., *Victor Pey Casado*, above n 134, 573–4.

[194] Mani, above n 57, 293; Mendelson, above n 14, 315–8; Dumbauld, above n 16, 160–1; but see Sztucki, above n 26, 97, 123, 259–60; Jerome Elkind, 'The *Aegean Sea* Case and Article 41 of the Statute of the International Court of Justice' (1979) 32 *Revue hellénique du droit international* 285, 332–3; Merrills, 'Substantive Jurisdiction', above n 121, 100–2.

[195] Above n 130, 28, 36 (Sep Op Shahabuddeen).

[196] Thirlway, 'Part Twelve', above n 59, 88–9.

[197] Above n 130, 18–19.

[198] See discussion in *MOX Plant*, ITLOS/PV.01/08, 11–15 (Daniel Bethlehem).

[199] See, e.g., Rosenne, *Provisional Measures*, above n 11, 196–201; 218–22.

[200] *Lockerbie*, above n 100, 11–15; see also *Arrest Warrant of 11 April 2000*, CR 2000/33, para 70 (Daniel Bethlehem).

[201] *Armed Activities on the Territory of the Congo* (2000) 39 ILM 1100; see also *Arrest Warrant*, CR 2003/33, para 69 (Daniel Bethlehem).

Other relevant activity might include the existence of a regional peace process,[202] or the negotiation of a ceasefire.[203] Fourth, an order for provisional measures should not prejudge any of the issues to be determined on the merits; in this sense, it cannot represent an interim judgment.[204] Fifth, international courts will often be careful to take account of the equal distribution of burdens in an order for provisional measures.[205] Finally, in accordance with their function in managing the dispute, international tribunals might also take into account the need to prevent the aggravation or extension of the dispute.[206]

C. Binding Quality of Provisional Measures

The constitutive instruments of international courts which expressly confer the power to grant provisional measures do not always provide that such measures have mandatory force. One constitutive instrument which does clarify the legal effect of provisional measures granted under it is UNCLOS. Under article 290(1) and 290(5) of UNCLOS, the ITLOS and arbitral tribunals constituted under UNCLOS have the power to 'prescribe' provisional measures, and article 290(6) makes it clear that states must 'comply promptly with any provisional measures prescribed under this article'.[207] But the statutes of many other international courts do not make similar provision. The question of whether provisional measures granted by the ICJ were legally binding was for many years one of the more controversial questions in public international law, and the issue engendered an extensive literature.[208] The uncertainty arose chiefly from the ambiguity of article 41 of the ICJ Statute, which provides that the ICJ has the power to 'indicate' provisional measures

[202] Merrills, 'Interim Measures/Recent Jurisprudence', above n 11, 125–30; *Military and Paramilitary Activities in and against Nicaragua (Provisional Measures)* [1984] ICJ Rep 169, 183–6.

[203] Merrills, ibid, 125–7; *Frontier Dispute*, above n 24, 10–11.

[204] Sztucki, above n 26, 93–102.

[205] Ibid, 124–6; Merrills, 'Interim Measures/Recent Jurisprudence', above n 11, 116–17.

[206] Merrills, ibid, 122–5; Thirlway, 'The Indication of Provisional Measures', above n 3, 12–16; Sztucki, above n 26, 127–9.

[207] UNCLOS, above n 1, art 290(6).

[208] See, e.g., Rosenne, *Law and Practice*, above n 174, 1377–8; Martin Mennecke and Christian Tams, 'The Right to Consular Assistance under International Law' (1999) 42 *German Yearbook of International Law* 192, 203–9; Eelko Szabó, 'Provisional Measures in the World Court: Binding or Bound to be Ineffective?' (1997) 10 *Leiden Journal of International Law* 475; Oda, above n 32, 554–6; Thirlway, 'The Indication of Provisional Measures', above n 3, 28–33; Fitzmaurice, *Law and Procedure*, above n 32, 548–50; Sztucki, above n 26, 260–302; Elkind, *Interim Protection*, above n 15, 153–66; Karin Oellers-Frahm, 'Interim Measures of Protection' in Rudolf Bernhardt (ed), *Encyclopedia of Public International Law* (1980) vol 1, 69; Karin Oellers-Frahm, *Die einstweilige Anordnung in der internationalen Gerichtsbarkeit* (1975) 107–15; V S Mani, 'Interim Measures of Protection: Article 94 of the UN Charter' (1970) 10 *Indian Journal of International Law* 359, 360–7; Lauterpacht, *Development*, above n 71, 254; Hambro, above n 31; Hudson, above n 31, 425–6; Åke Hammerskjöld, 'Quelques aspects de la question des mesures conservatoires en droit international positif' (1935) 5 *ZaöRV* 5, 26–7; Manley Hudson, *The Permanent Court of International Justice: A Treatise* (1934) 415; Sir Hersch Lauterpacht, *The Function of Law in the International Community* (1933) 208, fn 1; Dumbauld, above n 16, 168–9; Guggenheim, above n 16, 678–80; Niemeyer, above n 123, 38–44.

which 'ought' to be taken,[209] and that the parties and Security Council are to be notified of the provisional measures which have been 'suggested'.[210]

This uncertainty was finally resolved in *LaGrand* in 2001, where the ICJ held that its provisional measures were binding.[211] In *LaGrand*, the ICJ construed article 41 in accordance with the principle of effectiveness in treaty interpretation, holding that the purpose of provisional measures was 'to prevent the Court from being hampered in the exercise of its functions because the respective rights of the parties to a dispute before the Court are not preserved'.[212] Accordingly, it followed that:

> the power to indicate provisional measures entails that such measures should be binding, inasmuch as the power in question is based on the necessity, when the circumstances call for it, to safeguard, and to avoid prejudice to, the rights of the parties as determined by the final judgment of the Court.[213]

While it is likely that the decision in *LaGrand* is simply an example of the ICJ exercising its judicial functions in interpreting article 41 of the ICJ Statute, it might be suggested that another force may also have been at play. This is the introduction of inter-institutional competition into international adjudication. It might be speculated, for instance, that the decision was motivated in part by a desire for the ICJ to remain an attractive forum for cases involving requests for provisional measures, especially in light of the recent creation of the ITLOS, and the clear stipulations under UNCLOS that provisional measures granted by the ITLOS and other UNCLOS tribunals would be binding.[214] Indeed, when Australia and New Zealand commenced the *Southern Bluefin Tuna* cases against Japan in 1999, in which they requested provisional measures,[215] the ICJ was one of three possible fora for the dispute; the applicant states eventually chose to use the UNCLOS dispute settlement mechanisms.[216] This choice might have been partially motivated by the knowledge that if their request for provisional measures were successful, any provisional measures prescribed under UNCLOS would have binding effect; if the applicants chose to litigate before the ICJ, some uncertainty would attend this question. In reaching its decision in *LaGrand*, the ICJ was certainly not unaware of this issue; in its Counter-Memorial, the United States had argued that the ICJ's provisional measures were not binding, and compared the fact that provisional measures were 'prescribed' under UNCLOS, whereas they

209 ICJ Statute, above n 1, art 41(1).

210 Ibid, art 41(2).

211 Above n 56; see Jörg Kammerhofer, 'The Binding Nature of Provisional Measures of the International Court of Justice: The "Settlement" of the Issue in the *LaGrand* Case' (2003) 16 *Leiden Journal of International Law* 67; Martin Mennecke and Christian Tams, '*LaGrand* Case (*Germany v United States of America*)' (2002) 51 *ICLQ* 449; Xiodang Yang, 'Thou Shalt Not Violate Provisional Measures' (2001) 60 *CLJ* 441.

212 Above n 56, 1093.

213 Ibid; see also Rosenne, *Provisional Measures*, above n 11, 34–40.

214 UNCLOS, above n 1, art 290.

215 Above n 28.

216 See especially Cesare Romano, 'The *Southern Bluefin Tuna* Dispute: Hints of a World to Come... Like It or Not' (2001) *Ocean Development & International Law* 313.

were merely 'indicated' under the ICJ Statute.[217] Accordingly, the possibility cannot be dismissed that the ICJ's holding in *LaGrand* was encouraged by the fear that its case load might be lessened where cases might otherwise be referred to the ITLOS owing to the persistent uncertainty over the binding nature of its provisional measures.

There are, however, limitations to the impact of inter-institutional competition on the emergence of the common law of international adjudication. There is no objective or empirical evidence to substantiate the suggestion that it has had any influence on the decisions of international courts. Further, even if this consideration does play a role, the scope of its operation is limited to situations where international courts have overlapping jurisdictions, such as, primarily, the ICJ, the ITLOS, and other UNCLOS tribunals. This consideration arguably does not play a part as between many other international courts, due to their different jurisdictions.

The emergence of a common approach to the binding nature of provisional measures can also be found in the jurisprudence of other international courts. In *Mamatkulov and Abdurasulovic v Turkey*, for instance, a Chamber of the ECHR overturned previous authority and held that interim measures indicated by it had legal effect.[218] In its judgment, the Chamber referred to the principle of effectiveness in treaty interpretation, the evolutive approach, and also article 31(3)(c) of the VCLT.[219] In particular, with respect to article 31(3)(c) of the VCLT, the ECHR held that the European HR Convention was to be interpreted 'so far as possible consistently with the other principles of international law'.[220] It noted that other international courts had recently 'stressed the importance and purpose of interim measures and pointed out that compliance with such measures was necessary to ensure the effectiveness of decisions on the merits',[221] and made considerable reference to the practice of the ICJ, the IACHR, and other international human rights bodies.[222] The ECHR concluded that states parties to which interim measures had been indicated had to 'comply with those measures and refrain from any act or omission that will undermine the authority and effectiveness of the final judgment'.[223] In 2005, this decision was upheld by the ECHR's Grand Chamber, which likewise, by reference to the principle of effectiveness in treaty interpretation, an evolutive approach, and article 31(3)(c) of the VCLT,[224]

[217] *LaGrand*, Counter-Memorial of the United States, para 144 (27 March 2000), available at <http://www.icj-cij.org> (last visited 25 November 2006).

[218] *Mamatkulov and Abdurasulovic v Turkey*, above n 66; compare *Cruz Varas v Sweden*, above n 141; *Conka v Belgium*, above n 141; Bernhardt, above n 48, 100–3.

[219] *Mamatkulov*, ibid, paras 92–3 (referring to the principle of effectiveness), para 94 (applying an evolutive approach to treaty interpretation), paras 98–103 (referring to general principles of international law and article 31(3)(c) of the VCLT), and para 105 (referring to all three).

[220] Ibid, para 99. [221] Ibid, para 101. [222] Ibid, paras 39–51, 92–111.

[223] Ibid, para 110.

[224] *Mamatkulov and Askarov v Turkey* (ECHR, Judgment of 4 February 2005), paras 100–2, 121, 123 (principle of effectiveness), para 121 (evolutive approach), paras 110–11, 123–4 (general principles of international law, and article 31(3)(c) of the VCLT), available at <http://www.echr.coe.int> (last visited 30 November 2006).

made extensive reference to the practice of other international courts on the granting of provisional measures.[225]

The IACHR has also observed that compliance with provisional measures is mandatory, and necessary to ensure the effectiveness of its decisions on the merits.[226] In two orders granting provisional measures, it has also noted that states parties to the American Convention were required to 'comply in good faith (*pacta sunt servanda*) with all of the provisions of the Convention, including those relative to the operation of the two supervisory organs of the Inter-American system'.[227] Other international human rights bodies have also ruled that their provisional measures are binding, even those whose final reports are not binding, but merely recommendatory. These include the UN Human Rights Committee[228] and the Committee Against Torture.[229]

It should be remembered, however, that the general rule that international courts have the power to grant binding provisional measures does not apply if it is inconsistent with a particular court's constitutive instrument. This is arguably the case, for instance, with regard to the ICSID Convention, which provides in article 47 that ICSID tribunals merely have the power to 'recommend' provisional measures.[230] Yet ICSID tribunals have still treated provisional measures as having some legal relevance. First, tribunals have taken non-compliance with recommended provisional measures into account in awards on the merits;[231] and, second, the ICSID tribunal in *Maffezini* dramatically held that provisional measures granted under the ICSID Convention did, in fact, have binding effect:

> While there is a semantic difference between the word 'recommend' as used in Rule 39 and the word 'order' as used elsewhere in the rules to describe the Tribunal's ability to require a party to take a certain action, the difference is more apparent than real.... The Tribunal does not believe that the parties to the Convention meant to create a substantial difference in the effect of these two words. The Tribunal's authority to rule on provisional measures is no less binding than that of a final award.[232]

225 Ibid, paras 40–53, 99–129.

226 For example, *Constitutional Court (Peru)*, above n 140, 5–6; *Hilaire, Constantine, Benjamin v Trinidad and Tobago* (IACHR, Judgment of 21 June 2002), Ser C (No 94), paras 196–200; *Chunimá (Guatemala)* (IACHR Order of 15 July 1991), 6; see also Buergenthal, 'Interim Measures', above n 36, 84–8; Pasqualucci, *Practice and Procedure*, above n 61, 316–18.

227 *James* et al *v Trinidad and Tobago*, above n 138, 5.

228 *Piandiong v The Philippines*, Communication No 869/1999 (15 June 1999), UN Doc CCPR/C/70/D/869/1999 paras 5.1–5.4 (UN Human Rights Committee, 2000).

229 *TPS v Canada*, Communication No 99/1997 (19 September 1997), UN Doc CAT/C/24/D/99/1997 para 15.6 (UN Committee against Torture, 2000); *Cecilia Rosana Núñez Chipana (Venezuela)*, Communication No 110/1998, UN Doc CAT/C/21/D/110/1998 para 8 (UN Committee against Torture, 1998).

230 ICSID Convention, above n 1, art 47; Schreuer, above n 35, 757–8.

231 Schreuer, ibid, 761–2; Friedland, above n 23, 337; Lalive, above n 133, 137; ICSID Arbitration Rules, above n 35, Rule 39, Note B; *AGIP v Congo*, above n 24, 317–18 (1979); *MINE v Guinea*, 4 ICSID Rep 61, 77 (1988).

232 *Maffezini v Spain* (Provisional Measures), 5 ICSID Rep 393, 394 (1999).

It is suggested that this decision is incorrect. Regardless of the application of the principle of effectiveness or the adoption of an evolutive approach to treaty interpretation, the term 'recommend' should be properly understood as denoting a decision which is exhortatory rather than mandatory. Nevertheless, this decision has since been approved by two ICSID tribunals: first, the tribunal in *Victor Pey Casado*, which made extensive reference to the reasoning of the ICJ in *LaGrand* on this issue,[233] and second, the ICSID tribunal in *Tokios Tokeles*; this tribunal confirmed, as a 'well-established principle laid down by the jurisprudence of ICSID tribunals', that provisional measures 'recommended' under the ICSID Convention are binding.[234] These decisions thus represent a dramatic example of how common features in the practice of international courts with respect to a procedural issue can do more than merely fill a gap or influence the interpretation of an ambiguous provision. Rather, a common practice with respect to a question of procedure can even prevail over a clearly expressed provision in a constitutive instrument, such as that in article 47 of the ICSID Convention.

D. Power to Grant Provisional Measures *Ultra Petita* or *Proprio Motu*

The scope of the power to grant provisional measures is another aspect of the examination of common features in the exercise of the power. International courts generally consider themselves empowered to grant provisional measures *ultra petita*, or measures other than those which are requested, and have included such provisions in their rules of procedure.[235] Even if an international court does not have such a provision in its rules of procedure, it is suggested that all international courts have an inherent power to grant provisional measures *ultra petita*.[236] There are two justifications for this. Firstly, while the *ne ultra petita* rule restricts international courts to considering issues put forward by the parties in dispute, it does not restrict the manner in which international courts resolve those issues in dispute. An international court has 'the freedom to select the ground upon which it will base its judgment'.[237] Secondly, international courts are deemed to know the law (*jura novit curia*) and are not limited to the arguments put forward by the parties.[238]

233 *Victor Pey Casado*, above n 134, 578.

234 *Tokios Tokeles v Ukraine*, above n 102, (Procedural Order No 1 of 1 July 2003), para 4; (Procedural Order No 3 of 18 January 2005), paras 6–7, fn 12. See, however, *Biwater Gauff*, above n 24, where the ICSID Tribunal did not discuss the binding nature of its provisional measures, but expressed them as being 'recommended': (Procedural Order No 1 of 31 March 2006), paras 88, 98, and (Procedural Order No 3 of 29 September 2006), para 163, all available at <http://ita.law.uvic.ca> (last visited 25 November 2006).

235 ICJ Rules, above n 1, art 75(2); ITLOS Rules, art 89(5); ECHR Rules, above n 2, Rule 39(1); IACHR Rules, above n 1, art 25(1); see also ICSID Arbitration Rules, above n 35, Rule 39(3).

236 *Victor Pey Casado*, above n 134, 576.

237 *Convention Governing the Guardianship of Infants* [1958] ICJ Rep 55, 62.

238 Cheng, above n 46, 299–301.

Finally, there is substantial practice of international courts granting provisional measures other than those requested. Parties often present their requests in very detailed terms, and international courts often only grant interim relief in part.[239]

A separate question is whether international courts can grant provisional measures of their own motion, without there being any request at all (*proprio motu*). As with the power to grant provisional measures *ultra petita*, the rules of procedure of many international courts expressly confer this power.[240] As the exercise of this power is connected with the function of the international court in safeguarding its jurisdiction or ensuring that any judgment which it gives on the merits would be effective, it is suggested that all international courts can exercise this power *proprio motu*, unless to do so would be inconsistent with their constitutive instruments.

Conclusion

This chapter has reviewed the practice of international courts concerning the granting of provisional measures. It has suggested that international courts possess this power as an express power or one which can be implied from the text of the constitutive instrument, or as an inherent power, in the absence of agreement to the contrary. Importantly, international courts have made extensive reference to the jurisprudence of other international tribunals in exercising their powers over provisional measures. This has led to substantial common features in the granting of such measures; this even relates to issues which appear to be regulated by the express terms of constitutive instruments, such as the question concerning the binding nature of provisional measures under the ICSID Convention. The next chapter turns to a consideration of the level of commonality in the exercise by international courts of two post-adjudicatory powers; the power to interpret and the power to revise judgments.

239 Rosenne, *Provisional Measures*, above n 11, 175–7; Sztucki, above n 26, 158–60; see, e.g., *MOX Plant* (Procedural Order No 3), above n 159, 1195.

240 ICJ Rules, above n 1, art 75(1); ECHR Rules, above n 2, Rule 39(1); IACHR Rules, above n 1, art 25(1); I-ACommHR Rules, above n 4, art 25(1); see also ICSID Arbitration Rules, above n 35, Rule 39(3).

5

Power of International Courts to Interpret and Revise Judgments and Awards

Introduction

All international courts have certain functions, including the settlement of international disputes by adjudication and the proper administration of international justice. The decisions of international courts are final and binding on the parties to the dispute—that is, they have the force of *res judicata*, or *la chose jugée*—and only rarely is there the possibility of any recourse against the decision. Yet the rendering of a judgment might not be enough to settle the dispute, and some post-adjudication involvement might be necessary. One of the parties might allege, for instance, that the tribunal erred in law, that the tribunal was misled by fraudulent evidence, or that the international court was not properly constituted. To resolve these problems, post-adjudication procedures have been developed. This chapter examines two of these powers in detail: namely, the powers of international courts to interpret and to revise their judgments and awards, and it considers whether there is an emerging common law relating to the exercise of these powers.

I. Post-Adjudication Role of International Courts and Tribunals

A. Finality of Adjudication

There is a well-established principle in many domestic legal systems that where a final decision has been rendered by a court having jurisdiction over the parties and the subject-matter of the dispute, the parties may not dispute that decision—except on appeal—in subsequent litigation.[1] This principle is often expressed in the form of the rule of *res judicata*.[2] There are essentially two justifications for this rule. First, there is a public interest in the finality of litigation. It is not in the interests of the administration of justice for a matter to have been decided by one competent tribunal, only for that same matter to be re-litigated before the same, or even before another, tribunal. If it were otherwise, this would place an enormous burden on frequently overstretched judicial resources. Second, litigants have a right to be protected from a 'vexatious multiplication' of litigation, whether that be in the form of repeated identical civil claims, or multiple criminal prosecutions for the same alleged offence.[3]

[1] Yuval Shany, *The Competing Jurisdictions of International Courts and Tribunals* (2003) 164; Peter Barnett, Res Judicata, *Estoppel, and Foreign Judgments* (2001) 8; George Spencer Bower, AK Turner and KR Handley, *The Doctrine of* Res Judicata (1996) 9–10; Peter Herzog and Delmar Karlen, 'Attacks on Judicial Decisions', in International Association of Legal Science, *International Encyclopedia of Comparative Law* (1982) vol XVI, ch 8, 9–10.

[2] Barnett, ibid, 8; M Howard, *Phipson on Evidence* (15th ed, 2000) 988–9; Colin Tapper, *Cross & Tapper on Evidence* (9th ed, 1999) 80–2; Spencer Bower, Turner and Handley, ibid, 4.

[3] Barnett, ibid, 9; Spencer Bower, Turner and Handley, ibid, 10. These justifications are encapsulated in the Latin maxims, *interest reipublicae ut sit finis litium*, and *nemo debet bis vexari pro una et eadem causa*: Howard, ibid, 988–9.

As is the case with domestic courts, judgments of international courts are considered to be final and binding. This is expressly stated in the constitutive instruments of many international courts and tribunals.[4] In the WTO dispute settlement system, the principle of finality and the obligation on states parties to comply with the recommendations or determinations of a WTO panel or the Appellate Body are less clear;[5] nevertheless, the many separate clauses in the DSU imply the binding nature of reports adopted by the DSB.[6] Like final and binding decisions of domestic courts, such decisions of international courts have the effect of *res judicata*.[7] Various formulations of this rule have been proposed. In *Company General of the Orinoco*, the French-Venezuelan MCC held that:

> The general principle announced in numerous cases is that a right, question or fact *distinctly put in issue and directly determined* by a court of competent jurisdiction as a ground of recovery, cannot be disputed, etc.[8]

A somewhat wider formulation was put by the PCA tribunal in *Pious Fund of the Californias*:

> [A]ll parts of the judgment or the decree concerning the points debated in the litigation enlighten and mutually supplement each other, and . . . they all serve to render precise the meaning and the bearing of the *dispositif* (decisory part of the judgment) and to determine the points upon which there is *res judicata* and which thereafter cannot be put in question.[9]

The narrower test suggested by the French-Venezuelan MCC, which restricts the operation of *res judicata* to points directly determined in the judgment or award,

[4] See, e.g., *Statute of the International Court of Justice*, opened for signature 26 June 1945, 3 Bevans 1153 (entered into force 24 October 1945), arts 59–60; International Court of Justice Rules of Court, available at <http://www.icj-cij,org>, art 94; *United Nations Convention on the Law of the Sea*, 1833 UNTS 3, Annex VI ('ITLOS Statute'), art 33(1) and (2); *Convention for the Pacific Settlement of International Disputes*, opened for signature 29 July 1899, 1 Bevans 230 (entered into force 4 September 1900) ('1899 Convention'), arts 54 and 56; *Convention for the Pacific Settlement of International Disputes*, opened for signature 18 October 1907, 1 Bevans 577 (entered into force 26 January 1910) ('1907 Convention'), arts 81 and 84; *Convention for the Settlement of Investment Disputes between States and Nationals of Other States*, opened for signature 18 March 1965, 575 UNTS 159 (entered into force 14 October 1966) ('ICSID Convention'), art 53(1); *Convention for the Protection of Human Rights and Fundamental Freedoms*, opened for signature 4 November 1950, 213 UNTS 221 (entered into force 3 September 1953) ('European HR Convention'), arts 44 and 46; *American Convention on Human Rights*, opened for signature 22 November 1969, 1144 UNTS 123 (entered into force 18 July 1978) ('American Convention'), art 67.

[5] John Jackson, *The World Trading System* (2nd ed, 1997) 126.

[6] Ibid; Shany, above n 1, 253, fn 114; *Understanding on Rules and Procedures Governing the Settlement of Disputes*, opened for signature 15 April 1994, 1869 UNTS 101, 33 ILM 1226 (entered into force 1 January 1995) ('DSU').

[7] See, e.g., International Law Association ('ILA'), 'Interim Report: "Res Judicata" and Arbitration' (Berlin Conference, 2004) 19–24; Bin Cheng, *General Principles of Law as Applied by International Courts and Tribunals* (first published 1953, 1987 ed) 336–50; Michael Reisman, *Nullity and Revision* (1971) 14.

[8] 10 RIAA 184, 276 (French-Venezuelan MCC, 1905); Vaughan Lowe, '*Res Judicata* and the Rule of Law in International Arbitration' (1996) 8 *African Journal of International and Comparative Law* 38, 39.

[9] *Hague Court Reports* (1916) 1, 5; 9 RIAA 11, 12–13 (US–Mexico, 1902); Lowe, ibid, 39.

has been more widely adopted by international tribunals.[10] It is generally accepted, as suggested in the dissenting opinion of Judge Anzilotti in *Factory at Chorzów (Interpretation)*, that there are three conditions for the application of *res judicata*; these are identity of parties, identity of cause, and identity of object, or subject matter, in the proceedings.[11] As the arbitral tribunal in *Trail Smelter* held: 'There is no doubt that in the present case, there is *res judicata*. The three traditional elements for identification: parties, object, and cause are the same.'[12] The *res judicata* effect of judgments has been confirmed in the decisions of many different international courts.[13]

Res judicata can be characterized as a general principle of law;[14] it was even one of the examples cited by Lord Phillimore of the Advisory Committee of Jurists to describe the possible content of the provision in article 38(3) of the PCIJ Statute referring to the PCIJ's power to resort to 'general principles of law' as a source of international law.[15] It has also been suggested that *res judicata* can be regarded as a

[10] *SS Newchwang*, 6 RIAA 64, 65 (GB–US, 1921); *Polish Postal Service in Danzig*, Ser B, (No 11), 30 (PCIJ, 1925); *Factory at Chorzów (Interpretation)*, Ser A, (No 13), 20 (PCIJ, 1927); *Amco v Indonesia* (Resubmitted Case), 1 ICSID Rep 543, 549–50 (1988); *Waste Management v Mexico (No 2)* (2002) 41 ILM 1315, 1322–3 (NAFTA); Lowe, ibid, 39.

[11] *Factory at Chorzów (Interpretation)*, ibid, 23, 24, 27 (Diss Op Anzilotti) (PCIJ, 1927); Lowe, ibid, 40–7. See also ILA, above n 7, 21, where four preconditions are listed, the additional criterion being that the previous proceedings must have been conducted before a court or tribunal in the international legal order. However, it is suggested that the judgment of a domestic court will only rarely have *res judicata* effect before an international court due to the parties having different identity: Ian Brownlie, *Principles of Public International Law* (6th ed, 2003) 50.

[12] 3 RIAA 1938, 1952 (US–Canada, 1941) (references omitted).

[13] See, e.g., *Pious Fund of the Californias*, above n 9, 12–13; *Factory at Chorzów (Interpretation)*, above n 10, 20; see especially 23, 24, 27 (Diss Op Anzilotti); *Fabiani*, 10 RIAA 83, 109–10, 136–9 (French-Venezuelan CC, 1903); *Company General of the Orinoco*, above n 8, 276–80; *Land and Maritime Boundary between Cameroon and Nigeria (Interpretation)* (ICJ Judgment of 25 March 1999), para 12; *Continental Shelf (Revision and Interpretation)* [1985] ICJ Rep 192, 218–19; *Effect of Awards of Compensation of the UN Administrative Tribunal* [1954] ICJ Rep 47, 53; *Reynier v Commission* [1964] ECR 259, 266; *Amco v Indonesia* (Resubmitted Case), above n 10, 549–50; *CME Czech Republic BV v Czech Republic* (Final Award of 14 March 2003), para 435; see further August Reinisch, 'The Use and Limits of *Res Judicata* and *Lis Pendens* as Procedural Tools to Avoid Conflicting Dispute Settlement Outcomes' (2004) 3 *Law and Practice of International Courts and Tribunals* 37; Shany, above n 1, 248–53; Cheng, above n 7, 348–9. For a possible exception, see also *Argentina—Poultry*, WT/DS241/R (PR), paras 7.28–7.41 where a WTO panel rejected an argument by a third party intervening (Paraguay) that the decision of a Mercosur tribunal in a dispute between Argentina and Brazil was *res judicata*.

[14] For example, Shany, above n 1, 245–6; John Collier and Vaughan Lowe, *The Settlement of Disputes in International Law: Institutions and Procedures* (1999) 261; D W Bowett, '*Res Judicata* and the Limits of Rectification of Decisions by International Tribunals' (1996) 8 *African Journal of International and Comparative Law* 577, 577–9; Lowe, above n 8, 38–41; Herman Mosler, 'General Principles of Law' in Rudolf Bernhardt (ed), *Encyclopedia of Public International Law* (1995) vol II, 511, 522; Cheng, above n 7, 336; Georg Schwarzenberger, *International Law as Applied by International Courts and Tribunals* (1986) vol IV, 660–1; J L Simpson and Hazel Fox, *International Arbitration* (1959) 228–36. *Statute of the Permanent Court of International Justice*, PCIJ Publications, Ser D (No 1), 7 ('PCIJ Statute').

[15] PCIJ/Advisory Committee of Jurists, *Procès-Verbaux of the Proceedings of the Committee of Jurists* (1920) 335.

rule of customary international law.[16] For present purposes, it is not necessary to assess the strength of this claim; it is apparent that *res judicata* is a rule of international law, be it a general principle of law or a rule of customary international law.

B. Limits to the Principle of Finality

The rule concerning finality of litigation is, however, not absolute in domestic legal systems or in international adjudication.[17] Courts, like other human institutions, can make mistakes, and it is generally in the interests of international justice for the party aggrieved by an erroneous decision to have the means of correcting it.[18] Otherwise, the finality of proceedings might lead to 'perpetuating judicial errors' and may in fact hinder the proper administration of justice.[19] Early writers such as Pufendorf and Vattel also recognized the need for exceptions to the finality of litigation.[20] Accordingly, in most developed legal systems, procedures have evolved for challenging judicial decisions.[21] These procedures include 'appeal', which allows parties to bring a decision from a lower court, which the party believes has erred in law, before a higher court, which has the power to decide not only that the lower court has erred, but also to replace the lower court's decision with its own;[22] 'cassation', which refers to the procedure commonplace in civilian legal systems whereby a decision can be referred to a superior court, which then has the power to either let the decision stand, or *casser* (cancel, or void) the decision, and remand it to a lower court for a decision on the merits;[23] 'rehearing *de novo*', in which proceedings are completely recommenced in the original tribunal or a newly constituted tribunal, and none of the findings on fact or law from the first trial are relevant or binding on the second proceedings;[24] 'rectification', which involves the original tribunal correcting any clerical or arithmetical errors;[25] 'interpretation', in which the original tribunal clarifies obscurities in the judgment;[26] and 'revision', which involves a reopening of the case for the purpose of considering any newly discovered evidence which, had it been known to the court at the time of judgment, would have had a decisive effect on the award or

16 Shany, above n 1, 245.

17 Georges Scelle, 'Arbitral Procedure' [1950] *YbILC*, vol II, 114, 142, UN Doc A/CN.4/18.

18 Herzog and Karlen, above n 1, 4.

19 Shany, above n 1, 164.

20 For example, Samuel von Pufendorf, *De modo litigandi in libertate naturali*, (W Evans Darby trans), in W Evans Darby, *International Tribunals* (1899) 56, 60–1; Emmerich de Vattel, 'The Law of Nations or the Principles of Natural Justice' in James Brown Scott (ed), *Classics of International Law* (1916) 224–5.

21 Herzog and Karlen, above n 1, 69.

22 Ibid, 58–60.

23 Ibid, 63–4.

24 Ibid, 28–9.

25 Edward Tuttle (ed), *A Treatise on the Law of Judgments by A C Freeman* (5th ed, 1925) 281–303; in the context of international courts, see also Alan Redfern and Martin Hunter, *Law and Practice of International Commercial Arbitration* (3rd ed, 1999) 420; Stewart Baker and Mark Davis, *The UNCITRAL Arbitration Rules in Practice* (1992) 194–6; Reisman, above n 7, 186–92; Simpson and Fox, above n 14, 241–2.

26 Tuttle, ibid, 303–4; in the context of international courts, see also Baker and Davis, ibid, 192–4; Reisman, ibid, 192–208; Simpson and Fox, ibid, 245–7.

judgment.[27] Other post-adjudication procedures, which appear to be less commonly found in domestic legal systems, include requests for a 'supplementary' or 'additional' award, in which the tribunal is asked to decide any issues which were presented in the proceedings but which were omitted from the award;[28] and the 'annulment' or 'nullification' of an arbitral award, which generally involves a challenge to the award before a different tribunal.[29] There is some disagreement about the proper terminological classification of many of these post-adjudication proceedings.[30] Professor Reisman has commented that the powers of rectification, interpretation and revision 'share a startling number of procedural and material similarities'.[31] In addition, the term 'revision' is not understood uniformly in municipal legal systems; the terms 'revision', 'rehearing', 'cassation' and 'appeal' are sometimes used interchangeably, although they refer to quite different procedures.[32]

Some of these post-adjudication procedures have also been developed before international courts.[33] The question of whether international courts adopt a common approach to the exercise of all of these powers merits examination, but this task is beyond the scope of the present chapter.[34] Rather, this chapter considers two post-adjudication powers of international courts, being the powers of interpretation and revision, and examines whether these are applied consistently by international courts.

The purpose of the powers of interpretation and revision is to resolve disputes that arise after the rendering of the judgment by an international court. In the case of the power of interpretation, one or both parties to a judgment may consider the

[27] Herzog and Karlen, above n 1, 19–25; in the context of international courts, see also Reisman, ibid, 208–12; Simpson and Fox, ibid, 242–5; J C Witenberg, 'La théorie des preuves devant les juridictions internationales' (1936) 56 *Recueil des cours* 53, 71–8.

[28] For example PCA Optional Rules for Arbitrating Disputes between Two States, art 37; ICSID Convention, above n 4, art 49(2); UNCITRAL Arbitration Rules, art 37; Institut de Droit International, 'Projet de règlement pour la procédure arbitrale internationale' (1877) 1 *Annuaire de l'Institut de Droit International* 126, art 24.

[29] For example, Collier and Lowe, above n 14, 257; Reisman, above n 7, 265–634; Simpson and Fox, above n 14, 250–9; A Balasko, *Causes de nullité de la sentence arbitrale en droit international public* (1938); Witenberg, above n 27, 367–71.

[30] For example, J G Wetter, *The International Arbitral Process: Public and Private* (1979) vol II, 539.

[31] Reisman, above n 7, 188–9, 196; see, e.g., *Dewhurst v German Government*, 4 TAM 1 (Anglo-German MAT, 1924), which Reisman contends might have been considered as an application for the exercise of all three powers.

[32] Wetter, above n 30, vol II, 539; Durward Sandifer, *Evidence before International Tribunals* (2nd ed, 1975) 404, 407–8, 446–7; Reisman, above n 7, 212, 217–20; Simpson and Fox, above n 14, 242; Georges Scelle, 'Draft on Arbitral Procedure Adopted by the Commission at its Fifth Session, Report by Georges Scelle, Special Rapporteur' [1958] *YbILC*, vol II, 1, 12, UN Doc A/CN.4/113; ILC 'Memorandum Prepared by the Secretariat' [1950] *YbILC*, vol II, 157, UN Doc A/CN. 4/35, 177.

[33] For the history of these procedures, see Santiago Torres Bernárdez, 'A propos de l'interprétation et de la revision des arrêts de la Cour internationale de justice' in *Le Droit International à l'Heure de sa Codification: Etudes en l'honneur de Roberto Ago* (1987) vol III, 443, 444; Reisman, above n 7, 3–74.

[34] For in-depth studies, see Reisman, above n 7; Balasko, above n 29.

judgment obscure or contradictory in its reasons and operative provisions.[35] Such obscurities and inconsistencies might otherwise act as a bar to its execution, and the existence of the power of interpretation permits parties to seek clarification of the judgment in order to avoid the continuation of the dispute.[36] The purpose of an application for revision is to alter a judgment or award to take account of a decisive new fact which was unknown to the party and the court at the time of the judgment. Having discussed the limits to the principle of *res judicata* and the purpose of the powers of interpretation and revision, this chapter now turns to an examination of the source of those powers.

II. Source of the Powers of Interpretation and Revision

A. Constitutive Instruments of International Courts

1. Power of Interpretation

An express power to interpret awards or judgments is commonly conferred on international courts. The 1899 Convention did not provide for a general power of interpretation, but the power was included in article 82 of the 1907 Convention.[37] Under this provision, tribunals have the express power to interpret their awards, unless the parties agree otherwise.[38] Another early international court which was granted the power to interpret its judgments was the Central American Court of Justice.[39] The PCIJ was also conferred the power to interpret its judgments in article 60 of the PCIJ Statute.[40] The ICJ has retained this power in article 60 of the ICJ Statute, which provides in part that '[i]n the event of dispute as to the meaning or scope of the judgment, the Court shall construe it upon the request of any party'.[41]

Other international tribunals having an express power to interpret their judgments include the ITLOS, whose power was modelled on article 60 of the ICJ Statute,[42] UNCLOS tribunals,[43] ICSID tribunals,[44] the IACHR,[45] the Iran–US

[35] Schwarzenberger, above n 14, 680.

[36] Torres Bernárdez, above n 33, 445; Louis Cavaré, 'Les recours en interprétation et en appréciation de la légalité devant les tribunaux internationaux' (1953–4) 15 *ZaöRV* 482, 497–8; Witenberg, above n 27, 362.

[37] 1907 Convention, above n 4, art 82.

[38] See also Baron Schenk von Stauffenberg, *Le statut et règlement de la Cour Permanente De Justice Internationale* (1934) 424.

[39] *Convention for the Establishment of the Central American Court of Justice*, [1907] 2 *US Foreign Relations* 697, art 24; von Stauffenberg, ibid, 424.

[40] For the drafting history, see PCIJ/Advisory Committee of Jurists, above n 15, 744–5; Andreas Zimmermann and Tobias Thienel, 'Article 60', in Andreas Zimmermann, Christian Tomuschat, and Karin Oellers-Frahm (eds), *The Statute of the International Court of Justice: A Commentary* (2006) 1275, 1280–2; and Torres Bernardez, above n 33, 451.

[41] ICJ Statute, above n 4, art 60.

[42] ITLOS Statute, above n 4, art 33(3); Myron Nordquist (ed), *United Nations Convention on the Law of the Sea 1982: A Commentary* (1989) vol V, 396–7.

[43] *United Nations Convention on the Law of the Sea*, opened for signature 10 December 1982, 21 ILM 1261 (entered into force 16 November 1994) Annex VII, art 12; Nordquist (ed), ibid, vol V, 435–6.

[44] ICSID Convention, above n 4, art 50(1); Christoph Schreuer, *The ICSID Convention: A Commentary* (2001) 857.

[45] American Convention, above n 4, art 67.

Claims Tribunal,[46] and the ECJ.[47] Unlike these international courts, WTO panels and the Appellate Body do not have an express power under the DSU to interpret their reports.

2. *Power of Revision*

As for the power of revision, its history can be traced back at least to the late nineteenth century.[48] During the drafting of the 1899 Convention, the inclusion of the power of revision proved controversial, as the desire for finality in international arbitration was a significant factor for many delegates.[49] As a compromise, article 55 was included, which empowered arbitral tribunals to revise their awards, but only if the parties to the dispute reserved this power to the tribunal in the *compromis*. This provision was retained as article 83 of the 1907 Convention. In 1920, the power to revise judgments was specifically provided for in article 61 of the PCIJ Statute. The report of the Advisory Committee of Jurists reveals that the power of revision was considered an important power:

> Le droit de révision est un droit très grave, qui heurte, avec l'autorité des sentences rendues, ce qui, pour la paix des nations, doit être considerée comme acquis, mais la justice a cependant ses légitimes revendications. Tout bien pesé, le Comité a estimé que la révision devait être de droit.[50]

[46] Iran–US Claims Tribunal Rules of Procedure, 1 Ir–USCTR 57, art 30.

[47] *Protocol on the Statute of the Court of Justice, Consolidated Version of the Treaty estabilishing the European Economic Community*, OJ C 325/33, 167 (24 December 2002) ('ECJ Statute'), art 37; Daniel Bethlehem, 'Interpretation of Judgments' in Richard Plender (ed), *European Courts: Practice and Precedents* (1997) 743; Louis Cavaré, 'Quelques remarques sur les recours en interprétation des arrêts rendus par les Cours de justice internationales à propos de l'arrêt No 5–55 du 28 juin 1955 de la Cour de justice de la CECA' in *Hommage d'une génération de juristes au Président Basdevant* (1960) 96.

[48] For the suggestion that there were precedents of revision in ancient arbitration, see Robin Geiss, 'Revision Proceedings before the International Court of Justice' (2003) 63 *ZaöRV* 167, 167, fn 4. For Professor Corsi's *Projet de règlement pour les arbitrages internationaux* for the ILA, which included a power of revision, see A Corsi, 'Projet de règlement pour les arbitrages internationaux' (1896) 3 *Revue Générale de Droit International Public* 460, 465; W Evans Darby, *International Tribunals: A Collection of the Various Schemes Which Have Been Propounded; and of Instances Since 1815* (1900) 318–21; Balasko, above n 29, 14. For an early precedent, see *Traité d'Arbitrage général et permanent*, signed 23 July 1898 (Italy–Argentina), (1898) 5 *Revue Générale de Droit International Public* 868, art 13; and *General Treaty of Arbitration*, signed 18 September 1907 (Italy–Argentina), *Traités Généraux d'Arbitrage communiqués au Bureau International de la Cour Permanente d'Arbitrage* (2e Série, 1914), art 6 (entered into force 21 March 1910).

[49] For the debate between Mr Holls, the American delegate, and Dr Martens of Russia, see *Conférence internationale de la paix*, 4e partie, 3e commission, 5e séance, (1899) 36ff; Wetter, above n 30, vol II, 543–52; Geiss, above n 48, 171; Daniel Bardonnet, 'De l'équivoque des categories juridiques: la revision des sentences arbitrales pour "erreur de fait" ou "fait nouveau" dans la pratique latino-américaine', in *Liber Amicorum in Memoriam of Judge José María Ruda* (2000) 189, 193–4; Reisman, above n 7, 34–43; Scelle, 'Draft on Arbitral Procedure', above n 32, 12; Scelle, 'Arbitral Procedure', above n 17, 143; von Stauffenberg, above n 38, 431.

[50] PCIJ/Advisory Committee of Jurists, above n 15, 744; see also Torres Bernárdez, above n 33, 453; von Stauffenberg, ibid, 431–3. Another early precedent can be found in the *Convention for the Establishment of a Central American Court* of 1923: Louis Le Fur and Georges Chklaver, *Recueil de textes de Droit International Public* (1928) 626, art 1(4); Bardonnet, above n 49, 197; although this court was never established: Manley Hudson, *International Tribunals: Past and Future* (1944) 173.

The provision conferring the power of revision on the PCIJ was retained in 1945 in the ICJ Statute. In addition, several other international courts also have an express power to revise their judgments and awards under the terms of their constitutive instruments. These include the ECJ,[51] ICSID tribunals,[52] the ICTR,[53] the ICTY,[54] the International Criminal Court,[55] and the Cartagena Court of Justice.[56] The Pact of Bogotá of 1948 also provides for the power of revision.[57] Yet not all international courts are expressly granted the power of revision. As with the power of interpretation, for instance, WTO panels and the Appellate Body do not have an express power.

B. Rules of Procedure of International Courts

1. Power of Interpretation

Most of the post-First World War MATs included a power of interpretation in their rules of procedure,[58] as did the Mexican MCCs of the 1920s.[59] The ECHR is another international court which has included the power to interpret judgments in its rules of procedure.[60] This power was first invoked in *Ringeisen (Interpretation)* in 1972.[61] In this case, the ECHR held that article 52 of the Convention, which provides that 'the judgment of the Court shall be final' was solely aimed at preventing the ECHR's judgments from being subject to any appeal to another authority. The ECHR observed that in considering a request for interpretation, it was exercising 'inherent jurisdiction'.[62]

[51] ECJ Statute, above n 47, art 41; *Protocol of the Statute of Justice of the European Atomic Energy Community, Treaty establishing the European Atomic Energy Community*, signed 25 March 1957, 298 UNTS 167, art 42 (entered into force 1 January 1958); *Protocol of the Statute of Justice of the European Coal and Steel Community, Treaty establishing the European Coal and Steel Community*, opened for signature 18 April 1951, 26 UNTS 140, art 38 (entered into force 25 July 1952).

[52] ICSID Convention, above n 4, art 51(1).

[53] *International Tribunal for the Prosecution of Persons Responsible for Genocide in Rwanda*, adopted by SC Res 955 (1994), UN Doc S/RES/955 (1994) ('ICTR Statute'), art 25; Andrea Carcano, 'Requests for Review in the Practice of the International Criminal Tribunals for the Former Yugoslavia and Rwanda' (2004) 17 *Leiden Journal of International Law* 103, 103–4.

[54] *International Tribunal for the Prosecution of Persons Responsible for Serious Violations of International Humanitarian Law in Yugoslavia*, adopted by SC Res 827 (1993), UN Doc S/RES/827 (1993) ('ICTY Statute'), art 26; Carcano, ibid, 103–4.

[55] *Rome Statute of the International Criminal Court*, opened for signature 17 July 1998, 2187 UNTS 90 (entered into force 1 July 2002), art 84; Carcano, ibid, 110.

[56] See Decision 184 of the Commission of the Cartagena Agreement of 19 August 1983 concerning the Statute of the Court of Justice, cited in Bardonnet, above n 49, 198.

[57] Opened for signature 30 April 1948, 30 UNTS 55, art 48 (entered into force 6 May 1949).

[58] See, e.g., Franco-German MAT Rules of Procedure, 1 TAM 44, art 78.

[59] See, e.g., Rules of Procedure of the US–Mexican GCC, art XI(6), in A H Feller, *The Mexican Claims Commissions: 1923–34* (1935) 351.

[60] European Court of Human Rights, Rules of Court, Rule 79.

[61] *Ringeisen v Austria*, Ser A, (No 16), (ECHR, 1973).

[62] Ibid; see also 10 (Sep Op Verdross), 12 (Sep Op Zeika); approved in *Allenet de Ribemont v France*, ECHR Rep 1996–III, 903, 910; see also 912 (Sep Op Pettiti).

The rules of procedure of other international courts also provide for a power of interpretation. Some of these rules of procedure were prepared or selected by the states parties to the constitutive instrument, such as those of the Iran-US Claims Tribunal.[63] In addition, PCA tribunals operating under the Optional Rules of 1992 have the power to give an interpretation of their awards,[64] although those constituted under the 1907 Convention have the power by virtue of article 82 of that convention.

2. *Power of Revision*

The inclusion of the power of revision in rules of procedure of international tribunals can also be traced back to many of the MATs.[65] In addition, the Arbitral Commission and the Mixed Commission for the Agreement on German External Debts included the power in its Rules of Procedure,[66] as did the Arbitral Commission on Property, Rights and Interests in Germany.[67] The ECHR has also granted itself the power to revise its judgments in its Rules of Court',[68] as has the ITLOS;[69] Judge Eiriksson of the ITLOS has observed extrajudicially that the ITLOS regarded the power of revision as 'implicit in its judicial function',[70] and that 'this view was apparently shared by representatives in the Preparatory Commission', referring to the inclusion of the power in the draft rules prepared by that body.[71]

III. Powers of Interpretation and Revision as Inherent Powers

A. Possible Objections to the Powers as Inherent Powers

The fact that not all international courts have the express power to interpret or revise their judgments raises the question as to whether these bodies nonetheless have an inherent power to do so. Three chief objections may be made to the suggestion that these post-adjudication powers are inherent powers, which will now be examined.

The first objection is that the exercise of these powers possibly contravenes the principle of *res judicata* and the rule of finality. This, however, can be rejected. It is incorrect to say that the power of interpretation violates the principle of finality or

63 Ir–USCT Rules, above n 46, art 35.

64 PCA Optional Rules, above n 28, art 35(1).

65 See, e.g., Rules of Procedure of the Franco-German MAT, above n 58, arts 79–82.

66 Arbitral Tribunal and the Mixed Commission for the Agreement on German External Debts Rules of Procedure, art 48(a), (1958) 19 *ZaöRV* 728, also reprinted in Karin Oellers-Frahm and Norbert Wühler, *Dispute Settlement in Public International Law* (1984) 772, 779–80.

67 Arbitral Commission on Property, Rights and Interests in Germany Rules, Rule 68 [1957] *Bundesgesetzblatt*, vol II, 230, 249–50.

68 ECHR Rules, Rule 80.

69 ITLOS Rules of the Tribunal, art 179.

70 Gudmundur Eiriksson, *The International Tribunal for the Law of the Sea* (2000) 275.

71 Ibid.

res judicata, for this position misconceives the role of the request for interpretation: it is not a method of attacking a judgment, but a way of confirming it.[72] The power of interpretation can only be exercised to explain obscurities in a judgment, and not to replace it with a new judgment. In the case of the power of revision, this objection has more validity, as the power of revision does some violence to the principle of *res judicata*.[73] This might lead some international tribunals to be reticent in exercising the power. Nonetheless, both domestic and international judicial bodies exercise many post-adjudication powers, and the risk that the dispute might persist if this power is not available lends weight to its possible status as an inherent power. In this sense, it is suggested that some exceptions to finality are necessary in the interests of justice, as long as there are strict conditions on their use.[74] Indeed, there is much force in the proposition advanced by Mr Holls at the First Hague Peace Conference that 'nothing is settled until it is settled right'.[75] While this phrase might lend itself to subjective results—who, for example, is to decide whether a dispute has been 'settled right'?—it is nonetheless suggested that the rule of *res judicata* should not be permitted to protect a judgment which does not reflect the decision that the international court would have made had it been apprised of all the relevant facts.

The second objection is found in the argument that once an international tribunal has rendered its decision, the powers which were conferred on the arbitrators have expired; that is, the tribunal is *functus officio*.[76] In addition, as a practical matter, ad hoc arbitral tribunals are generally dissolved after the rendering of the decision.[77] Yet it is suggested that this objection is only applicable to ad hoc tribunals which are constituted for an individual dispute, and not to permanent bodies such as the ICJ or the ITLOS, or even semi-permanent bodies such as the Iran-US Claims Tribunal. But even the inability of ad hoc tribunals to interpret or revise an award is questionable. Tribunals can be reconstituted, and requests for interpretation or revision need not necessarily involve further oral proceedings. In effect, whether a tribunal is *functus officio* will depend on its terms of reference. If its terms of reference are to render an award in order to 'settle the dispute', it is suggested that this encompasses considering requests for interpretation or revision of that award. In any event, if the tribunal is unable to be reconstituted, then it might be possible to constitute another tribunal for the purposes of the request.

[72] Scelle, 'Arbitral Procedure', above n 17, 143; J C Witenberg, *L'Organisation Judiciaire: La Procédure et la Sentence Internationales* (1937) 362–3.

[73] Reisman, above n 7, 219–20; Witenberg, *L'Organisation Judiciaire*, ibid, 371–2; see also the unpersuasive view of Scelle, who argues that the power of revision does not affect the authority of *res judicata*: Scelle, 'Draft on Arbitral Procedure', above n 32, 12; Scelle, 'Arbitral Procedure', above n 17, 144; see also Elizabeth Zoller, 'Observations sur la révision et l'interpretation des sentences arbitrales' (1978) 24 *Annuaire Français du Droit International* 327, 345–6.

[74] Herzog and Karlen, above n 1, 4, 19; Zoller, ibid, 351.

[75] This mantra is attributed to Abraham Lincoln: *Conférence internationale de la paix*, above n 49, 36; see also Geiss, above n 48, 171; Scelle, 'Draft on Arbitral Procedure', above n 32, 12; Scelle, 'Arbitral Procedure', above n 17, 143.

[76] For example, Witenberg, *L'Organisation Judiciaire*, above n 72, 361.

[77] Ibid.

The third objection to the existence of inherent powers of interpretation and revision lies in the argument that international courts can only exercise powers expressly conferred on them.[78] This argument has been considered—and rejected—in chapter 2.[79] In the case of post-adjudication powers, however, there is some specific judicial authority for this proposition. This appears to be based on an early arbitral decision, the *Portendick*,[80] and on a dictum of the PCIJ in *Jaworzina Frontier*.[81]

The *Portendick* case concerned a dispute between the UK and France which was submitted to the King of Prussia as arbitrator.[82] The UK requested the King of Prussia to give an official interpretation of his award. He professed to be unable to interpret his award unless an interpretation was requested by both parties, but he nonetheless managed to satisfy the UK request for interpretation by stating how he had understood his terms of reference.[83] Accordingly, while this decision seems to support the proposition that the power to interpret decisions must be given expressly, the outcome actually tends to support the opposite conclusion.[84]

The PCIJ's advisory opinion in *Jaworzina Frontier* did not concern the court's power to interpret its judgments—this being expressly provided for in the PCIJ Statute—but rather, it concerned the finality of a decision of a body known as the Conference of Ambassadors, which had been entrusted with the task of delimiting certain frontiers. The Polish Government was dissatisfied with the location of a frontier, and sought a modification of the Conference's decision. The question whether the delimitation of the frontier was still open came before the PCIJ in the form of a request for an advisory opinion. In order to answer this question, the PCIJ considered that it had to decide whether the Conference had rendered a final and binding decision. It held that it was intended that the decision be final and have immediate effect.[85] Although the Conference was not established as a court or tribunal, the PCIJ considered that it filled a similar function to an adjudicative body. The PCIJ then turned to the issue of whether this decision was still open, and found that it was not, observing that the language of the Conference's decision was 'perfectly clear'.[86] Again likening the duties of the Conference to those of an Arbitrator, the PCIJ held that '[i]n the absence of an express agreement between the parties, the Arbitrator is not competent to interpret, still less to modify his

[78] Pieter Sanders, 'Arbitration' in IALS, *International Encyclopedia of Comparative Law*, above n 1, vol XVI, ch 12, 134; Schwarzenberger, above n 14, vol IV, 681; Simpson and Fox, above n 14, 245; Kenneth Carlston, *Process of International Arbitration* (1946) 241–2; Norman Hill, 'The Interpretation of the Decisions of International Courts' (1934) 22 *Georgetown Law Journal* 535, 535–6; see also Institut de Droit International, above n 28, art 24.

[79] See also Chester Brown, 'The Inherent Powers of International Courts and Tribunals' (2005) 76 *British Yearbook of International Law* 195, 210–11.

[80] Lapradelle and Politis, vol I, 512 (UK–France, 1843).

[81] Ser B, (No 8) (PCIJ, 1923).

[82] Above n 80.

[83] Ibid, 530–1.

[84] See also Reisman, above n 7, 193; Witenberg, *L'Organisation Judiciaire*, above n 72, 365.

[85] Above n 81, 29.

[86] Ibid, 36.

award by revising it'.[87] This statement has been referred to as denying international courts an inherent power of interpretation and revision.[88]

However, it is important not to read too much into this dictum,[89] for immediately after determining that the decision was no longer open, the PCIJ noted that the body entrusted with the task of implementing the decision, the Delimitation Commission, had 'a considerable amount of discretion' in fixing the boundary,[90] suggesting that the decision of the Conference of Ambassadors was in fact subject to some changes. In addition, support for the proposition that a restrictive view should be taken of the dictum of the PCIJ in *Jaworzina Frontier* can be found in the PCIJ's very next advisory opinion, *Monastery at Saint-Naoum*.

In this case, the PCIJ was asked to decide whether another decision of the Conference of Ambassadors, concerning the location of a monastery, was final.[91] The decision of the Conference was criticised, *inter alia*, on the grounds that 'it was based on erroneous information or adopted without regard to certain essential facts'.[92] The PCIJ held, however, that it was not called upon 'to give an opinion on the question whether such decisions can—except when an express reservation to that effect has been made—be revised in the event of the existence of an essential error being provided, or of new facts being relied on'.[93] The PCIJ went on to state that even if a power of revision could be implied, the necessary conditions were not present in *Monastery at Saint-Naoum*. The PCIJ then detailed the conditions which would need to be satisfied. These included whether:

> there existed new facts or facts unknown at the time when the decision was taken; in other words, as alleged by the Serbo-Croat-Slovene State and Greece, the Conference of Ambassadors allocated the Monastery to Albania simply because it was unacquainted with new facts, or unaware of facts already in existence, which, if taken into consideration, would have led to a contrary decision.[94]

The PCIJ held that in the absence of such new facts, there was no ground for the revision of the Conference's decision.[95] It is suggested that the dicta of the PCIJ in *Monastery at Saint-Naoum* can be interpreted as meaning that the power to interpret or revise a judgment or award might be implied from the terms of the constitutive instrument or *compromis*.[96] Had the PCIJ been clearly of the opinion—as it appeared to have been in *Jaworzina Frontier*—that the Conference of Ambassadors, or an arbitrator, retained no powers to interpret or revise its decision unless those powers had been expressly conferred on it, then the PCIJ had a clear opportunity to restate this view. However, it did not do so, and the PCIJ presented a more nuanced understanding of the post-adjudication powers of international adjudicatory

[87] Above n 81, 38.

[88] For example, see Bowett, above n 14, 590–1; Schwarzenberger, above n 14, vol IV, 683; Simpson and Fox, above n 14, 245.

[89] Shabtai Rosenne, *The Law and Practice of the International Court, 1920–2005* (2006) vol III, 1612; Reisman, above n 7, 199, 210.

[90] Above n 81, 38–9.

[91] Ser B, (No 9), 7 (PCIJ, 1924).

[92] Ibid, 21.

[93] Ibid, 21–2.

[94] Ibid, 22.

[95] Ibid, 22.

[96] See, e.g., Simpson and Fox, above n 14, 242.

bodies. By leaving the question open, the PCIJ clearly contemplated that situations may arise in which such powers might be implied, or that an international court might have an inherent power to interpret or revise decisions.

B. Practice of International Courts supporting the Existence of the Powers

There is also some practice of international courts exercising the powers of interpretation and revision as inherent powers. This practice can be found in situations where international courts have included these powers in their rules of procedure, which has already been referred to above; most international courts and tribunals frame their own rules of procedure, and can be understood to include in their rules provisions which they consider necessary for the performance of their functions. In addition, instances can be found where international courts have exercised the powers without any textual basis.

1. *Power of Interpretation*

Several early arbitral tribunals have exercised the power to interpret their awards where they had no express power. The King of Prussia's decision in the *Portendick* case, which has been referred to above, arguably provides one such example.[97] Another early instance of interpretation of an award can be found in the *Eliza* case, in which Peru made a claim against the United States for payment in gold of a sum owed under an award rendered by the Mixed Commission of Lima in 1863.[98] The US refused, arguing that it only had to pay in money, rather than gold; this difficulty of interpretation was submitted to a second Mixed Commission in 1870.[99] This body held that the claimant had the right to payment in gold, with interest.[100] The second Commission did not have an express power to interpret the earlier award, and its interpretation of it does not necessarily demonstrate a belief on its part that it had an inherent power to do so, for the request for interpretation of the first award appears effectively to have been submitted as a new dispute.[101] Nevertheless, it evinces the second body's recognition that it had a power to clarify the earlier award, despite the operation of the principle of *res judicata*.

The UNAT has also exercised the power in the absence of a provision in its Statute. In *Crawford*, it observed that although the UNAT Statute did not confer such a power, 'both Parties agreed during the oral proceedings to admit that competence to interpret was inherent in the judicial function which the International Court of Justice, in its advisory opinion of 13 July 1954, declared the Tribunal to possess'.[102]

97 See above nn 80–84 and accompanying text.

98 Lapradelle and Politis, vol II, 271 (Peru–US, 1863).

99 *E G Montano*, Lapradelle and Politis, vol II, 583, 601 (Peru–US, 1870).

100 Ibid; see also Witenberg, *L'Organisation Judiciaire*, above n 72, 365.

101 *Montano*, ibid.

102 (1955) 1 UNAT Rep 331, 335; *Statute of the Administrative Tribunal of the United Nations* UNGA Res 315–A(IV), 24 November 1949 ('UNAT Statute').

Finally, an example can be found in an award rendered by an ICC arbitral tribunal. *Case No 6233* of 1992 was heard under the pre-1998 ICC Arbitration Rules, which did not contain a provision on the interpretation of awards. The claimant made a request to the tribunal for the establishment of a new tribunal to give an interpretation of two awards which had been rendered. The tribunal agreed that it had the power of interpretation, holding that '[t]his power is based on the arbitral clause itself'.[103]

Considered together with the justifications for the existence of inherent powers, being the need of international courts to carry out their functions, it is suggested that this practice constitutes authority for the proposition that international courts have an inherent power to interpret their judgments.

2. *Power of Revision*

In addition to some international courts including the power of revision in their rules of procedure, some have made judicial pronouncements supporting the inherent nature of the power, with some even exercising the power in the absence of any textual basis. This arbitral practice can be confused by the characterization of the cases variously as applications for a 'rehearing' or for 'revision', and these are often made on several bases, including the discovery of new factual evidence or evidence that the award had been procured by fraud, and sometimes parties simply sought a rehearing *de novo*.[104] It is difficult to draw any general conclusions, in particular from the earlier practice. This will be considered first, before turning to the more recent jurisprudence of international courts.

The practice of the US-Mexican CC is quite inconsistent.[105] In 1876, it rejected a request for a rehearing, 'accompanied with some new evidence, and a reexamination of the old' in the *Weil* and *La Abra Silver Mining Co* cases.[106] The umpire, Sir Edward Thornton, refused the motion on a number of grounds; these included his understanding that he had no right to consider any evidence besides 'that which had already been before the commissioners, had been examined by them, and transmitted to the umpire'.[107] Notwithstanding Sir Edward's rejection of this and other applications for revision,[108] other decisions of the US-Mexican CC indicate the existence of a power to reopen cases for new evidence, such as *George Moore*,[109] *Shreck*,[110] and *Green*.[111]

[103] *Case No 6233* (1992), in Jean-Jacques Arnaldez, Yves Derains and Dominique Hascher (eds), *Collection of ICC Arbitral Awards 1991–1995* (1997) 332, 334.

[104] See, e.g., Sandifer, above n 32, 403–56, who describes the cases variously under the heading of 'rehearing' and 'revision'.

[105] See also Ibid, 414–16.

[106] Moore, vol II, 1324, 1329 (US–Mexican CC, 1876) (both cases).

[107] Ibid.

[108] See the cases listed in Moore, vol II, 1357, fn 2.

[109] Moore, vol II, 1357, 1357 (US–Mexican CC, 1871).

[110] Moore, vol II, 1357, 1358 (US–Mexican CC).

[111] Moore, vol II, 1358 (US–Mexican CC).

Decisions in two other early arbitrations, however, militate against the existence of an inherent power of revision. In the US–Spain arbitration in 1881, Umpire Loewenhaupt refused an application by the US arbitrator for a rehearing.[112] In the *Lazare* claim between the US and Haiti in 1886, the arbitrator, Judge Strong, refused a rehearing on the basis of newly discovered evidence, even though he acknowledged that 'the newly discovered evidence was of such a character that it would "materially have affected" his decision had it been presented to him pending the hearing of the case'.[113]

In 1933, the question of an inherent power of revision arose in the *Sabotage Claims* before the US–German MCC.[114] Here, the Commission was asked by the US to reopen a case on the basis that Germany had produced fraudulent evidence during the trial. The umpire, Justice Roberts, noted that the provision in article VI of the Agreement of 10 August 1922 stipulating that the decision of the Commission would be 'final and binding' did not prevent it from reopening any case.[115] Justice Roberts held that:

> [W]here the Commission has misinterpreted the evidence, or made a mistake in calculation, or where its decision does not follow its fact findings, or where in any other respect the decision does not comport with the record as made, or where the decision involves a material error of law, the Commission not only has the power, but is under the duty, upon a proper showing, to reopen and correct a decision to accord with the facts and the applicable legal rules.[116]

But he held that this did not empower the commission to reopen a case for the presentation of 'after-discovered' evidence. He held that 'in cases where a retrial is granted or a reopening and rehearing indulged for the submission of so-called after-discovered evidence, this is usually by a court', and that it was in the public interest 'that litigation be terminated'.[117] With respect to allegations that an award was founded on fraudulent evidence, however, the umpire held that:

> No tribunal worthy its name or of any respect may allow its decision to stand if such allegations are well-founded. Every tribunal has inherent power to reopen and to revise a decision induced by fraud. If it may correct its own errors and mistakes, *a fortiori* it may, while it still has jurisdiction of a cause, correct errors into which it has been led by fraud and collusion.[118]

In contrast to Justice Roberts' holding in the *Sabotage Claims*, the arbitral tribunal constituted to hear the *Trail Smelter* arbitration held, after reviewing the relevant arbitral practice, that the Convention of 15 April 1935 between the United States and Canada did not deny it the power to grant a revision for new facts, although it found that this did not extend to revision for error of law.[119]

112 Moore, vol III, 2190 (US–Spain, 1881).
113 Moore, vol II, 1749, 1801 (US–Haiti, 1886).
114 *Lehigh Valley Railroad Company*, 8 RIAA 160 (US–German MCC, 1933) ('*Sabotage Claims*').
115 Ibid, 187. 116 Ibid, 188. 117 Ibid, 188.
118 Ibid, 190; see also Alfred Verdross and Bruno Simma, *Universelles Völkerrecht* (3rd ed, 1984) 898.
119 Above n 12, 1953–6, 1957.

More recent international judicial practice supports the existence of the power of revision more consistently, but it is inconclusive as to the scope of the power. In *Effect of Awards of Compensation*, the ICJ gave a clear indication that it considers international courts to have an inherent power of revision.[120] In this advisory opinion, the ICJ considered the nature and powers of the UNAT,[121] and concluded that the UNAT was established as 'an independent and truly judicial body pronouncing final judgments without appeal within the limited field of its functions', and that its decisions were *res judicata*.[122] The ICJ noted the absence of a specific power of revision in the UNAT Statute, and also took note of evidence of the Supervisory Commission of the LNAT, on whose Statute the Statute was based, which indicated that the non-inclusion of a power of revision was a deliberate decision.[123] In spite of this evidence, the ICJ nonetheless essentially recognized that despite the finality of its judgments, the UNAT had an inherent power of revision:

> The rule contained in article 10, paragraph 2, cannot however be considered as excluding the Tribunal from itself revising a judgment in special circumstances when new facts of decisive importance have been discovered; and the Tribunal has already exercised this power. Such a strictly limited revision by the Tribunal itself cannot be considered an 'appeal' within the meaning of that Article and would conform with rules generally provided in statutes or laws issued for courts of justice, such as article 61 of the Statute of the International Court of Justice.[124]

Another international tribunal which has considered this question is the Iran-US Claims Tribunal.[125] In *Morris v Iran*, it held that:

> Whether a Chamber or the Full Tribunal, despite the absence of any express provision, has inherent power to review and revise an Award under exceptional circumstances—e.g., when an Award was based on forged documents or perjury—is a question which the Tribunal does not need to reach in this decision.[126]

The Iran–US Claims Tribunal did not specify what it meant by 'exceptional circumstances', such as whether it thought it was limited to evidence of fraud, or whether it also extended to any newly discovered evidence, irrespective of any evidence of fraud.[127] In two subsequent awards, *Dames and Moore v Iran*,[128] and

[120] *Effect of Awards*, above n 13. See also Bowett, above n 14, 590–1, fn 45. While the ICJ has never made similar statements with respect to its own power of revision, the power has certainly been characterized as an inherent power in oral argument before the ICJ: e.g., *Continental Shelf (Revision and Interpretation)* [1985] ICJ Pleadings 172, 174 (Professor Dupuy): the power of international courts to revise their judgments was 'une pièce inhérente de la fonction juridictionnelle', and 'un élément inhérent du système de l'arbitrage'.

[121] Above n 13, 51–3.

[122] Ibid, 53.

[123] Ibid, 54.

[124] Ibid, 55.

[125] David Caron, Lee Caplan and Matti Pellonpää, *The UNCITRAL Arbitration Rules: A Commentary* (2006) 914–26; Charles Brower and Jason Brueschke, *The Iran–United States Claims Tribunal* (1998) 242–60; Baker and Davis, above n 25, 200–5; Jacomijn van Hof, *Commentary on the UNCITRAL Arbitration Rules* (1991) 279–83.

[126] 3 Ir–USCTR 364, 365 (1983); see also *Dallal v Iran*, 5 Ir–USCTR 74, 75 (1984).

[127] Van Hof, above n 125, 281–2.

[128] 8 Ir–USCTR 107, 114, 117–18 (1985).

International Schools Services v Iran,[129] the Iran–US Claims Tribunal avoided ruling on the issue.

The most significant decision on the question of the power of the Iran–US Claims Tribunal to reopen and reconsider awards is *Ram International Industries, Inc v Air Force of Iran*.[130] In this case, Iran requested that the original award be reopened on grounds of fraud and perjury. In addressing the question of whether it had an inherent power to reopen the award, the Tribunal thoroughly reviewed how this question has been addressed in the constitutive instruments of other international courts,[131] and discussed the instances in which arbitral tribunals had exercised the power of revision, even though they had not been conferred an express power to do so, and concluded that these decisions had 'been accepted as sound in legal studies and writings discussing the circumstances under which revision can be sought'.[132] The Iran–US Claims Tribunal then expressed the view that:

> it might possibly be concluded that a tribunal . . . which is to adjudicate a large group of cases for a protracted period of time would by implication, until the adjournment and dissolution of the tribunal, have the authority to revise decisions induced by fraud.[133]

The Iran–US Claims Tribunal did not conclusively determine the question, as it considered that on the facts of the case, the allegations of fraud were not sufficient, even if proved, to have been a decisive factor.[134] Yet this is, nonetheless, persuasive authority for the proposition that international courts have the power, while they are still in operation, to revise judgments, albeit not for any newly discovered evidence, but solely for evidence of fraud.

A more definite result was reached by the UNCITRAL Tribunal in *Biloune and Marine Drive Complex Ltd v Ghana Investments Centre and the Government of Ghana*.[135] In its Award on Damages and Costs, it dealt with an argument by the respondents that aspects of its Award on Jurisdiction and Liability should be reconsidered. The Tribunal held that:

> [A] court or tribunal, including this international arbitral tribunal, has an inherent power to take cognizance of credible evidence, timely placed before it, that its previous determinations were the product of false testimony, forged documents, or other egregious 'fraud on the tribunal'. . . . Certainly if such corruption or fraud in the evidence would justify an international or a national court in voiding or refusing to enforce the award, this Tribunal also, so long as it still has jurisdiction over the dispute, can take necessary corrective action.[136]

[129] 14 Ir–USCTR 65, 70–1 (1987); van Hof, above n 125, 282.

[130] 29 Ir–USCTR 383 (1993); Brower and Brueschke, above n 125, 254–9.

[131] Ibid, 387–9.

[132] Ibid, 389. The Tribunal referred to the writings of Sir Elihu Lauterpacht, *Aspects of the Administration of International Justice* (1991) 100; Sandifer, above n 32, 426; Carlston, above n 78, 57–8, 224–8, 231–41; Reisman, above n 7, 208–12; Simpson and Fox, above n 14, 242.

[133] Above n 130, 390. [134] Ibid, 390–1. [135] 95 ILR 184 (1990).

[136] Ibid, 222, referring to the *Sabotage Claims* (see above n 114 and accompanying text), and also the ICJ Statute, above n 4, art 61, the ICSID Convention, above n 4, art 51, and the US Arbitration Act, 9 USC § 10; see also Caron, Caplan and Pellonpää, above n 125, 915–16.

In the arbitration concerning the *Heathrow Airport User Charges*, the US argued that international tribunals had 'inherent powers to revisit certain areas of an award', and that the principle of finality did not preclude the exercise of such powers.[137] The UK objected to the US requests, arguing that the US was effectively seeking to reopen a question on the merits.[138] The Tribunal noted that it could not 'exercise any power to the existence of which is inconsistent with the terms of the parties' agreement as a result of which alone the Tribunal has any being'.[139] It accepted that it had an inherent power to rectify clerical errors,[140] and further held that under Rule 22(2) of its Rules, it could reopen the proceedings *before* the award had been rendered 'on the ground that new evidence [was] forthcoming of such a nature as to constitute a decisive factor, or that there is a vital need for clarification on certain points'.[141] As it had an express power under its Rules to reopen a decision *before* the rendering of the award, the tribunal held that it was extremely doubtful that its inherent powers included 'the much wider and less qualified power to "revisit" its awards ... in circumstances such as have led the *other* Tribunals, to which [the US] refers, to revise awards that they had rendered'.[142] This award does not, therefore, militate generally against the inherent nature of the power of revision, as the tribunal was restricted from exercising the power by virtue of its rules of procedure.

By far the clearest pronouncement from an international court that the power of revision is an inherent power is that of the IACHR in *Genie Lacayo (Judicial Review)*.[143] In this case, the I-ACommHR requested the 'judicial review' of an earlier judgment. The IACHR recognized that it did not have the power of revision under the American Convention, the IACHR Statute or its Rules.[144] Referring to the practice of the ICJ and the ECHR, the IACHR discussed the power using the language of inherent powers, holding that:

> As stipulated in the Statute of the International Court of Justice and the Rules of the European Court, pursuant to the general principles of both domestic and international procedural law, and, in accordance with the criterion of generally accepted doctrine, the decisive or unappealable character of a judgment is not incompatible with the existence of the remedy of revision in some special cases.[145]

The IACHR thus made a finding that it could, in special cases, exercise the power to revise its judgments.[146]

While the early arbitral practice is inconclusive, the judicial pronouncements in the later case law are much more consistent with the existence of the power of revision as an inherent power. But the case law does not yet allow one to state confidently that every international court has accepted the existence of the power,

[137] *Heathrow Airport User Charges* (Supplemental Decisions and Clarifications) 102 ILR 564, 570 (US–UK, 1993).
[138] Ibid, 568
[139] Ibid, 579.
[140] Ibid, 571, 579.
[141] Ibid, 580.
[142] Ibid.
[143] Ser C, (No 45) (IACHR, 1997).
[144] Ibid para 6.
[145] Ibid, para 9.
[146] Ibid, para 12.

despite the relatively abundant practice on this issue. There is also inconsistent practice regarding the scope of the power; some international courts have confined its scope to discovery of evidence of fraud, rather than discovery of any new evidence. It is, therefore, difficult to conclude that there is a 'common law' with respect to the existence of a general power to revise judgments in light of newly discovered evidence. However, the arguments for the existence of the power as an inherent power are quite compelling. It might be suggested, for instance, that the functions of an international court in the settlement of the dispute and the proper administration of international justice are not carried out if there is no recourse against a judgment made in the absence of decisive evidence, or judgments procured by fraud; indeed, the procedural device of revision was introduced in order 'to avoid arbitral miscarriages of justice' which could be brought about by the exclusion of new facts.[147] Furthermore, if a state, after agreeing to submit a dispute to international adjudication, later discovers that evidence was hidden from it or that evidence was fraudulently submitted to the court, it is likely to be reluctant to comply with any judgment made against it. The proper administration of international justice, then, militates in favour of the admission of a procedure to take account of new evidence, subject to certain conditions discussed below, so long as the exercise of the power is not inconsistent with the terms of the constitutive instrument of each international court. It cannot yet be demonstrated, however, that there is universal acceptance of such a procedure; this is *a fortiori* the case with regard to the WTO dispute settlement system, which will now be considered.

C. Exercise of Post-Adjudication Powers in WTO Dispute Settlement

It has been observed above that WTO panels and the Appellate Body do not have an express power to interpret or revise their reports. In considering whether these post-adjudication procedures are available in WTO dispute settlement, it should be observed that several differences exist between the operation of WTO dispute settlement and other international courts. First, WTO dispute settlement reports are not binding on parties until they have been adopted by the DSB; it can be said that WTO reports are, at least in this respect, dissimilar to judgments or awards of other international courts which have the sole power to interpret their own pronouncements.[148] Second, under the DSU, the DSB is the body having authority, *inter alia*, to establish panels, adopt panel and Appellate Body reports, maintain surveillance of rulings and recommendations, and authorize suspension of concessions and other obligations under the covered agreements.[149] Given these differences, the question of whether these bodies can exercise post-adjudicatory powers is examined in a separate section. At the outset it is noted that the question

[147] Reisman, above n 7, 210.
[148] DSU, above n 6, arts 2(1), 16(4), 17(14).
[149] Ibid, art 2(1).

relating to the power of revision is really limited to the power of WTO panels; the Appellate Body does not determine questions of fact, but only questions of law,[150] therefore, it is more likely that a panel would be asked to revise its report for discovery of a new fact. This does not exclude the possibility that an application might be made to the Appellate Body for the revision of a report; depending on the timing of the discovery of the new fact; if the Appellate Body has already rendered its report and the report has been adopted, the initial request might be directed to that body.

The DSB's role in establishing panels, adopting reports, and maintaining surveillance of rulings and recommendations might suggest that it is the body with the power to interpret or revise panel and Appellate Body reports; or that it is the body with the power to reconstitute a panel (or constitute a new panel) to consider requests for the interpretation and revision of reports.[151] It might also be suggested that the power of interpretation is included in the scope of the implementation panels which may be constituted under article 21(5). Under this provision, if there is a disagreement regarding the consistency with a covered agreement of measures taken to comply with the recommendations of the DSB, it shall be decided through recourse to the WTO dispute settlement procedures, and, where possible, by the original panel.[152] Finally, in contrast to most other international courts, the WTO dispute settlement system has an appellate structure. It is not suggested that the power of interpretation or revision can be likened to the process of appeal, but merely that the availability of appeal ensures that a dissatisfied party to dispute settlement proceedings is not barred from further recourse. In these circumstances, it might be suggested that the WTO panels and the Appellate Body do not have powers of interpretation or revision.

Yet these considerations should not preclude the possibility that WTO panels and the Appellate Body might nonetheless have these powers. Although the DSB has considerable responsibility under the DSU, this does not necessarily deprive panels and the Appellate Body of post-adjudication competences. WTO panels have certainly exercised post-adjudication powers before; on numerous occasions they have exercised a power—which is not expressly provided for in the DSU—to rectify errors in their reports.[153] As for the procedure of implementation, this is distinct from that of interpretation; article 21(5) does not address disputes concerning the interpretation of panel or Appellate Body reports. Finally, the existence of an appellate structure has little bearing on the question of whether panels should be able to interpret or revise their reports. In particular, the Appellate

[150] Ibid, art 17(6).

[151] Such an approach was adopted on at least one occasion by the contracting parties to GATT 1947: Report of the Members of the Original Oilseeds Panel, *Follow-Up on the Panel Report 'EEC—Payments and Subsidies Paid to Processors and Producers of Oilseeds and Related Animal-Feed Proteins'* (BISD 39S/91) paras 3–4 (GATT, 1992).

[152] DSU, art 21(5).

[153] For example, *US—Corrosion-Resistant Carbon Steel*, WT/DS213/R/Corr.1 (PR); *Australia—Salmon*, WT/DS18/R/Corr.1 (PR).

Body's role in determining appeals cannot extend to deciding the decisive nature of new factual evidence. To admit of the powers of interpretation and revision would not undermine the role of the Appellate Body, and would be a more efficient and economical way of resolving such disputes.[154] It is suggested that WTO panels and the Appellate Body might possess the powers of interpretation and revision, and that these powers are not necessarily inconsistent with their functions or with the terms of the DSU.

D. Conclusion

Many international courts have the power to interpret and revise judgments and awards, regardless of whether this power is expressly conferred by the terms of their constitutive instruments. This is because these powers can be exercised as inherent powers, provided that they are not exercised in a fashion that is inconsistent with the functions or the terms of the constitutive instruments of international courts. The attention of this chapter now turns to whether international courts exercise these powers consistently.

IV. Issues relevant to the Exercise of the Powers of Interpretation and Revision

Judicial and arbitral practice on the exercise of the power of interpretation is somewhat limited, although instances of applications for the interpretation of judgments and awards can be found before most international courts, including the MATs,[155] the PCIJ,[156] the ICJ,[157] ICSID tribunals and tribunals constituted under bilateral investment treaties,[158] the ECHR,[159] the IACHR,[160] and PCA

[154] In *Canada—Aircraft*, DSR 1999–III, 1377, 1434–5, the Appellate Body appeared to suggest that Brazil could bring another claim should it discover a new fact concerning the consistency of Canada's measures with the SCM Agreement. Joost Pauwelyn, *Conflict of Norms in Public International Law* (2003) 111, regards this as similar to the procedure of revision, but it is suggested that it should be regarded more accurately as the submission of a new claim.

[155] For example, *Daville c État allemand*, 2 TAM 429 (Franco-German MAT, 1922); *Office allemand c Office français*, 4 TAM 441 (Franco-German MAT, 1924).

[156] *Factory at Chorzów (Interpretation)*, above n 10; *Treaty of Neuilly (Interpretation)*, Ser A, (No 4) (PCIJ, 1925).

[157] *Land and Maritime Boundary between Cameroon and Nigeria (Interpretation)*, above n 13; *Continental Shelf (Revision and Interpretation)*, above n 13; *Asylum (Interpretation)* [1950] ICJ Rep 395.

[158] *Marvin Feldman v Mexico* (ICSID Case No ARB(AF)/99/1, Decision on Correction and Interpretation of 13 June 2003) (NAFTA); *CCL v Kazakhstan* (SCC Case No 122/2001, Supplemental Award and Interpretation of 2004); and *Wena Hotels v Egypt* (ICSID Case No ARB/98/4, Decision on Application for Interpretation of Award of 31 October 2005), all available at <http://ita.law.uvic.edu> (last visited 25 November 2006).

[159] *Hentrich v France*, ECHR Rep 1997–IV, 1285; *Allenet de Ribemont v France*, above n 62; *Ringeisen v Austria*, above n 61.

[160] *Juan Humberto Sanchez (Interpretation)*, Ser C, (No 102) (IACHR, 2003); *Cesti Hurtado (Interpretation)*, Ser C, (No 86) (IACHR, 2001); *Ivcher Bronstein (Interpretation)*, Ser C, (No 84)

tribunals.[161] It appears that there have, to date, been no applications for the interpretation of a WTO report, an ITLOS judgment or an UNCLOS tribunal award.[162]

As with the power of interpretation, there is relatively little international judicial practice concerning the power of revision. No applications for revision were made before the PCIJ, but there is substantial practice from the MATs,[163] and the power has also been invoked before PCA tribunals,[164] the ICJ,[165] the IACHR,[166] and the ECHR.[167] There is, however, no practice emanating from the ITLOS, UNCLOS tribunals, the WTO dispute settlement system, or ICSID tribunals.[168]

In the available practice of international courts, two issues have emerged as being common to applications for interpretation and revision: the question of the jurisdiction of the international court to accede to such a request, and the composition

(IACHR, 2001); *Barrios Altos (Interpretation)*, Ser C, (No 83) (IACHR, 2001); *Cesti Hurtado (Interpretation)*, Ser C, (No 65) (IACHR, 2000); *Cesti Hurtado (Interpretation)*, Ser C, (No 62) (IACHR, 1999); *Blake (Interpretation)*, Ser C, (No 57) (IACHR, 1999); *Loayza Tamayo (Interpretation)*, Ser C, (No 53), (IACHR, 1999); *Suárez Rosero (Interpretation)*, Ser C, (No 51) (IACHR, 1999); *Loayza Tamayo (Intrepretation)*, Ser C, (No 47) (IACHR, 1998); *El Amparo (Interpretation)*, Ser C, (No 46) (IACHR, 1997); *Godínez-Cruz (Interpretation)*, Ser C, (No 10) (IACHR, 1990); *Velásquez Rodríguez (Interpretation)*, Ser C, (No 9) (IACHR, 1990).

[161] *Iron Rhine Railway* (Interpretation of Award of 20 September 2005); (see also *Iron Rhine Railway* (Correction of the Award of 20 September 2005)); Eritrea–Ethiopia Boundary Commission (Decision on Interpretation of 24 June 2002), available at <http://www.pca-cpa.org> (last visited 25 November 2006).

[162] However, Saint Vincent and the Grenadines apparently contemplated requesting the ITLOS for an interpretation of the judgment in *M/V 'Saiga'*: Eiriksson, above n 70, 213, 276.

[163] For example, *Heim et Chamant v Germany*, 3 TAM 50 (Franco-German MAT, 1922); *La Suédoise v Roller*, 4 TAM 315 (German-Belgian MAT, 1924); *Jules Créange v Paul Busch*, 5 TAM 114 (Franco-German MAT, 1924); *Baron de Neuflize v Diskontogesellschaft*, 7 TAM 629 (Franco-German MAT, 1927); *Epoux Ventense v State SHS*, 7 TAM 79 (German-Yugoslavian MAT, 1923); *Krichel v France* and *Krichel v Germany*, 8 TAM 757 (Franco-German MAT, 1928); *Office allemand v Office français*, 8 TAM 766 (Franco-German MAT, 1928); *Betz v Germany*, 9 TAM 654 (German-Belgian MAT, 1929); *Otzenberger v Germany*, 9 TAM 272 (Franco-German MAT, 1929); *Battus v Bulgaria*, 9 TAM 284 (Franco-Bulgarian MAT, 1929); *De Tayrac v Schmitz*, 9 TAM 492 (Franco-German MAT, 1929).

[164] *Pious Fund of the Californias*, above n 9; *North Atlantic Coast Fisheries*, 11 RIAA 167 (GB–US, 1910); *Orinoco Steamship Co*, 11 RIAA 227 (US–Venezuela, 1910). It should be noted that the application for revision in *Orinoco Steamship Co* centred on whether the umpire in that case had exceeded his jurisdiction or had made 'essential errors' involving errors of law. This is not the same as 'revision' on the grounds of a new fact. See discussion in *Klöckner v Cameroon* (Annulment), 114 ILR 243, 118–19 (1985).

[165] *Continental Shelf (Revision and Interpretation)*, above n 13; *Application of the Genocide Convention (Revision)* (ICJ Judgment of 3 February 2003); *Land Island and Maritime Frontier Dispute (Revision)* (ICJ Judgment of 18 December 2003), available at <http://www.icj-cij.org> (last visited 30 November 2006).

[166] *Genie Lacayo (Judicial Review)*, above n 143.

[167] For example, *Epple v Germany (Revision—Admissibility)*, Judgment of 15 December 2005, available at <http://www.echr.coe.int> (last visited 25 November 2006); *McGinley and Egan v United Kingdom (Revision—Admissibility)*, ECHR Rep 2000-I, 321; *Gustafsson v Sweden (Revision—Admissibility)*, ECHR Rep 1997–VI, 2152; *Gustafsson v Sweden (Revision—Merits)*, ECHR Rep 1998–V, 2085; *Pardo v France (Revision—Admissibility)*, ECHR Rep 1996–III, 860; *Pardo v France (Revision—Merits)*, ECHR Rep 1997–III, 735.

[168] But see the application for revision made in *American Manufacturing & Trading v DRC* (ICSID Case No ARB/93/1), which was discontinued by agreement of the parties on 26 July 2000: <http://www.worldbank.org/icsid> (last visited 25 November 2006).

of the international court hearing the request. These two issues will be considered before turning to the specific criteria for applications for interpretation and revision.

A. Jurisdiction of the International Court hearing the Request

Under the Institut de Droit International's *Projet de règlement* of 1875, any request for interpretation of an award had to be submitted jointly, in effect requiring both parties to consent to the jurisdiction of the international tribunal to give an interpretation.[169] But this position has not been maintained; international courts can give an interpretation or revision of their judgments without a separate act conferring jurisdiction. Article 60 of the ICJ Statute, for instance, does not expressly require a separate act of consent.[170] In 1926, when the PCIJ judges were revising the Rules of Court, this question engendered some debate. Several members of the PCIJ were of the opinion that the jurisdiction of the court over a request for interpretation was compulsory even if the original dispute had been referred to the PCIJ by special agreement.[171] This was finally clarified in the 1978 revision of the Rules; article 98(1) arguably makes it clear that no further act of consent is required of the parties.[172] The ICJ's power to consider a request for interpretation without the need for consent of both parties was confirmed by the ICJ in *Continental Shelf (Revision and Interpretation)*.[173] Likewise, it appears that its power of revision derives from article 61 of the ICJ Statute, and not from any separate basis of jurisdiction.[174]

As regards applications for the interpretation of PCA tribunal awards, article 82 of the 1907 Convention does not require that the dispute over the interpretation of the award be submitted by joint application.[175] The case is different for applications for revision; article 55 of the 1899 Convention and article 83 of the 1907 Convention require parties to include the power of revision to be consented to by the parties in the *compromis*.[176] Under the ITLOS Statute, article 33(3) merely provides that '[i]n the event of dispute as to the meaning or scope of the decision, the Tribunal shall construe it upon the request of any party';[177] the statement that 'any party' can request an interpretation suggests that a unilateral application will suffice. Likewise, article 12(1) of UNCLOS Annex VII, which confers the power of interpretation, does not require a new jurisdictional link.[178] Article 127 of the ITLOS Rules, which contains the power of revision, makes similar provision to article 61 of the ICJ Statute.[179] The provisions of the ICSID Convention conferring

169 Institut de Droit International, above n 28, art 24. 170 ICJ Statute, above n 4, art 60.
171 Ser D, No 2, Add, 174–80. 172 ICJ Rules of Court, art 98(1).
173 Above n 13, 216.
174 See, e.g., *Land, Island and Maritime Frontier Dispute (Revision)*, above n 165, paras 17–20; and *Application of the Genocide Convention (Revision)*, above n 165, para 14.
175 1907 Convention, above n 4, art 82.
176 1899 Convention, art 55; 1907 Convention, art 83 (both, above n 4).
177 ITLOS Statute, above n 4, art 33(3); ITLOS Rules, art 126.
178 UNCLOS, above n 43, Annex VII, art 12. 179 ITLOS Rules, art 127.

the power to interpret or revise awards similarly do not require separate bases of jurisdiction.[180]

This brief review of the statutory provisions and jurisprudence suggests that the jurisdiction of international courts over requests for interpretation or revision generally derives directly from the jurisdictional clause, and that no further act of consent is needed, unless there is agreement to the contrary.

B. Composition of the International Court hearing the Request

A second issue common to applications for interpretation and revision relates to the composition of the international court considering the request. Problems might arise particularly given that some ad hoc tribunals may be *functus officio* and disbanded after the rendering of the award. This issue is less significant in the procedure of standing courts such as the ICJ; the ICJ Statute and Rules do not contain any provisions concerning its composition for such requests. Under article 100(1) of the ICJ Rules, if the application for revision or interpretation concerns a judgment of the full Court, 'the request... shall be dealt with by the Court'; if a Chamber has been formed to hear the dispute, the request for interpretation or revision 'shall be dealt with by that chamber'.[181] This is consistent with the ICJ's approach to the question of third-party intervention which arose in *Land, Island and Maritime Frontier Dispute*; there, the ICJ decided that it was the Chamber formed in that case, rather than the full ICJ, which should determine Nicaragua's application to intervene.[182] This approach was followed by the ICJ Chamber when an application for revision was made in *Land, Island and Maritime Frontier Dispute* in 2002.[183]

The ITLOS Rules similarly provide that if the judgment to be interpreted or revised was given by the ITLOS, the request for interpretation or revision is to be heard by the ITLOS.[184] If the judgment was given by a Chamber, the request for interpretation or revision is, if possible, to be dealt with by that Chamber.[185] If it is not possible for the same ITLOS Chamber to be formed, the request is to be dealt with by another Chamber, and if this cannot be constituted, it is to be dealt with by the ITLOS.[186] The ICSID Arbitration Rules and the IACHR Rules make similar provision.[187]

[180] ICSID Convention, above n 4, art 50(1); ICSID Arbitration Rules, Rule 56(1).

[181] ICJ Rules, art 100(1).

[182] [1990] ICJ Rep 3, 5–6.

[183] *Land, Island and Maritime Frontier Dispute (Revision)*, above n 165, paras 3–5. Shabtai Rosenne has observed that 'not one of the members of the 2002 Chamber had been members of the 1992 Chamber', even though article 100(1) of the ICJ Rules requires that 'if the judgment... was given by a chamber, the request for its revision shall be dealt with by *that* chamber' (emphasis added): Rosenne, *Law and Practice*, above n 89, vol III, 1630.

[184] ITLOS Rules, art 129(1).

[185] Ibid, art 129(2).

[186] Ibid, art 129(2).

[187] ICSID Arbitration Rules, Rule 51; IACHR Rules of Court, article 59(3). On the IACHR Rules, see especially *Godínez- Cruz (Interpretation)*, above n 160, paras 12–13; and *Velásquez Rodríguez (Interpretation)*, above n 160, paras 12–13, where the IACHR interprets the provisions in light of ICJ and ECHR practice.

Where constitutive instruments and rules of procedure are silent on the question of composition, it is suggested that requests for interpretation and revision should be considered by the tribunal as originally composed, unless this is impossible, in which case a new tribunal should be constituted.

C. Scope of the Powers

International courts have made it clear that the power of interpretation is narrowly restricted to clarifying the terms of a judgment. This involves precisely defining the terms of the operative parts of the judgment, and specifying its scope, meaning and purpose. The confines of an interpretation were clearly spelled out by the PCIJ Chamber of Summary Procedure in *Treaty of Neuilly (Interpretation)*:

> [A]n interpretation—given in accordance with article 60 of the Statute—of the Judgment of September 12th, 1924, cannot go beyond the limits of that judgment itself, which are fixed by the special agreement.[188]

This has been accepted in the jurisprudence of many international courts, including the ICJ,[189] the ECHR,[190] the IACHR,[191] the Iran-US Claims Tribunal,[192] a NAFTA tribunal,[193] ad hoc arbitral tribunals,[194] and tribunals operating under institutional rules of commercial arbitration.[195] Importantly, interpretation cannot be used to seek a revision or rehearing of the original decision, and an interpretation cannot violate the principle of *res judicata*.[196] International courts are wary of parties who seek to achieve modification, revision or annulment of the judgment by means of interpretation; parties who have sought to do so have received mild judicial rebukes.[197]

188 Above n 156, 7; see also *Factory at Chorzów (Interpretation)*, above n 10, 21; von Stauffenberg, above n 38, 426.

189 *Continental Shelf (Revision and Interpretation)*, above n 13, 217; *Asylum (Interpretation)*, above n 157, 402.

190 *Ringeisen v Austria*, above n 61, para 13.

191 *Velásquez Rodríguez*, above n 160, para 26.

192 *PepsiCo Inc, v Iran*, 13 Ir–US CTR 328, 329 (1986); Baker and Davis, above n 25, 193–4; van Hof, above n 125, 278–84.

193 *Feldman v Mexico*, above n 158, paras 9–11.

194 *Dispute concerning the Course of the Frontier between Boundary Post 62 and Mount Fitzroy (Revision and Interpretation)*, 113 ILR 194, 229–31 (Argentina–Chile, 1995); *Delimitation of the Continental Shelf between the UK and the French Republic (Interpretation)*, 18 UNRIAA 271, 295–6 (UK–France, 1978).

195 See, e.g., Yves Derains and Eric Schwartz, *A Guide to the New ICC Rules of Arbitration* (1998) 300–1; Baker and Davis, above n 25, 194.

196 For example, *Land and Maritime Boundary (Interpretation)*, [1999] ICJ Rep 31, para 12; Rosenne, *Law and Practice*, above n 89, vol III, 1612; van Hof, above n 125, 280–3.

197 For example, *Feldman v Mexico*, above n 158, para 10; *Loayza Tamayo (Interpretation)*, above n 160, paras 15–16; *Hentrich v France*, above n 159, 1290; *Ford Aerospace and Communications Corporation v Air Force of Iran*, 12 Ir–USCTR 304, 304–5 (1986); *Ambatielos* [1953] ICJ Rep 10, 16–17; *Asylum (Interpretation)*, above n 157, 403; *Factory at Chorzów (Interpretation)*, above n 10, 21; *Treaty of Neuilly (Interpretation)*, above n 156, 7.

A further consideration surrounding the interpretation of judgments is that international courts are not 'bound by the formulae chosen by the parties', but will take an 'unhampered decision'.[198] Finally, a request for interpretation need not relate to the operative part of the judgment, but might extend to the reasoning in the judgment.[199]

International courts have also consistently construed the power of revision narrowly. As the power constitutes an exception to the principle of finality and *res judicata*, international tribunals are wary of applications for revision which are in reality attempts to appeal the decision or have it reviewed *de novo*.[200] As the Franco-Bulgarian MAT stated in *Battus v Bulgaria*, 'la procédure de révision instituée par le tribunal constitue une voie de recours extraordinaire... elle ne peut être considerée comme une voie indirecte, permettant de revenir par une nouvelle instance sur des décisions déclarées définitives'.[201]

D. Conditions for the Exercise of the Powers

1. *Power of Interpretation*

In *Factory at Chorzów (Interpretation)*, the PCIJ held that there were essentially two conditions for an application for interpretation under article 60. First, there had to be a dispute 'as to the meaning and scope of a judgment of the Court'.[202] The PCIJ observed that 'the manifestation of the existence of the dispute in a specific manner, as for instance by diplomatic negotiations, [was] not required',[203] but it was sufficient that 'the two Governments have in fact shown themselves as holding opposite views in regard to the meaning or scope of a judgment of the Court'.[204] Thus, a difference of opinion has to exist between the parties as to those points in the judgment in question which have been decided with binding force.[205] The PCIJ also accepted the possibility that a dispute regarding whether a particular point has or has not been decided with binding force might also constitute a case which comes within the terms of article 60.[206]

The second condition observed by the PCIJ was that 'the request should have for its object an interpretation of the judgment'.[207] The PCIJ held that its task of interpretation should be understood as meaning 'to give a precise definition of the meaning and scope which the Court intended to give to the judgment in question'.[208]

[198] *Factory at Chorzów (Interpretation)*, ibid, 15–16; Manley Hudson, *The Permanent Court of International Justice 1920–1942* (1943) 591.

[199] *Factory at Chorzów (Interpretation)*, ibid, 14; see also 23, 24 (Diss Op Anzilotti); see generally *Delimitation of the Continental Shelf*, above n 194, 295.

[200] See, e.g., Vittorio di Bucci, 'Revision' in Plender (ed), above n 47, 699, 702; *Epoux Ventense v State SHS*, above n 163, 82–3.

[201] Above n 163, 285.

[202] Above n 10, 10.

[203] Ibid.

[204] Ibid, 11; *Continental Shelf (Revision and Interpretation)* above n 13, 218; von Stauffenberg, above n 38, 425.

[205] *Factory at Chorzów*, above n 10.

[206] Ibid, 11–12.

[207] Ibid, 10.

[208] Ibid, 10; von Stauffenberg, above n 38, 426.

These conditions have been accepted by the ICJ, and by other international tribunals.[209]

An additional criterion which appears to differ among different international courts is the question of applicable time limits for making a request for interpretation. Before the ICJ, the ITLOS, ICSID tribunals, and the ECJ, there is no time limit. As regards PCA tribunals, article 82 of the 1907 Convention does not specify a time limit for requests for interpretation, but if the parties choose to adopt the PCA Optional Rules, article 35 of those Rules would require such requests to be submitted within 60 days of the receipt of the award. Before the ECHR, a request for interpretation must be made within one year of the judgment.[210] Under article 67 of the American Convention, a request for the interpretation of an IACHR judgment must be made within 90 days from the date of judgment.[211] Before the various Mexican MCCs, parties were able to request an interpretation within a period of between 15 and 60 days of the award being rendered.[212] Time limits also apply to requests for interpretation of awards made under the UNCITRAL Rules (30 days),[213] the ICC Rules (30 days),[214] the Iran–US Claims Tribunal Rules (30 days),[215] and the AAA Rules (30 days).[216] It is difficult to find any common ground on this question; the most that can be said is possibly that institutions having a permanent framework do not impose strict time limits on requests for interpretation, while ad hoc tribunals have much stricter time limits.

2. *Power of Revision*

Before addressing the necessary criteria for the power of revision, something must be said about the procedure for revision proceedings. Generally, revision proceedings are opened by a judgment of the international court, which expressly records the existence of the new fact, and recognizes that it has such a character as to lay the case open to revision, and declares the application admissible on this ground. Accordingly, applications for revision usually follow a two-stage procedure. First, the international court declares the application admissible. Second, the merits of the revision application are heard. This procedure is followed before the ICJ,[217] the ITLOS,[218] PCA tribunals,[219] the ECHR,[220] and the ECJ.[221] The ICSID

209 *Continental Shelf (Revision and Interpretation)*, above n 13, 217, 223; *Asylum (Interpretation)*, above n 157, 402; see also *Hentrich v France*, above n 159, 1290; *Allenet de Ribemont v France*, above n 62, 911; *Ringeisen v Austria*, above n 61, para 13.

210 ECHR Rules, art 79(1).

211 American Convention, above n 4, art 67.

212 For example, Franco-Mexican CC Rules of Procedure, art 46, in Feller, above n 59, 432 (15 days); US-Mexican GCC Rules, above n 59, art XI(6), in Feller, ibid, 351 (60 days).

213 UNCITRAL Rules, art 35(1).

214 ICC Rules of Arbitration, art 29(2).

215 Ir–USCT Rules, above n 46, art 35(1).

216 American Arbitration Association/ICDR Arbitration Rules, available at <http://www.adr.org>, art 30.

217 ICJ Statute, above n 4, art 61(2); see, e.g., *Land, Island and Maritime Frontier Dispute (Revision)*, above n 165, para 18.

218 ITLOS Rules, art 127(2).

219 1899 Convention, art 55, 1907 Convention, art 83 (both, above n 4).

220 ECHR Rules, Rule 80(1).

221 ECJ Statute, above n 47, art 41.

Convention does not state whether revision proceedings are to be heard in two stages, although it is suggested that it is likely that ICSID tribunals would also adopt this procedure.

There appear to be five conditions which are relevant to an application for revision. First, an application for revision of a judgment may be made only when it is based upon the 'discovery of a fact'.[222] The question of what constitutes a 'fact' is, however, one which is fraught with difficulty.[223] The absence of a clear distinction between legal and factual matters is a problem common to many legal systems.[224] This was recognized by the Franco-German MAT, which stated that:

> la notion de *fait* ne doit pas être mise en opposition absolue avec celle de droit, dont il n'est pas toujours facile de la distinguer, mais . . . elle doit s'entendre d'une façon plus large.[225]

There is further difficulty in defining what can be considered a 'new fact'. This was apparent to one delegate during the drafting of the 1899 Convention.[226] and examples suggested included new maps, or a new document of uncontested authenticity.[227] For instance, a document relating to the location of boundaries, being a Resolution of the Libyan Council of Ministers which determined the 'real course' of a boundary of a petroleum concession, known as 'Concession No 137', was put forward as a new 'fact' in *Continental Shelf (Revision and Interpretation)*.[228] In *Land, Island and Maritime Frontier Dispute (Revision)*, the new fact was scientific evidence, the discovery of a map, and the report of an expedition.[229] But the discovery of a new document or new evidence is not always sufficient. As the PCIJ observed in *Monastery at Saint-Naoum*, 'fresh documents do not in themselves amount to fresh facts'.[230] If the content of the document or evidence is already known, this does not constitute a new fact.[231] In *Application of the Genocide Convention (Revision)*, the Federal Republic of Yugoslavia ('FRY') argued that there were two new facts: that the FRY was not a state party to the ICJ Statute at

[222] For example, ICJ Statute, above n 4, art 61(1); ITLOS Rules, art 127(1); 1899 Convention, above n 4, art 55; 1907 Convention, above n 4, art 83; ICSID Convention, above n 4, art 51(1); ECHR Rules, Rule 80; ECJ Statute, above n 47, art 41; *Genie Lacayo (Judicial Review)*, above n 143, para 12.

[223] Bardonnet, above n 49, 198–200; Richard Bilder, 'The Fact/Law Distinction in International Adjudication' in Richard Lillich (ed), *Fact-Finding before International Tribunals* (1992) 95, 95–6; Jean Salmon, 'Le fait dans l'application du droit international' (1982) 175 *Receuil des cours* 257; Zoller, above n 73, 341–2; Reisman, above n 7, 426, fn 15; James Thayer, *A Preliminary Treatise on Evidence at the Common Law* (1898) 189–92, 201–4; Herzog and Karlen, above n 1, 46–7; Torres Bernárdez, above n 33, 473–9.

[224] Geiss, above n 48, 176; see especially *Application of the Genocide Convention (Revision)*, above n 165, 1–3 (Diss Op Dimitrijevic), 4–7 (Diss Op Vereshchetin).

[225] *Heim and Chamant v Germany*, above n 163, 55.

[226] 'On parle de fait nouveau, mais rien n'est plus difficile à definer': *Conférence Internationale de la Paix 1899*, above n 49, 40 (M le Jonkheer van Karnebeek); Geiss, above n 48, 176.

[227] *Conférence Internationale de la Paix 1899*, ibid, 37 (M Holls); Geiss, ibid, 174.

[228] Above n 13, 198. [229] Above n 165, para 25. [230] Above n 91, 22

[231] *Land, Island and Maritime Frontier Dispute (Revision)*, C6/CR 2003/2, 38–41 (Maurice Mendelson).

the time of the judgment, and that the FRY was not bound by the Genocide Convention at the time of the judgment.[232] The FRY argued that these facts were revealed by its admission to the UN on 1 November 2000.[233] The ICJ held that Yugoslavia's admission to the UN occurred well after the original judgment of 1996, and that this could not be regarded as a new fact within the meaning of article 61 of the ICJ Statute.[234] In response to the FRY's argument that its admission to the UN had simply 'revealed' two facts that existed at the time of the 1996 judgment,[235] the ICJ disagreed, holding that:

> In advancing this argument, the FRY does not rely on facts that existed in 1996. In reality, it bases its Application on the legal consequences which it seeks to draw from facts subsequent to the Judgment which it is asking to have revised. Those consequences, even supposing them to be established, cannot be regarded as facts within the meaning of article 61. The FRY's argument cannot accordingly be upheld.[236]

The second universally accepted condition of an application for revision is that the new fact must be of such a nature that it would have been a 'decisive' factor, had it been known at the time of the judgment.[237] Implicitly, this requires that the 'new fact' must have been in existence at the time of the judgment; if the fact was not in existence at the time of the judgment, there is no way that it could have influenced the outcome.[238]

The 'decisive' nature of a new fact has been interpreted in a consistent fashion. In *Continental Shelf (Revision and Interpretation)*, Tunisia submitted that a Resolution of the Libyan Council of Ministers determining the 'real course' of the boundary of a petroleum concession constituted a new fact which would have had a decisive influence on the ICJ's judgment.[239] The ICJ rejected the Tunisian application, and it held that its reasoning in the 1982 Judgment was 'wholly unaffected by the evidence now produced as to the boundaries of Concession No 137'.[240] In *Land, Island and Maritime Frontier Dispute (Revision)*, the ICJ held that the scientific evidence relating to the avulsion of a river 'would provide no basis for calling into question the decision taken by the Chamber in 1992 on wholly different grounds. The facts asserted in this connection by El Salvador are not "decisive factors" in respect of the judgment which it seeks to have revised.'[241] With regard to the second alleged new 'fact', the ICJ concluded that the new map only differed in minor details from the map which the ICJ had considered at the time of the

232 *Application of the Genocide Convention (Revision)*, above n 165, para 66.
233 Ibid, paras 18, 66. 234 Ibid, paras 66–8. 235 Ibid, paras 19, 69.
236 Ibid, para 69.
237 ICJ Statute, above n 4, art 61(1); ITLOS Rules, art 127; ICSID Convention, above n 4, art 51(1); 1899 Convention, above n 4, art 55; 1907 Convention, above n 4, art 83; ECHR Rules, Rule 80; *Genie Lacayo (Judicial Review)*, above n 143, paras 12, 15; *Ram International Industries v Air Force of Iran*, above n 130, 390; Franco-German MAT Rules, above n 98, art 79.
238 See, e.g., *Jules Créange v Paul Busch*, above n 163, 116; *Battus v Bulgaria*, above n 163, 286.
239 Above n 13, 201–2. 240 Ibid, 213. 241 Above n 165, para 40.

original judgment, as did the report of the expedition; the ICJ therefore held that these were not 'decisive factors' in respect of the 1992 judgment.[242]

The third condition relevant to revision proceedings is that the fact must have been unknown to the international court and also to the party claiming revision at a relevant point in time.[243] There is, however, some variation among international courts with regard to the timing of the discovery of the new fact. In applications for revision before the ICJ, the ITLOS, the ECHR, the IACHR and ICSID tribunals, the new fact must have been unknown at the time of the rendering of the judgment or award.[244] In contrast, in revision proceedings before PCA tribunals and the MATs, the new fact must have been unknown at the time of the end of the oral proceedings.[245]

The fourth condition is that the lack of knowledge of the new fact must not have been due to the negligence of the party requesting revision. This condition was not included in the Hague Conventions, but was first introduced by the Advisory Committee of Jurists into the PCIJ Statute in 1920, and is today recognized in the constitutive instruments and jurisprudence of most international tribunals.[246] In *Continental Shelf (Revision and Interpretation)*, the relevant fact, being the location of a Libyan concession, had been published in the Libyan Official Gazette. The ICJ held that 'the reasonable and appropriate course of action to be taken by Tunisia . . . would have been to seek to know the co-ordinates of the Concession', and that Tunisia had failed to prove why it had been impossible for it to do so, nor had it shown that it had in fact attempted to obtain this information.[247] Similarly, the ECHR rejected a request for revision in *McGinley v UK*, holding that the claimants had been 'manifestly on notice' of the existence of the relevant documents.[248]

The fifth condition relevant in revision proceedings before international courts is the time limit on such applications. This time limit is usually prescribed in the constitutive instruments, and differs somewhat between different tribunals. Applications for revision before the ICJ and the ITLOS must be made at the latest within six months of the discovery of the new fact, and no later than ten years from the date of judgment.[249] The Hague Conventions do not specify a time limit

[242] Ibid, paras 51–5.

[243] ICJ Statute, above n 4, article 61(1); ITLOS Rules, article 127; ICSID Convention, above n 4, article 51(1); 1899 Convention, above n 4, article 54; 1907 Convention, above n 143, article 83; ECHR Rules, Rule 80(1); *Genie Lacayo (Judicial Review)*, above n 143, para 12; *De Tayrac v Schmitz*, above n 163, 493–4.

[244] ICJ Statute, article 61(1); ITLOS Rules, article 127; ECHR Rules, Rule 80(1); *Genie Lacayo (Judicial Review)*, para 12; ICSID Convention, article 51(1).

[245] 1899 Convention, art 55; 1907 Convention, art 83; Franco-German MAT Rules, above n 58, art 79; see, e.g., *Baron de Neuflize v Diskontogesellschaft*, above n 163, 632.

[246] ICJ Statute, above n 4, art 61; ITLOS Rules, art 127; ICSID Convention, above n 4, art 51(1); see, e.g., *Ram International Industries v Air Force of Iran*, above n 130, 391.

[247] Above n 13, 205–7. [248] Above n 167, 324, 338.

[249] ICJ Statute, above n 4, art 61(4)-(5); ITLOS Rules, art 127(1); but see Rosenne, *Law and Practice*, above n 89, vol III, 1630, who is critical of the ten-year period, and suggests that 'from the

on requests for revision; this will depend on the terms agreed by the parties in the *compromis*.[250] Applications to the ECHR for revision must be made within six months of the discovery of the new fact, but no overall time limit is put on such applications.[251] Before arbitral tribunals, the time limits tend to be shorter; applications for revision before ICSID tribunals must be made within 90 days after the discovery of the fact, and within three years after the date on which the award was rendered.[252] Under the rules of the Franco-German MAT, no request for revision could be made more than one year after the rendering of the award.[253] In the absence of guidance from those tribunals which have considered the inherent nature of the power, it is suggested that an appropriate test might involve considering what a reasonable time would be in the circumstances. Before standing courts, it appears that it might be considered reasonable that a longer period should be allowed for applications for revision, such as within five to ten years of the date of the judgment. However, it is suggested that in disputes before ad hoc arbitral tribunals, a shorter time frame will be applicable, such as within one or two years of the judgment, due to the desire for greater speed in the settlement of the dispute, and the added practical problem of the disbanding of the tribunal. No firm conclusions can be drawn here, but it is suggested that there should be some temporal limitation on the power of revision; the *res judicata* of judgments cannot be subject to eternal suspense and uncertainty.[254]

There appears to be broad agreement among international courts that all five conditions must be met for a request for revision to be admissible; as the ICJ has stated, 'once it is established that the request for revision fails to meet one of the conditions for admissibility, the Court is not required to go further and investigate whether the other conditions are fulfilled'.[255]

Conclusion

This chapter has considered the power of international courts to interpret and revise their judgments. In the case of the power of interpretation, it is suggested that all international courts can exercise this power; if not conferred as an express

experience that has now been gained of revision cases, a shorter period, something between six and twelve months, would appear to be reasonable for the introduction of revision proceedings'.

250 1899 Convention, art 55; 1907 Convention, art 83 (both, above n 4).

251 ECHR Rules, Rule 80(1).

252 ICSID Convention, above n 4, art 51(2). The ICC, UNCITRAL and LCIA Rules make no provision for a power of revision.

253 Above n 58, art 80.

254 See especially comments of Rosenne, *Law and Practice*, above n 89, vol III, 1630.

255 *Land, Island and Maritime Frontier Dispute (Revision)*, above n 165, paras 20, 59; *Application of the Genocide Convention (Revision)*, above n 165, paras 17, 73; *Continental Shelf (Revision and Interpretation)* above n 13, 207; see, e.g., also ICSID Convention, above n 4, art 51; *McGinley v UK*, above n 167, 324, 338.

power, it can be exercised as an inherent power. This is because the power is necessary for international courts to be able to carry out their function in the settlement of international disputes by adjudication, for if a judgment or award is rendered which is ambiguous or contradictory, the dispute will not be settled. In addition, the interests of good administration of international justice are not served if courts are unable to assist parties in clarifying obscurities in judicial decisions. As for the power of revision, the case law is less conclusive on the existence of the power as one which can be exercised in the absence of express conferral in the constitutive instrument. But it is suggested that as a matter of principle, the power should be considered inherent, in order to safeguard the administration of international justice from unjust decisions made on the basis of incomplete or fraudulent evidence. This chapter has also suggested that existing international judicial practice on the powers of interpretation and revision demonstrates that they are generally exercised in a consistent manner by international courts. The next chapter turns to the practice of international courts regarding a possible outcome of international dispute settlement proceedings: the awarding of remedies.

6

Remedies in International Adjudication

Introduction

The subject of remedies is not one that fits within the concept of 'procedure'. Remedies are usually understood as the judicial relief which legal systems provide for the enforcement or defence of substantive rights.[1] In addition, unlike procedure, the constitutive instruments and rules of procedure of international courts make little provision for remedies. Most constitutive instruments are silent on the question, with some referring merely to the power of the international court to

[1] For example, Arwed Blomeyer, 'Types of Relief Available (Judicial Remedies)' in International Association of Legal Science, *International Encyclopedia of Comparative Law* (1982) vol XVI, ch 4, 3.

'decide the dispute'.[2] Thus the law of remedies has largely been left to be developed by international courts in their jurisprudence, and this practice has contributed to the formation of the secondary rules of international law concerning the legal consequences of an internationally wrongful act.[3] The absence of clear provision on remedies in conventions and constitutive instruments has led international courts to consider the practice of other international tribunals in the awarding of remedies. Additionally, the obtaining of a remedy is a significant reason for commencing international proceedings, placing the awarding of remedies at the heart of the adjudicative functions of international courts. In this sense, if there are some common features in the way that international courts approach the question of remedies, this will be significant in the examination of whether there is a common law of international adjudication.

The question of the existence of an international law of remedies has been posed before. In 1985, Professor Gray concluded that '[a]t present it is clear that the mass of arbitral and judicial practice has fallen somewhat short of producing an international law of remedies'.[4] Since this observation was made, there have been several developments, such as the phenomenon of proliferation, the increase in the resort by states and other non-state entities to international adjudication, and the adoption by the UN General Assembly of the ILC Articles on State Responsibility, which seek, *inter alia*, to codify the forms of reparation available in international law.[5] Thus, while judicial remedies in international law have previously been the subject of careful scholarship, it is timely that they be subjected to re-examination.

It is well established that a state responsible for an internationally wrongful act is under an obligation to make 'reparation', which is the remedy at international law. This is not coterminous with 'damages' or 'compensation'.[6] Rather, reparation is an umbrella concept, which can be represented in various forms. The three forms of reparation identified by the ILC are restitution, compensation and satisfaction. The law of reparation is to some extent independent of international judicial practice, for the obligation to make reparation arises as a result of state responsibility for an internationally wrongful act, regardless of whether this is determined in international

[2] For example, *Convention for the Settlement of Investment Disputes between States and Nationals of Other States*, opened for signature 18 March 1965, 575 UNTS 159 (entered into force 14 October 1966), art 42(1); *Statute of the International Court of Justice*, opened for signature 26 June 1945, 3 Bevans 1153 (entered into force 24 October 1945), art 38(1); see also Christine Gray, 'Is there an International Law of Remedies?' (1985) 56 *British Yearbook of International Law* 25, 35.

[3] The diplomatic practice of states has also played a part in the development of these rules: see, e.g., the instances referred to in James Crawford, *The International Law Commission's Articles on State Responsibility* (2002) 196–206.

[4] Gray, above n 2, 47; see also Christine Gray, *Judicial Remedies in International Law* (1987) 107–8.

[5] ILC Articles on State Responsibility, in Crawford, above n 3, 61–73 ('ILC Articles').

[6] ILC Articles, ibid, art 31; Crawford, ibid, 201–6; Ian Brownlie, *Principles of Public International Law* (6th ed, 2003) 442. On the terminological confusion in the law of remedies, see generally Suzan Haasdijk, 'The Lack of Uniformity in the Terminology of the International Law of Remedies' (1992) 5 *Leiden Journal of International Law* 245.

judicial proceedings or through diplomatic processes.[7] Once state responsibility is established, the responsible state is obliged to cease the unlawful act, to make assurances and guarantees of non-repetition, if circumstances so require, and to make full reparation to the injured state.[8]

As this chapter deals with subject matter which differs from that in preceding chapters, it is also structured somewhat differently. First, the source of the power of international courts to award remedies is briefly examined. The second part of this chapter examines the obligation to make 'full reparation', and briefly details the three different forms of reparation. The existence of these forms of reparation is relatively uncontentious, and there is much international practice supporting their existence. There is, however, some disagreement on the application of the three forms of reparation as judicial remedies, and some of these issues are highlighted. Certain questions related to the application of the three forms of reparation as judicial remedies are then considered. Controversial questions relate to the appropriateness of each remedy in particular disputes, the standard of compensation, the availability of compensation for future loss, and whether international courts can issue mandatory orders. Finally, the remedial regime in the WTO dispute settlement system is considered, which is traditionally regarded as a *lex specialis*. Nevertheless, it is suggested that although individual dispute settlement regimes have some special characteristics with respect to the awarding of remedies, the guiding principle of full reparation is generally applied, and it can even be seen to be exerting an influence on the WTO remedial regime.

I. Source of the Power to Award Remedies

It has been observed in chapter 2 that international courts having jurisdiction over a particular dispute have, as an essential part of that jurisdiction, the power to award remedies.[9] While many constitutive instruments are silent as to the power to award remedies,[10] others do make some provision for the power, and it is useful

[7] For example, Crawford, ibid, 222–3.

[8] ILC Articles, above n 5, arts 30–1; Crawford, ibid, 196–206; see also *Factory at Chorzów (Jurisdiction)*, Ser A, (No 9), 21 (PCIJ, 1927); *Gabcikovo–Nagymaros Project* [1997] ICJ Rep 7, 81.

[9] See above chapter 2, part III; *Factory at Chorzów*, above n 8, 21–5; *Corfu Channel (Merits)* [1949] ICJ Rep 4, 26; *Fisheries Jurisdiction* [1974] ICJ Rep 175, 203–5; *Nicaragua (Merits)* [1986] ICJ Rep 14, 142; *LaGrand (Merits)* (2001) 40 ILM 1069, 1082; *Avena* (2004) 43 ILM 581, 598; see also Chester Brown, 'The Inherent Powers of International Courts and Tribunals' (2005) 76 *British Yearbook of International Law* 195, 221.

[10] See, e.g., the ICSID Convention, above n 2, *Convention for the Pacific Settlement of International Disputes*, opened for signature 29 July 1899, 1 Bevans 230 (entered into force 4 September 1900) and *Convention for the Pacific Settlement of International Disputes*, opened for signature 18 October 1907, 1 Bevans 577 (entered into force 26 January 1910) none of which makes any provision for remedies. See also Petros Mavroidis, 'Remedies in the WTO Legal System: Between a Rock and a Hard Place' (2000) 11 *European Journal of International Law* 763, 764; Gray, *Judicial Remedies*, above n 4, 10–11; Gray, 'Is there an International Law of Remedies?', above n 2, 35.

to review these. The PCIJ Statute provided in article 36(2)(d) that states parties could declare that they recognize the PCIJ's jurisdiction in legal disputes concerning 'the nature or extent of the reparation to be made for the breach of an international obligation'.[11] This provision survives today in the ICJ Statute.[12] It only applies, however, in respect of disputes submitted to the ICJ under article 36(2), being the ICJ's optional clause jurisdiction. There are, of course, other ways in which the ICJ may take jurisdiction over a dispute; such as by special agreement (*compromis*) or compromissory clause in a multilateral convention,[13] by virtue of the transferred jurisdiction of the PCIJ,[14] or by *forum prorogatum*.[15] Article 36(2) does not apply to disputes referred to the ICJ under these heads of jurisdiction; thus the ICJ Statute is silent with respect to the power of the ICJ to award remedies in such cases. Of course, in cases referred to the ICJ by *compromis*, the parties themselves might specify the remedy which the ICJ is empowered to award. For instance, in *Continental Shelf (Tunisia/Libya)*, and *Continental Shelf (Libya/Malta)*, the ICJ was asked to declare 'the principles and rules of international law' applicable to the delimitation of the continental shelf in the disputed area.[16] In these cases, the ICJ would have exceeded the limits of its powers under the *compromis* had it ordered, say, the payment of compensation.

In contrast to the lack of provision in other statutes, the constitutive instruments of the ITLOS, the ECHR, the IACHR and the WTO dispute settlement system do contemplate the awarding of remedies. In article 304, UNCLOS provides simply that any provisions in UNCLOS regarding responsibility and liability for damage are without prejudice to the application of existing secondary rules regarding responsibility and liability under international law.[17] The European HR Convention provides that if the ECHR finds that there has been a violation of the convention or of its protocols, and if the domestic law of the state concerned 'allows only partial reparation to be made', the ECHR has the power, if necessary, to 'afford just satisfaction to the injured party'.[18] The American Convention provides that if the IACHR finds that there has been a breach of the convention, it has the power to 'rule that the injured party be ensured the enjoyment of his right or freedom that was violated', and, if appropriate, 'that the consequences of the measure or situation that constituted the breach of such right or freedom be remedied

[11] *Statute of the Permanent Court of International Justice*, PCIJ Publications, Ser D (No 1), 7 ('PCIJ Statute'), art 36(2)(d).

[12] ICJ Statute, above n 2, art 36(2)(d).

[13] Ibid, art 36(1).

[14] Ibid, arts 36(5), 37.

[15] International Court of Justice Rules of Court, available at <http://www.icj-cij.org>, art 38(5); see, e.g., Sienho Yee, '*Forum Prorogatum* Returns to the International Court of Justice' (2003) 16 *Leiden Journal of International Law* 701.

[16] [1982] ICJ Rep 18, 23; [1985] ICJ Rep 13, 16.

[17] *UN Convention on the Law of the Sea*, opened for signature 10 December 1982, 21 ILM 1261 (entered into force 16 November 1994), art 304.

[18] *Convention for the Protection of Human Rights and Fundamental Freedoms*, opened for signature 4 November 1950, 213 UNTS 221 (entered into force 3 September 1953), art 41.

and that fair compensation be paid to the injured party'.[19] Exactly what constitutes 'just satisfaction' under the European HR Convention, or 'fair compensation' under the American Convention, however, is left to be determined in the jurisprudence of these courts. In the case of the ECHR, the Committee of Ministers of the Council of Europe has a role in supervising the execution of judgments,[20] although this does not include awarding remedies in individual cases; it merely gives the Committee the role of ensuring that states comply with judgments. But the Committee expressed its views in its Recommendation No R(2000)2, where it approved of the relevance of the law of reparation, stating that in certain circumstances the obligation to abide by judgments of the ECHR 'may entail the adoption of measures . . . which ensure that the injured party is put, as far as possible, in the same situation as he or she enjoyed prior to the violation of the Convention (*restitutio in integrum*)'.[21]

The DSU of the WTO dispute settlement system makes extensive provision for its remedial regime.[22] This regime differs in several respects from the law of reparation in general international law. First, while the availability of reparation is usually contingent on the commission of an internationally wrongful act, dispute settlement proceedings may be commenced under the DSU if a member considers that benefits accruing to it are being 'impaired' by measures taken by another member;[23] there is no need for the breach of an international obligation. Second, while the aim under the law of reparation is, as far as possible, to 'wipe out' the consequences of the illegal act, the primary objective of WTO dispute settlement is 'usually to secure the withdrawal of the measures concerned if these are found to be inconsistent with the provisions of any covered agreements'.[24] The primacy of this objective is reinforced by the recommendations that can be made by WTO panels or the Appellate Body under article 19(1), which are that 'the Member concerned bring the measure into conformity with that agreement'.[25] As remedies in WTO dispute settlement can be considered a *lex specialis* and an exception to the obligation of reparation that arises under general international law, they are treated separately in a later section.

[19] *American Convention on Human Rights*, opened for signature 22 November 1969, 1144 UNTS 123 (entered into force 18 July 1978), art 63(1).

[20] *European HR Convention*, above n 18, art 54; *Statute of the Council of Europe*, opened for signature 5 May 1949, CETS No 001 (entered into force 3 August 1949), art 15.

[21] Recommendation No R(2000)2 of the Committee of Ministers to Member States on the Re-examination or Reopening of Certain Cases at Domestic Level Following Judgments of the ECHR, Adopted at 694th Meeting of Ministers' Deputies (19 January 2000).

[22] *Understanding on Rules and Procedures Governing the Settlement of Disputes*, opened for signature 15 April 1994, 1869 UNTS 401 (entered into force 1 January 1995) ('DSU'). See especially Patricio Grané, 'Remedies under WTO Law' (2001) 4 *Journal of International Economic Law* 755.

[23] DSU, ibid, art 3(3).

[24] Ibid, art 3(7).

[25] Ibid, art 19(1) (footnotes omitted).

II. 'Reparation' as the Remedy in International Law

A. Generally

The obligation to make reparation for the commission of an internationally wrongful act was accepted in many early arbitrations, and was affirmed by the PCIJ in *Factory at Chorzów*. In this case, it held that 'it is a principle of international law that the breach of an engagement involves an obligation to make reparation in an adequate form'.[26] In a later phase of *Factory at Chorzów*, the PCIJ elaborated on the content of the obligation of reparation, holding that:

> The essential principle contained in the actual notion of an illegal act—a principle which seems to be established by international practice and in particular by the decisions of arbitral tribunals—is that reparation must, as far as possible, wipe out all the consequences of the illegal act and re-establish the situation which would, in all probability, have existed if that act had not been committed. Restitution in kind, or, if this is not possible, payment of a sum corresponding to the value which a restitution in kind would bear; the award, if need be, of damages for loss sustained which would not be covered by restitution in kind or payment in place of it—such are the principles which should serve to determine the amount of compensation due for an act contrary to international law.[27]

As suggested by the PCIJ, reparation can take different forms. There are three forms which have been recognized in international practice, by writers, and by the ILC, being restitution, compensation, and satisfaction.

B. The Three Forms of Reparation

The availability of restitution as a form of reparation is widely accepted.[28] It consists of restoring the *status quo ante*, i.e. putting the claimant into the position it was in prior to the commission of the internationally wrongful act. The most authoritative judicial statement on the availability of restitution is the dictum of the PCIJ in *Factory at Chorzów*, excerpted above.[29] In that case, the PCIJ also confirmed

[26] Above n 8, 21; Crawford, above n 3, 201.

[27] Ser A, (No 17), 47 (PCIJ, 1928); Crawford, above n 3, 201.

[28] See, e.g., Brownlie, above n 6, 442; Crawford, above n 3, 213–17; Alfred Verdross and Bruno Simma, *Universelles Völkerrecht* (3rd ed, 1984) 873–5; F A Mann, 'The Consequences of an International Wrong in International and National Law' (1976–7) 48 *British Yearbook of International Law* 1, 3; J H W Verzijl, *International Law in Historical Perspective* (1976) vol VI, 742–5; D P O'Connell, *International Law* (2nd ed, 1970) 1114–15; Eduardo Jiminez de Aréchaga, 'International Responsibility' in Max Sørensen (ed), *Manual of Public International Law* (1968) 571, 565–7; J H W Verzijl, *The Jurisprudence of the World Court* (1965) vol I, 168–76; Friedrich Berber, *Lehrbuch des Völkerrechts* (1964) vol III, 23–6; Ladislas Reitzer, *La Réparation comme conséquence de l'acte illicite en Droit international* (1938) 171; Clyde Eagleton, *The Responsibility of States in International Law* (1928) 182; but see Gray, *Judicial Remedies*, above n 4, 13, 95–6; and *BP v Libya*, 53 ILR 297, 347–8 (1973).

[29] See above n 27 and accompanying text.

the primacy of restitution, stating that if it could not be awarded, or if it did not cover the loss sustained, a payment of compensation should be made.[30] The 'primacy' of restitution does not refer to it being the most frequently awarded form of reparation, but rather to its status as the most preferable remedy to restore the claimant to the position it was in prior to the internationally wrongful act; this primacy is generally accepted.[31] The ILC has affirmed that restitution should be awarded 'provided and to the extent that' it is not 'materially impossible', and that it does not place a disproportionate burden on the state responsible for the internationally wrongful act when compared with the possible benefit to the injured state.[32] Further, if a claimant elects another form of reparation, an international court would not award restitution, in pursuance of the *ne ultra petita* rule.[33] In addition, if an order for restitution does not achieve 'full reparation', it may also be accompanied by an order for other forms of reparation, such as compensation or satisfaction.[34]

Monetary compensation is perhaps the most commonly sought remedy in international adjudication.[35] Claims for monetary compensation are recognized in many domestic legal systems,[36] and the availability of compensation in international adjudication has been recognized by writers and most international courts.[37] The function of compensation is to provide judicially ascertained damages for a harm that is 'financially assessable'.[38] In *Lusitania*, Umpire Parker held that:

> The fundamental concept of 'damages' is satisfaction, reparation for a *loss* suffered; a judicially ascertained *compensation* for wrong. The remedy should be commensurate with the loss, so that the injured party may be made whole.[39]

The requirement that compensation cover loss which is 'financially assessable' operates so as to exclude 'moral damage' to a state from being the subject of compensation; the appropriate form of reparation for moral damage is satisfaction.[40]

30 Ibid.

31 Crawford, above n 3, 213; International Law Commission ('ILC'), 'Report of the International Law Commission on the Work of its Forty-fifth Session (3 May–23 July 1993)' [1993] *YbILC*, vol II, pt II, 1, 61–7, UN Doc A/48/10; Sir Hersch Lauterpacht, *Private Law Sources and Analogies of International Law* (1927) 149; but see Christine Gray, 'The Choice between Restitution and Compensation' (1999) 10 *European Journal of International Law* 413, 416; Gray, *Judicial Remedies*, above n 4, 13; Willem Riphagen, 'Second Report on the Content, Forms and Degrees of International Responsibility' [1981] *YbILC*, vol II, pt 1, 79, 88–9, UN Doc A/CN.4/344.

32 ILC Articles, above n 5, art 35.

33 For example, ILC Articles, ibid, art 43(2)(b); although see discussion in Crawford, above n 3, 262–3, noting that the injured state's right to elect the form of reparation is not unlimited.

34 ILC Articles, ibid, art 34; Crawford, ibid, 211–12.

35 Brownlie, above n 6, 442; Crawford, above n 3, 218; Gray, *Judicial Remedies*, above n 4, 18.

36 Blomeyer, above n 1, 26–30.

37 ILC Articles, above n 5, art 36; Crawford, above n 3, 218–30; Brownlie, above n 6, 446–7; Gray, *Judicial Remedies*, above n 4, 18–21, 77–92; Gaetano Arangio-Ruiz, 'Second Report on State Responsibility' [1989] *YbILC*, vol II, pt I, 1, 8–9, UN Doc A/CN.4/425; Eagleton, above n 28, 189; *Gabcikovo–Nagymaros Project*, above n 8, 81.

38 Crawford, ibid, 218–19.

39 7 RIAA 32, 39 (US–German MCC, 1923) (emphasis in original, footnotes omitted).

40 Crawford, above n 3, 218; Gray, *Judicial Remedies*, above n 4, 85–6.

In the event that an internationally wrongful act cannot be made good by restitution or compensation, the responsible state is under an obligation to give 'satisfaction' for the injury caused by that act. Satisfaction is an appropriate form of reparation in the case of injuries which are not financially assessable and amount to moral damage, or an affront to the state.[41] According to the ILC, satisfaction may consist of 'an acknowledgement of the breach, an expression of regret, a formal apology or another appropriate modality'.[42] A common modality in the case of moral or non-material injury is 'a declaration of the wrongfulness of the act by a competent court or tribunal'.[43] The importance of declaratory judgments—which are also found in domestic legal systems[44]—derives from the fact that the adjudication of a dispute can be of greater significance than the awarding of other remedies, especially for states committed to upholding the rule of law and meeting their obligations.[45]

C. Agreement and Disagreement in the Law of Remedies

There is much agreement on the availability of restitution, compensation, and declaratory judgments as remedies in international adjudication. This results from over two hundred years of development of the secondary rules of international law in the practice of interstate arbitrations, mixed claims commissions, ad hoc arbitral tribunals and permanent international courts. Despite the broad agreement on the guiding principles, there are also areas of contention.

First, although there is a large measure of acceptance of the availability of restitution, compensation and declaratory judgments in international adjudication, this does not mean that each form of reparation will be appropriate or even available as remedies in individual cases. The appropriateness of different remedies will depend on the nature of the court, the type of dispute, the identity of the parties, and, of course, the particular relief sought by the claimant in the proceedings. In addition, the express terms of the constitutive instrument of each international court may prescribe the remedies which are available. This is the case for WTO panels and the Appellate Body, whose remedial regime prescribed by the DSU can be regarded as a *lex specialis*.

The appropriateness of different forms of reparation in different disputes can be illustrated by several examples. For instance, in interstate disputes before the ICJ, PCA tribunals or ad hoc arbitral tribunals, which concern, say, the delimitation

[41] For example, Brownlie, above n 6, 443–5; Crawford, ibid, 231; Arangio-Ruiz, above n 37, 31–2; Aréchaga, above n 28, 572; Jean Personnaz, *La Réparation du Préjudice en Droit International Public* (1939) 277; J C Bluntschli, *Das moderne Völkerrecht der civilisirten Staten als Rechtsbuch dargestellt* (3rd ed, 1878, trans C Lardy, *Le droit international codifié*, 5th rev ed, 1895) 264, art 463.

[42] ILC Articles, above n 5, art 37.

[43] Crawford, above n 3, 233.

[44] Blomeyer, above n 1, 41–50.

[45] Edwin Borchard, *Declaratory Judgments* (1934) 10; Dinah Shelton, *Remedies in International Human Rights Law* (2nd ed, 2005) 255–7; see also Mann, above n 28, 10–11.

of a frontier, or the interpretation or application of a treaty, the appropriate remedy might be a declaratory judgment, and there might be no question of compensation. In a claim before the ECHR, the IACHR or the ACHPR, dealing with alleged violations of human rights, an appropriate remedy might be a declaration that the state has violated the rights of its citizens, and also an award of compensation for pecuniary and non-pecuniary loss relating to damage to property, personal injury, or emotional harm. In a trade dispute before a WTO panel, the appropriate remedy might be a declaration that the responsible state should bring its trade measures into conformity with its obligations. In a dispute before a quasi-judicial NCP regarding alleged breaches of duties arising under a multilateral environmental agreement, the appropriate remedy might also be a recommendation that the responsible state bring its legislation into conformity with its obligations, and possibly the imposition of sanctions.[46] Finally, in disputes arising out of an investment before the Iran–US Claims Tribunal, an ICSID tribunal, or a tribunal constituted under a bilateral investment treaty or chapter 11 of NAFTA, the appropriate remedy is more likely to be monetary compensation, for a declaratory judgment would probably be inadequate, and restitution of the claimant's property would be difficult to enforce. In any event, in such cases restitution would rarely be desirable due to a deterioration in the investor–host state relationship.[47]

Second, even where it is decided that a particular remedy is appropriate, difficulties might arise in the application of that remedy due to the unsettled state of the law. For instance, uncertainty persists surrounding the availability of compensation for future loss in claims relating to expropriation and damage to property.[48] In addition, disparities exist in the quantum of compensation awarded owing to disagreement on the standard of compensation and the method of valuation.[49]

Third, there is some uncertainty concerning the power of international courts to issue judgments in mandatory or consequential terms.[50] These might include judgments for restitution, specific performance, or negative injunctions. The dictum of the ICJ in *Haya de la Torre*, that it was not part of the judicial function to direct the parties on the manner in which they should comply with the judgment, suggested that international courts did not have the power to issue mandatory orders imposing an obligation on states to execute the judgment in a certain way.[51] Yet this assumption has been questioned by more recent decisions of international

[46] See, e.g., Malgosia Fitzmaurice and Catherine Redgwell, 'Environmental Non-Compliance Procedures and International Law' (2000) 31 *Netherlands Yearbook of International Law* 35.

[47] For example, Charles Brower and Jason Brueschke, *The Iran–United States Claims Tribunal* (1998) 473; see especially *BP v Libya*, above n 28, 323, 356–7; *LIAMCO v Libya*, 62 ILR 140, 198–200, 217 (1977); John Barker, 'The Valuation of Income-Producing Property in International Law' (PhD dissertation, University of Cambridge, 1998) 198.

[48] See part III(B)(2)(a) of this chapter below.

[49] See below nn 140–147 and accompanying text.

[50] Mann, above n 28, 13.

[51] [1951] ICJ Rep 71, 78–9.

courts,[52] which seem to suggest that international courts are increasingly assuming the power to issue judgments in mandatory form.[53]

There are also other issues which are of interest in an examination of judicial remedies in international law, which are not treated in detail in this book. One of these is the question whether punitive or exemplary damages are available in international law. The position which has been accepted by some international courts and many writers is that international courts do not have the power to order punitive damages.[54] Yet some international case law can be found which supports the availability of punitive damages,[55] and also writers have doubted the accepted position.[56] Another question connected with the awarding of remedies is whether international courts have the power to make orders for costs. There is inconsistent practice concerning this question.[57] The ICJ has stated that 'the basic principle regarding the question of costs in contentious proceedings before international tribunals... [is] that each party shall bear its own in the absence of a specific decision of the tribunal awarding costs'.[58] The ICSID Tribunal in *Generation Ukraine v Ukraine*, however, referred to 'the general rule that an unsuccessful litigant in international arbitration should bear the reasonable costs of its opponent'.[59] In *Waste Management v Mexico (No 2)*, however, the NAFTA Tribunal stated that '[t]here is

[52] See, e.g., *Enron Corporation and Ponderosa Assets v Argentina* (ICSID Case No ARB/01/3, Decision on Jurisdiction of 14 January 2004), paras 76–81; *Assanidze v Georgia* (2004) 39 EHRR 653; *Arrest Warrant (Merits)* (2002) 41 ILM 536, 556–7; *LaGrand*, above n 9, 1103; *Tanzania Electric Supply Co Ltd v Independent Power Tanzania* (ICSID Case No ARB/98/8, Award of 22 June 2001), 26; *Loayza Tamayo (Reparations)*, Ser C, (No 42) (IACHR, 1998); *Rainbow Warrior*, 82 ILR 499, 573 (New Zealand–France, 1990).

[53] See especially Shelton, above n 45, 280–9; Alexander Orakhelashvili, 'Judicial Competence and Judicial Remedies in the *Avena* Case' (2005) 18 *Leiden Journal of International Law* 31, 41–2, 44–5, 47–8; Christoph Schreuer, 'Non-Pecuniary Remedies in ICSID Arbitration' (2004) 20 *Arbitration International* 325, 326–32.

[54] See, e.g., Crawford, above n 3, 219; Stephan Wittich, 'Awe of the Gods and Fear of the Priests: Punitive Damages in the Law of State Responsibility' (1998) 3 *Austrian Review of International and European Law* 31, 54–7; Nina Jørgensen, 'A Reappraisal of Punitive Damages in International Law' (1997) 68 *British Yearbook of International Law* 247, 266; Aréchaga, above n 28, 571; *Re Letelier and Moffit*, 88 ILR 727, 737, 741 (Sep Op Orrego Vicuna) (Chile–US Int Com, 1992); *Velásquez Rodríguez*, 95 ILR 233, 315–16 (IACHR, 1989); *Lusitania*, above n 39, 39.

[55] For example, *Moke*, Moore, vol IV, 3411 (US–Mexican CC, 1871); *Janes*, 3 Annual Digest 256 (US–Mexican GCC 1925–6); *I'm Alone*, 7 Annual Digest 203, 206 (Canada–US 1933–4); *Sedco Inc v NIOC*, 10 Ir–USCTR 180, 189, 205, fn 40 (Sep Op Brower) (1986); see also Jørgensen, above n 54, 248–9.

[56] For a cautious expression of doubt, see Gray, *Judicial Remedies*, above n 4, 26–8; for the argument that punitive damages should be available in human rights claims, see Shelton, above n 45, 360–7.

[57] See, e.g., *International Thunderbird Gaming Corporation v Mexico* (NAFTA Tribunal Award of 26 January 2006), paras 124–47 (Sep Op Wälde), available at <http://ita.law.uvic.ca> (last visited 25 November 2006).

[58] *Application for Review of Judgment No 158* [1973] ICJ Rep 166, 212. For example, ICJ Statute, above n 2, art 64; ICJ Rules, above n 15, art 97; UNCLOS, above n 17, Annex VI ('ITLOS Statute'), art 34; Shabtai Rosenne, *The Law and Practice of the International Court, 1920–2005* (2006) vol III, 1279–81; Shabtai Rosenne, *Procedure in the International Court* (1983) 200.

[59] *Generation Ukraine v Ukraine* (ICSID Case No ARB/00/9, Award of 16 September 2003), para 24.1.

no rule in international arbitration that costs follow the event'.[60] Another controverted issue concerns the awarding of interest. The existence of a power to award interest does not appear to be in question; many international tribunals have held that they have the power to award interest, even in the absence of an express power, as interest forms part of the calculation of monetary compensation.[61] Yet uncertainties remain in the applicable method for calculation of interest, the applicable interest rate and the relevant dates.[62]

It is not possible to consider every issue pertaining to remedies in international adjudication in this chapter. Rather, this chapter considers the core issues in remedies, and assesses whether international courts deal with them in a broadly consistent fashion. These questions include the consistency of the awarding of remedies in particular types of disputes, whether international courts can award remedies in mandatory form, and the compatibility of remedies in the WTO dispute settlement system with the general international law of reparation. In addition, in order to ensure that this chapter does not overlook the significant differences that exist in the way that international courts and tribunals deal with questions of remedies, a short case study is included of an example when one international court seemingly ignored the case law of other international courts on a similar question.

III. Forms of Reparation in Particular Disputes

A. Restitution

It has been observed above that restitution is the primary form of reparation, although it might not be an appropriate remedy in all cases. Early practice of arbitral tribunals awarding restitution is scarce. This is probably due to the nature of many early arbitrations as claims for compensation which concerned expropriated property or injury to aliens. Nonetheless, instances can be found where tribunals have made awards for restitution, such as ordering the annulment of obligations of payment,[63] the provision of a consular residence to replace one destroyed by

[60] *Waste Management v Mexico (No 2)* (ICSID Case No ARB(AF)/00/3, Award of 30 April 2004), para 183, available at <http://ita.law.uvic.edu> (last visited 25 November 2006).

[61] For example, *Iran v US (Case A–19)*, 16 Ir–USCTR 285, 289–90 (1987); ILC Articles, above n 5, art 38; Crawford, above n 3, 235–9; Barker, above n 47, 207–47; Gray, *Judicial Remedies*, above n 4, 29–33.

[62] For example, on the awarding of compound rather than simple interest, see *Wena Hotels v Egypt* (2002) 41 ILM 896, 919–20; *Metalclad v Mexico* (2001) 16 *ICSID Review—FILJ* 168, 34, referring to *Asian Agricultural Products Ltd v Sri Lanka*, 4 ICSID Rep 245, 294–5 (1990); *Compañia del Desarrollo de Santa Elena* (Award), (2000) 15 *ICSID Review—FILJ* 169, 200–1, referring to arbitral practice and the writings of publicists; *Middle East Cement Shipping v Egypt*, (2003) 18 ICSID *Review–FILJ* 602, paras 174–5; John Gotanda, 'Compound Interest in International Disputes' (2004) *Villanova University School of Law Working Paper Series*, Working Paper 14; and Markham Ball, 'Assessing Damages in Claims by Investors Against States' (2001) 16 *ICSID Review—FILJ* 408, 429.

[63] *Martini*, 2 RIAA 975, 1002 (Italy–Venezuela, 1930).

government troops,[64] the revocation of governmental instructions to telegraphic authorities not to accept telegrams sent by a certain radio service,[65] and the restitution of money paid in taxes by operators of a mine which had to be abandoned due to political upheaval.[66] The Court of Justice of Central America also awarded restitution in *El Salvador v Nicaragua*, where it held that Nicaragua was under an obligation to re-establish and maintain the legal status that existed prior to the conclusion of the Bryan-Chamorro Treaty.[67]

The ICJ has also awarded restitution on several occasions. In *Temple of Preah Vihear*, the ICJ declared the location of the frontier between Cambodia and Thailand, and also ordered the return to Cambodia of certain objects removed from the temple by Thai authorities;[68] this order served to re-establish the *status quo ante*.[69] In *Tehran Hostages*, the ICJ ordered that Iran 'must immediately take all steps to redress the situation resulting from the events of 4 November 1979', and detailed what was required to do this;[70] this can also arguably be regarded as a form of restitution.[71] In *Passage through the Great Belt*, Finland sought, *inter alia*, the cessation by Denmark of the construction of a bridge over the Great Belt.[72] In the request for provisional measures, it was argued on behalf of Denmark that a remedy of restitution at the merits phase would be impossible, for Denmark intended to continue the construction of the bridge during the pendency of the proceedings.[73] The ICJ rejected this argument, stating that 'the possibility cannot and should not be excluded *a priori* of a judicial finding that such works must not be continued or must be modified or dismantled'.[74] Ultimately, Finland elected to seek compensation, and the dispute was the subject of a negotiated settlement.[75] Nevertheless, the ICJ's statement in its order on provisional measures makes clear that restitution would have been a possible remedy had the action proceeded to the merits.[76] In 2004, in *Avena*, while rejecting Mexico's request for restitution in the form of an order for the annulment of convictions of Mexican nationals which had been secured in the US in breach of obligations under the Consular Relations Convention,[77] the ICJ ordered that restitution would be achieved by the US

[64] *Rights of Britons in Morocco*, 2 RIAA 615, 722–7 (Spain–UK, 1925).

[65] *L'Affaire de la Société Radio-Orient*, 3 RIAA 1871, 1880–1 (France–Egypt, 1940).

[66] *Palmarejo and Mexican Goldfields*, 5 RIAA 298, 301 (GB–Mexican CC, 1931). See, however, *Casablanca*, 11 RIAA 119, 129–30 (France–Germany, 1909), and *Savarkar*, 11 RIAA 243, 254 (France–Great Britain, 1911), where PCA tribunals refused restitution: Reitzer, above n 28, 173. See further Crawford, above n 3, 214–17; O'Connell, above n 28, 1115.

[67] (1917) 11 *AJIL* 674, 730.

[68] [1962] ICJ Rep 6, 36–7.

[69] But see Gray, *Judicial Remedies*, above n 4, 67.

[70] [1980] ICJ Rep 3, 44–5.

[71] Crawford, above n 3, 214, fn 529; for the expression of doubt, see Gray, *Judicial Remedies*, above n 4, 95–6.

[72] [1991] ICJ Rep 12, 14.

[73] Ibid, 19.

[74] Ibid; Christine Gray, '*Passage through the Great Belt (Finland v Denmark)* Provisional Measures, Order of 29 July 1991' (1993) 42 *ICLQ* 705, 709.

[75] Martii Koskenniemi, 'L'affaire du passage par le Grand-Belt' (1992) 38 *Annuaire Français de Droit International* 905, 940.

[76] See also Crawford, above n 3, 262–3.

[77] Above n 9, 616; *Vienna Convention on Consular Relations*, opened for signature 24 April 1963, 596 UNTS 261 (entered into force 19 March 1967).

giving meaningful and effective 'review and reconsideration' of the convictions.[78] Furthermore, in *Legal Consequences of the Construction of a Wall in the Palestinian Occupied Territory*, the ICJ held that Israel must make full reparation, including returning land 'seized from any natural or legal person for the purposes of construction of the wall in the Occupied Palestinian Territory'.[79]

The ITLOS has not, as yet, ordered restitution as a remedy for a breach of an international obligation.[80] In *M/V 'Saiga' (No 2)*, Saint Vincent and the Grenadines did not expressly seek restitution, but rather, restricted its prayer for relief to compensation.[81] Restitution was probably materially impossible in this case; it would prove difficult to restore the situation that existed prior to the damage and unlawful arrest and detention of the *M/V 'Saiga'*. Yet the ITLOS clearly recognized the availability of restitution in its reference in that case to the PCIJ dictum in *Factory at Chorzów* and its citation of the forms of reparation recognized in the ILC Draft Articles on State Responsibility.[82] It is also possible that the remedy granted by the ITLOS in prompt release cases represents a form of restitution. Under article 292(1) of UNCLOS, if a state party detains a vessel flying the flag of another state party, and the detaining state does not promptly release the vessel or its crew after the posting of a reasonable bond or other financial security in accordance with article 73(2) of UNCLOS, then the flag state can apply to the ITLOS (or any other court or tribunal agreed upon by the parties) to have the question determined.[83] In such cases, the remedy is an order for the 'prompt release' of the detained vessel and its crew.[84] Such orders are arguably a form of restitution, as they re-establish the situation that existed prior to the internationally wrongful act, being the failure of the detaining state to release the vessel promptly upon the posting of a reasonable bond.

Human rights courts have also accepted that they can order restitution as an available remedy. In *Velásquez Rodríguez*, the IACHR referred to *Factory at Chorzów*, and held that:

> reparation of harm brought about by the violation of an international obligation consists in full restitution (*restitutio in integrum*), which includes the restoration of the prior situation,

[78] *Avena*, ibid, 616–19.

[79] *Legal Consequences of the Construction of a Wall* (ICJ Advisory Opinion of 9 July 2004), paras 152–3.

[80] At the time of writing, the ITLOS and other tribunals established under the UNCLOS had only rendered judgments or awards on the merits in two cases: *M/V 'Saiga' (No 2)*, 120 ILR 143, (ITLOS, 1999), and *Barbados/Trinidad and Tobago* (Award of 11 April 2006), a maritime boundary delimitation dispute, available at <http://www.pca-cpa.org> (last visited 25 November 2006). (This excludes applications for the prompt release of vessels, of which there have been seven applications and judgments: <http://www.itlos.org> (last visited 25 November 2006).)

[81] Ibid, 199.

[82] Ibid.

[83] UNCLOS, above n 17, art 292(1).

[84] Ibid, art 292(4). On such orders, see Anne-Katrin Escher, 'Release of Vessels and Crews before the International Tribunal for the Law of the Sea (Parts 1 and 2)' (2004) 3 *Law and Practice of International Courts and Tribunals* 205; Anne-Katrin Escher, 'Release of Vessels and Crews before the International Tribunal for the Law of the Sea (Part 3)' (2004) 3 *Law and Practice of International Courts and Tribunals* 411; and Chester Brown, '"Reasonableness" in the Law of the Sea: The Prompt Release of the *Volga*' (2003) 16 *Leiden Journal of International Law* 621.

the reparation of the consequences of the violation, and indemnification for patrimonial and non-patrimonial damages, including emotional harm.[85]

The ECHR has also applied the standard of 'complete reparation (*restitutio in integrum*)'. If this is not possible, 'just satisfaction' is required including 'full pecuniary indemnification'.[86] The ECHR made such an award in *Papamichalopoulos v Greece*, where it was confronted with a claim arising out of the seizure of privately owned property by the Greek government for the purpose of constructing a coastal resort for naval officers. Also referring to *Factory at Chorzów*, and 'international case-law, of courts or arbitration tribunals', the ECHR considered that restitution, in the form of 'the return of the land in issue', was the most appropriate remedy.[87] The ECHR did, however, observe that it did not have 'the power nor the practical possibility' of enforcing such a judgment.[88] In its Recommendation No R(2000)2, the Committee of Ministers also acknowledged the appropriateness of the standard of *restitutio in integrum* in awards of 'just satisfaction' in ECHR judgments.[89] In 2004, in *Assanidze v Georgia*, a case concerning the arbitrary detention of an individual, the ECHR held that Georgia was under an obligation to make reparation, which in this case involved 'secur[ing] the applicant's release at the earliest possible date'.[90]

B. Compensation

Compensation was the most commonly awarded remedy in early arbitral tribunals and claims commissions.[91] The PCIJ addressed issues of compensation on two occasions; in *SS Wimbledon*,[92] and in *Factory at Chorzów*,[93] although in the latter case, a settlement was ultimately reached between the parties.[94] The ICJ has only awarded compensation once, in *Corfu Channel*.[95] The ITLOS has also awarded compensation on one occasion, in *M/V 'Saiga' (No 2)*.[96] Human rights bodies, in particular the IACHR and the ECHR, frequently make awards of compensation,[97]

[85] *Velásquez Rodríguez (Compensation)*, 95 ILR 306, 314 (IACHR, 1989).

[86] For example, *König v FRG*, Ser A, (No 36), 14–15 (ECHR, 1980); *Artico v Italy*, Ser A, (No 37), 21 (ECHR, 1980).

[87] Ser A, (No 330–B), 59–60 (ECHR, 1995).

[88] Ibid, 59.

[89] Above n 21.

[90] Above n 52, 698–9. The ECHR also awarded the applicant €150,000 compensation.

[91] Gray, *Judicial Remedies*, above n 4, 18–21.

[92] Ser A, (No 1), 30–3 (PCIJ, 1923).

[93] Above n 8, 9.

[94] Barker, above n 47, 164.

[95] *Corfu Channel (Compensation)* [1949] ICJ Rep 244.

[96] Above n 80; see generally Crawford, above n 3, 221–2; Roger O'Keefe, 'ITLOS Flags Its Intent' (2000) 59 *CLJ* 428; Vaughan Lowe, 'The *M/V 'Saiga'*: The First Case in the International Tribunal for the Law of the Sea' (1999) 48 *ICLQ* 187.

[97] See, e.g., Shelton, above n 45, 294–316; Albrecht Randelzhofer and Christian Tomuschat, *State Responsibility and the Individual: Reparation in Instances of Grave Violations of Human Rights* (1999).

as do ICSID tribunals,[98] the Iran–US Claims Tribunal,[99] and tribunals constituted under bilateral investment treaties and under chapter 11 of NAFTA.[100]

This is not to say that every international court approaches questions of compensation in an identical fashion. Rather, there are three issues which need to be distinguished. These are, first, the availability of compensation as a remedy; second, the types of damage which can be compensated; and third, the method of assessing the quantum of compensation. The jurisprudence of international courts shows that there is widespread agreement concerning the availability of compensation as a remedy where there is financially assessable damage. There is also general agreement on the heads of damages which can be recovered, although, as noted by the ILC, the heads of damage recoverable in individual cases 'will vary, depending on the content of particular primary obligations, an evaluation of the respective behaviour of the parties, and a concern to reach an equitable and acceptable outcome'.[101] As for the third issue, there is some difference in the way that international courts approach the question of the assessment of compensation, but it is suggested that this might be due to the uncertainty in the applicable standard of compensation, and the validity of different methods of valuation, rather than any systemic differences between different international tribunals.[102]

Turning to the second issue, concerning the heads of damage which are recoverable, there are essentially three types of claim for compensable damage which have been identified by the ILC.[103] The first is where there is financially assessable damage to state interests, the second concerns damage to privately owned property, and the third relates to compensation claims for personal injury.

1. Compensation for Damage to the State

Damage to state interests might arise where harm is caused to an aircraft or ship, an attack is made on a state's diplomatic premises, or environmental damage is caused to the territory or property of a state. Incidental expenses might also arise

98 See, e.g., *ADC Affiliate Ltd and ADC & ADMC Management Ltd v Hungary* (ICSID Case No ARB/03/16, Award of 27 September 2006), paras 517–22; *CMS Gas Transmission Co v Argentina* (ICSID Case No ARB/01/8, Award of 12 May 2005), paras 468–71; *Asian Agricultural Products v Sri Lanka*, above n 62, 288–94; *Compañia del Desarrollo de Santa Elena SA v Republic of Costa Rica*, above n 62, 203.

99 For example, *Tippetts, Abbett, McCarthy, Stratton v TAMS–AFFA Consulting Engineers of Iran*, 6 Ir–USCTR 219, 225, 229 (1984); see generally Brower and Brueschke, above n 47; George Aldrich, *The Jurisprudence of the Iran–United States Claims Tribunal* (1996); Matti Pellonpää, 'Compensable Claims before the Tribunal: Expropriation Claims' in Richard Lillich and D McGraw (eds), *The Iran–United States Claims Tribunal: Its Contribution to the Law of State Responsibility* (1998) 185.

100 *CME Czech Republic BV v Czech Republic* (Award of 14 March 2003), para 620; *Sedelmayer v Russian Federation* (Award of 7 July 1998), 88–92, 106–11, 113, 118; *Metalclad Corporation v Mexico*, 5 ICSID Rep 212 (2000); *Marvin Feldman v Mexico* (ICSID Case No ARB(AF)/99/1, Award of 16 December 2002), paras 79–86.

101 Crawford, above n 3, 220.

102 See further below part III(B)(2)(b).

103 Crawford, above n 3, 221–30.

out of such damage, including the cost of paying medical expenses and pensions arising out of a wrongful act. These categories are not closed.[104] International courts have had relatively little occasion to consider the rules for compensation for such damage, for many disputes concerning damage to state interests are settled by diplomatic means.[105] The limited case law indicates that all financially assessable losses may be compensated. In *Corfu Channel*, the ICJ found that Albania was responsible for the destruction and damage caused to two British naval vessels in Albanian waters. Compensation was awarded for the replacement of the *Saumarez*, the damage sustained by the *Volage*, and costs associated with deaths and injuries of naval personnel; this latter head of damages included 'the costs of pensions and other grants made by [the UK] to the victims or their dependents, and for costs of administration, medical treatment, etc'.[106] Compensation for environmental loss includes costs resulting from the clean-up of pollution, the reduction in value of polluted property or other environmental damage. In *Trail Smelter*, Canada was ordered to pay compensation for damage to property caused by emissions from a Canadian smelter.[107] In addition, the UNCC has jurisdiction to assess Iraq's liability 'for any direct loss, damage, including environmental damage and the depletion of natural resources... as a result of its unlawful invasion and occupation of Kuwait'.[108]

2. *Compensation for Injury to Private Property*

In contrast with the paucity of jurisprudence on injury to the state, there is an immense body of case law considering compensation of loss or damage to private property. In *SS Wimbledon*, the PCIJ awarded damages in respect of demurrage, deviation, and expenditure of fuel; other claims in respect of repayment of a share of the vessel in the general expenses of the company were refused, as were claims for government stamp duty and other costs.[109] In *Factory at Chorzów*, the PCIJ ordered an expert inquiry regarding the compensation to be awarded, and requested information on the value of the factory at the date of expropriation; the predicted profits or losses of the factory up to the date of the judgment; and the value of the undertaking as at the date of judgment, including all 'lands, buildings, equipment, stocks, available processes, supply and delivery contracts, goodwill and future prospects', if they had remained in the hands of the German companies.[110] As noted above, the parties ultimately reached agreement on the amount of compensation. In *M/V 'Saiga' (No 2)*, the ITLOS awarded compensation with interest in respect of costs related to detention and repair of the

[104] Ibid, 221. [105] Ibid, 220–3. [106] Above n 95, 249.

[107] 3 RIAA 1938, 1980–1 (US–Canada, 1941).

[108] SC Res 687 (1991), available at <http://www.un.org> (last visited 24 April 2007) para 16; see also *Criteria for Additional Categories of Claims*, Decision 7 of the UNCC Governing Council, UN Doc S/AC.26/1991/7/Rev.1 (1992); Crawford, above n 3, 223.

[109] Above n 92, 30–3; Gray, *Judicial Remedies*, above n 4, 77. [110] Above n 27, 51.

M/V 'Saiga', losses suffered connected with its charter hire, and compensation for the value of the gasoil which had been discharged. Other damages were also awarded in respect of the detention of the captain and others on board, and compensation for medical expenses and pain and suffering.[111]

International case law has established that compensation generally falls under three heads, being compensation for the actual loss incurred (*damnum emergens*); compensation for future loss (*lucrum cessans*), and compensation for incidental expenses.[112] Much of the case law relates to claims for compensation arising out of the expropriation by states of foreign-owned property. There are two issues that have been disputed in the relevant jurisprudence. The first issue is whether compensation for future loss is only available if the expropriation is 'unlawful', in the sense that it does not comply with the requirements of public international law; those conditions are usually accepted as being that the expropriation must be for a public purpose, must not be discriminatory, and must be accompanied by compensation.[113] The second issue is the correct formulation of the relevant standard of compensation. These two issues will be addressed in turn.

a) Compensation for Future Loss

There have been suggestions in international arbitral and judicial practice that compensation for future loss might only be available if the expropriation is unlawful. The original authority for this proposition is the PCIJ's judgment in *Factory at Chorzów*, where it held that reparation 'must, as far as possible, wipe out all the consequences of the *illegal* act',[114] and its assessment of the compensable loss was affected by its finding that Poland's action in expropriating the factory had been unlawful as it had breached provisions of the Geneva Convention.[115] It followed from this that:

> the compensation due to the German government is not necessarily limited to the value of the undertaking at the moment of dispossession, plus interest to the day of payment. This limitation would only be admissible if the Polish Government had had the right to expropriate, and if its wrongful act consisted merely in not having paid to the two Companies the just price of what was expropriated.[116]

Accordingly, the PCIJ held that loss of profits and other heads of compensation could also be considered. In light of subsequent judicial and arbitral practice, however, it is questionable whether the rule still exists that compensation for future loss

[111] Above n 80, 200. [112] Crawford, above n 3, 225.

[113] See, e.g., Christoph Schreuer, 'The Concept of Expropriation under the ECT and other Investment Protection Treaties', in Clarisse Ribeiro (ed), *Investment Arbitration and the Energy Charter Treaty* (2006) 108, 109–10; see also Malcolm Shaw, *International Law* (5th ed, 2003) 737–51.

[114] Above n 27, 47 (emphasis added). [115] Ibid, 46.

[116] Ibid, 47; see especially Audley Sheppard, 'The Distinction between Lawful and Unlawful Expropriation', in Ribeiro (ed), above n 113, 169, 177–81.

can only be recovered where the expropriation is unlawful, for international jurisprudence on this issue has been far from consistent.[117] In an early decision, *Delagoa Bay Railway Co*, the tribunal awarded both *damnum emergens* and *lucrum cessans*; the award of lost profits was not for any illegal act, but was due to the mere interference with private rights.[118] In *May*, the tribunal also awarded lost profits, without discussing whether an illegal act was necessary.[119] The *Shufeldt* claim suggested that *damnum emergens* was always available, but that *lucrum cessans* had to be 'the direct fruit of the contract and not too remote or speculative'.[120]

Subsequent jurisprudence was also inconclusive. The arbitral tribunal in *LIAMCO v Libya* did not award lost profits, finding that the state of the law concerning their availability was unsettled, and, in any event, that states had the right to nationalize their wealth and natural resources.[121] The arbitral tribunal in *Kuwait v Aminoil* did not recognize any difference in the availability of remedies depending on whether the expropriation was lawful or not.[122] The practice of the three chambers of the Iran-NUS Claims Tribunal is also inconsistent. In *American International Group v Iran*, Chamber Three awarded lost profits, even though it had concluded that the expropriation was not unlawful.[123] Chambers of the Iran–US Claims Tribunal then applied the distinction between lawful and unlawful takings in *INA* (Chamber One),[124] *Amoco International Finance v Iran* (Chamber Three),[125] and *Phillips Petroleum* (Chamber Two),[126] and Judge Brower, in a separate opinion in *SEDCO*, also recognized the distinction.[127] However, in *Starrett Housing Corporation*, Chamber One of the Iran–US Claims Tribunal then failed to distinguish between lawful and unlawful takings.[128]

The practice of ICSID tribunals has also been inconsistent. In *AGIP v Congo*, the ICSID Tribunal awarded damages for loss of profits, noting that there had been illegality on the part of the government.[129] In *Amco Asia v Indonesia*, the ICSID Tribunal managed to sidestep the issue, as it found that the taking was in any event unlawful.[130] This lack of uniformity led Dr Barker to conclude in 1998 that the cases were 'diverse and often inconsistent in approach'.[131] Subsequent ICSID and NAFTA decisions shed little light on the problem, primarily because arbitral tribunals constituted under international investment treaties have usually had regard to the 'fair market value' of the property, assessed as of the date of the

[117] Crawford, above n 3, 225, fn 582; see especially Barker, above n 47, 135–206.

[118] *Delagoa Bay Railway Co*, in Henri La Fontaine, *Pasicrisie Internationale 1794–1900: Histoire Documentaire des Arbitrages Internationaux* (1997) 398 (GB and US–Portugal, 1900); Marjorie Whiteman, *Damages in International Law* (1943) vol III, 1694, 1698.

[119] 15 RIAA 47, 71–3 (US–Guatemala, 1900).

[120] 2 RIAA 1079 (US–Guatemala, 1930).

[121] Above n 47, 202–10, 217.

[122] 66 ILR 518, 600–1 (1982).

[123] 4 Ir–USCTR 96, 107–10 (1983).

[124] 8 Ir–USCTR 373, 378 (1985).

[125] 15 Ir–USCTR 189, 246–52, see, however, 289, 299–308 (Conc Op Brower) (1987).

[126] 21 Ir–USCTR 79, 122 (1989).

[127] Above n 55, 189, 203–6 (Sep Op Brower) (1986).

[128] 16 Ir–USCTR 112, see especially 237, 240–1 (Conc Op Holtzmann) (1987).

[129] 1 ICSID Rep 306, 326 (1979).

[130] 1 ICSID Rep 569, 612–13 (1990).

[131] Barker, above n 47, 203–4.

expropriation, as this standard of compensation is frequently specified in such treaties.[132]

However, in *ADC Affiliate Ltd and ADC & ADMC Management Ltd v Hungary*, the ICSID Tribunal, which was constituted under the Cyprus–Hungary bilateral investment treaty,[133] had occasion to revisit this question. In its award, the ICSID Tribunal rejected Hungary's submission that the relevant standard of compensation should be the one specified in the bilateral investment treaty—being 'the market value of the expropriated investments at the moment of expropriation'[134]—regardless of the lawfulness of the expropriation.[135] After a review of the relevant case law, the Tribunal held that 'there can be no doubt about the present vitality of the *Chorzów Factory* principle',[136] under which an unlawful expropriation gives rise to full reparation, being compensation not necessarily limited to the value of the undertaking at the moment of expropriation.[137] The Tribunal concluded that:

> The present case is almost unique among decided cases concerning the expropriation by States of foreign owned property, since the value of the investment after the date of expropriation (1 January 2002) has risen very considerably while other arbitrations that apply the *Chorzów Factory* standard all invariably involve scenarios where there has been a decline in the value of the investment after regulatory interference. It is for this reason that application of the restitution standard by various arbitration tribunals has led to use of the date of the expropriation as the date for the valuation of damages.
>
> However, in the present, *sui generis*, type of case the application of the *Chorzów Factory* standard requires that the date of the valuation should be the date of the Award and not the date of expropriation, since this is what is necessary to put the Claimants in the same position as if the expropriation had not been committed.[138]

132 Sheppard, above n 116, 184–93. For instances of the treaty standard, see, e.g., *North American Free Trade Agreement*, signed 17 December 1992, (1995) 32 ILM 289 (entered into force 1 January 1994), art 1110(2); *US Model Bilateral Investment Treaty* (November 2004), art 6(2)(b); *Energy Charter Treaty*, opened for signature 17 December 1994, (1995) 34 ILM 360 (entered into force 16 April 1998), art 13(1); *Agreement between the Government of Australia and the Government of the People's Republic of China on the Reciprocal Encouragement and Protection of Investments*, signed 11 July 1988 (entered into force 11 July 1988), art VIII(2). For other treaty standards, see, e.g., the *Agreement on Encouragement and Reciprocal Protection of Investments between the Kingdom of the Netherlands and the Czech and Slovak Federal Republic*, signed 29 April 1991 (entered into force 1 October 1992), art 5(c) requires 'just compensation' of the 'genuine value'; and the *Agreement between the Government of the United Kingdom of Great Britain and Northern Ireland and the Government of the Republic of Argentina for the Promotion and Protection of Investments*, signed 11 December 1990 (entered into force 19 February 1993), art 5(1): 'prompt, adequate and effective compensation' to amount to the 'genuine value' of the investment: all available at <http://www.unctadxi.org/templates/DocSearch_779.aspx> (last visited 25 November 2006).

133 *Agreement between the Government of the Republic of Cyprus and the Government of the Hungarian People's Republic on Mutual Promotion and Protection of Investments*, signed on 24 May 1989 (entered into force on 24 May 1989), available at <http://www.unctadxi.org/templates/DocSearch_779.aspx> (last visited 25 November 2006).

134 Ibid, art 4(2).

135 *ADC Affiliate Ltd and ADC & ADMC Management Ltd v Hungary*, above n 98, paras 480–3.

136 Ibid, para 493.

137 *Factory at Chorzów*, above n 27, 47.

138 *ADC Affiliate*, above n 98, paras 496–7.

The award in *ADC Affiliate Ltd and ADC & ADMC Management Ltd v Hungary* thus clearly reaffirmed the *Factory at Chorzów* principle that if an expropriation is unlawful, compensation for future loss will be available. However, it is likely that tribunals will remain reluctant to award lost profits where such profits are speculative, and that lost profits are more likely to be awarded 'on the basis of a contractually protected income stream than through the loss of income producing assets *per se*'.[139]

b) Standard of compensation

The applicable standard of compensation is another aspect of such claims that has proved controversial. This standard has been variously described as equivalent to 'full' compensation, 'adequate' compensation', 'fair' compensation, 'reasonable' compensation', and 'just' compensation.[140] The essential backdrop to this controversy is the tension between developed and developing states and the debates which took place in the UN in the 1960s and 1970s relating to decolonization and the declaration of permanent sovereignty over natural resources. Capital exporting states traditionally insisted on the 'Hull formula', which required compensation to be 'prompt, adequate and effective'.[141] However, developing states insisted that compensation should be 'appropriate', arguably enabling them to take into account national economic considerations.[142] Dr Barker has noted that 'full' compensation seems to rely solely on fair market value, while 'just' compensation appears to permit additional factors to be taken into account, including the ability of the host state to pay, the extent of economic reforms, and the conduct of the parties.[143] This debate is confused by the fact that developed states have claimed 'appropriate' and 'adequate' compensation to be the equivalent of 'full' compensation;[144] and the Iran–US Claims Tribunal has also regarded 'just' compensation as the equivalent of 'full' compensation.[145] In cases concerning the taking of property, the ECHR has also applied the standard of 'complete reparation (*restitutio in integrum*)'.[146] While the practice is inconsistent, it is not the case that one international court, such as the ICJ, applies one standard, while another type of international court, say, ICSID tribunals, applies another. Rather, there is no

[139] Barker, above n 47, 203; see also *ADC Affiliate*, ibid, para 515, where the Tribunal rejected the Claimants' claim relating to certain lost future developments, as they did not have 'firm contractual rights to those possible projects.'

[140] Barker, above n 47, 43.

[141] See, e.g., Brownlie, above n 6, 508–20; Shaw, above n 113, 743–7.

[142] For example, Declaration on Permanent Sovereignty over Natural Resources, GA Res 1803 (XVII), 17 UNGAOR, Supp 17, 15; Declaration on the Establishment of a New International Economic Order, GA Res 3201 (S–VI) (1974) 13 ILM 715; Charter of Economic Rights and Duties of States, GA Res 3281 (XXIX) (1975) 14 ILM 251.

[143] Barker, above n 47, 43.

[144] Ibid, 43–4; see also *INA Corporation v Iran*, above n 124, 378.

[145] *Amoco International Finance Corp v Iran*, above n 125, 252; Barker, above n 47, 43.

[146] *Papamichalopoulos v Greece*, above n 87, 59–60; *König v FRG*, above n 86, 14–15; *Artico v Italy*, above n 86, 21.

pattern that indicates that one international tribunal consistently applies the same standard. Indeed, as with the question relating to the availability of lost profits, different Chambers of the Iran–US Claims Tribunal have even reached different conclusions on these questions.[147] As has been discussed above, arbitral tribunals constituted under international investment treaties often apply the 'fair market value' of the property lost, as this standard of compensation is frequently specified in such treaties.[148] This standard has been defined by the Iran–US Claims Tribunal as:

> the amount which a willing buyer would have paid a willing seller for the shares of a going concern, disregarding any diminution of value due to the nationalisation itself or the anticipation thereof, and excluding consideration of events thereafter that might have increased or decreased the value of the shares.[149]

This standard of 'fair market value' has also been accepted by ICSID tribunals as the equivalent of 'full compensation',[150] 'full and effective compensation of the prejudice [the investor] suffered, as international law requires',[151] and 'full value'.[152] Yet doubt concerning the legal significance of the requirement for compensation persists even in recent arbitrations.[153] Dr Barker concluded that outside the context of bilateral or multilateral agreements, 'there is little prospect of meaningful agreement on standards of compensation'.[154] Moreover, even if a particular standard of compensation 'received universal acceptance', uncertainty still exists concerning the appropriate method of calculating the compensation.[155] Options include the determination of 'net book value' and the 'discounted cash flow' method; further discussion of valuation methods is not included in this chapter.[156]

[147] See, e.g., *American International Group v Iran*, above n 123, 109, where Chamber Three awarded full compensation; see also *INA Corporation v Iran*, above n 124, 377, where Chamber One suggested that in the case of large scale nationalizations, international law required less than full compensation (see especially Sep Ops Lagergren and Holtzmann).

[148] See above n 132; see further Sheppard, above n 116.

[149] *INA Corporation v Iran*, above n 124, 380, citing *American International Group Inc v Iran*, above n 123, 108–9; see also *Starrett Housing Corp v Iran*, above n 128, 201; *Phelps Dodge Corp v Iran*, 10 Ir–USCTR 121, 132 (1986); *Sedco Inc v NIOC*, above n 55, 187–9; NAFTA, above n 132, art 1110(2); Crawford, above n 3, 225–6; Jonathan Charney, 'Is International Law Threatened by Multiple International Tribunals?' (1998) 271 *Recueil des Cours* 101, 269–72; Barker, above n 47, 67–8.

[150] *AGIP v Congo*, above n 129, 326.

[151] *Amco v Indonesia (Award)*, 1 ICSID Rep 413, 504 (1984).

[152] *AAP v Sri Lanka*, above n 62, 288.

[153] See, e.g., *Tradex Hellas v Albania* (1999) 14 *ICSID Review—FILJ* 197, 224.

[154] Barker, above n 47, 57.

[155] Ibid.

[156] For discussion of different valuation techniques, see Crawford, above n 3, 226–30; Ball, above n 62, 417–27; Barker, above n 47; John Westberg, 'Applicable Law, Expropriatory Takings and Compensation in Cases of Expropriation; ICSID and Iran–US Claims Tribunal Compared' (1993) 8 *ICSID Review—FILJ* 1, 19–28; and John Westberg, 'Compensation in Cases of Expropriation and Nationalisation: Awards of the Iran–United States Claims Tribunal' (1990) 5 *ICSID Review—FILJ* 256.

3. *Compensation for Personal Injury*

As is the case in claims for damage to property, there is a large body of jurisprudence dealing with claims relating to compensation for personal injury.[157] According to the ILC, compensable personal injury encompasses:

> not only associated material losses, such as loss of earnings and earning capacity, medical expenses and the like, but also non-material damage suffered by the individual . . . Non-material damage is generally understood to encompass loss of loved ones, pain and suffering as well as the affront to sensibilities associated with an intrusion on the person, home or private life.[158]

Claims for personal injury have not come before the ICJ, but the ITLOS has awarded damages in respect of the detention of the crew of the *M/V Saiga*, as well as compensation for medical expenses and pain and suffering.[159] The ECHR and the IACHR both make awards of compensation to victims of human rights violations, for declaratory judgments often will not afford adequate redress.[160] In claims relating to personal injury, the ECHR awards compensation for pecuniary losses, non-pecuniary losses, and costs and expenses, and enjoys a certain discretion in the exercise of its power to award remedies.[161] Any award of compensation depends, of course, on a finding that a violation occurred, and that the violation caused the loss suffered.[162] In *Velásquez Rodríguez*, the IACHR held that 'reparation of harm brought about by the violation of an international obligation consists in full restitution (*restitutio in integrum*), which includes the restoration of the prior situation, the reparation of the consequences of the violation, and indemnification for patrimonial and non-patrimonial damages, including emotional harm'.[163]

Nevertheless, the observation that some international courts award compensation under the head of 'personal injury' cannot be made without acknowledging the differences that can be found concerning the amount of compensation that is ultimately awarded. Indeed, the method of calculating compensation—and the varying generosity of international courts—represents an area where relevant international jurisprudence may be of limited influence. One such instance can be found in *M/V 'Saiga' (No 2)*, a decision of the ITLOS.[164] In that case, Saint Vincent and the Grenadines sought compensation and damages from Guinea arising out of the pursuit, seizure and detention of a vessel flying the Saint Vincent and the Grenadines flag, and damage and injuries sustained by the vessel and crew.[165] It quantified its claims under four principal heads: a claim 'on behalf of the loss or damage to the vessel and owners arising from the detention and arrest and its subsequent treatment'; a claim 'for the benefit of the master and crew, including personal injury and deprivation of liberty'; a claim 'in respect of the

[157] See, e.g., Crawford, above n 3, 223–5.
[158] Ibid, 223.
[159] Above n 80, 200.
[160] Shelton, above n 45, 294–8, 299–301.
[161] Ibid, 297–8.
[162] Ibid, 296.
[163] Above n 85, 314.
[164] Above n 80.
[165] For a summary of the facts, see ibid, 167–70.

removal of the cargo from the vessel'; and a claim 'in respect of damages or loss suffered by the State of Saint Vincent and the Grenadines'.[166]

In making its second claim, Saint Vincent and the Grenadines argued that the Master and crew had been subjected to certain 'losses relating to personal injury and deprivation of liberty'.[167] These were their subjection by Guinea to the excessive use of force, their unlawful detention, the severe injuries suffered by two members of the crew due to the excessive use of force, and the theft of certain personal possessions belonging to the Master and crew.[168] In seeking compensation in respect of this claim, Saint Vincent and the Grenadines made extensive reference in their submissions to the jurisprudence of international arbitral tribunals, the IACHR and the ECHR.[169] In particular, it argued that although international law requires *restitutio in integrum*, 'in cases of human rights violations and personal injury a restorative act alone will usually be insufficient'.[170] On the basis of that jurisprudence, it argued that 'moral harm', such as that resulting from unlawful detention, was compensable.[171]

In order to quantify the 'moral harm', Saint Vincent and the Grenadines referred to decisions of the IACHR and ECHR, which had held that such quantification should be determined by principles of 'equity'.[172] It claimed the following amounts, 'in respect of damage suffered by the crew members occasioned by the excessive use of force against them and their unlawful detention': 'for the Master, US$50,750', being a *per diem* rate of $US250; 'for the five crew members detained for 123 days, US$12,300 each'; 'for the eight crew members detained for approximately 45 days, US$4,500 each'; and 'for the nine crew members detained for 21 days, US$2,100 each'; these represented a *per diem* rate of $US100.[173] Saint Vincent and the Grenadines argued that 'computation of damages for detention by using a daily rate is the norm in international claims'.[174] The relevant daily rates were reached by reliance on the jurisprudence of international arbitral tribunals, as well as the practice of the UNCC.[175] In *Faulkner*, for instance, the US-Mexican CC had calculated damages owed for the unlawful detention of a US national at US$150 per day.[176] In addition, in respect of the serious injuries

[166] *M/V 'Saiga' (No 2)*, Memorial of Saint Vincent and the Grenadines, para 178 (19 June 1998).

[167] Ibid, para 182. [168] Ibid. [169] Ibid, para 183–6. [170] Ibid, para 184.

[171] Ibid, para 185.

[172] Ibid; see also *M/V 'Saiga' (No 2)*, ITLOS/PV.99/1/Rev.1, 10–11 (Carl Joseph) (8 March 1999); see, e.g., *Godinez-Cruz (Compensatory Damages)*, Ser C, (No 8), para 25 (IACHR, 1989); *Velásquez Rodríguez (Compensatory Damages)*, Ser C, (No 7), para 27 (IACHR, 1989); *K-F v Germany* ECHR Rep 1997–VII, ECHR (Ser A) 2656, 2677; *van Mechelen v Netherlands (Article 50)* ECHR Rep 1997–VI, ECHR (Ser A), 2425, 2432; see further Shelton, above n 45, 295, 298, 306–9; Jo Pasqualucci, *The Practice and Procedure of the Inter-American Court of Human Rights* (2003) 265.

[173] *M/V 'Saiga' (No 2)*, Memorial, above n 166, para 187.

[174] *M/V 'Saiga' (No 2)*, Reply of Saint Vincent and the Grenadines, para 377 (19 November 1998).

[175] Ibid, paras 376–87. See, e.g., *Topaze*, 9 RIAA 387, 389 (GB–Venezuelan CC, date not reported); *Faulkner*, 4 RIAA 67 (US–Mexican GCC, 1926); see also UNCC Governing Council Decision No 3, UN Doc S/AC.26/1991/3 (23 October 1991), 109 ILR 574; and UNCC Governing Council Decision No 8, UN Doc S/AC.26/1992/8 (27 January 1992), 109 ILR 591.

[176] *Faulkner*, ibid, 71.

suffered by two crew members during the arrest of the *M/V 'Saiga'*, Saint Vincent and the Grenadines sought US$50,000 on behalf of each crew member,[177] arguing that this was 'consistent with sums awarded by the Inter-American Court of Human Rights and the European Court of Human Rights as moral or non-pecuniary damages in respect of similar violations'.[178]

The ITLOS, however, was unmoved by these submissions. Without referring to the ample international judicial and arbitral practice cited by Saint Vincent and the Grenadines, it simply awarded US$17,750 in respect of the detention of the Master, and US$76,000 with respect to the detention of all other members of the crew. Each of the crew was awarded the flat figure of US$3,300, with the exception of the injured crew members, Mr Klyuyev and Mr Niasse, who had been promptly removed from the vessel; they each received US$1,700. The ITLOS also awarded US$10,000 in respect of injury, pain and suffering for Mr Klyuyev, plus US$3,130 medical expenses; and US$25,000 for the injury, pain, suffering, disability and psychological damage to Mr Niasse, as well as US$6,315 to cover his medical expenses.[179]

Thus, the ITLOS implicitly rejected the arguments of Saint Vincent and the Grenadines that the jurisprudence of other international courts was relevant in determining the amount of compensation. Notably, it did not apply any principles of 'equity' in determining the compensation for each of the crew, and in awarding compensation to each crew member, no account was taken of the length of time that they were detained. This case demonstrates that referring to the practice of other international tribunals in comparable cases is not always destined to meet with success. It also suggests that in the field of compensation for personal injury, where one might assume that the jurisprudence of other international courts would be relevant, common practice is relatively limited.

C. Declaratory Judgments

The ILC states that declaratory relief is '[o]ne of the most common modalities of satisfaction provided in the case of moral or non-material injury to the state'.[180] In some cases, a declaration will be sufficient to settle the dispute; parties to dispute settlement proceedings often request a declaration of the applicable law and of their rights and duties, on the basis of which a settlement of the dispute can be reached.[181]

Although use of the declaratory judgment was not very widespread in early arbitral practice,[182] it is the most common form of remedy in litigation before the

[177] *M/V 'Saiga' (No 2)*, Memorial, above n 166, para 188.

[178] *M/V 'Saiga' (No 2)*, Reply, above n 174, para 372, referring to Memorial, above n 166, para 186, fn 42.

[179] Above n 80, 200–1.

[180] Crawford, above n 3, 233; James Crawford, 'Third Report on State Responsibility: Addendum', para 184, UN Doc A/CN.4/507/Add.1 (15 June 2000); Ian Brownlie, *System of the Law of Nations: State Responsibility Part I* (1983) 201.

[181] Shelton, above n 45, 255.

[182] Gray, *Judicial Remedies*, above n 4, 17–18; e.g. one arbitral tribunal held that it lacked the power to grant a declaratory judgment: *Cayuga Indians*, 6 RIAA 173, 189 (GB–US, 1926). Another case

PCIJ and ICJ.[183] The power to issue declaratory judgments is confirmed in the jurisprudence of other international courts, such as PCA tribunals,[184] ad hoc arbitral tribunals,[185] the ITLOS,[186] and ICSID tribunals,[187] although the latter are likely to accompany such declarations with an award of compensation. As for the human rights courts, in the past the ECHR has often restricted its judgments to a declaration of wrongdoing by the respondent state, even in the case of an ongoing violation of international law.[188] The IACHR has also held that it can grant declaratory relief.[189] Finally, in WTO dispute settlement, the primary remedy is a declaration that a trade measure is inconsistent with a WTO agreement, and a recommendation that the offending member state bring the measure into conformity.[190]

Declaratory judgments are appropriate remedies in interstate disputes concerning the interpretation or application of treaty provisions, or the location of frontiers, and this can be seen from the frequency with which the PCIJ and ICJ have issued such judgments. Where private interests are involved, such as damage to private property, declaratory judgments are less useful. While human rights courts sometimes restrict their judgments to declarations, such judgments are increasingly accompanied by awards of compensation, and consequential orders.

D. Mandatory or Consequential Orders

1. An available remedy in International Adjudication?

While there is widespread agreement on the availability of restitution, compensation and declaratory judgments as remedies in international adjudication, there is uncertainty concerning the power of international courts to issue judgments and awards in mandatory terms.[191] A 'mandatory' or 'consequential' order is one that directs the respondent state to take or abstain from some form of specific action. These may include orders for specific performance, negative injunctions, and orders indicating the conduct required of the unsuccessful state to comply with a judgment for restitution. While orders for specific performance and injunctive

cited by Gray does not provide clear authority for this proposition, as the tribunal held that there was inadequate evidence to make any declaration: *Sanchez*, 10 RIAA 754 (Spanish-Venezuelan CC, 1903).

183 Gray, ibid, 96; see, e.g., *Certain German Interests in Polish Upper Silesia (Jurisdiction)*, Ser A (No 6), 18 (PCIJ, 1925); *Corfu Channel*, above n 9, 35, 36; *Asylum* [1950] ICJ Rep 266, 288; *Anglo-Norwegian Fisheries* [1951] ICJ Rep 116, 143; *Right of Passage over Indian Territory* [1960] ICJ Rep 6, 45–6; *Fisheries Jurisdiction* [1974] ICJ Rep 3, 34–5; *Fisheries Jurisdiction* [1974] ICJ Rep 175, 205–6; *Arrest Warrant* above n 52, 557.

184 *Carthage*, 11 RIAA 449, 460 (France–Italy, 1913); *Manouba*, 11 RIAA 463, 475 (France–Italy, 1913).

185 For example, *LAFICO v Burundi*, 96 ILR 279, 329 (1991); *Rainbow Warrior*, above n 52, 576–7.

186 *M/V 'Saiga' (No 2)*, above n 80, 199, 201, 204.

187 *MINE v Guinea*, 4 ICSID Rep 61, 73 (1988); *AAP v Sri Lanka*, above n 62, 287.

188 Shelton, above n 45, 259–64. 189 Ibid, 266. 190 DSU, above n 22, art 19(1).

191 Gray, *Judicial Remedies*, above n 4, 12, 16–17, 95–6; Mann, above n 28, 10; Manley Hudson, *International Tribunals: Past and Future* (1944) 120–1.

relief are commonly available in domestic legal systems,[192] the power of international courts to make such orders is less clear. It might be observed that international courts make orders of a mandatory kind with relative frequency in the form of provisional measures, such as orders that states 'take all measures' at their disposal to ensure that prisoners on death row are not executed pending final decision;[193] orders that states are to observe a bilateral agreement;[194] and orders that states are to comply with the terms of a ceasefire.[195] But the uncertainty concerns their power to do so in final judgments.

There is some disagreement among writers concerning the proper classification of types of mandatory order.[196] The confusion is demonstrated in a statement of the arbitrator in *BP v Libya*, who considered that orders for restitution and specific performance were identical.[197] These orders certainly differ in their substantive effect: orders for restitution aim to put the claimant back into the position they were in prior to the unlawful act, orders for specific performance seek to ensure that the respondent state complies with an obligation arising under international law, and negative injunctions seek to prevent the respondent state from taking certain action. Yet the form in which such orders may be expressed is similar, and in this sense, they may sensibly be considered together.

The uncertainty surrounding the power of international courts to make such orders is undoubtedly linked to the dearth of relevant jurisprudence. Professor Gray observed in 1987 that '[t]here is apparently no instance of the award of a negative injunction by an international arbitral tribunal where no such provision was included in the *compromis*';[198] and that '[t]here is no clear instance in international arbitral practice of a tribunal ordering the specific performance of a treaty or of a contractual obligation'.[199] One might, however, point to the decision of the US-Mexican GCC in *George Hopkins*, where it arguably made an award for specific performance, ordering the Mexican government to pay the total amount of the postal orders held by the claimant, with interest.[200] Further, the decisions referred to above in the consideration of the early examples of restitution might be considered examples of mandatory orders.[201] Nonetheless, early international judicial practice remains limited.

It has also been suggested that mandatory orders might not be appropriate judicial remedies in international law.[202] This position appears to rest on judicial

192 Blomeyer, above n 1, 30–4, 50–6.

193 *LaGrand (Provisional Measures)* (1999) 38 ILM 308, 313; *Vienna Convention on Consular Relations* (1998) 37 ILM 810, 819; *Avena* (2003) 42 ILM 309, 319.

194 *Land and Maritime Boundary (Provisional Measures)* [1996] ICJ Rep 13, 24.

195 For example, *Frontier Dispute (Provisional Measures)* [1986] ICJ Rep 3, 12.

196 For example, Gray, *Judicial Remedies*, above n 4, 12, 16–17, 65–6; Mann, above n 28, 13.

197 Above n 28, 350–1; Gray, ibid, 12.

198 Gray, ibid, 12.

199 Ibid, 16.

200 4 RIAA 218 (US-Mexican GCC, 1927). See, however, Gray, ibid, 16, who argues that this should probably be regarded as an award of compensation.

201 See above nn 63–67 and accompanying text.

202 For example, Gray, *Judicial Remedies*, above n 4, 16–17, 159–60; Jackson Ralston, *International Arbitration from Athens to Locarno* (1929) 61.

pronouncements that the judicial function is subject to limitations which prevent the making of such orders. In *Factory at Chorzów*, for instance, the PCIJ observed that a court, in the exercise of its judicial function, 'neither can nor should contemplate the contingency of [a] judgment not being complied with'.[203] In accordance with this dictum, it is said that the question of the means of compliance is not the concern of international tribunals, but rather should be left to the state concerned; it is the tribunal's role merely to determine the rights and obligations in dispute. Further authority can be found in the ICJ's judgment in *Haya de la Torre*.[204] In that case, Colombia and Peru asked the ICJ for a decision regarding how they should implement its judgment in *Asylum*.[205] The ICJ noted that there were multiple ways in which Colombia might comply with the judgment, and refused to indicate the means to be employed to give effect to it. Specifically, the ICJ held that the courses open to Colombia were 'conditioned by facts and by possibilities which, to a very large extent, the parties are alone in a position to appreciate'.[206] It held that 'it is not part of the Court's judicial function to make such a choice', and the ICJ was 'unable to give any practical advice as to the various courses which might be followed with a view to terminating the asylum, since, by doing so, it would depart from its judicial function'.[207] This was endorsed in later ICJ jurisprudence.[208]

Decisions of other international courts provide further support for the proposition that international tribunals do not have the power to make orders as to how parties should implement their judgments. The ECHR, in particular, has been hesitant to grant mandatory orders, often restricting itself to issuing declaratory judgments; it held in *Marckx v Belgium* that it had no power to order the annulment or repeal of municipal legislative provisions, stating that 'the Court's judgment is essentially declaratory and leaves to the State the choice of means to be utilised in its domestic legal system for performance of its obligation [of compliance]'.[209] This reluctance to direct states in the method of compliance with a judgment can also be found in the practice of WTO dispute settlement organs. Under the DSU, WTO panels and the Appellate Body are authorized to make recommendations, and they can also 'suggest ways in which the Member concerned could implement the recommendations'.[210] A panel has held, however, that such

[203] Above n 27, 63. [204] Above n 51. [205] Ibid, 78; *Asylum*, above n 183.

[206] *Haya de la Torre*, ibid, 79. [207] Ibid, 79–83.

[208] *Northern Cameroons* [1963] ICJ Rep 15, 37–8; *Nuclear Tests (Australia)* [1974] ICJ Rep 253, 272; *Nicaragua (Jurisdiction and Admissibility)* [1984] ICJ Rep 392, 437–8; see also *Arrest Warrant*, CR 2001/9, 34 (Daniel Bethlehem).

[209] Ser A, (No 31), 25 (ECHR, 1979); Gray, *Judicial Remedies*, above n 4, 152; Alexander Orakhelashvili, 'Questions of International Judicial Jurisdiction in the *LaGrand* Case' (2002) 15 *Leiden Journal of International Law* 105, 126–9. For other cases where the ECHR refused to make a mandatory order, see, e.g., *Belilos v Switzerland*, Ser A, (No 132), 32–3 (ECHR, 1988); *Selmouni v France* (1999) 29 EHRR 403, 447–8.

[210] DSU, above n 22, art 19(1).

suggestions are not binding.[211] Another panel has also held that it was not within its mandate to direct states how they should implement its recommendations.[212]

2. *Practice of International Courts making such Orders*

Notwithstanding this general reluctance to issue mandatory orders, there is an increasing practice of international tribunals rendering judgments in such terms. The ICJ's decisions in *Temple of Preah Vihear* and *Tehran Hostages*, which included mandatory orders, have been referred to above.[213] It has been argued that the ICJ's discussion of its jurisdiction in *Temple of Preah Vihear* 'makes it quite clear that this judgment is . . . declaratory'.[214] If this is right, then, the ICJ is in fact doing exactly what it considered itself as being constrained from doing in *Haya de la Torre*, i.e. stating what Thailand was required to do in order to comply with the judgment.[215] Viewed in this light, the judgment can be regarded as containing a mandatory order.[216]

Decisions of other tribunals have lent support to the view that international courts can make mandatory orders. The question of principle was directly addressed by the arbitral tribunal in *Rainbow Warrior*. In its discussion of the possibility of issuing an order for the cessation or discontinuance of the internationally wrongful act, it held that:

> The authority to issue an order for the cessation or discontinuance of a wrongful act or omission results from the inherent powers of a competent tribunal which is confronted with the continuous breach of an international obligation which is in force and continues to be in force.[217]

It might be argued that this statement is of little import; states committing an internationally wrongful act are under an obligation to cease that act, just as they are under an obligation to make full reparation.[218] But it is the power of an international court to make such an order which is at issue. Here, the arbitral tribunal confirmed that in its view, there is such a power, and the power to make an order requiring the cessation of certain conduct goes beyond making a declaration that a state is in violation of its obligations at international law.

The IACHR has adopted a robust understanding of its remedial powers, and it has in several cases made mandatory orders requiring states to take specific action to remedy human rights violations.[219] In *Loayza Tamayo*, it ordered Peru to reinstate the claimant to her position of employment, to amend domestic legislation to conform to the American Convention, and to investigate the facts of the case

[211] *Guatemala—Cement I*, DSR 1998–IX, 3797, 4026 (PR).
[212] *Brazil—Aircraft*, DSR 1999–III, 1221, 1366 (PR); Grané, above n 22, 766–7.
[213] Above n 68; above n 70; see above nn 68–71 and accompanying text.
[214] Gray, *Judicial Remedies*, above n 4, 67.
[215] As indeed is recognized by Gray: ibid.
[216] Mann, above n 28, 13.
[217] Above n 52, 573.
[218] ILC Articles, above n 5, arts 30–1.
[219] Shelton, above n 45, 285–9; Pasqualucci, above n 172, 242–54.

and punish those responsible for breaches of the claimant's rights.[220] Similarly, in *Suarez Rosero*, it ordered Ecuador to carry out an investigation and punish those responsible for breaches of the convention.[221] The ECHR has also altered its view somewhat on its remedial powers since its holding in *Marckx*. In *Papamichalopoulos*, the ECHR referred to the 'precious source of inspiration' offered by the jurisprudence of other international courts,[222] and made an order that Greece return the requisitioned land in issue to the claimants.[223] In 2004, in *Assanidze*, the ECHR reiterated that 'its judgments are essentially declaratory in nature', and held that Georgia was under an obligation to make reparation. It held, however, that there was only one means of implementing the judgment, i.e. to 'secure the applicant's release at the earliest possible date'.[224] Two months later, the ECHR made a consequential order in *Broniowski*, a claim concerning a widespread property rights violation. It held that:

> the respondent state should... through appropriate legal and administrative measures, secure the effective and expeditious realisation of the entitlement in question in accordance with the principles for the protection of property rights laid down in Art. 1 of Protocol No 1, having particular regard to the principles relating to compensation.[225]

Several judgments of the ICJ also lend support to the view that mandatory orders may form part of judgments of international courts. In *LaGrand*, Germany asked the ICJ to adjudge and declare that the US give assurances and guarantees of non-repetition that, in future, German nationals would not be denied their rights under the Convention on Consular Relations.[226] The US argued that this relief 'has no precedent in the jurisprudence of this Court and would exceed the Court's jurisdiction and authority in this case'.[227] The ICJ took note of the actions of the US in seeking to ensure compliance with its obligations under the convention, and refrained from making such an order, but it clearly considered that it had the power to do so.[228] The ICJ also held that, should a German national be convicted in similar circumstances, the US was under an obligation, 'by means of its own choosing, [to] allow the review and reconsideration of the conviction and sentence'.[229] In *Arrest Warrant*, the DRC requested that the ICJ adjudge and declare that 'Belgium shall be required to recall and cancel the arrest warrant of 11 April 2000', which had been issued for the arrest of the DRC's former Foreign Minister.[230] Belgium argued that such a request could not be the subject of any judgment of the court, as such an order would be a direction by the ICJ to Belgium 'as to the method by

220 *Loayza Tamayo (Reparation)*, 116 ILR 388, 440–2 (IACHR, 1998).

221 *Suarez Rosero (Merits)*, 118 ILR 56, 90 (IACHR, 1997); (*Reparations*) 118 ILR 92, 113 (IACHR, 1999). See further Orakhelashvili, 'Questions of International Judicial Jurisdiction', above n 209, 126.

222 Above n 87, 59–60.

223 Ibid, 60.

224 Above n 52, 698–9.

225 (2005) 40 EHRR 495, 564. For discussion, see Shelton, above n 45, 284–5.

226 Above n 9, 1097.

227 Ibid, 1097–8.

228 Ibid, 1082.

229 Ibid, 1103.

230 Above n 52, 540.

which it should give effect to a judgment of the Court finding that the warrant had infringed the immunity of its Foreign Minister'.[231] The ICJ granted the DRC's request, holding that full reparation would not be made merely by a finding that the arrest warrant was unlawful under international law; it ordered that Belgium must 'by means of its own choosing, cancel the warrant in question and so inform the authorities to whom it was circulated'.[232] In *Avena*, Mexico requested the annulment of the convictions of Mexican nationals which were secured without rights under the Consular Relations Convention being afforded.[233] The ICJ refrained from making such an order,[234] but it found that the appropriate reparation was for the US to provide 'by means of its own choosing, review and reconsideration of the convictions and sentences'.[235] In *Legal Consequences of the Construction of a Wall*, the ICJ held that Israel was under an obligation to terminate its breaches of international law, by, *inter alia*, halting the construction of the wall, dismantling the structure already built, and repealing all related legislation.[236]

ICSID tribunals have also issued mandatory orders on at least two occasions.[237] In *Tanzania Electric Supply Co*, the Tribunal ordered the specific performance of contractual obligations; it did not discuss its competence to make such an order, simply assuming that it had this power.[238] Clearer affirmation of the existence of a power to make mandatory orders can be found in the ICSID Tribunal's decision on jurisdiction in *Enron Corporation and Ponderosa Assets v Argentina*. In this case, the claimants argued that the tribunal could order 'injunctive relief concerning the performance or non-performance of certain acts'. Further, the claimants argued, referring to international case law, that an award could deal with 'pecuniary and non-pecuniary determinations, including specific performance and an injunction'.[239] The ICSID Tribunal agreed, holding that '[a]n examination of the powers of international courts and tribunals to order measures concerning performance or injunction and of the ample practice that is available in this respect, leaves this Tribunal in no doubt about the fact that these powers are indeed available'.[240] The Tribunal found that it had jurisdiction to issue an order that 'the taxes assessed be declared expropriatory and in breach of the Treaty and unlawful, and that they be annulled and their collection permanently enjoined'.[241] Whether such an order would be issued in the circumstances of the case was an issue for the merits.

231 *Arrest Warrant*, CR 2001/9, 32 (Daniel Bethlehem).

232 Above n 52, 556–7.

233 Above n 9, 614.

234 Ibid, 615–16.

235 Ibid, 624; see especially Orakhelashvili, 'Judicial Competence', above n 53.

236 Above n 79, paras 150–1, 163(3)(B).

237 But see Schreuer, above n 53, 329–30, who also cites *Antoine Goetz v Burundi* (2000) 15 *ICSID Review—FILJ* 457, as possibly constituting authority for the proposition. However, as Professor Schreuer acknowledges, this is doubtful, principally because the award which directed Burundi to re-establish the free zone regime was based on the agreement of the parties.

238 *Tanzania Electric Supply Co Ltd v Independent Power Tanzania Ltd* (ICSID Case No ARB/98/8, Award of 22 June 2001), 19, 26. It should be noted that this tribunal was applying Tanzanian law, as opposed to international law.

239 *Enron v Argentina*, above n 52, paras 77–9.

240 Ibid, para 79.

241 Ibid, para 77.

International courts have, in recent years, adopted a more robust appreciation of their remedial powers. Many international courts have gone further than merely making a declaratory judgment, and have made orders which require states to take action within their domestic sphere. This may be due to international courts being more established, and the existence of a good record of compliance with international judgments.[242] Some caution is still required, however. There appears to be a certain reluctance among some international courts to issue judgments in mandatory terms, which possibly springs from the level of deference that some international courts have *vis-à-vis* the states parties before them, and the idea that states should be able to choose the method of implementing an international judgment. In this regard, the divergence in the practice of the ICJ and the IACHR is instructive. For instance, in *Avena*, referred to above, Mexico argued that the obligation on the US to provide *restitutio in integrum* required the annulment of the convictions and sentences of the 52 Mexican nationals which had been given in violation of their rights under the Convention on Consular Relations.[243] In its judgment, the ICJ restricted itself to requiring the US to 'review and reconsider' the convictions and sentences.[244] In doing so, it explained that:

> in the present case, it is not the convictions and sentences of the Mexican nationals which are to be regarded as a violation of international law, but solely certain breaches of treaty obligations which preceded them.[245]

In contrast, the IACHR has not refrained from ordering the annulment of convictions where they were made in violation of individual rights under the American Convention.[246] In *Hilaire, Constantine and Benjamin*, for instance, the IACHR ordered the retrial of petitioners whose convictions had been carried out in breach of various rights under the American Convention, including the right to be free from arbitrary deprivation of life (article 4), the right to humane treatment (article 5), and the right to be tried within a reasonable time (article 8(1)).[247] The greater readiness of the IACHR and other international human rights courts to grant mandatory orders against states demonstrates another apparent divergence in approach among different international courts.

The reluctance on the part of some international courts to issue consequential orders also possibly results from the difficulties inherent in enforcing such judgments in the absence of an enforcement mechanism. Yet some methods of enforcing

[242] See generally Constanze Schulte, *Compliance with Decisions of the International Court of Justice* (2004); and Colter Paulson, 'Compliance with Final Judgments of the International Court of Justice since 1987' (2004) 98 *AJIL* 434; see also C Wilfred Jenks, *The Prospects of International Adjudication* (1964) 663–726; Oscar Schachter, 'The Enforcement of International Judicial and Arbitral Decisions' (1960) 54 *AJIL* 1, 1.

[243] Above n 9, paras 116–17.

[244] Ibid, paras 121, 153(9).

[245] Ibid, para 123. On the approach of the ICJ in *Avena*, see especially Orakhelashvili, 'Judicial Competence', above n 53.

[246] See especially Pasqualucci, above n 172, 250–3.

[247] *Hilaire, Constantine and Benjamin*, Ser C (No 94), paras 214–15, operative paras 9, 11, 14 (IACHR, 2002).

international judgments do exist. In the case of ECHR judgments, such a mechanism exists in the form of the Committee of Ministers of the Council of Europe, and, in the case of *pecuniary* obligations arising under ICSID awards, this exists in the terms of article 54 of the ICSID Convention.[248] The enforcement of *non-pecuniary* obligations—such as mandatory or consequential orders—remains problematic. ICJ judgments can be enforced by the Security Council, which may 'make recommendations or decide on measures to be taken to give effect to the judgment',[249] but this provision has, to date, never been successfully invoked.[250] This might explain the ICJ's insistence on including the formula 'by means of its own choosing' in the judgments referred to above, which indicates a preference for leaving the state some discretion in how the judgment is implemented. For that matter, the ECHR also continues to insist that its judgments are 'essentially declaratory'.[251] Yet the reality in some cases, such as in *Arrest Warrant* before the ICJ, and *Assanidze* and *Broniowski* before the ECHR, that there may be only one method of implementing a judgment, permits the suggestion to be made that these judgments can be regarded as mandatory, and that despite some differences in approach, international courts are increasingly prepared to issue such judgments.

IV. Remedies in WTO Dispute Settlement

It was observed earlier in this chapter that in contrast to the constitutive instruments of most international courts, the DSU makes extensive provision for the remedies available in WTO dispute settlement.[252] These remedies are largely based on the past practice of GATT panels in awarding remedies; in GATT dispute settlement, the remedy was 'usually to secure the withdrawal of the measures concerned if these [were] found to be inconsistent with the General Agreement'.[253] Significant differences can be found between the remedies awarded under the GATT and the WTO dispute settlement systems, and those available under the law of reparation as applied by most other international courts. In this sense, the remedial regime may be regarded in large measure as a special regime, or *lex specialis*.

[248] ICSID Convention, above n 2, art 54; Christoph Schreuer, *The ICSID Convention: A Commentary* (2001) 1124–6.

[249] *Charter of the United Nations*, opened for signature 26 June 1945, 3 Bevans 1153 (entered into force 24 October 1945), art 94(2).

[250] See generally Schulte, above n 242; Bruno Simma (ed), *The Charter of the United Nations: A Commentary* (2nd ed, 2002) vol II, 1176–8.

[251] *Assanidze v Georgia*, above n 52, para 202.

[252] See above nn 22–25 and accompanying text.

[253] *Understanding Regarding Notification, Consultation, Dispute Settlement and Surveillance* (28 November 1979), Annex, para 4, GATT BISD (26th Supp), 210 (1980); Mitsuo Matsushita, Thomas Schoenbaum and Petros Mavroidis, *The World Trade Organization: Law, Practice and Policy* (2nd ed, 2006) 106.

A. WTO Remedies as *Lex Specialis*

An initial difference between the WTO and other dispute settlement systems, which affects the availability of remedies, lies in the three types of complaint that claimant states may make: namely, 'violation complaints', 'non-violation complaints', and 'situation complaints'. Each type of complaint relates to trade measures taken by other members which serve to 'nullify' or 'impair' any benefits which should accrue to it directly or indirectly under the covered agreements.[254] The concepts of 'nullification' and 'impairment' are specific to GATT and WTO dispute settlement, and are not coterminous with breaches of treaty obligations. The concepts were originally intended as 'procedural rules providing for legal remedies not only in case of treaty violations but also in situations where the commercial opportunities protected by those trade agreements were being nullified by other (e.g. purely domestic) measures'.[255] So, while there is no need for there to be a breach of a treaty obligation in order for there to be 'nullification or impairment', a breach of an obligation arising under a relevant treaty is considered prima facie to constitute a case of nullification or impairment.[256]

'Violation complaints' under article XXIII(1)(a) of GATT 1994 are, as might be expected, complaints that treaty obligations arising under the GATT have been breached. The DSU extends the reach of article XXIII(1)(a) to all covered agreements; under article 3(8), the infringement of obligations under any covered agreement 'is considered prima facie to constitute a case of nullification and impairment'.[257] A violation complaint can be made not only when harm is done to the economy of another member state, but simply when a trade measure is introduced which could cause harm. This was clarified by the WTO panel in *US—Sections 301–310 Trade Act*, where it held that:

> In treaties which concern only the relations between States, State responsibility is incurred only when an actual violation takes place. By contrast, in a treaty the benefits of which depend in part on the activity of individual operators the legislation itself may be construed as a breach, since the mere existence of legislation could have an appreciable 'chilling effect' on the economic activities of individuals.[258]

'Non-violation complaints' are provided for in article XXIII(1)(b) of the GATT 1994. Under article 26 of the DSU, where article XXIII(1)(b) is applicable to a covered agreement, a WTO panel can make rulings or recommendations when a party considers that benefits are being nullified or impaired as a result of any

[254] *General Agreement on Tariffs and Trade 1994*, opened for signature 15 April 1994, 1867 UNTS 190 (entered into force 1 January 1995) ('GATT 1994'), art XXIII(1).

[255] Ernst-Ulrich Petersmann, *The GATT/WTO Dispute Settlement System* (1997) 142–3.

[256] Ibid, 145–6; DSU, above n 22, art 3(8).

[257] DSU, art 3(8); David Palmeter and Petros Mavroidis, *Dispute Settlement in the World Trade Organisation* (2nd ed, 2004) 163.

[258] DSR 2000–II, 815, 1133–4 (PR).

measure, whether or not it is a violation of an agreement.[259] The purpose of non-violation complaints was stated by the WTO panel in *Japan—Film* as being to 'protect the balance of concessions under GATT by providing a means to redress government actions not otherwise regulated by GATT rules that nonetheless nullify or impair a Member's legitimate expectations of benefits from tariff negotiations'.[260] Non-violation complaints are very rare, as noted by the panel in *Japan—Film*, which observed that there had only been eight such claims in GATT and WTO practice. The panel stated that this suggested 'that both the GATT contracting parties and WTO Members have approached this remedy with caution and, indeed, have treated it as an exceptional instrument of dispute settlement'.[261]

Finally, 'situation complaints' are contemplated in article XXIII(1)(c) of the GATT 1994, and can be brought in respect of all covered agreements due to the operation of article 26(2) of the DSU.[262] A situation complaint involves an allegation of nullification or impairment of benefits which has not resulted from a violation complaint or non-violation complaint.[263] This provision is invoked very infrequently, and there have been no situation complaints which have resulted in GATT or WTO jurisprudence.[264]

As well as there being three types of complaint in WTO dispute settlement, the remedies available for each complaint differ. In the case of 'violation' complaints, article 3(7) of the DSU establishes a hierarchy of remedies; it stipulates that the first objective of the dispute settlement system is 'usually to secure the withdrawal of the measures concerned if these are found to be inconsistent with the provisions of any covered agreements'.[265] The primacy of this objective is reinforced by the recommendations that panels or the Appellate Body shall make under article 19(1), which are 'that the Member concerned bring the measure into conformity with that agreement'.[266] Another remedy contemplated in article 3(7) is 'compensation', which is to be invoked 'only if the immediate withdrawal of the measure is impracticable and as a temporary measure pending withdrawal of the measure which is inconsistent with a covered agreement'.[267] But 'compensation' under WTO law does not have the same meaning as in general international law.[268] WTO compensation is not 'an indemnity payment to repair damage or harm caused by an unlawful act', but is rather a prospective measure, since it offers relief for harm that the complainant will probably suffer pending the implementation

[259] DSU, above n 22, art 26(1). [260] DSR 1998–IV, 1179, 1652 (PR).

[261] Ibid, 1647–8. See also Palmeter and Mavroidis, above n 257, 163, who state that there were 14 instances in which non-violation complaints were alleged under the GATT 1947.

[262] Palmeter and Mavroidis, ibid, 164–5. [263] DSU, above n 22, art 26(2).

[264] WTO, *WTO Analytical Index: Guide to WTO Law and Practice* (2003) 382; GATT, *Guide to GATT Law and Practice*, (6th ed, 1994) 621–4. [265] DSU, above n 22, art 3(7).

[266] Ibid, art 19(1) (footnotes omitted). [267] Ibid, art 3(7).

[268] David Palmeter and Petros Mavroidis, *Dispute Settlement in the World Trade Organisation* (1st ed, 1999) 167; see also Marco Bronckers and Naboth van den Broek, 'Financial Compensation in the WTO: Improving the Remedies of WTO Dispute Settlement' (2005) 8 *Journal of International Economic Law* 101.

by the defendant of panel or Appellate Body recommendations.[269] Compensation is 'voluntary', meaning that the claimant state and defendant state must enter into negotiations 'with a view to developing mutually acceptable compensation',[270] and might entail concessions in the form of greater market access.[271] If no satisfactory compensation has been agreed within 20 days, the claimant state may request permission from the DSB to invoke the third remedy available under the DSU, being the suspension of concessions or other obligations under the covered agreements to the member concerned.[272] For instance, in *EC—Hormones*, the US and Canada requested authorization from the DSB to suspend concessions to the EC in the order of US$116.8 million and CAN$11.3 million per year respectively;[273] this authorization was duly granted,[274] and in *US—Section 110(5) of US Copyright Act*, the EC requested permission to suspend concessions or other obligations to the US in accordance with article 22(2) of the DSU, although in that case, the EC and the US eventually reached a mutually satisfactory temporary arrangement.[275]

WTO disputes can also be referred to arbitration, which is available as an alternative means of dispute settlement under article 25 of the DSU.[276] It is not clear that remedies available before WTO arbitration tribunals are limited by the terms of article 19(1), which relates exclusively to panel and Appellate Body recommendations. However, WTO arbitration tribunals remain bound by the terms of article 3(7). This provision, coupled with the fact that articles 21 and 22 of the DSU relating to compensation and the suspension of concessions also apply to WTO arbitration suggests that WTO arbitration tribunals are limited to the remedies which are available in panel proceedings.[277]

In the case of 'non-violation complaints', the remedies available are different. If a claim is successful, there is no obligation on the member to withdraw the measure, as, by definition, a non-violation complaint does not involve breach of a WTO agreement. In such cases, the panel or Appellate Body merely has the power to recommend that the members concerned make a 'mutually satisfactory adjustment'.[278] Finally, in the case of 'situation complaints', which, like non-violation complaints,

[269] Bronckers and van den Broek, ibid, 103; Grané, above n 22, 762. See, however, efforts by less developed countries to introduce retrospective monetary compensation as a WTO remedy in the DSU negotiations: Proposals by the LDC Group, TN/DS/W/17, paras 13–14 (9 October 2002).

[270] DSU, above n 22, art 22(2).

[271] Grané, above n 22, 758, fn 10; Matsushita, Schoenbaum and Mavroidis, above n 253, 119–21.

[272] DSU, above n 22, art 22(2).

[273] *EC—Hormones* (US), WT/DS26/21 (15 July 1999); *EC—Hormones* (Canada), WT/DS48/19 (15 July 1999).

[274] *EC—Hormones*, Minutes of Meeting held in the Centre Willem Rappard on 26 July 1999, WT/DSB/M65, 17–19.

[275] *US—Section 110(5) of the US Copyright Act*, WT/DS160/19 (11 January 2002); see especially Bernard O'Connor and Margareta Djordjevic, 'Practical Aspects of Monetary Compensation: The *US—Copyright* Case' (2005) 8 *Journal of International Economic Law* 127, 127–31.

[276] DSU, above n 22, art 25.

[277] For example, *US—Section 110(5) of the US Copyright Act* (Arbitration), WT/DS160/ARB25/1, paras 2.3–2.7.

[278] DSU, above n 22, art 26(1)(b); Grané, above n 22, 761.

do not involve an internationally wrongful act, any panel report, including any recommendations and rulings, must be adopted by consensus.[279] This contrasts with the position applicable in the adoption of panel reports in violation and non-violation complaints, which is the negative consensus rule: i.e. the report is adopted unless there is a consensus *not* to do so.

Aside from the absence of a requirement of injury in violation complaints, and the absence of a requirement of an internationally wrongful act in other complaints, the most striking difference is that the primary remedy in WTO dispute settlement is the recommendation that a member state bring its trade measures into conformity with its obligations. In other words, WTO remedies typically are not retrospective in nature; they do not put the injured state in the position it was in prior to the imposition of the inconsistent trade measure.[280] The other remedies contemplated by article 3(7), compensation and suspension of concessions, are also forward-looking. These remedies continue the regime existing under GATT dispute settlement, where a ruling by a panel that a legal violation had occurred would result in a 'recommendation' that the defendant government comply with its obligations.[281] Regardless of how long it took to secure compliance, there was, in general, no compensation for the harm done by the measure which constituted a violation.[282]

B. Influence of Reparation in WTO Dispute Settlement

Despite the prospective nature of WTO remedies, it is suggested that the law of reparation, including the concept that reparation should 'wipe out all the consequences of the illegal act', is nonetheless relevant to GATT and WTO dispute settlement.[283] In the pre-WTO era, GATT panels had recommended remedies with retroactive effect on six occasions.[284] Parties to WTO dispute settlement

[279] DSU, art 26(2); Decision of 12 April 1989 on Improvements to the GATT Dispute Settlement Rules and Procedures (BISD 36S/6), para G(3).

[280] See especially *US—Certain EC Products*, DSR 2001–II, 413, 473 (PR); Grané, above n 22, 766.

[281] Robert Hudec, 'Broadening the Scope of Remedies in the WTO Dispute Settlement System' in Friedl Weiss (ed), *Improving WTO Dispute Settlement Procedures* (2000) 369, 376.

[282] See especially *Norway—Procurement of Toll Collection Equipment for the City of Trondheim*, paras 4.17–4.26 (GATT BISD 40S/319, 13 May 1992); Grané, above n 22, 765.

[283] See also Christian Tams, 'Unity and Diversity in the Law of State Responsibility', in Andreas Zimmermann and Rainer Hofmann (eds), *Unity and Diversity in International Law* (2006) 437, 447–9; Joost Pauwelyn, *Conflict of Norms in Public International Law* (2003) 218–27; Matsushita, Schoenbaum and Mavroidis, above n 253, 185–7; Mavroidis, above n 10, 775; but see James Crawford, 'Third Report on State Responsibility: Addendum', para 420 UN Doc A/C N.4/507/Add.4 (4 August 2000).

[284] *US—Measures Affecting Imports of Softwood Lumber from Canada*, paras 413–15 (BISD 40S/358, 27 October 1993); *US—Anti-dumping Duties on Gray Portland Cement and Cement Clinker from Mexico*, paras 5.36–5.44, 6.2 (ADP/82, 7 September 1992) (unadopted); *US—Countervailing Duties on Fresh, Chilled and Frozen Pork from Canada*, paras 4.11, 5.2 (BISD 38S/30, 11 July 1991); *US—Imposition of Antidumping Duties on Imports of Seamless Stainless Steel Hollow Products from Sweden*, paras 5.21, 5.24 (ADP/47, 20 August 1990) (unadopted); *Canada—Imposition of Countervailing Duties on Imports of Manufacturing Beef from the EEC*, para 5.17

proceedings have also tested the prospective nature of WTO remedies in several cases by requesting retroactive remedies. The issue was raised, but not decided, in two disputes: *Guatemala—Cement I*,[285] and *Brazil—Aircraft*.[286] The issue arose again in *Australia—Leather*, a case concerning prohibited subsidies.[287] This case has already been discussed in chapter 4 in the context of the power to grant provisional measures. In this case, the US alleged that Australia was providing subsidies prohibited by the SCM Agreement to an Australian producer and exporter of automotive leather.[288] The panel found that the Australian subsidies were inconsistent with the SCM Agreement, and recommended that Australia withdraw them 'without delay'.[289] A panel was established to examine Australia's implementation of the recommendation, and both the US and Australia argued that article 4(7) of the SCM Agreement, which provides that panels shall recommend that offending subsidies be withdrawn without delay, was limited to purely prospective action.[290] The panel disagreed, and held that the phrase 'withdrawal of the subsidy' in article 4(7) of the SCM Agreement could also entail repayment of prohibited subsidies and therefore constituted a corrective measure with retrospective effect.[291] The panel held that it did not believe that:

> Article 19.1 of the DSU, even in conjunction with Art 3.7 of the DSU, requires the limitation of the specific remedy provided for in Article 4.7 of the SCM Agreement to purely prospective action.[292]

The panel rejected the position of both the parties and the EC, a third party intervening in the dispute, which had argued that permitting retroactive remedies under article 4(7) of the SCM Agreement would be contrary to article 19(1) of the DSU and previous practice of the GATT and WTO dispute settlement systems. The panel recalled that the recommendation to withdraw the subsidy was based on article 4(7) of the SCM Agreement, and not on article 19(1) of the DSU. It observed that article 4(7) of the SCM Agreement required a panel to recommend 'withdrawal of the subsidy'; whereas article 19(1) of the DSU required a panel to recommend the 'bringing of the measure into conformity' with WTO obligations.[293] The panel held that to interpret the words 'withdrawal of the subsidy' in article 4(7) as meaning prospective corrective measures would make this provision indistinguishable from article 19(1) of the DSU, and render article 4(7) redundant. In any event, the panel made no finding on whether retroactive remedies

(SCM/85, 13 October 1987) (unadopted); *New Zealand—Imports of Electrical Transformers from Finland*, para 4.11 (BISD 32S/55, 18 July 1985); see Palmeter and Mavroidis (2004), above n 257, 262–4; Grané, above n 22, 763–5; Hudec, above n 281, 384–5; Petersmann, above n 255, 139–40.

285 Above n 211. 286 Above n 212. 287 DSR 1999–III, 951 (PR).

288 Ibid, 953; Matshushita, Schoenbaum and Mavroidis, above n 253, 185; *Agreement on Subsidies and Countervailing Measures*, opened for signature 15 April 1994, 1869 UNTS 14 (entered into force 1 January 1995) ('SCM Agreement'). 289 Above n 287, 1104.

290 *Australia—Leather*, DSR 2000–III, 1189, 1200–3 (PR).

291 Ibid, 1205–11; Grané, above n 22, 768. 292 Above n 290, 1208.

293 Ibid, 1211, citing *Brazil—Aircraft*, DSR 1999-III, 1161, 1217–18 (AB).

were permitted under article 19(1) of the DSU.[294] Moreover, the panel noted that article 4(7) of the SCM Agreement was a new and specific provision under the WTO that had not been interpreted previously; this meant, in the view of the panel, that its interpretation of article 4(7) did not diverge from previous jurisprudence.[295]

The question was considered again in *Guatemala—Cement II*, an anti-dumping dispute.[296] Here, Mexico requested that the panel recommend that Guatemala 'revoke the anti-dumping measure adopted against imports of Mexican cement and refund the anti-dumping duties collected'.[297] Guatemala and the US, a third party, opposed this request.[298] The panel found that Guatemala was in breach of WTO antidumping rules, and stated that:

> we note that Guatemala has now maintained a WTO-inconsistent anti-dumping measure in place for a period of three and a half years. Thus, we fully understand Mexico's desire to see the anti-dumping duties repaid and consider that repayment might be justifiable in circumstances such as these.[299]

However, the panel declined to make such a suggestion:

> Mexico's request raises important systemic issues regarding the nature of the actions necessary to implement a recommendation under Article 19.1 of the DSU, issues which have not been fully explored in this dispute. Thus, we decline Mexico's request to suggest that Guatemala refund the anti-dumping duties collected.[300]

On the basis of these panel reports, it is suggested that the obligation on states responsible for an internationally wrongful act to make reparation has some relevance in the awarding of remedies in WTO dispute settlement, where the DSU and the relevant covered agreement leave gaps to be filled.[301] Its pertinence is supported by assertions of the Appellate Body and other panels that general international law has a role to play in WTO dispute settlement.[302] Professor Pauwelyn has even suggested that the past GATT practice of not awarding retroactive remedies is not due to the non-availability of such remedies, but arose simply because GATT parties did not usually request such remedies.[303] However, in view of the express terms of articles 3(7) and 19(1) of the DSU, it is suggested that retroactive remedies may be available only in trade disputes pertaining to covered agreements

[294] Above n 290, 1211. [295] Ibid, 1208; Grané, above n 22, 768.

[296] DSR 2000–XI, 5295 (PR). [297] Ibid, 5718. [298] Ibid, 5365–7.

[299] Ibid, 5719.

[300] Ibid, 5719. See also *US—Antidumping Measures on Certain Hot Rolled Steel Products from Japan*, WT/DS184/R, para 8.13 (PR), where the panel made an almost identical statement.

[301] See also Pauwelyn, above n 283, 220–7.

[302] See especially *Korea—Government Procurement*, DSR 2000–VIII, 3541, 3756 (PR); *US—Gasoline*, DSR 1996–I, 3, 16 (AB); see also Joost Pauwelyn, 'How to Win a World Trade Organisation Dispute Based on Non-World Trade Organisation Law?' (2003) 37 *Journal of World Trade* 997, 998, 1001–2, fnn 18–19; Joost Pauwelyn, 'The Role of Public International Law in the WTO: How Far Can We Go?' (2001) 95 *AJIL* 535; James Cameron and Kevin Gray, 'Principles of International Law in the WTO Dispute Settlement Body' (2001) 50 *ICLQ* 248.

[303] Pauwelyn, *Conflict of Norms*, above n 283, 223.

where there is a dispute settlement provision similar to article 4(7) of the SCM Agreement, from which a broader remedial competence might be inferred. The panel's reticence to rule on this question in *Guatemala—Cement II* suggests that retroactive remedies might also be available under the *Anti-dumping Agreement*, in which several provisions can be found indicating the possibility of retroactive compensation, such as provisions authorizing the complaining state to apply a provisional anti-dumping duty to the goods allegedly being dumped.[304] This question is likely to be revisited in future.[305]

Conclusion

This chapter has examined whether there are common practices among international courts concerning remedies, and a number of conclusions can be made. The first is that in the absence of express provision, there is agreement among international courts that states responsible for an internationally wrongful act resulting in injury are under an obligation to make reparation. A second conclusion that can be reached is that all international courts have the power to award remedies in dispute settlement proceedings. Indeed, the existence of the power to award remedies is so uncontroversial that most international courts do so without any discussion of the source of their authority. Third, in the absence of agreement to the contrary, there are three forms of reparation which are generally available as remedies in international adjudication: restitution, compensation, and declaratory judgments. These forms of reparation are not necessarily available in every dispute before every international court. The availability of remedies will depend on the type of dispute, the identity of the parties, the nature of the international court seised of the dispute, and the way in which parties frame their prayer for relief. A fourth conclusion is that although there is broad common ground in the availability of these remedies, there is less consistency in the manner in which they are awarded. Differences can be seen, for instance, in the approach of international human rights courts and the ITLOS concerning the award of compensation for personal injury. Fifth, despite suggestions to the contrary in early international judicial practice, international courts are increasingly recognizing that they have the power to issue judgments and awards in mandatory form. This appears to be an indispensable complement to the adjudicative function of international courts in settling disputes and awarding remedies; for if international courts can make an award, but cannot give directions to the parties on how that award is to be executed, then the dispute may persist, and the international

[304] *Agreement on Implementation of Article VI of the General Agreement on Tariffs and Trade 1994*, opened for signature 15 April 1994, 1868 UNTS 201 (entered into force 1 January 1995), art 7(3).

[305] See also Matsushita, Schoenbaum and Mavroidis, above n 253, 185–7, who also conclude that the question remains open.

court will not have carried out its function in settling the dispute. Nevertheless, some differences remain concerning the preparedness of international courts to issue mandatory orders without giving the state concerned discretion over how the judgment is implemented. Finally, the remedial regime applicable in WTO dispute settlement under the DSU is a *lex specialis*, and differs from the law of reparation in several respects, including its goal of prospective compliance with the obligations under the WTO agreements, and the non-availability of retroactive remedies to compensate the injured state for past harm. Nonetheless, some GATT and WTO practice suggests that the WTO remedial regime might not be hermetically sealed and impervious to the influence of the obligation to make reparation under general international law.

An overall conclusion is that, while there is general agreement among international courts on the availability of the different forms of reparation as judicial remedies, there is less common practice in what international courts are prepared to award—in particular, the varying standards of compensation, and the availability of mandatory orders—and the regime of remedies in the WTO dispute settlement system forms a distinct *lex specialis*, albeit one which might be susceptible to the influence of the general international law on reparation. There is, in this sense, less common ground than has been encountered in other areas, such as the applicable rules of evidence, and the power to grant provisional measures.

Having considered the existence of common practice in relation to rules of evidence, the power to grant provisional measures, the power to interpret and revise judgments, and the awarding of remedies in international adjudication, the next chapter considers the reasons for the emergence of a common law of international adjudication, and identifies limitations on its further development.

7

A Common Law of International Adjudication: Reasons and Limitations

Introduction

At the outset of this book, it was observed that proliferation has taken place in the context of concerns over the 'fragmentation' of international law.[1] It was also noted that arguably the multiplication of international courts and tribunals has exacerbated the possibility of fragmentation, and has, in addition, given rise to the creation of overlapping jurisdictions among international tribunals. The core question that has been examined in this book is whether, notwithstanding the several inconsistent decisions that have been rendered by international courts, one of the possible effects of proliferation is a trend towards norm-harmonization on issues of procedure and remedies, which is contributing to the emergence of what might be called a 'common law of international adjudication'. Through consideration of the sources of law relating to procedure and remedies, and the ability of international courts to have regard to the practice of other international tribunals, by, *inter alia*, principles of treaty interpretation and the exercise of implied and inherent powers, and after an examination of the approach of international courts to evidential issues, the granting of provisional measures, the interpretation and revision of judgments, and the awarding of remedies, common elements can indeed be identified in the approaches of international courts. This chapter turns to the question of the reasons for the emerging common law of international adjudication, and asks whether there are any limitations on its further development.

[1] See generally chapter 1.

I. Reasons for the Emerging Common Law of International Adjudication

It is not possible to identify one single explanation for the emergence of the common law of international adjudication. There is a wide range of factors that are relevant to the emergence of common approaches to issues of procedure and remedies, and it would be artificial to suggest that the each of those factors is applicable in every situation where an issue arises that might lend itself to the adoption of a common approach. Rather, the relevant factors—of which twelve can be identified—may only be applicable with respect to certain issues of procedure and remedies, and before certain international tribunals. It should also be emphasized that the twelve factors, which are described in the following paragraphs, are not necessarily self-contained; there is some degree of overlap among them.

The first of the factors that is relevant to the emergence of a common law of international adjudication is the fact that the constitutive instruments of international courts are frequently drafted in similar terms. This is the case, for instance, with regard to the ITLOS Statute, and the ECJ Statute, which were based on the ICJ Statute;[2] and the drafters of the ICSID Convention also drew on the ICJ Statute,[3] as did the framers of the European HR Convention.[4] The ICJ Statute, for its part, is almost identical to the PCIJ Statute,[5] which was, in turn, influenced by the first constitutive instruments of a permanent body for the settlement of international disputes, the 1899 Convention and the 1907 Convention, together with the Draft Convention Relative to the Creation of a Court of Arbitral Justice of 1907.[6] Given the common origins and similar drafting of these constitutive instruments, the common approaches which can be seen in the way these international courts interpret many of their provisions should not be unexpected. In

[2] See, e.g., in the case of the ITLOS, Barbara Kwiatkowska, 'The Future of the Law of the Sea Tribunal in Hamburg', in W P Heere (ed), *International Law and the Hague's 750th Anniversary* (1999) 417; and in the case of the ECJ, Jürgen Schwarze, 'Origins of the European Courts' Statutes and Rules of Procedure' in Richard Plender (ed), *European Courts: Practice and Precedents* (1997) 3, 4–5; and Richard Plender, 'Rules of Procedure in the International Court and the European Court' (1991) 2(2) *European Journal of International Law* 1, 2ff.

[3] See, e.g., Christoph Schreuer, *The ICSID Convention: A Commentary* (2001) 56, 59, 453–4, 545, 745–6, 766–7, 856–6, 869.

[4] See, e.g., *Loizidou v Turkey (Preliminary Objections)* (1995) 20 EHRR 99, 132, where the ECHR noted that various provisions of the European HR Convention had been modelled on the ICJ Statute.

[5] See, e.g., Ole Spiermann, *International Legal Argument in the Permanent Court of International Justice* (2005) 12; Ole Spiermann, '"Who Attempts too Much Does Nothing Well": The 1920 Advisory Committee of Jurists and the Statute of the Permanent Court of International Justice' (2002) 73 *British Yearbook of International Law* 187, 190; Shabtai Rosenne, *The Law and Practice of the International Court, 1920–2005* (2006) vol I, 52–76; *Statute of the Permanent Court of International Justice*, PCIJ Publications, Ser D (No 1), 7 ('PCIJ Statute').

[6] Manley Hudson, *The Permanent Court of International Justice: A Treatise* (1934) 109, 122–81; on the work of the Advisory Committee of Jurists in drafting the PCIJ Statute, see especially Spiermann, 'Who Attempts Too Much', ibid.

contrast, if a constitutive instrument is drafted differently, such as the DSU, this can make it less likely that an international tribunal constituted under that instrument—for instance, a WTO panel—will adopt approaches to questions of procedure and remedies which are similar to other international courts.[7]

It is difficult to identify with any certainty the reasons for similar drafting of different constitutive instruments without conducting an exhaustive review of the relevant *travaux préparatoires*, which is beyond the scope of this book. Yet it might be speculated that three factors play some role. First, the drafters of a constitutive instrument might have a degree of deference and respect for the tried and tested provisions of the constitutive instrument of an established international tribunal, such as the ICJ. Second, where a new international tribunal is being created to replace an old dispute settlement institution, there may be a desire on the part of the drafters to maintain a level of consistency with the pre-existing regime, as might be seen in the DSU, which adopts many aspects of the procedure applicable in GATT dispute settlement, and also the ICJ Statute, which is almost a direct replica of the PCIJ Statute. A third reason may simply be the principle that if a particular form of constitutive instrument has worked well before, a common-sense approach is to borrow the features of that statute which can be transplanted to the new institution.

If the constitutive instruments of international courts are drafted in similar terms, it should not be surprising that the provisions of those statutes are interpreted to have a broadly common meaning. Related to this is a second factor which is relevant to the emergence of a common law of international adjudication; namely, the principle that where an issue arises in one international court, the resolution of that issue is often aided by consideration of how that issue has been dealt with by other bodies with similar constitutive instruments. This practice is representative of the concept of precedent, or *stare decisis*, as it is natural for judges on international courts to ask whether the issue before them has been considered previously.[8] This is not to say that the doctrine of *stare decisis* is applicable in international law; article 59 of the ICJ Statute, for instance, makes it clear that it is not,[9] and many international tribunals have expressly stated that they are not bound by previous decisions.[10] Yet if the reasoning of one international court

[7] On the drafting of the DSU, see generally Ernst-Ulrich Petersmann, *The GATT/WTO Dispute Settlement System* (1997) 177–82; Terence Stewart and Christopher Callahan, *Dispute Settlement Mechanisms* (1993).

[8] For example, Mohamed Shahabuddeen, *Precedent in the World Court* (1996) 6.

[9] *Statute of the International Court of Justice*, opened for signature 26 June 1945, 3 Bevans 1153 (entered into force 24 October 1945), art 59: 'the decision of the Court has no binding force except between the parties and in respect of that particular case.'

[10] See, e.g., *Bayinder Insaat Turizm Ticaret Ve Sanayi AS v Pakistan* (ICSID Case No ARB/03/29, Decision on Jurisdiction of 14 November 2005), para 76: '[t]he Tribunal agrees that it is not bound by earlier decisions, but will certainly carefully consider such decisions whenever appropriate' (footnote omitted); *AES Corporation v Argentina* (ICSID Case No ARB/02/17, Decision on Jurisdiction of 26 April 2005), paras 30–3; see also *SGS v Philippines* (ICSID Case No ARB/02/6, Decision on Jurisdiction of 29 January 2004), para 97: 'although different tribunals constituted under the ICSID

which has considered a problem is persuasive, that will often encourage the same approach to be adopted by other international courts.[11] This is encapsulated most eloquently by Sir Hersch Lauterpacht, in explaining why the ICJ, although not bound by the doctrine of precedent, nonetheless follows its own decisions:

> The Court follows its own decisions for the same reasons for which all courts—whether bound by the doctrine of precedent or not—do so, namely, because such decisions are a repository of legal experience to which it is convenient to adhere; because they embody what the Court has considered in the past to be good law; because respect for decisions given in the past makes for certainty and stability, which are of the essence of the orderly administration of justice; and (a minor and not invariably accurate consideration) because judges are naturally reluctant, in the absence of compelling reasons to the contrary, to admit that they were previously in the wrong.[12]

A third reason for the emergence of common features in issues of procedure and remedies can be found in the ability of international courts to adopt approaches to the interpretation of their statutes and rules that permit them to take account of the practice of other international tribunals. While similarly drafted instruments are likely to be interpreted consistently, the analysis presented in this book shows that international courts have also managed to arrive at similar interpretations of differently worded provisions.[13] In order to facilitate such common interpretations, international courts have employed certain approaches to treaty interpretation which have been addressed in chapter 2.[14] These are, first, the principle of effectiveness in treaty interpretation, in accordance with which '[p]articular provisions are to be interpreted so as to give them the fullest weight and effect consistent with the normal meaning of the words and with other parts of the text'.[15] Second, international courts have adopted an evolutive approach to interpreting

system should in general seek to act consistently with each other, in the end it must be for each tribunal to exercise its competence in accordance with the applicable law': all available at <http://ita.law.uvic.ca> (last visited 25 November 2006).

[11] See, e.g., Yuval Shany, *The Competing Jurisdictions of International Courts and Tribunals* (2003) 110–11; see also Sir Elihu Lauterpacht, 'The Development of the Law of International Organisations by the Decisions of International Tribunals' (1976) 152 *Recueil des cours* 377, 396–402.

[12] Sir Hersch Lauterpacht, *The Development of International Law by the International Court* (1958) 14.

[13] On this point, see also Judge Rosalyn Higgins, 'A Babel of Judicial Voices? Ruminations from the Bench' (2006) 55 *ICLQ* 791, 797–8. See, e.g., the decisions of the ICSID tribunals in *Maffezini v Spain* (Provisional Measures), 5 ICSID Rep 393, 394 (1999); *Victor Pey Casado and Fondation Président Allende v Chile* (2001) 16 *ICSID Review—FILJ* 567, 578; and *Tokios Tokeles v Ukraine* (ICSID Case No ARB/02/18, Procedural Order No 1 of 1 July 2003), para 4; (Procedural Order No 3 of 18 January 2005), paras 6–7, fn 12, in which the ICSID tribunals interpreted the word 'recommend' consistently with ICJ jurisprudence to mean the same as 'order', available at <http://ita.law.uvic.ca> (last visited 25 November 2006); see, also, the judgment of the ECHR in *Mamatkulov and Abdurasulovic v Turkey* (Judgment of 6 February 2003), paras 39–51, 92–111, available at <http://www.echr.coe.int> (last visited 25 November 2006).

[14] See chapter 2, part I(C)(1).

[15] Sir Gerald Fitzmaurice, *The Law and Procedure of the International Court of Justice* (1986) 50; see also above ch 2, part I(C)(1).

their constitutive instruments, which recognizes that certain terms are not static, but their meanings may change with time.[16] Third, international courts have also taken account of international judicial practice by referring to article 31(3)(c) of the VCLT in interpreting provisions of their statutes and rules.[17]

A fourth reason for the adoption of common approaches by international courts in developing their procedures and remedies is that they have reference to customary rules developed in international judicial practice, and general principles of law, both of which are well established as sources of judicial procedure.[18] The application of customary rules and general principles of law has a harmonizing effect on issues of procedure and remedies precisely because they are not derived from any specific dispute settlement regime, but are rules and principles that are usually susceptible of general application. In applying such rules and principles, international courts will invariably have regard to the practice of other international tribunals, leading to the adoption of common approaches to these issues.

The fifth reason for the emergence of common approaches to issues of procedure and remedies is the ability of international courts to exercise inherent powers.[19] The constitutive instruments and rules of procedure of international courts do not always confer identical or similar powers on international courts, and contain *lacunae*.[20] If there are gaps on issues of procedure and remedies, international courts might have the ability to fill in such gaps by the exercise of inherent powers, which are powers that international courts possess in order to carry out their functions. In exercising such powers, which are not prescribed by the terms of their constitutive instruments and rules of procedure, international courts are likely to

[16] See, e.g., Sir Robert Jennings and Sir Arthur Watts (eds), *Oppenheim's International Law* (9th ed, 1992) vol I, 1282; see also *Gabcikovo–Nagymaros Project* [1997] ICJ Rep 7, 67–8; *Iron Rhine Railway* (Award of 24 May 2005), paras 79–81, available at <http://www.pca-cpa.org> (last visited 25 November 2006); see also above ch 2, part I(C)(1).

[17] See, e.g., Campbell McLachlan, 'The Principle of Systemic Integration and Article 31(3)(c) of the Vienna Convention' (2005) 54 *ICLQ* 279; Philippe Sands, 'Sustainable Development: Treaty, Custom and the Cross-Fertilisation of International Law' in Alan Boyle and David Freestone (eds), *International Law and Sustainable Development: Past Achievements and Future Challenges* (1999) 39; and Philippe Sands, 'Treaty, Custom and the Cross-Fertilisation of International Law' (1998) 1 *Yale Human Rights and Development Law Journal* 85, 95; see also above ch 2, part I(C)(1).

[18] See, e.g., Rosenne, *Law and Practice*, above n 5, vol III, 1022–8; Robert Kolb, 'General Principles of Procedural Law' in Andreas Zimmermann, Christian Tomuschat and Karin Oellers-Frahm (eds), *The Statute of the International Court of Justice: A Commentary* (2006) 793; Bin Cheng, *General Principles of Law as Applied by International Tribunals* (first published 1953, 1987 ed) 299–386; Georg Schwarzenberger, *International Law as Applied by International Courts and Tribunals* (1986) vol IV, 584–5; and Hugh Thirlway, 'Dilemma or Chimera? Admissibility of Illegally Obtained Evidence in International Adjudication' (1984) 78 *AJIL* 622, 623–4.

[19] See above chapter 2, parts II–V; see especially Chester Brown, 'The Inherent Powers of International Courts and Tribunals' (2005) 76 *British Yearbook of International Law* 195; Paola Gaeta, 'Inherent Powers of International Courts and Tribunals' in Lal Chand Vohrar *et al* (eds), *Man's Inhumanity to Man: Essays on International Law in Honour of Antonio Cassese* (2003) 353; Alexander Orakhelashvili, 'The Concept of International Judicial Jurisdiction: A Reappraisal' (2003) 3 *Law and Practice of International Courts and Tribunals* 501.

[20] See above chapter 2, part I(C); Brown, ibid, 202–5.

refer, instinctively, to the practice of other international tribunals. Accordingly, the exercise of inherent powers can result in an international court adopting an approach common to that found in the practice of other international tribunals.

The sixth reason for the emerging common law is that international courts essentially perform the same functions.[21] While there are competing conceptions of the different functions of international courts and tribunals,[22] there are two general functions shared by international courts: these are the settlement of disputes in accordance with law, and the proper administration of international justice. This is not to say that, in addition to these general functions, international courts necessarily share the same specific functions; indeed, the existence of specific functions can limit the relevance of the case law of other international courts, as will be noted below. Individual international courts might, in addition, have functions that require them to take into account other factors.[23] Yet the fact that international courts share two essential functions can serve to explain the increasing convergence in jurisprudence, for if an international court can identify other international courts with common functions, this arguably makes consideration of the practice of those courts more relevant.

The seventh reason might be found in the existence of a distinct group of international lawyers who regularly appear before different international courts. As Professor Cot has observed of those appearing before the ICJ:

> Le nombre d'avocats qui plaident régulièrement devant la Cour internationale de Justice peut être estimé à une douzaine. J'ai retenu six noms parmi ceux-ci: trois britanniques, un australien, deux français. Un ou plusieurs de ces avocats ont plaidé dans dix-neuf des vingt affaires contentieuses qui ont donné lieu à décision au cours de la décennie écoulée. Je ne connais pas de barreau national si restreint et de monopole mieux gardé que celui-là.[24]

In addition to this 'international bar', there are also a relatively limited number of people who comprise the 'international judiciary'; indeed, many international judges have served on more than one different international court.[25] It is suggested that the relatively small number of international lawyers and judges participating in international dispute settlement proceedings might also contribute to the emerging common law of international adjudication. This is because these

[21] See especially Brown, above n 19, 229–37.

[22] See above chapter 2, part V(A).

[23] See above chapter 2, part V(A).

[24] Jean-Pierre Cot, 'Le monde de la justice internationale', in Société Française pour le Droit International, *Colloque de Lille: La juridictionnalisation du droit international* (2003) 511, 513.

[25] There are many examples, of which only a few can be cited for reasons of space: Professor Georges Abi-Saab has served on the ICTY Appeals Chamber, the UNCC, as judge ad hoc of the ICJ, and is currently a member of the WTO Appellate Body; Stephen Schwebel has served as Judge and President of the ICJ, and has been appointed as an arbitrator on UNCLOS tribunals, an ICSID tribunal, a NAFTA tribunal, and two PCA tribunals; President Rosalyn Higgins of the ICJ has been appointed to two PCA tribunals, and has also served on an ICSID tribunal; Professor Sir Elihu Lauterpacht has served on ICSID, PCA, and NAFTA tribunals, and as judge ad hoc of the ICJ; Professor James Crawford has served on ICSID, NAFTA, PCA and UNCLOS tribunals; and Sir Arthur Watts has served on PCA, UNCLOS, and UNCITRAL tribunals.

international lawyers are frequently in contact, permitting them to exchange ideas related to international adjudication. In the words of Professor Cot:

> Ce petit monde vie en symbiose. Juges, agents, avocats, conseils se retrouvent aux mêmes bonnes tables de La Haye. Ils fréquentent les couloirs de la 42ème Rue et singulièrement de la VIème Commission. Les juges sont eux-mêmes d'anciens conseillers juridiques ou d'anciens avocats, souvent passés par la Commission du droit international.[26]

These same international lawyers, having appeared before or sat on different international tribunals, are also likely to bring a common legal experience to their work; experience gained with the procedure applicable before one international court is likely to be drawn on when appearing before—or serving on—another such body. The practice of international judges serving on the bench of more than one international court is by no means novel, or solely a product of the proliferation that has occurred over recent years; for instance, Judge Huber sat on a PCA tribunal while he was serving on the PCIJ,[27] and Sir Arnold McNair and Sir Gerald Fitzmaurice both served as judges of the ICJ and the ECHR.[28] Yet the frequency with which international lawyers are appearing before and serving on more than one judicial body appears to be increasing as a result of proliferation and the increase in volume of international litigation.

The eighth reason that might be suggested is that proliferation has arguably created a sense of competition among some international courts. This inter-institutional competition might, in some cases, lead to greater commonality in the approach of international courts to certain issues of procedure and remedies. It might be speculated, for instance, that international courts may wish to make their forum as attractive as possible to potential litigants; this could lead them to offer any procedural advantages that might be provided by other international courts with a similar jurisdiction. One possible example in this connection relates to the ICJ's judgment in *LaGrand* in 2001, in which it found that provisional measures indicated under the ICJ Statute were binding.[29] Although the ICJ's judgment was thoroughly reasoned, it might be speculated that it was at least partly motivated by a wish for the court to remain an attractive forum for cases involving requests for provisional measures, especially given that any provisional measures granted under UNCLOS would definitely be binding in view of the clear language of article 290(6) of that convention.[30] Indeed, following the entry

[26] Cot, above n 24, 514. [27] *Island of Palmas*, 2 RIAA 829 (US–Netherlands, 1928).

[28] See, e.g., John Merrills, *Judge Sir Gerald Fitzmaurice and the Discipline of International Law* (1998) 1.

[29] For discussion of this decision, see chapter 4, part III(C); Jörg Kammerhofer, 'The Binding Nature of Provisional Measures of the International Court of Justice: The "Settlement" of the Issue in the *LaGrand* Case' (2003) 16 *Leiden Journal of International Law* 67; Martin Mennecke and Christian Tams, '*LaGrand* Case (*Germany v United States of America*)' (2002) 51 *ICLQ* 449; Xiodang Yang, 'Thou Shalt Not Violate Provisional Measures' (2001) 60 *CLJ* 441.

[30] For the suggestion that it was not a 'mere coincidence' that the ICJ decision in *LaGrand* followed the express stipulation of the binding nature of provisional measures granted under UNCLOS, see,

into force of UNCLOS, the ICJ faced the real possibility that many new disputes over fisheries, the delimitation of maritime boundaries, or other issues concerning the law of the sea would not be referred to it, but rather to the ITLOS or other tribunals constituted under UNCLOS due to the certainty concerning the legal status of provisional measures under that convention.

However, there are limitations to the importance of this factor. It should be noted there is no objective or empirical evidence that inter-institutional competition has had any influence on the decisions of international courts, and in this sense, its significance is difficult to substantiate. In addition, even if this consideration is relevant, the scope of its operation is relatively limited. It can only have some effect in instances where international courts have overlapping jurisdictions such as the ICJ, the ITLOS, and other UNCLOS tribunals. There are many other cases where this consideration does not arise; for instance, the jurisdiction *ratione materiae* and *ratione personae* of the WTO dispute settlement system is very different to that of, say, the various international human rights tribunals. In this respect, the ECHR's judgment in *Mamatkulov* in 2003, in which it, too, held that its provisional measures had binding force, arguably was not influenced by any sense of inter-institutional competition with the ICJ, the ITLOS or UNCLOS tribunals; this is because the jurisdiction of these international courts does not overlap. It can be concluded, accordingly, that the emergence of common features in the jurisprudence of international courts that do not have overlapping jurisdictions is unlikely to have been motivated by inter-institutional competition.

A ninth reason for the emerging commonality could be that there is an underlying belief in the minds of many international judges that common practice is to be regarded as a positive development, and that they act on this belief and exercise procedural and remedial powers more or less consistently with the practice of other international courts. In this sense, some international tribunals might consciously strive to obtain similar outcomes. These efforts might result from a desire for systemic coherence in the administration of international justice, from a belief that commonality furthers the goal of 'security and predictability' in international adjudication,[31] or even from a sense of conformism to the practices of an international court which they regard as having the most prestige in the international legal order, such as the ICJ. Again, while it is difficult to substantiate the importance of this factor without extensive empirical research, this wish for relative consistency in the procedural and remedial aspects of international adjudication could also be a reason for the emergence of increasingly common practices.

A tenth reason is the existence of a similar relationship between international courts and the litigating parties before them. If a relationship exists between one

e.g., Ole Spiermann, 'Review of Shabtai Rosenne, *Provisional Measures in International Law: The International Court of Justice and the International Tribunal for the Law of the Sea*' (2005) 76 *British Yearbook of International Law* 554, 554.

[31] See, e.g., DSU, art 3(2): *Understanding on Rules and Procedures Governing the Settlement of Disputes*, opened for signature 15 April 1994, 1869 UNTS 401 art 3(2) (entered into force 1 January 1995) (DSU).

particular international court, say, the ICJ, and litigants which is similar to that found between another international court, say, the ITLOS, and the parties that appear before it, this might also mean that the second international court—here, the ITLOS—would be likely to adopt common approaches to procedural and remedial issues. For example, international courts might possess a coercive power, such as a power to issue mandatory orders. However, even though many international courts might possess that power, some international courts will not exercise it due to their deference to the parties.[32] Accordingly, if the relationship between the court and the parties is the same—as is arguably the situation in the case of, e.g., the ICJ, the ITLOS, and the WTO, where the parties are sovereign states[33]—then such a power is more likely to be exercised consistently.

An eleventh reason for the emergence of common practices might be found in the fact that the parties to international litigation have pleaded the relevance of the jurisprudence of other international courts. For although international courts can be presumed to know the law—*jura novit curia*—the submissions of litigants on the exercise of procedural and remedial powers will naturally have some influence on the international court's decision.

A twelfth relevant factor is that there may be norm-intrinsic reasons for the adoption of common approaches by international courts and tribunals, such as the perceived fairness or utility of the rule in question. This factor may have been influential in, for instance, the various findings by international tribunals on the binding nature of provisional measures,[34] and on the authority of international tribunals to permit non-governmental organizations to submit *amicus curiae* briefs in disputes having a public interest element.[35]

It can be seen that there are various forces at play that can contribute to the emerging common law of international adjudication. These forces are, however,

[32] See, e.g., the reluctance of many interstate courts, where the parties are sovereign states, to order the production of documents, or to issue mandatory or consequential orders as remedies: see above chapter 3, part III(B); see also above chapter 6, part III(D).

[33] See, e.g., ICJ Statute, above 9, art 34(1); *United Nations Convention on the Law of the Sea*, 1833 UNTS 3, Annex VI ('ITLOS Statute') art 20(1); DSU, above n 31, art 1(1). NB, however, that under ITLOS Statute, art 20(2), the ITLOS is open to entities other than states parties in any case expressly provided for in Part XI of UNCLOS, or in any case submitted pursuant to any other agreement conferring jurisdiction on the ITLOS which is accepted by all parties to that case.

[34] See, e.g., *LaGrand* (2001) 40 ILM 1069, para 102; *Mamatkulov and Abdurasulovic v Turkey* (Judgment of 6 February 2003), paras 101, 105.

[35] See, e.g., ICSID Arbitration Rules Rule 37(2), as amended on 10 April 2006, and discussion in *Biwater Gauff (Tanzania) Ltd v Tanzania* (ICSID Case No ARB/05/22, Procedural Order No 3 of 29 September 2006), para 122; see also *Aguas Provinciales de Santa Fe SA, Suez, Sociedad General de Aguas de Barcelona SA, and InterAguas Servicios Integrales del Agua SA v Argentina* (ICSID Case No ARB/03/17, Decision on *Amicus Curiae* of 17 March 2006), paras 9–16; *Aguas Argentinas SA, Suez, Sociedad General de Aguas de Barcelona SA, and Vivendi Universal SA v Argentina* (ICSID Case No ARB/03/19, Decision on *Amicus Curiae* of 19 May 2005), paras 8–16, all available at <http://ita.law.uvic.ca> (last visited 25 November 2006); *US—Shrimp*, DSR 1998–VII, 2755, paras 99–110 (ABR) (concerning the power of WTO panels to receive *amicus curiae* briefs); *US—Hot Rolled Steel*, WT/DS138/AB/R, para 36–42 (ABR) (concerning the power of the WTO Appellate Body to receive *amicus curiae* briefs).

not irresistible. There are limitations on the development of a common law of international adjudication, some of which are related to the reasons for its emergence. These are examined in the next section.

A final consideration is that it is apparent from the analysis presented in the foregoing chapters that some of the issues identified for examination are more likely to give rise to common approaches than others. For instance, a wide range of international courts has adopted common approaches to the granting of provisional measures, even on the basis of differently worded provisions in their constitutive instruments,[36] while with respect to the awarding of remedies, various approaches can be found,[37] to the extent that inconsistencies even exist within the jurisprudence of the same court, as is the case with the awarding of compensation by the different Chambers of the Iran-US Claims Tribunal.[38] These differences may be explained by the fact that remedies are awarded within a specific international regime, and the remedies awarded essentially represent the end product of the judicial or arbitral process. Given the varying particular functions of different international courts, it might not be unexpected to find some divergence in the available remedies. For instance, human rights courts are designed to grant remedies to individuals who have suffered human rights violations. What might be considered an appropriate remedy in such a claim arguably differs significantly from what would be an appropriate remedy in a claim brought by a multinational corporation under a bilateral investment treaty, or in a claim brought by a state under a covered agreement of the WTO. In the case of provisional measures, the adoption of common criteria may be due at least in part to the fact that provisional measures are not determinative of the claim on the merits, but are, rather, a procedural device designed to preserve the rights of the parties pending the resolution of the dispute; they are, therefore, less controversial.

II. Limitations to the Development of a Common Law of International Adjudication

In making the suggestion that there is an emerging common law of international adjudication, it is important to be mindful of the fact that this book has only considered in detail five specific issues that arise in international adjudication. It cannot be assumed that other aspects which have not been the subject of examination in this book equally receive consistent treatment. Nor, however, can it be assumed that the treatment of those issues by international courts and tribunals differs significantly. Yet it is important to identify the limitations which might curtail the further development of common practices in international adjudication.

[36] See above chapter 4. [37] See above chapter 6, part III(B)(3).
[38] See above chapter 6, part III(B)(2).

The most prominent limitation on the ability of international courts to reach out and engage in a cross-fertilization of rules relating to procedure and remedies lies in the particular drafting of the constitutive instruments and rules of procedure of international courts. Here, the level of detail provided for in an international court's statute and rules of procedure will serve as a limiting factor. One example of this which has been referred to in chapter 6 can be seen in the practice of the WTO concerning the availability of remedies. While most other international courts have adopted the general rule expressed by the PCIJ in *Factory at Chorzów*, that the appropriate remedy at international law is full reparation,[39] WTO panels and the WTO Appellate Body are limited by the clear terms of the DSU.[40] Although one WTO panel has allowed its remedies to be informed by the general international law of reparation,[41] arguably this is limited to certain disputes under the SCM Agreement and, possibly, the Anti-dumping Agreement; in the majority of WTO disputes, reparation will be unavailable.[42]

A second limiting factor on the development of a common law of international adjudication is the fact that international courts may have their own specific agendas and functions.[43] These specific functions can serve to limit—or enhance—an international tribunal's scope to exercise certain procedural powers. For example, if an international court has a constitutional function within a specific regime, which might be evidenced by a power to render advisory opinions in addition to its contentious jurisdiction, this might suggest that it will be prepared to take account of wider community interests, and accept *amicus curiae* briefs.[44] Ad hoc arbitral tribunals constituted for individual disputes, on the other hand, might be less likely to assert procedural powers in furtherance of any public function other than the settlement of the dispute. There is, however, a trend towards facilitating the greater participation of non-parties in international arbitration proceedings, as was recognized by the ICSID Tribunal in *Biwater Gauff (Tanzania) Ltd v Tanzania*,[45] and as is evidenced in the inclusion, as of 10 April 2006, of the new article 37(2) of the ICSID Arbitration Rules, which permits the submission of

[39] Ser A, (No 17), 47 (PCIJ, 1928); see, e.g., *ADC Affiliate Ltd and ADC & ADMC Management Ltd v Hungary* (ICSID Case No ARB/03/16, Award of 27 September 2006), paras 479–99; *Legal Consequences of the Construction of a Wall in the Palestinian Occupied Territory* (ICJ Advisory Opinion of 9 July 2004), paras 152–3; *M/V 'Saiga' (No 2)*, 120 ILR 143, 199 (ITLOS, 1999); *Velásquez Rodríguez*, 95 ILR 306, 314 (IACHR, 1989); *Papamichalopoulos v Greece*, Ser A, (No 330–B), 59–60 (ECHR, 1995); *Amoco International Finance Corp v Iran*, 15 Ir–USCTR 189 (1987); see further above chapter 6, part III.

[40] DSU, above n 31, arts 3(7), art 22; see above chapter 6, part IV.

[41] *Australia—Leather*, DSR 1999–III, 951 (PR). See discussion above in chapter 6, part IV(B).

[42] See, e.g., Marco Bronckers and Naboth van den Broek, 'Financial Compensation in the WTO: Improving the Remedies of WTO Dispute Settlement' (2005) 8 *Journal of International Economic Law* 101, 102–6.

[43] See above chapter 2, part V; see also Jonathan Charney, 'Is International Law Threatened by Multiple International Tribunals?' (1998) 271 *Recueil des Cours* 101, 371.

[44] See discussion above in chapter 2, part V.

[45] See, e.g., *Biwater Gauff (Tanzania) Ltd v Tanzania*, above n 35, para 122.

'non-disputing party' briefs,[46] and the practice of several ICSID and NAFTA tribunals.[47] In its Procedural Order No 3, the ICSID Tribunal in *Biwater Gauff (Tanzania) Ltd* noted the amendments to the ICSID Arbitration Rules, and it observed the 'overall trend in this field towards transparency'.[48] The Tribunal considered the rules on confidentiality and transparency which pertained to arbitrations conducted under the ICSID Additional Facility Rules, NAFTA chapter 11, and the UNCITRAL Rules.[49]

A third issue which might have a limiting influence on the development of a common law of international adjudication is the relationship between each particular international court and the parties litigating before it. It should be clarified that this is a factor which works both ways; if a practice or procedure is applied before an international court where there is considerable deference displayed by the court towards the parties, a similar procedure is likely to be applied before international tribunals where a similar relationship exists. However, if the relationship between the court and the parties is different, this would tend to make it less likely that the court would be minded to adopt the same approach.

Finally, one consideration which might be taken into account is whether it is indeed desirable from a normative viewpoint that the procedures and remedies applicable before different international courts should be the same. Here the practices of domestic courts are instructive. Different courts at the national level have differing procedures, such as degrees of formality that vary between, say, family law proceedings involving children, on one hand, and civil litigation before the High Court, on the other; these differences are seen as desirable. An illustration can be found in Lord Woolf's report on the UK civil litigation system, *Access to Justice*, which was published in July 1996.[50] In chapter 19, titled 'Specialist Jurisdictions', Lord Woolf stated that 'in chapter 26 of my interim report I stressed that the same general principles, rules and procedures need to apply as far as possible throughout the system'.[51] Nevertheless, he recognized the value of different procedures for certain matters. In his recommendations, he observed that 'a number of the special rules for intellectual property, Chancery and Admiralty proceedings should be retained'.[52] In addition to the perceived value of these differences which can be found in domestic court systems, alternative methods of

[46] ICSID Arbitration Rules Rule 37(2), as amended on 10 April 2006.

[47] See, e.g., *Aguas Provinciales de Santa Fe, etc*, above n 35, paras 9–16; *Aguas Argentinas SA, etc*, above n 35, paras 8–16, all available at <http://ita.law.uvic.ca> (last visited 25 November 2006); *United Parcel Services of America, Inc v Canada* (Decision on *Amici Curiae* of 17 October 2001), paras 59–73 (NAFTA Tribunal); *Methanex Corporation v United States* (Decision on *Amici Curiae* of 15 January 2001), paras 47–52, available at <http://www.naftalaw.org> (last visited 25 November 2006); for a discussion of the two NAFTA cases, see Loukas Mistelis, 'Confidentiality and Third Party Participation' (2005) 21 *Arbitration International* 211.

[48] Above n 35, para 122.

[49] Ibid, paras 123–32.

[50] Lord Woolf, *Access to Justice: Final Report* (1996), available at <http://www.dca.gov.uk/civil/final/index.htm> (last visited 25 November 2006).

[51] Ibid, ch 19, para 1.

[52] Ibid, ch 19, 'Recommendations', para 7.

dispute resolution, such as mediation, arbitration, adjudication, and expert determination, are increasingly popular for certain types of dispute at the domestic level;[53] these have been developed precisely because it was desirable to have different procedures.

As at the domestic level, there are arguably desirable limits to the increasing convergence in procedures and remedies before international tribunals. The differing functions of various international courts, together with the fact that some international courts are designed to confer standing on individuals (such as human rights courts and investment treaty tribunals), and others are solely designed for the participation of states (such as the ICJ, the ITLOS, and the WTO dispute settlement system), have given rise to differing approaches to certain issues. While it is arguably beneficial that there is broad agreement on, for instance, the power of international courts to order an expert report, the binding nature of provisional measures, and the availability of compensation for harm to personal property, it is less clear that international tribunals should apply the same standard of proof to, for instance, an allegation of state complicity in torture,[54] as to a claim made in a boundary dispute, where there is a lack of evidence, that the *uti possidetis* line was in a certain location.[55] In addition, it might be contended that it is desirable that the availability of the power of revision before ad hoc arbitral tribunals is different from the availability of the power before permanent international courts;[56] the practical problems that can result from having to reconstitute an ad hoc tribunal might serve to negate any benefits that once arose from the referral of the dispute to arbitration. Accordingly, while it is not a limitation it itself, the desirability of a common law of international adjudication is a question which nonetheless places some limitations on its further development.

Conclusion

This chapter has discussed the various reasons for the emerging common law of international adjudication, and the possible limitations on its further development. It remains to consider the practical and theoretical implications of this phenomenon, which is done in chapter 8.

[53] See, e.g., Alan Redfern and Martin Hunter, with Nigel Blackaby and Constantine Partasides, *Law and Practice of International Commercial Arbitration* (4th ed, 2004) 35–46.

[54] For example, *Velásquez Rodríguez (Merits)*, 95 ILR 259, 285 (IACHR, 1988).

[55] For example, *Land, Island and Maritime Frontier Dispute* [1992] ICJ Rep 351, 506.

[56] See the inconsistencies in international jurisprudence discussed above in chapter 5, part III(B)(2).

8

Implications of a Common Law of International Adjudication

Introduction

The emergence of a common law of international adjudication has significant practical and theoretical implications. Its practical effects include the establishment of a sound basis for parties to disputes before international courts to submit that the applicable procedure and remedies are not limited to those provided for in the court's constitutive instruments and rules of procedure. Rather, international courts have the competence to develop their procedures consistently with those applicable before other international judicial institutions, and this can be achieved by approaches to interpretation of the court's statute and rules, by the application of general principles of law, and also by the exercise of inherent powers, which operate as an important source of procedural and remedial competence. These practical effects are accompanied by theoretical implications, which are no less important. It was observed in chapter 1 that international courts do not form part of a formal hierarchy or 'system'. Writers have proposed various definitions of what constitutes a 'legal system', and have reached differing conclusions about whether the international legal order can be so regarded. The argument developed in this book suggests, however, that, regardless of whether international law satisfies the various criteria which have been proposed, a practice is emerging among international courts whereby the decisions of other international tribunals are often respected in the interests of comity and the good administration of international justice.

I. Practical Implications

A. Generally

The emerging common law of international adjudication in the areas identified in this book has significant practical implications for the resolution of disputes before international courts. In particular, this means that where the constitutive instruments and rules of procedure of international courts are silent on an issue of procedure or remedial competence, international courts which exercise similar functions might be able to refer to the practice of other international courts as a basis for the application of that procedure, subject to certain limitations. So, if a party applies for the exercise of a power which is not expressly conferred by the relevant international court's constitutive instrument, that party can argue that just because this procedure or power is not expressly provided for, does not mean that it is excluded. Rather, the party can argue that the international court might be able to apply the procedure, or exercise the power, either because the procedure is applicable as a general principle of judicial procedure, or because the power is an inherent power. Further, in determining whether the exercise of a particular power is necessary in order to carry out their functions, international courts might turn to the practice of other international tribunals for guidance. This practice represents an emerging body of jurisprudence to which international courts can refer, in much the same way that they refer to general principles of law and judicial decisions in order to avoid a *non liquet* and ensure that international law is not silent on issues of substantive law.[1]

Many examples of international courts referring to the practice of other international courts have been seen in earlier chapters. Instances include the report of the WTO Appellate Body in *US—Anti-Dumping Act of 1916*, where it examined the practice of the PCIJ, the ICJ, and the Iran—US Claims Tribunal, and found that it had the *compétence de la compétence*;[2] Procedural Order No 3 of the UNCLOS tribunal in *MOX Plant*, where it considered the practice of the ICJ and the ITLOS, and found that it too had the power to order provisional measures *ultra petita*;[3] the decision of the IACHR in *Genie Lacayo (Judicial Review)*, where it

[1] See especially Sir Hersch Lauterpacht, *Private Law Sources and Analogies of International Law* (1927); see also Prosper Weil, '"The Court Cannot Conclude Definitively..." *Non Liquet* Revisited' (1997) 36 *Columbia Journal of Transnational Law* 109, 109–14.

[2] WT/DS136/AB/R, para 54, fn 30 (ABR).

[3] (2003) 42 ILM 1187, 1195–7.

referred to the practice of the ICJ, the ECHR and 'the general principles of both domestic and international procedural law' in finding that it had the power to revise its judgments;[4] the judgment of the ECHR in *Mamatkulov*, where it considered the constitutive instruments and case law of the ICJ, the IACHR, and several UN human rights committees and held that it had the power to order binding provisional measures;[5] and the decision of the ICSID Tribunal in *Enron Corporation and Ponderosa Assets*, in which it referred to the jurisprudence of the ICJ, the Italian-Venezuelan CC, two ad hoc arbitral tribunals, and another ICSID tribunal, and found that it had the power to issue a judgment in mandatory terms.[6] In light of the reasons for the emergence of the common law of international adjudication suggested in the previous chapter, it is natural that international courts consider the practice of other international tribunals when facing issues of procedure and remedies which are not addressed in their statutes or rules of procedure, and this is particularly evident in these examples.[7]

The analysis of specific aspects of international adjudication in chapters 2–6 also suggests that in other areas which have not been covered in this book, international courts, when faced with questions of procedure and remedies not addressed in their constitutive instruments and rules of procedure, might equally adopt common approaches. In this respect, it is suggested that the analysis leading to the conclusion concerning the emergence of a common law of international adjudication also has some prescriptive value, and that there is a general trend towards a convergence in the practice of international courts and tribunals. This point may be illustrated with reference to three further questions, which have not been treated in detail. These questions might be thought to have increasing relevance in the new landscape of international dispute settlement, which is characterized by the existence of multiple international tribunals and the possibility of competing proceedings concerning the same parties, or subject matter, or both.

B. Practical Implications with respect to Problems posed by Proliferation

Mention was made in chapter 1 of several instances in which separate proceedings have been instituted before multiple international courts concerning the same

[4] *Genie Lacayo (Judicial Review)*, Ser C, (No 45), paras 6–10 (IAHCR, 1997).

[5] *Mamatkulov and Abdurasulovic v Turkey* (ECHR Judgment of 6 February 2003), paras 39–51, 101–3.

[6] *Enron Corporation and Ponderosa Assets v Argentina* (ICSID Case No ARB/01/3, Decision on Jurisdiction of 14 January 2004), paras 77–9.

[7] For instances where the ICJ has referred to the practice of other international courts, see Gilbert Guillaume, 'The Proliferation of International Judicial Bodies—The Outlook for the International Legal Order: Speech to the Sixth Committee of the General Assembly' (27 October 2000) 4–5, available at <http://www.icj-cij.org> (last visited 25 November 2006); Mohamed Shahabuddeen, *Precedent in the World Court* (1996) 23–9, 35–9; Sir Hersch Lauterpacht, *The Development of International Law by the International Court* (1958) 15–18.

subject matter. In the face of the increased number of jurisdictional overlaps, international courts may find that proceedings related to the dispute of which it is seised are also pending before another international court. The question of competing jurisdictions between international courts has been examined in detail by Professor Shany.[8] He concluded that the constitutive instruments of international courts do not, in general, make provision for competing proceedings, although a few exceptions can be found.[9] He also concluded that few jurisdiction-regulating rules can be found in customary international law or general principles of law which guide international courts confronted with instances of multiple proceedings.[10]

In the absence of relevant treaty provisions, rules of customary international law and general principles of law regulating jurisdictional competition, there are essentially two approaches that international courts might adopt. The first is for the international court to consider that it is a self-contained system, and to proceed on the basis that proceedings before another international court are irrelevant. Support for this approach might be gleaned from the language of some international tribunals, such as the ICTY Appeals Chamber in *Prosecutor v Tadic*, which held that '[i]n international law, every tribunal is a self-contained system (unless otherwise provided)';[11] the ECHR, in *Loizidou v Turkey*, where it held that '[t]he International Court is a free-standing international tribunal which has no links to a standard-setting treaty such as the Convention';[12] and the IACHR, which stated in *Right to Information on Consular Assistance* that 'this Court is an "autonomous judicial institution" '.[13] The second, and, it is submitted, the preferable approach, is for the international court to recognize that related proceedings before other international tribunals may impact on the proceedings before it. In recognizing this, the international tribunal might choose to exercise certain procedural powers to ensure the proper administration of international justice. Examples of these include: (1) the power to dismiss proceedings summarily; (2) the

[8] Yuval Shany, *The Competing Jurisdictions of International Courts and Tribunals* (2003).

[9] Ibid, 180–95; see, e.g., *Treaty Establishing the European Community*, (2002) OJ C325 (entered into force), art 292; *Understanding on Rules and Procedures Governing the Settlement of Disputes*, opened for signature 15 April 1994, 33 ILM 1226 (entered into force 1 January 1995) ('DSU'), art 23(2); *European Social Charter*, opened for signature 18 October 1961, 529 UNTS 89 (entered into force 26 February 1965), Pt III; *Convention for the Protection of Human Rights and Fundamental Freedoms*, opened for signature 4 November 1950, 213 UNTS 221 (entered into force 3 September 1953) ('European HR Convention'), art 55; *Convention for the Settlement of Investment Disputes between States and Nationals of Other States*, opened for signature 18 March 1965, 575 UNTS 159 (entered into force 14 October 1966) ('ICSID Convention'), art 26.

[10] Shany, above n 8, 229–45.

[11] *Prosecutor v Tadic* (Jurisdiction) (1996) 35 ILM 32, 39.

[12] *Loizidou v Turkey* (1995) 20 EHRR 99, 133.

[13] *Right to Information on Consular Assistance* (2000) 21 *Human Rights Law Journal* 24, 40, para 44, citing *'Other Treaties' Subject to the Advisory Jurisdiction of the Court (Art. 64 American Convention on Human Rights)*, (Advisory Opinion OC–1/82 of 24 September 1982), Ser A, (No 1), para 22, available at <http://www.corteidh.or.cr> (last visited 30 November 2006). For other instances where the IACHR has declared itself to be an 'autonomous institution', see *Right to Information on Consular Assistance* (2000) 21 *Human Rights Law Journal* 24, 40, para 44, fn 23.

power to suspend proceedings; and (3) the power to enjoin parties from pursuing other proceedings.

1. Power of Summary Dismissal

Possibly inspired by the competence of certain domestic courts to strike out proceedings,[14] in the past some international courts have recognized that they might possess the power to dismiss proceedings before reaching the phase of litigation where they ordinarily decide on their jurisdiction. Domestic courts in some common law systems have the power to strike out proceedings if they are an 'abuse of process'.[15] This concept is related to the doctrine of 'abuse of rights', a term more familiar in civilian legal systems.[16] The doctrine of abuse of process may operate, according to Dr Barnett, to preclude proceedings '*if it is necessary for a court to prevent a misuse of its procedure*', or 'to avoid the risk that the administration of justice might be brought into disrepute among right-thinking people'.[17] Significantly, as he explains, 'the doctrine is not limited to fixed categories: what constitutes an abuse of process will depend on all the circumstances of the case'.[18]

The suggestion that international courts have the power to dismiss international proceedings summarily was first made by Sir Gerald Fitzmaurice in his separate opinion in *Northern Cameroons*.[19] Referring to the screening procedure under the European HR Convention, under which claims could be declared 'inadmissible' and dismissed at an early stage of proceedings, Sir Gerald observed that:

> In the general international legal field there is nothing corresponding to the procedures found under most national systems of law, for eliminating at a relatively early stage, before

[14] See, e.g., Lawrence Collins (ed), *Dicey & Morris: The Conflict of Laws* (13th ed, 2000) vol I, 388, fn 18; *Civil Procedure Rules 1998* (UK), Rule 3.4(2)(b); *Nouveau Code de Procédure Civil*, (96e édition, 2004) art 32(1), 53–5. Common law courts have also exercised this power as an inherent power: e.g. *Connelly v DPP* [1964] AC 1254, 1301–2; *Neill v County Court of Victoria* (Unreported, Supreme Court of Victoria, Redlich J, 8 September 2003).

[15] See especially *Hunter v Chief Constable of the West Midlands* [1982] AC 529, 536; *Johnson v Gore Wood & Co* [2001] 2 WLR 72, 81–93, 117–20; Peter Barnett, Res Judicata, *Estoppel, and Foreign Judgments* (2001), 183–244.

[16] Michael Byers, 'Abuse of Rights: An Old Principle, A New Age' (2002) 47 *McGill Law Journal* 389, 391–5; on the application of the doctrine of abuse of rights to multiple proceedings, see further Shany, above n 8, 255–60.

[17] Barnett, above n 15, 185 (emphasis in original).

[18] Ibid (footnotes omitted); see also International Law Association ('ILA'), 'Interim Report: "Res Judicata" and Arbitration' (in ILA, *Report of the Seventy-First Conference, Berlin*, 2004) 9, referring to *Hunter v Chief Constable of the West Midlands*, above n 15, 536; *House of Spring Gardens Ltd v Waite* [1990] 3 WLR 347, 358; *Talbot v Berkshire County Council* [1993] 3 WLR 708, 712–15; *Walton v Gardiner* (1993) 177 CLR 378, 395; *Toronto (City) v Canadian Union of Public Employees* [2003] SCC No 63, paras 35–66; *Henderson v Henderson* (1844) 6 QB 288. For an argument that the rule in *Henderson v Henderson* should be abandoned, see Gary Watt, 'The Danger and Deceit of the Rule in *Henderson v Henderson*: A New Approach to Successive Civil Actions Arising from the Same Factual Matter' (2000) 19 *Civil Justice Quarterly* 287. The doctrine of abuse of process also exists as a tort in common law systems: see further Anthony Dugdale, *Clerk & Lindsell on Torts* (18th ed, 2000) 846–50; John Fleming, *The Law of Torts* (9th ed, 1998) 687–8.

[19] [1963] ICJ Rep 15, 97, 106 (Sep Op Fitzmaurice).

they reach the court which would otherwise hear and decide them, claims that are considered to be objectionable or not entertainable on some *a priori* ground. The absence of any corresponding 'filter' procedures in the [ICJ]'s jurisdictional field makes it necessary to regard a right to take similar action, on similar grounds, as being part of the inherent powers or jurisdiction of the court as an international tribunal.[20]

Most international courts, including the ICJ, do not have an express power to strike cases from their list. The ITLOS and other tribunals exercising jurisdiction under UNCLOS are exceptions;[21] in addition, the ECHR has retained the power to dismiss proceedings summarily,[22] and some other human rights bodies also have this power.[23] Yet there is some international judicial practice supporting the existence of the power, even in the absence of an express provision. No clear test has emerged from this practice, although it appears that relevant factors are that the international court 'manifestly lacks jurisdiction' to adjudicate on the merits, or that the claim should be considered an 'abuse of process'. It appears that it is not necessary that both these elements be present: proceedings may be dismissed on the basis of either one of them.

a) Manifest Lack of Jurisdiction to Adjudicate on the Merits

The ICJ has exercised a power to dismiss proceedings before reaching the jurisdiction phase of the dispute on several occasions. Its first experience was in cases where actions were brought by states which conceded that there was no basis of jurisdiction for their claim, but nonetheless invited the respondent government to agree to submit the dispute to the ICJ on a *forum prorogatum* basis.[24] After the respondent government declined to accept the ICJ's jurisdiction, the ICJ removed the cases from its list.[25]

The ICJ has also received requests from respondent states to remove cases from the list at the provisional measures phase on the grounds that it was 'manifestly not

20 Ibid, 106–7 (references omitted).

21 *United Nations Convention on the Law of the Sea*, opened for signature 10 December 1982, 21 ILM 1261 (entered into force 16 November 1994), art 294; see also art 300, which stipulates that parties shall meet in good faith the obligations assumed under the Convention and shall exercise the rights, jurisdiction and freedoms recognized in UNCLOS in a manner which would not constitute an abuse of rights.

22 European HR Convention, above n 9, art 35(3); Shany, above n 8, 256.

23 These include the UN HRC: *Optional Protocol to the International Covenant on Civil and Political Rights*, opened for signature 19 December 1966, 999 UNTS 302, art 3 (entered into force 23 March 1976); and the Committee against Torture: *Convention against Torture and Other Cruel, Inhuman or Degrading Treatment or Punishment*, opened for signature 10 December 1984, 1465 UNTS 85, art 22(2) (entered into force 26 June 1987); see also Shany, above n 8, 256.

24 For example, *Treatment in Hungary of the Aircraft and Crew of USA* [1954] ICJ Rep 103; *Aerial Incident of 7 October 1952* [1956] ICJ Rep 9; *Aerial Incident of 4 September 1954* [1958] ICJ Rep 158; *Aerial Incident of 7 November 1954* [1959] ICJ Rep 276.

25 The need for the ICJ to remove such cases from its list has been circumvented by ICJ Rules of Court, art 38(5), pursuant to which an application is not entered in the list until the respondent state has agreed to the ICJ's jurisdiction: e.g., *Certain Criminal Proceedings in France* (ICJ Order of 17 June 2003); Chester Brown, 'The Inherent Powers of International Courts and Tribunals' (2005) 76 *British Yearbook of International Law* 195, 195–6, fn 4; Sienho Yee, '*Forum Prorogatum* Returns to the International Court of Justice' (2003) 16 *Leiden Journal of International Law* 701, 701–2.

competent in the case'. It did not accede to several such requests,[26] but such a request was granted in two of the *Legality of Use of Force* cases brought by Yugoslavia against ten NATO member states in 1999. In its applications, Yugoslavia relied on article IX of the Genocide Convention to found the ICJ's jurisdiction. Both Spain and the US had made reservations to this provision.[27] Spain had also made an optional clause declaration in which it accepted the ICJ's jurisdiction, but excluded disputes referred to the ICJ by any state which had only accepted the ICJ's jurisdiction in the 12 months preceding the submission of that dispute; thus, Yugoslavia was precluded from relying on it to found the ICJ's jurisdiction.[28] In its pleadings in the provisional measures phase, Spain expressly requested that the case be removed from the list.[29] In ordering that the cases against Spain and the US be removed from the list, the ICJ explained that:

> the Court manifestly lacks jurisdiction to entertain Yugoslavia's Application ... it cannot therefore indicate any provisional measure whatsoever in order to protect the rights invoked therein; and ... within a system of consensual jurisdiction, to maintain on the General List a case upon which it appears certain that the Court will not be able to adjudicate on the merits would most assuredly not contribute to the sound administration of justice.[30]

What constitutes a 'manifest lack of jurisdiction' was not clarified by the ICJ. This question was considered by several judges in their separate opinions, however. Judge Higgins stated that 'if in considering whether there is jurisdiction *prima facie* for purposes of Article 41 of the Statute, it is clear beyond doubt that no jurisdiction exists in a particular case, good administration of justice requires that the case be immediately struck off the List *in limine*'.[31] Judge Oda took a particularly strict approach; he suggested that in any case where there was not a prima facie basis of jurisdiction, this 'should be interpreted as a ruling that it has no jurisdiction whatsoever to entertain the Applications, without leaving any room to retain these cases and to deal with the issue of jurisdiction in the future'.[32] Judge ad hoc Gaja's approach, outlined in his declaration in *Yugoslavia v Italy*, was slightly more cautious; he suggested that cases should be struck off the list only if no connection between the dispute and the treaty relied on to found jurisdiction could be established 'at subsequent stages of the proceedings'.[33]

[26] For example, *Nuclear Tests* [1973] ICJ Rep 99, 100; *Nuclear Tests* [1974] ICJ Rep 253, 257; *Aegean Sea* [1976] ICJ Rep 3, 5, see also 31, 32 (Sep Op Tarazi); *Nicaragua* [1984] ICJ Rep 169, 178, see also 190, 204 (Diss Op Schwebel).

[27] (*Yugoslavia v Spain*) [1999] ICJ Rep 761, 772; (Yugoslavia v Spain) [1999] ICJ Rep 916, 923.

[28] (*Yugoslavia v Spain*) ibid, 769–70. Yugoslavia had deposited its declaration accepting the ICJ's jurisdiction only three days prior to commencing the proceedings.

[29] *Legality of Use of Force*, CR 1999/22, para 4 (Aurelio Perez Giralda); CR 1999/33, 2 (Aurelio Perez Giralda); (*Yugoslavia v Spain*) ibid, 767–8.

[30] (*Yugoslavia v Spain*) ibid, 773–4; (*Yugoslavia v US*) above n 27, 925–6.

[31] Ibid, 798, 806 (Sep Op Higgins).

[32] Ibid, 781, 796 (Sep Op Oda); ibid, 933, 948 (Sep Op Oda).

[33] (*Yugoslavia v Italy*) [1999], ICJ Rep 481, 502, 502 (Decl Gaja).

The question also arose in *Armed Activities (New Application: 2002)*,[34] in which Rwanda requested that the Application of the Democratic Republic of the Congo ('DRC') be dismissed at the provisional measures stage. The Rwandan request was based on an argument that the Application should be considered an 'abuse of process',[35] but the alleged abuse of process related partly to the meagre jurisdictional grounds on which the claim was based. The ICJ rejected the Rwandan request,[36] although it found support in the separate opinion of Judge ad hoc Dugard.[37] He suggested that proceedings should be struck off where there was 'no reasonable possibility, based on the facts and circumstances of the unsuccessful Application, that the Applicant will at some future date be able to establish the jurisdiction of the Court on the instruments invoked for jurisdiction in the Application for provisional measures'.[38]

Yet it is suggested that the test espoused by the ICJ in its Orders on Provisional Measures in the *Legality of Use of Force* cases was in fact broader in scope than those proposed in any of the separate opinions in that case or in Judge ad hoc Dugard's separate opinion in *Armed Activities (New Application: 2002)*. In *Legality of Use of Force*, the ICJ observed that the power to dismiss proceedings summarily arose not only from a manifest lack of jurisdiction, but also if 'it appear[ed] certain' that the ICJ would 'not be able to adjudicate on the merits';[39] this suggests that even if the ICJ finds at the provisional measures stage that there is a prima facie basis of jurisdiction, but also finds that the claim would be ruled inadmissible, then it could dismiss the proceedings. This was confirmed in the ICJ's order rejecting the DRC's request for provisional measures in *Arrest Warrant*, where the ICJ held that 'mootness of the Application is one of the grounds which may lead the Court to remove a case from its List without further consideration'.[40]

The ICJ had a further opportunity to reconsider this issue in the preliminary objections phase of the *Legality of Use of Force* cases.[41] There, the ICJ confirmed that it has the power to strike cases from its List, but it held that this power was restricted;[42] this issue will be examined below.

b) Abuse of Process

Reference has already been made to the function of the doctrine of abuse of process in the courts of some common law systems.[43] The relevance of this doctrine in

[34] (2002) 41 ILM 1175, 1189; for comment, see Chester Brown, '*Armed Activities on the Territory of the Congo (New Application: 2002) (Democratic Republic of the Congo v Rwanda)* Provisional Measures, Order of 10 July 2002' (2003) 52 *ICLQ* 782.

[35] *Armed Activities (New Application: 2002)*, CR 2002/37, 24, 28 (Christopher Greenwood).

[36] Above n 34, 1196.

[37] Ibid, 1204, 1207 (Sep Op Dugard).

[38] Ibid, 1205 (Sep Op Dugard).

[39] (*Yugoslavia v Spain*), above n 27, 773–4; (*Yugoslavia v US*), above n 27, 925–6.

[40] *Arrest Warrant of 11 April 2000* (ICJ Order of 8 December 2000), para 55.

[41] (2005) 44 ILM 299; for comment, see Chester Brown, 'Access to International Justice in the *Legality of Use of Force* Cases' (2005) 64 *CLJ* 267.

[42] Ibid, 312.

[43] See above nn 14–18 and accompanying text.

international adjudication has been noted by several writers,[44] and there is also some international judicial practice on the question. The argument that a claim should be dismissed as an 'abuse of process' was made in *Certain Phosphate Lands in Nauru*,[45] in which Australia submitted that 'Nauru has failed to act consistently and in good faith' concerning the rehabilitation of the land which had been subjected to phosphate mining, and requested that the ICJ, 'in the exercise of its discretion, and in order to uphold judicial propriety', decline to hear the claims.[46] This objection was rejected by the ICJ, holding that 'the Application by Nauru has been properly submitted in the framework of the remedies open to it', and noted that 'such conduct does not amount to an abuse of process'.[47] A request that proceedings be dismissed as an abuse of process was also made in *Armed Activities (New Application: 2002)*, as has been noted above.[48] This allegation stemmed from two factors. First, it was submitted that the DRC had commenced similar proceedings against Rwanda in 1999, which were discontinued, and the DRC was initiating new proceedings, again with no real prospect of founding the ICJ's jurisdiction.[49] Second, in the 1999 proceedings (which were commenced by the DRC against Burundi and Uganda, as well as Rwanda), the DRC had alleged that all three states were responsible for the same violations of international law, such as the shooting-down of a Boeing 727 owned by Congo Airlines.[50] Rwanda noted that the DRC had given no 'indication whatever of the basis on which three different states were accused of one and the same action'.[51] In its 2002 Application the DRC renewed the allegation that Rwanda had shot down the aircraft which had been a subject—and remained a subject, in the case of the proceedings against Uganda—of the 1999 Application. Rwanda submitted that this was 'the clearest case of an abuse of process';[52] and that the case should be removed from the ICJ's list.[53] As observed above, the ICJ rejected the Rwandan request, but did not discuss the allegations of abuse of process, holding simply that 'in the absence of a manifest lack of jurisdiction, the Court cannot grant Rwanda's request that the case be removed from the List'.[54]

[44] Robert Kolb, 'General Principles of Procedural Law' in Andreas Zimmermann, Christian Tomuschat and Karin Oellers-Frahm (eds), *The Statute of the International Court of Justice: A Commentary* (2006) 793, 831–3; ILA, above n 18, 24; Shany, above n 8, 255–60; Robert Kolb, *La bonne foi en droit international public* (2000) 637–49; Vaughan Lowe, 'Overlapping Jurisdiction in International Tribunals' (1999) 20 *Australian Yearbook of International Law* 191, 202–3.

[45] [1992] ICJ Rep 240.

[46] Ibid, 255; see also *Certain Phosphate Lands in Nauru*, ICJ Pleadings, vol II, 164–6.

[47] Above n 45, 255.

[48] See above n 35 and accompanying text; above n 34, 1189.

[49] *Armed Activities (New Application: 2002)*, CR 2002/37, 10 (Gérard Gahima).

[50] *Armed Activities (DRC v Burundi)*, Application Instituting Proceedings (23 June 1999) 17–19; *Armed Activities (DRC v Uganda)*, Application Instituting Proceedings (23 June 1999) 16–19; *Armed Activities (DRC v Rwanda)*, Application Instituting Proceedings (23 June 1999) 18–19.

[51] *Armed Activities (New Application: 2002)*, CR 2002/37, 24 (Christopher Greenwood).

[52] Ibid.

[53] Ibid, 28.

[54] Above n 34, 1195. In its judgment of 3 February 2006, the ICJ held that it did not have jurisdiction to determine the merits of the dispute: *Armed Activities (New Application: 2002)*, (ICJ Judgment of 3 February 2006), paras 126–8.

The issue also arose in a claim brought under a bilateral investment treaty, *Bayindir Insaat Turizm Ticaret Ve Sanayi AS v Pakistan*. In that case, the respondent state argued that the claim should be dismissed on the grounds that it was an abuse of process.[55] Pakistan's argument was based on the claimant's abandonment of its original characterization of its complaints as contractual claims, and its 'dramatic' commencement of proceedings under the relevant investment treaty.[56] However, the ICSID Tribunal held that it had to 'distinguish between Bayindir's tactical choice to abandon the Contract Claims at the outset of the jurisdictional hearing and Bayindir's fundamental choice to pursue the Treaty Claims', and ruled that the claimant's pursuit of the treaty claims were not abusive.[57]

The question of dismissal for abuse of process has also arisen in arbitral disputes in which multiple claims were pursued. In *Waste Management v Mexico*, NAFTA proceedings were originally initiated by the US investor claimant in 1998, but these proceedings were dismissed due to a procedural defect in the claimant's Application.[58] It subsequently brought new proceedings in 2000. Apparently at the suggestion of the President of the NAFTA tribunal, Mexico argued that the new proceedings should be dismissed as an abuse of process.[59] The abuse of process apparently lay in the commencement of serial proceedings both under Chapter 11 of NAFTA, and also before domestic courts and tribunals in respect of the same claim. Mexico submitted that this power could be exercised 'not as a general legal principle, but as an inherent authority of the tribunal to safeguard the process'.[60] For its part, the claimant accepted that such an inherent power might exist in extreme cases, but denied that it was applicable in that case.[61] The Tribunal ultimately found that it was not necessary to decide whether NAFTA Chapter 11 tribunals possess any inherent power to dismiss a claim on grounds of abuse of process, or what circumstances might justify the exercise of any such power,[62] but it suggested that 'if such a power exists, it would only be for the purpose of protecting the integrity of the Tribunal's processes or dealing with genuinely vexatious claims'.[63]

The issue of abuse of process also arose in the context of two UNCITRAL arbitrations which saw the Czech Republic as the respondent in related proceedings.[64] These disputes emerged from the same set of facts concerning an agreement for television broadcasting services in the Czech Republic; one claim was brought by the Dutch-registered investor company, CME Czech Republic BV, under the

[55] *Bayindir Insaat Turizm Ticaret Ve Sanayi AS v Pakistan* (ICSID Case No ARB/03/29, Decision on Jurisdiction of 14 November 2005), paras 169–70, available at <http://ita.law.uvic.ca> (last visited 25 November 2006).

[56] Ibid, para 169.

[57] Ibid, paras 171–3.

[58] 5 ICSID Rep 443 (2000).

[59] Mexico's Post Hearing Brief on Jurisdiction (19 February 2002), paras 21–4, available at <http://www.naftalaw.org> (last visited 25 November 2006); (2002) 41 ILM 1315, 1324–5.

[60] Mexico's Post Hearing Brief, ibid, para 23; (2002) 41 ILM 1315, 1324, fn 53.

[61] (2002) 41 ILM 1315, 1324.

[62] Ibid.

[63] Ibid.

[64] *CME Czech Republic BV v Czech Republic* (Partial Award of 13 September 2001); *CME Czech Republic BV v Czech Republic* (Final Award of 14 March 2003); *Ronald Lauder v Czech Republic*, (Final Award of 3 September 2001), all available at <http://ita.law.uvic.ca> (last visited 25 November 2006).

Netherlands—Czech Republic bilateral investment treaty,[65] and the second claim was brought by a controlling shareholder of CME Czech Republic BV, Mr Ronald Lauder, a US national, under the US—Czech Republic bilateral investment treaty.[66] As Zachary Douglas explains:

> [I]n *CME Czech Republic BV (The Netherlands) v Czech Republic* ('CME') and *Ronald S Lauder v Czech Republic* ('Lauder'), two UNCITRAL tribunals established pursuant to different BITs considered the conduct of the same executive organ of the Czech Republic in relation to the same investment and came to quite different results on liability. The existence of these two proceedings was possible because the *CME* Tribunal recognised CME's 99 per-cent shareholding in a local Czech company with rights to operate a television licence as an investment for the purposes of the Netherlands/Czech Republic BIT, whereas the *Lauder* Tribunal deemed that Mr Lauder's (a US citizen) shareholding in the parent company of CME fell within the definition of an investment under the US/Czech Republic BIT.[67]

In the course of the arbitration brought by CME Czech Republic BV, the Czech Republic submitted that the claim could be dismissed as an abuse of process, on the grounds that CME Czech Republic BV and Mr Lauder were bringing virtually identical claims under two different treaties.[68] Without directly discussing the concept of abuse of process, the tribunal rejected this argument.[69] The Czech Republic subsequently challenged the award before the Swedish domestic courts on various grounds, including, *inter alia*, the argument that the arbitral proceedings were an abuse of process. Like the UNCITRAL Tribunal, the Svea Court of Appeals did not conclusively decide on the applicability of the doctrine, but it questioned its relevance, stating that:

> [T]he concept of abuse of process has no direct equivalent in Swedish law and it has also been questioned whether it can be applied in conjunction with international arbitration proceedings.[70]

[65] *Agreement on Encouragement and Reciprocal Protection of Investments between the Kingdom of the Netherlands and the Czech and Slovak Federal Republic*, signed 29 April 1991 (entered into force 1 October 1992), available at <http://www.unctadxi.org/templates/DocSearch_779.aspx> (last visited 25 November 2006).

[66] *Treaty with the Czech and Slovak Federal Republic concerning the Reciprocal Encouragement and Protection of Investment*, signed 22 October 1991, (entered into force 19 December 1992), available at <http://www.unctadxi.org/templates/DocSearch_779.aspx> (last visited 25 November 2006).

[67] Zachary Douglas, 'The Hybrid Foundations of Investment Treaty Arbitration' (2003) 74 *British Yearbook of International Law* 151, 174–5 (footnotes omitted); see also ibid, 202–4. See also the comments of the NAFTA Consolidation Tribunal in *Canfor Corporation v US, Tembec* et al *v US* and *Terminal Forest Products v US* (Order of the Consolidation Tribunal of 7 September 2005), para 132: 'experience shows that inconsistent results do occur as was unfortunately demonstrated by the conflicting outcomes in *Lauder/CME v The Czech Republic*. These cases are the more regrettable because, for all practical purposes, the parties and the claims were the same (even though the bilateral investment treaties in those cases were partly between different States Parties)' (footnote omitted), available at <http://ita.law.uvic.ca> (last visited 25 November 2006).

[68] *CME Czech Republic BV v Czech Republic* (Partial Award of 13 September 2001), paras 29, 302–10.

[69] Ibid, paras 412, 419; see also *CME Czech Republic BV v Czech Republic* (Final Award of 14 March 2003), para 431.

[70] *Czech Republic v CME Czech Republic BV* (2003) 42 ILM 919, 966.

It is suggested that the UNCITRAL Tribunal in *CME Czech Republic BV (The Netherlands) v Czech Republic* would have been well served by a more detailed examination of the concept of abuse of process. While it was correct to point out that the doctrine of *res judicata* was inapplicable in the proceedings as there was no identity of parties, it is suggested that the doctrine of abuse of process, as it is employed in the constitutive instruments of several international courts,[71] and as it has been discussed by the ICJ, ICSID and NAFTA tribunals, is relevant in international proceedings for the same justifications as it is in domestic legal systems. These are that the proper administration of international justice calls for courts to exercise powers to control the multiplicity of proceedings and the initiation of claims which, while they may not infringe any procedural rules, are nonetheless frivolous or vexatious, brought in breach of a forum selection agreement, or in all substantial respects identical to pending claims.[72]

The ICJ has apparently denied that it has the power summarily to dismiss claims which are an 'abuse of process'. In the *Legality of Use of Force* cases, referred to above, the ICJ ultimately held that its power in that regard was not a general power, but was restricted to two situations; namely, in cases where proceedings are instituted and no title of jurisdiction is relied on,[73] and in cases where it 'manifestly lacks jurisdiction'.[74] In her separate opinion, however, Judge Higgins begged to differ. Referring to the previous practice of the ICJ in removing cases from its List, she observed that:

> [T]hese were actions by the Court in the exercise of its inherent powers. The precedents on removal from the List cited by the Court—where from the outset no subsisting title of jurisdiction has been disclosed, or where the Court manifestly lacked jurisdiction—do not constitute two exclusive categories within which the Court has to fall if it wishes to exercise its inherent powers in the absence of discontinuance. There is nothing in the case law that so suggests. Indeed, it is hard to know what might be the legal source of a right to remove cases from the List provided only that this would be limited to those two examples.[75]

Judge Kooijmans expressed a similar view in his separate opinion:

> The fact that the Rules only speak of removing a case from the List by unilateral action of the applicant (Article 89) or joint action by the parties (Article 90) cannot deprive the Court of its inherent power, as master of its own procedure, to strike *proprio motu* a case from the List. . . . This power is not related to the intention of the parties but to the judicial task of the Court.[76]

[71] See above nn 21–23 and accompanying text.

[72] See also Shany, above n 8, 255–60.

[73] For examples of cases where this occurred, see, e.g., *Treatment in Hungary of the Aircraft and Crew of USA* [1954] ICJ Rep 99; ibid, above n 24; *Aerial Incident of 10 March 1953* [1956] ICJ Rep 6; *Aerial Incident of 7 October 1952* above n 24; *Antarctica* [1956] ICJ Rep 12; *Antarctica* [1956] ICJ Rep 15; *Aerial Incident of 4 September 1954*, above n 24; *Aerial Incident of 7 November 1954*, above n 24.

[74] *Legality of Use of Force*, above n 41, 312.

[75] Ibid, 341, 342 (Sep Op Higgins).

[76] Ibid, 345, 349 (Sep Op Kooijmans).

The approach of the Judges Higgins and Kooijmans is certainly preferable; it is suggested that international courts should be able summarily to dismiss claims on which it appears that they will not be able to adjudicate, either because of a manifest lack of jurisdiction, due to obvious bars to admissibility, or because the claim otherwise constitutes an abuse of process, and the exercise of that power should not be restricted to the categories listed by the ICJ.[77]

2. *Power to Suspend Proceedings*

A second power that international courts can exercise in cases of multiple proceedings is the power to order the suspension of the proceedings. This power is akin to that exercised by courts in many common law countries to stay proceedings on the ground that the forum is inappropriate (*forum non conveniens*).[78] In the present context, however, the power is not concerned with the permanent stay of proceedings, but the suspension of proceedings pending the decision of another international court. Some early arbitral practice can be found where an international tribunal acknowledged the existence of a power to suspend proceedings pending the resolution of issues before another tribunal.[79] This power was apparently exercised for the first time in the context of two related proceedings before international courts by the ICSID tribunal in *SPP v Egypt*.[80] In this dispute, SPP had previously commenced ICC arbitration, and the ICC award was the subject of proceedings in the French national courts. In the course of considering Egypt's three objections to its jurisdiction, the ICSID tribunal found that a preliminary question was whether the parties had agreed on another method of dispute resolution, in the form of ICC arbitration. The tribunal held that it was competent to answer this question, but observed that it was also currently under consideration in a different forum, being the Cour de cassation. The arbitral tribunal stated that the concurrent pursuit of a remedy 'entails certain practical problems of international judicial administration since it invites a clash between competing exercises of jurisdiction'.[81] Exercising its inherent power to suspend the proceedings, it explained that:

> When the jurisdictions of two unrelated and independent tribunals extend to the same dispute, there is no rule of international law which prevents either tribunal from exercising

[77] Brown, 'The Inherent Powers', above n 25, 243–4.

[78] For example, Andrew Bell, *Forum Shopping and Venue in Transnational Litigation* (2003) 149–69; *Spiliada Maritime Corporation v Cansulex Ltd* [1987] AC 460; for the application of the *forum non conveniens* doctrine in some other common law jurisdictions, see, e.g., Bell, ibid, 149, fn 108, citing, *inter alia*, *Mackay Refined Sugars NZ v NZ Sugar Co* [1997] 3 NZLR 476; *Amchem Products Inc v Workers' Compensation Board* [1993] 1 SCR 897; *The Adhiguna Meranti* [1988] 1 Lloyd's Rep 384; *Voth v Manildra Flour Mills Pty Ltd* (1990) 171 CLR 538. For the suggestion that a stay of proceedings might be available in some civil law jurisdictions, see Bell, ibid, 144, fn 72, 150, fn 112 and accompanying text.

[79] *Caire*, 5 RIAA 516, 525 (Franco-Mexican CC, 1929), where it was held that if a domestic court was seised of preliminary issues germane to the dispute before an international tribunal, the international court could stay its decision pending resolution of those issues.

[80] 3 ICSID Rep 112 (1985).

[81] Ibid, 129.

its jurisdiction. However, in the interests of judicial order, either of the tribunals may, in its discretion and as a matter of comity, decide to stay the exercise of its jurisdiction pending a decision by the other tribunal.[82]

A more recent example can be found in the Procedural Order No 3 of the UNCLOS tribunal in the *MOX Plant* dispute. In the course of the jurisdictional phase of the dispute, it became apparent that the resolution of issues arising under EC law would impact on the jurisdiction of the tribunal, in particular, the standing of the parties to bring and respond to UNCLOS proceedings, and the matters in dispute which are subject to the exclusive jurisdiction of the ECJ.[83] Given the real possibility that the European Commission would commence proceedings before the ECJ regarding questions which were pertinent to a decision of the UNCLOS Tribunal's jurisdiction—a possibility which was realised in late 2004—the UNCLOS Tribunal held that:

In the circumstances, and bearing in mind considerations of mutual respect and comity which should prevail between judicial institutions both of which may be called upon to determine rights and obligations as between two States, the Tribunal considers that it would be inappropriate for it to proceed further with hearing the Parties on the merits of the dispute in the absence of a resolution of the problems referred to. Moreover, a procedure that might result in two conflicting decisions on the same issue would not be helpful to the resolution of the dispute between the Parties.[84]

Accordingly, the Tribunal decided to suspend further proceedings on jurisdiction and the merits,[85] and those proceedings remain suspended.[86]

Yet another example is provided by the decision of the ICSID Tribunal in *SGS v Philippines*. In this dispute, the claimant argued that although there was a provision in the concession contract conferring exclusive jurisdiction on the domestic courts of the Philippines over disputes arising under the contract, the ICSID Tribunal was competent to adjudicate those claims due to the presence of an 'umbrella clause' in the Switzerland–Philippines bilateral investment treaty, which imposed an obligation on the Philippines to 'observe any obligation it has assumed with regard to specific investments in its territory by investors of the other Contracting Party'.[87] The Tribunal agreed that the umbrella clause made it a breach of the BIT 'for the host state to fail to observe binding commitments,

[82] Ibid, 129–30; Shany, above n 8, 263–4. [83] Above n 3, 1190. [84] Ibid, 1191.

[85] Ibid; Robin Churchill and Joanne Scott, 'The *MOX Plant* Litigation: The First Half-Life' (2004) 53 *ICLQ* 643, 649–50.

[86] *MOX Plant (UK v Ireland)* (Procedural Order No 4 of 14 November 2003 and Procedural Order No. 5 of 22 January 2007), both available at <http://www.pca-cpa.org> (last visited 30 May 2007).

[87] *Accord entre la Confédération suisse et la République des Philippines concernant la promotion et la protection réciproque des investissements*, signed 31 March 1997, art X(2) (entered into force 23 April 1999), available at <www.unctadxi.org/templates/DocSearch_779.aspx> (last visited 25 November 2006). On the history of 'umbrella clauses', see especially Anthony Sinclair, 'The Origins of the Umbrella Clause in the International Law of Investment Protection' (2004) 20 *Arbitration International* 411.

including contractual commitments, which it had assumed'.[88] But the Tribunal also held that a contractual claim brought under the bilateral investment treaty would be inadmissible, for the parties had agreed to include in the concession contract an exclusive jurisdiction clause which was not overridden by any provision of the treaty.[89] The effect of this finding was that 'SGS is bound by the terms of the exclusive jurisdiction clause, Article 12 of the CISS Agreement, in order to establish the quantum or content of the obligation which, under Article X(2) of the BIT, the Philippines is required to observe'.[90] In light of this finding, the ICSID Tribunal held, referring to the decision of the UNCLOS tribunal in *MOX Plant*, and the decision of another ICSID tribunal in *SGS v Pakistan*,[91] that it had the power to suspend its proceedings 'pending determination of the amount payable, either by agreement between the parties or by the Philippine courts in accordance with Article 12 of the CISS Agreement'.[92]

After a review of this case law, and as a matter of principle, it can be suggested that international courts, as masters of their procedure, have the power to suspend proceedings before them pending the determination of relevant issues before a domestic or international tribunal. As is the case with the power to dismiss proceedings, this power is based on the need of international courts to carry out their function in ensuring the good administration of international justice.

3. *Power to Enjoin Parties from pursuing Parallel Proceedings*

A third procedural power which international courts could exercise in order to regulate the increasing number of related proceedings is the power to issue an injunction enjoining parties from commencing or pursuing other proceedings before a different forum, including another international court. Such orders can be found in most Anglo-American domestic legal systems, and are known as 'anti-suit injunctions'.[93]

[88] *SGS v Philippines* (ICSID Case No ARB/02/6, Decision on Jurisdiction of 29 January 2004), para 128, available at <http://ita.law.uvic.ca> (last visited 25 November 2006).

[89] Ibid, paras 136–55.

[90] Ibid, para 170.

[91] (2003) 18 *ICSID Review—FILJ* 301, 371–2.

[92] Above n 88, para 175.

[93] See especially *Airbus Industrie GIE v Patel* [1999] 1 AC 119; *Société Nationale Industrielle Aerospatiale v Lee Kui Jak* [1987] AC 871. On their availability in other common law jurisdictions, see *Laker Airways Ltd v Sabena, Belgian World Airways*, 731 F 2d 909 (DC Circ, 1984), and Peter Hay, Russell Weintraub and Patrick Borchers, *Conflict of Laws: Cases and Materials* (11th ed, 2000) 183–6 (US); *CSR Ltd v Cigna Insurance Australia Ltd* (1997) 189 CLR 345, and Martin Davies, Sam Ricketson and Geoffrey Lindell, *Conflict of Laws: Commentary and Materials* (1997) 222–31 (Australia); and *Amchem*, above n 78 (Canada). Anti-suit injunctions are generally unknown in civil law systems; Dr Petrochilos writes that in such systems, 'they are . . . likely to be regarded as an affront to the jurisdiction of the court to determine its own jurisdiction': Georgios Petrochilos, *Procedure in International Arbitration* (2004) 105; e.g. Decision of 10 January 1996 of the Oberlandesgericht Düsseldorf [1996] *Recht der internationalen Wirtschaft* 237; see also Shany, above n 8, 160–1; and Lesley Jane Smith, 'Antisuit Injunctions, Forum non Conveniens und International Comity' [1993] *Recht der internationalen Wirtschaft* 802, 808. But see Markus Lenenbach, 'Antisuit Injunctions in England, Germany and the United States: Their Treatment Under European Civil Procedure and the Hague Convention' (1998) 20 *Loyola of Los Angeles International and Comparative Law Journal* 257, 273–5, who observes several instances in which German courts have issued anti-suit injunctions.

As described by Professors North and Fawcett:

> An English court cannot prohibit a foreign court from trying an action. However, it does have a discretionary power, in certain circumstances, to grant an injunction restraining a party from commencing or continuing as claimant in foreign proceedings.[94]

The categories of cases in which an anti-suit injunction may be issued are not closed, and the broad principle underlying its use is that the power should be exercised when the ends of justice require it.[95] At the same time, the power must be exercised with caution, as it entails an implicit interference with the jurisdiction of another court.[96] More specifically, 'an anti-suit injunction will not be granted in circumstances which amount to a breach of comity'.[97] The House of Lords has explained this requirement by stating that the English court should have 'a sufficient interest in, or connection with, the matter in question to justify the indirect interference with the foreign court which an anti-suit injunction entails'.[98] There is no clear consensus among writers as to the grounds on which an anti-suit injunction may be granted by English courts,[99] although most agree that an injunction can be ordered where the pursuit of other proceedings is vexatious or oppressive, and where the other proceedings are brought in breach of an agreement.[100] While there are several instances where international courts have issued orders to parties affecting claims before domestic courts,[101] there appears to be no

[94] Sir Peter North and J J Fawcett, *Cheshire and North's Private International Law* (13th ed, 1999) 359 (references omitted).

[95] *Airbus Industrie GIE v Patel*, above n 93, 133; *Société Aérospatiale v Lee Kui Jak*, above n 93, 892; John Collier, *Conflict of Laws* (3rd ed, 2001) 100–1; North and Fawcett, ibid, 361.

[96] Petrochilos, above n 93, 105; North and Fawcett, ibid, 360; see especially Decision of 10 January 1996 of the Oberlandesgericht Düsseldorf, above n 93.

[97] North and Fawcett, ibid, 361. The notion of 'comity' has been defined as 'those acts, practices and rules of goodwill, amity and courteous treatment habitually observed by states in their mutual intercourse without the conviction that any legal obligation is involved': Peter MacAlister-Smith, 'Comity' in Rudolf Bernhardt (ed), *Encyclopedia of Public International Law* (1992) vol I, 671, 671.

[98] *Airbus Industrie GIE v Patel*, above n 93, 138; *Castanho v Brown & Root (UK) Ltd* [1981] AC 557, 573.

[99] See Collins (ed), above n 14, 416–21; North and Fawcett, above n 94, 361–73; Jonathan Hill, *International Commercial Disputes* (2nd ed, 1998) 323–31.

[100] Collins (ed), ibid, 416–19; North and Fawcett, ibid, 362–67; Hill, ibid, 325–9; Trevor Hartley, 'Comity and the Use of Antisuit Injunctions in International Litigation' (1987) 35 *American Journal of Comparative Law* 487, 494–5, 497–500.

[101] See, e.g., *Electricity Company of Sofia and Bulgaria* (*Interim Measures*), Ser A/B, (No 79) (PCIJ, 1939), where Belgium sought to prevent Bulgaria from executing a municipal judgment; see Switzerland's request in *Interhandel* [1957] ICJ Rep 105, 106, that the US take no 'judicial' steps to part with the property allegedly owned by the Swiss corporation; see also *Occidental Exploration and Production Company v Ecuador* (Award of 1 July 2004), 73, where the tribunal directed the claimant to cease and desist from any local court proceedings; see, however, rejection of such a request in *SGS v Pakistan* (Procedural Order No 2) (2002) 17 *ICSID Review—FILJ* 293, 299–301; but see the recommendation that domestic arbitration be stayed pending decision by the ICSID tribunal on its jurisdiction: ibid, 305. See also the extensive practice of the Iran–US Claims Tribunal on ordering the stay of proceedings in other fora, especially in *E-Systems v Iran*, 2 Ir–USCTR 51, 57 (1983): Charles Brower and Jason Brueschke, *The Iran–United States Claims Tribunal* (1998) 229–35.

instance in which an international court has sought to enjoin a party from pursuing proceedings before another international court. It is suggested that given the increasing likelihood that international courts may be confronted with competing proceedings that could frustrate the resolution of the dispute of which they are seised, international courts might, in future, consider themselves competent to issue such orders.

Two objections to the issuing of anti-suit injunctions in international proceedings might be made: first, that anti-suit injunctions, like mandatory or consequential orders, are inappropriate orders for international courts to direct at sovereign states; and second, that such orders cannot in any event be enforced. The first objection can be rejected; while there is little practice of international courts issuing injunctions, recent jurisprudence suggests that international courts consider the issuing of mandatory orders to be included within their judicial functions.[102] As for the second objection, it is true that enforcement of such orders would pose difficulties. Even anti-suit injunctions issued by domestic courts are difficult to enforce; as Professors North and Fawcett note of English anti-suit injunctions, 'the reality is that, if the defendant neither lives in England nor has substantial assets there, the injunction is unlikely to be enforced except by the foreign court recognising and giving effect to the injunction'.[103] Yet it should be remembered that such orders are directed at a person who is subject to the jurisdiction of the court, and not at the court which is the venue of the second set of proceedings.[104] Thus, enforcement of domestic anti-suit injunctions may be effected by means of the court's inherent power to punish contempt of court.[105] Some international courts have also asserted an inherent power to deal with contempt. While this practice seems to be restricted to international criminal tribunals,[106] it may be open to other international courts to develop this procedure to assist in the enforcement of anti-suit injunctions. It is recognized, however, that there is a difference between enforcing an order against an individual by means of proceedings for contempt, and levelling the same charge against a state.

In light of the potential difficulties with issuing anti-suit injunctions, it can be concluded that this procedure is less likely to be adopted by international courts. Nonetheless, even if such injunctions cannot be enforced, the issuing of such an order would be a significant step which parties would not ignore lightly, and it is also possible that the other international court might recognize the order and suspend or dismiss any proceedings before it in the exercise of international judicial comity.

102 See above chapter 6, part III(D).

103 North and Fawcett, above n 94, 360.

104 Ibid; Bell, above n 78, 173–6; Collier, above n 95, 100–1.

105 Collier, ibid, 100; see especially *Prosecutor v Tadic* (Contempt), fn 16 (ICTY App Ch, 2000), reviewing the principles relating to the law of contempt as accepted by the UK House of Lords, Ontario Court of Appeal, High Court of Australia, and US Supreme Court.

106 See especially *Prosecutor v Tadic* (Contempt), ibid, paras 13–26; see also *Prosecutor v Simic* et al (Contempt), para 91 (ICTY App Ch, 2000); *Prosecutor v Blaskic* (Subpoena), 110 ILR 688, 722 (ICTY App Ch, 1997).

C. Conclusion

The emerging common law of international adjudication can have a significant impact on the resolution of procedural issues in international adjudication. The foregoing paragraphs have considered several specific issues which are increasingly likely to arise in international adjudication, and it is suggested that international courts might refer to the way these issues have been dealt with by other international courts to ensure the proper administration of international justice and to prevent the commencement of abusive claims. The preceding section does not represent an exhaustive consideration of these issues; yet the few instances of practice concerning these issues provided by several international courts represents a source of inspiration on which other international courts may draw, should they also be faced with such situations.

II. Theoretical Implications

The emergence of a common law of international adjudication is significant for reasons other than its practical effects, for it might inform answers to broader questions concerning the systemic coherence of the international legal order. It was observed in chapter 1 that international courts are not created as part of a formal system. Several international tribunals have expressly stated that they consider themselves to be self-contained regimes without any links to other international courts.[107] Yet the emergence of common standards in the procedure and remedies applied in international adjudication permits the suggestion to be made that despite the absence of formal institutional connections, international courts are beginning to operate as if they formed part of the same system.

Many attempts have been made in the past to define the term 'legal system', and to determine whether the international legal order meets the criteria.[108] An early

[107] See, e.g., the comments of the ICTY Appeals Chamber in *Prosecutor v Tadic* above n 11, 39: 'in international law, every tribunal is a self-contained system (unless otherwise provided)'; and in *Prosecutor v Delalic* (Judgment of 20 February 2001), para 24: 'this Tribunal is an autonomous international judicial body, and although the ICJ is the "principal judicial organ" within the United Nations system to which the Tribunal belongs, there is no hierarchical relationship between the two courts' (footnotes omitted), available at <http://www.un.org/icty/> under the name *Prosecutor v Mucic* et al (IT–96–21) ('Celibici') (last visited 25 November 2006); those of the ECHR in *Loizidou v Turkey*, above n 12, 133: '[t]he International Court is a free-standing international tribunal which has no links to a standard-setting treaty such as the Convention'; and those of the IACHR in *Consular Assistance*, above n 13, 40: 'this Court is an "autonomous judicial institution"'; see also *Argentina—Poultry*, WT/DS241/R, para 7.41 (PR), where the WTO panel ignored the ruling of a Mercosur arbitral tribunal in what was substantially the same dispute; and *CME Czech Republic BV v Czech Republic* (Final Award of 14 March 2003), paras 431–3.

[108] See especially the discussion in Shany, above n 8, 84–115; see also Benedict Kingsbury, 'Foreword: Is the Proliferation of International Courts and Tribunals a Problem?' (1999) 31 *New York University Journal of International Law and Politics* 679, 688–93; Georges Abi-Saab, 'Fragmentation

writer who considered the nature of international law, John Austin, considered that a law was 'a general command of a sovereign addressed to his subjects'; a legal system, then, existed if the common legislator of its laws was a sovereign, and if it was generally efficacious.[109] According to his definition of 'law', international law was no more than positive morality;[110] it could therefore scarcely be said that there was such a thing as an international legal system.[111]

Different approaches have been taken by other writers to this question. One who adopted a normative approach is Hans Kelsen. For Kelsen, a legal system is a system of legal norms; a plurality of norms constitutes a legal system 'if the validity of the norms can be traced back to a single norm as the ultimate basis of validity'.[112] He argued that the basic norm of international law is 'a norm that establishes custom—the reciprocal behaviour of states—as a law-creating material fact'.[113] Accordingly, he argued that international law met the requirements of structural hierarchy and qualified as a legal system.[114] However, he did note that international law was a primitive legal system, 'marked by wide-ranging decentralisation—at least in the field of general international law, and thus as it affects the entire international legal community'.[115] For instance, he observed that there were 'no organs, whose respective functions reflect a division of labour, for creating and applying legal norms'.[116]

Professor H L A Hart also adopted a normative approach to the idea of a legal system, and argued that 'a legal system is a complex union of primary and secondary rules'.[117] Primary rules are 'rules of obligation',[118] and secondary rules 'specify the ways in which the primary rules may be conclusively ascertained ... and the fact of the violation conclusively determined'.[119] For Professor Hart, two conditions were necessary and sufficient for the existence of a legal system. First, 'the rules of behaviour ... must be generally obeyed', and second, 'its rules of recognition ... and its rules of change and adjudication must be effectively accepted'.[120] Professor Hart argued that international law lacked effective secondary rules, and concluded that 'the rules which are in fact operative constitute not a system but a set of rules'.[121] Nevertheless, he did not dismiss the possibility that future developments might lead to the emergence of an international legal system.[122]

Other writers have presented definitions of what constitutes a legal system which stress the importance of normative coherence and institutional linkages. Professor Joseph Raz argued that a legal system should be understood as 'intricate

or Unification: Some Concluding Remarks' (1999) 31 *New York University Journal of International Law and Politics* 919.

[109] John Austin, *The Province of Jurisprudence Determined* (first published 1832, 1998 ed) 24–8; see also discussion in Joseph Raz, *The Concept of a Legal System* (2nd ed, 1980) 5–17.

[110] Austin, ibid, 12, 126–7.

[111] See especially Raz, above n 109, 16–17.

[112] Hans Kelsen, *Introduction to the Problems of Legal Theory* (first published 1934, 1992 ed) 55.

[113] Ibid, 108.

[114] Ibid.

[115] Ibid.

[116] Ibid.

[117] H L A Hart, *The Concept of Law* (2nd ed, 1994) 114; Shany, above n 8, 88.

[118] Hart, ibid, 94, 214.

[119] Ibid, 94.

[120] Ibid, 116.

[121] Ibid, 236.

[122] Ibid, 236–7.

webs of interconnected laws',[123] yet he also posited that the institutional enforcement of legal norms was an important feature in any legal system,[124] and referred to the 'essential role' of institutions in the law.[125] Professor Georges Abi-Saab also adopted a position which rejected the normative view of Professors Hart and Kelsen, but he also thought that writers who emphasized the role of institutions ignored the importance of norms in legal systems. Professor Abi-Saab argued that 'un ordre juridique sans normes... me paraît impossible... les institutions et les processus juridiques peuvent toujours être transcrits en termes normatifs.'[126] Thus, in his view, a strict institutional understanding of what constitutes a legal system failed to appreciate the importance of norms in the operation of the legal system.[127]

In the context of proliferation, it has also been asked whether the multitude of international dispute settlement bodies represents a system of international courts. In his Hague lectures, Professor Charney argued that the presence of a hierarchical structure to resolve inconsistent lines of authority is not necessary in order for a collection of courts and tribunals to be called a 'system'.[128] If a hierarchical structure is not essential for a collection of courts to exist as part of a system, is it necessary for them to apply the same norms? Professor Shany suggests that it is, but he also argues that merely because different courts apply the same norms 'does not suffice in order to view them as participating in the same legal system'.[129] For instance, he observes that English courts can apply French law, but this of course does not lead to the conclusion that English courts are part of the French legal system.[130] He also argues that although international judicial institutions share other common features, such as their establishment by international instruments, this is not enough for international courts to be considered as part of a system of international courts.[131] He sets the question as whether:

> these judicial bodies compose an institutional subsystem of their own, conceived through their reciprocal relations with each other, and not through their interaction with an overarching normative and political umbrella under which they, and other non-judicial institutions, function.[132]

In order for this question to be answered in the affirmative, Professor Shany argues that some sort of structural relations are needed between international courts; such structural relations might consist of the coordinated allocation of jurisdiction, rules on jurisdictional competition, and hierarchical structures.[133] Significantly, he

[123] Raz, above n 109, 183. [124] Ibid, 185–6. [125] Ibid, 194.

[126] Georges Abi-Saab, 'Cours général de droit international public' (1987) 207 *Recueil des cours* 9, 114. [127] Ibid.

[128] For example, Charney refers to the French legal system, which lacks a single reviewing court for its three separate court hierarchies, but the coherence of the French legal system cannot seriously be questioned: Jonathan Charney, 'Is International Law Threatened by Multiple International Tribunals?' (1998) 271 *Recueil des Cours* 101, 357–8; see also Michael Bogdan, *Comparative Law* (1994) 173–7. [129] Shany, above n 8, 105.

[130] Ibid, 104; see also H L A Hart, *Essays in Jurisprudence and Philosophy* (1983) 342.

[131] Shany, above n 8, 105. [132] Ibid, 106. [133] Ibid, 108.

argues that for international courts to constitute a system, '[a] similar role, procedure or applicable law is not enough'.[134]

It is agreed that similarities in the procedure and remedies applied by a group of courts is not sufficient for them to be considered as part of a system. For instance, just because damages are available as remedies in certain causes of action in the courts of New Zealand and Singapore does not mean that those bodies form part of the same legal system, even if they occasionally refer to each other's jurisprudence. As regards international courts, the absence of structural and hierarchical connections, and the absence of complete uniformity in the application of norms relating to procedure and remedies prevents designation of the assortment of international courts as an 'international legal system'. But what the analysis presented in this book suggests is that there is an increasing level of coherence in the application of norms relating to procedure and remedies in international adjudication. These conclusions suggest that international courts and tribunals, far from existing as a set of unconnected 'self-contained systems',[135] do amount to more than this. The evident convergence of practice by the constellation of international courts relating to procedure and remedies demonstrates the existence of systemic relations between these institutions, even though these may operate at an informal level.

It is suggested that this practice indicates that such bodies regard themselves as forming part of a community of international courts. Membership of this community may be said to imply for some, but not necessarily all bodies, a degree of acceptance of systemic relations, however informal they may be. International courts are increasingly aware of each other's judicial pronouncements and activities, they increasingly refer to each other's decisions, and they are frequently applying aspects of their law relating to procedure and remedies—as well as aspects of substantive law—consistently with other international tribunals.[136] On the basis of this practice of international courts, it is suggested that there is a 'community' of international courts,[137] which comprises an informal system of international dispute settlement.

Conclusion

This chapter has examined practical and theoretical implications of the emerging common law of international adjudication. These are that the procedural law and remedies applicable in international litigation are not limited to those expressly provided for in the constitutive instruments; often, these are silent on questions of

[134] Shany, above n 8, 107. [135] *Prosecutor v Tadic*, above n 11, 39.

[136] See also above n 7.

[137] See also, in this connection, Anne-Marie Slaughter, 'A Global Community of Courts' (2003) 44 *Harvard International Law Journal* 191.

procedure and remedies, and international courts can engage in the task of filling in the *lacunae* by adopting approaches to treaty interpretation, referring to general principles of law, and exercising inherent powers. In the context of proliferation, the emergence of a common law of international adjudication can have a significant impact on newer international courts which are in the process of developing their procedure and remedies, and also on more established international courts faced with complex issues of jurisdictional competition. It has been suggested that international courts faced with such issues might be able to exercise powers to suspend or dismiss proceedings, or to issue an order that other proceedings be discontinued. The theoretical implications of the common law of international adjudication include the realization that international courts, far from existing as self-contained systems—as suggested by the ICTY Appeals Chamber's dictum in *Tadic*[138]—actually operate as part of a community whose procedures and remedies have much in common. It is suggested that the practice of international courts reviewed in this book permits the suggestion to be made that there is much evidence of the existence of systemic features in international adjudication.

[138] Above n 11, 39.

Conclusion

This book has examined whether international courts and tribunals adopt common approaches to certain aspects of procedure and remedies. While the constitutive instruments of many international courts often make similar provision, they are not all identical, or, indeed, even similar, and often contain gaps, leaving procedural rules and remedies to be developed in international jurisprudence. As a result of the proliferation of international courts and tribunals, combined with the increase in resort by states and non-state entities to international litigation, many new international courts have had to develop their procedures, and in addition, many international tribunals have been confronted with challenging procedural issues—such as how to deal with an ever-increasing workload—which they have not previously faced. Against this background, this book has asked whether international courts have sought to resolve these issues by considering, and adopting, the practices of other international courts, leading to the emergence of a 'common law of international adjudication'.

This book has set about this task by examining the sources of the procedural and remedial competences of the principal international courts, and by analysing the tools available to international courts to engage in cross-fertilization on issues relating to procedure and remedies. The tools and methods employed by international courts to reach out to the practice of other international tribunals on these issues are manifold. Where their statutes and rules of procedure are drafted in similar terms, international courts can follow the rulings of other international tribunals. Where their constitutive instruments are inconsistent or contain *lacunae*, however, international courts can adopt methods of treaty interpretation which permit them to have regard to the practice of other international tribunals. These methods include the principle of effectiveness in treaty interpretation, the evolutive approach to treaty interpretation, and the rule contained in article 31(3)(c) of the VCLT, which requires that 'any relevant rules of international law applicable in the relations between the parties' be taken into account when interpreting a treaty. Further, in interpreting and devising their procedures and remedies, international courts can have regard to customary rules and general principles of law developed in international judicial and arbitral practice. In addition, where the statutes and rules of procedure of international courts are silent, international courts can adopt the practice of other international courts, in certain circumstances by the exercise of inherent powers.

Having considered the tools and methods available to international courts to reach out to the practice of other international tribunals, this book then proceeded to examine the degree of common practice with respect to several aspects of international adjudication. The areas considered were aspects of the rules of evidence; the power of international courts to grant provisional measures; the power of international courts to interpret and revise judgments; and the remedies available in international adjudication. Broad agreement could be discerned in the practice of different international courts and tribunals on these issues, although greater commonality existed with respect to some issues than others.

There are various factors which explain the emergence of a common law of international adjudication, in addition to the various methods which international courts can employ to harmonize their approaches to procedure and remedies. These include the fact that international courts essentially perform the same functions, which gives rise to the instinctive tendency to refer to the jurisprudence of similar adjudicatory bodies. In addition, members of the international judiciary—and the lawyers appearing before them—have often served on or appeared before several international tribunals, and also bring a common legal experience to their work. This, too, makes it more likely that procedural and remedial powers will be exercised consistently. In addition, with the advent of proliferation and the existence of multiple possible fora for the settlement of disputes by adjudication, it is possible that a sense of competition has emerged among some international courts, leading international courts to harmonize their procedures so that they provide the same advantages to potential litigants as other international tribunals. Further, there may also be a belief among members of the international judiciary that the emergence of a common set of standards applying to procedure and remedies is ultimately beneficial. Other factors might also be at play in determining the relevance of the practice of other international judicial bodies, such as the nature of the relationship between the respective international court and the parties before it, the question of whether the parties have pleaded the relevance of other international jurisprudence, and, of course, the perceived fairness or utility of the rule in question.

Despite these factors, which might militate in favour of a convergence of international judicial practice, there are limitations to the development of a common law of international adjudication. These relate to, *inter alia*, the differences in the drafting of each international court's constitutive instrument and rules of procedure; the different specific functions of international courts; the particular relationship between each international court and the parties; and the non-desirability of adopting common approaches to certain issues. Further, although there might be broad agreement among international courts with respect, for example, to the rule on the allocation of the burden of proof, the power to request the production of documents, the power to interpret judgments and awards, and the availability of compensation as a remedy for certain categories of harm, there are inconsistencies in the way that international courts deal with these questions. Thus, it cannot be said that there is a uniform approach to all of these issues. In this sense, it is unlikely that the emerging common law of international adjudication will crystallize into a single universally applicable set of rules.

This is not to say that the emerging broad commonality is not significant. On the contrary, it is suggested that it has substantial practical implications for the conduct of international litigation. These relate not only to procedural questions which already arise before many international courts, but also to other issues with which international courts are likely to be confronted and for which their statutes and rules of procedure make no clear provision. In this sense, the emerging common law of international adjudication can have some prescriptive effect. Examples considered relate to the way in which international courts deal with the existence of related proceedings before other international courts. Faced with such proceedings, several international courts have exercised a number of powers over their proceedings. Other international courts might adopt these practices, and international courts might also exercise inherent powers to devise new procedures.

The emerging common law of international adjudication also has theoretical implications. The proliferation of international courts and tribunals has occurred in the absence of an overarching systemic framework, such as a hierarchy of courts and a common court of appeal. What is demonstrated by the emerging common law of international adjudication, however, is that international courts do not operate in complete isolation from each other, and are increasingly demonstrating an appreciation of each other's jurisprudence on issues of procedure and remedies. This, then, suggests that while international courts might not form part of a formal system with structural relations and complete normative coherence, there is a distinct community of international courts, all of which exercise broadly similar functions in settling disputes and ensuring the proper administration of international justice. The suggestion that certain aspects of the process of international adjudication are approached in a similar fashion by international courts thus serves as a solid foundation for the further development of a harmonious system of international dispute settlement, and, it is suggested, the better administration of international justice.

Bibliography

Georges Abi-Saab, 'Fragmentation or Unification: Some Concluding Remarks' (1999) 31 *New York University Journal of International Law and Politics* 919

Georges Abi-Saab, 'Ensuring the Best Bench: Ways of Selecting Judges' in C Peck and R S Lee (eds), *Increasing the Effectiveness of the International Court of Justice* (1997) 165

Georges Abi-Saab, 'The International Court as a World Court' in Vaughan Lowe and Malgosia Fitzmaurice (eds), *Fifty Years of the International Court of Justice* (1996) 3

Georges Abi-Saab, 'Cours général de droit international public' (1987) 207 *Recueil des cours* 9

Georges Abi-Saab, *Les exceptions préliminaires dans la procédure de la Cour internationale* (1967)

A O Adede, *The System for the Settlement of Disputes under the United Nations Convention on the Law of the Sea* (1987)

M Aghahosseini, 'Evidence before the Iran–United States Claims Tribunal' (1999) 1 *International Law Forum du Droit International* 208

George Aldrich, *The Jurisprudence of the Iran–United States Claims Tribunal* (1996)

Stanimir Alexandrov, *Reservations in Unilateral Declarations Accepting the Compulsory Jurisdiction of the International Court of Justice* (1995)

Neill Alford, 'Fact finding by the World Court' (1958) 4 *Villanova Law Review* 37

Roger Alford, 'The Proliferation of International Courts and Tribunals: International Adjudication in Ascendance' [2000] *Proceedings of the 94th Annual Meeting of the American Society of International Law* 160

Jean Allain, *A Century of International Adjudication: The Rule of Law and Its Limits* (2000)

Chittharanjan Amerasinghe, *Evidence in International Litigation* (2005)

Chittharanjan Amerasinghe, 'Presumptions and Inferences in Evidence in International Litigation' (2004) 3 *Law and Practice of International Courts and Tribunals* 395

R P Anand, 'Role of International Adjudication' in Leo Gross (ed), *The Future of the International Court of Justice* (1976) vol I, 1

R P Anand, *International Courts and Contemporary Conflicts* (1974)

David Anderson, 'The International Tribunal for the Law of the Sea' in Malcolm Evans (ed), *Remedies in International Law* (1998) 71

Dionisio Anzilotti, *Corso di Diritto Internazionale* (4th ed, 1955)

Dionisio Anzilotti, *Cours de Droit International* (French trans Gilbert Gidel, of 3rd ed, 1929) vol I

Gaetano Arangio-Ruiz, 'Second Report on State Responsibility' [1989] *Yearbook of the International Law Commission*, vol II, pt I, 1, UN Doc A/CN.4/425

Eduardo Jiménez de Aréchaga, 'International Law in the Past Third of a Century' (1978) 159 *Recueil des cours* 1

Eduardo Jiménez de Aréchaga, 'The Amendments to the Rules of Procedure of the International Court of Justice' (1973) 67 *AJIL* 1

Eduardo Jiménez de Aréchaga, 'International Responsibility' in Max Sørensen (ed), *Manual of Public International Law* (1968) 571

Jean-Jacques Arnaldez, Yves Derains and Dominique Hascher (eds), *Collection of ICC Arbitral Awards 1991–1995* (1997)

Anthony Arnull, 'Does the Court of Justice Have Inherent Jurisdiction?' (1990) 27 *CML Rev* 683

Hervé Ascensio, 'La notion de juridiction internationale en question' in Société Française pour le Droit International, *Colloque de Lille: La juridictionnalisation du droit international* (2003) 163

Anthony Aust, *Modern Treaty Law and Practice* (2000)

John Austin, *The Province of Jurisprudence Determined* (first published 1832, 1998 ed)

James Bacchus, 'Table Talk: Around the Table of the Appellate Body of the World Trade Organisation' (2002) 35 *Vanderbilt Journal of Transnational Law* 1021

A Balasko, *Causes de nullité de la sentence arbitrale en droit international public* (1938)

Markham Ball, 'Assessing Damages in Claims by Investors Against States' (2001) 16 *ICSID Review–Foreign Investment Law Journal* 408

Stewart Baker and Mark Davis, *The UNCITRAL Arbitration Rules in Practice* (1992)

Daniel Bardonnet, 'De l'équivoque des categories juridiques: la revision des sentences arbitrales pour "erreur de fait" ou "fait nouveau" dans la pratique latino-américaine', in *Liber Amicorum in Memoriam of Judge José María Ruda* (2000) 189

John Barker, 'The Valuation of Income-Producing Property in International Law' (PhD dissertation, University of Cambridge, 1998)

Peter Barnett, Res Judicata, *Estoppel, and Foreign Judgments* (2001)

Lorand Bartels, 'Applicable Law in WTO Dispute Settlement Proceedings' (2001) 35 *Journal of World Trade Law* 499

John Basten, 'The Court Expert in Civil Trials: A Comparative Appraisal' (1977) 40 *MLR* 174

Mohammed Bedjaoui, 'La multiplication des tribunaux internationales, ou la bonne fortune du droit des gens' in Société Française pour le Droit International, *Colloque de Lille: La juridictionnalisation du droit international* (2003)

Mohammed Bedjaoui, 'La "Descente sur les Lieux" dans la Pratique de la Cour Internationale de Justice et de sa Devancière' in Gerhard Hafner *et al* (eds), *Liber Amicorum Professor Ignaz Seidl-Hohenveldern* (1998) 1

Rambod Behboodi, '"Should" means "Shall": A Critical Analysis of the Obligation to Submit Information under Article 13.1 of the DSU in the Canada—Aircraft Case' (2000) 3 *Journal of International Economic Law* 563

Andrew Bell, *Forum Shopping and Venue in Transnational Litigation* (2003)

Eyal Benvenisti, 'Margin of Appreciation, Consensus and Universal Standards' (1999) 31 *New York University Journal of International Law and Politics* 843

Friedrich Berber, *Lehrbuch des Völkerrechts* (1964)

Georges Berlia, 'Contribution à l'interprétation des traités' (1965) 114 *Recueil des cours* 287

Georges Berlia, 'Jurisprudence des Tribunaux Internationaux en ce qui concerne leur Compétence' (1955) 88 *Recueil des cours* 109

Santiago Torres Bernárdez, 'A propos de l'interprétation et de la revision des arrêts de la Cour internationale de justice' in *Le Droit International à l'Heure de sa Codification: Etudes en l'honneur de Roberto Ago* (1987) vol III, 443

Rudolf Bernhardt, 'Evolutive Treaty Interpretation, Especially of the European Convention on Human Rights' (1999) 42 *German Yearbook of International Law* 11

Rudolf Bernhardt (ed), *Encyclopedia of Public International Law* (1995)

Rudolf Bernhardt (ed), *Interim Measures Indicated by International Courts* (1994)

Rudolf Bernhardt, 'Interim Measures of Protection under the European Convention on Human Rights', in Rudolf Bernhardt (ed), *Interim Measures Indicated by International Courts* (1994) 95

Daniel Bethlehem, 'Submissions on Points of Fact and Law: Written and Oral Pleadings before the International Court of Justice' in Friedl Weiss (ed), *Improving WTO Dispute Settlement Procedures* (2000) 175

Daniel Bethlehem, 'Interpretation of Judgments' in Richard Plender (ed), *European Courts: Practice and Precedents* (1997) 743

Raj Bhala, 'The Myth about *Stare Decisis* and International Trade' (1999) 14 *American University International Law Review* 845

R Bierzanek, 'Some Remarks on the Function of International Courts in Contemporary World' (1975) 7 *Polish Yearbook of International Law* 121

Richard Bilder, 'The Fact/Law Distinction in International Adjudication' in Richard Lillich (ed), *Fact-Finding before International Tribunals* (1992) 95

Richard Bilder, 'International Dispute Settlement and the Role of International Adjudication' in Lori Damrosch (ed), *The International Court of Justice at a Crossroads* (1987) 155

Richard Bilder, 'Some Limitations of Adjudication as an International Dispute Settlement Technique' (1983) 23 *Virginia Journal of International Law* 1

Rudolf Bindschedler, 'Die Anerkennung im Völkerrecht' (1961–2) 9 *Archiv des Völkerrechts* 377

Sir William Blackstone, *Commentaries on the Laws of England* (first published 1765, Stanley Katz ed, 1979)

Xavier Blanc-Jouvan and Jean Boulois, 'France' in International Association of Legal Science, *International Encyclopedia of Comparative Law* (1972) vol I

Arwed Blomeyer, 'Types of Relief Available (Judicial Remedies)' in International Association of Legal Science, *International Encyclopedia of Comparative Law* (1982) vol XVI, ch 4

J C Bluntschli, *Das moderne Völkerrecht der civilisirten Staten als Rechtsbuch dargestellt* (3rd ed, 1878, trans C Lardy, *Le droit international codifié*, 5th rev ed, 1895)

Michael Bogdan, *Comparative Law* (1994)

Laurence Boisson de Chazournes (ed), *ASIL Proceedings: Implications of the Proliferation of International Adjudicatory Bodies for Dispute Resolution* (1995)

Laurence Boisson de Chazournes, Cesare Romano and Ruth Mackenzie (eds), *International Organisations and International Dispute Settlement* (2002)

Edwin Borchard, *Declaratory Judgments* (1934)

G Borchardt, 'The Award of Interim Measures by the European Court of Justice' (1985) 22 *Common Market Law Review* 203

D W Bowett, '*Res Judicata* and the Limits of Rectification of Decisions by International Tribunals' (1996) 8 *African Journal of International and Comparative Law* 577

D W Bowett, 'The Arbitration between the United Kingdom and France Concerning the Continental Shelf Boundary in the English Channel and South-Western Approaches' (1978) 49 *British Yearbook of International Law* 1

D W Bowett *et al* (eds), *The International Court of Justice: Process, Practice and Procedure* (1997)

Alan Boyle, 'Dispute Settlement and the Law of the Sea Convention: Problems of Fragmentation and Jurisdiction' (1997) 46 *ICLQ* 37

Alan Boyle, 'The Proliferation of International Jurisdiction and its Implications for the Court' in D W Bowett *et al* (eds), *The International Court of Justice: Process, Practice and Procedure* (1997) 124

Alan Boyle and David Freestone (eds), *International Law and Sustainable Development: Past Achievements and Future Challenges* (1999)

Boleslaw Adam Bozcek, *Historical Dictionary of International Tribunals* (1994)

Duncan Brack, 'The Shrimp-Turtle Case: Implications for the Multilateral Environmental Agreement–World Trade Organisation Debate' (1998) 9 *Yearbook of International Environmental Law* 13

Duncan Brack, 'Reconciling the GATT and Multilateral Environmental Agreements with Trade Provisions: The Latest Debate' (1997) 6 *Review of European Community and International Environmental Law* 112

Anders Bratholm and Jo Hov, *Sivil Retergang* (1973)

Mark Brealey, 'The Burden of Proof before the European Court' (1985) 10 *ELR* 250

J L Brierly, *The Law of Nations* (6th ed, 1963)

Herbert Briggs, 'The Incidental Jurisdiction of the International Court of Justice as Compulsory Jurisdiction' in FA v d Heydte, *Völkerrecht und Rechtliches Weltbild: Festschrift für Alfred Verdross* (1960) 92

British Institute of International and Comparative Law, *Evidence before International Tribunals* (2002)

Aron Broches, 'Convention on the Settlement of Disputes between States and Nationals of Other States of 1965: Explanatory Notes and Survey of its Application' (1993) 18 *Yearbook Commercial Arbitration* 627

Marco Bronckers and Naboth van den Broek, 'Financial Compensation in the WTO: Improving the Remedies of WTO Dispute Settlement' (2005) 8 *Journal of International Economic Law* 101

Charles Brower, 'Evidence before International Tribunals: The Need for some Standard Rules' (1994) 28 *International Lawyer* 47

Charles Brower, 'The Anatomy of Fact-Finding before International Tribunals: An Analysis and a Proposal Concerning the Evaluation of Evidence' in Richard Lillich (ed), *Fact-Finding Before International Tribunals* (1992) 147

Charles Brower and Jason Brueschke, *The Iran–United States Claims Tribunal* (1998)

Charles Brower and Ronald Goodman, 'Provisional Measures and the Protection of ICSID Jurisdictional Exclusivity Against Municipal Proceedings' (1991) 6 *ICSID Review—FILJ* 431

Bartram Brown, 'US Objections to the Statute of the International Criminal Court: A Brief Response' (1999) 31 *New York University Journal of International Law and Politics* 855

Chester Brown, 'The Inherent Powers of International Courts and Tribunals' (2005) 76 *British Yearbook of International Law* 195

Chester Brown, 'Access to International Justice in the *Legality of Use of Force* Cases' (2005) 64 *CLJ* 267

Chester Brown, 'Strasbourg Follows Suit on Provisional Measures' (2003) 62 *CLJ* 532

Chester Brown, ' "Reasonableness" in the Law of the Sea: The Prompt Release of the Volga' (2003) 16 *Leiden Journal of International Law* 621

Chester Brown, '*Armed Activities on the Territory of the Congo (New Application: 2002) (Democratic Republic of the Congo v Rwanda)* Provisional Measures, Order of 10 July 2002' (2003) 52 *ICLQ* 782

Chester Brown, 'The Evolution and Application of Rules Concerning Independence of the "International Judiciary"' (2003) 2 *Law and Practice of International Courts and Tribunals* 63

Chester Brown, 'The Proliferation of International Courts and Tribunals: Finding Your Way Through the Maze' (2002) 3 *Melbourne Journal of International Law* 453

Chester Brown, 'Provisional Measures before the International Tribunal for the Law of the Sea: The *MOX Plant* Case' (2002) 17 *International Journal of Marine and Coastal Law* 267

L Neville Brown and Tom Kennedy, Brown & Jacobs: *The Court of Justice of the European Communities* (5th ed, 2000)

James Brown Scott, *Sovereign States and Suits* (1925)

James Brown Scott (ed), *The Reports to the Hague Conferences of 1899 and 1907* (1917)

James Brown Scott (ed), *Classics of International Law* (1916)

James Brown Scott (ed), *Instructions to the American Delegates to the Hague Peace Conferences and their Official Reports* (1916)

Ian Brownlie, *Principles of Public International Law* (6th ed, 2003)

Ian Brownlie, *The Rule of Law in International Affairs* (1998)

Ian Brownlie, 'Remedies in the International Court of Justice' in Vaughan Lowe and Malgosia Fitzmaurice (eds), *Fifty Years of the International Court of Justice* (1996) 557

Ian Brownlie, 'The Rights of Peoples in Modern International Law', in James Crawford (ed), *The Rights of Peoples* (1988) 1

Ian Brownlie, 'Problems Concerning the Unity of International Law', in *Le droit international à l'heure de sa codification: Études en l'honneur de Roberto Ago* (1987) vol I, 153

Ian Brownlie, *System of the Law of Nations: State Responsibility Part I* (1983)

Ian Brownlie, 'Causes of Action in the Law of Nations' (1979) *British Yearbook of International Law* 13

Ian Brownlie, 'The Justiciability of Disputes and Issues in International Relations' (1967) 42 *British Yearbook of International Law* 123

Marcel Brus, *Third Party Dispute Settlement in an Interdependent World* (1995)

Vittorio di Bucci, 'Revision' in Richard Plender (ed), *European Courts: Practice and Precedents* (1997) 699

Thomas Buergenthal, 'Proliferation of International Courts and Tribunals: Is It Good or Bad?' (2001) 14 *Leiden Journal of International Law* 267

Thomas Buergenthal, 'Interim Measures in the Inter-American Court of Human Rights' in Rudolf Bernhardt (ed), *Interim Measures Indicated by International Courts* (1994), 69

Thomas Buergenthal, 'Judicial Fact Finding: Inter-American Human Rights Court' in Richard Lillich (ed), *Fact-Finding by International Tribunals* (1992) 271

Thomas Buergenthal, 'The Inter-American System for the Protection of Human Rights' in Theodor Meron (ed), *Human Rights in International Law: Legal and Policy Issues* (1984) 439

Thomas Buergenthal, 'The Inter-American Court of Human Rights' (1982) 76 *AJIL* 231

Thomas Buergenthal, 'The American and European Conventions on Human Rights: Similarities and Differences' (1980–1) 30 *American University Law Review* 155

William Burke-White, 'International Legal Pluralism' (2004) 25 *Michigan Journal of International Law* 963

Antonio Sanchez de Bustamante, *The World Court* (1925)

Michéle Buteau and Gabriël Oosthuizen, 'When the Statutes and Rules are Silent: The Inherent Powers of the Tribunal' in Richard May *et al* (eds), *Essays on ICTY Procedure and Evidence in Honour of Gabrielle Kirk McDonald* (2001) 65

William Butler (ed), *International Law in Comparative Perspective* (1980)

Michael Byers, 'Abuse of Rights: An Old Principle, A New Age' (2002) 47 *McGill Law Journal* 389

R C van Caenegem, 'History of European Civil Procedure', in *International Encyclopedia of Comparative Law* (1973) vol XVI, ch 1, 23

Lucius Calflisch (ed), *The Peaceful Settlement of Disputes Between States: Universal and European Perspectives* (1998)

James Cameron and Kevin Gray, 'Principles of International Law in the WTO Dispute Settlement Body' (2001) 50 *ICLQ* 248

James Cameron and Stephen Orava, 'GATT/WTO Panels between Recording and Finding Facts' in Friedl Weiss (ed), *Improving WTO Dispute Settlement Procedures* (2000) 195

Antonio Augusto Cançado Trindade, 'The Merits of Coordination of International Courts on Human Rights' (2004) 2 *Journal of International Criminal Law* 309

Mauro Cappelletti and Bryant Garth, 'Introduction—Policies, Trends and Ideas in Civil Procedure' in *International Encyclopaedia of Comparative Law, Civil Procedure* (1987) vol XVI, ch 1

Thomas Carbonneau, 'Arbitral Law-Making' (2004) 25 *Michigan Journal of International Law* 1183

Andrea Carcano, 'Requests for Review in the Practice of the International Criminal Tribunals for the Former Yugoslavia and Rwanda' (2004) 17 *Leiden Journal of International Law* 103

Kenneth Carlston, *Process of International Arbitration* (1946)

Chi Carmody, 'WTO Obligations as Collective' (2006) 17 *European Journal of International Law* 419

Chi Carmody, 'Remedies and Conformity under the WTO Agreement' (2002) 5 *Journal of International Economic Law* 307

Chi Carmody, 'Of Substantial Interest: Third Parties under GATT' (1997) 18 *Michigan Journal of International Law* 615

David Caron, 'Interim Measures of Protection: Theory and Practice in Light of the Iran-US Claims Tribunal' (1986) 46 *ZaöRV* 466

David Caron, Lee Caplan and Matti Pellonpää, *The UNCITRAL Arbitration Rules: A Commentary* (2006)

Juan Antonio Carrillo-Salcedo, 'The Inherent Powers of the International Criminal Tribunal for the Former Yugoslavia to Issue '*Subpoena Duces Tecum*' to a Sovereign State' in René-Jean Dupuy (ed), *Mélanges en l'honneur de Nicolas Valticos: Droit et Justice* (1999) 269

Janeen Carruthers, 'Substance and Procedure in the Conflict of Laws: A Continuing Debate in Relation to Damages' (2004) 53 *ICLQ* 691

Anthony Carty, 'The *Corfu Channel* Case—And the Missing Admiralty Orders' (2004) 2 *Law and Practice of International Courts and Tribunals* 1

Louis Cavaré, 'Quelques remarques sur les recours en inteprétation des arrêts rendus par les Cours de justice internationales à propos de l'arrêt No 5–55 du 28 juin 1955 de la Cour de justice de la CECA' in *Hommage d'une génération de juristes au Président Basdevant* (1960) 96

Louis Cavaré, 'Les recours en interprétation et en appréciation de la légalité devant les tribunaux internationaux' (1953–4) 15 *ZaöRV* 482

Antonio Cassese, *International Law* (2nd ed, 2005)

Antonio Cassese, Paola Gaeta and John D W D Jones (eds), *The Rome Statute of the International Criminal Court* (2002)

Jonathan Charney, 'The Impact on the International Legal System of the Growth of International Courts and Tribunals' (1999) 31 *New York University Journal of International Law and Politics* 697

Jonathan Charney, 'Is International Law Threatened by Multiple International Tribunals?' (1998) 271 *Recueil des cours* 101

Jonathan Charney, 'Third Party Dispute Settlement and International Law' (1997) 36 *Columbia Journal of Transnational Law* 65

Jonathan Charney, Richard Bilder, Bernard Oxman and Patricia Wald, 'The Horizontal Growth of International Courts and Tribunals: Challenges or Opportunities?' [2002] *Proceedings of the 96th Annual Meeting of the American Society of International Law* 369

Bin Cheng, *General Principles of Law as Applied by International Courts and Tribunals* (first published 1953, 1987 ed)

Christine Chinkin, *Third Parties in International Law* (1993)

Christine Chinkin, 'Third Party Intervention before the International Court of Justice' (1986) 80 *AJIL* 495

Christine Chinkin and Ruth Mackenzie, 'Intergovernmental Organisations as Friends of the Court', in Laurence Boisson de Chazournes, Cesare Romano and Ruth Mackenzie (eds), *International Organisations and International Dispute Settlement* (2002) 135

Robin Churchill, 'Dispute Settlement in the Law of the Sea—The Context of the International Tribunal for the Law of the Sea and Alternatives to it' in Malcolm Evans (ed), *Remedies in International Law* (1998) 85

Robin Churchill and Urfan Khaliq, 'The Collective Complaints System of the European Social Charter: An Effective Mechanism for Ensuring Compliance with Economic and Social Rights?' (2004) 15 *European Journal of International Law* 417

Robin Churchill and Vaughan Lowe, *The Law of the Sea* (3rd ed, 1999)

Robin Churchill and Joanne Scott, 'The *MOX Plant* Litigation: The First Half-Life' (2004) 53 *ICLQ* 643

Dan Ciobanu, 'Litispendence between the International Court of Justice and the Political Organs of the UN' in Leo Gross (ed), *The Future of the International Court of Justice* (1976) 209

Civil Procedure: The White Book Service (2002)

André Cocâtre-Zilgien, 'Les mesures conservatoires décidées par le juge ou par l'arbitre international' (1966) 70 *Revue Générale de Droit International Public* 5

John Collier, *Conflict of Laws* (3rd ed, 2001)

John Collier and Vaughan Lowe, *The Settlement of Disputes in International Law: Institutions and Procedures* (1999)

Lawrence Collins (ed), *Dicey & Morris: The Conflict of Laws* (13th ed, 2000)

Lawrence Collins, *Essays in International Litigation and the Conflict of Laws* (1994)

Lawrence Collins, 'Provisional and Protective Measures in International Litigation' (1992) 234 *Recueil des cours* 9

Jean Combacau, 'Le Droit International: Bric-à-Brac ou Système?' (1986) 31 *Archives de Philosophie du Droit* 85

L Condorelli, 'La Cour Internationale de Justice: 50 ans et (pour l'heure) pas une ride' (1995) 6 *European Journal of International Law* 388

Sydney Cone, 'The Asbestos Case and Dispute Settlement in the World Trade Organisation: The Uneasy Relationship between Panels and the Appellate Body' (2001) 23 *Michigan Journal of International Law* 103

Conférence internationale de la paix, 4e partie, 3e commission, 5e séance, (1899)

A Corsi, 'Projet de règlement pour les arbitrages internationaux' (1896) 3 *Revue Générale de Droit International Public* 460

Jean-Pierre Cot, 'Le monde de la justice internationale' in Société Française pour le Droit International, *Colloque de Lille: La juridictionnalisation du droit international* (2003) 511

Thomas Cottier, 'The WTO Dispute Settlement System: New Horizons' [1998] *Proceedings of the American Society of International Law* 86

Vincent Coussirat-Coustère, 'L'arrêt de la Cour sur le personnel diplomatique et consulaire américain à Téhéran' (1980) 26 *Annuaire Français de Droit International* 201

Vincent Coussirat-Coustère and Pierre-Michel Eisemann, 'La procédure devant les juridictions internationales permanentes' in Société Française pour le Droit International, *La juridiction internationale permanente* (1986) 103

Mireille Couston, 'La Multiplication des Juridictions Internationales: Sens et Dynamiques' (2002) 129 *Journal du Droit International* 5

Philippe Couvreur, 'L'organisation et les moyens des juridictions internationales face au contentieux international' in Société Française pour le Droit International, *Colloque de Lille: La juridictionnalisation du droit international* (2003) 467

James Crawford, *The International Law Commission's Articles on State Responsibility* (2002)

James Crawford, 'International Law as an Open System' in James Crawford, *International Law as an Open System* (2002) 17

James Crawford, 'Third Report on State Responsibility', UN Doc A/CN.4/507 (15 March 2000)

James Crawford, 'Third Report on State Responsibility: Addendum' UN Doc A/CN.4/507/Add.1 (15 June 2000)

James Crawford, 'Third Report on State Responsibility: Addendum' UN Doc A/CN.4/507/Add.2 (10 July 2000)

James Crawford, 'Third Report on State Responsibility: Addendum' UN Doc A/CN.4/507/Add.4 (4 August 2000)

James Crawford, Pierre Bodeau and Jacqueline Peel, 'The ILC's Draft Articles on State Responsibility: Toward Completion of a Second Reading' (2000) 94 *AJIL* 660

James Crawford and Simon Olleson, 'The Nature and Forms of International Responsibility' in Malcolm Evans (ed), *International Law* (2003) 445

Gennady Danilenko, 'The Economic Court of the Commonwealth of Independent States' (1999) 31 *New York University Journal of International Law and Politics* 893

W Evans Darby, *International Tribunals: A Collection of the Various Schemes Which Have Been Propounded; and of Instances Since 1815* (1900)

Scott Davidson, *The Inter-American Court of Human Rights* (1992)

Martin Davies, Sam Ricketson and Geoffrey Lindell, *Conflict of Laws: Commentary and Materials* (1997)

Emmanuel Decaux, 'Responsabilité et Réparation' in Société Française pour le Droit International, *Colloque du Mans: La Responsabilité dans le Système International* (1990) 147

Fernand Dehousse, 'L'Affaire des Eaux de la Meuse' (1937) 19 *Revue de Droit International* 177

Georges Delaume, 'ICSID Tribunals and Provisional Measures—A Review of the Cases' (1986) *ICSID Review—FILJ* 393

Georges Delaume, 'ICSID Arbitration Proceedings: Practical Aspects' (1985) 5 *Pace Law Review* 563

Gilbert Demez, 'La Cour de Justice Benelux' (1976) 12 *Cahiers de Droit Européen* 149

Yves Derains and Eric Schwartz, *A Guide to the New ICC Rules of Arbitration* (1998)

Baron Descamps, 'Report to the Conference from the Third Commission on Pacific Settlement of International Disputes' in James Brown Scott (ed), *The Reports to the Hague Conferences of 1899 and 1907* (1917) 42

P van Dijk and G H J van Hoof, *Theory and Practice of the European Convention on Human Rights* (2nd ed, 1990)

M S Dockray, 'The Inherent Jurisdiction to Regulate Civil Proceedings' (1997) 113 *LQR* 120

Christian Dominicé, 'La Réparation Non Contentieuse' in Société Française pour le Droit International, *Colloque du Mans: La Responsabilité dans le Système International* (1990) 191

Zachary Douglas, 'The Hybrid Foundations of Investment Treaty Arbitration' (2003) 74 *British Yearbook of International Law* 151

Michel Dubisson, *La Cour internationale de justice* (1964)

Anthony Dugdale, *Clerk & Lindsell on Torts* (18th ed, 2000)

E Dumbauld, *Interim Measures of Protection in International Controversies* (1932)

Pierre-Marie Dupuy, *Droit international public* (7e ed, 2004)

Pierre-Marie Dupuy, 'The Danger of Fragmentation or Unification of the International Legal System and the International Court of Justice' (1999) 31 *New York University Journal of International Law and Politics* 791

Alison Duxbury, 'Saving Lives in the International Court of Justice: The Use of Provisional Measures to Protect Human Rights' (2000) 31 *California Western International Law Journal* 141

Clyde Eagleton, *The Responsibility of States in International Law* (1928)

Werner Ebke and Matthew Finkin (eds), *Introduction to German Law* (1996)

Gudmundur Eiriksson, *The International Tribunal for the Law of the Sea* (2000)

Gudmundur Eiriksson, 'The Role of the International Tribunal for the Law of the Sea in the Peaceful Settlement of Disputes' (1997) 37 *Indian Journal of International Law* 347

Marc-André Eissen, 'Les mesures provisoires dans la Convention Européenne des Droits de l'Homme' (1969) 2 *Revue des Droits de l'Homme* 252

Marc-André Eissen, 'La Convention Européenne des Droits de L'Homme et les Mesures Conservatoires' (1967) 71 *Revue Générale de Droit International Public* 558

Jerome Elkind, *Non-Appearance before the International Court of Justice* (1983)

Jerome Elkind, *Interim Protection: A Functional Approach* (1981)

Jerome Elkind, 'The *Aegean Sea* Case and Article 41 of the Statute of the International Court of Justice' (1979) 32 *Revue hellénique du droit international* 285

Anne-Katrin Escher, 'Release of Vessels and Crews before the International Tribunal for the Law of the Sea (Parts 1 and 2)' (2004) 3 *Law and Practice of International Courts and Tribunals* 205

Anne-Katrin Escher, 'Release of Vessels and Crews before the International Tribunal for the Law of the Sea (Part 3)' (2004) 3 *Law and Practice of International Courts and Tribunals* 411

Malcolm Evans (ed), *International Law* (2003)

Malcolm Evans, 'The *Southern Bluefin Tuna* Dispute: Provisional Thinking on Provisional Measures?' (1999) 10 *Yearbook of International Environmental Law* 7

Malcolm Evans (ed), *Remedies in International Law: The Institutional Dilemma* (1998)

Jens Evensen, 'Evidence before International Courts' (1955) 25 *Nordisk Tidskrift for International Ret* 44

Alexander Fachiri, *The Permanent Court of International Justice* (1932)

A H Feller, *The Mexican Claims Commissions: 1923–34* (1935)

Andreas Fischer-Lescano and Guenther Teubner, 'Regime-Collisions: The Vain Search for Legal Unity in the Fragmentation of Global Law' (2004) 25 *Michigan Journal of International Law* 999

Owen Fiss, 'Against Settlement' (1983–4) 93 *Yale Law Journal* 1073

Sir Gerald Fitzmaurice, *The Law and Procedure of the International Court of Justice* (1986)

Sir Gerald Fitzmaurice, 'Hersch Lauterpacht and His Attitude to the Judicial Function' (1979) 50 *British Yearbook of International Law* 1

Sir Gerald Fitzmaurice, 'Hersch Lauterpacht—The Scholar as Judge: I' (1961) 37 *British Yearbook of International Law* 1

Sir Gerald Fitzmaurice, 'The Law and Procedure of the International Court of Justice, 1951–4' (1958) 34 *British Yearbook of International Law* 1

Malgosia Fitzmaurice and Catherine Redgwell, 'Environmental Non-Compliance Procedures and International Law' (2000) 31 *Netherlands Yearbook of International Law* 35

John Fleming, *The Law of Torts* (9th ed, 1998)

Caroline Foster, *The Adjudication of International Disputes Involving Scientific Uncertainty* (PhD dissertation, University of Cambridge, 2003)

Caroline Foster, 'The "Real Dispute" in the *Southern Bluefin Tuna* Case: A Scientific Dispute?' (2001) 16 *International Journal of Marine and Coastal Law* 571

Nigel Foster and Satish Sute, *German Legal Systems and Laws* (3rd ed, 2002)

Thomas Franck, 'Legitimacy in the International System' (1988) 82 *AJIL* 705

Thomas Franck, 'Icy Day at the ICJ' (1985) 79 *AJIL* 379

Felix Frankfurter and James Landis, 'Power of Congress over Procedure in Criminal Contempts in "Inferior" Federal Courts: A Study in Separation of Powers' (1924) 37 *Harvard Law Review* 1010

M D A Freeman, *Lloyd's Introduction to Jurisprudence* (7th ed, 2001)

David Freestone, 'Caution or Precaution: "A Rose By Any Other Name..."?' (1999) 10 *Yearbook of International Environmental Law* 25

Duncan French, 'Treaty Interpretation and the Incorporation of Extraneous Legal Rules' (2006) 55 *ICLQ* 281

Paul Friedland, 'Provisional Measures and ICSID Arbitration' (1986) 2 *Arbitration International* 335

Jochen Frowein, 'Fact-Finding by the European Commission of Human Rights' in Richard Lillich (ed), *Fact-Finding by International Tribunals* (1992) 237

Jochen Frowein und Wolfgang Peukert, *Europäische Menschenrechtskonvention-Kommentar* (1996)

Hisakazu Fujita, 'Chevauchements juridictionnels et tribunaux internationaux' in Nisuke Ando, Edward McWhinney and Rüdiger Wolfrum (eds), *Liber Amicorum Judge Shigeru Oda* (2002) 575

Louis Le Fur and Georges Chklaver, *Recueil de textes de Droit International Public* (1928)

Paola Gaeta, 'Inherent Powers of International Courts and Tribunals' in Lal Chand Vohrar *et al* (eds), *Man's Inhumanity to Man: Essays on International Law in Honour of Antonio Cassese* (2003) 353

Paola Gaeta, *La Giustizia Cautelare nel Diritto Internazionale* (2000)

Giorgio Gaja, 'Relationship of the ICJ with Other International Courts and Tribunals', in Andreas Zimmermann, Christian Tomuschat and Karin Oellers-Frahm (eds), *The Statute of the International Court of Justice: A Commentary* (2006) 532

GATT, *Guide to GATT Law and Practice* (6th ed, 1994)

GATT, Understanding Regarding Notification, Consultation, Dispute Settlement and Surveillance (28 November 1979), Annex, GATT BISD (26th Supp), 210 (1980)

Robin Geiss, 'Revision Proceedings before the International Court of Justice' (2003) 63 *ZaöRV* 167

Ruth Bader Ginsburg and Anders Bruzelius, *Civil Procedure in Sweden* (1965)

Claude Giverdon, 'The Problem of Proof in French Civil Law' (1956) 31 *Tulane Law Review* 29

Peter Goldsworthy, 'Interim Measures of Protection in the International Court of Justice' (1974) 68 *AJIL* 258

L Goldschmidt, 'Examen des Conclusions de la 2e Commission (Projet de Règlement pour la procédure arbitrale internationale' (1877) 1 *Annuaire de l'Institut de Droit International* 84

L Goldschmidt, 'Projet de règlement pour tribunaux arbitraux internationaux, présenté à l'Institut de Droit International (Session de Genève, 1874)' (1874) 6 *Revue de Droit International et de Législation Comparée* 421

Edward Gordon, 'The World Court and the Interpretation of Constitutive Treaties' (1965) 59 *AJIL* 794

John Gotanda, 'Compound Interest in International Disputes' (2004) *Villanova University School of Law Working Paper Series*, Working Paper 14

Patricio Grané, 'Remedies under WTO Law' (2001) 4 *Journal of International Economic Law* 755

Christine Gray, 'The Eritrea/Ethiopia Claims Commission Oversteps its Boundaries: A Partial Award?' (2006) 17 *European Journal of International Law* 699

Christine Gray, 'Types of Remedies in ICJ cases: Lessons for the WTO?' in Friedl Weiss (ed), *Improving WTO Dispute Settlement Procedures* (2000) 401

Christine Gray, 'The Choice between Restitution and Compensation' (1999) 10 *European Journal of International Law* 413

Christine Gray, '*Passage through the Great Belt (Finland v Denmark)* Provisional Measures, Order of 29 July 1991' (1993) 42 *ICLQ* 705

Christine Gray, *Judicial Remedies in International Law* (1987)

Christine Gray, 'Is there an International Law of Remedies?' (1985) 56 *British Yearbook of International Law* 25

Christine Gray, 'Remedies for Individuals under the European Convention on Human Rights' (1981) *Human Rights Review* 153

Christine Gray, 'Interim Measures of Protection in the European Court' (1979) 4 *ELR* 80

Christine Gray and Benedict Kingsbury, 'Developments in Dispute Settlement: Inter-state Arbitration Since 1945'(1992) 63 *British Yearbook of International Law* 97

Don Greig, 'The Balancing of Interests and the Granting of Interim Protection by the International Court' (1991) 11 *Australian Yearbook of International Law* 108

Forest Grieves, *Supranationalism and International Adjudication* (1969)

Leo Gross, 'Some Observations on Provisional Measures' in Yoram Dinstein (ed), *International Law at a Time of Perplexity: Essays in Honour of Shabtai Rosenne* (1989) 307

Hugo Grotius, *On the Law of War and Peace* (first published 1625, 1964 ed, Francis Kelsey trans)

Fabricio Guariglia, 'The Rules of Procedure and Evidence for the New International Criminal Court' in Antonio Cassese, Paola Gaeta and John DWD Jones (eds), *The Rome Statute of the International Criminal Court* (2002) vol II, 1111

Paul Guggenheim, 'Les mesures conservatoires dans la procédure arbitrale et judiciaire' (1932) 40 *Recueil des cours* 645

Gilbert Guillaume, 'Advantages and Risks of Proliferation: A Blueprint for Action' (2004) 2 *Journal of International Criminal Justice* 300

Gilbert Guillaume, 'The Current Situation of the International Court of Justice and its Future' (Address to the Lauterpacht Research Centre for International Law, University of Cambridge, 9 November 2001), available at <http://www.lcil.cam.ac.uk/lectures/lecture_papers.php>

Gilbert Guillaume, 'Speech to the General Assembly of the United Nations' (30 October 2001), available at <http://www.icj-cij.org> under 'Statements of the President of the Court'

Gilbert Guillaume, 'Speech to the Sixth Committee of the General Assembly of the United Nations' (31 Ocotober 2001), available at <http://www.icj-cij.org> under 'Statements of the President of the Court'

Gilbert Guillaume, 'The Proliferation of International Judicial Bodies—The Outlook for the International Legal Order: Speech to the Sixth Committee of the General Assembly' (27 October 2000), available at <http://www.icj-cij.org>

Gilbert Guillaume, 'Statement of the President of the Court to the UN General Assembly' (26 October 2000), available at <http://www.icj-cij.org> under 'Statements of the President of the Court'

Gilbert Guillaume, 'The Future of International Judicial Institutions' (1995) 44 *ICLQ* 848

Serge Guinchard *et al*, *Droit processuel: Droit Commun et droit comparé du procès* (2e edn, 2003)

Geneviève Guyomar, *Commentaire du règlement de la Cour internationale de justice* (1983)

Lakshman Guruswamy, 'Should UNCLOS or GATT/WTO Decide Trade and Environment Disputes? (1998) 7 *Minnesota Journal of Global Trade* 287

Suzan Haasdijk, 'The Lack of Uniformity in the Terminology of the International Law of Remedies' (1992) 5 *Leiden Journal of International Law* 245

Gerhard Hafner, 'Pros and Cons Ensuing from Fragmentation of International Law' (2004) 25 *Michigan Journal of International Law* 849

Gerhard Hafner, 'Risks Ensuing from the Fragmentation of International Law', *Official Records of the General Assembly, Fifty-fifth Session*, Supplement No 10, 321 (UN Doc A/55/10)

Gerhard Hafner, 'Should One Fear the Proliferation of Mechanisms for the Peaceful Settlement of Disputes?' in Lucius Caflisch (ed), *The Peaceful Settlement of Disputes Between States: Universal and European Perspectives* (1998) 25

Edvard Hambro, 'The Binding Character of the Provisional Measures of Protection Indicated by the International Court of Justice' in Walter Schätzel and Hans-Jürgen Schlochauer (eds), *Rechtsfragen der Internationalen Organisation—Festschrift für Hans Wehberg zu seinem 70. Geburtstag* (1956) 152

P Hamilton, H C Requena, L van Scheltinga and B Schifman (eds), *The Permanent Court of Arbitration: International Arbitration and Dispute Resolution* (1999)

Åke Hammerskjöld, 'Quelques aspects de la question des mesures conservatoires en droit international positif' (1935) 5 *ZaöRV* 5

Learned Hand, 'Historical and Practical Considerations Regarding Expert Testimony' (1901) 15 *Harvard Law Review* 40

Bernard Hanotiau, 'Satisfying the Burden of Proof: The Viewpoint of a "Civil Law" Lawyer' (1994) 10 *Arbitration International* 341

Elihu Harnon, '*Res Judicata* and Identity of Actions: Law and Rationale' (1966) 1 *Israel Law Review* 539

D J Harris, *Cases and Materials on International Law* (6th ed, 2004)

D J Harris, M O'Boyle, C Warbrick, *Law of the European Convention on Human Rights* (1995)

H L A Hart, *The Concept of Law* (2nd ed, 1994)

H L A Hart, *Essays in Jurisprudence and Philosophy* (1983)

Trevor Hartley, 'Comity and the Use of Antisuit Injunctions in International Litigation' (1987) 35 *American Journal of Comparative Law* 487

'Harvard Research Draft Convention on Judicial Assistance' (1939) *AJIL* Supplement 15

Peter Hay, Russell Weintraub and Patrick Borchers, *Conflict of Laws: Cases and Materials* (11th ed, 2000)

Moritaka Hayashi, 'The *Southern Bluefin Tuna* Cases: Prescription of Provisional Measures by the International Tribunal for the Law of the Sea' (2000) 13 *Tulane Environmental Law Journal* 361

W P Heere (ed), *International Law and the Hague's 750th Anniversary* (1999)

Laurence Helfer, 'Forum Shopping for Human Rights' (1999) 148 *University of Pennsylvania Law Review* 285

Debra Herz, 'Effects of International Arbitral Tribunals in National Courts' (1995–6) 28 *New York University Journal of International Law and Politics* 217

Peter Herzog and Delmar Karlen, 'Attacks on Judicial Decisions', in International Association of Legal Science, *International Encyclopedia of Comparative Law* (1982) vol XVI, ch 8

Rosalyn Higgins, 'A Babel of Judicial Voices? Ruminations from the Bench' (2006) 55 *ICLQ* 791

Rosalyn Higgins, 'The ICJ, the ECJ and the Integrity of International Law' (2003) 52 *ICLQ* 1

Rosalyn Higgins, 'Respecting Sovereign States and Running a Tight Courtroom' (2001) 50 *ICLQ* 121

Rosalyn Higgins, 'Remedies and the International Court of Justice: An Introduction' in Malcolm Evans (ed), *Remedies in International Law: The Institutional Dilemma* (1998) 1

Rosalyn Higgins, 'Interim Measures for the Protection of Human Rights' (1997) 36 *Columbia Journal of Transnational Law* 91

Rosalyn Higgins, *Problems & Process: International Law and How We Use It* (1994)

Rosalyn Higgins, 'The International Court and South West Africa' (1966) 42 *International Affairs* 573

Keith Highet, 'Evidence, the Chamber, and the *ELSI* Case' in Richard Lillich (ed), *Fact-Finding by International Tribunals* (1992) 33

Keith Highet, 'Evidence, the Court, and the Nicaragua Case' (1987) 81 *AJIL* 1

Keith Highet, 'Evidence and Proof of Facts' in Lori Damrosch (ed), *The International Court of Justice at a Crossroads* (1987) 355

Jonathan Hill, *International Commercial Disputes* (2nd ed, 1998)

Norman Hill, 'The Interpretation of the Decisions of International Courts' (1934) 22 *Georgetown Law Journal* 535

Deborah Horowitz, 'The Catch of Poseidon's Trident: The Fate of High Seas Fisheries in the *Southern Bluefin Tuna* Case' (2001) 25 *Melbourne University Law Review* 810

Jacomijn van Hof, *Commentary on the UNCITRAL Arbitration Rules* (1991)

M Howard, *Phipson on Evidence* (15th ed, 2000)

Robert Howse, 'Membership and its Privileges: The WTO, Civil Society, and the *Amicus* Brief Controversy' (2003) 9 *ELJ* 496

Robert Hudec, 'Broadening the Scope of Remedies in the WTO Dispute Settlement System' in Friedl Weiss (ed), *Improving WTO Dispute Settlement Procedures* (2000) 369

Robert Hudec, *Enforcing International Trade Law: The Evolution of the Modern GATT Legal System* (1993)

Manley Hudson, *International Tribunals: Past and Future* (1944)

Manley Hudson, *The Permanent Court of International Justice 1920–1942* (1943)

Manley Hudson, 'Visit by International Tribunals to Places Concerned in Proceedings' (1937) 31 *AJIL* 696

Manley Hudson, *The Permanent Court of International Justice: A Treatise* (1934)

ICJ, 'The International Court of Justice Revises its Working Methods to Expedite the Examination of Contested Cases' (Press Communiqué 2001/1, 12 January 2001)

ICJ, 'The International Court of Justice Revises its Working Methods to Expedite the Examination of Contested Cases' (Press Communiqué 1998/14, 6 April 1998)

ICJ, 'Response of the International Court of Justice to GA Resolution 52/161 of 15 December 1997' (1998) 37 ILM 1466

Institut de Droit International, 'Projet de règlement pour la procédure arbitrale internationale' (1877) 1 *Annuaire de l'Institut de Droit International* 126

Institut de Droit International, 'Procès-verbal de la session de Genève: Procès-verbal No 1: Séance du 31 août 1874' (1874) 6 *Revue de Droit International et de Législation Comparée* 583

International Law Association, 'Interim Report: "Res Judicata" and Arbitration', in International Law Association, *Report of the Seventy-First Conference: Berlin* (2004) 826, available at <http://www.ila-hq.org> (last visited 31 January 2007)

International Law Association, *Report of the Seventy-First Conference: Berlin* (2004)

International Law Association, *Report of the Committee on the Formation of Customary (General) International Law* (London Conference, 2000)

ILC, 'Fragmentation of International Law: Difficulties arising from the Diversification and Expansion of International Law', in ILC, *Report of the International Law Commission: Fifty-eighth Session (1 May–9 June and 3 July–11 August 2006)*, UNGAOR Sixty-first Session, Supplement No 10 (UN Doc A/61/10), available from <http://www.un.org>

ILC, 'Report of the Study Group on Fragmentation of International Law: Difficulties arising from the Diversification and Expansion of International Law', UN Doc A/CN.4/L.682 (4 April 2006)

ILC, 'Report of the Study Group on Fragmentation of International Law: Difficulties arising from the Diversification and Expansion of International Law', UN Doc A/CN.4/L.676 (29 July 2005)

ILC Articles on State Responsibility, in James Crawford, *The International Law Commission's Articles on State Responsibility* (2002)

ILC, 'Report of the International Law Commission on the Work of its Forty-fifth Session (3 May–23 July 1993)' [1993] *Yearbook of the International Law Commission*, vol II, pt II, 1 UN Doc A/48/10

ILC, 'Report of the Commission on the Work of its Eighteenth Session' [1966] *Yearbook of the ILC*, vol II, 172

ILC, 'Report of the Commission to the General Assembly on the Work of its Tenth Session' [1958] *Yearbook of the International Law Commission*, vol II, 78, UN Doc A/3859

ILC, 'Memorandum Prepared by the Secretariat' [1950] *Yearbook of the International Law Commission*, vol II, 157, UN Doc A/CN.4/35

Yuji Iwasawa, 'WTO Dispute Settlement as Judicial Supervision' (2002) 5 *Journal of International Economic Law* 287

John Jackson, 'The Varied Policies of International Juridical Bodies—Reflections on Theory and Practice' (2004) 25 *Michigan Journal of International Law* 869

John Jackson, 'Fragmentation or Unification Among International Institutions: The World Trade Organisation' (1999) 31 *New York University Journal of International Law and Politics* 823

John Jackson, *The World Trading System* (2nd ed, 1997)

I H Jacob, 'The Inherent Jurisdiction of the Court' (1970) 23 *CLP* 23

Francis Jacobs, 'Interim Measures in the Law and Practice of the Court of Justice of the European Communities', in Rudolf Bernhardt (ed), *Interim Measures Indicated by International Courts* (1994) 37

Mark Janis (ed), *International Courts for the Twenty-First Century* (1992)

Mark Janis, 'The Law of the Sea Tribunal', in Mark Janis (ed), *International Courts for the Twenty-First Century* (1992) 245

C Wilfred Jenks, *The Prospects of International Adjudication* (1964)

Sir Robert Jennings, 'The *LaGrand* Case' (2002) 1 *Law and Practice of International Courts and Tribunals* 13

Sir Robert Jennings, *Collected Writings of Sir Robert Jennings* (1998) 2 vols

Sir Robert Jennings, 'The Role of the International Court of Justice' (1997) 68 *British Yearbook of International Law* 1

Sir Robert Jennings, 'The Judiciary, International and National, and the Development of International Law' (1996) 45 *ICLQ* 5

Sir Robert Jennings, 'The International Court of Justice after Fifty Years' (1995) 89 *AJIL* 493

Sir Robert Jennings, 'The Proliferation of Adjudicatory Bodies: Dangers and Possible Answers', in Laurence Boisson de Chazournes (ed), *Implications of the Proliferation of International Adjudicatory Bodies for Dispute Resolution* (1995)

Sir Robert Jennings and Sir Arthur Watts (eds), *Oppenheim's International Law* (9th ed, 1992)

Philip Jessup, 'Foreword' in Durward Sandifer, *Evidence before International Tribunals* (rev ed, 1975) vii

Philip Jessup, 'The Palmas Island Arbitration' (1928) 22 *AJIL* 735
Marcelle Jokl, 'Aperçu sur l'Arrêt de la CPJI du 28 juin 1937' (1937) XLIV *Revue Générale de Droit International Public* 552
J A Jolowicz, *On Civil Procedure* (2000)
J A Jolowicz, 'Practice Directions and the Civil Procedure Rules' (2000) 59 *CLJ* 53
Nina Jørgensen, 'A Reappraisal of Punitive Damages in International Law' (1997) 68 *British Yearbook of International Law* 247
Leonid Kamarowskii, *Le Tribunal International* (1887)
Jörg Kammerhofer, 'The Binding Nature of Provisional Measures of the International Court of Justice: The "Settlement" of the Issue in the *LaGrand* Case' (2003) 16 *Leiden Journal of International Law* 67
P J G Kapteyn, 'Regional Courts' in W P Heere (ed), *International Law and the Hague's 750th Anniversary* (1999) 427
Syméon Karagiannis, 'La multiplication des juridictions internationales: un système anarchique?' in Société Française pour le Droit International, *Colloque de Lille: La juridictionnalisation du droit international* (2003) 7
Mojtaba Kazazi, *Burden of Proof and Related Issues: A Study on Evidence before International Tribunals* (1996)
Mojtaba Kazazi and Bette Shifman, 'Evidence before International Tribunals: Introduction' (1999) 1 *International Law FORUM du Droit International* 193
Hans Kelsen, *Introduction to the Problems of Legal Theory* (first published 1934, 1992 ed)
Hans Kelsen, *The Law of the United Nations* (1950)
Michel van de Kerchove and François Ost, *Legal System between Order and Disorder* (1994)
Benedict Kingsbury, Nico Krisch, and Richard Stewart, 'The Emergence of Global Administrative Law' (2005) 68 *Law and Contemporary Problems* 15
Benedict Kingsbury, 'Foreword: Is the Proliferation of International Courts and Tribunals a Problem?' (1999) 31 *New York University Journal of International Law and Politics* 679
Jan Klabbers, *An Introduction to International Institutional Law* (2001)
Charles H Koch, 'Judicial Dialogue for Legal Multiculturalism' (2004) 25 *Michigan Journal of International Law* 879
Robert Kolb, 'General Principles of Procedural Law', in Andreas Zimmermann, Christian Tomuschat and Karin Oellers-Frahm (eds), *The Statute of the International Court of Justice: A Commentary* (2006) 793
Robert Kolb, *La bonne foi en droit international public* (2000)
Abdul Koroma, 'The Interpretation of International Law' in *Contemporary International Law Issues: Proceedings of the Third ASIL/NVIR Joint Conference* (1996)
Martii Koskenniemi, 'Breach of Treaty or Non-Compliance? Reflections on the Enforcement of the Montreal Protocol' (1992) 3 *Yearbook of International Environmental Law* 123
Martii Koskenniemi, 'L'affaire du passage par le Grand-Belt' (1992) 38 *Annuaire Français de Droit International* 905
Martti Koskenniemi and Paivi Leino, 'Fragmentation of International Law? Postmodern Anxieties' (2002) 15 *Leiden Journal of International Law* 553
Johnnie Kovacevich, 'The Inherent Power of the District Court' [1989] *New Zealand Law Journal* 184
Peter Kovacs, 'Développement et limites de la jurisprudence en droit international' in Société Française pour le Droit International, *Colloque de Lille: La juridictionnalisation du droit international* (2003) 269

Hans Christian Krüger, 'The European Commission of Human Rights' (1980) 1 *Human Rights Law Journal* 66

Martin Kuijer, 'Voting Behaviour and National Bias in the European Court of Human Rights and the International Court of Justice' (1997) 10 *Leiden Journal of International Law* 49

Barbara Kwiatkowska, 'Case Report: *Southern Bluefin Tuna*' (2001) 95 *AJIL* 162

Barbara Kwiatkowska, 'The *Australian and New Zealand v Japan Southern Bluefin Tuna (Jurisdiction and Admissibility)* Award of the First Law of the Sea Convention Annex VII Arbitral Tribunal' (2001) 16 *International Journal of Marine and Coastal Law* 239

Barbara Kwiatkowska, 'The *Southern Bluefin Tuna* (New Zealand v Japan; Australia v Japan) Cases' (2000) 15 *International Journal of Marine and Coastal Law* 1

Barbara Kwiatkowska, 'The Future of the Law of the Sea Tribunal in Hamburg', in W P Heere (ed), *International Law and the Hague's 750th Anniversary* (1999) 417

Henri La Fontaine, *Pasicrisie Internationale 1794–1900: Histoire Documentaire des Arbitrages Internationaux* (1997)

Celso Lafer, *The World Trade Organisation Dispute Settlement System* (1996)

Jean-Flavien Lalive, 'Quelques remarques sur la preuve devant la Cour Permanente et la Cour international de Justice' (1950) 7 *Annuaire Suisse de Droit International* 77

Pierre Lalive, 'The First World Bank Arbitration (*Holiday Inns v Morocco*): Some Legal Problems' (1980) 51 *British Yearbook of International Law* 123

Heinrich Lammasch, *Die Rechtskraft internationaler Schiedsprüche* (1913)

K Lasok, *The European Court of Justice: Practice and Procedure* (2nd ed, 1994)

Sir Elihu Lauterpacht, ' "Partial" Judgments and the Inherent Jurisdiction of the International Court of Justice' in Vaughan Lowe and Malgosia Fitzmaurice (eds), *Fifty Years of the International Court of Justice* (1996) 465

Sir Elihu Lauterpacht, *Aspects of the Administration of International Justice* (1991)

Sir Elihu Lauterpacht, 'Oral Argument by Mr Lauterpacht, QC, on 8 May 1974, in *BP Exploration Company (Libya) Limited v Libya*' in J G Wetter, *The International Arbitral Process: Public and Private* (1979) vol II, 587

Sir Elihu Lauterpacht, 'The Development of the Law of International Organisations by the Decisions of International Tribunals' (1976) 152 *Recueil des cours* 377

Sir Hersch Lauterpacht, 'The Revision of the Statute of the International Court of Justice' (2002) 1 *Law and Practice of International Courts and Tribunals* 55

Sir Hersch Lauterpacht, *The Development of International Law by the International Court* (1958)

Sir Hersch Lauterpacht, 'Restrictive Interpretation and the Principle of Effectiveness in the Interpretation of Treaties' (1949) 26 *British Yearbook of International Law* 48

Sir Hersch Lauterpacht, 'The Legal Aspect' in C A W Manning (ed), *Peaceful Change: An International Problem* (1937) 135

Sir Hersch Lauterpacht, *The Development of International Law by the Permanent Court of International Justice* (1934)

Sir Hersch Lauterpacht, *The Function of Law in the International Community* (1933)

Sir Hersch Lauterpacht, 'The So-Called Anglo-American and Continental Schools of Thought in International Law' (1931) 12 *British Yearbook of International Law* 31

Sir Hersch Lauterpacht, *Private Law Sources and Analogies of International Law* (1927)

Markus Lenenbach, 'Antisuit Injunctions in England, Germany and the United States: Their Treatment Under European Civil Procedure and the Hague Convention' (1998) 20 *Loyola of Los Angeles International and Comparative Law Journal* 257

Richard Lillich (ed), *The United Nations Compensation Commission* (1995)
Richard Lillich (ed), *Fact-Finding Before International Tribunals* (1992)
Richard Lillich and D McGraw (eds), *The Iran–United States Claims Tribunal: Its Contribution to the Law of State Responsibility* (1998)
Per Henrik Lindblom, 'On the Distinction between Procedural and Substantive Law' (1974) 18 *Scandinavian Studies in Law* 109
Vaughan Lowe, 'The International Tribunal for the Law of the Sea: Survey for 2000' (2001) 16 *International Journal of Marine and Coastal Law* 549
Vaughan Lowe, 'Overlapping Jurisdiction in International Tribunals' (1999) 20 *Australian Yearbook of International Law* 191
Vaughan Lowe, '*The M/V 'Saiga'*: The First Case in the International Tribunal for the Law of the Sea' (1999) 48 *ICLQ* 187
Vaughan Lowe, '*Res Judicata* and the Rule of Law in International Arbitration' (1996) 8 *African Journal of International and Comparative Law* 38
Andreas Lowenfeld, *International Economic Law* (2002)
Andreas Lowenfeld, 'Remedies along with Rights: Institutional Reform in the New GATT' (1994) 88 *AJIL* 477
Peter MacAlister-Smith, 'Comity' in Rudolf Bernhardt (ed), *Encyclopedia of Public International Law* (1992) vol I, 671
Sir Henry Maine, *Dissertations on Early Law and Custom* (1883)
Peter Malanczuk, *Akehurst's Modern Introduction to International Law* (7th rev ed, 1997)
V S Mani, *International Adjudication: Procedural Aspects* (1980)
V S Mani, 'Interim Measures of Protection: Article 94 of the UN Charter' (1970) 10 *Indian Journal of International Law* 359
F A Mann, 'The Consequences of an International Wrong in International and National Law' (1976–7) 48 *British Yearbook of International Law* 1
Gabrielle Marceau, 'Conflicts of Norms and Conflicts of Jurisdictions: The Relationship between the WTO Agreement and MEAs and Other Treaties' (2001) 35 *Journal of World Trade* 1081
Gabrielle Marceau, 'A Call for Coherence in International Law' (1999) 33(5) *Journal of World Trade* 87
Gabrielle Marceau and Matthew Stilwell, 'Practical Suggestions for *Amicus Curiae* Briefs before WTO Adjudicating Bodies' (2001) 4 *Journal of International Economic Law* 155
G Marty, *La distinction du fait et du droit* (Toulouse, 1929)
Keith Mason, 'The Inherent Jurisdiction of the Court' (1983) 57 *Australian Law Journal* 449
A Masood, 'Provisional Measures of Protection in Arbitration under the World Bank Convention' (1972) 1 *Delhi Law Review* 138
Mitsuo Matsushita, Thomas Schoenbaum and Petros Mavroidis, *The World Trade Organisation: Law, Practice and Policy* (2nd ed, 2006)
Petros Mavroidis, 'Remedies in the WTO Legal System: Between a Rock and a Hard Place' (2000) 11 *European Journal of International Law* 763
R Macdonald, 'Interim Measures in International Law, with Special Reference to the European System for the Protection of Human Rights' (1992) 52 *ZaöRV* 703
Jacquelyn MacLennan, 'Evidence, Standard and Burden of Proof and the Use of Experts in Procedure before the Luxembourg Courts' in Friedl Weiss (ed), *Improving WTO Dispute Settlement Procedures* (2000) 265

Richard May, 'Evidence before the International Criminal Tribunal for the Former Yugoslavia: An Overview' (1999) 1 *International Law FORUM du Droit International* 197

Campbell McLachlan, 'The Principle of Systemic Integration and Article 31(3)(c) of the Vienna Convention' (2005) 54 *ICLQ* 279

Campbell McLachlan, 'Pinochet Revisited' (2002) 51 *ICLQ* 959

Sir Arnold McNair, *The Place of Law and Tribunals in International Relations* (1957)

Donald McRae, 'What is the Future of WTO Dispute Settlement?' (2004) 7 *Journal of International Economic Law* 3

Edward McWhinney, 'International Arbitration and International Adjudication: The Different Contemporary Lots of the Two Hague Tribunals' (1991) 29 *Canadian Yearbook of International Law* 403

Niall Meagher, 'The Sound of Silence: Giving Meaning to Omissions in Provisions of WTO Agreements' (2003) 37 *Journal of World Trade* 417

L Méchichi, 'Proliferation des juridictions internationales et unité de l'ordre juridique internationale', in Y Ben Achour and S Laghmani (eds), *Justice et Juridictions internationales* (2000) 77

Maurice Mendelson, 'Interim Measures of Protection in Cases of Contested Jurisdiction' (1972–3) 46 *British Yearbook of International Law* 259

Martin Mennecke and Christian Tams, '*LaGrand* Case (*Germany v United States of America*)' (2002) 51 *ICLQ* 449

Martin Mennecke and Christian Tams, 'The Right to Consular Assistance under International Law' (1999) 42 *German Yearbook of International Law* 192

Thomas Mensah, 'Provisional Measures in the International Tribunal for the Law of the Sea' (2002) 62 *ZaöRV* 43

A Mérignhac, *Traité théorique et pratique de l'arbitrage international* (1895)

John Merrills, 'The Contribution of the PCA to International Law and the Settlement of Disputes by Peaceful Means' in P Hamilton, H C Requena, L van Scheltinga and B Schifman (eds), *The Permanent Court of Arbitration: International Arbitration and Dispute Resolution* (1999)

John Merrills, 'Reflections on the Incidental Jurisdiction of the International Court of Justice' in Malcolm Evans (ed), *Remedies in International Law: The Institutional Dilemma* (1998) 51

John Merrills, *International Dispute Settlement* (3rd ed, 1998)

John Merrills, *Judge Sir Gerald Fitzmaurice and the Discipline of International Law* (1998)

John Merrills, 'Interim Measures of Protection in the Recent Jurisprudence of the International Court of Justice' (1995) 44 *ICLQ* 90

John Merrills, *The Development of International Law by the European Court of Human Rights* (2nd ed, 1993)

John Merrills, 'Interim Measures of Protection and the Substantive Jurisdiction of the International Court' (1977) 36 *CLJ* 86

Hans van Mierlo, 'The Future Development of Binding Dispute Settlement Mechanisms in International Law' in W P Heere (ed), *International Law and the Hague's 750th Anniversary* (1999) 445

Nathan Miller, 'An International Jurisprudence? The Operation of "Precedent" across International Tribunals' (2002) 15 *Leiden Journal of International Law* 483

Loukas Mistelis, 'Confidentiality and Third Party Participation' (2005) 21 *Arbitration International* 211

John Bassett Moore, *International Adjudications: Ancient and Modern—History and Documents* (1929) vol I

John Bassett Moore, *History and Digest of the International Arbitrations to which the United States has been a Party* (1898)

Herman Mosler, 'General Principles of Law' in Rudolf Bernhardt (ed), *Encyclopedia of Public International Law* (1995) vol II, 511

A S Muller, D Raic and J M Thuransky (eds), *The International Court of Justice: Its Future Role after Fifty Years* (1997)

Sean Murphy, 'Challenge of Iran–US Claims Tribunal Judge Bengt Broms' (2001) 95 *AJIL* 895

Kalypso Nicolaidis and Joyce Tong, 'Diversity or Cacophony? The Continuing Debate over New Sources of International Law' (2004) 25 *Michigan Journal of International Law* 1349

Hans Gerd Niemeyer, *Einstweilige Verfügungen des Weltgerichtshofs, ihr Wesen und ihre Grenzen* (1932)

Myron Nordquist (ed), *United Nations Convention on the Law of the Sea 1982: A Commentary* (1989)

Carl Aage Nørgaard and Hans Christian Krüger, 'Interim and Conservatory Measures under the European System of Protection of Human Rights' in Manfred Nowak, Dorothea Steuer and Hannes Tretter (eds), *Progress in the Spirit of Human Rights: Festschrift für Felix Ermacora* (1988) 109

Sir Peter North and J J Fawcett, *Cheshire and North's Private International Law* (13th ed, 1999)

D P O'Connell, *International Law* (2nd ed, 1970)

Bernard O'Connor and Margareta Djordjevic, 'Practical Aspects of Monetary Compensation: The *US—Copyright* Case' (2005) 8 *Journal of International Economic Law* 127

Shigeru Oda, 'Provisional Measures: The Practice of the International Court of Justice' in Vaughan Lowe and Malgosia Fitzmaurice (eds), *Fifty Years of the International Court of Justice* (1996) 541

Shigeru Oda, 'Dispute Settlement Prospects in the Law of the Sea' (1995) 44 *ICLQ* 863

Shigeru Oda, 'The International Court of Justice Viewed from the Bench (1976–93)' (1993) 244 *Recueil des cours* 12

Karin Oellers-Frahm, 'Article 41' in Andreas Zimmermann, Christian Tomuschat, and Karin Oellers-Frahm (eds), *The Statute of the International Court of Justice: A Commentary* (2006) 921

Karin Oellers-Frahm, 'Interim Measures of Protection' in Rudolf Bernhardt (ed), *Encyclopedia of Public International Law* (1980) vol 1, 69

Karin Oellers-Frahm, *Die einstweilige Anordnung in der internationalen Gerichtsbarkeit* (1975)

Karin Oellers-Frahm and Norbert Wühler, *Dispute Settlement in Public International Law* (1984)

Roger O'Keefe, 'ITLOS Flags Its Intent' (2000) 59 *CLJ* 428

Ben Olbourne, 'Independence and Impartiality: International Standards for National Judges and Courts' (2003) 2 *Law and Practice of International Courts and Tribunals* 97

Alexander Orakhelashvili, *Peremptory Norms in International Law* (2006)

Alexander Orakhelashvili, 'Judicial Competence and Judicial Remedies in the *Avena* Case' (2005) 18 *Leiden Journal of International Law* 31

Alexander Orakhelashvili, 'Peremptory Norms and Reparation for Internationally Wrongful Acts' (2003) 3 *Baltic Yearbook of International Law* 19

Alexander Orakhelashvili, 'Restrictive Interpretation of Human Rights Treaties in Recent Jurisprudence of the European Court of Human Rights' (2003) 14 *European Journal of International Law* 529

Alexander Orakhelashvili, 'The Concept of International Judicial Jurisdiction: A Reappraisal' (2003) 3 *Law and Practice of International Courts and Tribunals* 501

Alexander Orakhelashvili, '*Arrest Warrant of 11 April 2000* (Democratic Republic of the Congo v Belgium)' (2002) 96 *AJIL* 677

Alexander Orakhelashvili, 'Questions of International Judicial Jurisdiction in the *LaGrand* Case' (2002) 15 *Leiden Journal of International Law* 105

Francisco Orrego Vicuña, *International Dispute Settlement in an Evolving Global Society: Constitutionalization, Accessibility, Privatization* (2004)

Francisco Orrego Vicuña, 'From the 1893 *Bering Sea Fur-Seals* Case to the 1999 *Southern Bluefin Tuna* Cases: A Century of Efforts at Conservation of the Living Resources of the High Seas' (1999) 10 *Yearbook of International Environmental Law* 40

Marcos Orellana, 'The *Swordfish* Dispute between the EU and Chile at the ITLOS and the WTO' (2002) 71 *Nordic Journal of International Law* 55

Marcos Orellana, 'The EU and Chile Suspend the *Swordfish* Case Proceedings at the WTO and the International Tribunal of the Law of the Sea' in ASIL Insights, Issue 60, February 2001 <http://www.asil.org/insights/insigh60.htm#author>

Eugene O'Sullivan, 'Judicial Notice' in Richard May *et al* (eds), *Essays on ICTY Procedure and Evidence* (2001) 329

Bernard Oxman, 'Complementary Agreements and Compulsory Jurisdiction' (2001) 95 *AJIL* 277

Bernard Oxman, '*The M/V 'Saiga' (Saint Vincent and the Grenadines v Guinea)*, ITLOS Case No 1' (1998) 92 *AJIL* 278

Bernard Oxman, 'Jurisdiction and the Power to Indicate Provisional Measures' in Lori Damrosch (ed), *The International Court of Justice at a Crossroads* (1987) 323

Bernard Oxman and Vincent Bantz, '*The M/V 'Saiga' (No 2) (Saint Vincent and the Grenadines v Guinea)*, Judgment (ITLOS Case No 2)' (2000) 94 *AJIL* 140

David Palmeter, 'The WTO Appellate Body Needs Remand Authority' (1998) 32 *Journal of World Trade* 41

David Palmeter and Petros Mavroidis, *Dispute Settlement in the World Trade Organisation* (first published 1999, 2nd ed, 2004)

David Palmeter and Petros Mavroidis, 'The WTO Legal System: Sources of Law' (1998) 92 *AJIL* 398

William Park, *International Forum Selection* (1996)

Jo Pasqualucci, *The Practice and Procedure of the Inter-American Court of Human Rights* (2003)

Jo Pasqualucci, 'Provisional Measures in the Inter-American Human Rights System: An Innovative Development in International Law' (1993) 26 *Vanderbilt Journal of Transnational Law* 803

Colter Paulson, 'Compliance with Final Judgments of the International Court of Justice since 1987' (2004) 98 *AJIL* 434

Joost Pauwelyn, 'Bridging Fragmentation and Unity: International Law as a Universe of Inter-Connected Islands' (2004) 25 *Michigan Journal of International Law* 903

Joost Pauwelyn, *Conflict of Norms in Public International Law* (2003)

Joost Pauwelyn, 'How to Win a World Trade Organisation Dispute Based on Non-World Trade Organisation Law?' (2003) 37 *Journal of World Trade* 997

Joost Pauwelyn, 'The Use of Experts in WTO Dispute Settlement' (2002) 51 *ICLQ* 325

Joost Pauwelyn, 'The Role of Public International Law in the WTO: How Far Can We Go?' (2001) 95 *AJIL* 535

Joost Pauwelyn, 'Enforcement and Countermeasures in the WTO: Rules are Rules—Toward a More Collective Approach' (2000) 94 *AJIL* 335

Joost Pauwelyn, 'Evidence, Proof and Persuasion in WTO Dispute Settlement: Who Bears the Burden?' (1998) 1 *Journal of International Economic Law* 227

C Peck and R S Lee (eds), *Increasing the Effectiveness of the International Court of Justice* (1997)

Matti Pellonpää, 'Compensable Claims before the Tribunal: Expropriation Claims' in Richard Lillich and D McGraw (eds), *The Iran–United States Claims Tribunal: Its Contribution to the Law of State Responsibility* (1998) 185

PCA, 'Case Concerning Land Reclamation by Singapore in and around the Straits of Johor', (Press release dated 14 January 2005), at <http://www.pca-cpa.org>

PCIJ/Advisory Committee of Jurists, *Procès-Verbaux of the Proceedings of the Committee of Jurists* (1920)

Jean Personnaz, *La Réparation du Préjudice en Droit International Public* (1939)

Ernst-Ulrich Petersmann, 'Constitutionalism and International Adjudication: How to Constitutionalise the UN Dispute Settlement System?' (1999) 31 *New York University Journal of International Law and Politics* 753

Ernst-Ulrich Petersmann, *The GATT/WTO Dispute Settlement System* (1997)

Ernst-Ulrich Petersmann, 'The Transformation of the World Trading System through the 1994 Agreement Establishing the World Trade Organisation' (1995) 6 *European Journal of International Law* 161

Ernst-Ulrich Petersmann, 'Violation Complaints and Non-Violation Complaints in Public International Trade Law' (1991) 34 *German Yearbook of International Law* 175

Ernst-Ulrich Petersmann and M Hilf (eds), *The New GATT Round of Multilateral Trade Negotiations* (1988)

Georgios Petrochilos, *Procedure in International Arbitration* (2004)

Louis-Edmond Pettiti, Emmanuel Decaux and Pierre-Henri Imbert (eds), *La Convention Européenne des Droits de l'Homme: Commentaire article par article* (1999)

Jeffrey Pinsler, 'The Inherent Powers of the Court' (1997) *Singapore Journal of Legal Studies* 1

Mónica Pinto, 'Fragmentation or Unification Among International Institutions: Human Rights Tribunals' (1999) 31 *New York University Journal of International Law and Politics* 833

M C W Pinto, 'Pre-eminence of the International Court of Justice' in Connie Peck and Roy Lee (eds), *Increasing the Effectiveness of the International Court of Justice* (1997) 281

Charles Plant (ed), *Blackstone's Civil Practice* (2003)

Richard Plender, 'Procedure in the European Courts: Comparisons and Proposals' (1997) 267 *Recueil des cours* 9

Richard Plender (ed), *European Courts: Practice and Precedents* (1997)

Richard Plender, 'Intervention', in Richard Plender (ed), *European Courts: Practice and Precedents* (1997) 613

Richard Plender, 'Rules of Procedure in the International Court and the European Court' (1991) 2(2) *European Journal of International Law* 1

Richard Plender, 'The European Court as an International Tribunal' (1983) 42 *CLJ* 279

Fausto Pocar, 'The Proliferation of International Criminal Courts and Tribunals: A Necessity in the Current International Legal Community' (2004) 2 *Journal of International Criminal Justice* 304

Pitman B Potter, *The Wal Wal Arbitration* (1938)

Roscoe Pound, 'The Rule-Making Power of the Courts' (1926) 12 *American Bar Association Journal* 599

Dietmar Prager, 'Procedural Developments at the International Court of Justice' (2003) 2 *Law and Practice of International Courts and Tribunals* 175

Dietmar Prager, 'The 2001 Amendments to the Rules of Procedure of the International Court of Justice' (2002) 1 *Law and Practice of International Courts and Tribunals* 155

René Provost (ed), *State Responsibility in International Law* (2002)

Samuel von Pufendorf, *De modo litigandi in libertate naturali* (W Evans Darby trans), in W Evans Darby, *International Tribunals* (1899) 56

Robert Pushaw, 'The Inherent Powers of the Federal Courts and the Structural Constitution' (2001) 86 *Iowa Law Review* 735

Ernst Rabel, *The Conflict of Laws: A Comparative Study* (1958–64)

A Ræder, *L'arbitrage international chez les Hellènes* (1912)

Jackson Ralston, *Supplement to 1926 Revised Edition of The Law and Procedure of International Tribunals* (1936)

Jackson Ralston, *International Arbitration from Athens to Locarno* (1929)

Jackson Ralston, *The Law and Procedure of International Tribunals* (rev ed, 1926)

Manuel Rama-Montaldo, 'International Legal Personality and Implied Powers of International Organisations' (1970) 44 *British Yearbook of International Law* 111

Albrecht Randelzhofer and Christian Tomuschat, *State Responsibility and the Individual: Reparation in Instances of Grave Violations of Human Rights* (1999)

Pemmaraju Sreenivasa Rao, 'Multiple International Judicial Forums: A Reflection of the Strength of International Law or its Fragmentation?' (2004) 25 *Michigan Journal of International Law* 929

Joseph Raz, *The Concept of a Legal System* (2nd ed, 1980)

Alan Redfern and Martin Hunter with Nigel Blackaby and Constantine Partasides, *Law and Practice of International Commercial Arbitration* (3rd ed, 1999); (4th ed, 2004)

Catherine Redgwell, 'Universality or Integrity? Some Reflections on Reservations to General Multilateral Treaties' (1993) 64 *British Yearbook of International Law* 245

Andreas Reiner, 'Burden and General Standards of Proof' (1994) 10 *Arbitration International* 329

August Reinisch, 'The Use and Limits of *Res Judicata* and *Lis Pendens* as Procedural Tools to Avoid Conflicting Dispute Settlement Outcomes' (2004) 3 *Law and Practice of International Courts and Tribunals* 37

Michael Reisman (ed), *Jurisdiction in International Law* (1999)

Michael Reisman, 'The Supervisory Jurisdiction of the International Court of Justice: International Arbitration and International Adjudication' (1996) 258 *Recueil des cours* 9

Michael Reisman, *Systems of Control in International Adjudication and Arbitration* (1992)

Michael Reisman and Eric Freedman, 'The Plaintiff's Dilemma: Illegally Obtained Evidence and Admissibility in International Adjudication' (1982) 76 *AJIL* 737

Michael Reisman, *Nullity and Revision* (1971)

Ladislas Reitzer, *La Réparation comme conséquence de l'acte illicite en Droit international* (1938)

Clarisse Ribeiro (ed), *Investment Arbitration and the Energy Charter Treaty* (2006)

Willem Riphagen, 'Second Report on the Content, Forms and Degrees of International Responsibility' [1981] *Yearbook of the International Law Commission*, vol II, pt 1, 79, UN Doc A/CN.4/344

Josh Robbins, 'False Friends: *Amicus Curiae* and Procedural Discretion in WTO Appeals Under the *Hot-Rolled Lead/Asbestos* Doctrine' (2003) 44 *Harvard International Law Journal* 317

Cesare Romano, André Nollkaemper, and Jann Kleffner (eds), *Internationalized Criminal Courts: Sierra Leone, East Timor, Kosovo, and Cambodia* (2004)

Cesare Romano, 'PICT Synoptic Chart' at <http://www.pict-pcti.org>

Cesare Romano, 'The *Southern Bluefin Tuna* Dispute: Hints of a World to Come . . . Like It or Not' (2001) *Ocean Development & International Law* 313

Cesare Romano, 'The Proliferation of International Judicial Bodies: The Pieces of the Puzzle' (1999) 31 *New York University Journal of International Law and Politics* 709

Santi Romano, *L'ordre juridique* (L François and P Gothot, trans, 2nd ed, 1975)

Shabtai Rosenne, *The Law and Practice of the International Court, 1920–2005* (2006)

Shabtai Rosenne, *Provisional Measures in International Law* (2005)

Shabtai Rosenne, 'International Court of Justice: Practice Directions on Judges Ad Hoc; Agents; Counsel and Advocates; and Submission of New Documents' (2002) 1 *Law and Practice of International Courts and Tribunals* 223

Shabtai Rosenne, 'Updates to Law and Practice of the International Court of Justice' (2002) 1 *Law and Practice of International Courts and Tribunals* 129

Shabtai Rosenne, 'Controlling Interlocutory Aspects of Proceedings in the International Court of Justice' (2000) 94 *AJIL* 307

Shabtai Rosenne, 'Visit to the Site by the International Court' in Emile Yakpo and Tahar Boumedra (eds), *Liber Amicorum Mohammed Bedjaoui* (1999) 461

Shabtai Rosenne, *The World Court* (5th ed, 1995)

Shabtai Rosenne, *Intervention in the International Court of Justice* (1993)

Shabtai Rosenne, *Procedure in the International Court* (1983)

Shabtai Rosenne, 'Preliminary Rulings by the International Court of Justice at the Instance of National Courts: A Reply' (1988–9) 29 *Virginia Journal of International Law* 401

Shabtai Rosenne, *The Law and Practice of the International Court*, (1965) vol 1

Shabtai Rosenne, *The International Court of Justice: An Essay in Political and Legal Theory* (1957)

Charles Rousseau, *Droit International Public* (1953)

J M Ruda, 'Intervention before the International Court of Justice' in Vaughan Lowe and Malgosia Fitzmaurice (eds), *Fifty Years of the International Court of Justice* (1996) 487

Jean Salmon, 'Le fait dans l'application du droit international' (1982) 175 *Recueil des cours* 257

Mohamed Sameh M Amr, *The Role of the International Court of Justice as the Principal Judicial Organ of the United Nations* (2003)

Pieter Sanders, 'Arbitration' in International Association for Legal Science, *International Encyclopedia of Comparative Law* (1996) vol XVI, ch 12

Durward Sandifer, *Evidence before International Tribunals* (2nd ed, 1975)

Durward Sandifer, *Evidence before International Tribunals* (1939)

Philippe Sands, *Principles of International Environmental Law* (2nd ed, 2003)
Philippe Sands, 'Sustainable Development: Treaty, Custom and the Cross-Fertilisation of International Law' in Alan Boyle and David Freestone (eds), *International Law and Sustainable Development: Past Achievements and Future Challenges* (1999) 39
Philippe Sands, 'Treaty, Custom and the Cross-Fertilisation of International Law' (1998) 1 *Yale Human Rights and Development Law Journal* 85
Philippe Sands and Pierre Klein, *Bowett's Law of International Institutions* (5th ed, 2001)
Philippe Sands, Ruth Mackenzie and Yuval Shany (eds), *Manual on International Courts and Tribunals* (1999)
Danesh Sarooshi, 'The Powers of the United Nations International Criminal Tribunals' (1998) 2 *Max Planck Yearbook of United Nations Law* 141
Georges Scelle, 'Draft on Arbitral Procedure Adopted by the Commission at its Fifth Session, Report by Georges Scelle, Special Rapporteur' [1958] *Yearbook of the International Law Commission*, vol II, 1, UN Doc A/CN.4/113
Georges Scelle, 'Arbitral Procedure' [1950] *Yearbook of the International Law Commission*, vol II, 114, UN Doc A/CN.4/18
Oscar Schachter, 'The Enforcement of International Judicial and Arbitral Decisions' (1960) 54 *AJIL* 1
Harm Schepel and Erhard Blankenburg, 'Mobilizing the European Court of Justice' in Gráinne de Búrca and J H H Weiler, *The European Court of Justice* (2001) 9
J W Schneider, 'The Benelux Court' (1973) 4 *Netherlands Yearbook of International Law* 193
Christoph Schreuer, 'The Concept of Expropriation under the ECT and other Investment Protection Treaties', in Clarisse Ribeiro (ed), *Investment Arbitration and the Energy Charter Treaty* (2006) 108
Christoph Schreuer, 'Non-Pecuniary Remedies in ICSID Arbitration' (2004) 20 *Arbitration International* 325
Christoph Schreuer, *The ICSID Convention: A Commentary* (2001)
Constanze Schulte, *Compliance with Decisions of the International Court of Justice* (2004)
Jürgen Schwarze, 'Origins of the European Courts' Statutes and Rules of Procedure' in Richard Plender (ed), *European Courts: Practice and Precedents* (1997) 3
Georg Schwarzenberger, *International Law as Applied by International Courts and Tribunals* (1986) vol IV
Georg Schwarzenberger, *International Law as Applied by International Courts and Tribunals* (1976) vol III
Georg Schwarzenberger, *A Manual of International Law* (4th ed, 1960) vol I
Georg Schwarzenberger, *International Law* (3rd ed, 1957)
Stephen Schwebel, 'The Proliferation of International Tribunals: Threat or Promise?' in *Liber Amicorum in Honour of Lord Slynn of Hadley* (2000) vol II, 3
Stephen Schwebel, 'Address to the Plenary Session of the General Assembly of the United Nations' (26 October 1999), available at <http://www.icj-cij.org> under 'Statements of the President of the Court'
Stephen Schwebel, 'Address to the General Assembly of the United Nations' (27 October 1998), available at <http://www.icj-cij.org> under 'Statements of the President of the Court'
Stephen Schwebel, *Justice in International Law* (1994)
Stephen Schwebel, 'Three Cases of Fact-Finding before the International Court of Justice' in Richard Lillich (ed), *Fact-Finding before International Tribunals* (1992) 1

Iain Scobbie, 'The Theorist as Judge: Hersch Lauterpacht's Concept of the International Judicial Function' (1997) 8 *European Journal of International Law* 264

Iain Scobbie, 'Discontinuance in the International Court: The Enigma of the Nuclear Tests Cases' (1992) 41 *ICLQ* 808

Iain Scobbie, 'Legal Reasoning and the Judicial Function in the International Court' (PhD dissertation, University of Cambridge, 1990)

Ignaz Seidl-Hohenveldern, 'Die völkerrechtliche Haftung für Handlungen internationaler Organisationen im Verhältnis zu Nichtmitgliedstaaten' (1961) 11 *Österreichische Zeitschrift für öffentliches Recht* 497

Andrew Serdy, 'See You in Port: Australia and New Zealand as Third Parties in the Dispute between Chile and the European Community over Chile's Denial of Port Access to Spanish Vessels Fishing for Swordfish on the High Seas' (2002) 3 *Melbourne Journal of International Law* 79

A Sereni, *Principi generali di diretto e processo internazionali* (1955)

Finn Seyersted, *United Nations Forces in the Law of Peace and War* (1966)

Finn Seyersted, *Objective International Personality of Intergovernmental Organisations: Do their Capacities Really Depend on their Constitutions?* (1963)

Mohamed Shahabuddeen, 'Consistency in Holdings by International Tribunals' in Nisuke Ando, Edward McWhinney and Rüdiger Wolfrum (eds), *Liber Amicorum Judge Shigeru Oda* (2002) 633

Mohamed Shahabuddeen, *Precedent in the World Court* (1996)

Yuval Shany, *The Competing Jurisdictions of International Courts and Tribunals* (2003)

Malcolm Shaw, *International Law* (5th ed, 2003)

Malcolm Shaw, 'A Practical Look at the International Court of Justice' in Malcolm Evans (ed), *Remedies in International Law: The Institutional Dilemma* (1998) 11

Malcolm Shaw, 'The Security Council and the International Court of Justice: Judicial Drift and the Judicial Function' in A S Muller, D Raic and J M Thuransky (eds), *The International Court of Justice: Its Future Role after Fifty Years* (1997) 219

Sabrina Shaw and Risa Schwartz, 'Trade and Environment in the WTO—State of Play' (2002) 36 *Journal of World Trade* 129

Dinah Shelton, *Remedies in International Human Rights Law* (2nd ed, 2005)

Dinah Shelton, 'Legal Norms to Promote the Independence and Accountability of International Tribunals' (2003) 2 *Law and Practice of International Courts and Tribunals* 27

Dinah Shelton, 'Righting Wrongs: Reparations in the Articles on State Responsibility' (2002) 96 *AJIL* 833

Dinah Shelton, 'New Rules of Procedure for the Inter-American Commission on Human Rights' (2001) 22 *Human Rights Law Journal* 169

Dinah Shelton, 'The Participation of Nongovernmental Organisations in International Judicial Proceedings' (1994) 88 *AJIL* 611

Audley Sheppard, 'The Distinction between Lawful and Unlawful Expropriation', in Clarisse Ribeiro (ed), *Investment Arbitration and the Energy Charter Treaty* (2006) 169

Ibrahim Shihata, *The Power of the International Court to Determine Its Own Jurisdiction* (1965)

Ibrahim Shihata and Antonio Parra, 'The Experience of the International Centre for the Settlement of Investment Disputes' (1999) 14 *ICSID Review—FILJ* 299

Bruno Simma, 'Fragmentation in a Positive Light' (2004) 25 *Michigan Journal of International Law* 845

Bruno Simma (ed), *The Charter of the United Nations: A Commentary* (2nd ed, 2002) 2 vols

Bruno Simma, 'From Bilateralism to Community Interest in International Law' (1994) 250 *Recueil des cours* 217

Bruno Simma, 'Self-Contained Regimes' (1985) 16 *Netherlands Yearbook of International Law* 111

Bruno Simma and Dirk Pulkowski, 'Of Planets and the Universe: Self-Contained Regimes in International Law' (2006) 17 *European Journal of International Law* 483

J L Simpson and Hazel Fox, *International Arbitration* (1959)

Anthony Sinclair, 'The Origins of the Umbrella Clause in the International Law of Investment Protection' (2004) 20 *Arbitration International* 411

Nagendra Singh, *The Role and Record of the International Court of Justice* (1989)

Anne-Marie Slaughter, 'A Global Community of Courts' (2003) 44 *Harvard International Law Journal* 191

Blain Sloan, 'General Assembly Resolutions Revisited (Forty Years Later)' (1987) 58 *British Yearbook of International Law* 39

Göran Sluiter, *International Criminal Adjudication and the Collection of Evidence: Obligations of States* (2002)

Lesley Jane Smith, 'Antisuit Injunctions, *Forum non Conveniens* und International Comity' [1993] *Recht der internationalen Wirtschaft* 802

Société Française pour le Droit International, *Colloque de Lille: La juridictionnalisation du droit international* (2003)

Louis Sohn, 'International Arbitration in Historical Perspective: Past and Present' in A H A Soons (ed), *International Arbitration: Past and Prospects* (1990) 9

A H A Soons (ed), *International Arbitration: Past and Prospects* (1990)

George Spencer Bower, AK Turner and KR Handley, *The Doctrine of Res Judicata* (1996)

Ole Spiermann, 'Review of Shabtai Rosenne, *Provisional Measures in International Law: The International Court of Justice and the International Tribunal for the Law of the Sea*' (2005) 76 *British Yearbook of International Law* 554

Ole Spiermann, *International Legal Argument in the Permanent Court of International Justice* (2005)

Ole Spiermann, '"Who Attempts too Much Does Nothing Well": The 1920 Advisory Committee of Jurists and the Statute of the Permanent Court of International Justice' (2002) 73 *British Yearbook of International Law* 187

Baron Schenk von Stauffenberg, *Le statut et règlement de la Cour Permanente de Justice Internationale* (1934)

Debra Steger and Susain Hainsworth, 'World Trade Organisation Dispute Settlement: The First Three Years' (1998) 1 *Journal of International Economic Law* 199

E Stein, 'Lawyers, Judges and the Making of a Transnational Constitution' (1981) 75 *AJIL* 1

D Stewart, 'Compensation and Valuation Issues' in Richard Lillich and D McGraw (eds), *The Iran-United States Claims Tribunal: Its Contribution to the Law of State Responsibility* (1998) 325

Terence Stewart (ed), *The GATT Uruguay Round: A Negotiating History* (1993)

Terence Stewart and Christopher Callahan, *Dispute Settlement Mechanisms* (1993)

Terence Stewart and Amy Dwyer, 'The WTO/GATT World Trading System: An Overview' in Pierre Pescatore (ed), *Handbook of WTO/GATT Dispute Settlement* (2003) vol I, 3

M Straus, 'The Practice of the Iran–US Claims Tribunal in Receiving Evidence from Parties and from Experts' (1986) 3 *Journal of International Arbitration* 57

Subsidiary Body for Implementation, Procedures and Mechanisms Relating to Compliance under the Kyoto Protocol, 17 September 1999, UN Doc FCCC/SBI/1997/7 (1999)

Eelko Szabó, 'Provisional Measures in the World Court: Binding or Bound to be Ineffective?' (1997) 10 *Leiden Journal of International Law* 475

Jerzy Sztucki, *Interim Measures in the Hague Court* (1983)

Christian Tams, 'Article 49' in Andreas Zimmermann, Christian Tomuschat and Karin Oellers-Frahm (eds), *The Statute of the International Court of Justice: A Commentary* (2006) 1099

Christian Tams, 'Unity and Diversity in the Law of State Responsibility', in Andreas Zimmermann and Rainer Hofmann (eds), *Unity and Diversity in International Law* (2006) 437

Christian Tams, *Enforcing Obligations* Erga Omnes *in International Law* (2005)

Christian Tams, 'Interim Orders by the European Court of Human Rights: Comments on *Mamatkulov and Abdurasulovic v Turkey*' (2003) 63 *Zeitschrift für ausländisches öffentliches Recht und Völkerrecht* 681

Christian Tams, 'Recognizing Guarantees and Assurances of Non-Repetition: *LaGrand* and the Law of State Responsibility' (2002) 27 *Yale Journal of International Law* 423

Colin Tapper, *Cross & Tapper on Evidence* (9th ed, 1999)

C O'Neal Taylor, 'The Limits of Economic Power: Section 301 and the World Trade Organisation Dispute Settlement System' (1997) 30 *Vanderbilt Journal of Transnational Law* 209

James Thayer, *A Preliminary Treatise on Evidence at the Common Law* (1898)

Hugh Thirlway, 'The Proliferation of International Judicial Organs and the Formation of International Law' in W P Heere (ed), *International Law and the Hague's 750th Anniversary* (1999) 433

Hugh Thirlway, 'Procedural Law and the International Court of Justice' in Vaughan Lowe and Malgosia Fitzmaurice (eds), *Fifty Years of the International Court of Justice* (1996) 389

Hugh Thirlway, 'The Indication of Provisional Measures by the International Court of Justice' in Rudolf Bernhardt (ed), *Interim Measures Indicated by International Courts* (1994) 1

Hugh Thirlway, 'Procedure of International Courts and Tribunals', in Rudolf Bernhardt (ed), *Encyclopedia of Public International Law* (1992) vol III, 1128

Hugh Thirlway, 'The Law and Procedure of the International Court of Justice 1960–1989:
Part One' (1989) 60 *British Yearbook of International Law* 1
Part Three' (1991) 62 *British Yearbook of International Law* 1
Part Nine' (1998) 69 *British Yearbook of International Law* 1
Part Ten' (1999) 70 *British Yearbook of International Law* 1
Part Eleven' (2000) 71 *British Yearbook of International Law* 71
Part Twelve' (2001) 72 *British Yearbook of International Law* 37

Hugh Thirlway, *Non-Appearance in the International Court of Justice* (1985)

Hugh Thirlway, 'Dilemma or Chimera? Admissibility of Illegally Obtained Evidence in International Adjudication' (1984) 78 *AJIL* 622

Michael Tilbury, *Civil Remedies* (1990)

Marcus Niebuhr Tod, *International Arbitration amongst the Greeks* (1913)

Peter Tomka and Samuel Wordsworth, 'The First Site Visit of the International Court of Justice in Fulfilment of Its Judicial Function' (1998) 92 *AJIL* 133

Christian Tomuschat, 'International Courts and Tribunals' in Rudolf Bernhardt (ed), *Encyclopaedia of Public International Law* (1981) 92

Christian Tomuschat, 'International Courts and Tribunals with Regionally Restricted and/or Specialised Jurisdiction' in Max-Planck Institut für ausländisches öffentliches Recht und Völkerrecht, *Judicial Settlement of International Disputes—International Court of Justice, Other Courts and Tribunals, Arbitration and Conciliation: An International Symposium* (1974) 285

Joel Trachtman, 'The Domain of WTO Dispute Resolution' (1999) 40 *Harvard International Law Journal* 333

Tullio Treves, 'Le Tribunal International du Droit de la Mer et la Multiplication des Juridictions Internationales' (2000) 83 *Rivista di Diritto Internazionale* 726

Tullio Treves, 'Conflicts between the International Tribunal for the Law of the Sea and the International Court of Justice' (1999) 31 *New York University Journal of International Law and Politics* 809

Tullio Treves, 'Recent Trends in the Settlement of International Disputes' (1997) 1 *Bancaja Euromediterranean Courses of International Law* 395

Edward Tuttle (ed), *A Treatise on the Law of Judgments by A C Freeman* (5th ed, 1925) 3 vols

Georg Umbricht, 'An "Amicus Curiae" Brief on *Amicus Curiae* Briefs at the WTO' (2001) 4 *Journal of International Economic Law* 773

UN Secretary-General, *Survey of International Law in Relation to the Work of Codification of the International Law Commission* (1949) UN Doc A/CN.4/1/Rev.1 22

US Department of State, 'Statement on the US Withdrawal from the Proceedings Initiated by Nicaragua in the International Court of Justice' (1985) 24 ILM 246

Detlev Vagts, 'The International Legal Profession: A Need for More Governance?' (1996) 90 *AJIL* 250

Emmerich de Vattel, *The Law of Nations, or, Principles of the Law of Nature, Applied to the Conduct and Affairs of Nations and Sovereigns* (first published 1758, 4th ed, 1811)

Emmerich de Vattel, 'The Law of Nations or the Principles of Natural Justice' in James Brown Scott (ed), *Classics of International Law* (1916)

Alfred Verdross and Bruno Simma, *Universelles Völkerrecht* (3rd ed, 1984)

Alfred Verdross, *Die Verfassung der Völkerrechtsgemeinschaft* (1926)

J H W Verzijl, *International Law in Historical Perspective* (1976)

J H W Verzijl, *The Jurisprudence of the World Court* (1965)

Daniel Vignes, 'Concession des phares à l'Empire Ottoman' (1956) 2 *Annuaire Français de Droit International* 416

Jean Vincent and Serge Guinchard, *Procédure civile* (1999)

Michel Virally, 'The Sources of International Law' in Max Sørensen (ed), *Manual of Public International Law* (1968) 116

Charles de Visscher, *Theory and Reality in Public International Law* (1968)

Charles de Visscher, *Aspects Récent du Droit Procédural de la Cour Internationale de Justice* (1966)

Jeff Waincymer, *WTO Litigation: Procedural Aspects of Formal Dispute Settlement* (2002)

Richard Wainwright, 'Article 186 EEC: Interim Measures and Member States' (1977) 2 *ELR* 349

Sir Humphrey Waldock, 'Third Report on the Law of Treaties' [1964] *Yearbook of the International Law Commission*, vol II, 52

Sir Humphrey Waldock, 'General Course on Public International Law' (1962) 106 *Recueil des cours* 1

Gary Watt, 'The Danger and Deceit of the Rule in *Henderson v Henderson*: A New Approach to Successive Civil Actions Arising from the Same Factual Matter' (2000) 19 *Civil Justice Quarterly* 287

Sir Arthur Watts, 'The ICJ's Practice Directions of 30 July 2004' (2004) 3 *Law and Practice of International Courts and Tribunals* 385

Sir Arthur Watts, 'New Practice Directions of the International Court of Justice' (2002) 1 *Law and Practice of International Courts and Tribunals* 247

Sir Arthur Watts, 'Burden of Proof, and Evidence before the ICJ' in Friedl Weiss (ed), *Improving WTO Dispute Settlement Procedures: Issues and Lessons from the Practice of Other International Courts and Tribunals* (2000) 289

Gerhard Wegen, 'Discontinuance of International Proceedings: The Hostages Case' (1982) 76 *AJIL* 717

Hans Wehberg (ed), *Institut de Droit International: Tableau Général des Résolutions (1873–1956)* (1957)

Prosper Weil, '"The Court Cannot Conclude Definitively..." *Non Liquet* Revisited' (1997) 36 *Columbia Journal of Transnational Law* 109

Prosper Weil, 'Cours général de droit international public' (1992) 237 *Recueil des cours* 9

Joseph Weiler, 'Towards a Common Law of International Trade', in Joseph Weiler (ed), *The EU, the WTO and the NAFTA* (2000) 201

Friedl Weiss (ed), *Improving WTO Dispute Settlement Procedures: Issues and Lessons from the Practice of Other International Courts and Tribunals* (2000)

Friedl Weiss, 'Improving WTO Procedural Law: Problems and Lessons from the Practice of other International Courts and Tribunals' in Friedl Weiss (ed), *Improving WTO Dispute Settlement Procedures* (2000) 17

Karel Wellens, 'Fragmentation of International Law and Establishing an Accountability Regime for International Organisations: The Role of the Judiciary in Closing the Gap' (2004) 25 *Michigan Journal of International Law* 1159

Karel Wellens, 'Diversity in Secondary Rules and the Unity of International Law: Some Reflections on Current Trends' (1994) 25 *Netherlands Yearbook of International Law* 3

Marc Weller, *Iraq and Kuwait: The Hostilities and Their Aftermath* (1993)

John Westberg, 'Applicable Law, Expropriatory Takings and Compensation in Cases of Expropriation; ICSID and Iran–US Claims Tribunal Compared' (1993) 8 *ICSID Review—Foreign Investment Law Journal* 1

John Westberg, 'Compensation in Cases of Expropriation and Nationalisation: Awards of the Iran–United States Claims Tribunal' (1990) 5 *ICSID Review–Foreign Investment Law Journal* 256

J G Wetter, *The International Arbitral Process: Public and Private* (1979)

Gillian White, 'The Use of Experts by the International Court of Justice' in Vaughan Lowe and Malgosia Fitzmaurice (eds), *Fifty Years of the International Court of Justice* (1996) 528

Gillian White, *The Use of Experts by International Tribunals* (1965)

Nigel White, *The Law of International Organisations* (1996)

Nigel White, 'The UN Charter and Peacekeeping Forces: Constitutional Issues' (1996) 3 *International Peacekeeping* 43

Marjorie Whiteman, *Damages in International Law* (1943) 3 vols

John Wigmore, *A Treatise on the Anglo-American System of Evidence in Trials at Common Law* (1940)

Glanville Williams, 'The Evidential Burden: Some Common Misapprehensions' (1977) 127 *NLJ* 156

Sir John Fischer Williams, *Chapters on Current International Law and the League of Nations* (1929)

David Wirth, 'European Communities—Measures Affecting Asbestos and Asbestos-Containing Products' (2002) 96 *AJIL* 435

J C Witenberg, '*Onus probandi* devant les juridictions arbitrales' (1951) 55 *Revue Générale de Droit International Public* 321

J C Witenberg, *L'Organisation Judiciaire: La Procédure et la Sentence Internationales* (1937)

J C Witenberg, 'La théorie des preuves devant les juridictions internationales' (1936) 56 *Recueil des cours* 5

Stephan Wittich, 'Awe of the Gods and Fear of the Priests: Punitive Damages in the Law of State Responsibility' (1998) 3 *Austrian Review of International and European Law* 31

W van der Wolf and S de Haardt (eds), *International Courts and Tribunals: Selected Documents and Materials* (2nd ed, 2001)

Rüdiger Wolfrum, 'Kokurrierende Zuständigkeiten internationaler Streitentscheidungsinstanzen: Notwendigkeit für Lösungsmöglichkeiten und deren Grenzen' in Nisuke Ando, Edward McWhinney and Rüdiger Wolfrum (eds), *Liber Amicorum Judge Shigeru Oda* (2002) 651

Rüdiger Wolfrum, 'Means of Ensuring Compliance with and Enforcement of International Environmental Law' (1998) 272 *Recueil des cours* 25

Rüdiger Wolfrum, 'Provisional Measures of the International Tribunal for the Law of the Sea' (1997) 37 *Indian Journal of International Law* 420

Lord Woolf, *Access to Justice: Final Report* (1996), available at <http://www.dca.gov.uk/civil/final/index.htm>

WTO, *WTO Analytical Index: Guide to WTO Law and Practice* (2003) 2 vols

WTO, *The WTO Dispute Settlement Procedures* (2nd ed, 2001)

Xiodang Yang, 'Thou Shalt Not Violate Provisional Measures' (2001) 60 *CLJ* 441

Sienho Yee, '*Forum Prorogatum* Returns to the International Court of Justice' (2003) 16 *Leiden Journal of International Law* 701

Andreas Zimmermann, Christian Tomuschat and Karin Oellers-Frahm (eds), *The Statute of the International Court of Justice: A Commentary* (2006)

Andreas Zimmermann and Tobias Thienel, 'Article 60' in Andreas Zimmermann, Christian Tomuschat and Karin Oellers-Frahm (eds), *The Statute of the International Court of Justice: A Commentary* (2006) 1275

Andreas Zimmermann and Rainer Hofmann (eds), *Unity and Diversity in International Law* (2006)

Elizabeth Zoller, 'Observations sur la révision et l'interpretation des sentences arbitrales' (1978) 24 *Annuaire Français de Droit International* 327

Geert Zonnekeyn, 'The Appellate Body's Communication on *Amicus Curiae* Briefs in the *Asbestos* Case' (2001) 35 *Journal of World Trade* 553

Index